SpringerWienNewYork

mental ray® Handbooks

Edited by
Rolf Herken

Volume 1

SpringerWienNewYork

T. Driemeyer

Rendering with mental ray®

Third,
completely revised edition

SpringerWienNewYork

Thomas Driemeyer

mental images GmbH
Berlin, Federal Republic of Germany

Typesetting and page design by the authors
Printed by Manz Crossmedia, 1051 Wien, Austria
Printed on acid-free and chlorine-free bleached paper
SPIN 11313953

With 195 Figures (48 colored) and a CD-ROM

Library of Congress Control Number 2005925773

ISSN 1438-9835
ISBN-10 3-211-22875-6 SpringerWienNewYork
ISBN-13 978-3-211-22875-3 SpringerWienNewYork

ISBN-10 3-211-83663-2 2nd edn. SpringerWienNewYork

Series Editor's Foreword

The mental ray series of handbooks is conceived to provide concise and up to date general and technical information about the commercially available rendering software mental ray. The series addresses the needs of professional and non-professional users of the software as well as of software developers who intend to integrate the stand-alone version of mental ray or the mental ray component software into applications that require interactive photorealistic and high image quality programmable rendering. In addition, the series provides comprehensive information to students and researchers in computer graphics. mental ray is a valuable tool for teaching and demonstrating the fundamental concepts of photorealistic and programmable rendering as well as a benchmark and catalyst for further research.

The rendering software mental ray and many of its unique underlying concepts are the result of ongoing research and development at the company mental images since its incorporation in 1986. Leading vendors of 3D digital content creation and 3D CAD and product design software have made mental ray their rendering software of choice for all purposes of high end visualization and image synthesis ranging from digital special effects and 3D animation for motion picture, video film, and games production to 3D mechanical and architectural CAD and to industrial product design and automotive styling.

The development of mental ray was funded in part by the European Commission in ESPRIT projects 6173 (DESIRE) and 22.765 (DESIRE II). The publication of this series facilitates the dissemination of widely accessible information about the resulting software in a timely manner and in more technical detail than it could be achieved otherwise.

It is a great pleasure for me to thank Rudolf Siegle, Director of Springer-Verlag Wien/New York, and Silvia Schilgerius, Planning Department Manager, for their interest in the project and for their willingness to publish the series at Springer-Verlag Wien/New York as part of its distinguished publication program in computer graphics.

Rolf Herken
Berlin, September 1999

Table of Contents

Introduction

Organization of This Book

This book contains a general and comprehensive introduction to rendering with mental ray®, based on a complete definition of its input scene format. It is intended for beginners to learn about rendering techniques supported by mental ray, as well as for advanced users who need information on how to achieve certain effects with mental ray while maintaining maximum performance. It can also be read as an introductory course into computer graphics, with an emphasis on rendering and its underlying concepts.

Chapter 1	contains the general introduction.
Chapter 2	lists all features of mental ray, and explains the terms used. This chapter is organized by feature.
Chapters 3–21	are a cookbook-style collection of examples for using rendering techniques in an optimal way, and give hints for how to select and apply mental ray's features. These chapters are organized by technique.
Chapter 22	lists common problems and their solutions.
Glossary	is a glossary of terms.
Appendix A	lists the command line options of mental ray.
Appendix B	contains scene data samples too long for inclusion in the main text.
Appendix C, D, E	contain descriptions of shaders in the standard shader libraries.

Volume 2 of this series, **Programming mental ray** [PROG][1] is a technical reference manual intended for advanced users who write their own scene generators such as translators and modeling and animation applications, and users who write custom shaders. The reference manual

---

[1] The third edition of both volumes was extended to cover the new generation of mental ray, version 3.4, throughout the book. See page 23 for a list of changes in mental ray 3.x.

assumes a knowledge of the concepts described in this user manual, as well as knowledge of the C or C++ programming languages used for writing shaders.

Note that a large part of the material is presented three times, in different ways: chapter 2 of this book lists program features; chapter 3 shows how these features are used in combination to achieve certain effects, and the reference manual gives a complete specification including less-often used details that are omitted in this book.

mental ray does not contain built-in shaders but comes with separate shader libraries. Each library includes a separate document describing the shaders in the library. The main shader library that is used throughout this book is the base shader library, but physics shaders and contour shaders are also used.

	file	purpose
•	ray	standalone mental ray executable
	ivray	standalone mental ray executable with Inventor support
•	imf_disp	image display utility
•	imf_copy	image copying and conversion utility
	imf_info	image information utility
	imf_diff	image comparison utility
	mkmishader	utility to create C shader source skeletons
	mitoapi	utility to create C scene API source skeletons
•	base.so	base shader library
•	base.mi	shader declarations for base shader library
•	physics.so	physics shader library
•	physics.mi	shader declarations for physics shader library
•	contour.so	contour shader library
•	contour.mi	shader declarations for contour shader library
	shader.h	included by custom shaders written in C/C++
	shader.lib	for linking custom shaders, Windows NT only

The files marked "•" are required for the examples in this book.

mental ray is built into various modeling, animation, and CAD systems such as Avid/Softimage 3D and XSI, Alias Maya, Autodesk's 3D Studio MAX and Viz, Dassault Systèmes' CATIA, and Solidworks. These systems provide graphical user interfaces to mental ray functionality. This book is not specific to any of these systems and uses command line invocation and text file scenes, which is the common baseline "batch" mode that is always available. Refer to the application user manuals for information on accessing the features described here from the graphical user interface.

Typesetting Conventions

Roman   is used for explanations.

Teletype   denotes scene language or command line fragments that should be entered verbatim, as shown.

Italics   in scene language and command line fragments denote variable items that stand for certain application-dependent text or other insertions described in the following explanation. In a text, new terms being introduced are set in italics when they are first mentioned. Integer numbers are distinguished from floating-point numbers by an appended $_{int}$ subscript.

Boldface   is used in enumerations to emphasize the item being explained.

In scene fragments, these special symbols are used:

| the vertical bar separates alternatives. For example, " $x \mid y$ " means "either x or y ".

...   an ellipsis denotes omission, "zero or more of the preceding".

[ ]   optional parts are enclosed in tall square brackets. For example, " x [y]" means "either x, or x followed by y ".

Features that have become available in some versions are marked with a superscripted mental ray version number. For example, fine displacement[3.3] is supported by mental ray 3.3 and higher.

All scene examples are broken into lines and indented for easy reading. mental ray considers unquoted sequences of blanks, tabs, and newlines as interchangeable whitespace, so indentation and line breaks do not make a functional difference (except between double quotes, which enclose literal strings).

Chapters containing advanced material that can be skipped on first reading are marked with an asterisk (*). Chapters with technical details not required for using mental ray are marked with two asterisks (**).

This book uses the operating system name "Unix" for all members of the Unix-like family: Linux, MacOS X, FreeBSD, Irix, Solaris, AIX, HP/UX, etc. The name "Windows NT" refers to all Microsoft desktop operating systems, including Windows 2000 and Windows XP (in fact, Windows XP identifies itself as NT 5), except pre-2000 Windows versions (which support no adequate multithreading).

WWW Resources

mental images' homepage is `http://www.mentalimages.com`. For errata and changes that were made after this book went into print, and downloadable .mi scene file examples, see `http://www.mentalimages.com/books.html`.

The source code for the base and physics shader libraries described in appendix C and D is available on `ftp://ftp.mentalimages.com/pub/`. See the README file at this location for the exact path.

mental images runs several discussion mailing lists; see `http://www.mentalimages.com` for details and instructions for subscribing and posting (follow the *mental ray* and *Forum* links).

The Los Angeles mental ray user's group collects useful information on `http://www.lamrug.org/`.

Acknowledgements

I would like to thank Rolf Herken for his suggestions, and all members of the team at mental images who have taken the time to contribute to this edition: Juri Abramov, Pascal Amand, François Beaune, Per Christensen, Jennifer Courter, Susanna Fishel, Julia Flötotto, Albrecht Fritzsche, Bart Gawboy, Steffen Halme, Robert Hödicke, Henrik Wann Jensen, Kristjan Valur Jonsson, Alexander Keller, Andy Kopra, Jochen Kornitzky, Martin-Karl LeFrançois, Alexander Lobodzinski, Runa Löber, Jacopo Pantaleoni, Olivier Paugam, Slobodan Pavlić, Bernd Raabe, Stefan Radig, Steffen Römer, Thomas Schädlich, Karl Johann Schmidt, Tim Schröder, Dirk Schubert, Matthias Senz, Jürgen Singer, Gunter Sprenger, Tom-Michael Thamm, Max Wardetzky, Carsten Whimster, and Barbara Wolfers. We would also like to thank these and the other members of the team at mental images for providing support in numerous ways and for maintaining the creative environment in which the software described in this book was, and continues to be, developed.

Chapter 1

Overview

This chapter presents a brief overview of the features and concepts used by mental ray.

1.1 Photorealistic Rendering

The primary purpose of the mental ray rendering software is the generation of two-dimensional images from three-dimensional scene descriptions. Normally, the goal is to create photorealistic images, which means that they are indistinguishable from photographs taken in the real world. However, the programmability and extended feature set of mental ray support a wide range of looks, from cartoon-style contour images to physically correct lighting simulations used in architectural and CAD applications. The process of generating these images is called *rendering*.

1.2 Scenes and Animations

The scene descriptions upon which rendering operations are based are mathematical descriptions of geometric objects, surface and volume properties, light sources, cameras, and their spatial arrangement in a three-dimensional world. For example, an image of a cube requires a scene description consisting of the cube geometry, describing eight corner points and six faces, its surface material (plastic, metal, or fabric, texture, reflectivity, and so on), light sources that illuminate the cube, and a camera that looks at the cube from a certain position. Other elements of the scene description, called *instances*, define the locations and orientations of the cube, the lights, and the camera. There are also elements to group parts of the scene description.

Grouping is useful because it allows parts of the scene to be treated as a whole. For example, the wheel of a car might consist of many different objects: the tire, the hubcap, spokes, and other details. Placing all these components in a group allows easy manipulation of the entire wheel, such as rotating it or placing it in four different locations in the scene. Scene descriptions are hierarchical: once the wheel is in the scene, it can be used four times to build a car, which in turn may be used several times to create a car showroom.

mental ray stores scene descriptions in a database. New elements such as lights can be added to the database at any point in space; elements can be deleted or connected in different ways; instances can be modified to move objects, lights, or cameras; and surface properties such as object colors or light intensities can be modified. After the database has been set up, a render command can be given to let mental ray render the image. When rendering has completed, the database can be modified and the scene re-rendered without having to reload the database from scratch. Camera flythroughs, for example, simply become a matter of setting up the scene once and then only modifying the camera position for each frame.

Such database modifications are called *incremental changes* because once the scene description is set up in the database, it can be modified in incremental steps between frames. Only the differences between frames of an animation need to be given. All animations work by setting up the scene description for the first frame (image) of the animation, rendering it, then providing the difference to the next frame, rendering again, and repeating this until the last frame of the animation is finished. mental ray keeps track of modifications and avoids all rendering steps that can be reused from the previous frame. For example, complex curved objects are transformed into a triangle representation in a preprocessing step called *tessellation*. If an object was tessellated for the previous frame and has not changed since then, mental ray will cache the tessellation and reuse it.

mental ray's scene database is designed for parallel operation. Parallelism is the ability of the software to have multiple processors in a machine, or multiple machines on a network, or both, working simultaneously on a scene. mental ray is based on the concept of a *virtual shared database*, which means that any processor on the network can access scene data regardless of where on the network the data is actually located. See [Herken 94] for details on the design principles.

1.2.1 Geometric Objects

mental ray supports four fundamental ways to define geometric objects:

- **Polygonal geometry** consists of a closed shape defined by at least three vertices (corner points). The polygon is the shape bounded by the edges that connect successive vertices, and the edge that connects the last vertex back to the first. Vertices must be given in counter-clockwise order: when one is looking at the front side of the object, the vertices run in counter-clockwise order (front and back sides are different when computing illumination and during ray tracing).

  A polygon is called *convex* if, figuratively, a rubber band around the polygon touches all points on all edges (figure 1.1). The loop defined by the rubber band is also called the *convex hull* of the polygon. If an edge "caves in" from the convex hull it is called *concave*. Polygons may have holes and holes within holes. The outer boundary and hole boundaries may not intersect.

  Vertices are indicated by dots and edges by lines. The visible part is shaded. The rightmost polygon is illegal because its boundary is self-intersecting. Polygons must be planar (flat) or nearly planar.

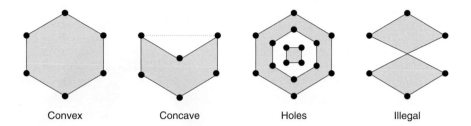

Figure 1.1: Convex and concave polygons.

- **Free-form surface geometry** consists of surface patches defined by a mesh of curves which are defined by control points. Control points are like polygon vertices, except that the surface does not necessarily run through the points. This depends on the type (more precisely, the "bases") of the curves. mental ray supports cardinal, Bézier, B-spline, Taylor, and arbitrary basis matrix bases. Figure 1.2 shows an example of a cardinal surface patch.

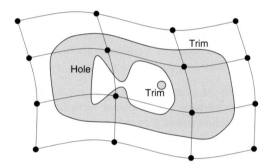

Figure 1.2: Surface control points.

Control points are indicated by dots. In addition to the curves that define the surface, the example uses two trimming curves to cut away parts of the surface, and a hole curve in one of them that cuts a hole. (The difference between a trimming curve and a hole curve is whether the part outside or inside is cut away.) Surfaces may consist of multiple patches. In this case the trimming and hole curves apply to the entire patch mesh. A *patch* is the smallest unit of a surface; every surface consists of at least one patch and may consist of multiple patches joined into a patch mesh. The number of control points per patch depends on the *surface degree*. Higher degrees allow more freedom of curvature in the patch.

mental ray also supports *rational surfaces* that give a weight to each control point. Weights allow local shape control, and control how surface coordinates are distributed over the patch surface. For example, a texture mapped on a 2×2 patch mesh would be mapped such that each patch receives one quarter of the texture. This can be adjusted with weights. For example, NURBS surfaces are a type of rational B-splines.

- **Subdivision surface geometry** is constructed from a base mesh consisting of triangles or quadrilaterals, plus optional detail vectors that provide more geometric detail inside those triangles and quads. This allows starting with a coarse mesh, and then adding detail where necessary, rather than beginning with enough control points to resolve the finest detail of the desired surface as freeform surfaces would.

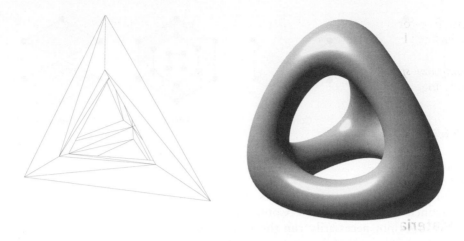

Figure 1.3: Subdivision surface.

The difference to a polygon mesh is that mental ray will further refine the provided mesh until a smooth *limit surface* is reached. Figure 1.3 shows an example of a base surface, and the limit surface automatically generated and rendered by mental ray.

- **Hair geometry**[3.1] consists of a series of vertices for each hair, which can be in linear, quadratic Bézier or cubic Bézier form. Various extra information can be associated with each hair strand, or with each vertex in a strand, as needed: normals, motion vectors, texture scalars, user scalars, and a radius. The radius can also be fixed for the entire hair object. All hairs in an object share the same material, an approximation, and two optimization parameters (size and depth).

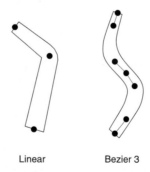

Linear   Bezier 3

Figure 1.4: Hair control points.

Hairs are normally treated as flat ribbons that always face the incoming ray, which makes them look like cylinders. However, the direction a hair is facing can be fixed by supplying a normal, making the hair primitive suitable for modeling flat blades of grass, for example. The hair primitive is designed to render fast, and assumes a small cross-section in screen space, in the range of one pixel wide or less. For larger widths, the flat nature of the hair primitive may become visible – they are not really cylinders, and there is no way to put a camera inside a hair or inspecting the end caps. Figure 1.4 shows two example hairs; note the rounded joints and flat ends.

Polygons, free-form surfaces, and subdivision surfaces can be displacement-mapped to introduce geometric detail based on a texture map such as an image.

Approximation specifications control the precision of the triangle mesh representation used for rendering. Various methods for regular, curvature-dependent, and view-dependent approximations are available. Although a large number of approximations is supported, in practice only three are needed for nearly every situation with mental ray 3.1 and higher. See page 337 for details.

This is only a quick overview of the available geometric primitives. For more details see the chapter on geometry on page 303.

1.2.2 Materials

In order to render a geometric object, its surface properties must be given in a *material definition*. Materials are defined separately and attached either to the geometric object directly, or to an instance above the geometric objects in the scene graph hierarchy. The latter case is called *material inheritance*, where objects do not define their own surface properties but inherit them from the scene graph. See page 379 for more information on material inheritance.

A material can be made up of nine different shader types. Shaders are short plug-in programs that can be chosen from one of the shader libraries bundled with mental ray. Custom shaders can be written in C or C++. Phenomenon scene elements can be used in place of shaders, and in place of materials. For more information on shaders and Phenomena see page 271.

- The **material shader** defines the appearance of the object surface to a visible ray, and handles illumination, reflection, transparency, and other surface effects. This shader is the only mandatory one in the material, all others are optional.

- The **shadow shader** controls how transparent objects cast shadows (like stained glass). Opaque objects do not need a shadow shader.

- The **photon shader** controls how the object affects incident light, implementing caustic and global illumination effects such as diffuse, glossy, and specular reflection and refraction, resulting in color bleeding, and other lighting effects. Photon shaders are only used if caustics or global illumination are enabled.

- The **volume shader** defines the coloring of a visible ray that passes through the empty space behind the object surface, assuming that it is transparent. This is useful for smoke-filled volumes, visible light beams, fur, and other volumic effects.

- The **photon volume shader** is similar to the volume shader, but acts on photons emitted by light sources rather than light rays from the camera (both are described in more detail later). It is used for global illumination effects such as participating media and volume caustics. It is used only if caustics or global illumination are enabled.

- The **displacement shader** introduces details into the geometric surface, such as embossing of text or other images. It is used during tessellation, not during rendering.

- The **environment shader** is used if the material shader applies environment mapping effects such as fake chrome reflections.

- The **contour shader** controls the style of contours if contour rendering is enabled. Contour rendering is used to render cartoon-style images, or to add glow to objects.

- The **lightmap shader**[1] creates a texture map by scanning the entire surface of the object, and stores the collected information in a texture map or other places, where it can be used during later rendering. Typical uses include light maps that capture illumination or irradiance.

- The **hardware shader**[3.3] can be used to override mental ray's automatic selection of a hardware shader for this material. It has an effect only for hardware rendering, which uses a graphics board installed in the machine to generate images.

1.2.3 Light Sources

One of the most important tasks of material shaders is to determine the illumination of the surface by light sources, and the effect of partial or full shadows. The mechanism is described on page 133. If global illumination is enabled, light sources are also used as sources of photons that are cast into the scene; mental ray follows the paths of the photons as they bounce around in the scene to determine indirect illumination.

Light sources are placed in the scene like objects, using instances that give them a position or orientation, or both, in 3D world space. There are three basic types:

- **Point lights** emit light uniformly in all directions. They have a position but no direction.

- **Infinite lights**, also called directional lights, emit parallel beams of lights from a given direction, such as sunlight. Up to mental ray 3.3, they have a direction but no position. With mental ray 3.4 and higher, directional lights may have an optional position defining a plane behind which no light will be emitted.

- **Spot lights** emit a cone of light from a point in a certain direction. They have a position, a direction and a spread.

Light sources can optionally be turned into area light sources, giving them a physical shape and extent. Supported shapes are rectangle, disc, sphere, and cylinder. Area light sources emit light from an area rather than from a single point or direction, and therefore give soft-edged shadows. See page 143 for details.

Light sources specify three shaders to control their characteristics:

- The **light shader** controls the intensity and color of the light emitted, based on the direction and distance to the illuminated point. It also checks whether that point is in shadow. This shader is mandatory.

---

[1] Light maps require mental ray 3.0 or later.

- A **light emitter shader** can be applied if caustics or global illumination are enabled. It controls the direction and energy of photons cast into the scene. It is rarely needed because mental ray supplies default emitters.

- The **hardware shader**[3.3] can be used to override mental ray's automatic selection of a hardware shader for this light. It has an effect only for hardware rendering, which uses a graphics board installed in the machine to generate images.

Finally, light definitions play an active role during shadow mapping. Shadow maps provide a fast way to compute shadows. See page 148 for details.

1.2.4 Cameras

The camera defines the viewpoint from which the scene is rendered. Multiple cameras can be defined but only one can be used for rendering at a time. The camera also defines various characteristics such as focal length and lenses (see page 39), as well as the sizes and types of rendered frame buffers and the image files they are written to. mental ray supports a wide range of image file types and formats, including depth maps, label channels, and different types of color file formats including formats with 8, 16, and 32 bits per color component and 1, 3, or 4 components per pixel (grayscale, RGB, or RGBA, respectively).

Cameras also employ shaders, all of them optional:

- The **lens shaders** define custom lenses that simulate physical lens types such as fisheye lenses or lenses causing depth of field focus blurring. More than one lens shader can be listed.

- The **output shaders** operate on the frame buffers after rendering completes. They may access the color image, the depth map, and other information, custom or standard, collected during rendering. They can be used for post effects and compositing. Multiple output shaders can be interspersed with image file output statements.

- The camera **volume shader** defines the characteristics of the entire 3D space, and can be used to simulate effects like a foggy atmosphere. (Object materials may also define volume shaders that override the camera volume shader when a ray enters the object.)

- The **environment shader** controls what is shown in directions where no objects are seen (where the camera looks into infinity). For example, they can be used to place objects into a procedural showroom without having to actually build geometry for the showroom.

1.3 Shaders

Shaders perform a variety of functions. Traditionally, shaders were used to determine the color and illumination of object surfaces (called *shading*), but mental ray extends the concept to make virtually all aspects of rendering customizable and programmable, and uses the term "shader" for all of them even if they do not actually shade anything.

A shader is a plug-in module written in C or C++ that is loaded by mental ray at runtime. Shaders can be provided as source code or object modules, but are most commonly collected into shared libraries (also called a Dynamic Shared Object (DSO) on Unix, or Dynamic Link Library (DLL) on Windows NT). Most of the shaders used in this book are taken from the base shader library that is provided with mental ray. See page 58 for details. Custom shaders can be written by users to extend the functionality of mental ray; see the mental ray Reference Manual [PROG] for instructions.

Shaders are divided into types. Some types have already been introduced; here is a complete list:

shader type	attached to	used for
material shader	material	surface shading
texture shader	anywhere	texture lookup
shadow shader	material	transparent shadows
photon shader	material	global illumination
volume shader	material	local volumic effects
	camera	global atmosphere, fog
photon volume shader	material	participating media
environment shader	material	reflection mapping
	camera	nongeometric procedural environment
hardware shader[3.3]	material	hardware shading override
	light	hardware light emission override
geometry shader	instance	procedural geometric objects
displacement shader	material	geometric surface detail
lightmap shader	material	bake illumination into object
light shader	light	light and shadow
light emitter shader	light	global illumination
lens shader	camera	depth of field, lens flares, etc
output shader	camera	image postprocessing, compositing
contour shader	material	draw contours
contour store shader	options	collect contour data for contour shader
contour contrast shader	options	determines where to put contours
inheritance shader	options	scene graph data inheritance

This table is only a rough overview. Shaders can produce a very wide range of effects; for example a combination of material, shadow, geometry, and volume shaders can produce an automatic volumic fur effect. Cooperating shaders that rely on each other and exchange data are common and often required for complex effects. For example, fur rendering depends on shadow shaders collecting data for volume shaders that actually produce the fur. Cooperating shaders are usually packaged in *Phenomena*; see below.

Shaders accept named parameters. For example, a material shader will normally have parameters that provide the colors of the surface, which the shader will use as the basis for computing proper illumination. Parameters may provide colors, scalars, flags, textures, lights, objects, structures and arrays of other parameters, subshaders, and many others. The writer of the shader decides which parameters (their names and types) the shader accepts. When the shader is used in the scene, values are provided for some or all parameters. For example, when a material shader is used in a material, its parameter named "ambient" may be set to the color green.

Instead of providing a literal value like green to a shader parameter, another shader may provide the value. mental ray will then call that other shader to obtain the parameter value for the first shader. This is called *shader assignment*. The "receiving shader" to whose parameter the other shader is attached can request the value, and mental ray performs all necessary actions to obtain it. mental ray uses hierarchical caching mechanisms to ensure that a shader that provides values to several parameters is called only once.

One common application for shader assignment is *texture mapping*. A material shader may have parameters such as ambient and diffuse color, but does not itself support texture mapping. The texture is applied by assigning a texture shader to both the ambient and diffuse parameters of the material shader. This encourages a "toolbox approach" to shader writing: instead of writing large monolithic shaders that can do everything, small shaders are written that each do only one thing. These small shaders can then be combined in arbitrary ways to build up more complex effects. mental ray comes with a *base shader library* that contains a number of such small shaders written for this purpose (see page 58). When building shader graphs (a generalization of shader trees) of this kind, it is usually advisable to package the graph into a Phenomenon.

1.4 Phenomena

A Phenomenon™ is a set of cooperating shaders and shader graphs and a set of requirements. On the outside, a Phenomenon looks just like a regular shader, with a name and external parameters called *interface parameters*, but on the inside it packages any number of internal shaders and rendering options that all work together to create an effect that would be too complex to achieve with a single shader.

Consider a candle flame. The flame itself is too ephemeral to be easily modeled as a geometric object, so a volume shader would be used to create it as a procedural volume effect. However, a material volume shader operates in a closed volume that delimits its effect, so a geometric container object such as a sphere is needed. The sphere itself must be invisible, so a fully transparent material shader is attached. A dancing light source in the flame would add appropriately flickering shadows. Finally, an output shader that creates a lens flare or halo may finish the effect, and certain mental ray options must be set to make it all work.

All of this can be done separately by creating the container sphere and its material and the light, and attaching the various shaders to the material, light, and camera, and setting the correct mental ray options, but all this is a lot of work. Phenomena™ provide a simple means to make complex effects like this as easy as white plastic — the Phenomenon takes care of all the geometry, lights, materials, shaders and other scene elements automatically, attaching them to the appropriate points in the scene without any user intervention.

Creating new Phenomena is simpler than writing shaders. No knowledge of the C or C++

languages is required. It is simply a matter of connecting existing shaders in shader graphs and setting the requirement flags. The parameters of any shaders inside a Phenomenon may also be assigned to the Phenomenon's interface parameters. Effectively, the interface acts as a gateway through which the user of the Phenomenon can pass parameter values to the shaders inside the Phenomenon. This is called *interface assignment*.

Phenomena are explained in more detail in chapter 11.

1.5 Scanline Rendering and Ray Tracing

mental ray, as the name implies, uses *ray tracing* to render images. Ray tracing is a rendering algorithm that computes the color for a given pixel by "shooting rays" from the camera into the scene, and seeing which objects are hit by the rays and what happens to the rays when they travel through empty space to that point. The object that was hit evaluates its color (more precisely, the appropriate material shader of the object is called), and it may cast secondary rays into the scene if it is reflective or refractive. Rays are also used to compute shadows, by discovering if there are any occluding objects between an illuminated point and a light source, and for final gathering to compute indirect illumination. Ray tracing is sometimes called *backwards ray tracing* because rays travel from the camera into the scene, whereas in the real world light rays originate at light sources. (Forward ray tracing is handled by mental ray also; see below.)

Ray tracing can handle reflections and refractions because they are simply a matter of casting another ray (called a *secondary ray*) from some point into some direction. For example, the material shader of a mirror may compute the mirror surface color by casting a secondary ray into the mirror direction and using the color returned by that ray. However, this flexibility comes at a cost — ray tracing has a certain amount of overhead because of the way it searches for objects in the path of a ray. For this reason, mental ray also supports another rendering approach called *scanline rendering*.

Scanline rendering operates in a different way. It projects all objects onto the two-dimensional viewing plane, and then sorts them according to their Y and X coordinates, in this order. Rendering then becomes simply a matter of looking up this sorted list, which in most cases is faster than ray tracing. This is possible if the camera (see chapter 3) is a pinhole camera without any distorting lens shaders that produce effects such as fisheye or depth of field distortion, and if there are no reflections or refractions in the scene. Sorting and selection (but not shaded rendering itself) may be accelerated using local OpenGL®[2] hardware if available. See page 446 for details.

mental ray 3.2 introduced an alternate scanline rendering algorithm called *Rapid Motion*, now renamed the *rasterizer*. As the name suggests, one of its main advantages is the ability to accelerate motion blurring, but it also manages scenes with high depth complexity much more efficiently. Depth complexity is high if a large number of objects line up behind a pixel to be rendered. The rasterizer can find the frontmost object faster, without considering the ones hidden behind it.

To ensure maximum performance, mental ray first uses scanline rendering to compute the color of an image sample, unless disabled because of distorting lenses. When a change of direction is

[2]OpenGL is a registered trademark of Silicon Graphics, Inc.

required due to reflections and refractions (but not plain transparency), mental ray switches to ray tracing on the fly.

mental ray's ray tracing feature is fully accessible to shaders, and can be used for features other than reflections and refractions. For example, one method for computing visible shafts of light in dusty atmospheres relies on ray tracing to detect objects in the path of the light beam in order to correctly compute shadows cutting into the beam, using a technique called *ray marching*.

The rendered image is computed by measuring the color at certain points of the image. Each such measurement is called a *sample*. If there are fewer samples than pixels in the rendered image this is called *infrasampling*; if there are more samples than pixels this is called *oversampling*. The decision whether to oversample or infrasample is made dynamically depending on local contrast. mental ray uses a variety of techniques such as edge following and jittering to detect and sample features in the image correctly without introducing sampling artifacts.

1.5.1   Transparency, Refractions, and Reflections

The choice between scanline rendering and ray tracing depends on the directional changes of rays. If there is no change in direction, scanline rendering can be used. After the first change in direction, ray tracing is used until the ray ends at a diffuse surface or at infinity. Once switched to ray tracing, mental ray does not return to scanline rendering until the next ray starts from the camera. Although scanline rendering, strictly speaking, deals with sorted geometry on a 2D plane and not with 3D rays in the sense of ray tracing, we use the term "ray" for both methods for simplicity because the difference is one of implementation only, and is not in any way visible to mental ray users or even shader writers.

Figures 1.5, 1.6, and 1.7 show examples for the methods mental ray uses for transparency, refraction, and reflection, respectively.

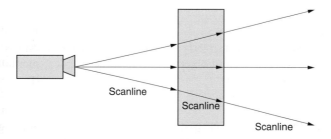

Figure 1.5: Transparency.

It is more efficient to use refraction only if necessary because scanline rendering is in most cases faster than ray tracing. As described later (page 123), transparency is refraction with an index of refraction of 1.0.

The ray directions are under control of the material shader of the object on the right side of each diagram. Typically they will cast the secondary rays in the directions shown, but are free to cast rays in any direction. For example, a shader may perturb the secondary ray direction to create glossy reflections instead of the normal specular reflections. Objects may also be refractive (or

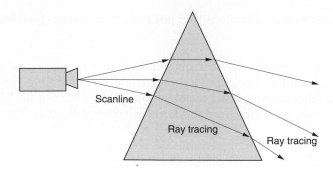

Figure 1.6: Refraction.

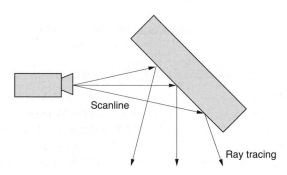

Figure 1.7: Reflection.

transparent) and reflective at the same time, and cast any number of rays of any type from any point, even from empty space.

1.5.2　Shadows

Shadows are important visual cues that greatly enhance the quality of rendered images. Without shadows, images look flat and unreal, and objects seem to float in space. mental ray supports two kinds of methods to compute shadows:

- **shadow map** shadows are precomputed depth maps attached to light sources that allow determination of whether any point in the scene is in shadow with respect to a given light source, without having to search for occluding (shadow-casting) objects. Shadow maps, once computed, can be used in multiple rendered images as long as the shadow does not move (due to movement of the light source, the occluding object, or the object in shadow). This algorithm is fast, but less precise and does not support transparent shadows cast by transparent objects. Shadow maps support soft shadows using various shadow map softness parameters. Computation of a shadow map does not require ray tracing; the algorithm is basically a variant of scanline rendering. See page 148 for details.

- **Ray tracing** additionally supports ray-traced shadows. They are always precise and physically correct and allow transparency, such as the colored shadows cast by a stained glass window, but often at a cost of a lower performance. Raytraced shadows support soft shadows from area light sources. See page 139 for details.

The choice of algorithm depends on the definition of the light source. Light sources may be marked to create shadow mapped shadows. This is independent of tracing visible lights as described in the previous section; any illuminated point may compute shadows either way. Even in pure ray-traced scenes that do not use scanline rendering at all, shadow map shadows are sufficient if none of the shadow-casting objects are transparent.

1.5.3 Motion Blur

Motion blurring is an effect caused by objects that move while the camera shutter is open, exposing the film. It causes the moving objects to be blurred. Motion blurring is often a very subtle effect, making movement in animations appear smooth where sharp snapshots would cause jerky movement. Like shadows, motion blur is supported for scanline rendering and ray tracing in different ways, but the difference is hidden and does not require any user interaction. The end result is indistinguishable regardless of the method.

The rasterizer[3.4], previously named Rapid Motion[3.2], variant of scanline rendering performs motion blurring faster by baking colors into triangles. If the triangle moves, the baked-in color is simply re-used for every pixel (or subpixel) it moves across without calling the material shader again to compute a new color, as regular scanline rendering and ray tracing do. This accelerates rendering, but it also has the effect of "dragging" effects like reflections and shadows with the moving object.

As a special performance optimization, it is possible to turn off motion blur for shadow mapped shadows to achieve maximum performance. By default, the shadow of a motion-blurred object is motion-blurred as well. See page 237 for details.

1.5.4 Lenses

Lens shaders are attached to the camera and can perform two functions: alter the origin and direction of the primary rays originating at the camera, or modify the color returned by the primary rays, or both. The first use allows distorting effects such as fisheye lenses and depth of field, and the second can be used to compute lens flares and other per-sample post effects. (Post effects that work on the entire finished image are performed by output shaders.)

Lens shaders that modify the origin or direction of primary rays require that scanline rendering is disabled, because altering ray directions requires ray tracing. Lens shaders may set options to disable scanline rendering automatically.

1.6   Caustics, Global Illumination, and Photon Maps

mental ray supports a class of algorithms simulating caustics and global illumination[2.1]:

- **Caustics** are light patterns formed by focused light. When light hits a reflective or refractive surface, it will be reflected or transmitted and form light patterns on other objects. An example would be a lens focusing light on a table, or waves of a swimming pool surface causing wavy light patterns to appear on the bottom of the swimming pool. Caustics are a subset of global illumination simulation but are handled separately to simplify modeling and increase performance. See page 190 for details.

- **Global illumination** simulation handles arbitrary diffuse, glossy, and specular reflection and transmission. The diffuse interreflection of light in a room of diffuse surfaces will indirectly light objects not directly illuminated by light sources. Objects close to a colored surface will receive colored indirect light, an effect known as *color bleeding*. Specular reflection and transmission occurs on smooth polished surfaces; glossy reflection and transmission occurs on non-polished frosted surfaces, and diffuse reflection and transmission occurs on rough surfaces such as wallpaper. See page 198 for details.

- **Final gathering** is a technique that improves on global illumination by gathering many illumination calculations at shading time, in order to make indirect illumination more smooth. Final gathering can also be used without enabling global illumination; this often improves performance and artistic control, at the cost of losing some light paths. Final gathering cannot replace caustics. Still, for film production work where physical correctness is not an important issue (unlike in CAD and physical simulation applications), final gathering is commonly used exclusively.

By default, mental ray renders both caustics and global illumination in a physically correct way, which means they will accurately simulate lighting situations in the real world in a way that can be proven. This is important in architecture visualizations, where it is necessary to make sure that all areas are properly lit, or in industrial design where poorly lit areas and unwanted glare must be avoided. However, explicit deviation from physical correctness is possible if only a visually pleasing effect is needed, for example by "turning off" or modifying the inverse-square falloff law for light energy.

mental ray's global illumination simulates *all* forms of light transport, including ray-traced reflections of caustics and any sequence of specular, glossy, and diffuse interactions on the path from the light to the camera, unlike classical mesh-subdivision radiosity methods that only support a subset of all possible interaction sequences.

Both caustics and global illumination involve a preprocessing step called *photon tracing*, also called *forward ray tracing*. This involves emitting simulated idealized photons from light sources and following them as they bounce around in the scene until they get absorbed by dark diffuse surfaces. The end result of this phase is a Photon Map™ data structure, which is then used during the subsequent scanline rendering or ray tracing pass to collect photons when calculating illumination. Photon maps can also be saved to and reloaded from files on disk.

1.7   Participating Media

Participating media are a variant of global illumination where photons interact with particles occupying a space, rather than with diffuse solid surfaces. The technique is called *participating media* because there are media, such as dusty air or water with floating particles, that participate in light transport by absorbing some of the light and hence becoming visible. Like regular surface-based caustics and global illumination, mental ray's participating media support is physically correct unless explicitly changed.

Examples include visible shafts of light when sunlight falls through a room with a dusty atmosphere, or underwater light beams caused by focused light patterns from the wavy surface traveling through murky water.

1.8   Parallelism

Parallelism refers to the ability to employ more than a single processor to render images. mental ray supports two modes of parallelism:

- **Thread parallelism** allows machines with multiple processors to cooperate when tessellating and rendering a scene. mental ray splits the entire job into many small tasks that are distributed to all available processors in a way that maximizes performance by load balancing. There is no configuration required to make use of multiple processors. If processors are available mental ray will use them unless told otherwise.

- **Network parallelism** allows multiple machines on a common network to cooperate when rendering an image. The same mechanisms are used as for thread parallelism, except that communication channels between machines are set up between all participating machines using TCP/IP socket protocols. The participating machines can be dissimilar; mental ray can connect machines regardless of CPU type, byte order, 32 or 64 bit architecture, and operating system (Unix or Windows NT). The mental ray versions must be reasonably close; mental ray will reject machines running incompatible mental ray versions. Typically, versions differing in the first two digits (like 3.2.1 amd 3.3.1) are not compatible; if the first two digits agree (like 3.3.1 and 3.3.2) they are probably, but not necessarily, compatible.

  On a network, the machine where mental ray is started by the user is called the *client machine*, and all other machines that help the client machine are called *server machines*. Before a machine can be used as a server machine, mental ray must be installed on it so that a certain TCP/IP port is waiting to accept connections from client machines. A server machine can simultaneously accept connections from multiple client machines while keeping both jobs separate.

Since network parallelism incurs a certain startup and communication overhead, there will be an optimal number of server machines depending on a number of variables such as the scene size and complexity, the network bandwidth, and the speed of the individual machines. mental ray attempts to balance the load across the machines and to conserve network bandwidth, but there is a point at which adding more machines does not significantly improve performance. Increasing the number of processors on a single machine may also incur some overhead, but mental ray scales very well to large machines with 16 processors and more. In general, it is more effective to have few machines with many processors each than many machines with few processors each.

The design of mental ray's virtual shared database for scene storage ensures that all connected processors, regardless of whether they are in the client machine or in one of the server machines, are equal in terms of the view of the scene database and the jobs to perform. No modifications to the scene or to shaders are necessary to take advantage of parallelism, as long as new custom shaders are written according to a few general rules for parallel programming.

1.9   Stages of Image Generation

Conceptually, the operation of mental ray 2.x can be divided into stages:

- Reading the scene from a scene file, or constructing it with a client application using the Application Programming Interface (API).

- Traversing the scene graph, building new geometric objects and other scene subgraphs using geometry shaders, and marking objects for tessellation (conversion to renderable triangles).

- Tessellation of all objects that have not yet been tessellated, or have changed since the last tessellation.

- Computation of shadow maps if there are light sources that specify shadow map rendering of shadows, and whose shadow maps cannot or should not be loaded from files on disk.

- Computation of the photon map if caustics or global illumination are enabled, and the photon map required for these features cannot or should not be loaded from an existing file on disk.

- Creation of acceleration data structures such as a BSP tree if ray tracing is enabled.

- Rendering the image, using a combination of scanline rendering and ray tracing, and making use of shadow maps and photon maps if available. For each image sample, the renderer proceeds with:

    { scanline rendering initially and for subsequent transparency, unless disabled explicitly or by certain lens shaders.

    { ray tracing for reflections and refractions, unless disabled.

- Running output shaders if specified, and writing output images.

In practice, these stages may overlap in certain cases. mental ray also exploits incremental changes to the scene database and cached information from earlier rendered frames of an animation in order to avoid redundancy and increase performance. For example, if an incremental change only involves a shader parameter, such as an object surface color, mental ray can re-render only the affected pixels while omitting all other stages normally leading up to rendering. This is useful for tuning shader parameters with minimum turnaround time.

mental ray 3.x does not use stages at all. As described on page 431, its dataflow architecture dynamically arranges the order of operations to minimize memory usage and runtime, and does not require that all operations in one of the above stages to be completed before the next stage can begin. Although the requirements of the algorithms can impose some implicit ordering, such as doing more tessellation than rendering initially, mental ray tends to show the first rendered pixel rectangles very early on, and often keeps on tessellating individual objects and rendering pieces of shadow maps all the time until image rendering finishes.

1.10   mental ray Configurations

There are several different ways of setting up a scene in the scene database. The simplest way, which is used in examples throughout this book, is loading a file on disk into the standalone mental ray program. The file describes the scene in a special language used in this book, and fully described in the mental ray Reference Manual [PROG]. Scene file names normally have the extension .mi and are called *mi files*. Rendering a scene then becomes a matter of typing a command line such as

```
ray scenefile.mi
```

at a shell prompt. mental ray also accepts a large number of command line options that can be inserted after the program name ray to override scene parameters or configure mental ray. The -help option provides a list of allowed options.

mental ray is also available as a library that is built into client applications that provide a graphical user interface and extended modeling and animation capabilities. In this configuration, no mi files are needed; the client application sets up the scene database directly using the Application Programming Interface (API) of mental ray. For information on how to load scenes and render them, refer to the client application's user manual.

For more information on the mental ray API refer to the second edition of volume 2 of this series, "Programming mental ray" [PROG].

Finally, the parts of the API that deal with scene database access (as opposed to network and library configurations) are also available to a type of custom shaders called *geometry shaders* that generate procedural geometry and other scene elements.

1.11   mental ray Versions

mental ray version numbers, as reported by ray -version at a shell prompt, consist of three or four parts:

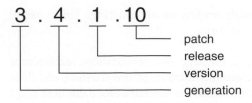

Generations identify different products. Scenes are generally backward compatible but not forward compatible (that is, older scenes work with newer versions but not vice versa), except in isolated cases (for example, contour rendering was completely redesigned in the second generation). Shaders need to be changed and recompiled for new generations.

Versions indicate major revisions, introducing new feature sets. Scenes are fully backward compatible. They are also forward compatible unless a feature was used that is only available in the newer version. Shaders need not be changed or recompiled, unless otherwise noted in the release notes. (mental ray 3.4 requires modifications to output shaders.)

Releases indicate minor upgrades. Minor new features are introduced, and miscellaneous changes and bug fixes are consolidated. Scenes are fully backward compatible. They are also forward compatible unless a feature was used that is only available in the newer version. Shaders need not be changed or recompiled.

Patches show the number of changes since the first release. These changes are usually made in response to bug reports, minor feature requests, or new platform ports. This number tends to increment quickly because every build gets a new patch number, including those that are not shipped to customers.

There are three generations of mental ray: 1.9 is obsolete, it was replaced with mental ray 2.0 in April 1996 and mental ray 2.1 in early 1999. The predominant generation now is mental ray 3.x, first available in Summer 2001. The current version, mental ray 3.4, became available in early 2005. This book does not apply to mental ray 1.9, which uses a simpler scene description language and lacks many features available in mental ray 2.0 and later. Although the concepts are similar, none of the scene examples in this book will work unchanged with mental ray 1.9. mental ray 2.x and 3.x will accept 1.9 scene files, falling back on language variants not described in this book.

1.11.1   Changes between Versions 2.0 and 2.1

Here is a list of new features in mental ray 2.1 that were added since mental ray 2.0:

- global illumination and multiple volume scattering (caustics are already supported in version 2.0),

- exclusion of objects from caustic processing using `caustic off` flags in object and instance definitions,

- exclusion of objects from global illumination processing using `globillum off` flags in object and instance definitions,

- support for space curves and subdivision surfaces,

- Delaunay triangulation and the "`any`" approximation modifier,

- quality control for the JPEG/JFIF image file format,

- user frame buffers,

- user data blocks and the `data` shader parameter type, and labels in instances and instance groups,

- OpenGL scanline rendering and shadowmap generation acceleration,

- Mitchell and Lanczos sampling filters,

- keystone distortion,

- sampling visualization,

- moving light sources (lights whose instances contain a motion transformation that motion-blurs the shadows and highlights from these lights),

- Motion blurring is up to five times as fast,

- parallelized output shaders, and

- explicit color clipping modes.

Shaders and scene files written for mental ray 2.0 work with mental ray 2.1 unchanged, with the exception of shaders (usually geometry shaders) that access internal data structures that are part of the geometry shader interface. The reverse is also true unless the shader or scene uses a feature only available in mental ray 2.1. Network rendering requires identical versions (generation, version, release, and patch) of mental ray 2.0 on both client and server machines; mental ray 2.1 uses a negotiation process to find out whether client and server versions are compatible.

1.11.2   Changes between Versions 2.1 and 3.0

Here is the list of new features in mental ray 3.0 that were added since mental ray 2.1:

- A new command line option `-jobmemory` controls mental ray 3.0's geometry cache. See page 431 for details on the geometry cache and new architecture.

- Geometric objects may specify bounding boxes, motion bounding boxes, and maximum displacement values. Object definitions may also be loaded on demand from .mi sub-scene files.

- Light mapping and writable textures allow creating texture maps that pack presampled illumination into texture maps.

- Floating-point TIFF is now supported for reading and writing.

- Instance materials may be marked with the `override` flag to override the material given in the object, or any instance material further down in the DAG.

- image output statements may specify `even` or `odd` modifiers for Softimage image files.

- Scanline rendering, motion blur, and final gathering use new algorithms that are faster and provide better quality. The parameters that control these features remain unchanged; however, optimal parameter values may differ between 2.1 and 3.0. It may be necessary to re-tune these features, such as reducing accuracies to achieve the same quality at better performance.

- A new final gathering mode called *fast lookup* stores irradiance information in the photon map, which slows down photon tracing but greatly accelerates final gathering.

Although mental ray 3.0 was designed to remain as compatible as possible to mental ray 2.1, it contains a number of incompatible changes:

- ray classification is no longer supported. It existed in mental ray 2.x only for backwards compatibility with mental ray 1.9.

- it is recommended that number-of-photons light statements for caustics and global illumination specify only the number of emitted photons (second argument) and leave the number of stored photons unspecified (first argument 0).

Shaders written for mental ray 2.x that depend on the number of threads or on direct access to shader user pointers will no longer work. mental ray 3.0 starts and stops threads dynamically, where 2.x always worked with a fixed set. There are also a number of minor changes that may affect shader writers; see [PROG] for details.

1.11.3   Changes between Versions 3.0 and 3.1

mental ray 3.1 is a new major version of mental rayand has a very similar interface. Very little upgrading work is necessary, but there are a number of additional features.

- A new hierarchical grid acceleration algorithm was introduced that allows much better control than the old static grid accelerator in mental ray2.1.

- Multipass rendering and merging is now supported. Render passes are independent renders of portions of the same scene, each generating a subsample-based layer file. Layer files can be merged back when rendering the last pass, or all layers can be merged as a separate process. Merging can be done in custom merging functions. Multipass rendering was introduced in mental ray 3.1.1, and was significantly enhanced (using an incompatible syntax extension) in mental ray 3.1.2.

- The `bsp shadow on` option enables the new shadow BSP tree, which holds all shadow objects. The main BSP tree then only holds trace objects. This is useful if the scene contains simplified shadow stand-in geometry and has very low shadow ray coherence, for example if a light dome computed from a chrome dome photograph is used.

- Objects may specify min and max sampling parameters that constrain the sampling range in the options. For eye rays that do not see any objects, the `samples` statement in the options block allows an optional default constraint.

- Multiple motion vectors are now possible, and may require changes to shaders that evaluate motion vectors. (Normally mental rayhandles motion vectors internally but post-motion output shaders might exist that access them directly.)

- A polygon vertex or free-form surface control point may have up to 15 motion vectors instead of only one. Multiple motion vectors define a path to allow curved motion blur. For motion transformations, a new `motion steps` option specifies the number of curve points to generate.

- Shutter statements may optionally define two values, a new shutter delay value defines the shutter open time in addition to the standard shutter close time.

- Two new types of area light source was introduced: one that uses any geometric object to define the shape of the light; and a user type that lets the light shader pick points on the light surface, and control integration in the material shader with *state* → *count*.

- A new hair geometry primitive was introduced that can efficiently render large numbers of hairs. These are assumed to be narrow in screen space, in the range of one pixel wide or less.

- The new fine approximation mode allows efficient tessellation of freeform surfaces and displacement to microtriangles, which allows extremely detailed displacement without the previous high memory demands. This works with all rendering modes, including shadows and self-shadowing, motion blurring, ray tracing, global illumination, etc. See page 337 for details.

- The new sharp approximation feature controls the sharpness of tessellations, by controlling the facet normals.

- New command-line options: `-approx`, `-approx_displace`, `-bsp_shadow`, `-diagnostic finalgather`, `-grid_depth`, `-grid_resolution`, `-grid_size`, `-nomaster`, `-motion_steps`, `-samples` with four arguments.

- New options block statements: `bsp shadow`, `diagnostic finalgather`, `grid depth`, `grid resolution`, `grid size`, `motion steps`, `pass`, `samples` with four arguments, `shutter` with delay argument, `traversal`. Image type `"rgbe"` in camera output statements, pass chain in the camera, `lightprofile` shader parameter type, `apply photonvol` in declarations, light profile blocks `lightprofile...end lightprofile`, `fine` and `sharp` attributes in approximations, and the `writable` attribute for texture statements. mental ray can use writable textures directly for rendering; mental ray 3.0 required a separate non-writable texture statement referencing the same file name.

- New image data types for RGBE (8-bit high dynamic range color data), and floating-point alpha and intensity channels including no-elliptic pyramid filtering for one-channel images. New image file formats IFF (Alias Maya), Radiance HDR, and HT (simple uncompressed HDR image).

- Inheritance functions are deprecated (but still supported), and replaced with the more powerful traversal functions that have full control over all forms of inheritance, including flags and materials.

1.11.4   Changes between mental ray 3.1 and 3.2

mental ray3.2 is a fully backwards-compatible feature upgrade of mental ray 3.1.

- Added Rapid Motion (now called the rasterizer since mental ray 3.4) rendering algorithm that performs very efficient motion blurring by shading geometry at a single point in time, and caching and re-using the results at multiple points that the object moves across. It is enabled with the `scanline rapid` statement in the options, or the `-scanline rapid` command-line option. A new `samples collect` option statement controls second-stage sample compositing.

- Implemented scene data swapping to disk, effectively extending available memory by a region on disk. It is enabled and set up with the `-swap_dir` and `-swap_limit` command-line arguments.

- Shadowmap files now contain extra information at the end of the regular depth data that defines a coordinate system for reloading the shadow map into a different scene.

- Subdivision surface rendering is supported without a separate mental matter library. (Subdivision surface *modeling* still requires mental matter.)

- Added `shadowmap rebuild merge` to light sources to read and add to existing shadowmap files.

- Added a `max displace` and `-maxdisplace` override option, useful for using mental ray 3.2 with older translators that do not generate maximum displacement distances.

- Added a `-texture_continue` command-line option that makes mental ray continue if a texture file cannot be found, instead of aborting immediately.

- Support for limited forward referencing of instances, objects, objects, lights, and cameras.

- Objects that are only visible but not traced are no longer visible to rays and photons. This is an issue for final gathering and all shaders that use ray tracing.

- The maximum length of mental ray tokens was increased to 4095 characters, and message length limits are increased as well.

- Camera output statements now accept the new image format png (Portable Network Graphics), and Alias IFF files accept "+rgba,z" as a data type string.

- New statements in the options block:

```
scanline rapid
samples collect N
shadowmap only
finalgather rebuild freeze
finalgather falloff N
finalgather depth N N N
finalgather filter N
displace presample on|off
acceleration large bsp
motion on|off
max displace N
filter clip lanczos
filter clip mitchell
photon autovolume on|off
```

New statements in objects and instances:

```
visible trace shadow globillum caustics approximate ...
approximate regular parametric N% N%
approximate ...   sharp N
```
(with a floating-point N)

New statements in instances:

```
override ...   approximate ...
```

New statements in light sources:

```
shadowmap rebuild merge
```

New statements in cameras:

```
pass "typelist" ...
```

New commands:

```
touch E
```

- New command-line options: `-scanline rapid`

```
-samples_collect N
-shadowmap_only
-finalgather_rebuild freeze
-finalgather_falloff N
-finalgather_depth N N N
-finalgather_filter N
-swap_dir S
-swap_limit N
-texture_continue
-memory N
```
(`-jobmemory` is obsolete and removed)
```
-displace_presample on|off
-acceleration largebsp
-echo incremental
-motion on|off
-maxdisplace N
```

1.11.5   Changes between mental ray 3.2 and 3.3

- Introduced detail shadowmaps that can multisample shadowmap pixels, and also call shadow shaders on shadow-casting geometry to obtain and store transparent shadows.

- Shadowmaps can now specify a shadowmap bias to replace the standard Woo trick, which stores the halfway distance between the first two shadow-casting objects, with a fixed distance. The bias can also be set in the options. Although Woo shadowmaps are generally superior, they are not compatible with shadowmap merging, which was also added to mental ray 3.3 to support shadows cast from one rendering pass on another. Note that mental ray 3.3 will read shadowmap files created with older versions of mental ray, but older versions cannot read the new 3.3 format.

- Shadowmaps also support extra fields supplied by a camera attached to the light source.

- Uncompressed HDR (High Dynamic Range) images are now supported in addition to compressed HDR images.

- Performance improvements: Light emitter shaders now work several times faster. Raytracing motion-blurred hair geometry, and hair rendering in general, is also several times faster. Significantly improved final gathering performance for surfaces with very strong bump mapping; for extreme bump mapping, performance can increase by a factor of 10. Scenes with very large numbers of instances are rendered much faster with far reduced memory overhead. Frame buffers now take about half as much space.

- Large finely displaced objects of which only a very small part is in the viewing frustum, and the bulk of the object to the side or behind the camera, are now handled much more efficiently. Much less subdivision effort is expended on invisible portions of such objects.

- For hyperthreaded Intel CPUs and Linux, the `-threads` command-line option now includes hyperthreaded pseudo CPUs. These pseudo-CPUs will not consume licenses.

- Autovolume mode no longer requires ray tracing.

- Multihosted rendering could get wedged in mental ray 3.2 under certain circumstances. mental ray 3.3 has a new networking algorithm that is completely stable, and also much faster, permitting more slave hosts to contribute efficiently.

- The multipass rendering file format was changed. Old files can be imported, but older versions of mental ray cannot read the new format.

- mental ray is now much more frugal with stack allocations. The default stack size was reduced from 4 MB to 512 KB. This reduces memory requirements and the risk of being unable to start another thread. If 512 KB is insufficient, it can be overridden with the `MI_STACKSIZE` environment variable.

- Detail shadowmaps introduce several new statements to light blocks: `shadowmap detail`, `shadowmap detail samples`, `shadowmap accuracy`, `shadowmap color`, and `shadowmap alpha`. Also, `shadowmap bias` was added for biased, non-Woo shadowmaps.

- ILM's OpenEXR 1.1 image file format is now supported. It is installed as an external library that is part of the mental ray distribution. The BW/A variant of Alias IFF image files is now supported. RGBE frame buffers are no longer gamma-corrected.

- Double-quoted strings may now contain the sequence
  ", which denotes a literal double quote. This makes it possible to put literal double quotes inside strings, which can be useful for `system` commands.

- Added conditionals to the language, such as `$ifdef` and `$ifeq`.

- Added an `offscreen` flag to approximations to disable coarse tessellations outside the viewing frustum.

- Added a `touch` statement to mark objects for re-evaluation.

- It is now possible to attach multiple finalgather file names to the options block.

- Shader parameters of type *light* now accept instances of light groups, in addition to instances of lights. The light group contains instances of lights that will be treated as if they were a single light.

- Added namespace support, using `namespace ... end namespace` brackets. Elements inside a namespace N can be referenced by prefixing their name with $N::$. Inside a namespace, a global symbol S can be referenced as $::S$.

- Hair geometry can now be rendered in Rapid Motion (called rasterizer since mental ray 3.4) mode.

- Numerical non-array shader parameters may be declared with defaults using a `default` keyword in the declaration block.

- The hard *max* limit of 7 for approximation subdivision has been removed for displacement approximations.

- Materials can omit the material shader, and objects and instances may specify the new flag `shadowmap off`. Both are useful for hull objects that are not visible themselves but enclose volume effects such as visible light cones.

1.11.6   Changes between mental ray 3.3 and 3.4

- Replaced the Rapid Motion algorithm with a new renderer called the *rasterizer*, which is an alternative to the regular scanline renderer. For backwards compatibility, the existing controlling options were mostly retained except as described below.

- Added color profiles.

- The `samples collect` statement, which sets the number of samples filtered by the rasterizer, now defaults to 4 (16 samples) instead of defaulting to a number derived from the oversampling parameters.

- The `shading samples` statement sets the number of shading points per pixel taken by the rasterizer.

- The `hardware samples` statement controls the supersampling and multisampling settings of the hardware renderer.

- The `finalgather trace depth` statement has another parameter to control the diffuse trace depth.

- The `lightmap` and `lightmap only` statements control light mapping.

- The `photonmap only` statements controls photon mapping.

- The `caustic scale`, `globillum scale`, and `finalgather scale` statements supply a scaling factor to the brightness of these effects.

- The `finalgather presample density` statement adjusts the number of finalgather points during finalgather preprocessing, as a correction factor.

- The `colorspace` statements, and their references in output and texture statements, control the color space (sRGB, CIE, etc) used for rendering, loading, and saving images.

- The `compress` modifier on output statements selects OpenEXR compression modes `none`, `piz`, `zip`, `rle`, or `pxr24`.

- The `trace` flag in instances and objects was replaced with separate `reflection`, `refraction`, `transparency`, and `finalgather` flags that follow the syntax of `globillum`. So does the `shadow` flag.

- The `shadowmap filter` statement in a light definition controls shadowmap filtering.

- A new variant of directional light can be specified by supplying both an `origin` and a `direction`, but not `spread` because that would turn the light into a spot light. A directional light with an origin does not illuminate points behind the plane defined by the origin and direction.

- The `volume group` statement in an object ties together all objects with the same object group number such that autovolume mode treats them as belonging to the same object with a single inside volume.

- The `nosmoothing` flag in approximations turns off a smoothing procedure which is otherwise used by default during fine polygon displacement.

- The `contour` and `contour normal` approximation modes were removed.

- The new command-line option `-fb_dir` *S* specifies a directory where mental ray can save frame buffer files while rendering. Frame buffers can be very large, and mental ray 3.4 has no upper limit on the number of frame buffers, so they are no longer permanently stored in memory but can be paged out to disk.

Chapter 2

Scene Construction

The purpose of the mental ray rendering software is the generation of images from scene descriptions. A scene description is a high-level 3D "blueprint" of elements such as geometric objects, lights, and a camera that looks at the scene. Scenes can be created by writing an appropriate text file using a text editor, but in general scenes will be too complex for that and are created by modeling, animation, and CAD tools instead. However, this book uses simple scenes that can be typed in with a text editor, or taken from the sample scenes provided with the mental ray distribution.

The images are generated by mental ray taking the place of the camera, looking out at the geometric and other objects in the scene, and taking into account lighting and a number of other effects. The end result are digital images, which are described as two-dimensional array of pixels. Often the goal is to generate photorealistic images, but other styles such as contour images for cartoon animation are also possible.

All aspects of rendering are controlled by the scene, including the surface properties (called "materials") of geometric objects, lighting, camera parameters such as the focal length, volume effects such as fog, and various rendering modes. Therefore, to generate an image from a scene file using the standalone mental ray renderer, it is sufficient to type the following command at a shell prompt:

    ray *scenefile.mi*

Here, ray is the name of the standalone mental ray program, and *scenefile.mi* is the name of a file containing the scene description. By convention, scene description files end with the extension .mi, and are often called "mi files". mental ray also accepts a large number of command line options that override some aspects of the scene. For example:

    ray -o output.pic -resolution 720 576 *scenefile.mi*

causes the rendered image to be named output.pic, at a resolution of 720×576 pixels, instead of the name and resolution specified in *scenefile.mi*. All command line options begin with a dash, and many have parameters. For a complete list of command line options, see appendix A.

The rest of this chapter introduces the features of mental ray, beginning with a trivial scene. The scene file examples shown do not list all possible permutations and options of each scene file element used; this is the purpose of the mental ray Reference Manual [PROG].

2.1   A Simple Scene

This chapter begins with a simple scene consisting of a camera, a light, a cube, and other elements. First, the elements of this scene will be discussed in general terms. This scene will then become the basis of the rest of the following chapters, which introduce various mental ray features using appropriate modifications to the simple scene.

```
verbose on
link "base.so"
$include <base.mi>

options "opt"
        samples         -1 2
        contrast        0.1  0.1  0.1
        object space
end options

camera "cam"
        frame           1
        output          "rgb" "out.rgb"
        focal           50
        aperture        44
        aspect          1
        resolution      800 800
end camera

instance "cam_inst" "cam"
        transform       0.7719  0.3042 -0.5582 0.0
                        0.0000  0.8781  0.4785 0.0
                        0.6357 -0.3693  0.6778 0.0
                        0.0000  0.0000 -2.5000 1.0
end instance

light "light1"
        "mib_light_point" (
            "color"     1 1 1,
            "factor"    0.75
        )
        origin          0 0 0
end light

instance "light1_inst" "light1"
        transform       1  0  0  0
                        0  1  0  0
                        0  0  1  0
```

```
                                -2  -3  -2   1
        end instance

material "mtl"
        opaque
        "mib_illum_phong" (
            "ambient"   0.5  0.5  0.5,
            "diffuse"   0.7  0.7  0.7,
            "ambience"  0.3  0.3  0.3,
            "specular"  1.0  1.0  1.0,
            "exponent"  50,
            "mode"      1,
            "lights"    ["light1_inst"]
        )
end material

object "cube1"
        visible trace shadow
        tag 1
        group
                -0.5 -0.5 -0.5
                -0.5 -0.5  0.5
                -0.5  0.5 -0.5
                -0.5  0.5  0.5
                 0.5 -0.5 -0.5
                 0.5 -0.5  0.5
                 0.5  0.5 -0.5
                 0.5  0.5  0.5

                v 0   v 1   v 2   v 3
                v 4   v 5   v 6   v 7

                p "mtl" 0  1  3  2
                p       1  5  7  3
                p       5  4  6  7
                p       4  0  2  6
                p       4  5  1  0
                p       2  3  7  6
        end group
end object

instance "cube1_inst" "cube1"
        transform       1  0  0  0
                        0  1  0  0
                        0  0  1  0
                        0  0  0  1
end instance

instgroup "rootgrp"
        "cam_inst" "light1_inst" "cube1_inst"
end instgroup

render "rootgrp" "cam_inst" "opt"
```

If you copy this text into a file `cube.mi` and render it with the command `ray cube.mi`, you will get an image file `out.rgb`, containing an image as shown in figure 2.1.

Figure 2.1: Simple cube.

This image file can be displayed on the screen with a viewer such as `imf_disp`. If you use other viewers or editing programs, you may have to convert the image to another format. The examples in this book use the SGI `rgb` format which is understood by many common utilities such as *xv*. To convert to another format, use the `imf_copy` utility, or use the `-file_type` command line option of mental ray with another file type. To summarize:

`imf_disp out.rgb`	*display the image on the screen*
`ray -file_type pic cube.mi`	*render a Softimage PIC image*
`imf_copy out.rgb out.jpg`	*convert to a JPEG image*

The imf_disp and imf_copy utilities are part of the mental ray distribution.

Note that the images in this book are shown on a white background, while display utilities like imf_disp will show a black background. mental ray computes an "alpha channel" that assigns an opacity value to each pixel, which makes it possible to distinguish objects from the background. This allows compositing the image. Not all image file formats support alpha channels: `rgb` and `pic` do, but `jpg` does not. For more information on image file formats, see page 296.

2.2   Anatomy of a Scene

Let's return to the scene file, `cube.mi`. It begins with two commands, `verbose` and `$include`, followed by the definition of toplevel elements (such as lights or instances), and ends with a `render` command. First, some general observations:

- The file consists of printable ASCII text, and can be edited with a standard text editor. However, mental ray also supports a binary extension to compress vectors, which make up the bulk of most scene files. The binary format can cause problems when trying to modify a scene file with some text editors that cannot handle binary data. All examples will use ASCII.

- Whitespace is not relevant. As long as keywords and numbers are separated, blanks, tabs, and newlines can be inserted anywhere without changing the scene, except between quotes.

- Numbers can contain periods, leading zeroes, and exponential notation. 1, 1.0, 0.5, .5, -.5, 1.609e-27 are all valid examples for numbers (the last one means $1.609 \cdot 10^{-27}$). mental ray distinguishes integers (no decimal point, no scientific notation) from real numbers. Integers can be used instead of real numbers (with one exception: weights in rational parameter lists), but not vice versa.

- Double quotes delimit strings. Any character except newline and double quote is valid in strings. When choosing names, avoid periods and colons because they have a special meaning in some contexts (namely, shader parameter names and namespaces[3.3]).

- Named elements must be defined before the element name can be used in another element. Forward referencing is not allowed, except in mental ray 3.3 and later, and there only for instances, groups, and instanced elements. Elements whose names are never used are stored, but do not take part in rendering.

- Scene files consist of simple *commands*, such as `verbose` and `$include`, and *top-level elements*. Top-level elements cannot be defined inside other elements. All top-level elements are defined with a double-quoted name, which can later be used to reference the element within other elements. Most top-level elements support many different substatements and have the form `X ... end X`, with `X` being the type of the top-level element. They are listed below.

- Scene files always contain procedural elements, called "shaders". A shader appears in the scene file as a double-quoted shader name, followed by a parenthesized list of shader parameters that control the behavior of the shader. For example, the `"mib_illum_phong"` shader[1] used in the material element specifies a set of surface properties, based on some shader-specific parameters such as the `"ambient"` color. Some basic shaders come with the mental ray distribution, but custom shaders written in C or C++ or other languages are also accepted. There are many different kinds of shaders for different purposes; see the second book of this series [PROG] for details.

- The `options` top-level element contains an `object space` statement. This statement specifies that geometric objects are specified in object coordinates, which means that each

---

[1] All shaders whose name begins with "mib" are found in the mental images base shader library, called `base.so`.

object, light, and camera has its own coordinate space, usually with the coordinate origin at the center of the object. mental ray also supports a `camera space` option which specifies that all objects, lights, and the camera share the same coordinate space with the camera at the origin, but this is less useful and not used in this book.

The top-level elements defined in the simple cube scene are:

options
: Options control the behavior of mental ray. They can be used to enable or disable features such as shadow casting or caustics, control the render quality, and modify global modes. Options stay constant for the entire rendering operation.

camera
: The camera simulates a real-world camera that looks at the scene. It is normally a pinhole camera (which means that everything is in focus), but can be changed by adding lenses (in the form of "lens shaders"). The camera also has a focal length and an aperture (which together define the field of view), and it specifies the image resolution, pixel aspect ratio, and the image file or files to write. See page 39.

light
: Lights illuminate the scene. Without lights, the scene would be very dark. Exactly how a light illuminates a geometric object depends on shaders attached to that object. For example, the `"mib_illum_phong"` shader used in the cube example above uses a light to calculate diffuse and specular illumination.

object
: Objects contain geometry, described by direct specification of polygons or free-form surfaces. The example specifies a single cube consisting of six simple polygons. See page 312.

instance
: Instances are the glue that hold a scene together. Since camera, light, and object definitions do not contain information about their relationship in the scene, instances must also be defined that reference them. The instances "add" information to the camera, light, and objects; primarily a transformation matrix but also optional visibility, material, and motion information. If the options specify `object space`, the transformation matrix in the instance specify the position and orientation of the instanced element in 3D space. See page 371.

instgroup
: Instance groups are simple containers that bundle multiple instances into one unit. Instance groups can themselves be instanced and bundled into another instance group. The top instance group, the only one that is not itself instanced, is called the *root group*; this is the group being named in the `render` command. The order of elements in an instance group does not matter.

material
: Materials define the surface and volume properties of geometric objects. Every polygon and free-form surface must have a material, either by naming it in the object definition or by inheriting it from an instance (for inheritance, see page 379). Every material references a material shader, which is responsible for the surface properties such as illumination and texturing. Materials may also reference other shaders that control volume properties, shadowing, photon map interaction, displacement, and others. It is important to distinguish materials

from material shaders. See page 49.

There are other top-level elements that are not used in the simple cube example. They will appear in later chapters, but are listed here for completeness:

texture   Top-level texture elements define images on disk that are used by material and other shaders for wrapping textures on objects, projector lights, environment reflection maps, and so on. The texture element merely loads the image file; how it is used depends on the shader that references the texture. See page 57.

shader   Shader definitions give a name to a parameterized shader. For example, "mib_illum_phong" and its parenthesized parameters in the cube example could be given the name "gray" using a shader statement. The "mtl" material would then only reference "gray" instead of "mib_illum_phong" and its parameters. This is useful if a parameterized shader is used many times.

declare   Before a shader like "mib_illum_phong" can be used, it must be declared so that mental ray knows what type it is and what the names and types of all its parameters are. For example, the declaration for "mib_illum_phong" specifies that it returns a color, can be used as material, shadow, and photon shader, and has many parameters such as "ambient", which is a color, and "shiny", which is a scalar (real number). All shaders must be declared before their first use. The declaration does not appear in the example because it is in a separate file, base.mi, that is loaded in ("included") at the beginning of the example with a $include command. See page 272.

userdata   is a container for arbitrary data that is not used by mental ray, but can be passed to shaders by parameter.

Defining top-level elements with a name, and then using these names in the subsequent definition of other elements, which themselves have names that may be referenced in other elements, introduces a hierarchy into a scene. The hierarchy of the cube example scene is very simple (figure 2.2). The material and the shader are not shown.

The three instances all have different instance transformation matrices that move the instanced elements and their inherent object coordinate spaces to different locations in world space. The camera is moved backwards by 2.5 units on the world Z axis (which points towards the viewer) and has a rotation component in the upper $3{\times}3$ part which makes it point slightly down and to one side while looking at the world space origin. The light is shifted to world space coordinate $(2, 3, 2)$; and the cube is centered at the world space origin.

All matrices operate from parent to local space. In the case of the cube, for example, the local space is the object space of the cube used to define all its vertices, and the parent space is world space because the cube instance is directly attached to the root group. For example, if the cube instance transformation matrix had no rotation or scaling but a translation (first three values of the last row) of (230), its object space vertex coordinates $(0.5\ 0.5\ 0.5)$ would be translated to $(-1.5\ -2.5\ 0.5)$ in world space, effectively moving the cube two units to the left and three units down.

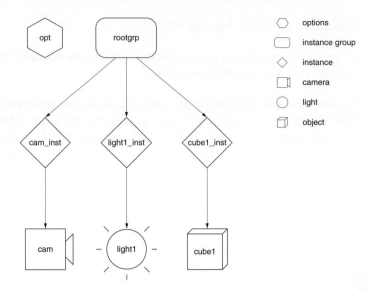

Figure 2.2: Simple cube scene hierarchy.

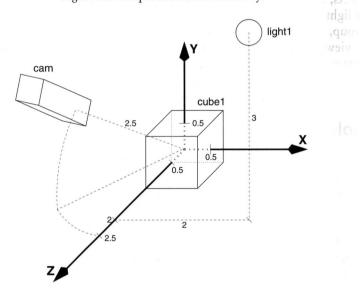

Figure 2.3: Coordinate space of a cube.

In figure 2.3 the cube's local coordinate system and the world coordinate system coincide because the cube's instance transformation matrix is the identity matrix.

Chapter 3

Cameras

Rendering a scene means looking at the scene from the viewpoint of a camera, calculating the view, and recording it in an image file. The camera is part of the scene, just like lights and geometric objects, and has its own instance that defines its position and orientation in 3D space, again just like lights and objects. Unlike objects, however, the camera instance must be attached to the root group, to prevent multiple instancing of the camera. The scene cannot be rendered from multiple viewpoints simultaneously. It is, however, possible to define multiple cameras and attach their camera instances to the root group; the one to be used must be passed to the `render` statement. See the simple cube example on page 32 for a very simple scene setup.

3.1   Pinhole Cameras

The default camera is a pinhole camera. The name derives from the *camera obscura*, a dark box with a tiny hole in one wall that lets light enter to project an image on the opposite wall. Unlike a real pinhole camera, however, the mental ray rendering software does not render images upside-down. One important property of a pinhole camera is that its imaging properties can be described by only one parameter, the *field of view*. By convention, the field of view is actually described by two parameters, the *aperture*, which is the width of the image on the viewing plane, and the *focal length*, which is the distance from the pinhole camera to the viewing plane. The viewing plane is a conceptual plane that the image "seen" by the camera is projected onto, and later written out to disk. Figure 3.1 shows a pinhole camera, seen from the top.

The point where the rays enter the camera is the origin (coordinate $(0, 0, 0)$) of camera space. See section 14.4 for more details on coordinate spaces.

3.2   Image Resolution

mental ray needs some additional parameters to describe the camera. First, it needs to know the image resolution, in pixels, which becomes the size of the image to render. Since the horizontal

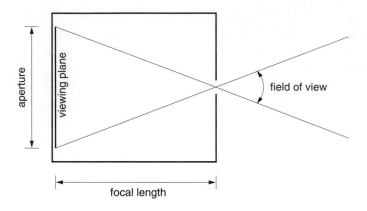

Figure 3.1: Pinhole camera.

and vertical image resolution need not be the same, by convention the aperture corresponds to the horizontal resolution. The "vertical aperture" is not relevant, but could be computed by dividing the aperture by the horizontal pixel resolution and multiplying it by the vertical pixel resolution. In other words, aperture and horizontal resolution describe the same thing, but the former is in camera space and the latter in raster space (measured in pixels on the resulting rendered image). Camera space is related to world space by the camera instance.

Although the image resolution must be given in pixels, mental ray does not normally measure things in pixels. Object dimensions, distances, aperture and focal length, and nearly everything else is in camera, world, or object space, using abstract measurement units. (There is one exception: pixels come into play during view-dependent approximation, which adjusts the precision of geometry to the number of pixels it occupies in the image; see page 337.) The different spaces — camera, world, and object — differ mainly by their respective origins, positions, and orientations, as defined by instance transformations. Also, they are all 3D coordinates, while raster space is 2D, without depth.

3.3   Aspect Ratio

mental ray can control the aspect ratio, which is the width of the image divided by its height. This does not alter the number of pixels, which are defined by the resolution. If the viewing plane has an aspect ratio of 4:3, which means it is 1/3 wider than it is tall, its numerical aspect ratio is 1.33. This 4:3 ratio is commonly used in traditional PAL and NTSC video production (PAL plus and HDTV use a 16:9 aspect ratio), which is why mental ray's default for the aspect ratio is 1.33.

If the aspect ratio is 1.33, and the image resolution is 720×540 pixels ($\frac{720}{540} \approx 1.33$), the pixels are assumed to be square. Pixels are square on most computer screens, but analog video standards use nonsquare pixels. For example, to render a PAL image at a resolution of 720×576 pixels, at an image ratio of 4:3, pixels are slightly wider than tall, by a factor of $\frac{576}{720} \cdot \frac{4}{3} \approx 1.067$. Therefore, a sphere that looks round on a computer screen with square pixels would look squashed, slightly wider than tall, on a PAL monitor because PAL crowds 576 scanlines into the same space that is filled by 540 scanlines on the computer screen.

Therefore, to render a 720×576 pixel image to be displayed on a PAL monitor, an aspect ratio of $\frac{4}{3} \cdot 1.067 \approx 1.422$ should be used. The sphere now looks round on the PAL monitor but stretched on the computer screen. In general, larger aspect ratio values will make rendered objects look taller. The width is not affected. Here are the aspect ratio values for a few common video formats:

standard	width	height	aspect
PAL	720	576	1.422
	768	576	1.333
	702	576	1.459
NTSC	720	486	1.2
	768	486	1.125
	702	486	1.231

3.4   Keystone Distortion

Normally the viewing plane camera is centered on the viewing direction. A camera offset allows shifting the viewing plane sideways and up or down such that it is no longer centered. The resulting distortion is called *keystone distortion*[2.1]. It effectively renders extra pixels on one edge of the rendered image and drops pixels on the opposite side. The camera offset is specified in pixels, or fractions of pixels, in the camera statement:

```
offset x y
```

The default is 0.0 for both x and y, which means that the image will be centered on the camera's Z axis. Positive values translate the viewing plane up and to the right, which has the effect that objects in the rendered image move down and to the left. The offset is measured in pixel units. Figure 3.2 shows a camera with a positive offset that shifts the viewing plane up.

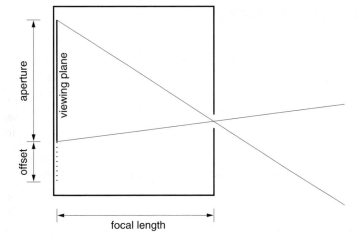

Figure 3.2: Camera offset.

3.5   Rendering Subwindows

Often it is not necessary to render the entire image. A subwindow can be specified that defines, in pixel coordinates, the lower left and the upper right corner of the section of the image to render. A subwindow is specified in the camera with a `window` statement:

> `window` xl_{int} yl_{int} xh_{int} yh_{int}

The integer pixel coordinates xl_{int} yl_{int} specify the lower left corner of the subwindow to render, and xh_{int} yh_{int} specify the upper right corner, as shown in figure 3.3.

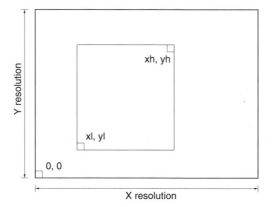

Figure 3.3: Camera window.

Only the pixels in the inner rectangle will be rendered. If the window exceeds the resolution, it is clipped back to the resolution, which means that subwindow cropping can be turned off by setting it to values like 0 0 99999 99999.

3.6   Orthographic Camera

In addition to the standard pinhole camera, mental ray also supports an orthographic camera. An orthographic camera is like a pinhole camera with an infinite focal length. A pinhole camera is switched to an orthographic camera with the statement `focal infinity` in the scene file. This means that the field of view becomes zero, and all rays are parallel, as shown in figure 3.4.

If the camera in the simple cube scene on page 32 is changed to an orthographic camera by replacing the camera definition with the following definition (identical except for the `focal` statement and the aperture, which is reduced to a size slightly larger than the object diameter as seen from the camera angle):

```
camera "cam"
        frame           1
        output          "rgb" "out.rgb"
        focal           infinity
```

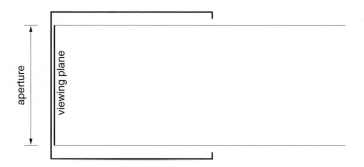

Figure 3.4: Orthographic camera.

```
        aperture        2
        aspect          1
        resolution      800 800
    end camera
```

the result would be the image on the right of figure 3.5, next to the standard pinhole camera image. The orthographic image lacks perspective. All its faces are exact parallelograms, with opposing edges being parallel.

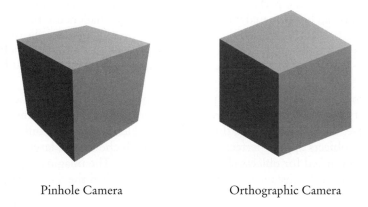

Pinhole Camera   Orthographic Camera

Figure 3.5: Pinhole and orthographic camera.

3.7   Clipping Planes *

The clipping planes define the smallest and largest distance from the camera. Only geometrical objects between these planes will be rendered; geometry outside this range will be ignored. Like the focal plane, the clipping planes are perpendicular to the camera view direction. The arguments are the distance to the near and far plane in camera space, respectively, and are also called the *hither* and *yon* planes. The defaults are 0.001 and 1 000 000.0. Smaller hither planes will be rejected for technical reasons (the perspective transformation becomes unstable). Calculations also become inaccurate if the yon plane is chosen too large.

The purpose of clipping planes is to define the valid range of geometry used by the scanline rendering algorithm. They should be chosen such that only geometry is clipped away that is too close or too distant to be visible anyway, not to create cut views of the scene. mental ray only treats them as a hint.

Normally the default clipping planes work well. However, if the camera is zoomed very close to an object, so that the coordinate size of the scene becomes very large compared to the coordinate size of the part that is visible, artifacts such as cracks can appear. For example, if the visible scene is placed on a huge ground plane, almost all of which is outside the rendered image, the ground plane may crack. In this case the clipping planes should be moved, using the statement

        clip *hither yon*

Good values are 0.1 for *hither* and 10 000 for *yon*. If a scene shows artifacts that disappear when a `scanline off` statement is added to the options block, this is a strong indication of unsuitable clipping planes.

3.8   Lenses: Depth of Field

Pinhole cameras are often too perfect — they are perfectly in focus at any distance, and there are no distortions. This can be corrected with lens shaders. Lens shaders can be added to the camera to modify ray direction and origin, so that rays can take more realistic paths through the camera instead of passing through a perfect point. Lens shaders can also modify the color that reaches the viewing plane and produce lens effects such as color correction.

As an example, consider a lens shader that produces depth of field. Depth of field is a visual effect that makes objects very close or very far from the camera appear blurry, giving an added sense of depth to the image. Like a real camera, the depth of field lens shader has only one distance from the camera where objects appear perfectly sharp, although choosing a larger focal length makes the effect less pronounced for objects close to that distance. The imaginary plane perpendicular to the view direction at the distance of perfect sharpness is called the *focus plane*.

Figure 3.6 shows that the only place where a single point in the scene gets projected on a single point on the viewing plane is the focus plane. The farther an object is from the focus plane, the more blurry it will appear because larger portions of it are projected onto a single point on the viewing plane.

For details on how to write lens shaders that achieve effects like this, see volume 2 of this series, "Programming mental ray" [PROG]. Here is an example using the standard mental ray physics shader *physical_lens_dof*. Replace the options and the camera in the simple example on page page 32 with:

```
options "opt"
        samples         1 3
```

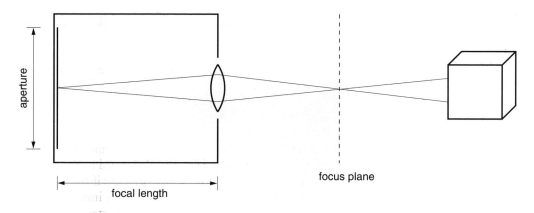

Figure 3.6: Depth of field.

```
            contrast          0.05   0.05   0.05
            scanline          off
            object space
    end options

    camera "cam"
            frame             1
            output            "rgb" "out.rgb"
            lens              "physical_lens_dof" (
                                      "plane"  -1.65,
                                      "radius"  0.1
                              )
            focal             50
            aperture          44
            aspect            1
            resolution        800 800
    end camera
```

The only difference in the camera is the introduction of a `lens` statement naming the *physical_-
lens_dof* lens shader, along with its parameters. The `plane` parameter positions the focus plane
at the Z coordinate −1.65 (remember that the camera always looks down the negative Z axis in
camera space). This is roughly the distance of the frontmost corner of the cube to the camera.
The other shader parameter is `radius`, which specifies the radius of the lens. Larger numbers
make the scene more blurry. The relatively small value of 0.1 is chosen to prevent the result from
becoming too myopic despite the rather large field of view of the camera and the closeness of the
cube.

The options were changed to increase oversampling, using larger values for the `samples`
parameter. Depth of field, like many features that introduce blurriness, often requires higher
quality settings such as an increased oversampling density; see page 440 for details. The other
new option is `scanline off`, which switches mental ray to pure ray tracing mode because the
physical_lens_dof shader is written such that it does not function in scanline mode. In fact
this statement is redundant because the shader declaration has already informed ray about this
requirement.

Figure 3.7: Depth of field blurring.

Since the center corner of the cube in figure 3.7 is at the focus plane it appears sharp; more distant parts of the cube are blurred. In the chapter on output shaders on page 291, another method for depth of field that relies on postprocessing is introduced.

3.9   Full Camera Example

This completes the discussion of camera specifications. Later, more features are introduced that deal with postprocessing and file formats (see page 296), which do not directly control the view of the scene but are also defined as part of the mental ray camera. Here is an example of a camera that makes use of all available options:

```
camera "cam"
        output          "rgba" "rgb" "out.rgb"

        lens            "physical_lens_dof" (
                                "plane"     -1.65,
                                "radius"     0.02
                        )
        volume          "soft_fog" (
                                "transmit"   .9 .9 .7,
                                "start"      1.7,
                                "stop"       3.0
                        )
        environment     "soft_env_sphere" (
                                "rotate"     1.0
                        )
        focal           50
        aperture        44
```

```
            aspect          1.1
            offset          0 0
            resolution      900 600
            window          0 0 999999 999999
            clip            0.001 1000000
            frame           1 0.0
    end camera
```

This example combines features that have been described in this chapter, features that will described in later chapters, and a few odds and ends:

output
: This statement specifies the image file to write when rendering finishes, with (optional) data type, file format type, and file name. Output statements can also name output shaders, which can perform postprocessing on the rendered frame buffers. Multiple output statements can be given; they are executed in the order they are listed in the camera. For more information, see page 291.

pass[3.3]
: Multipass renderingmultipass rendering statements and pass shaders. Render passes are used to render different parts of the scene separately, and compositing the results. Results are saved as pass files containing subpixel samples, not pixels.

lens
: The lens shader or list of lens shaders, as described above. If more than one lens statement is given, the lens shaders are executed in order.

volume
: Specifies a volume shader that operates in the global volume, also known as the *atmosphere*, that fills the entire scene except where overridden by object volume shaders (see page 165). In this example heavy fog is introduced.

environment
: An environment shader that colors any rays that leave the scene without hitting an object. This can be used as a cheap way of defining background images without creating geometry. See page 108. The environment shader in the example is actually nonfunctional because most of its parameters are left unspecified; it is listed for completeness only.

focal
: The focal length of the camera, which is the distance between the camera's origin and the viewing plane. The default is 1.0 if the focal length is never specified. See page 39. Instead of a numeric parameter, the keyword infinity may be given to switch to an orthographic camera, see page 42.

aperture
: The aperture of the camera, which is the width of its viewing plane in camera coordinates. The default is 1.0 if the aperture is never specified. See page 39.

aspect
: The aspect ratio of the camera, which is the ratio between the image width and height. If it does not match the ratio between the X and Y resolution, pixels are nonsquare. The default is 1.33. See page 40 for rules to calculate aspect ratios.

offset
: The camera offset would shift the viewing plane if parameters other than 0/0 pixels were specified.

resolution   The resolution of all files written by output statements; and also the resolution of all frame buffers, in pixels. The default is 768 576 (768 pixels wide by 576 pixels tall; $\frac{768}{576} \approx 1.33$, which is the aspect default, so pixels are square by default). In the example, $\frac{600}{400} = 1.5 > 1.1$, so pixels are taller than wide by a factor of $\frac{1.5}{1.1}$ and the image looks stretched horizontally when displayed on a square-pixel computer screen.

window   The subwindow to render. All pixels outside this window will be black. See page 42.

clip   The clipping planes limit the scanline rendering algorithm to geometry between the hither and yon planes.

frame   The frame number and optional frame time of the frame to render. The defaults are both 0. The frame number is an integer and is normally used to sequentially number rendered frames of an animation, beginning with 0 or 1. The frame time is a floating-point number normally taken to mean seconds; it is useful if a shader needs to know the elapsed time. Elapsed time cannot be derived from the frame number — there may be 24, 25, 30, or some other number of frames per second. Neither one of the numbers is used in any way by mental ray, but they are available for any shaders that need to know the current position on the time axis. It is a good idea to at least specify the frame number, in case some shader expects it.

data   This statement allows attaching user data[2.1] to the camera. User data is not used by mental ray but can be accessed by shaders. See page 287 for details. If the null keyword is used instead of the name of a user data block, any existing user data block reference is removed from the camera; this is useful for incremental changes. If more than one data statement is specified, they are connected to a chain in the order specified.

Figure 3.8 shows the image resulting from the camera example, on a computer screen with square pixels.

Figure 3.8: Full camera example.

Chapter 4

Surface Shading

This chapter discusses surface properties of geometric objects. When the camera sees a geometric object in the scene, the mental ray rendering software needs to determine the color of every point on the object. In addition to the object color this may include:

- illumination: objects lit by light sources appear brighter, and unlit objects and objects in shadow appear darker. See page 52.

- texture mapping: instead of a constant object color, images can be wrapped around objects, like wallpaper or decals. Textures can be image files or procedural textures. See page 57.

- environment mapping: this is a reflection simulation. Reflections of other objects are not visible, only reflections from an "environment" that wraps the entire scene like wallpaper on the inside of an infinite sphere around the scene. See page 108.

- reflection: reflections allow general mirror effects. Reflections of other objects in the scene are seen on the surface. See page 118.

- transparency and refraction: this allows see-through objects. See page 123.

- bump mapping alters the surface normal to make the object surface appear as if it had more geometric detail than it actually does. See page 85.

Traditionally, illumination models, materials, and textures are explained by showing how a sphere using the illumination model looks to the viewer. Here is a new example scene that is used throughout this chapter:

```
verbose on
link "base.so"
$include <base.mi>

light "light1"
        "mib_light_point" (
```

```
            "color"      1 1 1,
            "factor"     0.75
        )
        origin           10 10 10
end light

instance "light1_inst" "light1"
end instance

options "opt"
        samples          0 2
        contrast         0.1  0.1  0.1
        object space
end options

camera "cam"
        frame            1
        output           "rgb" "out.rgb"
        focal            1
        aperture         1
        aspect           1
        resolution       800 800
end camera

material "mtl"
        opaque
        "mib_illum_phong" (
            "ambient"    0.5  0.5  0.5,
            "diffuse"    0.7  0.7  0.7,
            "ambience"   0.2  0.2  0.2,
            "specular"   1.0  1.0  1.0,
            "exponent"   50,
            "mode"       1,
            "lights"     ["light1_inst"]
        )
end material

$include "sphere.mi"              # see appendix for a listing of sphere.mi

instance "sphere1_inst" "sphere"
        material         "mtl"
end instance

instance "cam_inst" "cam"
        transform        1  0  0  0
                         0  1  0  0
                         0  0  1  0
                         0  0 -12  1
end instance

instgroup "rootgrp"
        "cam_inst" "light1_inst"  "sphere1_inst"
end instgroup
```

```
render "rootgrp" "cam_inst" "opt"
```

The scene is similar to the cube scene, except that the identity matrices in instances have been removed, and the camera position and field of view have been adjusted. The camera is now at position $(0, 0, 12)$ in world space and looking toward the world space origin, where the sphere is centered, and the light is at position $(10, 10, 10)$, to the left and above the camera.

The sphere itself is not a polygonal model like the cube (this would have required too many polygons for a reasonably smooth sphere), but a free-form surface. Free-form surfaces will be dealt with in chapter 13.3, so only a brief description is given: free-form surfaces are defined by two bases, such as Bézier or B-spline, that define curves that are swept along the U and V parameter space to span a curved surface. The example scene defines a texture space using a `texture surface` statement; this is in preparation for the next chapter which deals with textures. For the complete sphere object definition, refer to appendix B.

On surfaces, UV coordinates are planar coordinates — every point on the surface has a pair (U and V). In the case of a sphere, lines of constant V form the latitude circles that run once around the sphere, and lines of constant U form longitude half-circles that run from pole to pole. On the sphere, U and V form polar coordinates with the bottom pole at V=0 and the top pole at V=1. U begins at some point on the sphere, then circles around until it meets itself at the same point, as shown in figure 4.1.

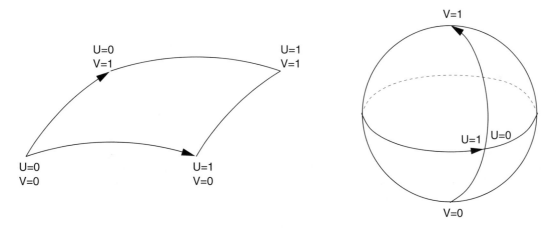

Figure 4.1: UV parameter space.

The sphere on the right of figure 4.1 uses the same principle as the patch on the left, except that the U axis has been stretched and wrapped around until the left edge is perfectly aligned with the right edge, which turns the patch into a cylinder. Then the top and bottom edges, which now form circles, are shrunk until the radius is zero and the circles become poles of a sphere.

UV coordinate spaces are very important for texture mapping. When a texture image, which is inherently 2D (it has a width and a height but no depth), is pasted onto a surface, it can be easily aligned with the UV coordinates, which are also 2D. UV coordinates are inherent in free-form surfaces, but mental ray also allows UV coordinates to be attached to polygonal geometry.

Typically, UV coordinates undergo various kinds of transformations to position the texture correctly.

4.1 Color and Illumination

Illumination is an important aspect of computing the color of a surface. It adds the effects of lighting to the base color of an object. There are many different models for direct illumination of a surface:

Flat

All lights are ignored. The object has the same color regardless of illumination. By convention, this color is called the object's *diffuse color*.

Lambert

The part of the object facing away from the light is flat-shaded and has a constant color that is called *ambient color*. On the side of the object facing the light, the object color is the sum of the ambient color and the contribution from the light source. To compute this contribution, the light color is multiplied by the object's *diffuse color* and a factor that depends on the orientation of the surface towards the light: points directly facing the light are brightest, and points pointing less directly towards the light receive less illumination. The falloff is very smooth (linear), giving a dull plastic appearance.

Phong

Phong shading is similar to Lambert shading, except that there is a third color contribution that is also added on the side of the object that faces the light. This additional contribution is the product of the light color and the object's *specular color* multiplied by a factor. Unlike the diffuse factor, the specular factor does not fall off linearly but much faster, with the power of a cosine. This creates a specular highlight whose size can be controlled with the *specular exponent*. The result is a shiny-looking surface, such as polished plastic.

Blinn

Blinn shading improves on Phong shading by making the highlight depend not only on the direction to the light, but also on the view direction. The result looks much like Phong shading, except when the view direction is almost in the surface plane, in which case the highlight looks bigger because the surface scatters more light. Blinn shading requires specification of a surface roughness parameter; rougher surfaces scatter more light at glancing angles and hence increase the effect.

Cook-Torrance

Cook-Torrance shading further improves on Blinn shading by making surface scattering wavelength-dependent. Instead of specifying the surface roughness as a single parameter, three separate parameters for the red, green, and blue ranges of the visible spectrum are given. This causes colored fringes at the edges of the highlight at glancing viewing directions, simulating the lighting on certain brushed metals or plastics.

Ward   Ward shading simulates glossy surfaces whose light reflection depends on
                         a "brushing direction". Highlights on brushed aluminum, for example,
                         are stretched against the brushing direction. More precisely, the direction
                         is based on surface derivatives, which provide directional information in
                         UV coordinates on the surface. This is also called *anisotropic shading*.
                         (See the texture section below on page 57 for details on UV coordinates,
                         and page 104 for anisotropic shading.)

The "specular" contribution used in the Phong and Blinn shading models is actually named
incorrectly. The term "specular" implies a mirror direction, but what these shaders really do is
a direct glossy reflection of light (with the specular exponent specifying the glossiness), as well
as mirror reflection of indirect light. However, the literature on these shading models uses the
term "specular" in this sense, so we do too. For a discussion of the precise meaning of diffuse,
glossy, and specular reflection, see the description of the *dgs_material* shader on page 127, and
[Hanrahan 93].

All these illumination models (with the exception of flat shading, which does not actually involve
illumination) are collectively known as BRDFs — bidirectional reflectance distribution functions.
They are not built into mental ray itself but are implemented as material shaders. For example, the
standard *mib_illum_phong* shader, which implements the Phong shading model, has the following
parameters:

```
"mib_illum_phong" (
    "ambient"   0.5  0.5  0.5,
    "diffuse"   0.7  0.7  0.7,
    "ambience"  0.2  0.2  0.2,
    "specular"  1.0  1.0  1.0,
    "exponent"  5,
    "mode"      1,
    "lights"    ["light1_inst"]
)
```

The parameters are:

ambient   The ambient color is a constant RGB color added to the lighting result, so that
                the parts of the object facing away from the light are not completely black.
                This parameter should be set to black if global illumination (indirect lighting) is
                enabled.

ambience   This is an RGB multiplier for the *ambient* parameter. It allows deriving both
                the ambient and diffuse colors from the same source, such as a texture, and then
                reducing the effect of the ambient illumination component.

diffuse   This RGB color is added to the object color based on the illumination direction,
                with a smooth falloff.

specular   This is the RGB color of the highlight. The specular color is similar to the diffuse
                color but falls off much more rapidly, depending on the exponent parameter.

exponent   The sharpness of the highlight. Smaller values increase the size.

mode   Specifies the interpretation of the light list: mode 0 uses all lights in the light list, mode 1 uses all lights in the scene that are in the light list (this is different from mode 0 if there are lights that are multiply instanced; see page 371), and mode 2 uses all lights in the scene except those that are in the light list.

lights   This is the list of lights (actually, the names of the light instances which provide the position and orientation of the lights necessary for computing illumination). The example on page 49 lists only a single light, but a comma-separated list of multiple lights is possible. If multiple lights are given, multiple diffuse and specular contributions are taken into account, one from each light. The angle brackets indicate that this parameter accepts lists; they may not be omitted.

mental ray represents colors as RGBA colors, giving red, green, blue, and alpha components as four floating-point numbers, in RGBA order. The RGB components specify the color; (0, 0, 0) is black and (1, 1, 1) is white. Colors are not restricted to this range and can have any value, even negative; this can be used for special effects like extra-bright light sources or negative light sources (sometimes called *darklights* or *light suckers*). However, most image file formats on disk only allow colors in the standard 0…1 range; see page 296.

The alpha component specifies transparency. Value 0 is transparent and 1 is opaque. For example, the RGBA value (1, 1, 0, 1) is opaque yellow. All color computations use premultiplication, which means that the RGB components have been scaled by A and can therefore never exceed A. This would be stored as $(R_1 \cdot A, G_1 \cdot A, B_1 \cdot A, A)$, with $R_1 G_1 B_1$ being the color that would be used in the opaque case. For example, 70% transparent white is represented as (0.3, 0.3, 0.3, 0.3), not as (1, 1, 1, 0.3). This format allows simple and efficient compositing operations such as alpha blending (where background colors "shine through" transparent foreground colors, a very useful operation when texturing), and is almost universally used in computer graphics. Premultiplication can be turned off with the premultiply option, but this only affects mental ray's frame buffer and image files written to disk to ensure that shader color computations do not need to check this option. If turned off, color clipping should generally be switched to raw mode.

Premultiplication selects the method for storing transparent colors. A second problem concerns color clipping[2.1]. An 8-bit or 16-bit frame buffer supports only color component values between 0 and 1, which means that color components outside this range must be clipped by reducing all values greater than 1 to 1, and all values less than 0 to 0. There are three methods to do this:

rgb   indicates that the RGB color and brightness must be preserved. If premultiplication is enabled, this means that the alpha component must be increased to the maximum of R, G, and B.

alpha   indicates that the transparency must be preserved. If premultiplication is enabled, this means that the alpha component stays unchanged and the R, G, and B components that exceed alpha are reduced to alpha.

raw   turns color clipping and premultiplication off. This allows color values that do not normally make sense, such as $R = 1, G = 1, B = 1, A = 0$ (no amount of premultiplication will get any opacity into this nonblack color), but it assumes that all affected shaders can deal with such colors. This mode should be used with care because the standard shaders cannot deal with it.

The premultiplication and color clipping modes are set in the options block (see page 417), or on the command line. Figure 4.2 shows the flow of color values from shaders to the frame buffer and back. Sample filtering, which combines multiple samples into one pixel in the frame buffer, is not shown. The default path is shown in a darker shade. The return path shown at the bottom applies mainly to output shaders, which also need to read the frame buffers.

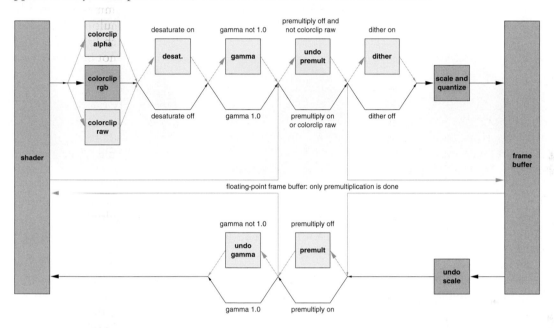

Figure 4.2: Sample value data flow.

The *mib_illum_phong* shader, and all other illumination shader used in this section, ignore the alpha components of their color parameters. Transparency is handled by different shaders; see page 123. Therefore, it is sufficient to specify three numbers (red, green, blue). Figure 4.3 shows examples for various illumination models supported by the base shader library. (Illumination models are implemented by material shaders; additional ones besides the basics shown below can be implemented in custom shaders.)

Half of each sphere faces the light, and the other does not. The dividing line between them is called the *terminator*. On a sphere the terminator is a circle. Note that if the exponent parameter, if chosen too small, can make the highlight so large that it touches the terminator, but since it will never be able to cross it, a sharp contrast can appear.

The following table shows the shaders and shader parameters used for the spheres above:

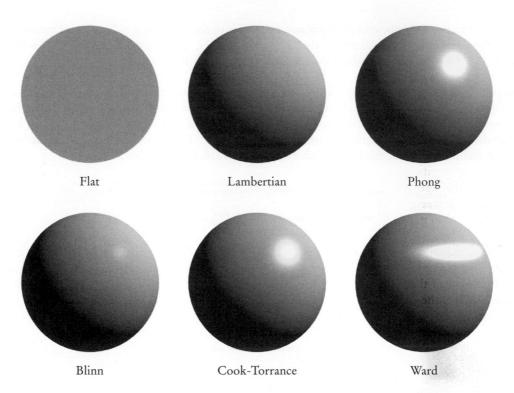

Figure 4.3: Illumination models.

	Flat	Lambert	Phong	Blinn	Cook-T.	Ward
*mib_illum_*	*lambert*	*lambert*	*phong*	*blinn*	*cooktorr*	*ward_deriv*
ambient	.5 .5 .5	.5 .5 .5	.5 .5 .5	.5 .5 .5	.5 .5 .5	.5 .5 .5
ambience	1 1 1	.2 .2 .2	.2 .2 .2	.2 .2 .2	.2 .2 .2	.2 .2 .2
diffuse	–	.7 .7 .7	.7 .7 .7	.7 .7 .7	.7 .7 .7	.7 .7 .7
specular	–	–	1 1 1	1 1 1	1 1 1	–
exponent	–	–	50	–	–	–
roughness	–	–	–	.18	.18	–
ior	–	–	–	3	4 80 8	–
glossy	–	–	–	–	–	1 1 1
shiny_u	–	–	–	–	–	2
shiny_v	–	–	–	–	–	9
mode	–	1	1	1	1	1
lights	–	*yes*	*yes*	*yes*	*yes*	*yes*

Note that there is no specific shader for flat shading, so *mib_illum_lambert* was used without a diffuse component. Omitting a parameter (indicated by a dash in the table) is equivalent to setting it to null values (or whatever defaults[3.3] the shader declaration specifies). The *mib_illum_-ward_deriv* shader requires surface derivatives; see page 104 for a definitions and how to specify them, or instruct mental ray to provide them. The light list must contain only light instances, all of which must also be part of the scene graph (by listing them in the root group or some other instance group in the scene).

The `roughness` parameter of the Blinn and Cook-Torrance shading models specifies the surface roughness, which controls how much light is scattered in directions other than the mirror direction. Shiny surfaces produce small highlights while rough surfaces produce large highlights. Note that the Phong `exponent` parameter works the opposite way: larger exponents produce a smaller highlight. Unlike the Phong exponent, the Ward roughness has a physical foundation.

The `ior` parameter specifies the index of refraction of the surface, which simulates the light reflection of metals. An `ior` value of 1.0 indicates the perfect mirror direction, while values greater than 1.0 bend the reflected light direction towards the mirror direction. Since the index of refraction is specified separately for the red, green, and blue components, this allows highlights with colored fringes. In the example, the highlight is white at the center, then fades to blue-green, and has a soft green fringe because $ior_r < ior_b < ior_g$. See [Foley 96] for more information on the mathematical principles behind the various shading models.

The top right sphere above uses a Phong `exponent` value of 50. The spheres in figure 4.4 use `exponent` values of 5, 20, and 200, respectively; the highlight touches the terminator if the value is 5. Note that if the exponent parameter is accidentally omitted, it defaults to 0 and causes the highlight to fill the entire object with the constant highlight color, up to the terminator.

`"exponent" 5`   `"exponent" 20`   `"exponent" 200`

Figure 4.4: Highlight size depending on Phong exponent.

4.2 Texture Mapping

The materials used in the previous chapter to render examples of the various illumination models had simple, uniform colors specified by their ambient, diffuse, and specular colors. However, normal, real-world objects almost never have uniform colors — they resemble wood, stone, or fabric, or they may have decals or text, or dirt on them. It would be clearly impractical to model a paved road with geometry and carefully adjust the individual colors. Instead, these objects are texture mapped.

There are two basic types of textures: 2D textures and 3D textures. A 2D texture is flat, it has a width and height but no depth, like a photograph (albeit one that can be stretched and folded infinitely). 2D textures appear shrink-wrapped around objects like wallpaper. 3D textures are defined in three dimensions, making the object appear as if it were carved from the texture. For example, wood can be applied as a 2D texture the way one glues veneer on an object, but wood looks much more believable on objects with complex shapes when applied as a 3D texture which defines a color for every point in 3D space. If one were to follow a single wood grain fiber through 3D space, the fiber would provide the color for any point of the object surface that passes through the fiber.

3D textures are fairly easy to apply because they are defined in 3D coordinates (that is, each point has X, Y, and Z coordinates) — the same in which geometric objects are defined. 2D textures do not have this advantage; one must map the object's 3D coordinates to the texture's 2D coordinates. By convention, 3D coordinates are named X, Y, and Z, and 2D coordinates are named U and V. In other words, one must decide where to paste on the wallpaper, and with which orientation. Several ways of doing this are presented in this section.

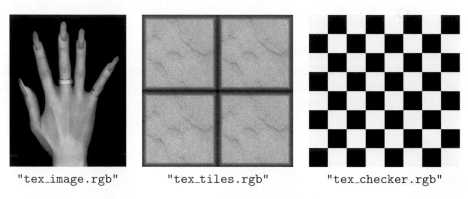

"tex_image.rgb"   "tex_tiles.rgb"   "tex_checker.rgb"

Figure 4.5: Texture images.

The texture images used in this chapter are shown in figure 4.5. These files must exist for the following examples to work. If they are not available, any image will do. The "tex_image.rgb" image contains an alpha channel, which means that every pixel has an alpha component. This is used in some examples for compositing but the scenes will still render if no alpha channel is available.

4.2.1 Texture Projections

Textures are material properties, so applying textures to the sphere in the scene example in appendix B involves changing the material definition. Although in principle texture support could be built into the material shader, this is not what is normally done; instead a separate shader is used to handle the texture and is referenced by the material shader. The reason is modularization: it is easier to write a new illumination model if one does not have to worry about texturing, and it is easier to introduce new texture shaders without worrying about illumination.

This chapter uses the mental images base shader library. This library contains a set of small shaders that are designed to do single tasks, such that they can be combined with one another or with user-written shaders to perform complex tasks. To make the base shader library available, two lines must be used in the scene file:

```
link <base.so>
```

```
$include <base.mi>
```

The extension .so applies to Unix systems. Windows NT uses .dll, but mental ray automatically converts one to the other as needed. The first line links the actual shader implementation into mental ray. The file base.so is a shared library (also called a Dynamic Shared Object (DSO), or Dynamic Link Library (DLL) on Windows NT) that contains code that mental ray can run. The second line loads the declaration file base.mi, which describes the interface of the function to mental ray so it knows how to call the functions in base.so, and with which parameters. Linking must precede declarations. The base shaders are described in detail in appendix C.

4.2.1.1   Simple XY Projection

The following example applies a simple texture projection to the sphere. This requires a new material and a new material shader. The material shader is written as a *Phenomenon* that performs four tasks:

1. Coordinate projection (using the *mib_texture_vector* base shader),

2. Coordinate remapping (using the *mib_texture_remap* base shader),

3. Texture image lookup (using the *mib_texture_lookup* base shader), and

4. Phong illumination, using the *mib_illum_phong* base shader.

These shaders are bundled into the Phenomenon textured_mtl_sh, and call each other using *shader assignments* and *interface assignments*. The new material and the Phenomenon it uses will be mentioned here only briefly because this chapter is mainly about textures; Phenomena are described in chapter 11.

Texturing in this scene is a four-step process: an image file is referenced using a color texture statement; one or more texture shaders (here, three) pick a color from it, a material shader adds illumination, and finally a material references the material shader:

```
color texture "pic1" "tex_image.rgb"

declare phenomenon
        color "textured_mtl_sh" (
                color texture   "texture",
                array light     "lights"
        )
        shader "coord" "mib_texture_vector" (
                "select"        -1,
                "project"       2,
                "selspace"      1
        )
        shader "remap" "mib_texture_remap" (
                "input"         = "coord",
```

```
                    "transform"        .0999 0     0    0
                                       0     .0999 0    0
                                       0     0     0    0
                                       .5    .5    0    1
              )
         shader "tex" "mib_texture_lookup" (
                    "tex"              = interface "texture",
                    "coord"            = "remap"
         )
         shader "mtl" "mib_illum_phong" (
                    "ambient"          = "tex",
                    "diffuse"          = "tex",
                    "ambience"         .1 .1 .1,
                    "specular"         1 1 1,
                    "exponent"         50,
                    "mode"             1,
                    "lights"           = interface "lights"
         )
         root = "mtl"
    end declare

    material "mtl"
         opaque
         "textured_mtl_sh" (
              "texture"    "pic1",
              "lights"     ["light1_inst"],
         )
    end material
```

This fragment replaces the material definition in the sphere example on page 49. The material itself is basically unchanged except that it uses the Phenomenon *textured_mtl_sh* instead of the shader *mib_illum_phong*. The Phenomenon has only two parameters, texture and lights, which are called the *Phenomenon interface*. A Phenomenon has no contact to the rest of the scene file except through its interface. The Phenomenon body consists of four shaders:

mib_illum_phong	This shader is called first because the last line marks it as the *root shader* (again, for more information on what that means, see page 271). It obtains its ambient color and diffuse color from the tex shader, which is a reference to *mib_texture_lookup* together with that shader's parameters.
mib_texture_lookup	This is a straightforward color texture lookup function. The texture (here, the tex_image.rgb file) is looked up at the UV coordinate coord, which must be in the range [0, 1) (a range including 0 but excluding 1).
mib_texture_remap	This is an intermediate shader that accepts a raw texture coordinate coord and performs scaling, repetition, alternation, and various other operations on it. It operates on 3D coordinates, but here only X and Y (called U and V in the 2D case) are used. A transformation

matrix is used to remap XYZ space:

$$\begin{pmatrix} 0.0999 & 0 & 0 & 0 \\ 0 & 0.0999 & 0 & 0 \\ 0 & 0 & 0 & 0 \\ 0.5 & 0.5 & 0 & 1 \end{pmatrix}$$

The upper left 3×3 rotation matrix is used for scaling only, and the bottom translation row shifts the texture. The incoming coord is in the range $[-5, 5]$, which means that multiplying by 0.0999 and adding 0.5 brings it into the desired range $[0, 1)$. The value 0.0999 is used instead of 0.1 to make sure that the UV coordinates are less than 1; as described above texture coordinates must be in the range $[0, 1)$ to avoid overflows.

mib_texture_vector   This shader generates raw texture coordinates. Its mode -2 generates XY coordinates, in object space because selspace is 1. This is the object coordinate with Z removed, and since the object is defined in the range $[-5, 5]$ this is also the returned texture coordinate range.

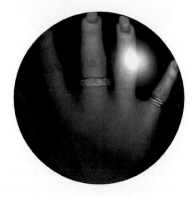

Figure 4.6: XY texture projection.

Figure 4.6 shows the resulting image. It is seen head-on because the object's X and Y axes happen to be aligned with the camera's X and Y axes. If the camera would be moved to a different viewpoint, the hand would stay in place on the sphere and would be seen from a different angle because the texture generator *mib_illum_lookup* was set up to return object coordinates.

4.2.1.2 Repeated XY Projection

Since all coordinate transformations, mappings, and texture lookups are under the control of shaders, the projection of textures can be changed arbitrarily. The *mib_texture_remap* shader used in the example on page 59 also has parameters that allow repetition and alternation (flipping around every other texture copy). For example, if the remap shader definition is replaced with

```
shader "remap" "mib_texture_remap" (
        "input"         = "coord",
        "repeat"        6 6 0,
        "alt_x"         on,
        "alt_y"         on,
        "transform"     .1  0   0   0
                         0  .1  0   0
                         0   0  0   0
                        .5  .5  0   1
)
```

the texture is replicated six times in each direction, and every other copy is alternated. The rendered image changes to figure 4.7.

Figure 4.7: Repeating texture.

4.2.1.3   Other Projections

Note that these projections are not hardwired features of mental ray, but rather features of the specific base shaders that come with mental ray. Other texturing projections and modes can be easily implemented using mental ray's shader interface, described in volume 2 of this series [PROG].

The standard projections supported by the base shaders are XY, XZ, YZ, spherical, and cylindrical projections, selected by the `select` parameter of *mib_texture_vector*. Figure 4.8 shows the same sphere, plus a smaller extra one in front that shows the top view (the large sphere rolled 90 degrees towards the camera), for each of the projections.

The XY, XZ, and YZ projections are also called *orthographic projections* because they work like a slide projector with perfectly parallel light rays. Unlike a slide projector, the projection is not stopped by occluding surfaces, so the back side is a mirror image of the front side. These projections basically use object space coordinates as texture coordinates, by taking two coordinates and dropping the third (XY drops Z, XZ drops Y, and YZ drops X). This means that they work best if the object coordinates are in the range $[0, 1)$, but the `transform` parameter of

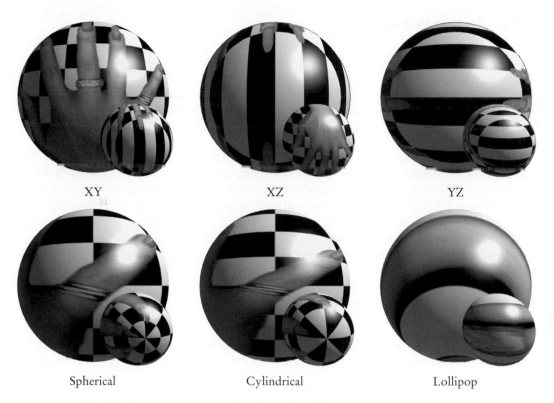

XY	XZ	YZ
Spherical	Cylindrical	Lollipop

Figure 4.8: Texture projections.

the *mib_texture_remap* shader can be used to convert the object space parameters into the [0, 1) range (see page 60).

Spherical projection shrink-wraps a sphere around the object (easy on a spherical object, but it works with any shape) by using polar coordinates as UV texture coordinates. The result is always in the range [0, 1) regardless of object coordinates.

Cylindrical projection shrink-wraps a cylinder with the object-space Y axis of the object onto the object. This is a mixture of spherical projection (for the U coordinate) and orthographic projection (for the V coordinate). Hence, U is in the range [0, 1) but V is in whatever object-space Y range the object is defined with.

Lollipop projection puts the center of the texture on top of the object, and folds the edges of the texture down towards the bottom of the object, like the wrapping paper of a lollipop candy stick. Since the texture is folded down smoothly, only a round (or elliptical) disc in the texture is actually used, and the corners are ignored.

Instead of object space, the *mib_texture_vector* shader also allows other spaces; see below (page 69).

4.2.1.4 **Texture Vectors**

Until now, texture coordinates have been computed on the fly from object coordinates. The advantage is that they can be computed exactly for any given coordinate, but they cannot handle all situations. For example, if a wood grain texture is mapped on a stick using cylindrical mapping, and the stick is bent into a circle, the texture does not follow the bend, but turns around on itself. If textures do not stay glued to their objects, they are said to be *swimming*.

Texture vectors provide an alternative. mental ray tessellates objects into triangles before rendering. Each triangle has three *vertices* (corners), each of which is at a known location in 3D space (usually object space). Vertices can optionally have texture vectors attached to them, which contain XYZ or UV coordinates that can be picked up during rendering and used as texture coordinates. If the point-in-space coordinates in the vertex change (that is, the triangle moves) but the texture vectors do not, then the texture will stay glued to the triangle regardless of its motion. The projections from the previous chapter cannot guarantee this because they are derived from the points in space.

However, texture vectors have two disadvantages:

- The scene creator must put them into the object definition. If they are missing, texture mapping that relies on texture vectors will fail (more precisely, it will get random garbage).

- Since texture vectors exist only at triangle vertices, they must be derived by bilinear interpolation on the rest of the triangle. If the object is highly curved or has singularities, this will cause artifacts. For example, a spherical projection on a cube implemented with texture vectors will not resolve the center of the top face correctly because there is no vertex there, and interpolation from the cube corners will result in diagonal lines instead of converging lines. (More about this later.)

When areas of high curvature and near singularities are tessellated finely enough, texture vectors provide a very flexible way of mapping textures in arbitrary ways. Here is an example:

```
color texture "pic1" "tex_image.rgb"

declare phenomenon
        color "textured_mtl_sh" (
                color texture    "texture",
                array light      "lights"
        )
        shader "coord" "mib_texture_vector" (
                "select"         0,
                "selspace"       1
        )
        shader "remap" "mib_texture_remap" (
                "input"          = "coord",
        )
        shader "tex" "mib_texture_lookup" (
                "tex"            = interface "texture",
```

```
                    "coord"            = "remap"
            )
        shader "texmix" "mib_color_mix" (
                    "num"              2,
                    "weight_0"         1,
                    "color_0"          0.3 0.3 0.3,
                    "weight_1"         1,
                    "color_1"          = "tex",
            )
        shader "mtl" "mib_illum_phong" (
                    "ambient"          = "texmix",
                    "diffuse"          = "texmix",
                    "ambience"         .1 .1 .1,
                    "specular"         1 1 1,
                    "exponent"         50,
                    "mode"             1,
                    "lights"           = interface "lights"
            )
        root = "mtl"
end declare

material "mtl"
        opaque
        "textured_mtl_sh" (
            "texture"    "pic1",
            "lights"     ["light1_inst"],
            )
end material

object "cube1"
        visible trace shadow
        tag 1
        group
                -0.5 -0.5 -0.5
                -0.5 -0.5  0.5
                -0.5  0.5 -0.5
                -0.5  0.5  0.5
                 0.5 -0.5 -0.5
                 0.5 -0.5  0.5
                 0.5  0.5 -0.5
                 0.5  0.5  0.5

                 0.0       0.0       0.0
                 0.99999   0.0       0.0
                 0.0       0.99999   0.0
                 0.99999   0.99999   0.0

                 v 0 t 8   v 1 t 9   v 3 t 11  v 2 t 10
                 v 1 t 8   v 5 t 9   v 7 t 11  v 3 t 10
                 v 5 t 8   v 4 t 9   v 6 t 11  v 7 t 10
                 v 4 t 8   v 0 t 9   v 2 t 11  v 6 t 10
                 v 5 t 8   v 1 t 9   v 0 t 11  v 4 t 10
                 v 3 t 8   v 7 t 9   v 6 t 11  v 2 t 10
```

```
            p "mtl"   0   1   2   3
            p         4   5   6   7
            p         8   9  10  11
            p        12  13  14  15
            p        16  17  18  19
            p        20  21  22  23
        end group
    end object
```

The Phenomenon is similar to the simple texturing Phenomenon on page 59, with two changes:

- The select parameter of the *mib_texture_vector* shader was changed from -2 to 0. This shader can generate texture vectors from many sources; negative values compute it from the point in space or other intersection parameters (-2 is an orthographic XY projection, -3 is XZ, -4 is YZ, and so on; see appendix C), and value 0 or greater select texture spaces built into the geometry. The selspace parameter is not used in this case.

- A new shader *mib_color_mix* was introduced that uses an alpha blending operation to paste the image returned by *mib_texture_lookup* on top of a constant gray (0.3 0.3 0.3) background. The background from the image is pure transparent black, which makes it difficult to see the edges of the cube. The same shader was used in the orthogonal examples above to paste the texture image on top of a checkerboard image. This is only an aesthetic change that is unrelated to texture vertices.

The material is unchanged from page 59. The interesting change to the scene is in the object definition. It is the cube from the example on page 32 with texture vectors added.

Each of the polygon vertices defined with v statements were extended with a t statement that specifies a vector that becomes the texture coordinate for the vertex. Up to 64 t statements can be attached to every v statement. All vertices should have the same number of t statements because shaders like *mib_texture_vector* rely on them. Vectors in mental ray always have three components (X, Y, Z), so the third component is set to 0.0. See page 312 for more information on the definition of vectors, vertices, and polygons.

The cube example above has six polygons with four vertices each. At each vertex, three polygons meet. In the simple, untextured example on page 32, this was used to specify one vertex for each of the eight corners of the cube, and building the polygons from these vertices by using each one in the three polygons that meet at that corner. However, the example on page 64 cannot do this because each face has its own texture, as shown in figure 4.9.

Consider the cube corner in the center of this image. It is the top left corner (U=0, V=0.99999) of the texture image on the front wall of the cube, the top right corner (U=0.99999, V=0) of the texture image on the left wall, and the bottom left corner (U=0, V=0) of the texture image on the ceiling of the cube. Since the texture vectors referenced in vertices control the UV coordinates of the texture, it is necessary to use different vertices in these three cases, each with a different texture vector, even though they are all located at the same point in space.

Figure 4.9: Texture vertices.

In figure 4.10, each polygon is shown with its corners labeled with letters A, B, C, and D that show the texture image alignment: A is bottom left, B is bottom right, C is top right, and D is top left.

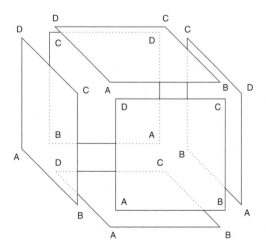

Figure 4.10: Texture alignment on a cube.

The cube corner in the center of the image consists of three vertices, all at the same point in space $((-0.5, 0.5, -0.5)$, or vector number 2) but with different texture coordinates:

Texture corner	U	V	Texture vector number
A	0.0	0.0	8
B	0.99999	0.0	9
C	0.99999	0.99999	11
D	0.0	0.99999	10

The number in the last column is the number listed in the t statements.

Effectively, the texture is defined only at the vertices. When mental ray needs a texture coordinate between vertices, it uses bilinear interpolation between vertices. Since all geometry is tessellated into triangles before rendering, this can lead to surprising results. Consider the polygon defined by the vertices A, B, C, and D, which has a texture consisting of a horizontal stripe in the center mapped onto it, as shown in figure 4.11.

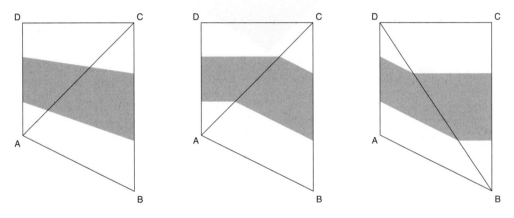

Figure 4.11: Texture vertex interpolation.

What one would expect is the leftmost image, but that is not what happens. Instead, either the middle or right image is rendered, depending on the vertex definition order. The reason for this behavior is the interpolation. Consider the middle image: the distance A-D is interpolated smoothly, which means that the stripe correctly appears centered on A-D. Since the distance A-C is also interpolated smoothly, the stripe must also be centered on A-C. This is the case in the middle and right images, but not the left one.

To avoid this situation, triangles with a right angle should be used, or pairs of triangles that form parallelograms, that is, each pair of opposing edges is parallel, like a skewed rectangle. In general, it also helps to increase the number of polygons to increase the number of texture vectors to allow finer interpolation, especially in areas of high curvature or distortion.

The same problem appears on free-form surfaces because they are also tessellated into triangles before rendering. For example, the texture projections on page 63 would not look as smooth with texture vectors, especially the spherical and cylindrical cases, because the projection onto the curved area of the sphere introduces a curvature into the texture that cannot be achieved with linear interpolation of a small number of texture vectors. In practice, this is not a problem because mental ray 3.1 and higher support *fine approximation*[3.1] mode for free-form surfaces and displacement, which efficiently generates a sufficient number of triangles without filling up memory. Older versions of mental ray can address this with curvature-dependent adaptive tessellation that automatically creates more triangles in areas of high curvature.

4.2.1.5 Texture Generation from Coordinate Spaces

All the above examples have used simple projections based on object space or texture coordinates. However, the *mib_texture_vector* base shader used in the preceding example supports more coordinate modes, listed here without sample scenes:

- If the `selspace` parameter is changed from 1 (object space) to 2 (world space), the texture no longer sticks with the object but stays in place. If the object moves, it "swims" through the texture.

- If the `selspace` parameter is changed from 1 to 3 (camera space), the texture shifts to face the camera (if the `select` parameter is −2, for XY projections). This is sometimes called "billboard mapping".

- If the `selspace` parameter is changed from 1 to 4 (screen space), and the `select` parameter is −2 (XY), the texture is anchored to the screen, no matter where the object and the camera is. This is useful for compositing with background plates if the texture is mapped on an object without any illumination shader (effectively using flat shading) at any depth in the scene, or if the texture is used by an environment shader.

4.2.2 Local Textures: Avoiding Network Transfers

All previous examples contained scene file statements like

```
color texture "name"
            [ colorprofile "profilename"³·⁴]
            "filename"
```

This statement loads the given *filename* as a texture image, and makes it available to shaders under the name *name*. The entire texture is loaded before mental ray proceeds to the next statement. If mental ray renders in a network of machines, the image is sent across the network to any remote machine that needs it, when it needs it. Textures are transmitted on demand only.

If rendering is performed in a color space[3.4] selected by a color profile, then textures may optionally be qualified with a color profile describing in which color space the texture is given. See page 162 for details on color profiles.

Yet, if there is a large number of textures, or if the textures are large (typically resolutions of 1000 pixels in any direction are considered large), there is a large overhead involved when loading the textures, and transmitting them to other machines. Since large textures are measured in megabytes or tens of megabytes, this introduces a heavy load on the network, which limits the number of machines that can usefully contribute to rendering before network overload slows down rendering so much that fewer machines would actually be faster.

If an animation is rendered and the same image is used in several frames, one `color texture` statement before the first frame definition in the scene file suffices. It does not have to be repeated for every successive frame. This has the advantage that the texture is still in memory on all machines that have used it in the previous frame, reducing the impact of loading and transmission overhead. But often textures change frequently, such as live-action background plates or if multiple scenes using the same textures are rendered separately (and so cannot share data), which can make texture handling unacceptably slow.

Local textures solve the problem of network transmissions by delaying loading of a texture from disk until it is actually needed. If it turns out that the texture is never needed because the texture-mapped object is occluded or otherwise invisible, then there is no overhead from this texture. Local textures are prefixed with the keyword `local`:

```
local color texture "name"
                    [ colorprofile "profilename"³·⁴]
                    "filename"
```

```
local color texture "name" "filename"
```

The addition of the `local` keyword makes mental ray load *filename* from disk when it first needs it. In particular, remote machines on the network also load it from their local disks (hence the name "local" texture). This means that the user must manually copy the texture to the disks of all machines that participate in rendering. Local disk loading is fast and can happen in parallel on all machines, unlike network transfers, because the network is a shared resource.

When using the `local` keyword, it is also possible to place textures on network file servers (NFS servers), and let all machines access their local textures from there. This creates some network overhead, but there is still a performance advantage if the file server is a fast machine on a fast network because texture loading is deferred to the time when the texture is actually needed.

It is important to ensure that the given *filename* is valid on all machines. File names are passed through a registry substitution mechanism that allows different interpretation of the given filename on different machines; for example by applying path translation from Unix paths to Windows NT paths. See page 412 for details of the mental ray registry.

4.2.3 Memory Mapped Textures: Reducing Memory Usage

Memory mapping takes local textures one step further. Instead of allocating memory and reading the texture when it is first accessed, mental ray merely creates a "window" in virtual memory into the file directly. The result is that the texture does not reserve a large block of memory up front, but lets the operating system read small pieces of the texture whenever and wherever it is needed, and discard these pieces when memory is needed elsewhere. A non-memory mapped texture would have to be read in its entirety, and paged out to temporary swap space on disk when memory runs out, which is expensive.

If a machine is said to have a certain amount of memory, say, 512 megabytes (MB, 1 MB is 1048576 bytes) installed, it has 512 MB of *physical memory*. Physical memory is hardware, memory chips that are plugged into the machine. The user address space of the machine, which is the amount of memory it *could* use for user processes, is much larger — typically 2 gigabytes (2048 MB or 2 GB; the other 2 GB are usually reserved for the operating system) on a 32-bit machine and something much larger, for all practical purposes infinite, on 64-bit machines[1]. (mental ray is available in 32-bit and 64-bit versions.) This larger address space is called *virtual memory* space, and the operating system assigns physical memory to virtual memory as needed. If more virtual memory is needed than physical memory is available, the operating system "pages out" data that has not been accessed for a long time onto the swap space on disk, and reuses the physical memory. Swap space is limited (try the `swap -1` command at a shell prompt under Unix), and using it is very expensive in terms of run time. Paging to swap space should be avoided if possible, and memory mapped textures help because they are, by definition, never paged out.

Memory mapping pays off especially if the textures are large, because it avoids the time-consuming process of reading them into memory. Memory mapping takes practically no time at all. However, a texture image file must first be converted to a special format before it can be used for memory mapping. mental ray comes with a utility `imf_copy` for this purpose:

> `imf_copy` *filename*`.rgb` *filename*`.map`

This requires version 2.1 of `imf_copy` (as reported by `imf_copy -v`) or later. The first argument is a file to convert (any format), and the second argument is the new memory mappable file to create. By convention, the extension of memory mappable image files is `.map`, but mental ray will recognize a memory mappable file no matter what the extension is. However, `imf_copy` looks at the extension to decide which file type to create, so if the extension is not `.map` a third argument `map` must be appended to the command line:

> `imf_copy -r` *filename1*`.rgb` *filename2*`.rgb map`

This allows converting image files to map files without changing the name, to avoid having to change all `color texture` statements in the scene file. Note that the first two arguments of `imf_copy` may not be identical. Use a different directory for the target files in this case. (See also page 77, which introduces pyramid textures created with the `-p` command line option of `imf_copy`.)

The `-r` option was introduced in `imf_copy` and mental ray 3.2. It rearranges the pixels in the map file into a rectangular layout that improves texture caching performance. Textures created with the `-r` option work only with mental ray 3.2 and higher.

A memory mappable file created on one machine is portable to any other machine of the same byte order. Once created, it can be copied to other machines that have the same byte order. There are two different byte orders: Windows NT and all Intel Pentium CPUs and DEC Alpha CPUs are *little-endian*, and most others are big-endian. These terms refer to the way a (hexadecimal) number 1234 is stored in consecutive bytes of memory: little-endian architectures store 34 followed by 12, and big-endian architectures store 12 followed by 34. mental ray takes care of these technical details automatically, with one exception — memory mapped texture files must have the right byte order. If a map file with the wrong byte order is supplied, mental ray cannot memory-map it and must load it like a non-map image file instead. `imf_copy` always creates files with the byte order of the machine where the copying is done.

---

[1]SGI MIPS R1x000 CPUs, AMD Athlon-64 and Opteron CPUs, and Intel Pentium 4 CPUs with the EM64T extension support both 32-bit and 64-bit modes; Intel Itanium CPUs support 64 bits only, and Intel Pentium CPUs without EM64T support 32 bits only.

When mental ray finds a statement such as

```
color texture "name" "filename"
```

in the scene file, no matter what *filename* is and what extension it has, if it finds that *filename* is a memory mappable file, it will memory map it. This turns the texture into a local texture (see page 69) even without the `local` modifier in the `color texture` statement. The benefit of memory mapping is so significant that this is done regardless of whether `local` is present, under the assumption that if the user has taken the trouble to convert the textures they should be used that way.

Like regular local textures, memory mapped textures can be read from network file servers (NFS servers), but this slows down reading even more than with regular textures because the texture is read in small pieces as needed and not all at once. It is recommended to place memory mappable texture files on fast local disks.

To estimate the memory usage by textures, add up all the file sizes of the memory mappable versions of all textures, rounding up each one to the next higher multiple of 16 kilobytes (KB, 1 KB is 1024 bytes) or 14 KB (depending on the type of machine)[2]. As a rule of thumb, a memory mappable texture file is about twice as large as a regular image file such as a SGI .rgb file because they are uncompressed. Add another 35% if the texture is filtered (see below). Note that the process size, as indicated by certain operating system tools such as `top` on Unix, always show virtual memory — the sum of physical memory used, memory swapped out to disk, and virtual memory that is used for memory mapped textures. This number cannot be compared to the amount of physical memory (512 MB, for example) without subtracting the total size of memory mapped textures from the process size first.

Unix systems limit the number of file descriptors. A file descriptor is an operating system structure that describes an open file, and with mental ray 3.1 or earlier, each memory-mapped texture uses one. The default limit is usually near 200. If a very large number of textures are memory-mapped, the error message "Too many open files" indicates that the limit was exceeded. To increase the limit, use the statement

```
limit descriptors number
```

at a shell prompt with an appropriately large *number* such as 2000. This must be done before starting mental ray (or the application it is built into). The `limit -h` command shows the hard limits set by the system administrator. mental ray 3.2 and higher manage system resources more efficiently and do not depend on setting high limits.

4.2.4 Aliasing in Unfiltered Textures

Local textures and memory mapping textures control how mental ray accesses texture files on disk. Filtering is an independent technique (although it works especially well with memory mapping) that controls how the texture is sampled during tessellation and rendering.

The following scene is perfectly pathological. It creates a tiled floor with 102400 tiles (the 8×8 checker texture repeated 40×40 times), and places the camera to look at it at a grazing angle

---

[2]mental ray 3.2 and higher may decide to not memory-map very small files if rounding would create more overhead than memory-mapping avoids.

such that the tiles size becomes microscopic at the horizon, and it becomes very hard to resolve correctly in the rendered image. No lighting is done, the floor uses flat shading (see page 52).

```
verbose on
link "base.so"
$include <base.mi>

options "opt"
        samples         -2 -2
        object space
end options

camera "cam"
        frame           1
        output          "rgb" "out.rgb"
        focal           1
        aperture        2
        aspect          1
        resolution      800 800
end camera

color texture "pic" "tex_checker.rgb"

declare phenomenon
        color "flat_checker" (
                color texture     "texture"
        )
        shader "coord" "mib_texture_vector" (
                "select"        0,
                "selspace"      1
        )
        shader "remap" "mib_texture_remap" (
                "input"         = "coord",
                "repeat"        40 40
        )
        shader "tex" "mib_texture_lookup" (
                "tex"           = interface "texture",
                "coord"         = "remap"
        )
        root = "tex"
end declare

material "mtl"
        opaque
        "flat_checker" (
            "texture"   "pic"
        )
end material

object "plane"
        visible trace shadow
        tag 1
```

```
        group
                -50   0   -50
                -50   0    50
                 50   0   -50
                 50   0    50

                  0   0   0
                  0   1   0
                  1   0   0
                  1   1   0

                v 0 t 4   v 1 t 5   v 2 t 6   v 3 t 7

                p "mtl" 0  1  3  2
        end group
end object

instance "plane_inst" "plane"
end instance

instance "cam_inst" "cam"
        transform        -0.9501 -0.1946  0.2439  0
                          0.0000  0.7817  0.6237  0
                         -0.3120  0.5925 -0.7427  0
                          0.0000  0.7682 -2.5739  1
end instance

instgroup "rootgrp"
        "cam_inst" "plane_inst"
end instgroup

render "rootgrp" "cam_inst" "opt"
```

Note the camera parameter samples -2 -2, which instructs mental ray to use infrasampling, sampling only one pixel out of sixteen. Obviously the result is going to be highly blocky and aliased. The term *aliasing* refers to high-frequency sampling problems, typically unwanted hard edges that should be smooth. At larger distances, pixels become unpredictable as the chance of a ray hitting a white tile becomes equal to the chance of hitting a black tile. The advantage of texture sampling at render time is that the regular oversampling algorithms are effective for resolving texture details, but the huge number of tiles at the horizon in this example quickly overwhelms any sampling density.

The image on the left of figure 4.12 was rendered with one sample for every 16 pixels, the one in the middle with up to one sample per pixel, and the right one with up to 16 samples per pixel. The oversampling parameters specify the minimum and maximum number of samples as powers of two: $2^{-2} = \frac{1}{4}$ horizontal and vertical, for a total of $\frac{1}{16}$ sample per pixel; $2^0 = 1$ sample per pixel; and $2^2 = 4$ for a total of 16 samples per pixel.

The situation gets worse in an animation because any movement of the camera or the plane will cause the samples to shift, causing them to switch abruptly from black to white or vice versa.

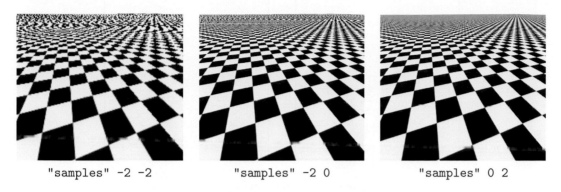

`"samples" -2 -2`   `"samples" -2 0`   `"samples" 0 2`

Figure 4.12: Texture mapping without filtering.

This is called texture flashing or flickering.

Quite obviously unfiltered texture lookup is not sufficient for this scene. It works well for scenes where the texture size is approximately the size of the object it was mapped, and where the mapped object surface is roughly perpendicular to the viewing direction. It also helps if there are no repeating areas of high contrast in the texture. The example is a worst-case violation of all these assumptions.

4.2.5 Simple Filtered Textures: Reducing Texture Aliasing

Unfiltered texture lookups perform point samples in the texture. The point where a ray hits the texture is calculated, and four neighboring pixels are weighted to find the color of the texture at that point. (As usual in mental ray, this is implemented in a shader; in this case in *mib_texture_lookup*.) As the plane recedes into the distance, the samples are spaced farther apart, which means that they not only miss all the detail between texture samples but also cause flickering because shifting samples hit formerly unsampled texture pixels (also called texels).

Texture filtering is an approach that is not based on point sampling, which considers only four texture pixels, but on sampling larger areas of the texture at greater distances, as shown in figure 4.13.

The circles in the left figure shows unfiltered lookups in texture space, and a representative selection of the samples taken. Samples are spaced farther apart at greater distances from the camera because more tiles of the texture cover less image space. The right figure shows how texture samples grow at greater distances, considering more than just four texels and missing less detail in unsampled areas.

Texture filtering is enabled by specifying a `filter` keyword in the `color texture` statement:

```
filter 120.0 color texture "pic" "tex_checker.rgb"
```

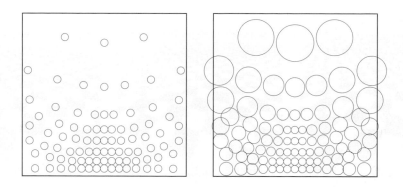

Figure 4.13: Texture sampling locations.

The `filter` keyword has an optional floating-point argument that changes the filter size. The default is 1.0; a value of 3.0 triples the filter size, which makes the texture softer. The value 1.0 corresponds to mental ray's best guess about the proper filtering — it assumes that the texture is parallel to the viewing plane, is not scaled or repeated or otherwise transformed (that is, object space corresponds roughly to texture space), and that there is no magnifying lens; then scales the filter such that one texture pixel roughly corresponds to one image pixel and calls that "`filter 1.0`".

If these assumptions are not true, the filter constant must be adjusted. For example, if the texture is replicated 100 times on the object, it will appear at 1/100 of the size that mental ray expects, which can be compensated with "`filter 100`". Since texture projections are handled by shaders and not by the mental ray core, mental ray cannot do this automatically. The filter statement was used in the following example, which repeats the previous example with filtering. The filter size was tripled because filters are round and become spaced farther apart vertically faster than horizontally, a problem that is fully addressed only with elliptical texture filtering, described in the next section.

Figure 4.14 shows the improved images, using the filter constant of 120 — 3 to make it softer than the default, multiplied by 40 because the texture is replicated 40 times across the plane.

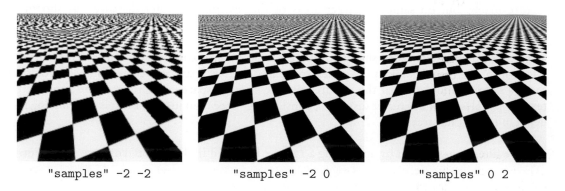

Figure 4.14: Texture mapping with filtering.

Texture filtering causes larger and larger areas to be covered by samples at greater distances, eventually turning the checkerboards near the horizon into a uniform gray. The halftoning raster used to print this book makes it difficult to distinguish the random pixel scattering on page 75 from the uniform gray in the above images, especially the rightmost one, but the effect is very obvious on a display screen.

Computing large filter lookups requires adding up many texels. mental ray does this by pre-filtering the texture into successively lower resolutions, each one-half the previous one, and interpolating small texel samples on two successive levels. Prefiltered multiresolution textures are called *pyramid textures* because they can be visualized as stacks of textures that are smaller at higher levels. The mip-map textures implemented in graphics systems such as OpenGL are a form of pyramid textures. mip-map textures are popular because they are simple to implement in hardware. mental ray works with RGBA textures (containing an alpha channel) and imposes no restriction on the horizontal and vertical resolution.

When loading a texture image from disk, mental ray prefilters it into a pyramid texture if a filter statement is present. This increases the memory requirements by approximately 35%, and can take a while to compute. However, pyramid textures are especially well suited for memory mapping (see page 70) because this not only avoids the memory penalty and the time-consuming prefiltering stage, but also might never or rarely touch any of the higher-resolution levels of the texture pyramid. This is a great advantage because each level requires four times the memory space of the next higher, lower-resolution level.

To create a memory mappable pyramid texture in advance, use version 2.1 (or later) of the imf_copy command with the -p option, in addition to the -r option described above:

    imf_copy -rp *filename*.rgb *filename*.map

This filtering technique is very easy to use — all it takes is the addition of `filter` statements in the scene file. The only drawback is the assumption that filters can be round, which gives good results in most images but fails if textures are seen at glancing angles, like in the checkerboard example. This remaining problem is addressed by elliptical texture filtering, described in the next section.

4.2.6 Elliptic Filtered Textures: Even Better Texture Anti-Aliasing

Simple filtered textures as described in the previous section work well if the viewing angle is not too small, but there are often areas near the sides of objects, or surfaces vanishing in the distance like the checkerboard example, where textures need to be filtered in one direction more than in another direction. The checkerboard example requires more texels to be considered in the vertical direction than in the horizontal direction, which turns the round texture samples into ellipses. In the example, the ellipse is taller than wide, but ellipses can be oriented at any angle.

Ellipses allow covering the entire texture as shown in figure 4.15, without leaving gaps or requiring overlaps such as those caused by the `filter` value 3.0 in the previous example. Overlaps helped to filter distant areas where the filters are sparse but cause unwanted blurring close to the camera where filters are closely spaced. Ellipses cover the texture much better without resorting to uniform scaling.

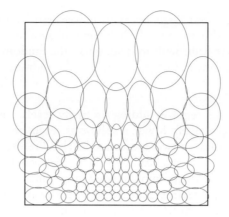

Figure 4.15: Elliptical texture sampling locations.

In order to do this, elliptical texture filtering requires more knowledge about the texturing situation than simple texture filtering. The following example replaces the *mib_texture_lookup* base shader in the example on page 73 with the *mib_texture_filter_lookup* base shader, which implements elliptical texture filtering:

```
filter color texture "pic" "tex_checker.rgb"

declare phenomenon
        color "flat_checker" (
                color texture    "texture"
        )
        shader "coord" "mib_texture_vector" (
                "select"         0,
                "selspace"       1
        )
        shader "remap" "mib_texture_remap" (
                "input"          = "coord",
                "repeat"         40 40
        )
        shader "tex" "mib_texture_filter_lookup" (
                "tex"            = interface "texture",
                "coord"          = "remap",
                "remap"          "remap",
                "eccmax"         20,
                "maxminor"       6,
                "space"          0
        )
        root = "tex"
end declare
```

This material is similar to the original one on page 73, except that it uses *mib_texture_filter_lookup* instead of *mib_texture_lookup*. This new base shader performs elliptical texture filtering. It has the following parameters:

tex   The texture to map; in this case, the checkerboard image.

coord   The coordinate to map at.

remap   The shader that was used for remapping. Note that this is not an assignment, but the shader itself is passed. It will be called multiple times to establish the texture viewing angle, which depends on the texture scaling, rotation, and whatever else happens during remapping. The shader must accept external texture coordinates (using its fourth argument; see [PROG]).

eccmax   The maximum eccentricity of the sphere; that is, the ratio between its large and small radius. This prevents runaway projections that can cause extremely long and thin ellipses. It is optional.

maxminor The largest allowed value for the smaller radius of the ellipse. This can be used to limit the maximum filter size. This is also optional.

space   Elliptic filtering only works together with texture vectors; see page 64. It does not work with projections. This parameter controls which texture space to use. Here, it must agree with the value of the select parameter of the *mib_texture_vector* shader; and it must be 0 or greater.

If elliptical texture filtering fails for any reason, for example because the remap parameter is missing or the referenced shader fails, it falls back on regular non-elliptical texture filtering. Figure 4.16 shows the result with elliptical filtering.

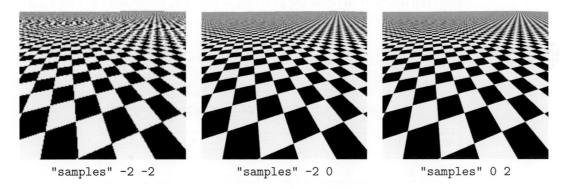

"samples" -2 -2   "samples" -2 0   "samples" 0 2

Figure 4.16: Texture mapping with elliptical filtering.

4.2.7 Summary: Selecting Optimal Texturing Methods

The choice of texturing methods affects quality, speed, and memory usage.

Quality: Worst with unfiltered textures, better with filtered textures, and best with elliptical texture filtering. It is often convenient to begin with unfiltered textures, but occasionally texturing situations exist that cause bump mapping artifacts, motion artifacts (flickering), and aliasing when viewing textures at grazing angles.

Speed: With no other factors considered, filtered textures (and more so elliptical filtered textures) are slightly slower than unfiltered textures at the same sampling rate. However, artifacts may be introduced by unfiltered textures, especially when the texture is used for bump mapping and displacement mapping. This can increase the number of triangles and the number of samples because mental ray tries to better resolve spurious artifacts, so in general the choice of filtering methods is of little concern for performance.

              Local textures are significantly faster than nonlocal textures if multiple machines are used for rendering (network parallelism) because the textures do not have to be downloaded at runtime. Textures are large and can quickly overwhelm a network, which means that remote machines spend too much time loading textures and get less or no chance to actually contribute useful work.

              Memory mapped textures are faster than non-mapped textures, even faster than local non-mapped textures, because they do not have to be read into memory in their entirety and they do not have to be uncompressed when loaded.

Memory: Memory usage can become an overriding concern in film production, which often uses hundreds of very large textures. In these cases memory mapping should no longer be considered an option, but becomes essential. If any kind of filtering is used, the corresponding memory mapped textures **must** be a pyramid textures created in advance with `imf_copy -rp` (see page 71 and page 77) because otherwise mental ray is forced to build the pyramid at runtime, which does not only take a very long time but also defeats memory mapping.

To summarize:

	nonlocal nonmapped	local nonmapped	local mapped	local mapped pyramid
unfiltered	●	○	●	○
filtered	○	○	○	●
elliptical	○	○	○	●

- A recommended combination of features. Unfiltered, nonlocal, and nonmapped textures are sufficient for small textures in simple situations (texture size matches size in the rendered image, not seen from grazing angles, no high contrast, not used for bump or displacement mapping).

- A possible but discouraged combination of features. Filtered and elliptically filtered textures should always use local mapped pyramid files because the pyramid texture would have to be built at runtime otherwise. If local textures are installed, one should use the memory mapped format. Local nonmapped is only acceptable for low-resolution (video) film strips where local disk space becomes a concern. (Memory mappable texture files are larger because they are uncompressed.)

Note that a memory mappable texture file automatically assumes that it is a local texture even if the color texture statement in the scene file does not specify the local modifier.

4.2.8 3D Textures

The previous examples all dealt with 2D textures, which pasted a flat image on the object. Since objects are defined in three dimensions, this involves a projection. In contrast, 3D textures are defined in three dimensions, so no projection is necessary. A 3D texture fills the space; it is defined for every point of 3D space. Applying a 3D texture to an object means that for every point on the surface of the object, the corresponding color provided by the 3D texture is used.

For example, consider a 3D texture that models wood grain applied to an object. On the surface of the object, the wood texture is evaluated and applied to the object. The effect is that the object appears carved from wood; a single wood fiber is visible on both sides of the object, and at any point in between where the object surface happens to intersect that fiber.

Consider the cube in the scene on page 32, instanced three times and scaled differently to add more edges to the scene, with a new material Phenomenon that constructs a 3D texture from the *mib_texture_turbulence* coherent noise generator:

```
verbose on
link "base.so"
$include <base.mi>

light "light1"
        "mib_light_point" (
            "color"     1 1 1,
            "factor"    0.75
        )
        origin          0 0 0
end light

instance "light1_inst" "light1"
        transform       1  0  0  0
                        0  1  0  0
                        0  0  1  0
                       -2 -3 -2  1
end instance

options "opt"
        samples         -1 2
        contrast        0.1  0.1  0.1
        object space
end options
```

```
camera "cam"
        frame           1
        output          "rgb" "out.rgb"
        focal           50
        aperture        44
        aspect          1
        resolution      800 800
end camera

declare phenomenon
        color "textured_mtl_sh" (
                array light     "lights",
        )
        shader "coord" "mib_texture_vector" (
                "select"        -1,
                "selspace"      2
        )
        shader "tex" "mib_texture_turbulence" (
                "coord"         = "coord",
                "iteration"     4,
                "strength"      12,
                "power"         .3
        )
        shader "map" "mib_color_interpolate" (
                "input"         = "tex",
                "num"           2,
                "color_0"       .1 .3 1,
                "color_1"       1 1 1
        )
        shader "mtl" "mib_illum_phong" (
                "ambient"       = "map",
                "diffuse"       = "map",
                "ambience"      .1 .1 .1,
                "specular"      1 1 1,
                "exponent"      50,
                "mode"          1,
                "lights"        = interface "lights"
        )
        root = "mtl"
end declare

material "mtl"
        opaque
        "textured_mtl_sh" (
            "lights"    ["light1_inst"],
        )
end material
```

The *mib_texture_vector* is used to extract the point in space (select -7) in world space (selspace 2), which is fed to the turbulence shader. The turbulence shader returns a scalar noise value, which is mapped to a color range from white to blue. Figure 4.17 shows the resulting image.

Figure 4.17: 3D texture.

Note how the bubbles and curls of the texture fold around the edges, giving the impression that they continue inside the object and have been brought to the surface by carving the object from a solid material. Since the turbulence is based on world space, the texture is consistent on the three scaled "cubes" even though they are three different objects which happen to share the same material.

Note that, being textures, 3D textures are evaluated only on the surface of the object. If the object were transparent, the carved appearance is lost because the object looks hollow, with the texture visible only at the surface. Textures are always surface effects; shaders that fill a volume to produce volumic effects are discussed on page 165.

4.3 Transparency Mapping

The previous chapter introduced texture mapping as a method to paste a "wallpaper" on objects by obtaining a surface color from a texture. Transparency mapping does the same but uses the texture to control the transparency of the surface of an object rather than its color. This can be used to punch holes into an object, but also to place cutouts of objects such as trees or water spray in a scene.

The most common method to determine the portions of an object that should be opaque or transparent is to use the alpha channel of a texture as the material color. Colors consist of red (R), green (G), blue (B), and alpha (A) components. Alpha specifies the opacity of the color: 0.0 is fully transparent and 1.0 is fully opaque. Due to premultiplication, the red, green, and blue components may never exceed the alpha component, even if premultiplication was switched off with a command line option (this was done so that shader writers do not have to implement two different modes). For example:

R	G	B	A	
1.0	1.0	1.0	1.0	fully opaque white
0.4	0.4	0.4	1.0	fully opaque 40% gray
0.4	0.4	0.4	0.4	60% transparent white
0.2	0.2	0.2	0.4	60% transparent 50% gray
1.0	1.0	1.0	0.4	illegal because RGB exceed A

Color values outside the 0...1 range are legal and can be used, but they must be either clipped or desaturated when stored in an 8-bit or 16-bit frame buffer, which is the last step after the last shader for the current sample has finished (usually a lens shader or material shader). The texture image used in the following image does have an alpha channel; without it no transparency mapping would take place.

The following example is identical to the texture vertex example on page 64, except that the Phenomenon has been replaced with:

```
declare phenomenon
    color "textured_mtl_sh" (
            color texture    "texture",
            array light      "lights"
    )
    shader "coord" "mib_texture_vector" (
            "select"         0,
            "selspace"       1
    )
    shader "remap" "mib_texture_remap" (
            "input"          = "coord"
    )
    shader "tex" "mib_texture_lookup" (
            "tex"            = interface "texture",
            "coord"          = "remap"
    )
    shader "mtl" "mib_illum_phong" (
            "ambient"        = "tex",
            "diffuse"        = "tex",
            "ambience"       .1 .1 .1,
            "specular"       1 1 1,
            "exponent"       50,
            "mode"           1,
            "lights"         = interface "lights"
    )
    shader "alpha" "mib_color_alpha" (
            "input"          = "tex",
            "factor"         1
    )
    shader "opacity" "mib_opacity" (
```

```
            "input"          = "mtl",
            "opacity"        = "alpha"
        )
      root = "opacity"
  end declare
```

This Phenomenon is more complex than the previous ones. Figure 4.18 shows a chart of all the connections between shaders, not showing the constant parameters:

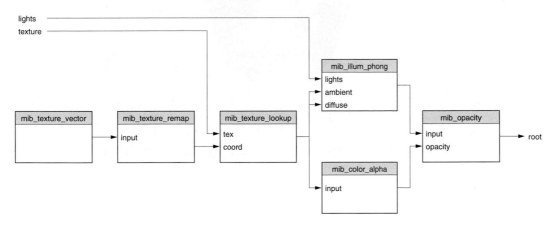

Figure 4.18: Texturing Phenomenon graph.

Since this Phenomenon defines a material shader, and material shaders are responsible for casting transparency rays if other objects behind the shaded object are visible, the *mib_opacity* shader was introduced which takes the alpha component of the texture, extracted by the *mib_color_alpha* shader, indicates where the object should be opaque, and casts transparency rays further on into the scene where the object is transparent. These transparency rays then hit the back side of the cube.

4.4   Bump Mapping

Bump mapping is a technique that introduces apparent surface deviations from its original shape, based on a texture. It can make a surface look as if a texture were engraved or raised in the geometric surface without actually changing the geometry. This is achieved by changing the surface normals. Surface normals are vectors that point perpendicular to the surface and define how the surface is oriented. Bump mapping perturbs the surface normals in a way *as if* the engraving or raises actually existed, as shown in figure 4.20.

The upper diagram shows a surface where the local geometric detail is modeled, and the lower diagram shows the same surface where the displacement is simulated with bump mapping. Visually, the effect is the same because the lighting calculations operate with the same normals in both cases — except that the shape of the object did not actually change, and no extra vertices (shown as circles) are needed.

Figure 4.19: Cube with transparency map

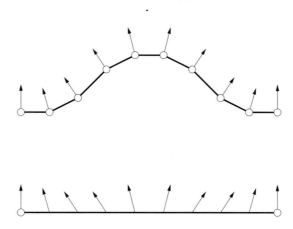

Figure 4.20: Bump mapping normals.

The advantages of bump mapping are:

- usage. Also, the extra normals are easily computed during rendering and need not be stored.
- tessellated, the acceleration data structures are smaller, and because the computation is performed only where the bump map is visible.
- the precision of the tessellation.

The disadvantages are:

- bump-mapped surface is seen edge-on, the illusion is lost.

- actual geometric bump that could cast a shadow back on the surface.

- match at the seam, or unexpected sharp lines appear.

Note that mental ray also supports *displacement mapping*, which has a similar effect as bump mapping but achieves it by actually deforming and introducing geometry. See page 90 for details.

Here is a bump mapping example. Again, the scene from page 64 is changed by replacing the Phenomenon declaration with the following one:

```
declare phenomenon
        color "textured_mtl_sh" (
                color texture    "texture",
                array light      "lights"
        )
        shader "coord" "mib_texture_vector" (
                "select"         0,
                "selspace"       1
        )
        shader "remap" "mib_texture_remap" (
                "input"          = "coord"
        )
        shader "mtl" "mib_illum_phong" (
                "ambient"        .3 .3 .3,
                "diffuse"        .7 .7 .7,
                "ambience"       .1 .1 .1,
                "specular"       1 1 1,
                "exponent"       50,
                "mode"           1,
                "lights"         = interface "lights"
        )

        shader "basis" "mib_bump_basis" (
                "project"        -1,
                "ntex"           0
        )
        shader "bump" "mib_passthrough_bump_map" (
                "tex"            = interface "texture",
                "u"              = "basis.u",
                "v"              = "basis.v",
                "coord"          = "remap",
                "step"           -.01 .01,
                "factor"         -4
        )
        root = "bump"
              = "mtl"
    end declare
```

This example uses two new Phenomenon features that have not been discussed before:

- The *mib_bump_basis* shader has two outputs, *u* and *v*, that can be connected to different shaders but here happen to be connected to the same one.

- The *mib_passthrough_bump_map* and *mib_illum_phong* shaders are connected in a shader list, which means that mental ray will call them one after the other. The root statement above lists both shaders in the order in which they will be called. The call order is important; *mib_passthrough_bump_map* must get the chance to modify the normal vector before *mib_illum_phong* uses it for shading. Note that the "=" sign is a prefix that refers to a named shader, not an assignment operator.

See page 271 for more details on Phenomena. Most of the work in this Phenomenon goes into perturbing the normal. Graphically, the Phenomenon is similar to figure 4.21. Again, only shader connections but not constant values are shown.

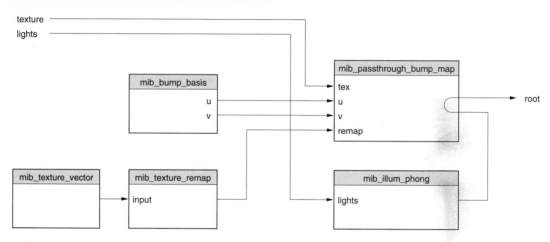

Figure 4.21: Bump mapping Phenomenon graph.

The texture coordinate calculation using the *mib_texture_vector* and *mib_texture_remap* shader is familiar, except that the resulting coordinate is not used for a color lookup but fed into *mib_passthrough_bump_map*, which looks up the texture at the current coordinate, slightly above that coordinate (in UV space), and slightly to the right of that coordinate. These three lookups provide *mib_passthrough_bump_map* with the gradient of the texture in the U and V directions, by subtracting the center lookup from the top and right lookups, respectively, and calculating the differences ΔU and ΔV. These differences measure how strongly the texture changes both horizontally and vertically.

The next step taken by *mib_passthrough_bump_map* is to convert these horizontal and vertical differences into a normal vector perturbation, by bending the normal in two directions multiplied by ΔU and ΔV. These directions are called *bump basis vectors*. They control how texture UV space relates to the surface of the object. Bump mapping is similar to texture mapping except that two vectors perpendicular to each other and to the normal vector are needed, instead of a single coordinate. As an equation, with $\vec{n}$ being the normal vector and $\vec{u}$ and $\vec{v}$ being the bump basis vectors, the new normal is calculated as

$$\vec{n}' := \vec{n} + \Delta U \cdot \vec{u} + \Delta V \cdot \vec{v}$$

After this computation, $\vec{n}'$ is normalized (so it has unit length as before) and becomes the new normal vector which is then used in shading computations.

Two parameters of *mib_passthrough_bump_map* are especially interesting: step is a vector that specifies how far in texture space the shader should look above and to the right of the center lookup. Good numbers for this parameter are small integers (say, 1...9) divided by the image resolution. The other is factor, which controls the strength of the effect; it is a multiplier for the bump basis vectors. Note that *mib_passthrough_bump_map* differs from the standard *mib_bump_map* shader by its color return parameter, which it leaves unchanged, rather than returning a vector. This allows it to be inserted into the color root shader list; hence the name "passthrough".

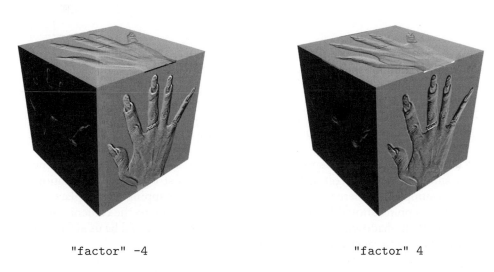

"factor" -4   "factor" 4

Figure 4.22: Bump mapping images.

One notable effect is that the sign of the factor determines whether the bump map is depressed or raised on the surface. Figure 4.22 shows the scene with a factor value of -4 and with a factor value of 4. The texture appears raised on the left image and depressed in the right image. Additionally, the sign of the step parameter values can be used to correct the sign of the bump basis vectors.

Note how the bump map looks good in the center, but that it does not change the edges in any way (this is especially visible at the bottom right edge). The left face of the cube receives some light because shadowing is not enabled; see page 133 for a discussion of shadows.

4.5   Displacement Mapping

Displacement mapping deforms object geometry by applying local offsets to the surface, which involves moving and introducing new vertices and triangles accordingly. The offsets are derived from texture lookups. For example, from the brightness of a texture image. Positive offsets displace the surface in the direction of the normal (effectively raising the surface), and negative offsets displace in the opposite direction (carving).

Figure 4.23 shows an undisplaced surface (top) and a surface with displacement (bottom). The displacement in the direction of the original surface normals is shown with dashed arrows. The normal vectors (solid arrows) are recomputed to fit the displaced surface.

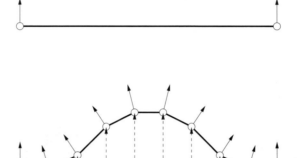

Figure 4.23: Displacement mapping.

Unlike bump mapping, displacement mapping actually alters geometry and hence results in a correct silhouette and correct self-shadowing, at the cost of slower tessellation and higher memory consumption. There is a tradeoff between bump mapping and displacement mapping: displacement mapping should be used when the object is close to the camera where details like silhouettes and self-shadowing are visible, and bump mapping should be used for distant or small objects where the difference does not matter.

Using high-quality displacement mapping indiscriminately can lead to unnecessarily large triangle counts, long tessellation times, and large memory consumption. The rules are:

- Use displacement mapping only when bump mapping is unacceptable.

- If using mental ray 3.1 or higher, always use fine approximation modes; either "fine length" or "fine view length" with an appropriate argument. The latter is recommended; use a pixel diagonal like 0.5 or 0.25.

- mental ray 3.0 and earlier do not handle displacement detail very well because they do not support fine approximation modes and must create all triangles for a displacement-mapped object in memory. Avoid noisy textures with fine detail, and choose the surface approximation carefully. More about this on page 93; also see page 346 for performance issues.

In the previous sections, all texture mapping effects were shading effects, which were handled by a material shader. Displacement mapping is different because it happens during geometry tessellation, not during rendering. Therefore, it is handled not by the material shader but by a special shader called a displacement shader. Like material shaders, displacement shaders are attached to the material of an object. Materials are "containers" that always contain a material shader, but may contain several other types of shaders.

The displacement mapping example in this section is again based on the texture mapped cube on pages 64 and 87, but here both the Phenomenon and the material are replaced with

```
declare phenomenon
        color "mtl_sh" (
                array light     "lights"
        )
        shader "mtl" "mib_illum_phong" (
                "ambient"       .3 .3 .3,
                "diffuse"       .7 .7 .7,
                "ambience"      .1 .1 .1,
                "specular"      1 1 1,
                "exponent"      50,
                "mode"          1,
                "lights"        = interface "lights"
        )
        root = "mtl"
end declare

declare phenomenon
        scalar "displace_sh" (
                color texture   "texture"
        )
        shader "coord" "mib_texture_vector" (
                "select"        0,
                "selspace"      1
        )
        shader "remap" "mib_texture_remap" (
                "input"         = "coord"
        )
        shader "tex" "mib_texture_lookup" (
                "tex"           = interface "texture",
                "coord"         = "remap"
        )
        shader "displace" "mib_color_intensity" (
                "input"         = "tex",
                "factor"        .2
        )
        root = "displace"
end declare

material "mtl"
        opaque
        "mtl_sh" (
```

```
        "lights"     ["light1_inst"]
    )
    displace "displace_sh" (
        "texture"    "pic1"
    )
end material
```

The "mtl_sh" Phenomenon which implements the material shader has shrunk to a single shader; it does not perform any texture mapping. The material "mtl" acquired a new shader, introduced with the displace keyword, that references the new Phenomenon "displace_sh" which implements the displacement shader. It performs the usual texture mapping steps: calculate a texture vector, remap it, and look it up in the texture image. The pixel that was looked up is converted to grayscale based on intensity using the *mib_color_intensity* shader, and the result is returned.

Note that the displacement Phenomenon returns a scalar value, not a color, as indicated with the scalar keyword after the declare phenomenon statement. However, mental ray accepts colors where scalars are expected, simply by taking the first component of the color (red). The *mib_color_intensity* shader was designed with this in mind.

mental ray 3.0 and higher require that displacement-mapped objects specify the maximum displacement using a max displace N statement in the object definition, with N being the maximum distance a point is displaced from its non-displaced 3D position in object space. Since mental ray 3.0 tessellates objects on demand, it must know when a ray comes close enough to the object to require tessellation, *including* the space around the object bounding box that contains the displacement. Bounding boxes always describe the shape of the object without taking displacement into account.

Before the scene can be rendered, it is necessary to add the statement

```
approximate fine view length 0.5
```

for mental ray 3.1 and higher, or

```
approximate angle 5 2 10
```

for mental ray 3.0 or lower, just before the end group statement in the object definition. Although mental ray 3.1 continue to support angle approximation, fine view length or fine length approximations are nearly always superior and far easier to adjust. The approximation statements control the precision of the approximation, and will be explained below. The resulting images, again with different factor values, are shown in figure 4.24.

Displacement mapping and bump mapping are very different approaches to the same problem, so the factor parameters in both cases have to be chosen differently. In the bump mapping case on page 87, the factor is applied to a normal-vector perturbation, while displacement mapping

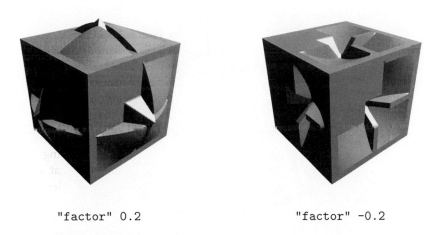

"factor" 0.2   "factor" -0.2

Figure 4.24: Approximation of displacement maps.

uses the factor as a multiplier for the distance a given point should be moved. The left image of figure 4.26 shows the image that was used for displacing the cubes.

The right image of figure 4.26 is a complex displacement map. Figure 4.25 shows the resulting displacement on a sphere, using the approximation "fine view length 0.1":

Care must be taken to use images with little noise because noisy images cause large numbers of irregular peaks and dents in the displacement that correspond to specks in the displacement map. The resolution must be sufficiently high so that displacement does not pick up and reproduce the individual square pixels; anti-aliased displacement maps can be counterproductive. Displacing, like any other form of mapping, is subject to sampling. Sampling is controlled by the approximation specification of the surface. For the same reason, it is often necessary to use 16-bit or floating-point textures for large displacement, because a difference of 1/256 can show up as a small but visible step on the displaced surface.

mental ray normally presamples displacement maps to improve displacement performance. However, in some cases the time spent for presampling cannot be amortized during rendering, for example because only a small section of a complex displaced object is visible. If mental ray seems to spend too much time with presampling, mental ray 3.2 allows turning it off with a displace presample off statement in the options block.

4.5.1 Simple Displacement Approximation[3.1]

mental ray supports a large number of approximation algorithms that allow detailed control over the conversion of geometry and displacement to triangles. However, in nearly all cases only three variants are necessary and useful. The following statements apply to polygonal geometry:

    approximate fine view length *length*

Figure 4.25: Fine approximation of a complex displacement map.

Figure 4.26: Displacement map textures.

This approximation subdivides the geometry until no triangle has an edge longer than *length* pixel diagonals. Typical *length* values are 0.5 or 0.25, although sometimes values as low as 0.1 are needed to resolve sharp corners properly. Since this can generate a large number of triangles, mental ray tessellates the geometry in small batches and maintains only the triangles it currently needs. Since mental ray 3.0 and earlier were not able to do this, they would need to keep all resulting triangles simultaneously, probably causing it to run out of memory and abort.

    approximate fine length *length*

This approximation is similar, except that *length* is measured in object space units, not pixel diagonals. This is sometimes more efficient if the object is multiply instanced, because then all instances can share the same tessellation, or if the scene is an animation using incremental changes to move the camera between frames, but does not change the geometry. Approximations using the keyword view depend on the relative position and orientation of the camera.

    approximate regular parametric *u v*

This approximation simply subdivides each triangle in a regular mesh of 4^u triangles. It is sometimes useful for very smooth displacements with no sharp edges. It does not cause the object to be split into fragments like the fine approximations do. Typically, it is more often used as a base surface approximation for free-form surface geometry, with one of the other two approximations used for displacement.

Approximations for free-form surface geometry is similar, but distinguish the approximation of the base surface, and the approximation of the displacement. Since surfaces are named, the (double-quoted) names must be appended to the statements:

    approximate fine view length *length names*
    approximate displace fine view length *length names*

    approximate fine length *length names*
    approximate displace fine length *length names*

    approximate regular parametric *u v names*
    approximate displace regular parametric *u v names*

The base surface typically has far less detail than the displacement, and will typically use a regular parametric approximation, while the displacement typically uses a fine view length approximation.

4.5.2 Advanced Displacement Approximation *

Although the three approximation algorithms presented in the previous section are nearly always sufficient, some applications need finer control over the tessellation. This is especially the case for industrial CAD applications. This section lists the complete set of approximation features provided by mental ray.

Quality and performance of displacement mapping greatly depend on the number of triangles used to approximate the displaced surface. It is important to use triangles wisely: many in areas of high curvature but few in nearly flat areas. This can be controlled with approximation statements.

If no approximation is given, mental ray will displace the vertices that would have been created anyway, and not add any for the displacement. Since the cube in the example above has only four vertices per face, and none are near a point on the texture that causes any displacement, displacement would have no effect without an approximation statement.

Approximation statements will be described in detail on page 337. Here the effect of approximation statements on displacement will be described. Approximation statements for displacements have the form

> approximate *flags technique limits*

when applied to polygons, and

> approximate displace *flags technique limits*

when applied to free-form surfaces such as the one on page 49 and appendix B because free-form surfaces also have other types of approximation statements that need to be distinguished. The components of the statement are:

flags   is an optional sequence of single words. This is described in more detail on page 337; for displacement mapping there are only two useful flags:

> view   enables view-dependent approximation, which causes the *d* parameters of the length and distance techniques to be interpreted as pixels, not 3D units. This causes distant objects to be tessellated less finely because they cover fewer pixels. It is less efficient for multiply-instanced objects because each instance may be tessellated differently (see page 371).

> any[2.1]   Normally, tessellation continues until all *technique*s are satisfied. The any keyword changes this policy to stop tessellation if any *technique* is satisfied. For example, if both angle and length techniques are specified together with any, the angle technique will only create triangles until the triangle edge lengths drop below the limit imposed by the length technique. This can be used to prevent runaway angle approximation by stopping the subdivision when the triangle edge length drops below one pixel diagonal (using the view keyword also).

> fine[3]   This keyword can be combined with the length technique to cause mental ray to split the object into small fragments that are tessellated separately. This makes it possible to generate extremely large numbers of very small triangles without the memory penalty that this would normally involve, making very fine approximations practical.

technique   specifies the criteria that guide mental ray when subdividing triangles to resolve details more finely. The technique is either parametric, regular parametric, or

---
[3]The fine keyword is available only in mental ray 3.1 and later.

any combination of one or more of the length, distance, and angle techniques. Parametric techniques cannot be mixed with others.

parametric *u v*   subdivides the edge into 2^u edges. Note that this differs from the interpretation of *u* in surface approximations, and that *v* is ignored.

length *d*   subdivides until the length of any triangle edge is less than *d* units (or *d* pixel diagonals in the view-dependent case).

distance *d*   subdivides until the difference between the displacement of all pairs of neighboring vertices is less than *d* units (or *d* pixel diagonals in the view-dependent case). This is different from distance approximation on the base free-form surface, where the distance to the true analytical surface is considered.

angle *d*   subdivides until no two normal vectors of neighboring triangles form an angle of more than *d* degrees along an edge. This technique should be used with care because displacement mapping can introduce arbitrarily sharp edges, which makes the final number of triangles difficult to predict unless it is limited with the any keyword and another technique such as length.

limits   consists of two integers that limit approximation subdivision. The first specifies the minimum number of times a triangle should be subdivided, and the second the maximum number of times it should be subdivided. This is done recursively, which means that increasing an integer by 1 quadruples the maximum allowed number of triangles. If the *limit* is omitted, the default is 0 5, for fine the default is 0 7. Limits have no effect on parametric techniques because they apply fixed subdivision.

Tessellation of free-form surfaces is performed in two stages. First the base approximation is applied. Then the displacement map is sampled at all vertices that were generated in the process, and the mesh is refined by introducing new vertices and samples as dictated by the displacement approximation. This means that a displacement approximation can never create fewer triangles than required by the base approximation, it can only add new triangles. It is often a good idea to make the base approximation weaker when the displacement approximation is introduced, and increasing the base approximation again if the displacement map sampling is insufficient. Polygonal and subdivision surface approximations only use a single stage.

Here are some examples that show different approaches to displacement approximation. All of them use large constants and no fine[3.3] flag to better show the strengths and weaknesses of the different techniques. In real scenes better constants would be chosen to remove the remaining artifacts; here they were chosen so that individual triangles remain visible in the wireframe images. Real scenes often require a number of triangles that is close to the number of pixels covered in the rendered image.

The simplest approach is parametric approximation, which creates a regular grid of triangles. This works well for soft wavy displacements with no sharp edges or large flat areas. Figure 4.27 shows the rendered image and the parametric triangle mesh. The mesh consists of 7200 triangles (all approximations in this section were tuned to result in approximately 7200 triangles for comparison). Figure 4.28 shows the texture image used for displacement.

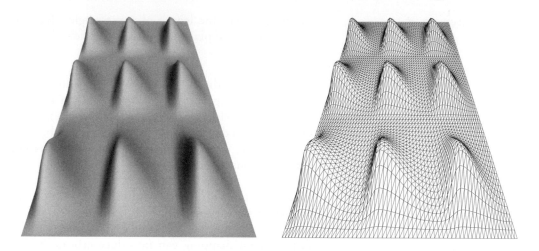

Figure 4.27: Parametric displacement map approximation.

Figure 4.28: Displacement map texture.

Here is the complete scene file for this scene. The `approximate surface` statement chooses parametric subdivision of the base surface into $(10 \cdot degree) \times (10 \cdot degree)$ triangle pairs. The *degree* of the base surface is 3 (as defined by the `bez` basis), so the base surface is divided into 1800 triangles. Every vertex of this surface becomes an initial sample point for the displacement map. The `approximate displace` approximation statement then controls whether the surface resulting from this displacement requires further subdivision. As described above, the parametric displacement approximation parameter 1 specifies constant subdivision into a $2^1 \cdot 2^1$ mesh, resulting in a total triangle count of 7200.

```
link "contour.so"
link "base.so"
$include <contour.mi>
$include <base.mi>

options "opt"
        samples         -1 2
```

```
            contrast         0.1   0.1   0.1
            jitter           0
            object space
    end options

    camera "cam"
            frame            1
            output           "rgb" "out.rgb"
            focal            3
            aperture         1
            aspect           1
            resolution       800 800
    end camera

    instance "cam_inst" "cam"
            transform 1 0 0 0  0 1 0 0  0 0 1 0  0 0 -14.5 1
    end instance

    light "light1"
            "mib_light_point" (
                "color"      1 1 1
            )
            origin           50 150 400
    end light

    instance "light1_inst" "light1" end instance

    color texture "pic1" "tex_wave.rgb"

    declare phenomenon
            color "displace_sh" (
                    color texture    "texture"
            )
            shader "coord" "mib_texture_vector" (
                    "select"         0,
                    "selspace"       1
            )
            shader "remap" "mib_texture_remap" (
                    "input"          = "coord",
                    "repeat"         3 3
            )
            shader "tex" "mib_texture_lookup" (
                    "tex"            = interface "texture",
                    "coord"          = "remap"
            )
            root = "tex"
    end declare

    material "mtl"
            opaque
            "mib_illum_phong" (
                "ambient"    0.3   0.3   0.3,
                "diffuse"    0.7   0.7   0.7,
```

```
                    "ambience"   0.3   0.3   0.3,
                    "specular"   0.2   0.2   0.2,
                    "exponent"   50,
                    "mode"       1,
                    "lights"     ["light1_inst"]
              )
              displace "displace_sh" (
                    "texture"    "pic1"
              )
       end material

       object "plane"
              visible trace shadow tag 1
              max displace 1.0
              basis "bez" bezier 3
              basis "lin" bezier 1
              group
                         -2 -2  2         -1 -2  2          1 -2  2         2 -2  2
                         -2  0 -4         -1  0 -4          1  0 -4         2  0 -4
                         -2  2 -10        -1  2 -10         1  2 -10        2  2 -10
                         -2  4 -16        -1  4 -16         1  4 -16        2  4 -16

                          0 .99  0          0  0  0        .99 .99 0        .99  0  0

                         v 0 v 1 v 2 v 3 v 4 v 5 v 6 v 7 v 8 v 9 v 10
                         v 11 v 12 v 13 v 14 v 15 v 16 v 17 v 18 v 19

                         surface "surf" "mtl"
                                  "bez" 0 1        0. 1.
                                  "bez" 0 1        0. 1.
                                  0 1 2 3    4 5 6 7    8 9 10 11    12 13 14 15

                         texture "lin"            0. 1.
                                  "lin"           0. 1.
                                  16 17 18 19

                         approximate surface   parametric 10 10 "surf"
                         approximate displace parametric 1 1    "surf"
              end group
       end object

       instance "plane_inst" "plane" end instance

       instgroup "rootgrp"
              "cam_inst" "light1_inst" "plane_inst"
       end instgroup

       render "rootgrp" "cam_inst" "opt"
```

Note that with parametric approximation, it is always possible to increase the grid density until the desired quality is achieved, but the number of triangles grows quickly, and there are other techniques that create fewer triangles by adaptively subdividing surfaces.

Next, length approximation is applied to the displacement:

```
approximate surface  parametric 4 4 "surf"
approximate displace length 0.412 1 5 "surf"
```

The parametric subdivision of the base surface was reduced to 4 4 or 144 triangles, and it was left to the edge length limit to reduce the triangle size. In particular, diagonal triangle edges were reduced, especially where the surface was stretched by the displacement map. Since the displacement approximation forces at least one subdivision, the same effect could have been achieved with approximating the base surface with `parametric 4 4` and decreasing both limits of the displacement approximation. View dependency further improves the tessellation:

```
approximate surface  parametric 4 4 "surf"
approximate displace view length 22.5 1 5 "surf"
```

View dependency measures the edge length in pixel diagonals projected on the viewing plane. This means that triangles at greater distances, which appear smaller in the rendered images, are tessellated less finely. The right image in figure 4.29 shows that the distant bumps are tessellated with far fewer triangles, and that the flat areas of the base surface also requires fewer triangles at greater distances. View-dependent edge length approximation is useful to achieve a desired ratio of triangles to pixels in the rendered image.

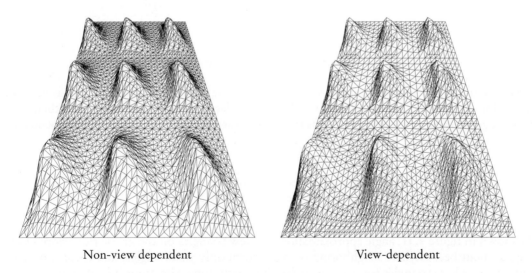

Non-view dependent   View-dependent

Figure 4.29: Edge length displacement map approximation.

Distance approximation measures the difference between displacements at neighboring vertices. This increases the number of triangles in areas of high curvature because more triangles are required to approximate a curved surface closely with linear triangle edges. Distance approximation also allows view dependency:

```
approximate surface   parametric 4 4 "surf"
approximate displace distance 0.119 1 5 "surf"


approximate surface   parametric 4 4 "surf"
approximate displace view distance 6.86 1 5 "surf"
```

Figure 4.30 shows that distance approximation uses very few triangles in flat areas, and concentrates on areas of high curvature. Again, view dependency uses more triangles for bumps close to the camera and few triangles for distant bumps.

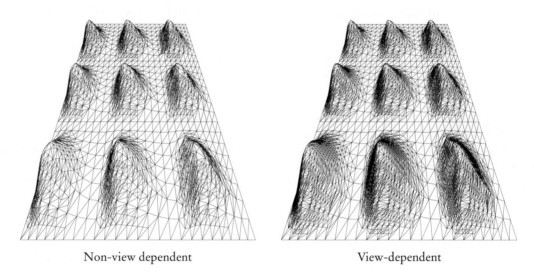

Non-view dependent   View-dependent

Figure 4.30: Distance displacement map approximation.

Finally, angle approximation considers the angle that neighboring triangles form. It is very well suited for displacements where large parts of the displacement are nearly flat and others show sharp edges because it specifically spends triangles in the areas of high curvature and spends little effort on the nearly flat areas.

```
approximate surface   parametric 4 4 "surf"
approximate displace angle 38.4 1 5 "surf"
```

As shown in figure 4.31, angle approximation uses few triangles on the gentle right slopes of the displacement because here neighboring triangles form only small angles, and focuses on edges and creases where triangles form sharp angles. For angle approximations it is often necessary to specify either an upper tessellation limit (here 5) to avoid very large numbers of triangles at sharp discontinuities, or to use the any flag[2.1] together with a length technique to stop subdivision when a minimum triangle edge length is reached.

The last three techniques can also be combined to ensure that the tessellation satisfies multiple criteria, but one suffices in most cases. If multiple criteria are given, the resulting triangle count is

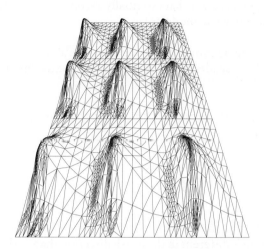

Figure 4.31: Angle displacement map approximation.

equal to or higher than with any of the criteria alone because subdivision continues until all criteria are satisfied. If techniques are combined and the any keyword is added, tessellation stops when *any* criterion is satisfied, resulting in at most as many triangles as the least demanding technique alone. Typically subdivision limits can be set lower with the any keyword than without.

All techniques other than parametric allow approximation subdivision limits. The first number should be small enough to not cause unnecessary "minimum" subdivision where no displacement detail requires it, and large enough to make sure that there are sufficient initial samples near displaced areas. Typically it is set to 0. However, it is generally the wrong strategy to first perfect the free-form surface approximation and then add displacement detail with the displacement approximation. Instead, the surface approximation should be as coarse as possible, and the displacement approximation should be used to improve the mesh. In this case the minimum subdivision limit is helpful to increase detail uniformly over the pretessellated base surface.

The second number limits the maximum subdivision to prevent runaway tessellation. For example, a sharp edge resulting from high-contrast lines in the displacement texture image can cause a great deal of subdivision when the angle approximation technique is used with a sufficiently small parameter because each new triangle would form some large angle between the "horizontal" and the "vertical" side of the edge.

Remember that the limits operate recursively — increasing the lower limit number by 1 quadruples the minimum number of triangles, and increasing the maximum limit quadruples the maximum number of triangles.

Displacement mapping is an excellent tool to introduce geometric detail, but in general it cannot replace a modeling program. Especially texture-based non-fine displacement mapping (as opposed to procedural displacement mapping, which is possible with appropriate custom shaders) is restricted by the limited sample resolution to images with little noise. Fine approximations[3.1] can deal with noisy displacement, but it still slows down rendering. The wireframe images show that texture-based displacement that essentially reconstructs geometry from images cannot achieve the precision of a geometric modeler.

Note that displacement mapping moves points on a surface along their normal, perpendicular to the surface, but displacement shaders have the option of controlling the direction along which points are displaced.

Displacement of polygonal meshes results in smooth surfaces if the polygons have shared vertex normals, and in faceted surfaces otherwise.

4.6   Anisotropic Shading

Anisotropic shading means that the shaded surface is "not the same" in different directions. For example, brushed aluminum is different in the brush direction than in the perpendicular direction, which affects shading. Directions on a surface are closely tied to UV coordinates on the surface (see page 51 for examples and diagrams), except that they are not defined by the absolute UV coordinates but the *rate of change* of the UV coordinates, called the *first surface derivatives*. The first surface derivative is a pair of vectors defined in UV space that define the local UV axes: one vector points in the direction in which the U coordinates increase, and the other in the direction in which the V coordinates increase.

mental ray also supports *second surface derivatives*, which specify the rate of change of the first derivative. Second derivatives are defined by the three vectors, $\partial^2 \vec{P}/\partial U^2$, $\partial^2 \vec{P}/\partial V^2$, and $\partial^2 \vec{P}/(\partial U \partial V)$. However, they are not important for anisotropic shading and are mentioned here only for completeness.

Anisotropic shading is possible only on surfaces that have surface derivatives built into them (a shader could compute them at render time, but that is less efficient and less precise, and none of the base shaders that come with mental ray do it). For polygons, the translator that generated the scene must provide them using appropriate d statements in every vertex definition. Free-form surfaces are easier; mental ray automatically generates derivatives if the `derivative` statement is specified once in the surface definition. The sphere scene on page 49 and appendix B contains such a statement specifically for anisotropic shading.

At the beginning of this chapter, a simple form of anisotropic shading was introduced: the *mib_illum_ward_deriv* shader (see page 53) creates an anisotropic highlight. Figure 4.32 shows an example. The left sphere simulates metal brushed vertically from pole to pole; the right sphere is brushed horizontally in circles around the circumference.

The scene is similar to the scene shown on page 49 and in appendix B, with the sphere at the position (0, 0, 0) and rotated around the X axis by 45 degrees, and four light sources at t,he positions (0, 20, 5), (0, -20, 5), (-20, 20, 40), and (10, 20, 10). The sphere material uses the *mib_illum_ward_deriv* material shader:

```
material "mtl"
        opaque
```

```
"shiny_u" 5                          "shiny_u" 60
"shiny_v" 60                         "shiny_v" 5
```

Figure 4.32: Anisotropic shading.

```
"mib_illum_ward_deriv" (
        "ambient"          .1 .1 .1,
        "diffuse"          .2 .2 .2,
        "ambience"         .1 .1 .1,
        "glossy"           .3 .3 .3,
        "shiny_u"          5,
        "shiny_v"          60,
        "lights"           ["light1_inst", "light2_inst",
                            "light3_inst", "light4_inst"]
)
end material
```

This material was used for the left image in figure 4.32. The right image uses the same material but with shiny_u and shiny_v reversed. These parameters specify the extent of the highlight in the U (longitude) and V (latitude) directions.

Next, the concept is extended with a texture map to rotate the surface derivatives. Instead of controlling the extent of the highlights directly from the surface derivatives, a special shader is used to rotate the surface derivative directions based on the brightness of a texture image. The following material creates anisotropic reflections when used in the standard sphere scene on page 49 (this time with an unrotated sphere and only one light):

```
color texture "pic0" "tex_aniso.rgb"

declare phenomenon
        color "anis_mtl_sh" (
                color texture   "texture",
                array light     "lights"
        )
```

```
shader "coord" "mib_texture_vector" (
        "select"        -1,
        "project"        6,
        "selspace"       1
)
shader "remap" "mib_texture_remap" (
        "input"         = "coord",
        "repeat"         6  3  1,
        "transform"      1  0  0  0
                         0 .1  0  0
                         0  0  0  0
                         0 .5  0  1
)
shader "tex" "mib_texture_lookup" (
        "tex"           = interface "texture",
        "coord"         = "remap"
)
shader "uderiv" "mib_texture_vector" (
        "select"        -5
)
shader "rotate" "mib_texture_rotate" (
        "input"         = "uderiv",
        "angle"         = "tex",
        "min"            0,
        "max"            1
)
shader "mtl" "mib_illum_ward" (
        "ambient"       = "tex",
        "diffuse"        .7 .7 .7,
        "ambience"       .1 .1 .1,
        "glossy"         1  1  1,
        "u"             = "rotate.u",
        "v"             = "rotate.v",
        "shiny_u"        2,
        "shiny_v"        9,
        "mode"           1,
        "lights"        = interface "lights"
)
root = "mtl"
end declare

material "mtl"
        opaque
        "anis_mtl_sh" (
            "texture"   "pic0",
            "lights"    ["light1_inst"],
        )
end material
```

The material Phenomenon consists of three parts:

Texture   The *mib_texture_vector*, *mib_texture_remap*, and *mib_texture_lookup* shaders implement a standard texture map that tile an image on the sphere, using spherical projection. Except for slight numerical parameter adjustments this is no different from the texture projection example on page 63.

Anisotropy   The second *mib_texture_lookup* and the *mib_texture_vector* and *mib_texture_rotate* shaders read the U surface derivative and rotate it around the surface normal, by an angle that depends on the brightness of the texture image. The *mib_texture_rotate* shader only requires a single derivative vector, because the other one is implicitly given by the fact that this vector, the other one, and the normal are all perpendicular to one another (or, in mathematical terms, are vector cross products of one another).

Illumination   The *mib_illum_ward* shader is similar to the *mib_illum_ward_deriv* shader used in the simple Ward shading example on page 53, except that it accepts explicit surface derivative vectors (as u and v parameters) instead of taking them from the render state. The dot notation in the u and v assignments is necessary because the *mib_texture_rotate* shader has two return values u and v (all other shaders only have a single return value). In the example, the texture is also mapped on the ambient color to better show the effect of the brightness of the texture.

The min and max parameters of *mib_illum_ward* determine which texture brightness correspond to no (0 degrees) and full (360 degrees) rotation, in the range [0..1]. The texture image used for this example (figure 4.33) contains only black (0) and 25% gray (0.25) values, that get translated to rotations of 0 and 90 degrees.

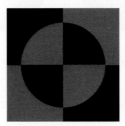

Figure 4.33: Anisotropic control texture.

Anisotropic reflection makes the strongest visual impression when it is animated. The sequence in figure 4.34 shows the anisotropic scene above with a light moving from the (10, 10, 10) position (to the right and above the camera) to the (0, 0, 0) position (directly in the line of sight):

The texture image determines the movements of the highlights. This texture image contains only two perpendicular brushing directions, but arbitrary brushing can be implemented simply by using an appropriate texture image. Concentric brushing such as the brushing found in some frying pans requires a different texture (figure 4.35).

Note that white indicates the same direction as black because 0 and 360 degrees are equivalent. Here is the result when mapped on the same spheres as above, with higher values for the repeat count and a constant (0.3 0.3 0.3) ambient illumination, as shown in figure 4.36.

Figure 4.34: Patterned anisotropic shading.

Figure 4.35: Another anisotropic control texture.

Figure 4.36: Concentric anisotropic shading.

Care should be taken to avoid anti-aliasing in the control texture that could cause tiny "brushing vortices" in areas of high contrasts.

4.7 Environment Mapping

Environment mapping, sometimes called reflection mapping, is a technique that maps a texture on an infinite sphere, cube, or other similar "large" enclosing shape, and calculates what this mapped shape would look like when reflected in the environment-mapped object. The enclosing shape is not an object itself, it is merely an abstraction, calculated analytically taking only the viewing direction and (sometimes) the viewing location into account.

Environment mapping is a local effect, which means that no other object is involved, only the environment-mapped object. In fact, environment maps are attached to the material of the environment-mapped object. This means that two different objects can have different environment maps, if any at all. Environment mapping is a cheap alternative for real reflection.

True raytraced reflections show the reflection of other objects in the scene; environment mapping does not. However, unlike true reflections which require ray tracing, they are simple and very fast to compute.

Environment maps are not a good way to model mirrors or other precise reflectors that are expected to properly reflect other objects in the scene, but they can be very effectively used to give objects a shiny appearance by letting the environment map make only a small contribution. They are also useful to simulate chrome on highly curved surfaces because reflections on such surfaces are highly distorted, which makes it less important to accurately reflect other objects. Attaching a blurry image to an object as an environment map makes the object appear glossy, at very low computational cost.

Here is an example for a material with an environment shader and a material shader that reflects the environment map. The following scene fragment replaces the Phenomenon and the material in the simple sphere scene on page 49:

```
color texture "pic0" "tex_tiles.rgb"
color texture "pic1" "tex_checker.rgb"

declare phenomenon
        color "mtl_sh" (
                array light      "lights"
        )
        shader "mtl" "mib_illum_phong" (
                "ambient"        .3 .3 .3,
                "diffuse"        .7 .7 .7,
                "ambience"       .1 .1 .1,
                "specular"       1 1 1,
                "exponent"       50,
                "mode"           1,
                "lights"         = interface "lights"
        )
        shader "env" "mib_reflect" (
                "input"          = "mtl",
                "reflect"        .3 .3 .3 .3,
                "notrace"        true
        )
        root = "env"
end declare

declare phenomenon
        color "env_sh" (
                color texture    "ceil_env",
                color texture    "floor_env",
                color texture    "wall_env"
        )
        shader "state-point" "mib_texture_vector" (
                "select"         -1,
                "selspace"       2
        )
        shader "state-dir" "mib_texture_vector" (
```

```
                    "select"           -4,
                    "selspace"          2
            )
        shader "tex" "mib_lookup_cube6" (
                    "point"           = "state-point",
                    "dir"             = "state-dir",
                    "size"            100 100 100,
                    "tex_mx"          = interface "wall_env",
                    "tex_px"          = interface "wall_env",
                    "tex_my"          = interface "floor_env",
                    "tex_py"          = interface "ceil_env",
                    "tex_mz"          = interface "wall_env",
                    "tex_pz"          = interface "wall_env"
            )
        root = "tex"
    end declare

    material "mtl"
            opaque
            "mtl_sh" (
                "lights"     ["light1_inst"],
            )
            environment "env_sh" (
                "ceil_env"  "pic0",
                "floor_env" "pic0",
                "wall_env"  "pic1"
            )
    end material
```

The material Phenomenon uses the *mib_reflect* shader to blend the result of the *mib_illum_phong* shader with the environment map. The reflectivity is constant; it could have been textured by attaching an appropriate texture shader to the *reflect* parameter. The *notrace* parameter ensures that only the environment map is sampled; for true reflections see section 4.9.

Note that the environment itself is not part of the material Phenomenon. A separate environment attached to the material provides the lookup function. This type of environment is called a *local environment* because it applies only to the material to which it is attached. If the material is attached to an instance, material inheritance is applied to other objects in the tree, which then use this environment as well. See page 379 for details on material inheritance. When mental ray evaluates environments, it also takes atmospheric effects (implemented as volume shaders, see page 165) into account. Figure 4.37 shows the image, which shows the environment being reflected in the sphere.

The alternative to local environments are *global environments* that are not attached to a material but to a camera. The global environment does not apply to individual objects but to parts of the rendered image where no object is seen (more precisely, for primary rays that leave the scene). Camera definitions accept the same environment statements as materials. If the camera definition is replaced with

```
    camera "cam"
```

Figure 4.37: Local environment map.

```
        frame           1
        output          "rgb" "out.rgb"
        focal           1
        aperture        1
        aspect          1
        resolution      800 800
        environment "env_sh" (
            "ceil_env"  "pic0",
            "floor_env" "pic0",
            "wall_env"  "pic1"
        )
    end camera
```

The camera and its camera instance need to be moved after the environment Phenomenon definition for this to work, because scene entities cannot be used before they are defined. The result is shown in figure 4.38. The sphere looks the same as before because its material did not change in any way, but the background now also shows the environment.

Figure 4.38: Global and local environment map.

4.8 Light Mapping

Light mapping is a new feature in mental ray 3.0 and is not supported in mental ray 2.x. It is basically a new way of dealing with textures. Standard textures contain patterns wrapped on an object while lightmap textures contain entire illumination solutions. This is especially useful for computationally expensive indirect light simulations. The basic idea is that the simulation is done once and then "baked" onto the object. When rendering, the illumination can simply be taken from the light map instead of being computed by sampling light sources or global illumination irradiance.

During rendering, light maps are not very different from regular textures, except that they make illumination computations unnecessary. However, light maps must be created first, and this is where mental ray's light mapping support comes in. Creating a light map means that information is sampled for each point on the surface of the object, even those not visible from the camera, and stored in the light map.

mental ray creates light maps before rendering begins. For every object that references or inherits a material that contains a light map shader, mental ray calls that lightmap shader in "vertex mode" for each triangle vertex of the object. The shader may sample and record information for each call. When all vertices have finished, the lightmap shader is called once more in "output mode" to write the texture using the recorded information. Lightmap shaders in output mode typically project and paint triangles into the texture.

The vertex and output mode distinction is a very general mechanism that allows various different approaches to light map generation. In vertex mode, the lightmap shader may sample illumination to be interpolated during lightmap texture creation, or it may just record point and normal information and do the illumination sampling in output mode. The first case is useful for vertex lighting, while the second case is useful for illumination texture mapping. The second approach is taken by the *mib_lightmap_** shaders in the base shader library.

Here are the necessary steps for creating a light map for an object:

- ☑ Add a lightmap shader to a material of the object, or that is inherited by the object. One is enough, even if the material is attached to only a subset of triangles. Lightmap shaders always apply to the entire object.

- ☑ If the lightmap shader generates a light map texture (this is the normal case), declare a writable texture.

Lightmap shaders are added to a material using the `lightmap` statement:

```
material "material_name"
    ...
    lightmap shader
end material
```

Writable textures have been introduced in mental ray 3.0 to allow a shader to create a texture image during rendering. A new keyword `writable` turns standard texture definitions into writable texture definitions:

$$\text{writable [local] } \textit{type} \text{ texture "}\textit{name}\text{" "}\textit{filename}\text{"} \quad [\textit{xres yres [zres]}]$$

Writable textures must specify the horizontal and vertical resolution of the texture in pixels, in square brackets at the end of the definition. The *type* is one of color, vector, and scalar. If the type is color, the number of bytes per component (1 for bytes, 2 for 16-bit words, or 4 for 32-bit floating-point numbers) may be specified also as *zres*; the default is 1. Writable textures are created in memory as transparent black images, null vectors, or null scalars, even if the texture file already exists on disk. They are then written to by the shader, then saved to disk, and can finally be used like any other texture for the remainder of rendering.

The following example uses the *mib_lightmap_sample* and *mib_lightmap_write* shader pair in the base shader library to collect vertex information during the vertex stage, and to sample each point of the texture surface from this information during the output stage, respectively:

```
verbose on
link "base.so"
link "physics.so"
$include <base.mi>
$include <physics.mi>

light "light1"
        "physical_light" (
            "color"     60000 60000 60000
        )
        origin          20 20 20
        energy          60000 60000 60000
        globillum photons 100000
end light

instance "light1-i" "light1" end instance

options "opt"
        samples         0 2
        globillum       on
        globillum accuracy 4000 2.0
        object space
end options

camera "cam"
        frame           1
        output          "rgb" "out.rgb"
        focal           1
        aperture        1
        aspect          1
        resolution      800 800
end camera

material "mtl" opaque
        "dgs_material" (
            "diffuse"   0.7 0.7 0.7,
            "glossy"    0.2 0.2 0.2,
            "shiny"     5,
```

```
               "lights"      ["light1-i"]
        )
        photon "dgs_material_photon" ()
end material

$include "sphere.mi"              # see appendix for a listing of sphere.mi

#--------------------------------------------------------------------------

local writable color texture "pic" "lightmap.map" [ 800 800 4 ]

declare phenomenon
        material "lightmap_mtl" (
                color texture    "texture",
                array light      "lights"
        )
        shader "coord" "mib_texture_vector" (
                "select"         -1,
                "project"        7,
                "selspace"       1
        )
        shader "tex" "mib_texture_lookup" (
                "tex"            = interface "texture",
                "coord"          = "coord"
        )
        shader "mtlsh" "mib_illum_lambert" (
                "ambient"        = "tex",
                "ambience"       0.318 0.318 0.318      # 1/pi
        )
        shader "lm_sample" "mib_lightmap_sample" (
                "indirect"       on,
                "lights"         = interface "lights"
        )
        shader "lm_write" "mib_lightmap_write" (
                "texture"        = interface "texture",
                "coord"          "coord",
                "input"          "lm_sample"
        )
        material "mtl" opaque
                = "mtlsh"
                lightmap         = "lm_write"
                photon "dgs_material_photon" (
                        "diffuse"        0.7 0.7 0.7,
                        "lights"         = interface "lights"
                )
        end material
        root material "mtl"
end declare

shader "texmtl" "lightmap_mtl" (
        "texture"        "pic",
        "lights"         ["light1-i"],
)
```

```
instance "center-i" "sphere"
        material "texmtl"
end instance

instance "sph0-i" "sphere"
        transform       2 0 0 0   0 2 0 0   0 0 2 0   20 0 0 1
end instance

instance "sph1-i" "sphere"
        transform       2 0 0 0   0 2 0 0   0 0 2 0   -20 0 0 1
end instance

instance "sph2-i" "sphere"
        transform       2 0 0 0   0 2 0 0   0 0 2 0   10 -8 10 1
end instance

instance "sph3-i" "sphere"
        transform       2 0 0 0   0 2 0 0   0 0 2 0   -10 -8 10 1
end instance

instance "sph4-i" "sphere"
        transform       2 0 0 0   0 2 0 0   0 0 2 0   10 8 -10 1
end instance

instance "sph5-i" "sphere"
        transform       2 0 0 0   0 2 0 0   0 0 2 0   -10 8 -10 1
end instance

instgroup "spheres"
        "center-i" "sph0-i" "sph1-i" "sph2-i" "sph3-i" "sph4-i" "sph5-i"
end instgroup

instance "sevenspheres" "spheres"
        material        "mtl"
        transform       1 0 0 0   0 1 0 0   0 0 1 0   0 0 12 1
end instance
#-------------------------------------------------------------------------

instance "cam_inst" "cam"
        transform       1 0 0 0   0 1 0 0   0 0 1 0   0 0 -14 1
end instance

instgroup "rootgrp"
        "cam_inst" "light1-i"  "sevenspheres"
end instgroup

render "rootgrp" "cam_inst" "opt"
```

The *mib_lightmap_write* lightmap shader computes texture pixel from both direct and indirect illumination. Indirect illumination comes from final gathering, which is enabled in the options block. Note that the *mib_illum_lambert* material shader is used to generate flat shading, by leaving the diffuse color undefined (black). The ambient color is derived from the light map. No light is passed to the material shader — this is not necessary because *mib_lightmap_write* has already computed all illumination and stored it in the light map texture.

The six spheres around the center sphere are not light-mapped; they use a standard Phong shading material to cast some reflected light on the central sphere. The front two small spheres are lowered, while the back spheres are raised. The small spheres inherit their Phong materials from the group that contains all spheres (sevenspheres), while the central sphere inherits its lightmapping material from its own instance (center-i). The material shader Phenomenon uses a "lollipop" projection method (mode 7) that puts the center of the texture at the top pole of the central sphere, and folds the edges so they all meet at the bottom pole.

Figure 4.39: Created light map

Figure 4.39 shows the computed light map (the file lightmap.map), and figure 4.40 shows the rendered image. The light map shows the direct illumination as a large white patch on the bottom left. Light received indirectly from the small spheres appears as smaller patches at the top right of the light map. Note that the rendered image shows correct highlights and soft indirect illumination from the small sphere even though its shader performs no illumination calculations whatever — it's all in the light map texture.

Note that the light map contains *irradiance*, which describes the incoming light, and must be converted to illumination in order to be mapped onto the object. This is done by dividing the values in the light map by π, which is why the material shader uses 0.318 (1 divided by π) for its ambience parameter. See the subsection on Illumination Models on page 225 for more information on irradiance vs. illumination, and the reason for the π factor. Also note that the light map is stored in floating-point format (specified by the 4 in the writable texture statement, which means 4 bytes per component) to permit storing irradiance values outside the 0..1 range. (This is also why the .map format was chosen in the example — .rgb would have clamped to the 0..1 range.)

The light map texture projection is important. It should be chosen to cover the entire surface and have no ambiguities or singularities. The lollipop texture mode is a boundary case: it is

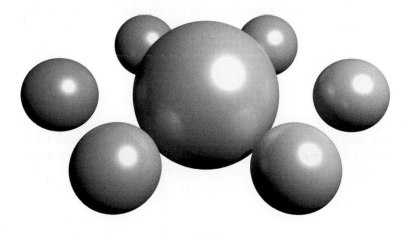

Figure 4.40: Image rendered with light map

continuous and free of singularities only from the center, where it maps to the north pole of the sphere, to a ring that maps to the south pole. The *mib_texture_vector* shader is programmed to reject singularity coordinates (it returns "false"). This prevents the *mib_lightmap_write* lightmap shader from painting huge triangles from one edge of the texture to the opposite edge, which would overwrite otherwise valid illumination data and cause large and nearly flat texture images. Texture vertices often allow more control over mapping than procedural texture projections like lollipop or spherical projections. They were not used here to keep the example scene short.

The example scene both creates and uses the light map. Typically the light map is created once and then used for many subsequent rendering operations, which then do not need the final gathering or other illumination calculations that are "frozen" into the light map and not required by other elements in the scene. Light mapping is especially useful to create textures for real-time entertainment scenes where scenes are rendered on game consoles that are not powerful enough to support global illumination. Obviously, a light map remains useful only as long as the scene does not change too much.

A material containing a lightmap shader should not be applied to more than one object instance. In the example it was applied only to the center sphere and not to the six smaller spheres. If a lightmap shader is applied to multiple objects, or a group of objects, or to an object that is multiply instanced, it would run once for each object, each time clearing the light map and painting into it, overwriting the light maps for the other object instances. On multiprocessor systems, this happens in parallel, causing the shaders to fight over the light map texture, which would end up as an unpredictable mixture of illumination contributions from multiple object instances.

Note that mental ray's light map mechanism is very general. It basically provides access to all vertices and all triangles of an object, and leaves the actual illumination computation and data storage to the lightmap shader. Instead of generating a light map texture, the shaders might also write out geometric or illumination data to a file for external game development projects, or sample non-illumination data such as visibility or scene geometry properties.

4.9 Reflection

Environment mapping is a fast method for showing reflections from textures mapped on simple procedural shapes such as infinite spheres around the scene, but it cannot handle reflections of other objects. mental ray handles reflections (as well as refraction, see below) using a ray tracing algorithm. Note that ray tracing is an optional algorithm that can be switched off using the -trace off command line option, or the trace off statement in the options block of the scene. If this is done no reflections appear.

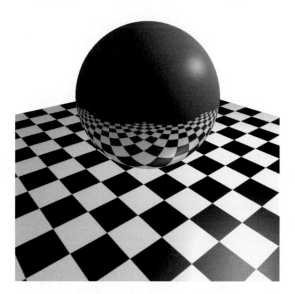

Figure 4.41: Reflective sphere.

It is a tradition to demonstrate reflections with a reflective sphere on a checkerboard ground plane at this point (figure 4.41). Schematically, the scene consists of a camera, a sphere with a reflective material shader, and a ground plane with a checkerboard texture mapped on it, as shown in figure 4.42.

The interesting object is the sphere. It uses a regular Phong illumination shader (*mib_illum_-phong*), whose output is passed through a shader that applies the reflection (*mib_reflect*). Reflections are handled by material shaders. The shader must determine the direction in which the incoming ray is reflected, cast a reflection ray, and apply the returned color to the material

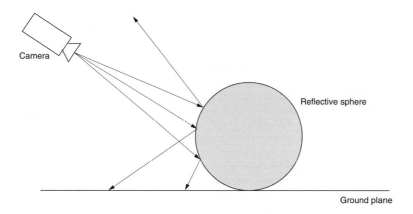

Figure 4.42: Schematic view of reflective sphere.

color. mental ray offers shader interface functions to help with direction calculation and to cast rays but does not handle reflection by itself. Reflections, just like ambient and diffuse colors, are handled by shaders, which have full control over how many secondary rays are cast and in which direction, and how the result is applied to the shader result.

In this case, *mib_reflect* always casts a single ray in the mirror direction of the incoming ray, and blends that result with the illumination color.

The scene that created the above image is lengthy, but it will be used for refraction and caustics also, so here is the entire scene file. Only the definition of the sphere object was omitted; refer to appendix B.

```
link "base.so"
$include <base.mi>

light "light1"
        "mib_light_point" (
            "color"      1 1 1,
            "factor"     0.75
        )
        origin           10 10 10
end light

instance "light1_inst" "light1"
end instance

options "opt"
        samples          0 2
        contrast         0.1  0.1  0.1
        trace depth      2 2 4
        trace            on
        face             both
        object space
end options
```

```
camera "cam"
        frame           1
        output          "rgb" "out.rgb"
        focal           1
        aperture        1
        aspect          1
        resolution      800 800
end camera

instance "cam_inst" "cam"
        transform       0.7719  0.3042 -0.5582 0.0
                        0.0000  0.8781  0.4785 0.0
                        0.6357 -0.3693  0.6778 0.0
                        0.0000  5.0000 -27.000 1.0
end instance

#-------------------------------------------------- ground

color texture "pic0" "tex_checker.rgb"

declare phenomenon
        color "textured_mtl_sh" (
                color texture   "texture",
                array light     "lights"
        )
        shader "coord" "mib_texture_vector" (
                "select"        -1,
                "project"       3,
                "selspace"      1
        )
        shader "remap" "mib_texture_remap" (
                "input"         = "coord",
                "repeat"        2 2 0,
                "transform"     1  0  0  0
                                0  1  0  0
                                0  0  0  0
                                .5 .5  0  1
        )
        shader "tex" "mib_texture_lookup" (
                "tex"           = interface "texture",
                "coord"         = "remap"
        )
        shader "mtl" "mib_illum_phong" (
                "ambient"       = "tex",
                "diffuse"       = "tex",
                "ambience"      .1 .1 .1,
                "specular"      .5 .5 .5,
                "exponent"      50,
                "mode"          1,
                "lights"        = interface "lights"
        )
        root = "mtl"
```

```
        end declare

material "g-mtl"
        opaque
        "textured_mtl_sh" (
            "texture"    "pic0",
            "lights"     ["light1_inst"]
        )
end material

object "ground"
        visible trace shadow
        tag 1
        group
                -.5  0   .5
                 .5  0   .5
                 .5  0  -.5
                -.5  0  -.5
                v 0   v 1   v 2   v 3
                p "g-mtl"   0  1  2  3
        end group
end object

instance "ground_inst" "ground"
        transform    .02  0    0    0
                     0   .02   0    0
                     0    0   .02   0
                     0   .15   0    1
end instance

#---------------------------------------------- sphere

declare phenomenon
        color "mtl_sh" (
                array light     "lights"
        )
        shader "mtl" "mib_illum_phong" (
                "ambient"      1 1 1,
                "diffuse"      1 1 1,
                "ambience"     .1 .1 .1,
                "specular"     1 1 1,
                "exponent"     50,
                "mode"         1,
                "lights"       = interface "lights"
        )
        shader "refl" "mib_reflect" (
                "input"        = "mtl",
                "reflect"      .6 .6 .6,
                "notrace"      false
        )
        root = "refl"
end declare
```

```
material "s-mtl"
        opaque
        "mtl_sh" (
            "lights"      ["light1_inst"],
        )
end material

object "sphere" visible shadow trace tag 2
# ... same as before
end object

instance "sphere_inst" "sphere"
        transform        0.7 0    0    0
                         0   0.7  0    0
                         0   0    0.7  0
                         0   0    0    1
end instance

#----------------------------------------------------

instgroup "rootgrp"
        "cam_inst" "light1_inst" "ground_inst" "sphere_inst"
end instgroup

render "rootgrp" "cam_inst" "opt"
```

Two new statements were added to the options block, trace depth and trace. The latter is redundant because ray tracing is enabled by default unless turned off on the command line, but it serves as a reminder that this scene will work only in ray tracing mode. See page 417 for a discussion of rendering modes.

The trace depth specifies the number of reflections and refractions (see below) that a ray can go through. In the example, rays emitted by the camera go through one reflection before they terminate at the ground plane, but if multiple objects in the scene are reflective the ray can bounce back and forth many times. The trace depth specification can be used to limit the number of reflections (first number), refractions (second number) and the sum of both (third number). When the trace depth is reached, any attempt to cast a reflection or refraction ray is ignored, or uses the environment shader if one is defined in the material. The trace depth statement in the example is actually redundant because 2 2 4 is the default, and in fact 1 0 1 would have been sufficient because no ray is reflected more than once.

There is nothing remarkable about the ground plane Phenomenon and material (texturing is discussed at length on page 57). The sphere was extended to support reflections using the *mib_reflect* shader. After the regular Phong shader has computed the illumination of the sphere under the assumption that it is not reflective, its result is added to the result of a reflected ray cast by *mib_reflect*. The *reflect* parameter specifies that the final sphere color consists of 60% reflection and 40% surface color from *mib_illum_phong*. Although the *reflect* parameter is an RGBA color, it is a good idea to only set RGB and leave alpha at zero because a reflector is normally not considered transparent just because it reflects a transparent part of the scene.

Note that mental ray computes true reflections including self-reflections, which means that a curved object can reflect other parts of itself.

4.10 Transparency and Refraction

Refraction is very similar to reflection — rays that hit a surface are propagated in a new direction, and the result from that ray is merged with the surface color. However, refraction rays are sent *into* the object, not reflected away from it. The new direction of the refraction rays is controlled by the *index of refraction* of the refractive object.

The index of refraction is a physical material property. Dense materials such as water or glass have a higher index than air. When a ray enters a material with a different index, it is bent according to the quotient of the index of the material it came from and the index of the material it enters. When a ray crosses from air into glass, this causes the ray direction to be bent towards the surface normal. This is what makes water pools appear shallower than they really are. Typical index values are 1.0 for air, 1.33 for water, and 1.5 for glass.

In some cases, this bending of the angle is such that the ray ends up not crossing the boundary at all but reflecting back to the side it came from. This happens at grazing angles when the materials at both sides of the surface have different indices. For example, when looking up towards a water surface the surface is transparent up to a certain distance from the viewer, where the water surface becomes reflective because the viewing direction is sufficiently close to the water surface plane. This effect is called *total internal reflection* (figure 4.43).

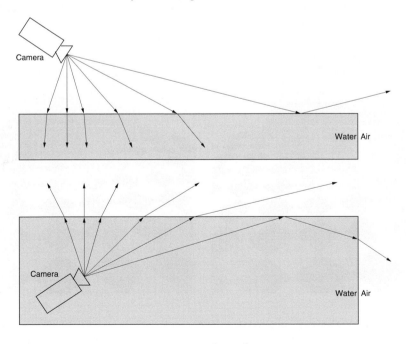

Figure 4.43: Refracted rays.

mental ray distinguishes between refraction and transparency. Transparency is defined as refraction with an index quotient of 1.0, which means that the index of refraction on both sides of the surface is the same and the ray does not change direction when it crosses the surface. Since the scanline rendering algorithm for primary rays supports transparency but not refraction, because it cannot bend rays, there is a performance advantage in using indices of refraction of 1.0. For all other indices, shaders automatically switch to ray tracing for the current ray, which may take longer. Every ray that leaves the camera is first handled by the scanline algorithm until something happens that the scanline algorithm cannot handle, such as reflection or refraction, at which point mental ray continues with ray tracing. Once in ray tracing mode, mental ray does not switch back to scanline mode for this ray. For this reason it is advisable to model window panes or other flat objects that do not cause obvious refraction effects as simple transparent surfaces, not two-walled closed refractive objects.

The *mib_refract* shader casts transparency rays if *ior* is 1.0 or 0.0 (or missing), and refraction rays otherwise. It also allows specification of the refraction fraction (*refract*) as an RGBA color. The alpha component should be set to blend with the alpha component of the refraction ray. This makes a difference if the ray leaves the scene without hitting anything, as is the case near the top.

Another parameter that must be set correctly is the `face` option, which must be set to `face both`. This is the default, and causes mental ray to consider ray intersections that hit the back side of an object too. The back side is defined to be the side that the surface normal points away from, seen from the incoming ray. The `face both`, `face front`, and `face back` cause mental ray to consider both sides, only the front side, and only the back side, respectively.

If the reflective sphere on page 119 is changed to a refractive sphere, the image on the left of figure 4.44 is rendered. The image on the right was rendered from the scene, except with an *ior* parameter of 1.0. Figure 4.45 shows a schematic view.

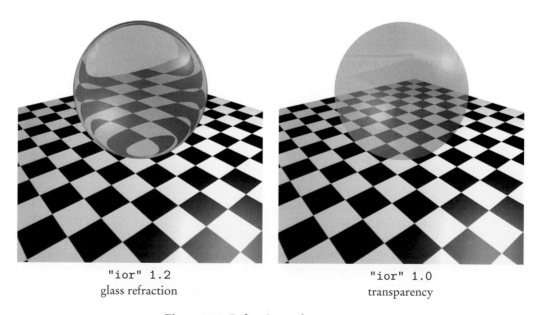

`"ior" 1.2`   `"ior" 1.0`
glass refraction   transparency

Figure 4.44: Refraction and transparency.

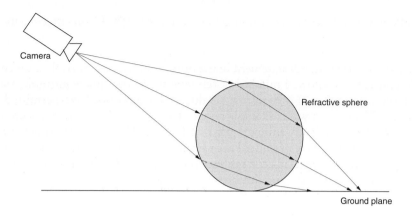

Figure 4.45: Schematic view of refraction rays.

Effectively, the sphere acts as a very strong lens that distorts the checkerboard ground plane behind it. This was achieved by changing the sphere material Phenomenon in the scene on page 119 to

```
declare phenomenon
        color "mtl_sh" (
                array light     "lights"
        )
        shader "mtl" "mib_illum_phong" (
                "ambient"       1 1 1,
                "diffuse"       1 1 1,
                "ambience"      .1 .1 .1,
                "specular"      1 1 1,
                "exponent"      50,
                "mode"          1,
                "lights"        = interface "lights"
        )
        shader "ior" "mib_refraction_index" (
                "mtl_ior"       1.2
        )
        shader "refl" "mib_refract" (
                "input"         = "mtl",
                "refract"       .7 .7 .7 .7,
                "ior"           = "ior.ior"
        )
        root = "refl"
end declare
```

The *mib_refract* shader is similar to the *mib_reflect* shader, but has an *ior* (index of refraction) quotient parameter that is used to compute the new ray direction. The quotient is computed by the *mib_refraction_index* shader, which can distinguish rays that enter the sphere and rays that leave the sphere. On entering, it returns 1.2 (its ior parameter), and on leaving it returns $\frac{1}{1.2}$. It can also handle nested refractive objects; in general it returns $\frac{inner\_ior}{outer\_ior}$ on entering and $\frac{outer\_ior}{inner\_ior}$ on leaving.

As for reflections, the trace depth statement in the options block (see the reflection code example on page 119) controls the allowed number of refractions. In the sphere example, the refraction trace depth (second number, 2) is required; a value of 1 would not have permitted the rays to leave the sphere. The second water example above shows the importance of specifying the sum of reflection and refraction depth; a trace depth of 1 1 1 would have permitted either reflection or refraction, but it would not have permitted the rightmost ray undergoing total internal reflection to leave the right side of the water object by refraction. The trace depth sum can be left unspecified; in this case it is assumed to be the sum of the first two numbers.

4.11   Glossy Reflection

Glossy reflection is a ray tracing effect. It is achieved by using a shader that chooses reflection ray directions near the mirror direction, but according to the distributions shown in the middle diagram on page 179. The following scene uses the *dgs_material* material shader:

```
link "base.so"
link "physics.so"
$include <base.mi>
$include <physics.mi>           # for dgs_material

camera "cam"
        frame           1
        output          "rgb" "out.rgb"
        focal           115
        aperture        42
        aspect          1
        resolution      800 800
end camera

options "opt"
        trace           on
        trace depth     2 2
        shadow          on
        samples         -1 2
        contrast        0.1     0.1     0.1
        object space
end options

light "source"
        "physical_light" (
            "color"     16000 16000 16000
        )
        origin          -4 10 -15
end light

instance "source-i" "source" end instance
```

```
material "teapotmat" opaque
        "dgs_material" (
            "diffuse"   0.7 0.7 0.7,
            "glossy"    0.2 0.2 0.2,
            "shiny"     25,
            "lights"    ["source-i"]
        )
end material

material "reflector" opaque
        "dgs_material" (
            "diffuse"   0.2 0.2 0.2,
            "glossy"    0.8 0.8 0.8,
            "shiny"     1000,
            "lights"    ["source-i"]
        )
end material
```

The objects and instances are not shown in this listing. The scenes in this chapter are generally too complex to be listed in their entirety; the Utah teapot object group alone requires 300 lines (see the listing in appendix B).

The reflection types of the *dgs_material* material shader are:

- Diffuse (Lambertian)

- Glossy (Ward model)

- Specular (ideal mirror)

(Hence its name, DGS material.) It can simulate mirrors, glossy paint or plastic, diffuse materials, transparent materials with and without refraction, translucency, and combinations of these. It requires the reflection parameters to be physically plausible: they must be energy preserving, that is, the sum of the reflection coefficients of diffuse, glossy, and specular reflection in each color band (red, green, and blue) must not exceed 1.

Specular reflection is modeled as ideal mirror reflection. Note that the Phong shading model traditionally uses the term "specular illumination" to indicate what is more correctly described as direct glossy illumination combined with reflection from the mirror direction. The parameter shiny determines how wide the glossy reflection is, in a manner similar to the Phong reflection exponent shiny: 5 is very wide and 100 is very narrow. The reflectivity is always assumed to be $1 - \texttt{transp}$.

Glossy reflection and transmission can either be *isotropic* or *anisotropic*. Anisotropic materials have the property that the reflection changes when the surface is rotated about its normal. Examples of anisotropic materials are brushed metals or butterfly wings. See page 104 for more information.

Figure 4.46 shows the rendered images with different values for the `"shiny"` parameter of the *dgs_material* shader on the reflecting table.

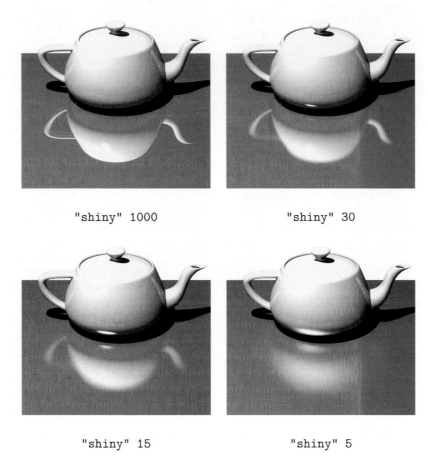

"shiny" 1000   "shiny" 30

"shiny" 15   "shiny" 5

Figure 4.46: Glossy reflection.

In the first image, the glossy reflection is so narrow that it is indistinguishable from specular (mirror) reflection. In the following images the glossy reflection gets wider, creating a "softer" reflection. For the wide glossy reflection, the sampling rate was increased to 1 4 to avoid noise. Note how the highlight near the bottom of the teapot becomes wider as the reflection becomes more fuzzy; this is the reflection of the glossy reflection of the teapot itself, and the highlight is again glossily reflected on the floor.

4.12 Glossy Transmission (Translucency)

Translucency is another name for glossy or diffuse transmission. The following example again uses the *dgs_material* material shader:

```
material "frosted_glass"
        "dgs_material" (
                "transp"    1.0,
                "ior"       1.2,
                "glossy"    1.0 1.0 1.0,
                "shiny"     1000.0,
                "lights"    ["light1_inst"],
        )
end material
```

The sphere in the example shows varying degrees of glossy translucency, becoming more and more frosted. In the first image, the glossy transmission (refraction) is so narrow that it is hard to distinguish from (specular) refraction. In the images in figure 4.47, the glossy distribution gets increasingly wide.

4.13 Summary of Illumination Models

Six illumination models have been introduced in this chapter:

Direct specular
> makes area light sources in the mirror direction visible, if the light source is marked visible. Non-area light sources have zero size and are therefore never visible. This requires ray tracing.

Direct glossy
> creates a fuzzy reflection of a light source, area or not. The Ward and Cook-Torrance shading models simulate direct glossy illumination in a physically correct way; the Phong and Blinn shading models do not attempt correctness and offer an incorrectly named parameter "specular" for the highlight color, which is simply spread out.

Direct diffuse
> is Lambert shading, causing a soft brightening of the side of the object facing towards the light source.

Indirect specular
> is ray-traced reflection in the mirror direction, showing other objects in the scene as a reflection on the surface. Environment mapping is a simple substitute that does not require ray tracing.

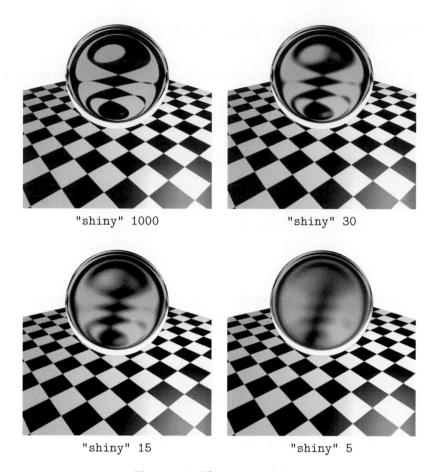

"shiny" 1000   "shiny" 30

"shiny" 15   "shiny" 5

Figure 4.47: Glossy transmission.

Indirect glossy

   is a variation on indirect specular illumination, but the reflection directions are chosen according to a distribution function centered around the mirror direction, such that the reflection becomes blurred. This also requires ray tracing.

Indirect diffuse

   is the combined illumination caused by diffuse reflection of light from the entire scene. Effectively, a brightly lit nearby object begins to act like an area light source itself, for example. Indirect diffuse illumination requires global illumination, which is the topic of chapter 7. Some shaders, such as the Phong and Blinn shaders, simulate this with a constant ambient color.

The features introduced in this chapter make different use of these illumination models:

	D.S.	D.G.	D.D.	I.S.	I.G.	I.D.
Flat shading	○	○	○	○	○	★
Lambert shading	○	○	●	○	○	★
Phong shading	○	●	●	●	○	★
Blinn shading	○	●	●	●	○	★
Cook-Torrance shading	○	●	●	●	○	★
Ward shading	○	●	●	●	○	★
Reflection	○	○	○	●	○	○
Refraction, transparency	○	○	○	●	○	○
Glossy reflection	○	○	○	○	●	○
Glossy transmission (translucency)	○	○	○	○	●	○
dgs_material shader	●	●	●	●	●	●

● means the lighting model is supported, ○ means it is not, and ★ means it is not supported but faked with a constant ambient color.

Chapter 5

Light and Shadow

All scene examples in the preceding Surface Shading chapter defined light sources that illuminate objects in certain ways. A light source provides light whose effect is taken into account when illuminating surfaces or volumes. Two main kinds of illumination are distinguished:

local illumination

    is handled by material and volume shaders by computing the color of an illuminated surface or volume simply by considering the direction, strength, and color of incoming light and how it is reflected towards the viewer. Incoming light always comes directly from the light source (which can optionally be blocked by occluding objects, causing shadows). The examples in chapter 4.1 on page 52 demonstrate various kinds of local illumination.

global illumination

    complements local illumination by allowing material shaders to take into account indirect illumination from other lighted objects in the scene. It cannot be computed by directly adding up incoming light from light sources but requires a special preprocessing step that emits photons from light sources and follows them as they bounce around in the scene. This allows simulating natural effects that go far beyond local illumination. Global illumination is described in chapter 7.7 on page 198.

Local and global illumination complement each other: local illumination only considers light that arrives directly from the light source, and global illumination only considers light that is indirectly received from other lighted objects. Together they result in a physically correct lighting solution, if set up correctly, that can be used for architectural and other simulations where the rendered illumination must match real-world illumination.

However, it is also possible to deviate from physical correctness to achieve certain effects. For example, lights can have negative color (sometimes called *darklights* or *light suckers*) because negative light, when added to a lighting solution, *decreases* the result. Also, the light from physically correct point and spot lights falls off with the square of the distance, but some scenes use lights without falloff, which makes modeling easier because it does not matter how far away the light source is. To achieve physical correctness, it is necessary to choose shaders that support it, and to set their parameters correctly. This is covered in more detail on page 198.

Lights have the following characteristics:

- The **light shader** is the central part of a light. It is a function, either custom or from one of the standard shader libraries, that controls the color of the light, directional and distance attenuation, projector light capabilities (which determine the light color by looking up a texture map), and controls shadow casting.

- The **origin**, **direction** and **spread** specify the light type, and where the light is in 3D space. If only an origin is specified the light is a point light; if only a direction is specified the light is an infinite light (also called a directional light). Up to mental ray 3.3, if both are specified, the light is a spot light. With mental ray 3.4 and higher, if both are specified but no **spread** is given, the light is an infinite light with origin: the origin defines a plane whose normal is aligned with the light direction, and behind which no light is emitted; if **origin**, **direction** and **spread** are specified, the light is a spot light. Point lights emit light in all directions; spot lights are a variant of point lights that emit light only in a cone of light; and infinite lights emit light only in one particular direction with all light rays being parallel, like, for all practical purposes, sunlight. Both the origin and direction are subject to instancing (page 371) as if they were geometric objects with only a single vertex. For spot lights, the **spread** value is the cosine of the opening angle of the spot light.

- The **area** parameters specify whether the light is an area light source, and if so, its shape and orientation. Area light sources allow soft shadows. See below for more detail.

- The **shadow map** parameters control a set of features that implement the shadow map algorithm, which allows fast, non-raytraced shadows at the cost of lower precision and lack of transparency. This is also described in more detail below.

- The **visible** flag makes point and spot light sources directly visible to the camera. This only has an effect if the light is an area light source because otherwise it is infinitely small. This is important for physical correctness because it makes sure that light rays that hit the camera directly are not lost, but if only the visual effect is important, appropriate lens flare shaders give a better result.

- The optional **label** and **data blocks** can be used for identification purposes. The mental ray rendering software does not use them but makes them available to shaders, which can alter their behavior based on the label and user data. If more than one user data block is specified, the blocks are chained. See section 11.6.

In the scene file, a light has the following syntax:

```
light "light_name"
    "light_shader_name" (parameters)
    [ origin     x y z ]
    [ direction  x y z ]
    [ spread     angle ]
    [ visible    [ on|off ]]
    [ tag        label_int ]
    [ data       "data_name" | null ]
    [ shadow mapping statements ]
```

> [*area light source statements*]
> [*global illumination statements*]
> end light

The following sections discuss the purpose of these features, beginning with simple lights, then lights with shadows, area lights, and shadow maps. Shadow mapping statements are listed on page 151. Area light statements are on page 143. Lights that provide global illumination are discussed separately in chapter 7.

5.1   Point, Spot, and Infinite Lights

Here is a simple scene that will be used in this chapter. It consists of a light, a cube that is instanced twice (see page 371) to form a "floor" and a cube that touches the floor, a camera, and rendering options:

```
verbose on
link "base.so"
$include <base.mi>

light "light1"
        "mib_light_point" (
            "color"      1 1 1
        )
        origin           .6  .4   0
end light

instance "light1_inst" "light1"
end instance

options "opt"
        samples          -1 2
        contrast         0.1  0.1  0.1
        object space
end options

camera "cam"
        frame            1
        output           "rgb" "out.rgb"
        focal            50
        aperture         20
        aspect           1
        resolution       800 800
end camera

material "mtl"
        opaque
        "mib_illum_phong" (
            "ambient"    0.5  0.5  0.5,
            "diffuse"    0.7  0.7  0.7,
```

```
                "ambience"   0.4   0.4   0.4,
                "specular"   1.0   1.0   1.0,
                "exponent"   50,
                "mode"       1,
                "lights"     ["light1_inst"]
            )
    end material

    object "cube1"
            visible trace shadow
            tag 1
            group
                    -0.5 -0.5 -0.5
                    -0.5 -0.5  0.5
                    -0.5  0.5 -0.5
                    -0.5  0.5  0.5
                     0.5 -0.5 -0.5
                     0.5 -0.5  0.5
                     0.5  0.5 -0.5
                     0.5  0.5  0.5

                    v 0   v 1   v 2   v 3
                    v 4   v 5   v 6   v 7

                    p "mtl" 0  1  3  2
                    p       1  5  7  3
                    p       5  4  6  7
                    p       4  0  2  6
                    p       4  5  1  0
                    p       2  3  7  6
            end group
    end object

    instance "floor_inst" "cube1"
            transform        .5   0    0    0
                             0   10    0    0
                             0    0   .5    0
                             0   .5    0    1
    end instance

    instance "cube1_inst" "cube1"
            transform        5    0    0    0
                             0    5    0    0
                             0    0    5    0
                            -1  -.5    0    1
    end instance

    instance "cam_inst" "cam"
            transform        0.7719  0.3042 -0.5582 0.0
                             0.0000  0.8781  0.4785 0.0
                             0.6357 -0.3693  0.6778 0.0
                             0.0000  0.0000 -2.5000 1.0
    end instance
```

```
instgroup "rootgrp"
        "cam_inst" "light1_inst"  "floor_inst"  "cube1_inst"
end instgroup

render "rootgrp" "cam_inst" "opt"
```

The rendering options contain the statement shadow on, which is redundant because shadows are enabled by default. It will be discussed below (see page 147). The subject of this chapter is the light near the top of the scene file. It defines a point light because there is an origin but no direction or spread. The absence or presence of these parameters determine the light type:

origin	direction	spread	type
●	○	○	point light
○	●	○	infinite light
●	●	○	infinite light with origin[3.4]
●	●	●	spot light

To turn the light into a spot light, a direction and a spread must be given:

```
light "light1"
        "mib_light_spot" (
            "color"     1 1 1,
            "cone"      0.9
        )
        origin          .6  .4   0
        direction      -.6 -.6   0
        spread          0.8
end light
```

The spot light is at the same origin as the point light, just above and to the right of the top right edge of the cube. The spot opening angle is rather wide with an outer spread of 0.8 (arc cos $0.8 \approx 37$ degrees) and an inner cone of 0.9 (arc cos $0.9 \approx 26$ degrees). Between these angles, the spot edge fades from full white (color 1 1 1) to black. The closer a spread or cone angle is to 1.0, the *narrower* the beam becomes.

Infinite lights only require a direction:

```
light "light1"
        "mib_light_infinite" (
            "color"      1 1 1
        )
        direction      -.6 -.6   0
end light
```

Optionally, starting with mental ray 3.4, an infinite light may have an origin that defines a plane behind which no light is emitted:

```
light "light1"
        "mib_light_infinite" (
            "color"      1 1 1
        )
        origin           .3  .2   0
        direction        -.6 -.6   0
end light
```

Figure 5.1 shows the result when rendering the scene with each of the four lights.

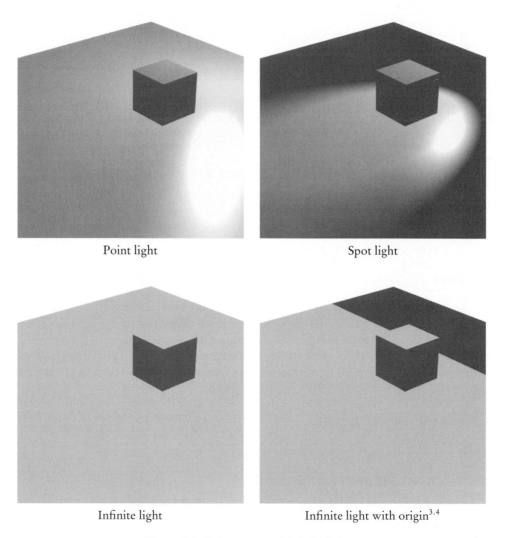

Point light   Spot light

Infinite light   Infinite light with origin[3.4]

Figure 5.1: Point, spot, and infinite lights.

These scenes do not look especially interesting because there is only one light and one material in the scene, which means that all points not lit by the light have the same uniform dark gray, as defined by the ambient color of the light source. Note, however, that the highlight on the floor near the right edge of the point and spot light images is missing in the infinite light images.

There is no limit to the number of lights that can be used in a scene, or to the number of lights that can be named in a material shader's light list. For example, in this scene another light shining from a different origin or direction could be used to contrast the cube faces and the floor that are not lit by the primary light, or a "darklight" with a negative `color` parameter could be used to soften the highlight on the floor.

The computational cost of lighting, which strongly determines the performance of the entire rendering operation, is nearly proportional to the number of lights in the material shader light lists. The total number of lights in the scene also influences performance, but to a much lesser degree. mental ray will quickly reject lights on the wrong side of the illuminated surface, spot lights whose cone does not contain the illuminated point, and infinite lights pointing in the wrong direction, but even in those cases a small overhead remains.

5.2 Raytraced Shadows

mental ray can use ray tracing to compute shadows cast by objects on other objects and onto themselves. Several conditions must be met:

☑ Shadows must be enabled. This is the default. Shadows can be explicitly disabled with a `shadow` statement in the options block in the scene file, or the `-shadow` command line option.

☑ The light source must specify a light shader that supports shadows, and if this light shader requires a special option to enable shadows it must be explicitly set. Light shaders typically default to no shadows. This is the case for the light shaders used in this chapter.

☑ If caustics are cast by the object, or if global illumination is enabled, do not use shadow shaders; the photon shader will take care of propagating light. Otherwise:

☑ For transparent shadows (see below), a shadow shader must be attached to the material of the object that casts the transparent shadow, and the material may not contain the `opaque` flag.

☑ Some shadow shaders require a particular shadow mode, which is either set implicitly by the shader in its shader declaration, or explicitly in the options block in the scene file, or as a command line option. See page 147 for details.

Since shadows are rendered by default, it is sufficient to enable shadow casting in the light shaders by adding the `shadow` and, if available, `factor` shader parameters to the *mib_light_point*, *mib_light_spot*, and *mib_light_infinite* shaders, for example:

```
light "light1"
        "mib_light_point" (
```

```
        "color"      1 1 1,
        "shadow"     on,
        "factor"     0.25
    )
      origin           .6  .4   0
end light
```

The factor parameter blends the shadow-casting result with the light color, effectively letting light bleed onto places that are occluded. This makes shadows look less stark. In this example, 25% of the light reaches the illuminated floor directly and only 75% is subject to shadowing. Without this parameter, the areas in shadow would only show the ambient color of the material. Figure 5.2 shows the resulting images.

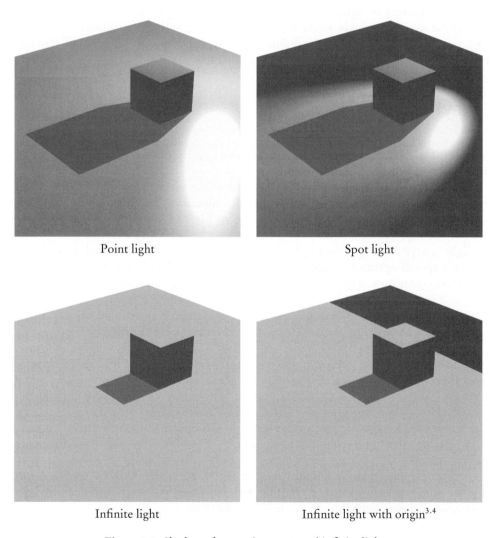

Point light   Spot light

Infinite light   Infinite light with origin[3.4]

Figure 5.2: Shadows from point, spot, and infinite lights.

mental ray shadow casting supports self-shadowing, which means that curved objects with protrusions or dents cast shadows on themselves. This is also true of the bumps and dents introduced with displacement mapping (see page 90). However, mental ray takes special care to avoid a common problem called *surface acne* that results from a surface incorrectly shadowing itself due to numerical imprecision. Note, however, that shadow maps created with OpenGL hardware acceleration are more susceptible to surface acne due to the limited precision of the hardware.

5.2.1 Transparent Shadows with Shadow Shaders

Without transparent shadows, objects can either be in shadow from a given light source or not. Transparent shadows allow transparent objects to cast softer shadows because some of the light passes through the object and reaches the illuminated object that receives the shadow. This can be combined with texture mapping to produce effects like colored stained glass windows.

Since color and transparency are controlled by the material shader (see page 123), and are not known to mental ray, transparent shadows need cooperation from the shadow-casting material to determine whether and how an object transmits light. This is handled by the material's *shadow shader*.

Shadow shaders are different from material shaders because they do much less — they need to check the object transparency, perhaps evaluate a texture map, but they do not need to (and are, in fact, not allowed to) cast secondary rays or light rays themselves. However, many material shaders detect when they are being called as shadow shaders and act like shadow shaders in this case.

The next example adds the *mib_shadow_transparency* shader as shadow shader in the material in the scene on page 135:

```
material "mtl"
     "mib_illum_phong" (
         "ambient"   0.5  0.5  0.5,
         "diffuse"   0.7  0.7  0.7,
         "ambience"  0.4  0.4  0.4,
         "specular"  1.0  1.0  1.0,
         "exponent"  50,
         "mode"      1,
         "lights"    ["light1_inst"]
     )
     shadow "mib_shadow_transparency" (
         "color"     0.7  0.7  0.7  1.0,
         "transp"    0.5  0.5  0.5,
         "mode"      3
     )
end material
```

Also, the first polygon was removed so that the left side of the cube is open, which means that some light rays pass through two faces (the top and front or rear, for example) and others pass only through one face. Since the *mib_shadow_transparency* shader parameters specify a transparency of 0.5 (50%) for the material, the shadows are darker where they pass through cube faces twice, as shown in figure 5.3.

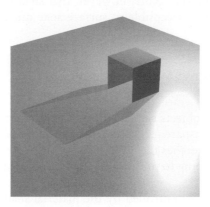

Figure 5.3: Transparent shadow.

Typically, the shadow shader's `color` parameter is chosen to be identical to the material shader's diffuse color, and the shadow shader's transparency is chosen to be identical to the material shader's transparency (which may use *mib_transparency*, for example; see page 123). This is not the case in the example scene — the material is left opaque — which is why the shadow is transparent but the camera cannot see through the cube faces.

Sometimes, shadow shaders accept the same parameters as the corresponding material shader, and in fact can be the same function as the material shader — with different behavior depending on the incoming ray type. Since material shader parameter lists can be quite long, mental ray allows a special optimization: if the shadow shader in the material has no parameters (opening parenthesis immediately followed by a closing parenthesis), it receives the material shader parameters instead. (The same, incidentally, is true for photon shaders.) This also applies if the "=" notation is used to reference a parameterless named shadow (or photon) shader by shader assignment; see page 271.

Note that if global illumination or caustics are cast from a transparent object, the material should have no shadow shader or the opaque flag. In these cases, light from light sources passes through the object in the form of photons that can be focused and dispersed, not by determining the reduction of light traveling on a straight path as the shadow shader method assumes. Using both methods at the same time would cause the light to reach the shadow behind the object twice — as direct illumination from the shadow shader and as indirect illumination from the photon shader, resulting in incorrect illumination.

This is related to the difference between refraction and transparency for visible rays from the camera: refraction involves changing the direction of rays, and transparency does not. Similarly, if the light from the light source travels through a transparent object such as flat window glass, the transparent shadows should be handled by a shadow shader, but if the light must be refracted because the glass has varying thickness like a lens then it is a case for caustics created by a photon shader. Using both at the same time should be avoided because otherwise light contributes twice, once directly and once indirectly. See page 190 for more details on caustics.

5.2.2   Soft Shadows with Area Light Sources

Point and spot lights create shadows with hard edges because the light is infinitely small, so a point on an illuminated surface can either "see" the light or not, so it is either wholly or not at all in shadow. In reality, there are no infinitely small light sources, so it is possible that an illuminated point "sees" only a part of the light source while the rest is hidden by some occluding shadow-casting object. This is what causes soft shadows (shadows that have soft edges).

Extended light sources are called *area light sources*. Any point or spot light in mental ray can be turned into an area light source by adding area light statements to the light source in the scene file. Four types of area light sources are supported: rectangle, disc, sphere, and cylinder. They act like geometric rectangles, discs, spheres, or cylinders centered on the light origin, which emit light uniformly from their surfaces. In figure 5.4, a rectangular area light source is shown that casts a soft shadow on an illuminated object.

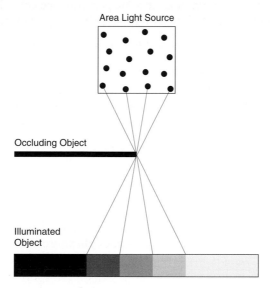

Figure 5.4: Area light sampling.

Area lights are sampled, which means they behave as if consisting of an array of pseudo-randomly spaced lights (only much more efficiently). In figure 5.4, the rectangle area light is subdivided into approximately four by four samples, for a total of 16 samples. For four of them, the shadow edges are shown, which results in a soft shadow edge.

The syntax of the area light source statements that extend the light source block in the scene file (see page 134) is:

```
light "light_name"
    ...
    [rectangle   [u_edge_{x,y,z}  v_edge_{x,y,z}  [sampling]]]
    [disc        [normal_{x,y,z}  radius  [sampling]]]
    [sphere      [radius  [sampling]]]
    [cylinder    [axis_{x,y,z}  radius  [sampling]]]
```

```
[ object      "object_instance_name" [ sampling ]]3.1
[ user        [ sampling ]]3.1
   ...
end light
```

Object and user area light sources are available only for mental ray 3.1 and higher. Object light sources reference the instance of an object whose surface is assumed to uniformly emit light, and is fully transparent so that it does not cast shadows on itself. This is slower than the other shapes, especially for complex objects with many triangles. User area light sources leave the determination of the shape to the light shader, which must have been custom-built to implement the shape.

Only one of the six shapes may be specified, and a light source is an area light source if exactly one is specified. The notation $X_{x,y,z}$ means that X is a vector and that three numbers must be given. The optional sampling parameters specify the sampling precision; numbers greater than 3 increase the quality by reducing graininess, at some performance cost. The *sampling* parameters are optional, and consist of up to five integer numbers that control sampling quality:

$$u\_samples_{int} \quad v\_samples_{int} \ [\ level_{int} \ [\ low\_u\_samples_{int} \quad low\_v\_samples_{int} \ ]]$$

If the optional *level* exists and is greater than 0, then mental ray will use *low_u_samples* and *low_v_samples* instead of *u_samples* and *v_samples*, respectively, if the sum of the reflection and refraction trace level exceeds *level*. The level default is 3, and the low sampling defaults are 2. The effect is that reflections and refractions of soft shadows are sampled at lower precision than directly visible soft shadows, which can improve performance significantly. The low levels are also used for final gathering rays used when sampling global illumination regardless of the specified level; see page 206 for details. mental ray 2.1 will multiply the U and V resolutions, and then choose the next lower power of two as the number of samples. For example, 3 3 will sample the light source 8 times, and 8 3 will sample 16 times.

If the rectangle, disc, sphere, or cylinder keyword is specified without any of the following arguments, then the light source reverts to a non-area light source. This is useful for incremental changes.

If the point light source in the example scene on page 135 is replaced with one of the following four lights:

```
light "light1"
      "mib_light_point" (
          "color"     1 1 1,
          "shadow"    on,
          "factor"    0.25
      )
      origin          .6  .4  0
      rectangle       .1   0  0        # U size
                       0  .1  0        # V size
                       5 5             # subdivision
end light


light "light1"
```

```
              "mib_light_point" (
                  "color"      1 1 1,
                  "shadow"     on,
                  "factor"     0.25
              )
              origin       .6  .4   0
              disc         -.6 -.6 -.6      # direction
                           .05              # radius
                           5 5              # subdivision
       end light


   light "light1"
              "mib_light_point" (
                  "color"      1 1 1,
                  "shadow"     on,
                  "factor"     0.25
              )
              origin       .6  .4   0
              sphere       .05              # radius
                           5 5              # subdivision
       end light


   light "light1"
              "mib_light_point" (
                  "color"      1 1 1,
                  "shadow"     on,
                  "factor"     0.25
              )
              origin       .6  .4   0
              cylinder     0   0   .3       # axis
                           .01              # radius
                           25 2             # subdivision
       end light
```

the cube in the image on page 138 gets a soft shadow. Figure 5.5 shows area light sources with each of the four lights. In the first three cases, the area light size is slightly smaller than the cube, and is very close to the cube. The cylinder light is 50% wider than the cube. The disc light faces towards the camera. The disc and sphere shadows are softer than the rectangle shadow because the side of the rectangle comes into view almost at the same time when moving out of the shadow. The difference between disc and sphere lights depends on the illumination direction — it does not matter for the sphere, but a disc light is two-dimensional and appears smaller if seen from the edge.

Note that the shadow has a hard edge where it touches the cube, and gets softer with increasing distance.

The subdivision parameters, here 5 5, should be as small as possible to improve performance, but if they are chosen too small the shadow becomes grainy. Square rectangle area light sources typically have same subdivision parameters for U and V, but they can be adjusted independently

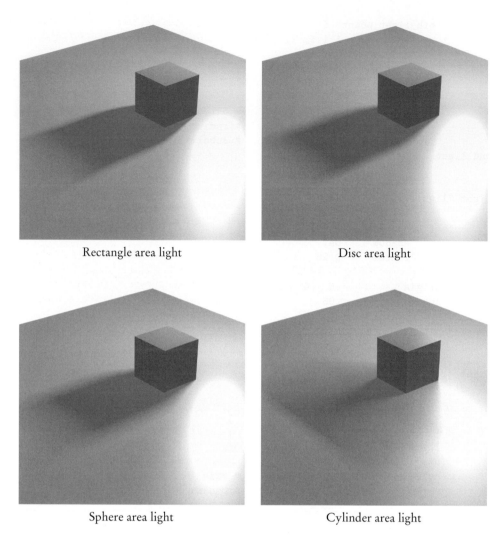

Rectangle area light   Disc area light

Sphere area light   Cylinder area light

Figure 5.5: Area light source types.

to match the ratio of the lengths of the rectangle edges. A subdivision of 5 5 is quite high and needed only to resolve shadows near the camera accurately. If there are no shadows at all, even 1 1 often produces accurate and smooth illumination.

For example, neon tube light sources, sometimes called linear light sources, can be simulated with a cylinder area light source.

The closer an occluding object is to the illuminated surface, the sharper its shadow will be. Conversely, a distant occluding object close to the area light source will cast a very soft shadow. Very soft shadows tend to require larger subdivision parameters to reduce graininess. Since a spot light is conceptually a point light with a housing that blocks light except in a certain direction, and since the light-blocking housing is equivalent to an occluding object close to the light (even if no geometry for it exists in the scene), area spot lights generally require much larger subdivision parameters than area point lights. If possible, area spot lights should be avoided and replaced with non-area spot lights or area point lights if possible to improve quality and performance.

5.2.3 Shadow Modes: Regular, Sorted, Segmented

Shadow modes are global modes that apply to all raytraced shadows in a scene. They control how and in which order occluding objects that cast shadows are found. Shadow modes do not apply to shadow map shadows. There are three different modes:

Regular   This is the default. When the light source traces shadow rays in order to find out how much light reaches the illuminated point, mental ray searches for occluding objects between the light source and the illuminated point. When one is found, its shadow shader is called, which gets the opportunity to reduce the amount of light if the object is less than fully transparent. If no light is left, or if the object does not have a shadow shader, the search stops because no other occluding object can make a difference now. All shadow rays go from the light source to the occluding object. The order in which occluding objects are found is unpredictable.

Use this mode for simple, fast shadows.

Sorted   This mode is similar to regular mode, except that mental ray first searches for *all* occluding objects, then sorts the resulting list, and then begins calling shadow shaders from the list, the one closest to the light source first, until no light is left or all shadow shaders on the list have been called. This mode can be slower than the regular mode because all occluding objects had to be found; there is no way to terminate the search early if an occluding object turns out to be opaque.

Use this mode only if some shadow shaders in the scene that keep track of bounded volumes require it. In most cases, segmented shadows are more appropriate for these applications; sorted shadows are deprecated.

Segmented   This mode is different from the other two. Shadow rays are treated like visible rays, and mental ray begins the search for occluding objects at the illuminated point, shooting a ray towards the light source. When an object is found, its shadow shader is called as usual, but the shadow shader is responsible for casting the next shadow ray towards the light source. This allows volumetric effects between any two occluding objects (which may actually be the front and back side of the same object) because shadow rays always hop from one occluding object to the next. The performance of this mode is slightly lower than the performance of sorted shadows.

Use this mode to trace shadows in volumes, for example to allow procedural smoke to cast a shadow on the ground.

Off   Listed for completeness only. This mode turns shadows off altogether by disabling all searching for occluding objects. If a light source asks mental ray to find occluding objects, mental ray immediately returns with an unchanged light color, effectively telling the light shader that all its light reaches the illuminated point. This can increase performance significantly if there are many shadow-casting light sources.

Use this mode for quick preview rendering when shadow casting is not relevant.

Shadow modes are controlled either by the `shadow` statement in the scene file (see the scene example on page 135) or the command line option `-shadow`:

shadow mode	options statement	command line option
off	`shadow off`	`-shadow off`
regular	`shadow on`	`-shadow on`
sorted	`shadow sort`	`-shadow sort`
segmented	`shadow segment`	`-shadow segment`

Regular shadows are the default. From the above discussion it is clear that the choice between regular, sorted, and segmented shadows depends on the requirements of the shaders used in the scene. mental ray allows shaders to "upgrade" the shadow mode from regular to sorted or segmented by giving an appropriate statement in their shader declaration, which means that when shaders are properly designed it is sufficient to use the `shadow on` and `shadow off` statements or command line options and let mental ray take care of sorting and segmenting.

Materials attached to occluding objects may specify the `opaque` flag. This is a hint to mental ray that this object is fully opaque, and no texture alpha channels or other forms of transparency are taken into account by either its material shader or shadow shader. mental ray is then free to ignore the shadow shader because it knows that the shadow shader can only shut off all light transmission. However, the `opaque` flag is only a hint to increase performance, not a command. To ensure maximum performance for opaque materials, it is best to not specify a shadow shader at all.

5.3   Fast Shadows with Shadow Maps

Shadow maps work in a completely different way than normal raytraced shadows. The situation is similar to true raytraced reflections vs. reflection maps — ray tracing correctly takes other scene elements into account, while the non-raytraced shadow and environment mapping algorithms are shortcuts that trade correctness for performance.

The advantages of shadow mapping are:

- Shadow maps are very fast. The cost of computing shadow maps grows slowly with scene complexity, and the cost of using shadow maps is almost independent of scene complexity. The reason for this behavior is that shadow maps can be both computed and used with the fast scanline algorithm and do not require any form of ray tracing.

- Shadow maps can take advantage of OpenGL hardware acceleration (see page 446).

- Shadow maps, once computed, can be used in multiple frames of an animation if the shadows do not change.

- Shadow mapping is a light attribute, so it can be applied only to those light sources that do not require the full precision of raytraced shadows.

The disadvantages of standard shadow mapping are:

- Only opaque shadows are supported. Transparent (and colored) shadows are not possible. This also means that the distinction of regular, sorted, and segmented shadows does not apply. For the same reason, no shadow shaders are called. (This is not the case for detail shadowmaps[3.3]; see below.)

- While shadow-mapped shadows are not as precise as those from raytraced area light sources, soft shadows are supported with a special shadow map softness parameter. However, the resulting softness does not depend on the distance to the shadow-casting object.

- Shadow maps are not spatially precise. If the shadow touches the object that is casting the shadow, as in figure 5.6, two problems can appear: either the shadow sets in too late, not quite touching the object, or it sets in early and a narrow shadow edge appears on the lighted side of the object that is not in shadow. This can be alleviated with a higher shadow map resolution. See below.

To use shadow maps, the following steps must be taken:

☑ Shadows must be enabled in the options block with a `shadow on` statement. This is the default.

☑ Shadow maps must be enabled in the options block with a `shadowmap on` or `shadowmap opengl` statement. Shadow maps are disabled by default.

☑ All light sources that should generate shadow-mapped shadows must be flagged with the `shadowmap on` statement. (If `shadowmap` is specified without argument, on is the default.)

The remaining steps are optional:

☑ The light source may provide a shadow map resolution, which specifies the number of shadow samples taken in the U and V directions when the shadow map is computed. 500 is a good number; it computes a shadow map containing 500×500 depth samples. The default is 256. If the number is too low, the shadow becomes blocky, grainy, or banded; if it is too high, shadow map computation performance is reduced and memory demands increase. Shadow maps for point lights consist of six images instead of one, and mental ray will adjust their resolution such that the total number of pixels in all six roughly corresponds to the specified shadow map resolution.

☑ If shadow mapping may be greatly accelerated with the OpenGL acceleration algorithm (using `shadowmap opengl` instead of `shadowmap on`), but only if the shadow map resolution does not exceed the smaller screen resolution, typically 1024. See page 446.

☑ Remove the shadow flag from objects which do not need to cast shadows. For an object which is farthest away from the shadow-casting light source, there is no farther object onto which a shadow could be cast, so the flag is not needed. For example, in a simple scene with an overhead light and some objects on the floor, the objects should cast shadows on the floor but the floor does not need to cast a shadow since nothing is below it. This is particularly important when using shadow maps, because the shadow map will be computed to cover the region containing all shadow-casting objects. If this region is unnecessarily expanded by a large object and the shadow map resolution is held constant, it effectively reduces the usable resolution of the shadow map. Shadow artifacts would appear unless the sampling rate were increased, but this impacts performance.

☑ If a soft shadow is desired, the light source should also specify a shadow map softness. This number controls the range of nearby depth values in the shadow map, essentially filtering the shadow map at render time. Filtering at render time, as opposed to prefiltering during shadow map computation, allows soft shadows whose softness depends on the lighting direction (but not the distance to the shadow-casting object). Larger numbers produce softer shadows but often require a higher shadow map resolution or a higher number of shadow map samples.

☑ If a soft shadow is desired, the light source should also specify the number of shadow map samples. Softness is achieved by averaging several samples in the shadow map, in an area whose size is controlled by the shadow map softness parameter. The number of shadow map samples controls the grainyness of the shadow; higher values average more samples but also reduce performance when rendering. Good numbers are between 4 and 10; more if the result is noisy. Changing the softness does not require recomputation of the shadowmap itself.

Note that ray tracing does not have to be enabled for shadow map shadows, and in fact has been explicitly turned off in the scene example. However, raytraced and shadow-mapped shadows can coexist in a scene. For a more detailed description of the computation and sampling of shadow maps, see page 158.

The key to good shadows with shadow maps is good framing. A shadowmap is basically a picture taken from the viewpoint of the light, recording depths of shadow-casting objects. If the shadow-casting objects occupy just a small portion of the image, with lots of empty space around them, the map is said to be poorly framed, and most of its pixels are wasted. This results in shadows that are coarser and more boxy than the shadowmap resolution would seem to permit. The `shadowmap file` statement can be used to save the shadowmap to a file, which can be viewed with the *imf_disp* image viewer program. It will show near depths dark and distant depths bright, as shown in figure 5.6. Note that the stored depth is not identical to the depth of the frontmost surface; it is adjusted to prevent self-shadowing. (Detail shadowmaps cannot be visualized in this way.) Unless the map files are required for other purposes, they should only be written while working on the framing, because writing shadowmap files forces mental ray to compute the entire shadowmap even if only a partial map is needed for rendering.

Automatic framing works well for spot lights, because the spot spread limits the illuminated geometry, and directional lights, because the shadowmap can be aligned easily with the bounding box of the shadow-casting geometry. (This relies on the shadow or shadow cast[3.4] flags being set only on objects or instances that actually cast shadows.) Point lights are more difficult to frame because they cast lights in all directions. Manual framing can be performed by supplying a shadowmap camera[3.3], see below.

The syntax of the extra shadow-mapping statements that can be added to the light source block in the scene file (see page 134) is:

```
light  "light_name"
    ...
    [ shadowmap on|off ]
    [ shadowmap resolution resolution_int ]
    [ shadowmap softness softness ]
    [ shadowmap samples samples_int ]
    [ shadowmap file "filename" ]
    [ shadowmap merge [ on|off ]³·³ ]
    [ shadowmap bias bias ]³·³
    [ shadowmap camera "camera_name" ]³·³
    ...
end light
```

mental ray 3.3 introduces shadowmap merging, which both reads and computes the shadowmap. The computed shadowmap and the one found on disk (a file statement must be present) are merged so that the smaller distance is stored in the resulting map. This is useful for multipass rendering, where the scene is rendered in multiple passes that are later composited together. However, this introduces a problem: shadowmaps normally do not contain the exact distance of a shadow-casting object to the light source, but the halfway point between the *next two* shadow-casting objects to avoid self-shadowing artifacts. (This is known as the Woo trick.) But if the scene is rendered in multiple passes, the second object may be unknown because it lives in a different pass. Therefore, mental ray 3.3 also implements biased shadowmaps where the stored depth is a little behind the shadow-casting surface, by a distance called the *bias*. Biased mode is enabled if a bias greater than 0 is specified in the light block. This mode works well with shadowmap merging. For more details, see page 158. The default bias is 0, which enables the Woo trick.

mental ray 3.3 also allows attaching a shadowmap camera to a light definition. The camera is basically a container for additional information that is not needed most of the time, but allows finer control over the shadowmap computation process:

- The camera **resolution** overrides the `shadowmap resolution` statement in the light source. It also allows nonsquare resolutions.

- The camera **window** selects a subrectangle of the shadowmap resolution. Shadowmap pixels outside the window are not computed.

- The camera **aperture**, **focal**, and **aspect** fields define the field of view of the camera. These parameters allow framing the shadowmap so that it covers only the area of the scene that will receive shadowmap shadows. The default normally computed by mental ray may be too large because it considers the entire bounding boxes of shadow-casting and receiving objects, which sometimes results in shadowmaps with large unused margins.

- The camera **clip** planes define hither and yon planes. Occluding objects should be no closer than the hither plane and no further than the yon plane. It is almost never necessary to change the defaults.

The other camera fields are ignored. Using a camera to define these parameters makes it simple to put a camera on the light source position in a modeling application, and using normal GUI tools to optimally frame the area of the scene that should receive shadowmap shadows.

Here is the definition of a shadow-mapped light source, along with an options block that enables shadow maps:

```
options "opt"
        samples         -1 2
        contrast        0.1  0.1  0.1
        shadowmap       on
        trace           off
        object space
end options

light "light1"
        "mib_light_spot" (
            "color"    1 1 1,
            "cone"     0.9,
            "shadow"   on,
            "factor"   0.25
        )
        origin                      .6  .4   0
        direction                  -.6 -.6   0
        spread                      0.8
        shadowmap                   on
        shadowmap resolution        500
        shadowmap softness          0.05
        shadowmap samples           12
        shadowmap file              "out.zt"
end light
```

If the above options block and shadow map light source are inserted into the scene file on page 135, the left image in figure 5.6 is rendered. The resulting shadowmap is saved to the file out.zt, shown on the right.

Note how the softness of the shadow at the left edge is higher than at the sides, as it should be, but nowhere near the correct softness that can be achieved with the raytraced method as shown on page 146. Also, the shadow edge does not quite meet the lower right corner of the cube where it should, but doesn't, lose all softness at the corner. In the real world, shadows become softer with distance from the shadow-casting object; shadow-mapped shadows do not.

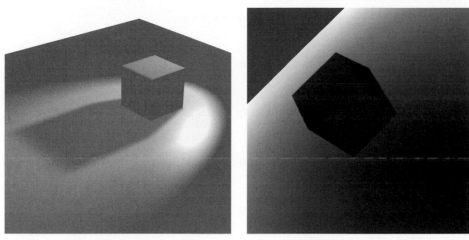

Rendered image.   Shadow map contents.

Figure 5.6: Rendering with shadow maps.

Shadow map rendering is controlled by a number of statements in the options block or command line options, and the light source definition. The command line options is

> `-shadowmap` *options* `--`

options is a sequence of optional command words, terminated with a double minus sign:

`on`	enables shadow maps. They are disabled by default.
`opengl`	enables shadow maps, which will be rendered with OpenGL hardware acceleration.
`off`	disables shadow maps. This is the default.
`motion`	enables motion-blurred shadows (that is, if an occluding object moves and is motion-blurred, so is its shadow). This is the default.
`nomotion`	disables motion-blurred shadows. This improves rendering performance.
`rebuild`	forces mental ray to always rebuild all shadow map files, even if a file with the name specified in the light source is found on disk.
`reuse`	allows mental ray to read shadow map files.
`only`	performs shadow map preprocessing but does not render an image. This is useful to create shadow map files to be used in future rendering because it is often possible to create shadow map files once and then use them throughout an animation. This does not work with detail shadowmaps[3.3] because detail shadowmap files only store shadowmap tiles that were needed during rendering.

The options block in the scene file supports similar options:

```
shadowmap on
```
                is equivalent to `-shadowmap on`.

```
shadowmap opengl
```
                is equivalent to `-shadowmap opengl`.

```
shadowmap off
```
                is equivalent to `-shadowmap off`.

```
shadowmap motion on
```
                is equivalent to `-shadowmap motion`.

```
shadowmap motion off
```
                is equivalent to `-shadowmap nomotion`.

```
shadowmap rebuild on
```
                is equivalent to `-shadowmap rebuild`.

```
shadowmap rebuild off
```
                is equivalent to `-shadowmap reuse`.

As always, command line options override specifications in the options block. Finally, the relevant statement in light definitions are:

```
shadowmap on|off
```
                is a flag that must be turned on to enable shadow maps for this light source. A light source without this flag uses ray tracing to compute shadows.

```
shadowmap resolution n
```
                specifies that the shadow map should consists of $n \times n$ depth values. Larger values take longer during preprocessing but allow more precision during rendering. The default is 256.

```
shadowmap softness f
```
                If f is larger than zero, n different samples (see next statement) will be taken from the shadow map, on a square region with size f. This will make the boundaries of the shadows appear softer. The size f is in internal space units on the shadow map projection plane. For directional lights, an orthographic projection is used, and therefore the softness will be constant in the scene, and the soft region will roughly have size f. For other lights, because of the projective projection used, apparent softness will increase with distance from the light. This means that much smaller f values are usually required for spot lights than directional lights. The default for f is 0.0.

```
shadowmap samples n
```
                specifies the number of samples to take in the shadow map when rendering

soft shadows. The default is one sample. This must be increased when `shadowmap softness` is used.

`shadowmap file "`*s*`"`

is the name of the shadow map file that will be used to load and save the shadow map for this light source. By default, no name is set, and the shadow map is neither loaded nor saved. The suggested extension for *filename* is `.zt`.

5.4   Detail Shadowmaps$^{3.3}$

Detail shadowmaps are like shadowmaps, except that extra information is stored for each shadowmap pixel: multisampling is used to discover partial occlusion of a pixel, and transparent shadows are supported. Regular shadowmaps only take one sample per shadowmap pixel, and assume that all shadow-casting objects are opaque.

Transparency is computed by calling the shadow shaders of occluding (shadow-casting) objects, if it has one. If the shadow shader reports transparency, the next occluding object is evaluated as well, and so on. All this information is stored in the detail shadowmap. This makes detail shadowmaps larger and slower than regular shadowmaps, but they are often faster than raytraced shadows and, unlike raytraced shadows, they can be written to disk and reused in the next frame.

Detail shadowmaps work with all of the regular shadow map statements, except shadowmap merging. Detail shadowmaps support several extra statements in the light source definition (see page 134) that are ignored by regular shadowmaps:

```
light "light_name"
    ...
    [ shadowmap detail ]
    [ shadowmap detail samples samplesint ]
    [ shadowmap accuracy accuracy ]
    ...
end light
```

The `shadowmap detail` statement enables detail shadowmaps. It replaces the `shadowmap on` statement, which switches back to regular shadowmaps.

The `shadowmap detail samples` statement controls multisampling: a value of *n* instructs mental ray to use $n \times n$ samples for each shadowmap pixel during the computation of this map. If set to a value greater than 1, this smoothes jagged edges at shadow boundaries.

The `shadowmap accuracy` parameter determines how far two depth values have to be apart to be stored as separate depth values. Depth values too close to each other will be combined into one depth value. The units for this parameter are the same internal space units used for the `bias` and `softness` parameters. The default value of zero instructs mental ray to use a heuristic to compute an accuracy parameter internally. If the accuracy is too large, then shadow artifacts will appear since values from surfaces too far apart will be combined. If the accuracy value is selected too small, then there will be no further improvements in image quality, but memory and time resources will be wasted, since many more depth points per detail shadow map pixel will have to be stored and queried during lookup.

If a light is switched to detail shadowmap mode with the `shadowmap detail` statement, the `file` statements in the light source is assumed to refer to detail shadowmap files. It is not possible to mix detail and regular mode, and files are not automatically converted.

Detail shadow maps stored in files behave slightly different from regular shadow maps. The latter files always contain a complete shadow map. Detail shadow maps files contain only those tiles that needed to be computed during the rendering of the previous and current frames. New tiles will be dynamically added when needed. This has the advantage that when the frame is finished, mental ray will not stay busy by filling up all the gaps in the shadowmap, rendering shadowmap tiles after rendering has already reached 100%. On the other hand, the `shadowmap only` mode no longer has an effect because without rendering the detail shadowmap remains empty.

Detail shadowmaps also do not support the `softness` statement, there is no support for the segmented shadow mode (including per-segment volumes), and area light source settings are ignored.

5.5 Internals: How Shadows are Computed **

This section describes the algorithms that mental ray uses to compute shadows. This is advanced material and not required for using shadows in a scene, but it helps to understand how shaders cooperate to produce advanced effects such as shadow-casting procedural volumes.

5.5.1 Raytraced Shadows

This subsection describes the steps that mental ray takes to compute raytraced (that is, non-shadow map) shadows, and how the various types of shaders cooperate to generate shadows. First, here is a scene with an illuminated object whose material shader has a list of light source instances. Shaders like *mib_illum_phong* have a parameter `lights`; see page 135 for an example. The material shader will query, or "trace", each light in the list to add its light contribution, which results in the light shader of each traced light to be called.

Light shaders that support shadows (such as the *mib_light_point* shader used on page 135), and have a `shadow on` parameter, will ask mental ray to find occluding objects. As described on page 147, mental ray will then search for occluding objects and call shadow shaders for each one found until no light is left or all relevant occluding objects have been considered.

When a material shader traces a light source, it casts a ray from the illuminated point to the light source, which is called a *light ray* (even though, strictly speaking, no ray tracing is involved; this is simply a shader call). When an occluding object is found, mental ray constructs a *shadow ray*. This is relevant for the diagrams below, and for the shader writer because each shader can access information about the "current ray", such as start and end point, type, and length. This is how light shaders compute distance attenuation, for example. See volume 2 of this series for details.

Finally, a volume shader, if available, is called for the visible ray and the light ray. Volume shaders are stored in materials. Their purpose is to attenuate light, for example to simulate a hazy atmosphere that fades colors towards white depending on the length of the ray (the distance traveled through the haze). However, regular shadows and sorted shadows can only deal with simple homogeneous atmospheres, not volumic shadows, because the volume shader is only called for the distance from the illuminated point to the light source, which is not sufficient for a shadow-casting cloud between occluding objects, for example.

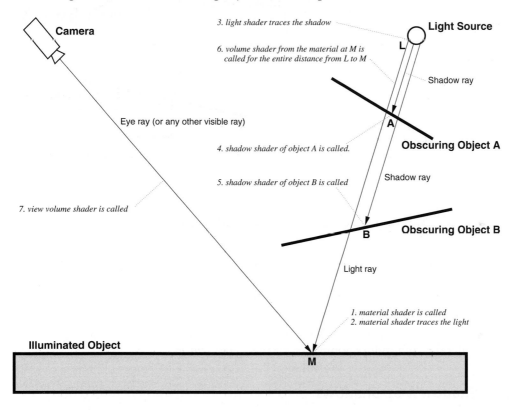

Figure 5.7: Regular and sorted shadow modes.

Figure 5.7 illustrates the events in regular and sorted shadow mode. In regular shadow mode, it is unpredictable whether object A or object B is found first, so steps 4 and 5 may be reversed. In sorted shadow mode, A is always evaluated before B, so step 4 always comes before step 5.

The segmented shadow mode differs from regular and sorted shadows by treating shadow rays like visible rays that travel from the illuminated point towards the light source. They are called *segmented* because each new shadow ray begins where the previous one ended. The advantage is that for each such segment, a volume shader is called, so if there is a shadow-casting cloud between A and B, B's volume shader will be called to produce the appropriate shadow without any extra effort (the volume shader is also called when visible rays from the camera travel through the cloud, and does the same thing). This is called *volumic shadows*. Figure 5.8 is the diagram for segmented shadow mode.

Note that the shadow rays run in the opposite direction than in the regular and sorted shadow

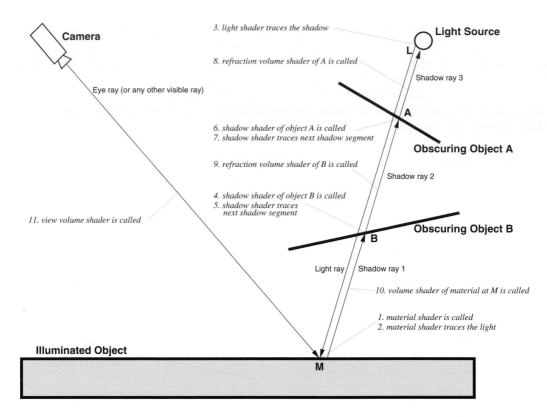

Figure 5.8: Segmented shadow mode.

cases, and that the shadow shader closest to the illuminated point is called first. Shader writers must consider this, but it does not matter for the scene creator.

5.5.2 Shadow Map Shadows

Shadow mapping uses a very different algorithm. Before the actual image is rendered, mental ray automatically performs a preprocessing step to create a shadow map for every light source that has the `shadowmap` flag set. The shadow map is a square array of depth values, as seen from the light source; see figure 5.9. (If a shadowmap camera[3.3] is provided, it may specify nonsquare shadowmaps and a window in the shadowmap.)

The Woo trick consists of not storing the actual depth (2, 3, or 4), but the halfway point between this and the next occluding object. This solves a difficult problem: if an occluding object itself is shaded, say the one at depth 2, it too would look up the shadowmap and would find that everything at a distance of 2 and greater is in shadow. Comparing two depths in this way is not numerically stable, so sometimes it would decide that it is in shadow (from itself, but it doesn't know that), and sometimes it would decide that it is not in shadow. This results in an irregular pattern called *shadow acne*. It can never happen if the Woo trick is applied because 2.5 is safely greater than 2. It might appear strange that the occluding object at depth 4 never stores a value because there is no "next" occluder that the halfway point could be computed from, so it stores

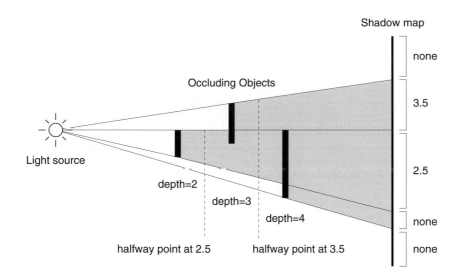

Figure 5.9: Shadow map algorithm with Woo trick.

"none", but that's ok – if there is no "next" object, then there is nothing that could find itself in shadow from the occluder at depth 4 so the contents of the shadowmap do not matter there.

mental ray 3.3 also supports shadowmap merging, where shadowmaps rendered from multiple passes are combined. Since each pass renders like a normal scene, which contains only a subset of all objects, the Woo trick often fails because the "next" object may be in a different pass and not present in the current pass. This would result in an incorrect halfway point. Therefore, mental ray 3.3 also supports biased shadowmaps, where each occluder stores its depth plus a constant bias, as shown in figure 5.10. The figure assumes a bias of 0.2. The bias can be set in the light source block. Biased shadowmaps should be avoided unless required for merging because the bias value must be chosen carefully to avoid artifacts such as holes in the shadow, or speckles resulting from self-shadowing. Note that shadowmaps rendered with OpenGL always use the bias method, because hardware rendering cannot implement the Woo trick since there is no notion of a "next" occluder.

A shadow map need not be preprocessed if the light source contains a shadow map file name to read the shadow map from, and if the mental ray options do not disable file reading. For point lights, six image files instead of one are generated, one for each side of a cube centered on the point light. The six files are distinguished by appending an extension 1...6 to the file names. If the shadow map file name contains the character "#", it is replaced with an eight-digit (hexadecimal) hash code that encodes the light's transformation. This makes it possible to have unique file names for multiply-instanced light sources, but care must be taken to keep these file names from accumulating and filling all available disk space.

After preprocessing, there is one shadow map for every shadow-mapped light source, and image rendering can begin. When a light shader asks mental ray to compute shadows, mental ray checks each shadow-mapped light source in turn. For each one, it checks whether the distance of the illuminated point to the light source is greater than the corresponding shadow map value. If yes, the search is stopped and mental ray returns "no light" to the light shader.

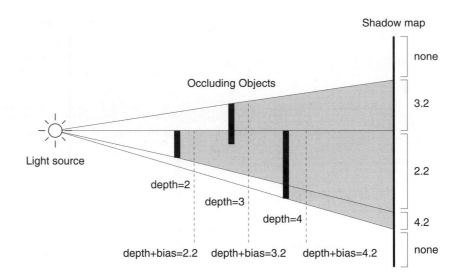

Figure 5.10: Biased shadow map algorithm[3.3].

If a nonzero shadow map softness value is given, mental ray checks nearby shadow map values too (as many as specified by the shadow map samples parameter) and filters them such that the light value returned to the light shader can be higher than completely black even for an illuminated point in shadow if it is found that some shadow map values in the range checked are representing points not in shadow.

5.6 Shadow Summary and Performance

Here is a checklist of necessary preparations for shadow casting:

	raytraced			shadow mapped		
	normal	transp.	area	normal	soft	detail
light: enable shadows	●	●	●	●	●	○
light: enable shadow maps	○	○	○	○	○	●
light: enable detail shadow maps	○	○	○	●	●	●
light: specify shadow map resolution	○	○	○	●	●	●
light: specify shadow map softness	○	○	○	○	●	○
light: specify shadow map samples	○	○	○	○	●	●
light: specify shadow map accuracy	○	○	○	○	○	●
material: shadow shader	○	●	○	○	○	●
material: do not use opaque flag †	○	●	○	○	○	●
options: enable shadows †	●	●	●	●	●	●
options: choose shadow mode †	○	○	○	○	○	○
options: enable ray tracing †	●	●	●	○	○	○
options: enable `face both` †	○	●	○	○	○	○
options: enable shadow maps	○	○	○	●	●	●

Options that are the default are marked "†". Required settings are marked "●", while settings marked "○" are not required. Choosing a shadow mode is not required because well-written shadow shaders do this automatically. In the case of the material opaque flag, specifying it where allowed (that is, if no transparent shadows are cast) improves performance. Enabling the `face both` option is not strictly necessary but a good idea when transparency is involved because with `face front` the back side of objects are invisible. No additional special preparations are necessary for volumic shadows; they fall in the *transparency* category.

The rules for achieving maximum performance are:

- Keep the number of lights evaluated by material shaders short (that is, keep the light lists in each shader parameter list short unless the light list is in exclusive mode). The absolute number of lights in the scene has little impact on performance.

- Only enable shadow casting on lights that are expected to cast shadows. Do not enable shadow casting on "fill-in lights" such as darklights or lights that only brighten up colors or highlights in the scene but do not correspond to real light sources.

- Materials attached to opaque objects that always cast opaque shadows should have the opaque flag set, and should have no shadow shader.

- If all shadows from a light are opaque, use shadow map mode for that light. Moreover, if the shadows do not move, specify a shadow map file name in the light so mental ray can re-use the computed shadow map in multiple frames. For best performance, choose the lowest shadow map resolution that gives acceptable results, or use a shadowmap camera[3.3] to optimally frame the area that receives shadows.

- When using shadow maps together with motion blurring, turn off shadow map motion blur if the movement is small and normal shadow map softness can achieve sufficient blurring.

- Use softness for shadow maps only when necessary.

- Use area light sources only where necessary to achieve soft shadows. If the soft shadow appears only on a single object but the light source illuminates many others too where soft shadows are not necessary, use two light sources in the same location, one with area parameters and the other without, and use the area light source in the light list of the material that must have soft shadows and the other light everywhere else.

- Use small sampling values for area light sources.

- Complex and inefficient shaders can dominate rendering time; always use the simplest one you can get away with. If possible, split lights in the way suggested for area light sources.

- You may have to turn off OpenGL shadow map acceleration if dark spots (surface acne) appear on illuminated objects.

5.7   Color Profiles[3.4]*

Colors are a product of human perception. In nature there are no colors, only electromagnetic radiation. By default, mental ray operates with a single color representation (also called a "color space") that works with red, green, and blue channels that are manipulated by shaders, written to frame buffers, and saved to output images.

Color spaces can also be selected explicitly, separately for rendering and for each output image. The most common color space for computer screens is sRGB, which is normally also the appropriate output color space for mental ray. Which color space to select for the actual rendering is a more difficult question. The space that comes closest to the physical reality is mental ray's boxRGB space, which averages the electromagnetic power distribution within three separate ranges of the visible spectrum. Though this is the physically most correct color representation for rendering purposes, it does not always result in the aesthetically most pleasing images. This has to do with the fact that the reaction of a material to light is commonly also expressed as a color with components between zero and one. Those colors are often selected in a color space associated with a computer display. They are only very rarely derived from a measured spectral response of a material to a light source. For this reason mental ray offers separate color spaces for rendering, output, and texture input.

The choice of color space is not sufficient. The human eye can adapt to varying illumination situations. Even the perception of "white" is variable: the color of the most dominant light source tends to be identified as white. When the computed images are later viewed under different lighting conditions, the colors in the image look wrong. This can be remedied by performing a white point adaption. The white point of an sRGB display is defined to correspond to a standardized illuminant called D65, which represents the average daylight illumination under an overcast sky. The number 65 says that this illuminant has a color temperature of 6500 Kelvin.

One more problem is the question of gamma correction. The response of a CRT or LCD display to the applied voltage is not linear. Therefore, the viewing program should correct for this non-linearity of the display. However, if this correction is applied to images with a resolution of less than ten bits per color channel, artifacts like color banding may result. Therefore, if the output image format has such a limited resolution, then it is better to apply the gamma transform within mental ray before the image is written out. However, ideally the image should be written with unmodified floating point resolution for each color channel, while the device dependend gamma correction should be performed by the viewing program. TV cameras or digital cameras perform this gamma correction before the image is created on the storage medium. For this reason it may be necessary to "ungamma" correct textures read into mental ray.

The sRGB and HDTV standards require gamma correction. However, mental ray does not apply this gamma correction by default when such an output color space is selected. The requested gamma correction has to be explicitly stated in the color profile associated with the color space. mental ray's color spaces refer only to the color properties, not to the intensity changes induced by gamma correction. Here are the sRGB and HDTV color profiles including gamma correction as required by the standard, in .mi syntax:

```
colorprofile "sRGBg"
    color space "hdtv"
    white D 65
    gamma 2.4 0.0313080
end colorprofile

colorprofile "HDTVg"
    color space "hdtv"
    white D 65
    gamma 2.22 0.018
end colorprofile
```

The standards specify a slightly more complicated formula for the gamma correction than $t^{1/\gamma}$, which explains the deviation of the gamma values from the commonly used values of 2.2 and 2.0 for sRGB and HDTV, respectively. The first number after the gamma statement is the exponent and the second number is a threshold below which the power function is replaced by a linear interpolation.

mental ray supports the following color spaces:

space	render	output	application
sRGB/HDTV	+	++	viewing
NTSC	o	+	viewing
sharp RGB	+	−	rendering
box RGB	++	−	rendering
CIE XYZ	−	++	generic device independent
CIE Luv	−	+	quantitative, perceptionally uniform
CIE Lab	−	+	quantitative, perceptionally uniform

The suitability for the purpose ranges from unsuitable (−) to neutral (o) to recommended (++)

The most generic of theses color spaces is the CIE XYZ space. It contains all colors, while the other spaces, at least with color coefficients restricted to the range from zero to one, are restricted to a subset of all colors. The perceptionally uniform spaces CIE Luv and CIE Lab are intented only for quantitative output purposes, like measuring the results of illumination simulations.

By default mental ray does not perform any gamma correction on images written to a file. Gamma correction is not needed for rendering, only to adjust for distortions introduced by output devices such as CRT or LCD displays. Gamma correction is also used to perform minor color corrections due to the expected environment lighting condition when an image is viewed. This is why sRGB and HDTV, though they use the same color representation have been standardized to use different gamma values: The former is appropriate to office viewing conditions, while the latter is intended for watching television in a darkened room.

The color profile selected for rendering is specified in mental ray's options block:

```
options "opt"
    ....
    colorprofile "sRGB"
end options
```

The color profile to be used for the output is specified within the camera

```
camera "cam"
    output colorprofile "sRGBg" "rgb" "jpg" "out.jpg"
    ....
end camera
```

These statements assume that the color profiles sRGB and sRGBg have been defined previously with colorprofile blocks, like those shown at the beginning of this section. If a texture statement is qualified with a colorprofile statement, then the texture is assumed to contain colors conforming to the specified color profile. It will be transformed to the rendering color space.

```
color texture "tex" colorprofile "CIE XYZ" "texture.tif"
```

Again, the color profile (here CIE XYZ) must have been previously defined.

Chapter 6

Volume Rendering

The material shaders introduced on page 49 determine the color of the surface of a geometric object. The mental ray rendering software can also take into account the space between objects, with procedural *volume shaders* that control what happens when looking through it. In the simplest case, this can be a uniform fog that fades distant objects towards white. Volume shading is also the method of choice for

- anisotropic fog, non-uniform fog banks

- smoke and clouds

- fire

- visible light beams

- fur and feathers

and all other effects that either have no solid substance or are otherwise difficult to model geometrically. In principle, volume shaders can be used for any interaction with rays, including geometric models. It is possible to write volume shaders that act as sub-renderers in their domain of space, performing object and volume intersection tests like mental ray does. However, in practice volume shaders are used for effects like those in the above list; mental ray can handle solid object intersections much more efficiently.

There are two basic applications for volume rendering: global volumes that fill all outside space, like fog and other atmospheric effects, and local volumes that fill the inside of a geometric object. Both use the same method of volume shading but are attached to the scene in different ways.

Note that volume shaders only apply to visible primary and secondary rays that originate at the camera, including reflections, refractions, and environment hits, and light rays emitted by light sources or segmented shadow rays (this is configurable in some volume shaders), to compute local illumination. For photons there is a separate kind of volume shader, called a *photon volume shader*, which is described in chapter 7.7.

6.1   Global Volumes: Atmospheres and Fog

Global volumes apply to the space that contains all objects and the camera, outside all objects. They can be used for atmospheric effects that are not bounded by a specific object. Global volume shaders are attached to the camera, using the volume statement in the camera definition.

Consider the reflective sphere on page 119. If the camera is extended with a volume statement, like this:

```
link "softimage.so"
$include <softimage.mi>

camera "cam"
        frame           1
        output          "rgb" "out.rgb"
        focal           1
        aperture        1
        aspect          1
        resolution      800 800
        volume          "soft_fog" (
                                "transmit"  .9 .9 .7,
                                "start"     10,
                                "stop"      40
                        )
end camera
```

the generated image changes from the one on page 118 to the one in figure 6.1.

Figure 6.1: Global volume: fog.

The start and stop parameters control the distances where the fog sets in and where it becomes fully opaque. Volume shaders are applied to *all* rays, both primary rays from the camera and secondary rays caused by reflections and refractions. The effect becomes cumulative as rays bounce around in the scene, becoming more and more opaque as each successive secondary ray is faded on its own, independently of the others that preceded it.

Volume shaders are also called during shadow casting. Volume effects, like visible rays, cast shadows unless the volume shader is explicitly written not to. The time when volume shaders are called during shadow computations depends on the shadow mode; see page 147 for details.

Some volume shaders have a boolean parameter that allows turning off the effect of volume rendering for light rays. Normally, volume shaders also apply to light rays, which means that distant lights are dimmed by the fog.

6.2   Local Volumes: Fur, Fire, Smoke

Local volumes work like global volumes, except that the volume shaders are attached to object materials, not the camera. This means that when a refraction ray enters a geometric object whose material at that point specifies a volume shader, the volume shader now controls what happens to the ray as it travels inside the object. When the ray exits the other side of the object (another refraction), the outside volume shader is restored. Object inside/outside calculations and the decision of whether to use the object's interior volume shader or the one from the outside is up to the material shader.

Consider the scene shown in figure 6.2, consisting of a camera and two nested transparent objects that have materials A and B assigned to them, respectively. When the camera looks at this scene, the following sequence of events happens (the bottom diagram shows the sequence; the solid arrows indicate rays cast and the dotted arrows indicate finalization of rays):

1a.   The camera casts the ray. Since the camera has the volume shader C attached to it, the ray state contains a reference to volume shader C.

2a.   The ray hits the outer object at point **2**, and the material shader in material A is called. The shader places the volume shader in material A into the ray state, and casts a transparency ray.

3a.   The transparency ray hits the inner object at point **3**, and the material shader in material B is called. The shader places the volume shader in material B into the ray state, and casts another transparency ray.

4a.   The ray hits the back side of the inner object at point **4**, and the material shader in material B is called again. It notices that this time the ray is leaving, and restores the ray state to the previous volume shader from material A before casting a third transparency ray.

5a.   The same thing happens at point **5**, and the volume shader C is restored by the material shader of material A before casting the fourth transparency ray.

6a.   The fourth transparency ray does not hit further objects (if it did, the same thing would

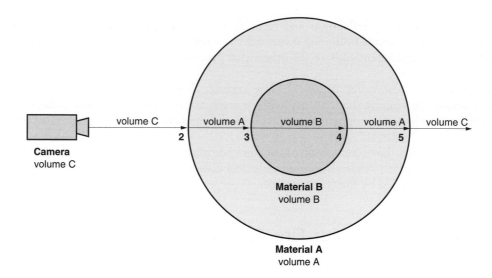

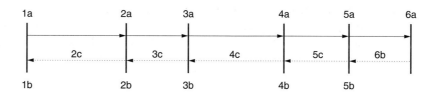

Figure 6.2: Nested volumes.

happen all over), and an environment shader, if present, is called. Otherwise, the ray returns black.

6b.   The volume shader C selected in step 5a is called for the distance between points **5** to infinity, and modifies the color from step 6a.

5b.   The material shader that cast the ray in step 5a applies the color returned in step 6a and modified in step 6b to its result color, and returns.

5c.   The volume shader A selected in step 4a modifies the result color from step 5b, and returns it.

4b.   The material shader that cast the ray in step 4a applies the color returned in step 5b and modified in step 5c to its result color, and returns.

4c.   The volume shader B selected in step 3a modifies the result color from step 4b, and returns it.

3b.   The material shader that cast the ray in step 3a applies the color returned in step 5b and modified in step 4c to its result color, and returns.

3c.   The volume shader A selected in step 2a modifies the result color from step 3b, and returns it.

2b.   The material shader that cast the ray in step 2a applies the color returned in step 3b and modified in step 3c to its result color, and returns.

2c.   The volume shader C from the camera modifies the result color from step 2b, and returns it.

1b.   The end result from step 2c is the sample color to be merged into the frame buffer.

The sequence may seem complicated, but it follows two simple rules: rays carry references to volume shaders with them, and material shaders select which one to use before casting the transparency or refraction ray. After a material shader or environment shader returns, the volume shader (if present) of the ray leading to that point is called for the distance to that point.

Nesting of objects with interior volumes is rarely done. The main application for local volumes is to use geometry to delimit the effects of a volume shader. Consider fire: it occurs in a small bounded volume, and the volume shader that produces it should be attached to the material of a simple geometric object that is otherwise fully transparent. This ensures that the fire volume shader is called only for rays that have a chance to intersect the fire because it requires hitting and entering the bounding object. In principle, the fire volume shader could have been attached to the camera, but then it would be called for all rays in the scene, which would lead to very poor performance. The better the bounding object fits the volume effect, the higher the performance will be.

Several steps must be taken to implement fire in this way:

☑   the bounding object must be created,

☑   a material for the bounding object must be created,

☑   a fully transparent material shader must be attached to the material,

☑   the fire volume shader must also be attached to the material, and

☑   the refraction trace depth must be set to at least 2 in the options block.

The following example demonstrates a fire effect, using two concepts introduced later in this book: *Phenomenon* scene elements (page 271), which are used to represent the effect as a single easy-to-use package, and *geometry shaders* (page 365), which create geometry procedurally.

Here is a very simple Phenomenon that produces a disembodied flame inside a procedural sphere. The base shader library contains a number of geometry shaders that produce simple geometric objects such as spheres and cones that are useful for bounding volume effects. The flame example replaces the sphere and its material, Phenomenon, and instance in the scene on page 118 with the following Phenomenon and instance:

```
code "fire.c"

declare shader
        color "fire" (
                color           "filter"
        )
        version 1
end declare

declare phenomenon
        geometry "fire_phen" (
                color           "filter"
        )
        shader "mtl_sh" "mib_transparency" (
                "transp"        1 1 1 1
        )
        shader "vol_sh" "fire" (
                "filter"        = interface "filter"
        )
        material "ballmat"      = "mtl_sh"
                volume          = "vol_sh"
        end material
        shader "sphere" "mib_geo_sphere" (
                "u_subdiv"      10,
                "v_subdiv"      10
        )
        shader "sphere_inst" "mib_geo_instance" (
                "object"        "sphere",
                "material"      "ballmat",
                "matrix"        1 0 0 0  0 1 0 0  0 0 1 0  0 0 0 1
        )
        root = "sphere_inst"
end declare

instance "sphere_inst"
        geometry "fire_phen" (
                "filter"        1.0 0.9 0.8
        )
        transform       .125 0    0    0
                        0    .125 0    0
                        0    0    .125 0
                        1   -.1  -1    1
end instance
```

This Phenomenon acts like a geometry shader, which means that it computes a geometric object at runtime. The actual geometry is created by the *mib_geo_sphere* shader, and an instance for it is created by the *mib_geo_instance* shader, which also accepts a material parameter that will be inherited by the sphere during rendering (see material inheritance on page 379). The material references a material shader, which makes the sphere surface completely transparent, and a volume shader that computes the actual fire. Figure 6.3 shows the structure of the Phenomenon.

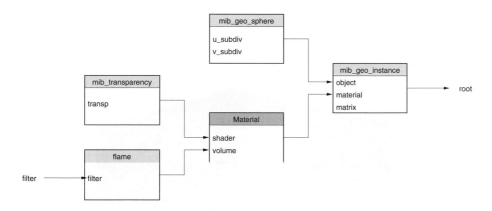

Figure 6.3: Structure of fire Phenomenon.

This Phenomenon is still rather simple. A real fire might also contain an animated light source, which is missing here, and the fire shader is very minimalistic and does not handle overlapping volumes. There is, however, no limit to the complexity of a Phenomenon; it can be extended with lights without disturbing scenes using the Phenomenon in any way.

The Phenomenon is placed into the scene with an instance, much like geometric objects defined with `object ... end object` blocks are. The `geometry` keyword followed by a shader definition (consisting of a shader or Phenomenon name plus parameters) replaces the regular object name:

```
instance "instance_name"
    geometry "name" (parameters)
    ...
end instance
```

See page 371 for more information on instancing. Figure 6.4 shows the rendered image.

6.3 Ray Marching

Ray marching is a technique used by volume shaders to integrate illumination or other effects over a distance by point sampling, if analytical methods do not work because the shader does not have the necessary information. A typical example are light shafts in a dusty room. The room would be filled with a volume shader that needs to find out how many illuminated dust particles are encountered by any given ray crossing the volume, and brighten the ray accordingly. Any analytical method would require a list of occluding objects that interrupt the shafts, but usually such a list is not available so a ray marcher that point-samples the volume is the only option.

The ray marcher does this by considering various points along the length of the ray, and evaluating the situation at each of them. It may choose points in regular intervals, and add more points between any two points that came up with very different results to improve sampling resolution, or use variable spacing depending on the distance to the light source or other factors. Figure 6.5 shows a schematic view.

Figure 6.4: Fire.

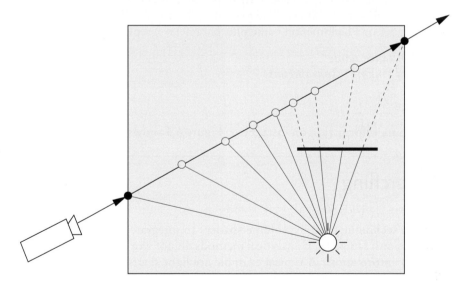

Figure 6.5: Ray marching in a volume.

The volume shader in the bounding box, which controls the shaded volume, chooses sample points and evaluates the direct illumination at each of them. Some of them receive light, others do not because of the shadow-casting object or an inhomogeneous atmosphere. If the volume shader assumes a homogeneous atmosphere, it would add up all point illuminations and divide by the number of points to determine the average brightening of the ray, or it may apply some distribution function if the atmosphere is not homogeneous.

Here is a simple scene that uses the *parti_volume* shader, which uses ray marching to determine the lighting in a participating medium such as homogeneous or nonhomogeneous fog:

```
link "base.so"
link "physics.so"
$include <base.mi>
$include <physics.mi>

camera "cam"
        output          "rgb" "out.rgb"
        focal           270.0
        aperture        30.0
        aspect          1.0
        resolution      800 800
end camera

options "opt"
        object space
end options

light "light1"
        "physical_light" (
            "color"     1000 1000 1000
        )
        visible
        origin          0 1 -50
        sphere          0.1  5 5
end light

instance "light-i" "light1" end instance

material "volsurf"
        "transmat" ()
        volume "parti_volume" (
            "scatter"           0.1 0.1 0.1,
            "extinction"        0.1,
            "nonuniform"        0.0,
            "min_step_len"      0.03,
            "max_step_len"      0.2,
            "lights"            ["light-i"]
        )
end material

object "box" visible trace tag 1
        group
                    -3       3       -51.5
                    -3       3       -48.5
                    -3      -3       -48.5
                    -3      -3       -51.5
                     3       3       -51.5
                     3       3       -48.5
                     3      -3       -48.5
```

```
                  3        -3        -51.5

              v 0 v 1 v 2 v 3 v 4 v 5 v 6 v 7

              p "volsurf"       0 1 2 3
              p                 4 5 6 7
              p                 3 7 4 0
              p                 2 6 5 1
              p                 5 4 0 1
              p                 6 7 3 2
        end group
  end object

  instance "cam-i" "cam" end instance
  instance "box-i" "box" end instance

  instgroup "all"
        "cam-i" "light-i" "box-i"
  end instgroup

  render "all" "cam-i" "opt"
```

The *parti_volume* volume shader in the physics.so shader library has various parameters to control the step size between sample points, and is used here to simulate a homogeneous (uniform) atmosphere. Non-homogeneous atmospheres can be specified with the nonuniform parameter:

```
  material "volsurf"
        "transmat" ()
        volume "parti_volume" (
            "scatter"          0.1 0.1 0.1,
            "extinction"       0.1,
            "nonuniform"       0.9,
            "min_step_len"     0.03,
            "max_step_len"     0.2,
            "lights"           ["light-i"]
        )
  end material
```

The images (figure 6.6) rendered with this scene and both volumes show the light glare introduced by rays passing close to the light source. The sample points that are very close to the light source receive a lot of light, while more distant sample points receive less light. The use of the *physical-light* light shader ensures correct inverse-square light energy falloff with distance.

To work correctly, this scene requires ray tracing and shadows, both of which must be turned on in the options block.

Note that ray marching is often a compute-intensive volume effect. If the scene also uses global illumination, it may be necessary to turn off the final gathering feature that improves global illumination quality, because it relies on ray tracing and can reduce rendering performance if individual rays become very expensive. See page 206 for details on final gathering.

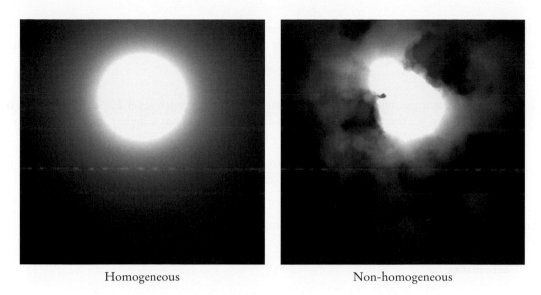

Homogeneous   Non-homogeneous

Figure 6.6: Fog and clouds rendered with ray marching.

6.4 Automatic Volumes[3.3]

autovolumeProper volume shading like in figure 6.2 on page 168 depends on mental ray knowing which volumes a ray enters and leaves. In particular, the method would break down if the camera would move into one of the objects containing a volume shader, like sphere A in the figure. It would then apply the volume C shader that is attached to the camera to the inside of sphere A. If the sphere represents a visible light cone, like that of a street light in the fog, the cone would disappear.

mental ray 3.3 introduces automatic volume detection, which finds out which volumes the camera is in, and adding that volume to the volume stack so that the situation shown in figure 6.2 is correctly represented, complete with all five arrows representing the nested volumes.

In addition, automatic volume detection supports multiple volumes. Each volume shader declaration can be assigned an integer number called a *level*. Volumes with equal numbers mix, like two different gases, and volumes with higher numbers displace volumes with lower numbers, like glass displaces fog. For example, the declarations of two shaders implementing glass and fog might look like this:

```
declare shader "glass" (...)
        ...
        volume level 20
end declare

declare shader "fog" (...)
        ...
        volume level 10
end declare
```

The volume levels need not be consecutive, and negative numbers can be used as well. A declaration without a level specification defaults to level 0. To return to figure 6.2, assuming that volume shader C has level 0:

- Material A is a gas with level 10 and material B is glass with level 20: inside volume B, shown as step 4c, the volume shader B is called because it has a higher level and therefore displaces the gas.

- Material A and B are both gases that mix, and both have level 10: inside volume B, in step 4c, both the volume shader A and volume shader B are called.

Automatic volume detection is enabled by adding the statement

```
autovolume on
```

to the options block in the scene file. The statement

```
photon autovolume on
```

enables automatic volume detection for photons, see Chapter 7.

If this mode is enabled, volume shaders can also use API facilities to detect inside/outside conditions. See the mental ray manual for details on programming shaders that take advantage of automatic volume detection. This can greatly simplify programming volume shaders, but also refractive material shaders that need to knbow the direction in which to bend the ray based on the inside and outside index of refraction.

Chapter 7

Caustics and Global Illumination

All previous scenes used local illumination: every rendered point on an object surface or in a volume computes the amount of light that reaches it by querying each light source in turn, and adding up the contributions. This method only considers direct illumination because the light travels directly, in a straight path, from the light source to the illuminated point. Occlusion by shadow-casting objects in that path are considered.

Indirect illumination occurs if light travels from the light source to the illuminated points via reflection or transmission by other objects, for example a mirror reflecting the light to the illuminated point, or a diffuse reflective white wall. The technique to also capture indirect illumination is called *global illumination*. Global illumination is the simulation of *all* light interreflection effects in a scene. Global illumination permits indirect lighting effects such as caustics and color bleeding.

Caustics are created by focusing and dispersion of light by specular reflection or refraction, onto a diffuse surface. For example, an illuminated (refractive) water bottle casts a focused caustic on a diffuse table, as does a (reflective) mirror. A typical example is the light pattern cast on the bottom of a swimming pool by the wave pattern on the (refractive) water surface. By the above definition, caustics are a form of global illumination; however, mental ray treats them independently from other global illumination effects to allow finer control and to improve performance. Caustics and global illumination are treated as separate features by mental ray — and in the chapter title — even though, theoretically, one is a subset of the other.

Color bleeding is caused by colored diffuse objects that color the light they reflect onto other objects, which then receive indirect colored light and therefore appear colored themselves. If a diffuse white wall is next to a diffuse red wall, the white wall gets a pink tint. Note, however, that bleeding red onto a pure green diffuse wall will not have an effect because the green wall does not reflect any of the incident red light to the viewer. Colors in nature rarely have such pure colors.

Simulation of caustics and global illumination has at least two distinct uses:

- Physically accurate simulation of the illumination in an environment, for example the light distribution inside an office building or the light emanating from the headlights of a car.

- Visually credible lighting effects for applications in the entertainment industry. Artistic control is more important than physical accuracy, the images just have to look realistic.

mental ray supports two approaches for computing global illumination, photon maps and final gathering, which will be described in detail below. Although final gathering, strictly speaking, is a technique that improves on photon mapping, it can be used alone too.

Photon mapping	Final gathering	Application
off	off	direct illumination only.
on	off	Physically accurate simulation.
on	on	Physically accurate simulation with improved smoothness. There are extra parameters in addition to photon mapping to adjust, but they are easier to tune.
off	on	Visually credible lighting effects, but not physically accurate because some multi-bounce light paths are missing. Diffuse effects only; no caustics. Fast, needs less memory, easy to control. This is most often used in non-CAD digital entertainment content production. Higher degree of physical correctness can be achieved with increasing the number of bounces taken into account, which significantly slows down the rendering making it slower than final gathering in combination with photon mapping.

Caustics always require photon mapping. They are not related to final gathering at all, because caustics are a specular (mirror-like) effect and final gathering is inherently a diffuse solution.

7.1   Photon Mapping vs. Final Gathering

Full global illumination effects are not possible with ordinary ray tracing algorithms because ray tracing "needs to know" where to look (that is, in which directions to cast the rays). Global illumination is characterized by flooding the entire scene with interreflected light coming from many directions that depend on the arrangement of objects in the scene. Ray tracing could attempt to sample in all directions, hoping to catch the indirect light by chance (a method called *distribution ray tracing*), but this approach is extremely inefficient and hence very slow. Instead, mental ray supports a much faster approach, called the *photon map* method.

mental ray computes global illumination in a two-phase process. In the first phase, light in the form of small energy packets (conveniently called *photon*s) is emitted into the scene, and the paths the photons take as they bounce around in the scene are followed. At some point each photon is either absorbed by an object, or escapes into infinity without hitting another object. When a photon hits an object, it can be reflected, transmitted, or absorbed. Each photon is stored at all surfaces with a diffuse component that it hit on its path (except for the first hit, which is the direct illumination). Photons are stored in a three-dimensional data structure called a *photon map* [Jensen 96]. Photons are emitted until a specified number has been stored, or (optionally) until a maximum number was emitted.

The photon map is independent of geometry storage, which means that global illumination performance is largely independent of scene complexity. While radiosity algorithms using subdivision meshing become progressively slower as the number of triangles in the scene rises, the photon map method does not appreciably slow down rendering large scenes and works with millions of triangles and instanced geometry. Photon mapping imposes no inherent complexity limit and works with any scene that can be raytraced.

In the second phase, during normal rendering, the material shaders compute the direct local illumination as usual, and also add the indirect global illumination by collecting nearby photons in the photon map and adding their contribution. The roles are cleanly separated: direct illumination is handled by local illumination, and indirect illumination is handled by global illumination. Whereas local illumination only deals with light that travels directly from the light source to the illuminated point in a straight line (possibly attenuated by shadow shaders), the global illumination feature is only used for interreflected light.

The quality and smoothness of photon mapping depends on the second phase finding enough nearby photons to compute an accurate estimate. Sometimes this is hard to achieve, for example when a room is lit only by indirect light through a very small window. If there are not enough photons that find their way through the window, there will be a very sparse photon distribution in the room, and the illumination computation will have very few photons to work with. This shows up as low-frequency noise.

Figure 7.1 shows this situation, where a light in the left room is well-covered by the photons emitted by the light source, but the right room can only be rendered with low precision because very few photons have managed to find their way there.

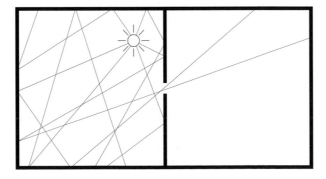

Figure 7.1: Sparse photon distribution.

To address this problem, final gathering can be enabled. Final gathering does not look for photons at the illuminated point, but casts a large number of rays into the hemisphere over the illuminated point. Each of these rays measures the illumination at its endpoint (by calling the material shader there). All results are averaged, so even if many results are imprecise or noisy, the errors are averaged out. Figure 7.2 shows a single final gathering operation, with the final gathering rays over the hemisphere shown as dotted lines.

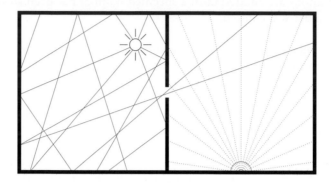

Figure 7.2: Sparse photon distribution with final gathering.

In practice, there are many more photons and many more final gathering rays than shown here. The default for a final gathering step is 1000 rays. At first, this would appear to make rendering very expensive – every illuminated point explodes into a bundle of 1000 rays. In practice, mental ray does this only rarely. Final gathering is by its nature a diffuse effect, so it is enough to space the final gathering operations widely, and re-use each result for many illuminated points in the vicinity.

Figure 7.2 also shows that final gathering without photon mapping is possible but will miss light. None of the dotted lines in the figure have managed to cross over into the left room that is brightly lit, and even if some do, the photon paths with multiple bounces cannot be reproduced. However, for simple single-bounce effects like color bleeding from a neighboring wall, or darkening near a contact shadow, final gathering without photon mapping can give excellent results.

This can be taken one step further, by limiting the maximum length of the final gathering rays, which can be done in shaders using a feature called ray falloffs. (It is called *falloff* because rays are not truncated abruptly but fade out when they get close to their maximum length, to avoid edge artifacts.) This works because effects like color bleeding and contact shadows are quite local, resulting from nearby objects only. Limiting ray lengths is very effective because the final gathering rays no longer cross large distances and pull distant objects into memory, and many final gathering rays terminate before they can even cause a material shader call. Limiting final gather ray lengths can greatly improve speed in large scenes. Obviously, the result is not physically correct, but this trick is commonly used in entertainment content creation.

Final gathering with ray falloffs is related to another technique called ambient occlusion that is often used in digital content production. Ambient occlusion also casts many short rays, but is only interested in the percentage of rays that got stopped by a nearby object. The higher the percentage, the more the point is darkened because the nearby objects are assumed to block part of the ambient light. This does not support color bleeding because no shaders are called, and it gives wrong results if the ambient light is not the same from all directions, but it does increase realism. mental ray shaders can implement ambient occlusion by not computing color if called for the endpoint of a final gather ray, and the shader at the illuminated point considers only the alpha component of the result. See the mental ray manual for details.

7.2   Local Illumination vs. Caustics vs. Global Illumination

Although the term "global illumination", strictly speaking, includes all forms of illumination including local illumination, mental ray's global illumination photon maps are used only in cases that the traditional local illumination models cannot handle. This allows mental ray to use the faster local illumination methods whenever possible and fall back on the slower photon maps only where necessary. Turning the global illumination features of mental ray on or off only affects these additional non-local illumination methods. In this sense the term "global illumination" becomes an extension to, rather than a superset of, local illumination. It is used in this sense in this book.

Caustics are a special (specular) case of global illumination, but mental ray treats them separately also because they are usually used in different ways and require different parameters: global illumination is a global effect involving most objects in the scene and is caused by diffuse light interactions, while caustics are typically small localized effects and are caused by specular light interactions. Both are based on the same photon map approach, but have separate parameters in the scene file to control them. Therefore, mental ray distinguishes three ways of dealing with illumination:

- Local illumination travels from the light source to the illuminated point in a straight line. Neither the caustics nor the global illumination features of mental ray are needed.

- Caustics introduce specular reflections and transmission of light onto diffuse surfaces or volumes. They require the caustics feature but not the global illumination feature.

- Full diffuse global illumination requires the global illumination[2.1] feature.

Although, as explained above, all three are special cases of the strict interpretation of the term "global illumination", mental ray distinguishes them for efficiency reasons and requires turning on the global illumination feature only if non-direct and non-caustic illumination must be computed. Note also that the list does not imply an inclusive order — if global illumination is enabled but caustics are not, then there will be no caustics in the rendered image. Global illumination does not "take over" the specular modes.

7.3   Diffuse, Glossy, and Specular Reflection and Transmission

Reflection of light from a surface can be divided into three types: diffuse, glossy, and specular. Diffuse reflection scatters all reflected light evenly in all directions on the hemisphere above the surface point. Specular reflection reflects only in the mirror direction, where the angle of incidence equals the angle of reflectance. Glossy reflection is directional but not restricted to a single direction, as with unpolished metal reflecting mostly but not exclusively in the mirror direction.

In computer graphics, glossy reflection is typically modeled by applying microfacet theory. The assumption is that glossy reflection is actually the same thing as specular reflection, and the reflecting surface is not planar but consists of a large number of invisibly small microfacets that form a small angle to the macroscopic plane of the surface, thus reflecting in directions that differ from the mirror direction of the surface. This results in a glossy look.

Figure 7.3 illustrates the three types of light reflection. The reflective floor in the bottom row of images has diffuse, glossy, and specular characteristics, respectively.

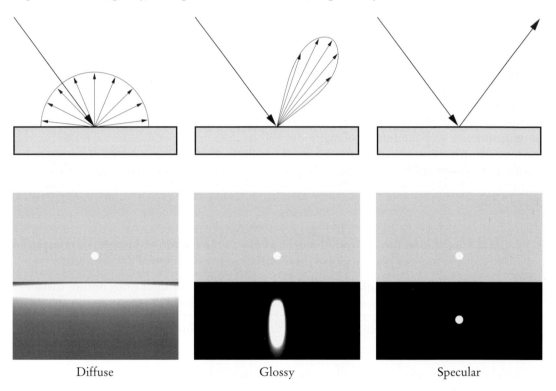

Diffuse   Glossy   Specular

Figure 7.3: Diffuse, glossy, and specular reflection.

This also applies to the three types of transmission, in which case the outgoing arrows are on the opposite side of the surface, as shown in figure 7.4. Note that the diffuse transmission image on the bottom left of figure 7.4 is uniformly dark gray because the light is scattered uniformly.

The examples use the *physical_light* light shader and the *dgs_material* material shader in the physics.so shader library. The reflective material definitions are:

```
material "mat" opaque                          # diffuse reflection
        "dgs_material" (
            "diffuse"   0.8 0.8 0.8,
            "lights"    ["light1-i"]
```

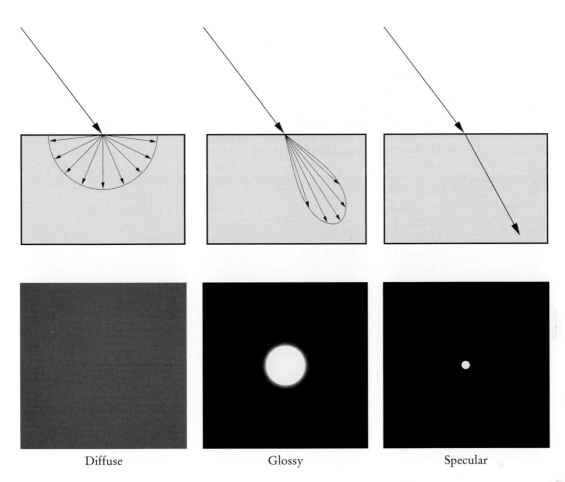

Figure 7.4: Diffuse, glossy, and specular transmission.

```
        )
end material

material "mat" opaque                              # glossy reflection
        "dgs_material" (
            "glossy"    0.8 0.8 0.8,
            "shiny"     30.0,
            "lights"    ["light1-i"]
        )
end material

material "mat" opaque                              # specular reflection
        "dgs_material" (
            "specular"  0.8 0.8 0.8,
            "lights"    ["light1-i"]
        )
end material
```

And the transmission materials are:

```
material "mat" opaque                           # diffuse transmission
        "dgs_material" (
            "ior"      1.0,
            "diffuse"  0.8 0.8 0.8,
            "transp"   1.0,
            "lights"   ["light1-i"]
        )
end material

material "mat" opaque                           # glossy transmission
        "dgs_material" (
            "ior"      1.0,
            "glossy"   0.8 0.8 0.8,
            "shiny"    20.0,
            "transp"   1.0,
            "lights"   ["light1-i"]
        )
end material

material "mat" opaque                           # specular transmission
        "dgs_material" (
            "ior"      1.0,
            "specular" 0.8 0.8 0.8,
            "transp"   1.0,
            "lights"   ["light1-i"]
        )
end material
```

See page 127 for more information on the *dgs_material* shader.

7.4   Classification of Light Paths

The paths that light can take as it travels from the light source to the camera are normally written in a shorthand notation using letters, introduced first in [Heckbert 90]:

L	light source
E	camera (eye)
S	specular reflection or transmission
G	glossy reflection or transmission
D	diffuse reflection or transmission

To identify a light path, these letters are combined, beginning with an L, ending with an E (because photons travel from the light source to the camera), and with optional specular (S), glossy (G), and diffuse (D) interactions in between. The notation $\{D|G|S\}$ means "exactly one of D, G, or S", and an asterisk ("*") means "zero or more of the preceding".

Reflection and transmission are not distinguished in this notation; the difference is simply a matter of outgoing light direction. Specular transmission is called *transparency* if the index of refraction is 1.0 and *refraction* otherwise, while glossy and diffuse transmission is known as *translucency*.

Here is a list of some common paths:

LE	Light travels directly from the light source to the camera. The light source itself becomes visible. It must be an area light source since all others have zero size and therefore do not actually show up. See page 134 for a description of visible light sources, and page 143 for area light sources.
$L\{D|G|S\}E$	All direct illumination involves one reflection or transmission between the light source and the camera. It can be specular, glossy, or diffuse. Simple illumination models such as Phong shading simulate specular/glossy and diffuse illumination using specular and diffuse color parameters, respectively, with a special Phong exponent parameter controlling the glossiness.
$L\{D|G|S\}S^*E$	These paths define classical ray tracing without global illumination. Note that ray tracing, unlike photon map generation, works backwards: the rays begin at the camera (E), then may undergo specular (S) reflections and transmissions, until they finally hit an object where direct illumination is computed. (Actually the path could be written $ES^*\{D|G|S\}L$ to emphasize that the rays travel backwards, but by convention this is not done.)
LD^*E	This is what classical radiosity using subdivision meshing can do. Only diffuse interactions are possible, which includes effects like color bleeding (where a colored wall can tint an adjacent white wall because the light it reflects is colored), but not specular and glossy effects or caustics.
LD^*S^*E	Some radiosity renderers add a ray tracing pass after rendering the radiosity image. The two passes are independent and cannot handle specular and glossy interactions before diffuse interactions.
LSS^*DE	This is a caustic: the light is first specularly reflected or refracted one or more times, and then reflected to the camera by a diffuse surface. For example, the water surface of a swimming pool refracts light onto the diffuse floor of the pool, where it is seen by the camera. (See page 190 for information on adding caustics to a scene.)
$L\{D|G|S\}^*E$	This expression covers all possible light paths, and defines all interactions that can be handled by local illumination together with global illumination. Here are some simple examples:

visible light source	*LE*
mirror image of light source	*LSE*
glossy highlight	*LGE*
diffuse reflection of light source	*LDE*
mirror image of mirror image of light source	*LSSE*
glossy highlight of mirror reflection of light source	*LSGE*
simple caustic	*LSDE*
mirror image of glossy highlight	*LGSE*
glossy reflection of glossy highlight	*LGGE*
diffuse reflection of glossy highlight	*LGDE*
mirror image of diffusely reflected light	*LDSE*
glossy reflection of diffusely reflected light	*LDGE*
diffuse reflection of diffusely reflected light	*LDDE*
⋮	⋮

Figure 7.5 shows examples of light paths. The scene consists of two perpendicular diffuse planes and a glass sphere with specular reflection and refraction.

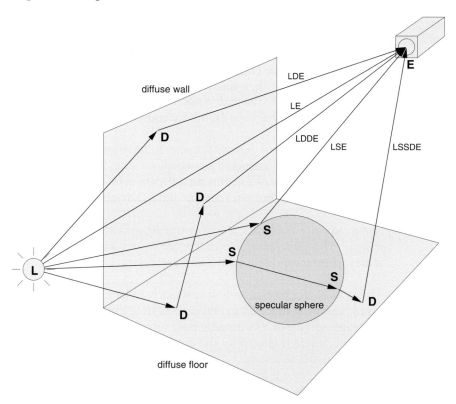

Figure 7.5: Light paths.

Five things can happen to photons: emission, reflection, transmission, absorption, and storing. A photon is emitted first at the light source, and then reflected, transmitted, or absorbed when it hits a surface. The emission of a photon is conceptually similar to casting a ray, except that the path begins at the light source and not at the camera, and that photons have energies but rays have colors. Absorption happens at surfaces and in volumes when the photon is *not* reflected or transmitted, its path ends where it is absorbed.

A photon is stored by a special shader called a *photon shader*. Photon shaders are attached to the material of all objects that reflect, transmit, or absorb photons. Photon shaders store photons only if the surface has a diffuse component. The photon can then be reflected or transmitted by the photon shader (in a direction determined by the photon shader). If the photon is not re-emitted, it is said to be absorbed. Indirect illumination of completely specular surfaces (that is, surfaces with no diffuse component) is computed with ray tracing, so no photons are stored at these surfaces. Storing means that a record of the incoming energy of the photon is put into the photon map, where it can be used to compute indirect illumination at the later shading stage. As an exception to the rule that photons may be stored where they bounce, photons are never stored at the first reflection or transmission location because that location is handled by direct illumination, not global illumination, so the light would incorrectly be taken into account twice.

Reflection, transmission, absorption, and storing are all under complete control of the photon shader (or photon volume shader in 3D volumes; see below) attached to the material of the surface or volume, respectively. Absorption is forced by mental ray when the photon trace depth limit set in the options block is reached (see page 232).

Consider figure 7.6. Two photon paths are shown. The first photon is emitted at the light source, hits a diffuse wall and is reflected at point A but not stored (because it is the first reflection), and finally hits point B where it is stored and absorbed. The second photon is reflected at the diffuse floor (C), then reflected and stored at the wall (D), transmitted but not stored at the specular (non-diffuse) sphere surface points E and F, and finally stored and absorbed on the floor (G).

7.5   Caustic and Global Illumination Lights

Light sources that provide local illumination are discussed in detail in the chapter 5. Lights that provide global illumination must specify extra information. The syntax of the extra global illumination and caustics statements in the light source block in the scene file is:

```
light "light_name"
    ...
    [ emitter              "emitter_shader_name" ( parameters) ]
    [ energy               r  g  b ]
    [ exponent             exp ]
    [ caustic photons      store_int [ emit_int ]]
    [ globillum photons    store_int [ emit_int ]]
    ...
end light
```

See page 134 for the rest of the light syntax. The photon emitter shader, if present, controls the emission of photons from the light source; without this shader the photons are emitted uniformly in all directions that have a chance of hitting objects. Possible directions are bounded by the direction and spread parameters, depending on the light type (point, spot, or directional).

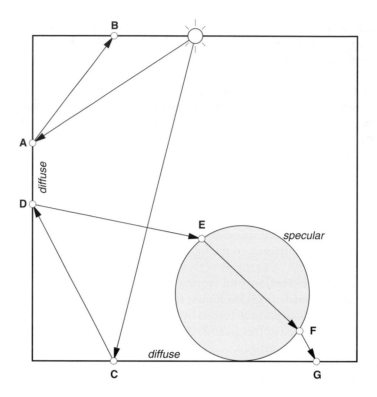

Figure 7.6: Emitting, absorbing, and storing photons.

The light energy, specified as red, green, and blue components, is the total amount of radiated energy. If 1000 photons are emitted, each carries away $\frac{1}{1000}$th of the energy. This is a different concept than the light color passed to the light shader (although the RGB *hue* will usually agree), because the light color is a nonphysical concept of light contribution while the energy is a physically correct energy contribution. Here, physical correctness means that mental ray will ensure conservation of energy: all energy sent into the scene by a light source will correctly appear as illumination in the rendered image, and none will be lost or duplicated. Note that the common method of using dim lights with large diffuse and specular coefficients for the material shaders does not work for caustics and global illumination — the diffuse, glossy, and specular coefficients must add up to at most 1.0 to preserve physical accuracy, so the correct choice of light energy values is important.

The light energy is different from the light shader color in another respect too: while most light shaders, such as the *mib_light_point* shader used in many examples in this book, are not distance-dependent, energy falls off with the square of the distance, which is what happens in nature. This means that the energy must be chosen quite high when distant objects are to be illuminated: an object twice as far away than another will receive only one quarter of the radiated energy. Think of it as the wattage of a light bulb: a sixty-Watt light bulb works well for a desk lamp but much higher energies are needed to light a large room, or a football stadium. In practice, that means that energy RGB values often range in the thousands or tens of thousands, while light shader color parameters normally do not far exceed the 0...1 range. The color parameter of the *physical_-light* light shader is an exception when the shader is applied to point or spot lights; it performs physically correct falloff and accepts the same RGB values given in the energy statement. (Note that directional light, by definition, does not disperse and therefore has no falloff.) mental ray does not cast any photons if the light has zero energy.

However, sometimes physical correctness can become a nuisance if only a "nice effect" must be achieved and the distance dependency just makes scene creation harder. While CAD applications insist on correctness, entertainment applications emphasize art direction. In these cases, the exponent statement allows overriding the inverse-square falloff law. An exponent *exp* of 2.0 is the default, providing inverse-square ($\frac{1}{r^2}$) falloff. A value of 1.0 selects ($\frac{1}{r}$) falloff. A value of 0.0 disables the falloff. Values less than 1.0 should be avoided because they tend to flood the scene with excessive amounts of light, as the light appears to become rapidly stronger with distance.

Finally, the `caustic photons` and `globillum photons` parameters control the number of photons stored in the photon map for caustics and global illumination. A photon is stored at every diffuse or partially diffuse surface it hits, including the surface where it is absorbed. In other words, storing at some location means that the photon deposited energy (or more precisely, contributed to the energy flux) there.[1] The word "photon" is not used in the quantum-mechanical sense here, but as an abstraction to model energy flux.

Caustics and global illumination are controlled separately because caustics tend to be more localized and often look good with smaller numbers of photons. Good values for the numbers of photons range from tens of thousands for quick previews to millions for high-quality global illumination simulations of building interiors or other complex scenes.

Care should be taken to ensure that emitted photons really hit objects that store them. A point light in a scene that only has one small hidden photon absorber will cause most photons to be lost, which can severely reduce performance since new photons need to be emitted. After 10 000 unsuccessful emissions, mental ray will print a warning; after 1 000 000, emission from that light is aborted with an error message. The reason why the number of *stored* photons is specified, rather than the number of *emitted* photons, is that the image quality directly depends only on the number of stored photons. Stored photons enter the illumination computation during rendering, unstored photons do not.

However, the maximum number of emitted photons may also be specified as a second argument to the `caustic photons` and `globillum photons` statements[2.1] to limit the emission in cases where very few photons can be stored, perhaps to prevent long render times if a few frames of an animation intentionally "lose" most photons. This parameter is intended to prevent runaways, not to control render quality.

---

[1] A technical note: photons are always stored with full energy; the material shader that collects them during shading will multiply the photon energy by the material's diffuse color. This is consistent with the way material shaders deal with direct illumination. The stored energy is also direction-independent; if photons strike a surface at a grazing angle the stored density (photons per surface area) is smaller, leading to the desired smaller average illumination when shading.

7.6 Caustics

Caustics are a highly visible indirect illumination effect. A caustic is created by light emitted from a light source, going through one or more specular reflections or refractions, and then hitting a diffuse surface and being diffusely reflected to the eye. The specular surface is said to *cast* a caustic, and the diffuse surface is said to *receive* a caustic. Figures 7.7 and 7.8 show the mental images swimming pool, first without and then with caustics. To create a caustic, several steps must be taken:

Figure 7.7: Swimming pool without caustics.

Figure 7.8: Swimming pool with caustics.

☑   Caustics must be enabled in the options block with the statement `caustic on`, or the `-caustic on` command line option.

☑ The light source must have an energy statement. It is advisable to use a light shader like *physical_light* that ensures physical correctness. The energy is distance-dependent and often has to be chosen quite large.

☑ Both the caustic-casting and caustic-receiving objects must have a material, either directly in the object or inherited from its instance, that contains a photon shader statement. Photon shaders may store and either absorb, reflect, or transmit photons. If the photon shader is missing on the casting object the photons are never reflected or transmitted by it, and if it is missing on the receiving object no photons are stored.

☑ The material should not have a shadow shader to avoid having light pass through the object twice, once directly and once indirectly. (Shadow shaders can also be disabled by setting the opaque flag in the material.) See the note on page 142 for a discussion of this.

☑ The caustic-casting material should not be diffuse because diffuse objects spread the light rather than focus it. Attempts to make a diffuse object cast caustics by increasing the light energy usually turns the object into a fireball without obtaining a caustic, so keep the diffuse component to a minimum or avoid it.

☑ The caustic-receiving material must be diffuse, because otherwise no photons are stored there. Its material shader must support collecting stored photons.

☑ If the caustic-casting object is refractive, its index of refraction should be greater than 1.0 to create a focusing effect.

The following optional steps help controlling quality and performance:

☑ To increase the precision of the caustic, the number of photons emitted and stored from a light source can be adjusted with `caustic photons` statements. The number of photons is typically between 10 000 and 1 000 000; smaller values cause blurry caustics. The default is 10 000.

☑ By default, all objects both cast and receive caustics. This can be optimized by adding a `caustic 0` statement to the options block, and adding `caustic` statements to individual objects. The caustic-casting object must then be marked with the statement `caustic 1 or 3`, and the caustic-receiving object must be marked with the statement `caustic 2 or 3`. Objects out of the way of all caustic photons should be marked `caustic off` to exclude them from all caustic photon tracing. Alternatively, the flags may be applied to the object's instance, to be inherited by the object (see page 389 for flag inheritance).

☑ If the caustic looks grainy, the statement `caustic accuracy` acc_{int} *radius* can be added to the options block. The accuracy *acc* controls how many photons are considered during rendering. The default is 100; larger numbers like 200 make the caustic less noisy but also more blurry. The *radius* controls the maximum distance in which mental ray considers photons to compute the indirect illumination or caustic. The default radius is computed from the scene extent. Graininess is best reduced by increasing *acc* or *radius*.

If an object has more than one material, they must all meet the requirements listed above.

Accuracy parameters can be used to select two fundamentally different photon sampling policies. If the radius is relatively large (as is the default) the overall limiting factor is is the number of photons The radius then only catches runaway situations with very few photons. Since darker areas have stored fewer photons than brighter areas, the effective radius within which the photons are found is larger in dark areas. The effect is that low intensity areas will have less detail than high intensity areas. Also, increasing the number of photons in the scene will result in the effective radius becoming smaller (because mental ray does not have to look for photons as far away as before), so if the number of photons is not adjusted to compensate the same amount of noise will be seen, only on a smaller scale.

The other policy is to select a small radius, on the scale of the desired geometric detail. The number of photons can then be chosen high. In this case, a constant radius is examined which results in the scale of the detail remaining constant between light and dark areas. Increasing the number of photons in the map will have the effect of reducing noise. In practice, one will often use a combination of the two policies, with a small radius to get detail in dark areas, and moderate numbers of photons to speed up rendering. Regardless of the chosen policy, a large effective radius gives less noise but a more blurred result. To decrease the noise without blurring detail, it is necessary to increase the number of photons in the photon map using a `photon` statement in the light source definition. It is very instructive to explore the effect of setting these options with the aid of the `diagnostic photon` option in the options block since the false color image it generates show the difference in estimated density more clearly. For fast previewing of caustics it can be useful to set the number of photons in thew accuracy statements to small values like 20.

The following scene is similar to the scene used to show shadowing (see page 135). The lines marked with #<<< have been modified to allow caustics, and the light has been moved to the front of the cube to show how the cube reflects the light. Here is the entire scene file:

```
verbose on
link "base.so"
link "physics.so"
$include <base.mi>
$include <physics.mi>

options "opt"
        samples         -1 2
        contrast        0.1  0.1  0.1
        caustic         on                      # <<<
        caustic         0                       # <<<
        caustic accuracy 1000                   # <<<
        object space
end options

camera "cam"
        frame           1
        output          "rgb" "out.rgb"
        focal           50
        aperture        20
        aspect          1
        resolution      800 800
end camera
```

```
light "light1"
        "physical_light" (                          # <<<
            "color"      400 400 400
        )
        origin           -2 2 1
        direction        .667 -.667 -.333
        spread           .9
        sphere           0.3  7 7
        energy           400 400 400                 # <<<
        caustic photons 200000                       # <<<
end light

instance "light1_inst" "light1" end instance

material "specular_mtl"
        opaque
        "dgs_material" (                             # <<<
            "specular"  0.8 0.8 0.8,                 # <<<
            "diffuse"   0.1 0.1 0.1,                 # <<<
            "lights"    ["light1_inst"]
        )
        photon "dgs_material_photon" ()              # <<<
end material

material "diffuse_mtl"
        opaque
        "dgs_material" (                             # <<<
            "diffuse"   0.8 0.8 0.8,                 # <<<
            "lights"    ["light1_inst"]
        )
        photon "dgs_material_photon" ()              # <<<
end material

object "cube1"
        visible trace shadow
        tag 1
        group
                -0.5 -0.5 -0.5
                -0.5 -0.5  0.5
                -0.5  0.5 -0.5
                -0.5  0.5  0.5
                 0.5 -0.5 -0.5
                 0.5 -0.5  0.5
                 0.5  0.5 -0.5
                 0.5  0.5  0.5

                v 0   v 1   v 2   v 3
                v 4   v 5   v 6   v 7

                p 0  1  3  2
                p 1  5  7  3
                p 5  4  6  7
```

```
                        p 4   0   2   6
                        p 4   5   1   0
                        p 2   3   7   6
             end group
      end object

      instance "floor_inst" "cube1"
             material        "diffuse_mtl"              # <<<
             caustic         2                          # <<<
             transform       .5   0    0    0
                              0   10    0    0
                              0    0   .5    0
                              0   .5    0    1
      end instance

      instance "cube1_inst" "cube1"
             material        "specular_mtl"             # <<<
             caustic         1                          # <<<
             transform        5    0    0    0
                              0    5    0    0
                              0    0    5    0
                             -1  -.5    0    1
      end instance

      instance "cam_inst" "cam"
             transform        0.7719   0.3042  -0.5582 0.0
                              0.0000   0.8781   0.4785 0.0
                              0.6357  -0.3693   0.6778 0.0
                              0.0000   0.0000  -2.5000 1.0
      end instance

      instgroup "rootgrp"
             "cam_inst" "light1_inst"  "floor_inst"  "cube1_inst"
      end instgroup

      render "rootgrp" "cam_inst" "opt"
```

The file physics.mi contains declarations of material shaders and light shaders that support caustics and global illumination. The caustic on statement in the options enables caustic generation. The light source *physical_light* is a physically accurate light shader. The energy light statement is used to simulate global illumination during photon map generation; the color shader parameter is used to compute direct illumination.

The caustic accuracy statement in the options block and the caustic photons statement in the light definition are optional. They increase the quality by raising the defaults of 100 and 10 000, respectively. Accuracy statements control how many photons in the photon map are considered when computing indirect illumination. They do not affect the photon map itself, so it need not be rebuilt after changing accuracy statements.

The caustic 3 statement repeats the default, it can be omitted. The default caustic 3 specifies that all objects are both caustic casters and caustic receivers. Values 0 specifies neither, 1 is cast only, 2 is receive only, and 3 is cast and receive. The scene can be optimized by specifying `caustic 0` in the options block and adding `caustic` statements to the individual objects that cast or receive caustics. This helps mental ray to choose better photon emission directions. In the scene example, three statements are added: `caustic 0` to the options block, `caustic 2` to the instance `floor_inst`, and `caustic 1` to the instance `cube1_inst`.

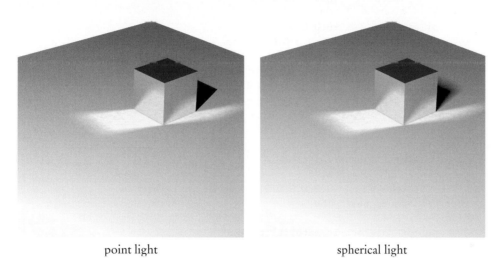

point light   spherical light

Figure 7.9: Reflection caustics from a cube.

The rendered image is shown on the right of figure 7.9, and the same image without the area light source attribute (the `sphere` statement was removed) on the left. The reflective cube is the caustic generator, and the diffuse ground plane is the caustic receiver. The caustics are the two trapezoid-shaped bright regions on the ground plane. The example uses the *dgs_material* shader, a material shader that can simulate diffuse, glossy, and specular reflection, and that collects photon map light contributions.

The typical example for a focused caustic, which is no different in principle from the parallel caustic cast by the cube, requires a curved caustic-casting object such as a filled wine glass or sphere that acts as a lens. An empty glass does not work well because although the glass is curved, its inner and outer wall are very close and the glass has constant thickness, which does not look much like a lens and has little power to focus light. The focal point of strongly curved lenses such as the sphere is very close to the lens, which means that careful positioning is important just like with a real glass lens.

Here are the options block, light source, and materials of a scene consisting of a refractive sphere and a diffuse ground plane, with an area light source that casts both a soft shadow and a caustic:

```
options "opt"
        trace depth      2 4
        shadow           on
        caustic          on
        samples          -1 2
        caustic accuracy 400
```

```
            object space
    end options

    light "source"
            "physical_light" (
                "color"      1600 1600 1600
            )
            origin           -5.0 5.0 -20.0
            rectangle        0.3 0.3 0.0
                             0.0 0.0 0.3
                             10 10
            energy           1600.0 1600.0 1600.0
            caustic photons 200000
    end light

    material "glass"                          # dense flint glass
            "dielectric_material" (
                "ior"        1.75,
                "col"        0.9 0.9 0.9,
                "phong_coef" 150
            )
            photon "dielectric_material_photon" ()
    end material

    material "paper" opaque                   # diffuse white material
            "dgs_material" (
                "diffuse"    0.8 0.8 0.8,
                "lights"     ["source-i"]
            )
            photon "dgs_material_photon" ()
    end material
```

The *dielectric_material* shader is another physically correct material shader in the physics.so shader library. It is designed for highly realistic glass materials. Figure 7.10 shows the rendered image.

Figure 7.11 is another example, showing a curved reflector that casts a caustic on a diffuse floor, rendered with 10 000 and with 100 000 photons. The inside wall of the ring shows a focused specular reflection of the caustic, and there is another dispersed caustic outside in front of the ring. Note how the caustics become sharper with more photons.

These caustics are surface effects — patterns of light cast onto object surfaces. See page 212 for an example of volume caustics that create shafts of caustic light in foggy air.

The most common problem encountered when creating caustics is the lack of photon shaders in the materials. In this case mental ray will spend a long time casting photons into the scene until the required number has been stored. If the number of unsuccessful photons grows suspiciously large, the warning message

```
no photons stored after emitting 10000 photons
```

Figure 7.10: Caustic from a refractive sphere.

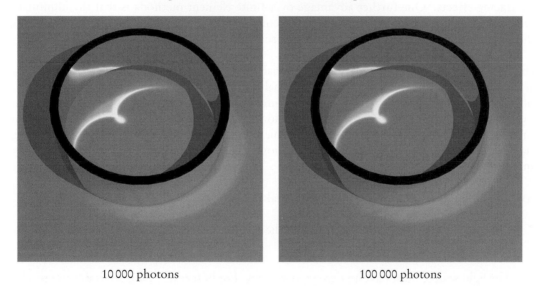

| 10 000 photons | 100 000 photons |

Figure 7.11: Reflection caustic from a ring.

is printed. This can also happen if the receiving object has an awkward shape (long and thin, for example) as seen from the light source, which makes it more difficult for mental ray to cast photons in the directions where they have a chance of being stored. It can also be caused by objects in the path of the photons that have no photon shader, or a photon shader that always absorbs photons, because an absorbed photon that never got stored will cause a new photon to be emitted. After one million photons have been emitted and none of them have been stored, an error message is printed and mental ray gives up and proceeds with the next light source.

7.7　Global Illumination

Global illumination simulates all possible forms of light transport: diffuse, glossy, and specular. This section begins with diffuse global illumination, then introduces glossy effects, and finally specular effects.

7.7.1　Diffuse Global Illumination (Radiosity)

"Radiosity" is the traditional term for global illumination simulation in purely diffuse environments: it simulates all LD^*E paths. Diffuse global illumination has traditionally been solved with subdivision meshing (finite element) methods, also known in computer graphics circles as "radiosity methods". These methods have a large overhead for areas of high contrast such as shadow edges, and only work efficiently for very small scenes up to some tens of thousands of triangles; they handle curved surfaces poorly. The photon map method can handle this case much more efficiently, and is fully integrated with all other possible global illumination and ray tracing effects. One further advantage over finite element methods is that the illumination computation is decoupled from the geometric complexity. With the photon map method, global illumination can be simulated in very complex scenes with many millions of triangles.

The ambient color parameter of many material shaders such as the Lambert or Phong base shaders is a cheap replacement for diffuse global illumination. It assumes that there is uniform diffuse light reaching all points with equal intensity, with absolutely no attempt to achieve physical correctness. These simple ambient color methods are fast to compute but look flat and unrealistic compared to global illumination, which actually computes the amount of diffuse light that reaches each point. When global illumination is used, any ambient color parameters are best omitted or set to black (0 0 0).

For global illumination, several steps must be taken:

☑ Global illumination must be enabled in the options block using the statement `globillum on`.

☑ The light source must have an `energy` statement. For best results, it is advisable to use a light shader like *physical_light* that ensures physical correctness. The energy is distance-dependent and often has to be chosen quite large.

☑ Each participating object must have a material, either directly in the object or inherited from its instance, containing a photon shader statement. Photon shaders may store photons, and either absorb, reflect, or transmit photons.

☑ Materials with photon shaders used for transmitting global illumination should not have a shadow shader to prevent light from crossing the object twice.

The remaining steps are optional:

☑ The light source may have a `globillum photons` statement that overrides the default of

100 000. The number of photons is typically between 10 000 and 1 000 000; smaller values cause fuzzy "puddles" of light. If final gathering is turned on, lower values are generally sufficient.

☑ By default, all objects both cast and receive global illumination. This can be optimized by adding a `globillum 0` statement to the options block, and adding `globillum` statements to individual objects. The casting object must then be marked with the statement `globillum 1` or `3`, and the receiving object must be marked with the statement `globillum 2 or 3`. ("Globillum casting" objects can reflect photons and "globillum receiving" objects can store photons.) Objects out of the way of all global illumination photons should be marked `globillum off` to exclude them from all global illumination photon tracing. Alternatively, the flags may be applied to the object's instance, to be inherited by the object (see page 389 for flag inheritance).

☑ If the global illumination looks grainy, the statement `globillum accuracy` acc_{int} *radius* can be added to the options block. The accuracy *acc* controls how many photons are considered during rendering. The default is 500; larger numbers like 2000 make global illumination smoother but slower. The *radius* controls the distance from the current point in which mental ray considers photons. The default radius is computed from the scene extent.

For a discussion of accuracy parameters, see the discussion of caustic accuracies on page 191.

The classical test scene for global illumination is the Cornell box. It was first built at Cornell University to allow physical measurements in different lighting situations, which could then be compared to computer simulations. In the real Cornell box, the left wall is red and the right wall is blue; in the following examples all walls have the same white color. Here is the scene:

```
verbose on
link "base.so"
link "physics.so"
$include <base.mi>
$include <physics.mi>

options "opt"
        globillum        on                        # <<<
        globillum accuracy 4000 2.0                 # <<<
        samples          -2 1
end options

camera "cam"
        output           "rgb" "out.rgb"
        focal            50
        aperture         34
        aspect           1
        resolution       800 800
end camera

light "light1"
        "physical_light" (
              "color"    600 600 600
```

```
            )
            origin          0.0 4.999 -20.0
            rectangle       1 0 0  0 0 1  6 6
            visible                                  # <<<
            energy          600 600 600              # <<<
            globillum photons 200000                 # <<<
    end light

    instance "light1-i" "light1" end instance

    material "paper" opaque                          # diffuse white material
            "dgs_material" (
                "diffuse"   0.8 0.8 0.8,             # <<<
                "lights"    ["light1-i"]
            )
            photon "dgs_material_photon" ()          # <<<
    end material

    object "box" visible shadow trace tag 1
            group
                    -5      -5      -25
                    -5       5      -25
                     5       5      -25
                     5      -5      -25
                    -5      -5      -15
                    -5       5      -15
                     5       5      -15
                     5      -5      -15
                    v 0 v 1 v 2 v 3 v 4 v 5 v 6 v 7
                    p "paper" 3 2 1 0                # back wall
                    p         0 1 4 5                # left wall
                    p         2 3 7 6                # right wall
                    p         4 7 3 0                # floor
                    p         1 2 6 5                # ceiling
            end group
    end object

    instance "cam-i" "cam" end instance
    instance "box-i" "box" end instance
    instgroup "rootgrp" "cam-i" "light1-i" "box-i" end instgroup
    render "rootgrp" "cam-i" "opt"
```

The interesting lines are marked #<<<. The steps required to enable global illumination are very similar to the steps required for caustics, but the keyword globillum is used instead of caustic. Of course, both can be combined if a scene or light source uses both global illumination and caustics. (Remember that mental ray splits off caustics from global illumination and treats them like an independent feature.)

Note that the front wall of the box is missing to allow the camera to look into the box. Also, the area light source is marked visible, which makes it show up as a white rectangle on the ceiling. Figure 7.12 shows the rendered image, without and with global illumination.

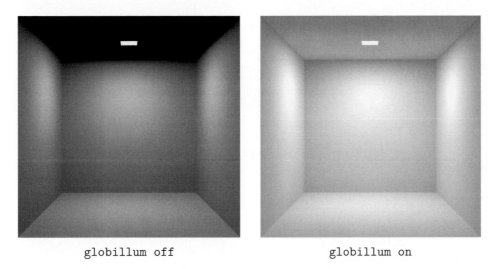

globillum off   globillum on

Figure 7.12: Empty Cornell box with white walls and diffuse global illumination.

Without global illumination, the ceiling is completely black because no light can reach it directly; with global illumination it is indirectly illuminated by diffuse reflections from the floor and the walls. Indirect illumination also brightens the walls and the floor.

If one of the walls had been colored — for example red — the light reflected off that wall would be red. This would give a pink hue to the nearby white walls. This effect is known as *color bleeding*. If the pink tint is lacking in an image, the image looks "wrong", even though it might be hard to point out precisely why. Such global illumination effects can be subtle but add a significant degree of realism to an image.

7.7.2 Glossy Global Illumination

In addition to pure diffuse global illumination (radiosity), global illumination can also be computed in scenes with glossy reflection and transmission (translucency). As described on page 127, glossy reflection and transmission can be either *isotropic* or *anisotropic*.

The Cornell box on page 199 now gets a glossy floor. Furthermore, two spheres are added, one with glossy transmission (translucency) and reflection and one with anisotropic glossy reflection. Here is the list of materials:

```
material "frosted_glass" opaque              # glossy transmission/reflect
        "dgs_material" (
            "ior"       1.75,
            "transp"    1.0,
            "glossy"    1.0 1.0 1.0,
            "shiny"     20.0,
            "lights"    ["light1-i"]
        )
```

```
            photon "dgs_material_photon" ()
     end material

     material "rough_metal" opaque                # isotropic glossy
            "dgs_material" (
                  "glossy"     1.0 1.0 1.0,
                  "shiny"      10.0,
                  "lights"     ["light1-i"]
            )
            photon "dgs_material_photon" ()
     end material

     material "brushed_metal" opaque              # anisotropic glossy
            "dgs_material" (
                  "glossy"     1.0 1.0 1.0,
                  "shiny_u"    5.0,
                  "shiny_v"    20.0,
                  "lights"     ["light1-i"]
            )
            photon "dgs_material_photon" ()
     end material

     material "paper" opaque                       # diffuse white material
            "dgs_material" (
                  "diffuse"    0.8 0.8 0.8,
                  "lights"     ["light1-i"]
            )
            photon "dgs_material_photon" ()
     end material
```

The box itself is the same as before, except that the floor polygon got the material "rough_metal" instead of "paper". Figure 7.13 shows the rendered image, again without and with global illumination.

7.7.3 General Global Illumination

General global illumination simulates all six combinations of diffuse, glossy, and specular reflection and transmission.

The following example is similar to the previous, with three changes:

- The floor is diffuse again, as in the first example.

- The material of the glass sphere in front is clear glass, introducing a specular reflector and refractor.

- The material of the metal sphere in the back is rough metal, turning it into an isotropic glossy reflector.

globillum off   globillum on

Figure 7.13: Cornell box with a glossy floor.

Figure 7.14 shows the changed image, with direct illumination only, with caustics only and global illumination only, and with both to illustrate the various light contributions. Note how the specular light paths are handled by the caustics feature and the rest by the global illumination feature. Note also the soft global illumination on the ceiling caused by the sphere focusing the bright caustic on the floor back to the ceiling (an *LSSDSSDE* path), and the subtle pattern on the left wall caused by the sphere focusing the image of the opposite wall. Secondary effects like this can be controlled with the photon trace depth settings in the options block.

Here is the entire scene file for the caustic and global illumination version (the others were generated by simply changing the caustic and globillum statements in the options block). The Cornell box definition was omitted (see page 199), as was the sphere (see page 327):

```
min version "2.1"
verbose on
link "physics.so"
$include <physics.mi>

options "opt"
        caustic             on
        caustic accuracy    100 1.0
        globillum           on
        globillum accuracy 4000 2.0
        samples             -1 2
        trace depth         5 5 5
        object space
end options

camera "cam"
        output          "rgb" "out.rgb"
        focal           50
        aperture        34
```

Direct illumination only   Caustics only

Global illumination only   All combined

Figure 7.14: Cornell box with caustics and general global illumination.

```
        aspect          1
        resolution      800 800
end camera

light "light1"
        "physical_light" (
            "color"      600 600 600
        )
        origin          0.0 4.999 -20.0
        rectangle       1 0 0  0 0 1  6 6
        visible
        energy          600 600 600
        caustic photons    10000   # (the default)
```

```
        globillum photons 500000
end light

instance "light1-i" "light1" end instance

#-------------------------------- materials

material "glass" opaque                        # clear glass material
        "dielectric_material" (
              "ior"         1.75,
              "col"         0.99 0.99 0.995,
        )
        photon "dielectric_material_photon" ()
end material

material "rough_metal" opaque                  # isotropic glossy
        "dgs_material" (
              "glossy"    1.0 1.0 1.0,
              "shiny"     10.0,
              "lights"    ["light1-i"]
        )
        photon "dgs_material_photon" ()
end material

material "paper" opaque                        # diffuse white material
        "dgs_material" (
              "diffuse"   0.8 0.8 0.8,
              "lights"    ["light1-i"]
        )
        photon "dgs_material_photon" ()
end material

#-------------------------------- objects

object "box" visible shadow trace tag 1
        # ...
end object

object "sphere" visible shadow trace tag 2
        # ...
end object

instance "cam-i" "cam" end instance
instance "box-i" "box" end instance
instance "sphere1-i" "sphere"                  # left sphere
        transform .5 0 0 0   0 .5 0 0   0 0 .5 0   1 1.5 9 1
        material "glass"
end instance
instance "sphere2-i" "sphere"                  # right sphere
        transform .5 0 0 0   0 .5 0 0   0 0 .5 0   -1 1.5 11 1
        material "rough_metal"
end instance
```

```
instgroup "rootgrp"
        "cam-i" "light1-i" "box-i" "sphere1-i" "sphere2-i"
end instgroup

render "rootgrp" "cam-i" "opt"
```

This example contains specular reflection and refraction, glossy reflection, and diffuse reflection. Generating scenes that also include glossy and diffuse transmission (translucency) is trivial, for example by adjusting the glass sphere material.

7.7.4 Final Gathering

Final gathering means that at each shaded point, the hemisphere above that point is sampled to compute indirect illumination, in addition to direct illumination. The hemisphere is sampled by sending rays into appropriate directions. Only a single generation of final gathering rays is traced. However, these final gathering rays cause material shaders to be called when they hit geometry, and these material shaders may cast secondary reflection, refraction, or transparency rays. These secondary rays will be traced also if they are specular or glossy, but (in most cases) not if they are diffuse[2]. This makes final gathering a simple method for computing "one-generation" indirect illumination by computing an LDDE contribution: color bleeding and other diffuse illumination from the next diffuse surfaces are computed, but not illumination involving multiple diffuse surfaces. Since it also traces secondary specular and glossy rays, it can handle the more general $L\{D|S|G\}\{S|G\} * D\{S|G\} * E$ case where light can be gathered through glass panes and mirrors, either polished or frosted.

mental ray 3.4 and higher can trace multiple diffuse bounces as well, but this makes rendering significantly slower. If multiple diffuse bounces are required, for example to pass through an otherwise irrelevant glass wall, final gathering in combination with photon mapping may improve performance. Photon mapping requires additonal work for setting up photon emitting lights, but in most cases delivers a better performance if three or more diffuse bounces are required. The performance of final gathering in combination with photon mapping is almost independent on the number of diffuse bounces, while the performance of final gathering without photon mapping grows at least linearly with the number of diffuse bounces.

A final gather step is computationally expensive: typically 500–2000 rays are cast to sample the indirect illumination. (The default is 1000; mental ray 3.4 and higher works well with half these numbers.) However, it is not necessary to do this every time a material shader computes illumination. Global illumination, unlike caustics, is a diffuse effect whose illumination contribution changes slowly, which means that it is sufficient to do final gathering only at selected locations on the illuminated diffuse surface. Between these locations, the results can be interpolated and extrapolated. (See [Ward 92] for a technical description of the underlying principle.)

Final gathering is disabled by default. Final gathering can be enabled and controlled by adjusting default values with optional statements in the options block:

---

[2]Tracing specular and glossy secondary rays means that final gathering will work through glass panes or mirrors, and stopping secondary diffuse rays prevents redundant sampling of "directionless" diffuse light.

`finalgather on|off`

> Final gathering is off by default but can be turned on with this statement. If turned on, it is possible and desirable to decrease the number of global illumination photons in all light source definitions, specified by `globillum photon` statements. Typically, one tenth as many photons are required with final gathering.
>
> Turning final gathering on works best in scenes with diffuse illumination that changes slowly without bright contrast edges. It should not be turned on in scenes with complex volumic effects, for example using ray marching, because these effects make each final gather ray expensive.

`finalgather fastlookup`[3.x]

> This mode is available in mental ray 3.0 and later only. It enables final gathering, and also arranges irradiance to be stored with global illumination photons in the photon map. Caustic photons are not considered. If there are no global illumination photons, perhaps because no light source specifies a globillum photon count or because globillum is disabled, fast lookup mode is ignored and falls back on on mode. Fast lookup mode slows down globillum photon tracing but accelerates final gathering because final gather rays no longer need to collect a large number of photons to estimate irradiance; a single lookup is sufficient.
>
> The break-even point for fast lookups varies, but as a rule of thumb it pays off if there are more than three times as many final gather rays as there are stored photons. If the photon map is read from disk or already present from the previous frame (this is controlled by the `photonmap file` and `photonmap rebuild` option statements), fast lookup gets the benefits without the cost. Note that for optimum performance, fast lookup should be enabled both for photon map creation and rendering, but a saved photon map created without fast lookup enabled will also work because mental ray detects this case and computes the missing irradiance information automatically.

`finalgather accuracy [ view`[3.x]`] nrays`$_{int}$ `[ maxdist [ mindist ]]`

> The *nrays* parameter specifies the number of rays in each final gather step. The default is 1000. Higher numbers increase the precision but reduce performance. If the number is too low, soft patterns of light and shadow appear. Note that mental ray 3.4 has changed the final gathering algorithm. It normally achieves better quality at higher speed with approximately one-half the number of rays. It is necessary to modify the accuracy statements though, for example reducing 1000 to 500, or rendering times will increase.
>
> The optional `view` statement requires mental ray 3.0 and higher. It modifies the sampling algorithm so that nearby objects are sampled more finely than distant objects. This is achieved by interpreting the *maxdist* and *mindist* parameters as pixel distances, effectively covering the image raster space evenly with finalgather results. Its use is recommended.

The optional *maxdist* parameter specifies the maximum distance in scene units at which another final gather step result may be used for interpolation or extrapolation. Lower numbers increase the number of final gathering steps, and increase precision in areas where diffuse illumination changes rapidly (which is rare) at the cost of lower performance. The default distance is computed from the scene extent, which is a very rough guess; it is better to specify the maximum distance explicitly.

The optional *mindist* parameter specifies that a final gather result must be used for interpolation or extrapolation if it is within this distance. The default distance is 10% of *maxdist*. The minimum distance tends to have less influence on the rendering quality than the maximum distance.

finalgather falloff [*start*] *stop*[3.2]

If final gathering is enabled, limit the length of final gather rays to *stop*. If the ray has not hit anything before this distance, it returns no indirect light. To avoid sharp boundaries, the ray starts to fade out at the *start* distance, which must be less than the *stop* distance. This option is very important to prevent finalgather rays to pull in distant geometry. Careful use can greatly improve rendering performance and memory usage.

finalgather file "*filename*"[3.x]

This statement requires mental ray 3.0 or later. Like photon maps, final gathering results are stored in a file if a file statement is given. This allows later frames to reuse final gathering results from earlier frames. However, unlike photon maps, mental ray will not only reuse data but also add to the data loaded from the file if it is insufficient, perhaps because the camera has moved or changed (unlike photon maps, final gathering results depend on the camera) or due to other changes. The additional final gather points will be appended to the file.

mental ray keeps track of the accuracy at the time the final gather file is written. If the currently specified accuracy is materially different from the accuracy at the time the final gather file was written, the file will be ignored, all points will be recomputed, and a new file will be written.

finalgather file ["*filename*" ...][3.4]

mental ray 3.4 also allows giving a list of finalgather file names instead of a single file name. The list must be enclosed in angle brackets. mental ray will read and use all files listed if they exist, and the end result will be written to the first one. This can be used to precompute multiple map files in finalgather only mode, perhaps for different lighting passes or portions of the animations, and then putting them all together for the final beauty pass.

finalgather only[3.3]

The only mode is supported by mental ray 3.3 and higher. It enables final gathering, but disables all other rendering modes. In particular, no color image is rendered. This is useful to just create a finalgather map file, possibly for an entire animation, which is then used for the final beauty pass where finalgather rebuild mode is turned off to make sure that all frames use the exact same finalgather points. Preprocessing finalgather map files in this way can pay off if the animation is tuned and rendered many times, and it eliminates animation flickering of finalgather solutions, especially in cases where the camera moves into areas that were not visible in earlier frames. There is little point to use this mode without a finalgather file.

finalgather rebuild on|off[3.x]

This statement also requires mental ray 3.0 or later. Turning the rebuild option on forces mental ray to ignore previous final gathering results stored in memory or in a file, and rebuild all final gathering results from scratch. This is useful if the lighting or geometry has changed. Since mental ray appends new final gathering results the final gathering file, if specified, it may be useful to periodically "flush" the file by forcing a rebuild, especially if the camera has moved such that few or none of the originally visible objects are still visible, to eliminate useless final gathering results. However, final gathering files tend to be much smaller than photon map files and do not normally grow excessively. The default is finalgather rebuild on. (Note that the default for photonmap rebuild is off to maintain compatibility with mental ray 2.1).

finalgather rebuild freeze[3.3]

This mode suppresses finalgather preprocessing, so that *only* finalgather points from the file are used. No new finalgather points are added to the finalgather map. However, if an interpolation among finalgather points is not possible for certain parts of a scene, mental ray can create some new temporary finalgather points. This mode makes it possible to precompute finalgather maps for an animation, using the "finalgather only" option, and then rendering with that map to reduce flickering.

finalgather trace depth $refl_{int}$ [$refr_{int}$ [$diff_{int}$[3.4][sum_{int}]]][3.2]

This statement requires mental ray 3.2 or later. It allows multi-generation final gathering: when a final gather ray hits an object whose material shader casts secondary rays, these rays are not truncated if the finalgather trace depth is greater than 0. A count of 0 only allows the final gather ray itself, and every increase by 1 allows one further generation of rays. It can be specified separately for reflection and, refraction/transparency rays, for the sum of reflection and refraction rays, as well as for diffuse rays (i.e. secondary finalgather rays) for mental ray 3.4 and above.

For example, if final gathering should see a wall behind a glass surface, set the refraction count and sum to 2; if the glass is double-sided, 3 is needed. The default is 0 0 0 (0 0 0 0 for mental ray 3.4 and above). Secondary finalgather rays are never cast in mental ray 3.3 and earlier versions. Large depth numbers can reduce performance, especially if shaders trace more than one ray. If a single argument is specified, it is taken as a value for reflection and refraction depths. If two arguments are specified, they are taken as values for reflection and refraction depths, respectively. The sum is set to the sum of reflection and refracton depths in those cases. If (for mental ray 3.4 and higher) three arguments are specified, they are taken as reflection, refraction, and diffuse depths; the sum is set to the value of the diffuse depth.

`finalgather scale` $r\,g\,b\,[a]^{3.4}$

This statement requires mental ray 3.4 or later. The indirect illumination obtainied from final gathering is multiplied with that color. This allows fast artistic tuning of indirect illumination. If just this option is changed, it is correct to re-render scene with `finalgather rebuild freeze`, saving the finalgather preprocessing step. Note that values different fromt the default 1 1 1 1 do not produce physically correct results.

`finalgather presample density` $T^{3.4}$

This statement requires mental ray 3.4 or later. It increases (or decreases if $T < 1$) the number of finalgather points computed in the final gathering preprocessing stage approximately T times. mental ray increases the presample density automatically if the number of rays (*nrays* in the `finalgather acuracy`) is increased, so this option is not strictly necessary. It can be used for performance tuning for high quality tuning, or for improving performance for the preview images.

Note that if increasing of the density of finalgather points is desired, this option should be used instead of *maxdist* and *mindist* in the `finalgather acuracy`. Lowering of the *maxdist* and *mindist* distances may decrease the number of finalgather points used for interpolation, which may result in a spotchy look, especially for high contrast scenes.

To optimize final gathering in scenes with area light sources, the direct illumination at each point that a final gather ray hits can be computed with less accuracy than directly visible light. The lower accuracy is masked by the diffuse effect of final gathering. As described on page 143, area light source definitions may specify both a regular and a "low" sampling density. The low density is used for secondary rays, exploiting the fact that secondary rays contribute less to the overall image quality and can be sampled at a lower density with little or no quality loss. Rays cast by final gathering are considered secondary rays.

For example, a rectangle area light source definition may contain the following statement:

```
rectangle  1 0 0  0 0 1      # rectangle size
           5 5               # regular sampling density
           3                 # trace depth threshold for low density
           1 1               # low sampling density
```

The trace depth controls the number of reflection and refraction levels at which sampling switches from regular to low, and does not affect final gathering, which always uses the low sampling density. The low density 1 1 reduces the default 2 2 to a single sample.

If a final gather step is done from a point that is exactly on the edge between two polygons, the final gather rays may entirely miss both polygons because rays never hit a plane from which they were cast. This causes results that are too dark. Because final gathering uses interpolation at the distances specified by the `finalgather accuracy` statement in the options block, this can cause neighboring samples to appear too dark also. Normally, this only happens in very simple and symmetric scenes. It can be prevented by adding the statement

```
jitter 1.0
```

to the options block. Decreasing the accuracy distances would only reduce the size of the artifact, and possibly greatly increase the rendering time and average image quality in other areas.

Final gathering can be combined with global illumination. In this case, final gathering is the simulation of one last light bounce after the global illumination simulation. The effect is similar to pure global illumination but works with far fewer global illumination photons (typically one tenth as many as without final gathering) because final gathering involves averaging many photon lookups. This combination works well if the diffuse illumination is soft and changes slowly.

The advantages of final gathering are:

- Fewer photons need to be cast in the photon tracing phase since the demands on irradiance estimate accuracy are much lower (because 500–2000 of them are averaged). This makes photon tracing faster, and reduces the amount of memory required for the photon map.

- The illumination accuracy is higher than for a direct photon map lookup, especially near edges and corners of objects.

The disadvantages of final gathering are:

- Without global illumination, rendering takes much longer than with just direct illumination.

- With global illumination, depending on the accuracy settings, the rendering pass can take longer than without final gathering, depending on the required accuracy of the solution and the number of photons used to estimate irradiance. The performance increase or decrease is a trade-off between faster photon map generation and higher quality, and slower rendering.

When a material shader computes the illumination at a given diffuse point, it uses different methods for caustic and global illumination effects if final gathering is on:

- **Caustics** directly look up the photon density on the diffuse illuminated surface (only photons that come from a specular reflection or transmission contribute). This involves finding the nearest photons stored at the surface and weighting their contributions. This is controlled by the `caustic accuracy` statement in the options block.

- **Global illumination** does not directly look up the photon density. Instead, a final gather step is performed every time the material shader computes indirect illumination at a diffuse surface. It involves shooting many rays to sample the incident illumination on the hemisphere above the point. When one of these rays hits a diffuse surface, the direct illumination is computed at that point (by sampling light sources) and the indirect illumination is computed from the photon density there.

There are good reasons why final gathering is not used to compute caustics: if the caustic stems from a non-area light source, the rays employed by final gathering would never hit it (since it has no size), so there would be no caustic. If the light source is an area light source, some rays will hit it, but since the caustic intensity is very dependent on the number of rays that do so, the resulting caustic would be very noisy. Using final gathering to compute global illumination from diffuse surfaces does not suffer from this problem because it considers only illumination from geometric objects, not light sources. Final gathering relies on the smooth variation of indirect illumination to avoid noise.

7.8   Participating Media

In the previous sections, the medium that the scene is in has been assumed to be clear air over short distances, so that the medium does not affect the light traveling through it. However, this assumption does not hold when the medium is smoke, fog, clouds, dusty air, silty water, or even air over long distances: these media do affect the light traveling through them. In other words, these media *participate* in the light transport. The participating medium can be homogeneous (like uniform fog) or nonhomogeneous (like swirling smoke) and exhibit isotropic or anisotropic scattering (that is, scatters more in some directions than others). Details on participating media can be found in [Glassner 95]. The use of photon maps for participating media is described in [Jensen 98].

Just as photon shaders complement material shaders to support global illumination, *photon volume shaders* complement volume shaders to support participating media. Like photon shaders, photon volume shaders do not deal with rays (like material and volume shaders) but with photons. Basically, photon volume shaders transmit, scatter, or absorb photons traveling through empty space (that is, space free of geometry), just as photon shaders do on surfaces. Illuminated smoke, for example, lights up because it scatters photons. All four types of shaders (material, photon, volume, and photon volume) are attached to materials. In the volume case, the shaders are attached to the material of the bounding object that encloses the volume.

mental ray distinguishes two types of participating media effects: *volume caustics* and *multiple volume scattering*.

7.8.1   Volume Caustics

Volume caustics are caused by light that has been specularly reflected or refracted by one or more surfaces and is then scattered by a participating medium in a volume. Examples are:

- Sunlight refracted by a wavy water surface and then scattered by silt particles in the water.

- Car headlights: light emitted by a bulb filament, reflected by a parabolic reflector, transmitted through glass, and scattered by fog.

To compute volume caustics, photons are stored in the volume, but the volume does not re-emit photons. This effect is called volume caustics because some object is reflecting or refracting photons into the volume which lights up. Regular surface caustics work the same way, except that it is a solid surface that lights up. The result is a glare or beam of light, as shown in figure 7.15.

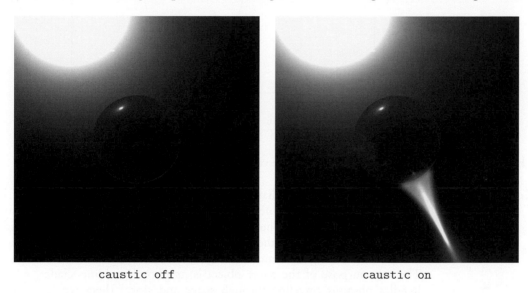

caustic off   caustic on

Figure 7.15: Volume caustic.

This scene consists of a camera, a light source, a sphere that focuses light, and two invisible objects (a bounding box and a cover polygon), as shown in figure 7.16.

Note that there is no background — the light, shadow and beam exist in empty 3D space. The situation is rather complex because both direct illumination and indirect illumination need to be considered:

- **direct illumination** takes care of the glare around the light source and the shadow under the sphere. This is done by ray marching, a standard ray tracing technique that "walks" along a ray and checks in certain intervals whether a light source is visible, and if so, the result of the ray is brightened accordingly. This is handled by a volume shader attached to the material of the bounding box around the scene. See page 171 for an example.

- **indirect illumination** adds the light beam underneath the sphere. The light is indirect because the ray marcher cannot see it by looking directly at the light source; the light must travel through the sphere first. The ray marcher collects stored photons from the photon map in addition to the direct contribution from the light source.

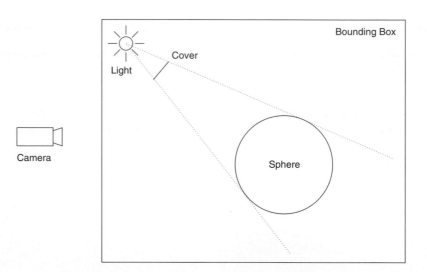

Figure 7.16: Schematic volume caustic scene.

The objects in the scene interact to provide the volume caustics:

Cover   Has a photon shader that merely transmits all photons that hit it, undiminished and in the same direction. Its material shader (*transmat*) always claims full transparency. These two combined make sure that all photons and visible rays pass through the cover object unchanged. Direct illumination also passes unchanged because the object does not have the `shadow` flag set. The sole purpose of the cover object is its photon volume shader, which handles photons traveling through space and stores them where needed. It is small, just covering the beam, to let mental ray better predict useful photon directions. To avoid wasting photons on space in front of the sphere, which is handled by direct illumination, a `min_level` parameter counts down transmissions. The cover object has a `caustic 1` flag because it is a caustic generator.

Bounding box   Also uses *transmat* as the material and shadow shader, ensuring full transparency to make the bounding box invisible. The important shader is the volume shader *parti_volume*, which is the ray marcher that does all the work during rendering.

Sphere   The sphere is straightforward — an almost-transparent material shader (*dgs_material*), and a photon shader (*dgs_material_photon*) that focuses the photons in the beam. There is no shadow shader; this ensures that the ray marcher does not see any light behind the sphere — all light in the shadow cone is handled by indirect illumination. The sphere has a `caustic 3` flag because it casts a caustic.

Here is the complete scene file. The sphere was omitted; see appendix B for a listing of a simple NURBS unit sphere.

```
link "physics.so"
$include <physics.mi>

camera "cam"
        output          "rgb" "out.rgb"
        focal           270.0
        aperture        30.0
        aspect          1.0
        resolution      800 800
end camera

options "opt"
        caustic             on
        caustic             0
        photonvol accuracy 500 0.15
        shadow              on
        samples             -1 2
        contrast            0.05 0.05 0.05 0.1
        dither              on
        trace depth         2 3 4
        photon trace depth 0 3 3
        object space
end options

light "pointlight"
        "physical_light" (
            "color"     1000 1000 1000
        )
        origin          -1.5 2.999 -50.0
        energy          1000 1000 1000
        caustic photons 100000
end light

instance "light-i" "pointlight" end instance

material "covermat"                         #-------- light cover
        "transmat" ()
        photon "transmat_photon" ()
        volume "parti_volume" (
            "scatter"               0.3 0.3 0.3,
            "extinction"            0.3,
            "min_step_len"          0.03,   # for ray marching
            "max_step_len"          0.2,    # for ray marching
            "no_globil_where_direct"  true, # optimization
            "lights"                ["light-i"]
        )
        photonvol "parti_volume_photon" (
            "scatter"               0.3 0.3 0.3,
            "extinction"            0.3,
            "min_level"             3       # only store after 3 refracts
        )
end material
```

```
object "cover" visible trace tag 0 caustic 1
        group
                -1.4    2.0      -49.6
                -1.4    2.0      -50.4
                -0.5    2.0      -50.4
                -0.5    2.0      -49.6
                v 0 v 1 v 2 v 3
                p "covermat"    0 1 2 3
        end group
end object

material "volsurf"                          #--------- bounding box
        "transmat" ()
        shadow "transmat" ()
        volume "parti_volume" (
            "scatter"                   0.3 0.3 0.3,
            "extinction"                0.3,
            "min_step_len"              0.03,
            "max_step_len"              0.2,
            "no_globil_where_direct"    true,
            "lights"                    ["light-i"]
        )
end material

object "bbox" visible trace tag 1
        group
                -3  3 -51.5    -3  3 -48.5    -3 -3 -48.5    -3 -3 -51.5
                 3  3 -51.5     3  3 -48.5     3 -3 -48.5     3 -3 -51.5
                v 0 v 1 v 2 v 3 v 4 v 5 v 6 v 7
                p "volsurf"    0 1 2 3       # left wall
                p              4 5 6 7       # right wall
                p              3 7 4 0       # back wall
                p              2 6 5 1       # front wall
                p              5 4 0 1       # ceiling
                p              6 7 3 2       # floor
        end group
end object

material "glass"                            #--------- sphere, radius 1
        "dgs_material" (
            "ior"     1.5,
            "transp"  0.9,
            "specular"  1.0 1.0 1.0
        )
        photon "dgs_material_photon" (
            "ior"     1.5,
            "transp"  1.0,
            "specular"  1.0 1.0 1.0
        )
end material

object "sphere" visible shadow trace caustic 3
        # ...
```

```
end object

instance "cam-i"    "cam"     end instance        #--------- instancing/rendering
instance "cover-i"  "cover"   end instance
instance "bbox-i"   "bbox"    end instance
instance "sphere-i" "sphere"
        transform 1 0 0 0   0 1 0 0   0 0 1 0   0 0 50 1
end instance

instgroup "all"
        "cam-i" "light-i" "cover-i" "bbox-i" "sphere-i"
end instgroup

render "all" "cam-i" "opt"
```

The caustic 0 statement in the options block is necessary to disable caustic casting and receiving by default, and allows adding individual caustic statements to objects. Without this statement, the default of caustic 3 would override all object caustic statements, and rendering would take longer.

The necessary steps for volume caustics are similar to the steps needed for regular surface caustics, with the addition of a photon volume shader:

☑   Caustics must be enabled in the options block using the statement caustic on.

☑   The light source must have an energy statement. For best results, it is advisable to use a light shader like *physical_light* that ensures physical correctness. The energy is distance-dependent and often has to be chosen quite large.

☑   If photon autovolume mode is not enabled, the light from the light source must pass through an object with a photon volume shader (like the cover object in the example above). This object typically also has completely transparent material and shadow shaders, and a pass-through photon shader.

☑   The rays from the camera must pass through an object that bounds the effect (the bounding box in the example), which is also completely transparent and contains a ray-marching volume shader that can collect photons. Attaching the volume shader to the camera as a global volume is possible but much less efficient because it controls too much space.

☑   The caustic-casting object (the sphere) must have a material, either directly in the object or inherited from its instance, that contains a photon shader statement. The material should not be diffuse to prevent it from spreading rather than focusing light.

The remaining steps are optional:

☑   The light source may have a caustic photons statement that overrides the default of 10 000. The number of photons is typically between 10 000 and 1 000 000; smaller values cause blurring.

☑ To improve performance, the statement `caustic 0` can be added to the options block if a `caustic 1` flag is added to the cover object. Removing the `shadow` flag further improves performance.

☑ If `caustic 0` is added to the options block, the caustic-casting object (the sphere in the example) must be marked with the statement `caustic 1`. Alternatively, this flag may be applied to the object's instance, to be inherited by the object (see page 389 for flag inheritance).

☑ If `caustic 0` is added to the options block, there must be at least one object in the scene between the light and the caustic that is marked with the statement `caustic 2` or `caustic 3`.

☑ If the volume effect looks grainy, the statement `photonvol accuracy` acc_{int} $radius$ can be added to the options block. The accuracy acc controls how many photons are considered during rendering. The default is 30; larger numbers like 200 make the effect smoother. The $radius$ controls the maximum distance at which mental ray considers photons. Again, the default radius is computed from the scene extent.

For a discussion of accuracy parameters, see the discussion of caustic accuracies on page 191.

7.8.2   Multiple Volume Scattering: Global Illumination in Volumes

Multiple volume scattering is global illumination in volumes, that is, self-illuminating participating media. This is done by scattering photons within the medium. For example, this can be used to model multiple volume scattering in clouds or car headlight beams, where multiple volume scattering widens the beam and softens its edges.

The following scene is a variation of the previous, containing the same scene elements (a light, a camera, a bounding box, and a cover polygon, but no sphere). It also uses ray marching inside the bounding box to collect direct illumination. However, the photon shader attached to the cover polygon supports multiple volume scattering. Figure 7.17 shows the rendered image.

The ray marcher creates the main beam in both cases, but in the second case scattering causes a glow around the beam, especially close to the light source. The glow is caused by photons being scattered inside the beam and leaving the beam, where they light up the fog around the light source. Here is the entire scene:

```
min version "2.1"
verbose on
link "physics.so"
$include <physics.mi>

options "opt"
        samples          -2 1
        dither           on
        globillum        on
        photonvol accuracy 500 0.5
        object space
end options
```

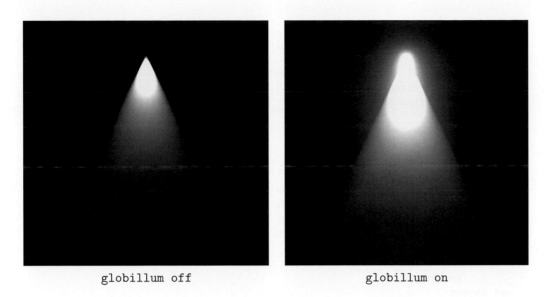

globillum off   globillum on

Figure 7.17: Multiple volume scattering from a light beam.

```
camera "cam"
        output          "rgb" "out.rgb"
        focal           270.0
        aperture        30.0
        aspect          1.0
        resolution      800 800
end camera

light "light" visible
        "physical_light" (
            "color"     1000 1000 1000
        )
        origin          0.0 2.0 -50.0
        direction       0.0 -1.0 0.0
        spread          0.9
        energy          10000 10000 10000
        globillum photons 100000
end light

instance "light-i" "light" end instance

#-------------------------------- light cover (to enter volume)

material "covermat"
        "transmat" ()
        photon "transmat_photon" ()
        volume "parti_volume" (
            "scatter"     0.3 0.3 0.3,
            "extinction"  0.4,
            "min_step_len" 0.01,           # for ray marching
```

```
                "max_step_len" 0.1,           # for ray marching
                "lights"        ["light-i"]
            )
            photonvol "parti_volume_photon" (
                "scatter"      0.3 0.3 0.3,
                "extinction"   0.4
            )
    end material

    object "cover" visible trace tag 0
            group
                    -0.1    1.999   -49.99
                    -0.1    1.999   -50.01
                     0.1    1.999   -50.01
                     0.1    1.999   -49.99
                    v 0 v 1 v 2 v 3
                    p "covermat"     0 1 2 3
            end group
    end object

    #------------------------------- box

    material "volsurf"
            "transmat" ()
            photon "transmat_photon" ()
            volume "parti_volume" (
                "scatter"      0.3 0.3 0.3,
                "extinction"   0.3,
                "min_step_len" 0.01,
                "max_step_len" 0.1,
                "lights"        ["light-i"]
            )
    end material

    object "box" visible trace tag 1
            group
                    -3      -3      -51
                    -3       3      -51
                     3       3      -51
                     3      -3      -51
                    -3      -3      -49
                    -3       3      -49
                     3       3      -49
                     3      -3      -49
                    v 0 v 1 v 2 v 3 v 4 v 5 v 6 v 7
                    p "volsurf"     0 1 2 3         # back wall
                    p               7 6 5 4         # front wall
                    p               0 1 4 5         # left wall
                    p               2 3 7 6         # right wall
                    p               1 2 6 5         # ceiling
                    p               0 3 7 4         # floor
            end group
    end object
```

```
#------------------------------- instances and rendering

instance "cam-i"   "cam"   end instance
instance "cover-i" "cover" end instance
instance "box-i"   "box"   end instance

instgroup "all"
        "cam-i" "light-i" "cover-i" "box-i"
end instgroup

render "all" "cam-i" "opt"
```

The light energy was set to ten times the color parameter of the *physical_light* shader to magnify the effect.

7.8.3 Global Illumination in Volumes and Surfaces

Global illumination can also occur in both volumes and surfaces in the same scene. In the following scene, the Cornell box is filled with homogeneous smoke; see figure 7.18.

caustics off   caustics on
globillum off   globillum on

Figure 7.18: Cornell box with global volume illumination.

The Cornell box is similar to the previous ones, except that

- the left wall is red and the right wall is blue;

- a transparent front wall with a ray marching volume shader was added;

- the rear wall was also made transparent (the light beam effect would not be as apparent in front of a white wall), and also delimits the fog so it does not extend into infinity; and

- the customary transparent cover polygon that puts the photon volume shader into the path of the photons was added directly in front of the ceiling light. Finally,

- both spheres are made of glass, and the front sphere was raised to show the caustic beam.

The options block and the materials used in this scene are:

```
options "opt"
        samples         -1 2
        contrast        0.1 0.1 0.1 1.0
        trace depth     7 7 7
        shadow          on
        dither          on
        caustic         on
        globillum       on
        caustic accuracy    500 1.0
        globillum accuracy 1500 1.0
        photonvol accuracy  100 0.5
        finalgather     off
        object space
end options

#------------------------------- light cover

material "volsurf"
        "transmat" ()
        photon "transmat_photon" ()
        volume "parti_volume" (
            "scatter"       0.05 0.05 0.05,
            "extinction"    0.05,
            "min_step_len" 0.13,
            "max_step_len" 1.0,
            "light_dist"    2.0,
            "lights"        ["light-i"]
        )
        photonvol "parti_volume_photon" (
            "scatter"       0.05 0.05 0.05,
            "extinction"    0.05
        )
end material

#------------------------------- Cornell box

material "diffusewhite" opaque
        "dgs_material" (
            "diffuse"   0.8 0.8 0.8,
            "lights"    ["light-i"]
        )
```

```
        photon "dgs_material_photon" ()
end material

material "diffusered" opaque
        "dgs_material" (
            "diffuse"    0.8 0.0 0.0,
            "lights"    ["light-i"]
        )
        photon "dgs_material_photon" ()
end material

material "diffuseblue" opaque
        "dgs_material" (
            "diffuse"    0.0 0.0 0.8,
            "lights"    ["light-i"]
        )
        photon "dgs_material_photon" ()
end material

#------------------------------- sphere

material "mirror" opaque         # ideal mirror: specular reflection
        "dgs_material" (
            "specular"  1.0 1.0 1.0,
            "lights"    ["light-i"]
        )
        photon "dgs_material_photon" ()
end material

material "glass" opaque          # clear glass: specular reflection/refraction
        "dielectric_material" (
            "ior"        1.75,
            "col"        0.990 0.990 0.995
        )
        photon "dielectric_material_photon" ()
end material
```

7.9   The Importance of Physically Correct Shaders

Traditional computer graphics worked in a cartoon-like magic universe where all material color parameters were just that, colors, with values between 0 and 1. Because light did not have physical properties, it could never get brighter than 1. This allows for very simple and intuitive mathematics: set a light to a brightness of 0.5, set a material diffuse color to 1, and the rendered object will show a color of 0.5 (or less if attenuated by the surface orientation). Sadly, the real world does not work like that. Such a material, put into the real world, would be emitting over three times as much energy as it is receiving.

When creating scenes containing physically correct lighting simulations, including indirect illumination effects such as caustics, global illumination, and final gathering support physically correct lighting simulations, but only if the shaders used in the scene — especially the light, material, and photon shaders — are also physically correct. If they are not, the lighting of the scene is incorrect, and typically becomes much brighter. Unfortunately, many of the classical shading models such as Phong and Lambert, and constant-result light shaders, that have traditionally been used in computer graphics for simple direct illumination rendering fall into this category.

Physical correctness means that three conditions are met:

1. Light emitted by light sources follows an inverse-square distance falloff law.

2. Materials may not amplify light by emitting more energy than was received.

3. Material and photon shaders should agree and implement the same illumination model.

This section describes the two main pitfalls.

7.9.1   Light and Distance

Light from point lights in nature follows an inverse-square falloff law, which means they appear to get dimmer with distance quickly. It is important to recognize this fact when working with mental ray's global illumination functions. This requires some explanation:

Consider a 100-watt point light inside a sphere with a radius of one meter. The 100 watts are distributed evenly over the inside of the sphere, which has an area of about 12.6 square meters. A sheet of paper stuck to the inside of the sphere covers about 1.5% of this area, and so receives 1.5 watts. Now double the radius of the sphere to two meters. The inside will have four times the area, so the same sheet of paper stuck to the inside of the sphere would cover only one quarter as much of the total area as before. Since the number of watts did not change and is now distributed over four times the old area, the sheet of paper would receive only one quarter of the previous energy, 0.375 watts. This is what inverse square falloff means: one quarter the energy at twice the distance, one ninth at three times the distance, and so on.

Now consider the same setup with a point light that does not obey the inverse square law, and applies no falloff at all. After doubling the sphere radius, the sheet of paper would receive the same energy as before, 1.5 watts. Since you need four times the number of such sheets to wallpaper the larger sphere, the total energy received by the sphere is four times as large as before, 400 watts! The energy appears to get stronger with distance. At three times the distance it increases by a factor of nine, and at ten times by a factor of one hundred. This is clearly not physically correct.

mental ray's photons and final gather rays are intrinsically physically correct. If a light source emits 1000 photons, each carries 1/1000th of the light energy (0.1 watts in this example). If the sphere gets larger, they are distributed over a larger area, but they do not increase in number or energy. Hence only one quarter the number of 0.1 watt photons hit the sheet of paper in the larger sphere, amounting to one quarter of the previous incident energy.

However, classical Phong shaders assume a different model. The same light energy gets multiplied by the diffuse (and specular) terms regardless of the distance to the light, which causes the strange situation of total light emission getting stronger with distance. If mental ray uses only photon mapping, it just looks at physically correctly distributed photons, but if final gathering is enabled, it samples and integrates (which means summing over an area visible from a sampling point) direct light. If that direct light is not physically correct because it follows the classical Phong model, there will be too much of it, and the area sum will be too bright.

If you turn on final gathering and your scene becomes much brighter, you may have a problem with lack of inverse square falloff in your light shaders. The hallmark of incorrect light shaders are "color" values in the range 0..1, or not much more, where the light energy parameter has a far higher value, perhaps in the thousands or more.

To prevent this kind of problem, it is important to ensure that the direct light follows the same falloff as the indirect light. Since photon irradiance falls off with the square of the distance (for point and spot lights), so must the direct light. In mental ray, distance falloff is handled by light shaders. The *physical_light* shader in the physics shader library does this; the Phong and other shaders in the base shader library do not.

Note that directional light does not follow the inverse-square falloff law because all light rays are parallel, and hence do not disperse. The sphere example above does not apply; since all rays go in the same direction there is no way to illuminate the inside of a sphere evenly. In this sense mental ray's directional lights with their infinite size (extent) cannot exist in nature; however, they are a good approximation for extremely large and abundant light sources like the sun illuminating, in comparison, extremely small geometry. Strictly speaking, directional light shaders should not apply inverse-square falloff; here the Phong model happens to be correct. Note however that in mental ray the exponent $exp = 2.0$ should be specified even for a physically correct directional light. For a directional light, mental ray subtracts 2.0 from the exponent exp before the falloff computation. This is done to unify the exponent value for all types of lights.

Note also that specifying exponent different from 2.0 for a directional light without origin (origin can be specified for a directional light in mental ray 3.4 and higher) is an error. This leads to unpredicateble results: if origin is not given, mental ray chooses some location outside of the scene bounding box internally, and the falloff factor depends on where that location is chosen.

7.9.2   Illumination Models

Another problem with some material shaders is that they can be easily made to violate the laws of nature. A Lambert shader, for instance, takes the incoming color, adjusts for the surface orientation and multiplies with a parameter called "diffuse" and returns the result. Physically correct shaders cannot simply make the same old Phong and Lambert assumptions, which are basically ad-hoc approximations that sort of happen to look good with direct illumination but may emit more energy than they received, and so become light amplifiers. Since global illumination includes light going through many diffuse paths in the scene, the total light content of the scene is amplified, depending on the number of light paths computed, and will never reach an equilibrium.

Instead, equations that implement the optical laws of nature must be used. Since the photon shaders and material shaders used in the same material should agree on the lighting equations, this implies that Phong and Lambert are not good choices for material shaders either. The physics shader library that comes with mental ray contains some matched sets of physically-correct material and photon shaders that avoid all these problems. (It contains a *physical_light* light shader also that avoids the inverse-square falloff problem explained above as well.)

Global illumination and especially final gathering not only permit physical correctness, but also *depend* on physically correct shaders. If the shaders do not calculate light in a physically correct way, preservation of energy in the scene no longer holds, and typically the whole scene becomes much brighter for no apparent reason when global illumination and final gathering are enabled.

In technical terms, these shaders incorrectly equate incoming *flux density* from the hemisphere around the illuminated point with the outgoing *flux per solid angle per unit area* in the ray direction, with the end result that they appear too bright by a factor of exactly π (about 3.14159). Writing correct shaders is beyond the scope of this book, but if a scene looks much brighter than expected if global illumination or final gathering are enabled, it may be a good idea to try the shaders in the base and physics libraries (especially the DGS shader) that come with mental ray. If that fixes the brightness, there is a bug in the original material and photon shaders. (The unexpected brightness increase is not necessarily a factor of three — it may be less if only parts of the scene have the problem, or more if a single light path goes through multiple incorrect interactions.)

7.10 Frequently Asked Questions

This section answers some frequently asked questions about caustics, global illumination, and final gathering.

Should I use photon tracing, final gathering, or both?

Photon tracing without final gathering estimates the indirect illumination at a point by computing the photon density in a disc around that point. This computation inherently gives a low-pass filtering of the indirect illumination, so a lot of stored photons are required to get sharp edges in the indirect illumination (or few photons within a small disc, but that gives noise which is also undesirable). For many scenes this is not a problem, since the indirect illumination often has only slow variation.

Final gathering alone computes a single bounce (unless modified with a finalgather trace depth statement[3.2]) of indirect light to diffuse surfaces. It can be used in scenes with lots of direct light (rule of thumb: at least 50% of the surfaces illuminated by direct light). If there is less direct light, the image with final gathering will be rather dark — in which case it is necessary to use both photon tracing and final gathering to get more indirect light. Typically, entertainment content projects use final gathering only, because the results are visually pleasing and artistic control is easier to handle than for photons, while industrial CAD projects require photon mapping.

Photon tracing combined with final gathering gives the benefits of multiple bounces of indirect light and high resolution on the indirect illumination. Unfortunately, it also takes longer to compute (although the number of stored photons and the globillum accuracy can be reduced significantly compared to computations with photon tracing alone). Final gathering without global illumination is not physically correct because some light paths are missed. With multiple bounces (set by finalgather trace depth statement[3.2], including the number of diffuse bounces[3.4]), images close to physically correct ones can be rendered, but the rendering time grows significantly with the number of bounces. In general, best physically accurate results are achieved if final gathering and global illumination are both enabled. The number of photons should be chosen as memory permits[3]. Then, the final gathering accuracy should be tuned to achieve optimum quality.

Why is final gathering so slow?

Final gathering can become slow in some situations: if there is a very large number of light sources or other very bright spots (such as strong light shining through a large array of lenses), or if a large number of area light sources are visible (have the `visible` attribute in their definition, see page 134), it becomes expensive to resolve the illumination properly with final gathering. In these cases, it can become faster to use only global illumination, with a higher number of photons.

mental ray 3.4 usually gives better and much faster results with far fewer finalgather rays, so the number of rays in the accuracy statements should be reduced. A good first approximation is halving the previous number of rays. If this is not done, final gathering in mental ray 3.4 is significantly slower than earlier versions. (The accuracy diameters can be left unchanged.)

How can finalgather flickering be avoided in camera animations?

Final gathering relies on interpolating nearby finalgather points that measure incident indirect light. If there are not enough nearby points, mental ray adds some. If the camera moves, the points will be added in different locations. If parts of the scene are dark or there are large illumination contrasts, so that the variance of finalgather points is high, this might show up as flicker.

Increasing the accuracy ray count and diameters usually fix the problem, at some performance cost regarding the ray count. It is also possible to run the animation in `finalgather only`[3.3] mode to record all finalgather points in one or more[3.4] finalgather files[3.x]. Depending on the scene and camera movement speed, it may be sufficient to render every second, or even every tenth frame. Then, run the same animation again to compute the beauty pass. The beauty pass should specify `finalgather rebuild freeze` to make sure that all frames use exactly the same finalgather points. This procedure is more time-consuming but is a safe way to eliminate all flickering.

Finalgather files can grow too large because they accumulate points and never lose any, especially if the image resolution is large, the accuracy radii are small, and the animation consists of many frames with fast camera motion that brings large parts of the scene in view. Multiple per-object finalgather files[3.4] for portions of the animation can help here.

What is a photon?

The photons in photon tracing are not the photons known from physics. In physics, a photon is an indivisible energy quantum with a specific wavelength. Here it is a divisible packet of

---

[3] mental ray 2.1 uses 32 bytes; mental ray 3.0 uses data compression to reduce the size to 24 bytes.

energy with several wavelengths. The photons used in photon tracing can be thought of as a representation of many physical photons.

What is the relationship between light source power, irradiance, and pixel color?

The irradiance value picked up by the material shader from the photon map proportional to the power of the light source, but the constant of proportionality depends on reflection and transmission coefficients and the geometry of the scene. The pixel color represents irradiance, which is power per projected area per steradian. The units of irradiance depend on the units of the light power and scene sizes. If the light power is in Watts [W] and the scene lengths in meters, the pixel colors are $[W/(m^2 sr)]$. If, on the other hand, the light power is in milliwatts [mW] and the scene lengths are in centimeters [cm], the pixel colors are in $[mW/(cm^2 sr)]$.

Why must the reflection coefficients be less than 1?

Energy conservation for a surface implies that within each color band, the amount of reflected light can be at most equal to the incident light. Therefore, the scattering coefficients have to fulfill the following condition for each color component (red, green, and blue):

$$diffuse + glossy + specular \leq 1$$

In nature, reflection coefficients are less than 1 while light sources can be arbitrarily bright. Computer graphics has traditionally done it the other way around: light sources have intensity 1, and in order not to get very dark images the reflection coefficients are higher than 1, typically up to 10 or 100. This does not actually make a lot of sense, but for direct illumination it doesn't matter, since the reflected light is simply the product of light source color and reflection coefficients.

But for indirect illumination calculations, where the light may go through multiple reflections, it unfortunately does matter. The reflection coefficients are used to determine the probability of reflection and absorption. If the reflection coefficients are larger than one, the probability for reflection also becomes larger than one, breaking one of the fundamental laws of probability calculus. Furthermore, the photons will contain more energy for each bounce so the indirect illumination will be too bright relative to the direct illumination. To avoid such disasters, the coefficients are automatically reduced to be at most 1 in the photon shaders. The result of this clipping is that the indirect illumination might be darker than expected relative to the direct illumination, but at least the laws of probability and energy preservation are obeyed.

Why is there no caustic or global illumination in my image?

There can be many different reasons why there ends up being no photons stored in the scene. The most common are:

- Caustics or global illumination is not turned on in the options or on the command line.

- The objects are not flagged as caustic or global illumination on. Photons fly straight through such objects.

- The objects are not flagged as caustic or global illumination generators and/or receivers, and the options block does not override them (as is the default). Photons are absorbed without being added to a photon map at object surfaces that are neither generators nor receivers.

- The specified photon trace depth is too small.

- The objects have no photon shaders (photons get absorbed by objects without photon shaders).

- The (photon) material shaders do not have the right reflection parameters — for example purely diffuse reflection for a caustic generator.

- Light source may simply point in the wrong direction, or is hidden behind another object that does not transmit photons.

When there are no photon shaders at all in the scene, no photons get stored — since one of the jobs of photon shaders is to store photons. Wrong object flags can also prevent storing photons. If the light source specifies a maximum number of photons to emit, the emission will stop when that number has been emitted. If there is no maximum number specified, mental ray could emit photons forever without getting anywhere. To catch this situation, there is a check that gives a warning if 10 000 photons have been emitted but not a single one of them has been stored. When 1 000 000 photons have been emitted to no avail, mental ray gives up and aborts this light source with an error message.

Finally, it can also happen that there are indeed caustic or global illumination photons stored in the scene, but their energy is so low that they are not visible in the image. See below for a description of this problem.

Why is the indirect illumination too dark?

Photons from a point, spot, or area light source are emitted in diverging directions, so the photon density falls off with the inverse square of the distance from the light source. This is also how physical photons in nature behave. (The density of photons from a directional light does not change with distance.)

However, many shaders do not implement a similar inverse-square falloff. (The *physical_light* shader does it correctly.) In general, the *color* of a light source has a different falloff than the *energy*, and these values have to be adjusted accordingly. If *physical_light* is used, the *color* and *energy* should be the same and everything should work out right.

The photon density falloff can not be changed, but the photon energy can be increased based on distance. This can to some extent compensate for the falloff. The photon energy increase is done "behind the scenes" and is specified with the *exponent* keyword. This feature should not be abused by setting the *exponent* too low, because then the most far-flying photons will have extremely large energy.

For debugging global illumination, it is often a good idea to temporarily change the *color* of all light sources to $(0, 0, 0)$ to turn off the direct illumination.

Why is the indirect illumination too bright?

If the light shaders do not implement inverse-square distance falloff, or if the material or photon shaders are not energy-preserving, that is, they do not fulfill the inequalities discussed above, final gathering, caustics, and global illumination can be too bright. For a detailed discussion, see the section "The Importance of Physically Correct Shaders" on page 223.

Why does the photon pass take longer when I remove some photon shaders?

If the scene specifies a number of photons to store, but not a maximum number of photons to emit, emission will continue until the specified number of photons have been stored (unless one of the cases described above apply).

If some of the objects have photon shaders and others do not, more photons get absorbed without being stored (a photon gets absorbed if it hits an object without a photon shader). This means that more photons have to be emitted and traced before the specified number of photons succeed in getting stored. This is why the photon tracing step takes longer if only some of the objects have photon shaders. However, the solution is not to attach "dummy" photon shaders to everything, but to remove caustic and global illumination flags from objects that do not participate in photon tracing, and disabling the override flags in the options block.

Similarly, if the objects are small and far from each other, photons from one object have only a small chance of hitting other objects, so it will take a long time before the specified number of photons have been stored.

Why are there more "emitted photons" than "light photons"?

The projection map rejects some photons before they are even traced from the light source. These photons still count as emitted, since the energy of the light source has to be divided by the total number of emitted photons (including the ones that got rejected immediately by the projection map) to find the energy of each emitted photon.

Why are a few more photons stored than I asked for?

This is to avoid truncating the path of the last photon from each photon emission task. If it were truncated, a small amount of indirect illumination would be lost. For an extreme example, assume that the light source specifies that there should be only one photon stored. If photon tracing were allowed to store only *exactly* 1 photon, there would be no photons stored that had been through multiple bounces, introducing a bias in the solution.

Why is my image splotchy?

If the accuracy radius r (either specified in the file or command line or estimated automatically based on scene extent) for computation of caustics or global illumination is too small, the disc with that radius will either contain a photon or not. This gives a very abrupt border between the regions of surfaces where there is a photon within distance r (the splotches) and the other parts of the surface. The solution is to increase the number of emitted photons or to increase the radius using accuracy statements.

How do I prevent light leaks?

Light leaks are a common problem of classical subdivision meshing radiosity, where illumination is computed only at triangle vertices, and interpolated across the triangle even if another triangle (perhaps a wall dividing the floor into rooms) intersects it and should be blocking the light. mental ray's global illumination algorithms do not suffer from this problem. However, if a wall is thinner than the maximum radius specified by the globillum accuracy, it is possible that the radius can reach through the wall and fetch photons from the other side. This causes a narrow band of light where the floor and the wall meet, where light from the other side of the wall appears to leak. This can usually be fixed by avoiding zero-thickness walls. It can also be avoided by reducing the maximum accuracy radius, but this increases noise in the scene.

7.11 Summary

For caustics, global illumination, and participating media effects, statements have to be added to the options block, materials, objects, and light sources. In the following table, ● means that the statement must be added, ○ means that it need not be added and has no effect, and ⋆ means that it may be added to change defaults. C means caustics, GI means global illumination, VC means volume caustics, and VGI means volumic global illumination. Final gathering is listed here as an extension to global illumination but can also be used alone without enabling globillum.

where	statement to add	C	GI	VC	VGI
options	caustic on	●	○	●	○
	globillum on	○	●	○	●
	finalgather on	○	⋆	○	⋆
	finalgather fastlookup	○	⋆	○	⋆
	finalgather file "$filename$"$^{3.x}$	○	⋆	○	⋆
	finalgather file ["$filename$" ...]$^{3.4}$	○	⋆	○	⋆
	finalgather only$^{3.3}$	○	⋆	○	⋆
	finalgather rebuild off	○	⋆	○	⋆
	finalgather trace depth $refl_{int}$ [$refr_{int}$ [$diff_{int}$$^{3.4}$[sum_{int}]]]$^{3.2}$	○	⋆	○	⋆
	caustic $mode_{int}$	⋆	○	⋆	○
	globillum $mode_{int}$	○	⋆	○	⋆
	caustic accuracy acc_{int} [r]	⋆	○	○	○
	globillum accuracy acc_{int} [r]	○	⋆	○	○
	finalgather accuracy acc_{int} [d_{max} [d_{min}]]	○	⋆	○	○
	photonvol accuracy acc_{int} [r]	○	⋆	○	○
	caustic filter box|cone $size$	⋆	○	⋆	○
	photon trace depth $refl_{int}$ [$refr_{int}$ [sum_{int}]]	⋆	⋆	⋆	⋆
	photonmap file "$filename$"	⋆	⋆	⋆	⋆
	photonmap rebuild on	⋆	⋆	⋆	⋆
material	photon $photon\_shader$	●	●	●	●
	photonvol $photon\_volume\_shader$	○	○	●	●
instance, object	caustic [on|off|$mode_{int}$]	⋆	○	⋆	○
	globillum [on|off|$mode_{int}$]	○	⋆	○	⋆
	finalgather [on|off|$mode_{int}$]$^{3.4}$	○	⋆	○	⋆
	finalgather file "$filename$"$^{3.4}$	○	⋆	○	⋆
	finalgather file ["$filename$" ...]$^{3.4}$	○	⋆	○	⋆
light	energy r g b	●	●	●	●
	caustic photons $nstore_{int}$ [$maxemit_{int}$]	⋆	○	⋆	○
	globillum photons $nstore_{int}$ [$maxemit_{int}$]	○	⋆	○	⋆
	exponent exp	⋆	⋆	⋆	⋆
	emitter $emitter\_shader$	⋆	⋆	⋆	⋆

Final gathering may reduce performance, especially in scenes with multiple volume scattering. However, turning it on allows a drastic reduction of the number of globillum photons, and it can also be used effectively without global illumination. Here is a brief summary of the main statements in the table:

accuracy
: The *acc* argument specifies the number of photons (or rays, in the final gathering case) considered by a material or other shader that looks at the photon map to obtain the caustics or global illumination contribution. The default is 100 for caustic accuracy, 500 for globillum accuracy, 30 for photonvol accuracy, and 1000 for final gathering accuracy. The radius r specifies a maximum distance within which mental ray will look for photons; if omitted the default is computed based on the scene extent. The distance d_{max} limits the distance at which previous final gathering results may be considered, and the distance d_{min} prevents final gathering steps too close together.

caustic filter
: By default, a box filter is used to filter photons to generate a caustic. The caustic filter option allows replacing the box filter with a cone filter, which generates smoother caustics. Also, the filter size may be changed: larger filters cause softer caustics. The default size is 1.1.

photon trace depth
: The photon trace depth limits the number of "bounces" (re-emissions) that a photon can undergo before it is absorbed, separately for reflections, refractions (transmissions), and the sum of reflection and refractions. This improves performance because photons that are reflected or transmitted many times often have little effect on the final image. The defaults are 5 5 5. If *refr* is omitted, it defaults to *refl*; if *sum* is omitted, it defaults to *refl* + *refr*.

finalgather trace depth[3.3]
: Similar to the photon trace depth, but applies to finalgather rays. In addition, mental ray 3.4 accepts the number of diffuse bounces. The default is 0 0 0 (0 0 0 0 for mental ray 3.4), meaning first generation finalgather rays only.

photonmap file
: If a file name is specified, mental ray will save the photon map into a file with this name after creating it, or reload it from that file instead of creating it if possible. This improves performance, and can be used if the scene does not change significantly. The suggested file name extension is .pmap.

finalgather file[3.x]
: Similar to photonmap files, except that finalgather points are stored. mental ray 3.4 also allows specifying a list of files, where all are read if they exist, but only the first is written to. Note that in an animation, finalgather points will be appended to the (first) file indefinitely and none will ever be discarded; care must be taken to prevent the file from growing unmanageably large in long animations. mental ray 3.4 also allows specifying per-object finalgather files or file lists for some objects.

`photonmap rebuild`	If set to on, mental ray will always rebuild the photon map even if a photon map file is specified and could be loaded. The default is `off`.
`photon`	The photon shader is responsible for absorbing or re-emitting photons on object surfaces.
`photonvol`	The photon volume shader is responsible for absorbing or re-emitting photons in participating media (empty space, that is, space free of geometry, containing a volume effect).
`caustic`	The caustic mode can be specified both in the options block and in objects. When considering an object, mental ray uses the logical OR of both. The resulting mode must be 1 or 3 for caustic-casting materials and 2 or 3 for caustic-receiving materials. If set to `off` in objects, the objects does not participate in caustic photon tracing at all, which improves performance. This flag may also be inherited from the instance instead of being specified in the object. The default is 3 in the options block and 0 in objects.
`globillum`	These statements are analog to the corresponding `caustic` statements, but apply to global illumination.
`energy`	The light energy is the "wattage" of the light source that determines the total energy of all emitted photons, and hence the strength of the effect. Frequently, large numbers in the hundreds or tens of thousands are required to properly illuminate distant objects. If a physically correct light shader such as *physical_light* is used, its color parameter should be set to the same values.
`photons`	The number of photons stored in the photon map, and optionally the maximum number of photons to emit. Storing between 10 000 and 1 000 000 photons is common. Larger numbers increase sharpness. Graininess is best reduced by increasing the accuracy, not by changing the number of photons.
`exponent`	The exponent can be used to override the inverse-square law that ensures physical correctness. The default is 2. A value of 1, for example, causes $(\frac{1}{r})$ falloff.
`emitter`	A custom photon emitter shader allows casting photons with programmable energy and direction. Normally, mental ray will predict optimal directions.

For a description of the shader syntax (quoted name followed by parenthesized parameters, or an equal sign followed by the quoted name of a named shader; either a single shader or a shader list), see page 275. For more information on light sources that enable caustics and global illumination, see page 187.

7.12 Performance

If it is sufficient to achieve a visually pleasing result but not physical correctness, consider using only final gathering without any photons (globillum or caustics) at all and no multiple bounces. Preferrably use a large accuracy radius such as 1/10 of the scene diameter (the default) and tune the number of rays in the accuracy statement. To reduce flickering, it may help to use the finalgather-only mode to precompute a finalgather map file for the entire animation, instead of jacking up the accuracy too high. If you write your own material shaders, it helps to design them so that they compute simplified results when hit by a finalgather ray. (Refer to the mental ray manual for information on how to do this.)

For more complex effects, photons are needed. To achieve maximum performance if physical correctness is not required, only turn those light sources that actually contribute global illumination into photon emitters. Small lights that only brighten or darken ("darklights") small areas might not make much of a difference and do not need to emit photons. Begin with a small number of photons, such as the default of 10 000 or 50 000, and increase until the light effects stop being "splotchy" and achieve the desired sharpness at the edges. If this causes graininess, increase the accuracy number (or accuracy radius) from their defaults. In general, start with a large radius and reduce until artifacts become visible.

If there are many light sources that emit photons, it is often possible to reduce the number of photons cast by each of them.

Use `caustic` and `globillum` modes to mark only those objects that cast or receive caustics or global illumination, respectively. Objects that do not participate in caustics and global illumination computation at all should be marked `caustic off` or `globillum off`, respectively. Photons will then no longer intersect with these objects, and mental ray will avoid sending photons in directions where there are only objects marked with `off` flags. However, note that `off` flags effectively make the object transparent to the corresponding type of photon, which means that non-`off` objects behind them may become lit inappropriately.

The fewer objects are marked to be photon receivers or casters, the better mental ray can predict photon emission directions, and fewer photons will be lost or stored in places where they do not change illumination.

The message

```
no photons stored after emitting 10000 photons
```

is a warning sign that something may be wrong or inefficient — either the photons are never stored because there are no caustic or globillum receivers, no diffuse materials, no specular materials in the caustic case, or because receivers exist but are difficult to reach, or because reflectors bend the photons away from them such that few reach them and get stored, or if objects in the path of the photons have no photon shaders, causing the photons to be absorbed by default and be new photons to be emitted. In these cases, the photon map preprocessing phase can significantly reduce performance. A few such messages may be acceptable, but if nothing happens for a long time and messages like

```
no photons stored after emitting 1000000 photons (canceling emission job)
```

appear, the scene definitely has problems that prevent photons from being stored. If this second message appears, mental ray keeps trying for a very long time, perhaps hours, but will most likely not produce usable images. In this case the scene must be checked to make sure that photons emitted by the light sources hit objects or volumes where they can be stored. For example, spot lights that point the wrong way, or intervening reflectors that reflect photons out of the scene or otherwise away from the receiving objects, can cause this problem.

If the caustic caster is a thin diagonal or curved line from the viewpoint of the light source, perhaps because it is seen edge-on when the light source is almost at the edge of a plane, many more photons need to be emitted before the requested number of photons is stored.

If there are objects that do not participate in photon tracing at all, they should be marked "`caustic off`" and "`globillum off`" to prevent mental ray sending photons in directions where they will not be stored — photons that hit objects without photon shaders get absorbed by default, and photons that get absorbed without having been stored are re-emitted.

Chapter 8

Motion Blur

Physical cameras expose their film for some period of time, during which moving objects in the scene may change their position, orientation, size, or shape. Moving objects leave a blurry "trail" on the film. In particular, the edges of moving objects become semi-transparent because the object was only occupying the blurred region for some fraction of the shutter open time. Motion blurring simulates these effects.

All types of motion blur require a specification in the options block of how long the camera shutter stays open:

> shutter [$delay^{3.1}$] $time$

(There is also a command line option -shutter with the same effect.) If the shutter specification is missing, the shutter open time is assumed to be zero, and no motion blur takes place. Note that the shutter open time does not affect the brightness of the rendered image, even though one might think that more light has time to expose the "film".

To achieve motion blur, it is also necessary to specify how objects are moving. There are two methods to do this: motion transformations and motion vectors, both described below. Both can be combined in a scene and even in a single object. The movement specified by both methods is assumed to take place within one time unit. If the $time$ argument of the shutter specification is 1.0, the motion transformation and/or motion vectors determine the endpoints of the motion blur "trails"; if the shutter time is 0.5, the trails are only half as long.

Normally, the shutter opens at time 0, which is defined as the time at which the scene is defined. At time 0, all objects will appear in the position and shape they were defined in, disregarding their motion vectors and motion transformations. This opening time can be changed by defining the $delay^{3.1}$ value. The shutter stays open until the closing time defined by the $time$ parameter.

Motion blur is always "forward". The scene specifies the situation at the shutter open time, and the motion transformations and motion vectors specify the situation one time unit later.

Motion blur is available both in ray tracing and (non-OpenGL) scanline rendering modes. The same rules apply for non-blurred and blurred objects; the same algorithm is used for both. See page 14 for a discussion of rendering algorithms.

Motion blurring comes at a cost that is directly proportional to the number of blurred pixels for the standard scanline and raytracing algorithms, but is significantly lower for the rasterizer (formerly known as Rapid Motion mode), which is a first-generation renderer similar to scanline rendering, but specially optimized for fast motion blurring by re-using shading results. Effectively, objects are shaded only once (or a small user-defined number of times during the shutter time interval), and the shading results are re-used at every point that the moving point passes over. This has side effects, such as a moving mirror dragging its reflection with it, but it is much faster than reshading at every time sample.

8.1   Motion Transformations

Geometry is positioned in the scene using scene entities called instances. (A simple example is on page 32.) Among other things, instances contain a transformation matrix that specifies the position, orientation, and scale of the instanced object by transforming the next higher space, which in the example is world space to the object's local space ("object space"). As will be shown in chapter 14.1, instances can also be nested to form hierarchies of spaces.

Consider the displaced cube on page 93, which is based on the simple cube on page 32. Its camera instance moves the camera to the left and above the cube, looking down on it, while the cube itself has an empty instance (which is equivalent to an instance with an identity transformation). To add motion blur in the cube's $-X$ direction, replace the instance with the following one, and add a shutter statement to the options block:

```
options "opt"
        samples         -1 2
        contrast        0.1  0.1  0.1
        time contrast   0.2  0.2  0.2
        shutter         1.0
        object space
end options

instance "cube1_inst" "cube1"
        transform           1   0   0   0
                            0   1   0   0
                            0   0   1   0
                            0   0   0   1

        motion transform  1   0   0   0
                           0   1   0   0
                           0   0   1   0
                           0.1 0   0   1
end instance
```

The regular identity transformation is spelled out (this is optional), and a motion transformation matrix is added that tells the mental ray rendering software that one time unit later, the instanced cube is 0.1 units to the left, in object coordinates. Like regular instance transformations, motion transformations transform from object space to the next higher space (world space if this is a toplevel instance). A common approach for animations is to specify the next frame's transformation as this frame's motion transformation. The vertices of the cube move in a straight line from the position at the beginning of the shutter interval, specified by the regular instance transformation, to the position at the end of the shutter interval, specified by the motion transformation.

The number of segments that a curved transformation motion path is divided into is configurable. The default is 1, which means that only the endpoint of the motion is calculated. It can be increased to values up to 15 with the motion steps statement in the options block.

Here is a replacement for the instance that rotates the cube by 20 degrees clockwise:

```
instance "cube1_inst" "cube1"
        transform          1    0    0    0
                           0    1    0    0
                           0    0    1    0
                           0    0    0    1

        motion transform .94   0  -.34   0
                           0    1    0    0
                         .34    0  .94    0
                           0    0    0    1
end instance
```

20 degrees is a very large rotation. At 24 frames per second, for example, this corresponds to 80 revolutions per minute. Normally, objects move much slower than this, and the blur effect is much less pronounced. Still, even small amounts of motion blur give the visual impression of smooth movement that would look jerky without motion blur. Figure 8.1 shows the rendered images.

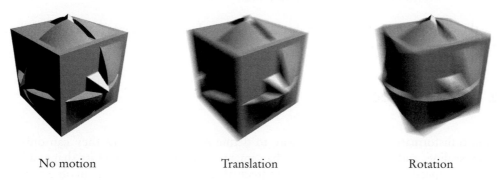

No motion   Translation   Rotation

Figure 8.1: Transformation motion blurring.

As discussed in the advanced geometry chapters later in this book (see page 379), instances can be nested, and the final transformation of an object relative to the camera is a concatenation of all instance transformations from the root of the tree to the object. This is also true for the motion transformations, which means that the final motion blur is determined by all the relative movements in the hierarchy combined.

The camera, too, has an instance that places it in the scene, and that instance may also have a motion transformation. This creates object motion blur from camera movements: if a camera moves past a "stationary" object the object will appear motion-blurred. Note, however, that camera motion blurring will cause *all* objects in the scene to be motion-blurred (unless explicitly disabled), which will increase rendering time.

Light sources also have instances, which may have motion transformations[1]. Moving light sources cause shadows and highlights from the light source to be blurred.

The `motion` statement in instances takes one of three forms:

`motion transform` *matrix*

> specifies the transformation at the end point of the movement, as in the examples above. For animations, the motion *matrix* in this statement is normally the instance transformation matrix of the next frame.

`motion transform`

> means that this instance does not have a motion transformation, but may inherit one from other instances (for inheritance, see page 379). This has the same effect as specifying a copy of the instance transformation as motion transformation, but is more efficient. It is also the default, but can be used in incremental changes to remove a previously specified motion transformation.

`motion off`

> does not specify a motion transformation, and turns off any motion transformations inherited from above. This can be used to explicitly turn off motion transformation-type motion blur (but not motion vector-type motion blur, see the next section) for the instanced object. However, instances lower in the instance tree can re-introduce motion transformation motion blur.

These three are mutually exclusive; if any of these is used in an incremental change it replaces the previous setting in the instance.

8.2   Motion Vectors

Motion transformations are a simple way to define motion paths, but they can only handle moving, scaling, and rotating objects or the camera. If an object changes its shape, it becomes necessary to specify the direction for each individual vertex or control point, in object space. The direction vectors are called motion vectors.

Motion vectors specify the difference between the position of a vertex or control point at the shutter open time and the position one time unit later. If a vertex moves one unit in the +X

---

[1] mental ray 2.0 ignores the motion transformation in light instances.

direction in object space in one time unit, its motion vector would be 1 0 0. Motion vectors are specified in vertex definitions by adding an m statement after the v statement that begins the vertex definition:

> v $index_{int}$
> m $index_{int}$

With mental ray 3.0 or higher, up to 15 m statements can be attached to each v vertex to create curved motion paths. If there are, say, *10* motion vectors, the first shows the distance the object moved after a time of 0.1, the second shows the distance the object moved after a time of 0.2, and so on. The last m statement always describes the movement at time 1. Note that each motion vector is relative to the position defined by the v statement, not the preceding motion vector. All vertices of an object must have the same number of motion vectors.

Vertices may have other information attached too, such as normal vectors (n statements) or texture vectors (t statements, see page 64). Here is an example that replaces the options block and object definitions on page 32:

```
options "opt"
        samples         -1  2
        contrast        0.1   0.1   0.1
        time contrast   0.2   0.2   0.2
        shutter         0.5
        object space
end options

object "cube1"
        visible trace shadow
        tag 1
        group
                -0.5 -0.5 -0.5
                -0.5 -0.5  0.5
                -0.5  0.5 -0.5
                -0.5  0.5  0.5
                 0.5 -0.5 -0.5
                 0.5 -0.5  0.5
                 0.5  0.5 -0.5
                 0.5  0.5  0.5

                -1.0  0.0  0.0
                 1.0  0.0  0.0

                v 0 m 8    v 1 m 8    v 2 m 9    v 3 m 9
                v 4 m 8    v 5 m 8    v 6 m 9    v 7 m 9

                p "mtl" 0  1  3  2
                p       1  5  7  3
                p       5  4  6  7
                p       4  0  2  6
                p       4  5  1  0
                p       2  3  7  6
        end group
```

```
    end object
```

Each vertex definition got an extra m statement that provides a motion vector. The bottom face of the cube is made to move left and the top face moves right, making the cube change shape to a rhomboid; see figure 8.2.

Figure 8.2: Vector motion blurring.

Motion vectors should only be used to specify shape changes, not motion in the scene. While it would be possible to express movement of the entire object in world space by attaching the same motion vector to all vertices, this would be more difficult to do because such vectors would have to reflect all motion of instances higher up in the scene graph and in the camera. Worse, it defeats multiple instancing (see page 371) because each instance may be moving in a different way, but motion vectors are "baked into" the object and apply to all instances in the same way.

Finally, changing motion vectors requires an incremental change to the entire object, causing overhead such as retessellation, while changing an instance motion transformation is a cheap operation. If the object changes shape it needs to be rewritten anyway because all its vertices change, but for linear motion the overhead of changing nothing but the motion vectors would be unacceptable.

Motion vectors and motion transformations can be combined. If both are present, the resulting motion blur is the sum of the individual motions.

8.3 Summary and Performance

The following steps are necessary to use motion blurring:

☑ Set the shutter time to a nonzero value, such as 1.0, using the shutter statement in the options block or the -shutter command line option.

☑ Define the movement using one or more of the following methods:

- Define motion transformations in object or instance group instances. The transformation provides movement information for all objects below the instance in the scene graph, except when explicitly turned off. This is useful for motion caused by changing instance transformations (translate, rotate, scale only).

- Define a motion transformation in the camera instance. This is useful for camera flythroughs.

- Define motion vectors in objects. This is useful for objects that change shape rapidly enough to require blurring.

☑ For large amounts of motion blur it is necessary to increase the sampling limits with a `samples` statement in the options block or with the `-samples` command line option to values such as 0 2 or 0 3. Sampling visualization (see page 443) helps to determine the effect of motion blurring on oversampling.

☑ When adjusting the image quality, use the time contrast statement in the options block, not the regular contrast statement.

The performance is determined by the number of pixels being blurred, and the smoothness of the blur defined by the time contrast and sampling limits. Follow these rules for maximum performance:

☑ Keep the blurred trails short by using low shutter values.

☑ Use the rasterizer (formerly called Rapid Motion mode) instead of regular scanline rendering if possible. The rasterizer is enabled with a `scanline rasterizer` statement in the options block. The rasterizer works with ray tracing just as regular scanline rendering does.

☑ If not using the rasterizer, use higher values like 0.3 for the time contrast than for the regular contrast. This makes the motion blur more grainy (without compromising non-blur antialiasing), but this does not reduce perceived quality as much as it would in a still image. As usual, tune quality with contrast settings, not with sampling limits.

☑ Use motion blurring only for fast-moving objects, but not for stationary objects or objects too slow to cause noticeable motion blur. Use `motion off` statements in the instance definition to exempt such objects from motion blur caused by motion transformations in the camera instance or instances higher up in the scene graph. Camera motion transformations are inherently more expensive because they blur all objects that have not been explicitly exempted. Moving lights can also be expensive because they are often sampled very frequently.

☑ If motion transformation matrices almost or exactly match the regular instance transformation matrix, or if the motion vectors are almost or exactly zero, no or very little motion blurring occurs, but the performance is lower than as if no motion transformations and no motion vectors exist. In other words, it takes time to detect that the motion is negligible or nonexistent.

☑ If motion vectors or motion transformations are present but the camera shutter is zero, no motion blur is computed. However, motion vectors are still interpolated and made available to shaders. This allows postprocessing motion blur, motion frame buffers, and other motion modes, but is also slows down rendering slightly compared to a scene without motion vectors and motion transformations.

☑ If using BSP ray tracing acceleration, it often significantly improves performance to reduce the BSP tree depth using a `bsp depth` statement in the options block. While 40 may be a good depth for non-motion blurred scenes, 28 might be several times as fast with motion blur if the blurring is large compared to the triangle size.

Chapter 9

Hardware Rendering

Hardware rendering refers to leveraging hardware graphics acceleration boards installed in PCs or workstations, available from vendors such as NVIDIA, ATI, 3Dlabs, Matrox, SGI, Sun, and others, that can draw 3D geometry at very high speed. This document uses the term "hardware" to refer to 3D graphics hardware.

mental ray versions prior to 3.3 already supported OpenGL rendering for a limited form of hardware acceleration, primarily for 3D projection and visibility calculations for rendering and shadow mapping. The scene was painted using OpenGL, but not with its true surface colors but pseudo colors that encode addressing information that tells mental ray for every pixel which object and which triangle is in front. mental ray then only needs to perform shading, but not intersection calculations. For actual color rendering, the visual quality of hardware shading was not acceptable so this was done in software.

Hardware capabilities have grown significantly since then. It is now possible to perform hardware shading with a simple form of procedural shaders. Shaders allow visual effects that go far beyond the "plastic look" limitations of older designs. It is now becoming practical to use graphics hardware for actual color shading at very high speeds without compromising image quality in unacceptable ways.

9.1 Hardware vs. Software Rendering

Ideally, software rendering algorithms should be translatable directly to hardware. However, this is not possible because hardware and software rendering use two very different approaches:

- Software rendering (like ray tracing) has direct access to the entire 3D scene to be rendered in memory, and samples it subpixel by subpixel and tile by tile. In other words, the scene is static and always present, but the renderer deals with one subpixel at a time.

- Hardware rendering operates the opposite way. All pixels are present at all times, but rendering consists of considering the scene one triangle at a time, "painting" each one into the frame buffer. The hardware has no notion of a scene; only a single triangle is known at any one time.

Software is completely unconstrained, except by performance considerations, and can perform any algorithm whatever. The subpixel loop method is chosen because it allows rendering nonlocal effects that require considering different portions of the scene in order to compute a single pixel or subpixel. For example, reflections require access to both the reflecting and the reflected object. A more complex example is global illumination, which considers the indirect light from all surrounding objects to compute the brightness of the subpixel being rendered. Hardware can do none of this because it only ever knows one triangle at a time, and has no notion of other objects.

Hardware rendering uses a several workarounds to address some of these limitations. These workarounds typically involve pre-rendering objects into "maps", which are rectangular pixel rectangles encoding properties of other objects and are stored in the graphics hardware in the form of texture images. While graphics hardware cannot deal with multiple objects, it can deal very efficiently with texture images. Examples for such mapping techniques are:

- Shadow mapping renders the scene from the viewpoint of each light source, recording only the depth of the frontmost object. This can later be used during final rendering to decide whether a point is in shadow, if it is farther away from the light than the recorded depth. This approach does not work well for area lights that cast soft shadows (shadows with fuzzy edges), and it cannot handle transparent shadow-casting objects such as stained glass or smoke.

- Reflection maps render the scene from the viewpoint of a mirror. This image is then "pasted in" when the final render needs to know what is seen in the mirror. This works only for flat or near-flat mirrors.

- Environment maps contain a hemispherical or otherwise complete view of the surroundings as seen from the rendered scene. Nearby objects are not normally included. Although environment maps represent the scene poorly, and cannot capture the arrangement of nearby objects at reasonable computational cost, they are acceptable for highly curved reflectors such as chrome trims.

Workarounds like this have one difficulty: they require a lot of manual preparation and fine-tuning to work; like creating on a good environment map. The computer cannot do this because while computing a correct map is possible, it would be very expensive and easily defeat the expected time savings.

The driving force behind graphics hardware design is gaming, which involves rendering as many triangles per second as possible to a video screen. Also, procedural shading is still quite primitive and requires workarounds as described above. This creates some limitations of hardware rendering:

- Rendered images go to a video screen. Retrieving them to the main memory for further processing is often poorly optimized and slow. This can be the main factor limiting frame rates.

- To achieve full speed, the entire renderer must be carefully hand-crafted to the scene being rendered. This cannot be done for a general-purpose renderer.

- Many effects beside the mapping workarounds described above require rendering the scene multiple times because the complexity of the effect exceeds the capacity of the hardware. This is called "layering" and described in more detail below. This reduces the achievable frame rates.

- Multiple frame buffers are unavailable. Rendering to video only requires RGBA video with low bit depth and a depth (Z) buffer. General-purpose production rendering requires many frame buffers with high bit depths.

- Oversampling to reduce "staircase" aliasing is more restricted than software filtering. mental ray offers both *multisampling* in the hardware pixel pipeline, and *supersampling* which involves rendering at a higher resolution and downfiltering. Both can be combined. Transparency turns multisampling off automatically.

- There is no good approach to motion blurring. This is critically important for film production.

- Pixel resolutions are limited. The hardware is designed to drive a video display with limited resolution. Film production typically uses images 2000 or 4000 pixels wide.

- Textures must be stored in the video hardware before use. The available memory is usually between 128 or 512 MB. Film production often uses tens of gigabytes of textures, which requires very slow data transfers between main memory and hardware memory.

- Compatibility between the hardware from different vendors, and even between successive hardware generations from the same vendor, is often poor. Although the OpenGL library used by mental ray hides many differences, the most advanced features and the fastest speed paths generally have not found an abstraction in OpenGL yet. Hardware development cycles are extremely rapid.

None of this is mentioned in the literature and sales material for graphics hardware boards. In general, it is unrealistic to expect to attain advertised realtime frame rates, often over 100 frames per second, for general-purpose rendering without spending the years of custom development that game designers generally require.

Yet, despite all the limitations of hardware rendering, the things it can do are done at extremely high speed, sometimes more than a hundred times faster than software for very similar visual quality – provided that no features such as ray tracing or motion blurring that exceed the capabilities of the hardware are used.

Since most scenes contain some aspect that exceed hardware capabilities, mental ray can automatically separated the scene in hardware and software parts, which are both rendered and then merged. Performance degrades gracefully with the number of software-rendered effects, instead of rendering simple effects at full speed with hardware only, and then hitting a wall and dropping to a hundredth of the former speed when any effect that requires software rendering enters the scene.

9.2   Layering

The key concept for combining hardware with software rendering is layering. It refers to building a final image from multiple sub-render passes. The concept is already common in pure hardware rendering: a surface might be too complex to be rendered in one pass, so a first render pass may lay down the base color, another adds glossy, glow, or fur effects, and a final pass puts highlights on top. Each layer accumulates color in the frame buffer. Newer hardware also permits combining successive layers in ways other than accumulation of the frame buffer by providing a feedback path from the previous layer result to the current layer calculation.

Here, the term Layering is extended to also cover pre-rendering of shadow maps and other maps as describe above. Although the result is stored as textures and not accumulated in the image frame buffer, the feedback paths in recent hardware designs are beginning to blur this distinction.

Layering does not necessarily involve rendering the entire scene. It is more common to group sections of the scene by object or by material. Many objects contain multiple materials, and it is fairly expensive to switch materials in the graphics hardware because that may involve reloading of textures, lights, shaders, transformation matrices, and other context information. Reloading is *far* slower than rendering triangles. For this reason, object sections are automatically sorted by material.

Effectively, hardware rendering is a fairly long sequence of rendering separate object portions, many of them multiple times, each time resulting in some form of pixel rectangle. The rendering operations form a dependency graph, with pixel rectangles flowing along the edges of the graph, shown in figure 9.1.

Rendering begins at the bottom of the graph because all inputs to a node must be available before beginning to calculate the node. Object 1 consists of two layers, one computing illumination (and hence needing to know which points are in shadow) and the other adding some extra information such as glows. Object 2 is only a single pass illuminated only by one light, but using a chrome reflection model that requires an environment map. Both objects are combined to calculate the final output image. In practice, such graphs are far larger than this trivial example.

Some of the graph nodes are computed in software, and others in hardware. For example, to add global illumination to the above graph, a software node would compute the global illumination map (using final gathering or photon mapping), then another software node would create a light map to bake the indirect light into a texture, which is then used by a hardware node to add to the direct light contribution computed by hardware shading.

The shaded nodes in figure 9.2 are software nodes; the unshaded nodes are hardware nodes. Note that it is often possible, as in the case of global illumination maps, to compute the map once and re-use it for multiple frames.

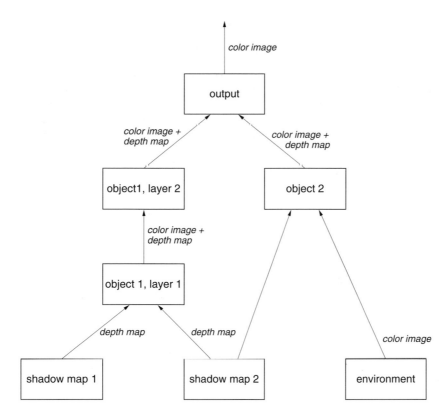

Figure 9.1: Hardware rendering flowchart.

9.3   Speed vs. Quality Tradeoffs

Since the graphs in figures 9.1 and 9.2 consist of distinct nodes that communicate only by frame buffers, it is possible to switch nodes between hardware and software. This has several applications:

- **Switching by shader**: whenever a hardware variant of a shader is available, use it, even if it has reduced functionality. This is useful for fast previews. For example, while the user interacts with the scene by moving an object, fast preview rendering is done; when the interactions stops a high-quality image is rendered and displayed.

- **Switching by functionality**: specific effects can be achieved by switching functional node groups between hardware and software rendering. For example, an object may be rendered in software with accurate transparent ray-traced shadows, or it may be rendered in hardware with nontransparent shadowmapped shadows. In general, any effect that requires surface mapping can be switched in this way by rendering the map in software and the mapped object in hardware.

- **Switching by object**: entire objects and all their associated shaders can be switched. This is useful for scenes that are well suited for hardware rendering, except for a small number

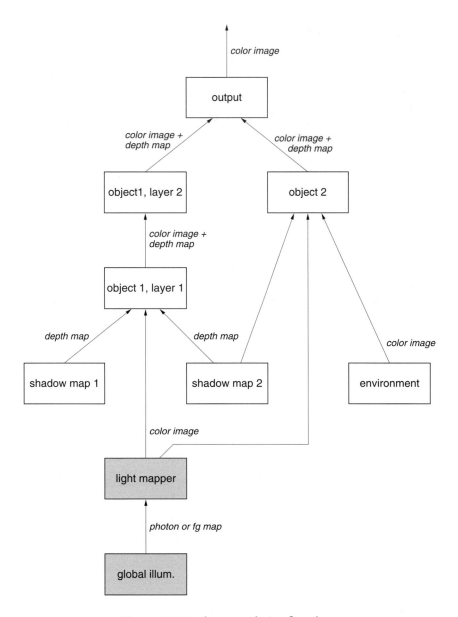

Figure 9.2: Hardware rendering flowchart.

of objects that require the flexibility of software.

Traditionally, hardware rendering was considered to generate images with poor quality, good enough for fast games but not for professional video or film production. But in fact not all aspects of a scene have equally high demands on rendering complexity – some parts of a scene can easily be rendered in hardware, while others absolutely require software. mental ray combines the benefits of both.

9.4   Shader Interfaces

The smallest unit that can be switched between hardware and software is a single shader. If a shader has two implementations, one in hardware and one in software, mental ray can choose automatically depending on options in the scene file, but will generally choose the hardware version. Examples for such shaders are local shading models like Phong and Blinn, or transparency shaders. If a hardware version is unavailable, mental ray will render it in software; examples for this type of shader are true reflections and refractions. Normally mental ray chooses hardware rendering only if there is no degradation of quality, but it can be switched to use hardware rendering unconditionally for fast preview rendering.

To realize the goal of providing inaccurate but fast previews, it is important to replace any software node with a hardware node, or omit it altogether, and still obtain a reasonable simplified image. Global illumination has no hardware equivalent, but a software shader that renders an object layer (such as the three object nodes in the above graphs) may have an equivalent or simplified hardware version. This requires that a shader interface is introduced that allows defining hardware and software shaders that provide a similar interface to the scene. The following intrinsic differences need to be abstracted:

All shaders have inputs and outputs. It is possible to create graphs of shaders where shaders obtain their inputs from the outputs of other shaders. Such graphs can be used to create Phenomena, which encapsulate one or more shader graphs and other information such that the Phenomenon appears like a monolithic shader. This allows a separation of functions: different components of a complex effect may be built from simple shaders, each taking care of some aspect of the effect. (See page 271 and [LeFrançois 05] for more details on Phenomena.)

Hardware shaders are interchangeable with individual nodes of a shader graph or Phenomenon only if they are implemented in a language that supports plugging shaders together. At this time only NVIDIA's Cg 1.2 language does. Hardware shaders written in another language or assembly code can only replace entire shaders or Phenomena. Shaders written in Cg are not limited to NVIDIA hardware; they support generic OpenGL ARB standards as well. mental ray takes care of properly compiling the Cg code for the available hardware.

Software shaders have no inherent limit on the number of lights and textures. Hardware shaders do, because the number of hardware resources such as uniform variables, registers or number of instructions are limited. Effects that would exceed this limit require layering. For example, if there is only room for ten lights in the uniform variables but the shader's light list contains twenty, the shader must be called twice to layer the effect. The design does not attempt to automate this at this time because it is not known how lights and other parameters interact. If a hardware shader is rejected by the hardware loader, it will be replaced with the software version (unless the options enforce pure hardware rendering).

9.5   Shader Declarations

Shaders are both declared with a declaration statement in the scene file or an include file. A
software shader declaration is little more than a list of the parameters accepted by the shader and
their data types, without the actual values (they are defined later when the shader is used). Such
a declaration might look like this, using mental ray's .mi scene definition syntax:

```
declare shader
    color "mib_illum_lambert" (
        color           "ambience",
        color           "ambient",
        color           "diffuse",
        integer         "mode",
        array light     "lights"
    )
    version 2
end declare
```

The declaration is the same for hardware and software shaders. This makes it simple to substitute
a hardware shader for a software shader if both are written with the same interface parameters.
mental ray will use the declaration as a template to convert and pass parameter values to the
format that the hardware or software shader requires.

The declaration is the gateway between the shader and the hardware. The declaration may be
fairly complex, but once written by the shader writer, the intricacies of hardware and software
shaders and their differences are taken care of automatically by mental ray. The burden of writing
the shader and declaring it is shifted to the programmer in a way that the artist, who later uses
the shader, does not have to care about the complexities of hardware shader writing at all.

The only exception is that shaders might have built-in limitations not usually found in software
shaders, such as accepting only a limited number of lights or textures; but these limitations are
all in the domain of scene design and not in the domain of programming. Since the artist and
the programmer require different skill sets, and are not normally the same person, mental ray
maintains a strict separation of these two roles.

Hardware shaders come with additional information that is hidden behind the parameter
declaration, in ways that only the programmer but not the artist needs to understand. A hardware
shader declaration needs to contain the following information:

- The implementation of the vertex shader, if required. (Almost no shaders require vertex
  shaders.)

- The implementation of the fragment shader.

- An optional C/C++ function that can perform extra OpenGL setup and shutdown. (Most
  hardware shaders do not need this.)

• Hardware requirements, such as the availability of a certain OpenGL version of a feature. mental ray will reject the shader if the requirements are not met.

9.6   Loading Hardware Shaders

mental ray uses OpenGL not only for defining a scene, but also to load hardware shaders[1]. Hardware shaders include the vertex and fragment shaders, precompiled uniform variables, and additional parameters. Just as mental ray relies on external shared libraries (DSOs on Unix or DLLs on Windows) containing precompiled C/C++ software shaders, it relies on external libraries containing hardware shaders. The libraries are created by external compilers such as NVIDIA's Cg compiler from source code provided by the shader writer, as shown in figure 9.3.

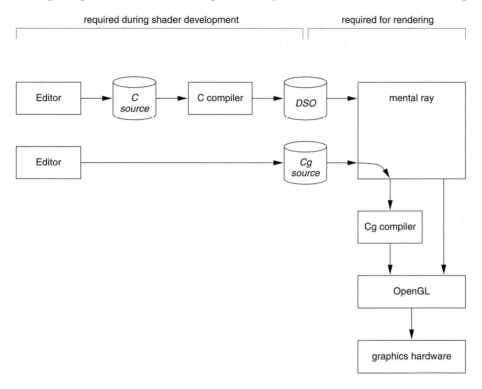

Figure 9.3: Shader execution flowchart.

The hardware shader pipeline mirrors mental ray's software pipeline, except that the end result is not a DSO executed within mental ray, but a Cg hardware shader library. Hardware shaders are collected, processed, compiled, and sent to OpenGL for installation on the graphics hardware where they are executed.

---

[1]Some application integrations of mental ray use Microsoft's DirectX instead of OpenGL, but DirectX not portable so such versions are available for Windows only.

NVIDIA's Cg compiler is only one example of a shader compiler. It accepts a high-level source code format that is designed to look like C code, with various restrictions and extensions. It is not limited to graphics hardware designed by NVIDIA, but can also generate code for other graphics architectures such as OpenGL ARB through the use of *profiles*. All graphics vendors accept shader source code written in a form of specialized low-level assembly language, all specific to the vendor's graphics hardware; in this case the Cg or other compiler is not required. The OpenGL 2.0 standard will accept shaders in a high-level language common to all vendors.

Since the hardware shader source code and libraries currently differ greatly from vendor to vendor, and from hardware generation to hardware generation, mental ray does not attempt to integrate a compiler. If it did, it would become subject to the rapid change in the hardware industry, and would have to be modified each time any graphics hardware vendor designed a new board or language feature. mental ray is hardware-agnostic and compatible with all graphics hardware from any vendor.

9.7   Using Hardware Rendering

Hardware rendering requires the following components and configurations:

☑ **mental ray.**
Hardware rendering requires mental ray 3.3.1 or higher.

☑ **Driver library.**
A shared library that acts as the "driver" for mental ray to connect to graphics hardware. This library must match the installed hardware. For example, there is `mi_opengl.so` (or `mi_opengl.dll` on NT) for OpenGL rendering. This includes Cg, OpenGL Shader Language, and generic OpenGL shaders. Special versions of mental ray (like the Solidworks visualization component) also support Microsoft's proprietary DirectX technology with the `mi_directx.dll` library.

☑ **Hardware shaders.**
NVIDIA hardware shaders are usually written in a hardware shading language called Cg, version 1.2 or later; assembly assembly language may also be used. Each software shader that implements an algorithm supported by hardware rendering must have a corresponding file containing the hardware fragment shader. (Software shaders that implement algorithms that cannot be handled in hardware, such as ray tracing, have no corresponding hardware shader.) There may also be another optional file for the vertex shader, if required. Transparently switching from software to hardware rendering is possible only if software shaders have properly named hardware equivalents.

☑ **Shader support library.**
Some hardware shaders may be augmented with a C/C++ function that performs special setup before the hardware begins rendering, although most hardware shaders do not need a C/C++ companion. However, if the graphics hardware does not support programmable hardware shaders at all, such as hardware that implements OpenGL 1.3 or earlier, the C/C++ function must handle the entire shading configuration by setting hardwired BRDF parameters. The

C/C++ function name and filename of the library containing these functions must be formed by prefixing the shader or library name:

function prefix	library prefix	language
micg_	—	NVIDIA Cg shader language
migl_	migl_	native OpenGL, no programmable shaders
mifx_	—	Microsoft HLSL (High Level Shader Language), also known as *.fx*; DirectX only
midx_	midx_	native DirectX, no programmable shaders

☑ **Configuration.**

Certain statements in the mental ray startup file (rayrc or .rayrc) configure mental ray for the available hardware.

☑ **Options.**

mental ray rendering options must be modified to use hardware rendering. In the simplest case, this can be a simple -hardware all option on the command line or in the scene file. Hardware rendering is turned off by default. See below. for more options.

The configuration in the startup file must first specify the hardware board to use, by setting the _MI_REG_VENDOR registry key. (Note that mental ray's registry is not related to the various Unix and Windows NT system registries.) To use OpenGL hardware, add these lines to the startup file:

```
registry "{_MI_REG_VENDOR}"
    value "OpenGL"
    link "mi_opengl.so"
end registry
```

The value is for informational uses only. Since OpenGL provides the basic rendering functionality, even if NVIDIA shaders are used instead of the native OpenGL shaders, mental ray will also load the OpenGL system library, called libGL.so on Unix and opengl32.dll on NT. However, it is optionally possible to choose a different OpenGL library by setting the _MI_REG_OPENGL registry key:

```
registry "{_MI_REG_OPENGL}"
    value "custom OpenGL"
    link "my_libGL.so"
end registry
```

Effectively, OpenGL requires two libraries: one that is part of the mental ray distribution (*mi_opengl.so*), and one that comes with the operating system (*libGL.so*). This allows upgrading mental ray for different or updated hardware capabilities by replacing *mi_opengl.so* instead of requiring installation of a new mental ray version. At this time, *mi_opengl.so* supports a wide range of OpenGL versions (1.3 and later) and hardware capabilities, including NVIDIA's Cg language extension.

Finally, mental ray needs to be told where to look for hardware shaders written in NVIDIA's Cg language, or the graphics board's assembly language. Cg shader files have the extension .cg (as opposed to the extension .so or .dll for software shaders). A search path for these files can be set with the _MI_REG_HARDWARE registry key:

```
registry "{_MI_REG_HARDWARE}"
    value "/tmp;/usr/local/cgshaders"
end registry
```

Note that the path is set in a value field, not a link field, since these files are Cg files, not DSO or DLL libraries that can be linked into mental ray. This is equivalent to other search paths like _MI_REG_LIBRARY (for software shaders) or _MI_REG_TEXTURE (for texture image files). The hardware search path can also be given on the command line with the -hardware_path option.

It is not necessary to configure the names of the optional hardware libraries like migl_base.so (for OpenGL) that provide extra setup code for the software shaders in base.so. For example, after the OpenGL driver library mi_opengl.so is loaded, it will automatically look for the migl_ prefix, and from then on mental ray will automatically construct hardware library names from this prefix and any software shader library being loaded, and try to find and load the hardware library as well. This prefix is set by mi_opengl.so and does not need to be configured in the startup file.

9.7.1 Enabling Hardware Rendering

All of the following command-line options are also available in the options block in the scene file, using the same syntax but without the leading hyphen. The configuration procedure is designed such that once the system is configured, switching to hardware rendering is very simple. To enable hardware rendering wherever possible, specify

```
-hardware all
```

on the command line. mental ray will try to find a hardware replacement for every software shader in the scene, but if none can be found, mental ray falls back on software rendering. This is useful to render a scene with hardware without any modifications to the scene file.

To gain more control over individual shaders and objects, use

```
-hardware on
```

instead. In this mode, only those objects are rendered in hardware that specify the `hardware` flag, and only those materials that explicitly specify a hardware shader. No automatic mapping is performed like `hardware all` does.

All hardware shading can be disabled with

```
-hardware off
```

This is the default.

9.7.2   Choosing Hardware Shader Categories

mental ray supports options that modify hardware shader selection:

```
-hardware cg
```

will use Cg shaders if available, to achieve the highest quality. Alternatively,

```
-hardware native
```

will use OpenGL 2.0 (or DirectX HLSL, if supported and available) shaders, but not Cg shaders. This improves performance, but complex effects may not be available, and Phenomena will not be automatically dissected and translated to hardware shader graphs. (Only Cg supports shader graphs at this time.) Finally,

```
-hardware fast
```

will use the fixed illumination shading models in OpenGL (or DirectX). This is very fast, but only very simple shading models are supported. This is useful for preview rendering. The default behaviour will try all shader types in turn: Cg, native, and fast.

Normally mental ray falls back on software if no hardware shader can be found. This can be disabled with

```
-hardware force
```

All of these options can be combined. This example will render the entire scene with hardware. If an error occurs or the Cg shader is not found, the object will be rendered with a default material instead of falling back on software:

```
-hardware all cg force
```

9.7.3   Enabling Hardware Rendering per Object

With -hardware on, it is possible to turn hardware rendering on or off for individual objects:

```
object "obj"
    hardware on
    ...
end object
```

specifies that this object should be rendered in hardware. If set to off, it will be rendered in software (unless the global hardware mode is all, which always renders everything in hardware for maximum speed). The default is off. Like all other boolean object flags, these flag statements can also be added to instances, and will be inherited down the scene graph.

option	object	object is rendered with
off	*	software
on	off	software
on	on	hardware if the shader is available, otherwise software
all	*	hardware

Asterisks (*) mean that the setting is ignored. The next section shows how mental ray looks for hardware shaders.

9.7.4   Hardware Shaders in Materials

Hardware shaders can be explicitly specified in material definitions:

```
material "mtl"
    "mib_illum_phong" (...)
    hardware "my_hardware_phong" (...)
end material
```

If the hardware mode is off, the hardware statement will be ignored. If it is on or all, the hardware version of the shader *my_hardware_phong* will be used. If the material does not contain an explicit hardware shader, the rules change: if the hardware mode is on, the material is rendered in software; if it is all mental ray tries to locate a hardware shader corresponding to *mib_illum_phong*, or failing that, a built-in default hardware shader. Effectively, mode all always uses hardware shading even if this compromises quality or accuracy, while mode on only uses hardware where a hardware shader is explicitly supplied.

mode	material SW shader	material HW shader	shader being used
off	S	*	software S
on	S	none	software S
on	S	H	hardware H
all	S	none	hardware miXX_S if found, or default hardware shader if not
all	S	H	hardware H

Again, asterisks (*) mean that the setting is ignored. S and H stand for software and hardware shader names such as *mib_illum_phong* or *myphong*, respectively. The XX part of the prefix depends on the hardware language, and may be *cg*, *gl*, *dx*, *sl*, or *fx*. Note that the choice of a name for H is not bound by the miXX_S convention; that is just what mental ray uses to automatically find hardware substitutes. It is a good idea to follow that convention though to avoid confusion.

The off/on modes are the end result of option and object flags as described in the previous table; the all mode is active if the global hardware all option is specified regardless of object flags.

9.7.5 Extracting Cg Shader Code

mental ray will use the Cg compiler to build hardware shaders from Phenomena or shader graphs. This involves collecting and preparing the Cg code that implements the subshaders that form the Phenomenon, passing this to the Cg compiler, and sending the resulting assembly code to the graphics board. This process is normally invisible and automatic.

However, it is sometimes useful to extract the Cg compiler input and output for debugging purposes, or to transplant the shader into a game platform. This allows mental ray to be used as a prototyping system for shader development with the full benefit of Phenomenon construction; and then extracting the resulting hardware shaders for use in a game engine. This is done with the command-line options

```
-hardware_echo "path" --
-hardware_echo error "path" --
```

The first variant saves all shaders into the directory *path*; the second saves only those shaders for which the Cg compiler has reported an error. The latter mode is intended for debugging by shader authors. Saving a shader means creating four files per material that uses a Cg hardware shader:

- *materialname.cg* contains the Cg input to the compiler.

- *materialname.asm* contains the assembly output of the Cg compiler.

- *materialname.C* contains sample C++ code that installs the shader with the appropriate OpenGL calls.

- *materialname.txt* contains informational messages about the construction of the shader graph with all its connections.

Note that the file names are constructed from the name of the material containing the hardware shaders, not from the name of a shader, because many shaders are usually collected to build a Cg input file, and because two materials using the same shader with different parameters will result in different Cg files.

9.8   Hardware Shader Implementation

Hardware shader names can be explicitly specified in materials, or automatically constructed from software shader names by adding a vendor prefix like `migl_`. Once the shader name is known, mental ray will perform two operations:

- First, mental ray will attempt to call a software function whose name is constructed by adding the prefix to the shader name. For example, if the hardware shader name is *myphong* and the hardware shader is implemented in Cg, mental ray will try to call the software function *micg_myphong*. This is not a hardware or software shader but a C/C++ function that can be used to do special setup operations needed for the shader, such as copying data to the graphics board or calling special GL functions needed by the shader. This function is optional and rarely necessary.

    This function is normally implemented in the shader support library. For example, the software shader library `base.so` might have a support library `migl_base.so` for Cg hardware shaders.

- Second, the actual shader is loaded from files on disk into the graphics board. Files are searched for with the hardware search path configured with the `_MI_REG_HARDWARE` registry key in the startup file, or the `-hardware_path` command-line option. The file name must exactly match the shader name, plus a postfix:

postfix	contents
`_v.cg`	Cg vertex shaders
`_f.cg`	Cg fragment shaders

    Either one may be missing if the shader does not require this type of shader. (Most shaders do not require a vertex shader and provide only a fragment shader.) For example, if the hardware shader name is *myphong*, mental ray will load the Cg files `myphong_v.cg` and `myphong_f.cg`.

- If no such Cg shader can be found, or `-hardware native` or `-hardware fast` is specified on the command line to turn off all programmable shaders, mental ray will use plain hardwired OpenGL shading. This requires a C/C++ function that performs the necessary OpenGL calls to load colors etc. This function follows the same conventions as the support functions in the first item: the shaders get the prefix *migl_*, for example *migl_myphong*, and they are loaded from the library *migl_base.so*. The only difference is that they are loaded instead of, rather than in addition to, any hardware shaders.

Chapter 10

Contours

Contour lines, also called *ink lines*, are used in cartoon animation to provide visual cues to distinguish objects and accentuate their shape, illumination, and spatial relations. Contour rendering in the mental ray rendering software supplements standard color rendering. It works by making decisions during rendering about where and how contour lines should be placed, and then, during postprocessing, drawing contours based on the results. Drawing can take place on top of the rendered color image, or in a blank color frame buffer (if only the contours are desired), or to a PostScript file. All stages of contour rendering are programmable with shaders.

More precisely, four stages are necessary for contour rendering, each represented by a shader:

1. The **contour store shader** defined in the options block is called for every image sample (see page 440). It stores information that the decision whether to place a contour, and the contour itself, are based on. This usually includes the color, depth, normal vector, and other information.

2. Whenever mental ray compares two samples, it calls the **contour contrast shader**, also defined in the options block, with the information that was collected by the contour store shader for the two samples. The contour contrast shader decides whether the two sets of information are different enough to require a contour between them.

3. If the contour contrast shader wants a contour, the **contour shader** in the material definition is called to decide on the color, width, and other attributes of the contour between the two points. mental ray then connects these contour points into contour segments, each consisting of two end points. Each end point has a coordinate, color, width, depth, label, motion vector, and normal vector. The segments are stored in a special segment list that is independent of the frame buffers.

4. After rendering completes, a **contour output shader** is called. It has access to all the contour line segments and can draw lines into the color frame buffer, perhaps after clearing it first, or create a PostScript file.

All four types of shaders are user-programmable. However, C/C++ programming is beyond the scope of this book (see volume 2 of this series), and all examples will use shaders from the `contour.so` shader library that is part of the mental ray distribution. The `contour.mi` file contains the declarations for the shaders in `contour.so`.

To create contours, the following steps are necessary:

- ☑ add a contour store shader statement to the options block.

- ☑ add a contour contrast shader statement to the options block.

- ☑ add a contour shader statement to all materials that should get contoured.

- ☑ add an output statement referencing a contour output shader to the camera definition.

- ☑ use a `samples 0 2` (or similar) statement in the *options block* to set the oversampling limits sufficiently high to avoid precision problems at contour intersections. A maximum sampling density of 2 or 3 is generally sufficient.

The first three types of shaders should form a matching set. For example, they must all agree what kind of information is stored by the contour store shader so they can interpret it correctly.

10.1   Outline Contours

Two questions must be answered for contouring: where should the contours be placed, and what should they look like. The first question determines the choice and parameters of the contour contrast shader in the options block, and the second determines the choice and parameters of the contour shader in the material.

The `contour.so` shader library contains one matching pair of contour store shader (*contour_store_function*) and contour contrast shader (*contour_contrast_function_levels*). The latter has a variety of shader parameters that can be used for many different effects, some of which are presented in this chapter. Both shaders, like all shader types used by mental ray, can be replaced with custom-written shaders for creating other contouring styles — for example for mixing different contouring styles on different objects in the same scene depending on the object label.

The first example uses *contour_contrast_function_levels* to select contours at the outer edges of objects by placing a contour segment where the depth difference (Z coordinate delta) is large. Here is a complete scene file, with only the teapot geometry missing because of its size (see appendix B for the teapot definition):

```
link "base.so"
link "contour.so"
$include <base.mi>
$include <contour.mi>

options "opt"
```

```
        samples           0 3
        contour store     "contour_store_function" ()
        contour contrast "contour_contrast_function_levels" (
                          "zdelta"     2.0,
                          "ndelta"     180.0,
                          "max_level"  1
                    )
        object space
end options

camera "cam"
        output            "rgb" "out.rgb"
        output            "contour,rgba" "contour_composite" ()
        output            "rgb" "out.1.rgb"
        focal             120.0
        aperture          42.0
        aspect            1.66
        resolution        800 480
end camera

light "light"
        "mib_light_point" (
            "color"      1 1 1
        )
        origin           -5 5 -18
end light

instance "light-i" "light" end instance

shader "illum" "mib_illum_phong" (
            "ambient"    0.5 0.5 0.5,
            "ambience"   1.0 1.0 1.0,
            "diffuse"    0.8 0.8 0.8,
            "specular"   1.0 1.0 1.0,
            "exponent"   50.0,
            "lights"     ["light-i"]
        )

material "white" opaque
        = "illum"
        contour "contour_shader_simple" (
            "color"      0.0 0.0 0.0 1.0,
            "width"      0.5
        )
end material

$include "teapot.mi"     # 300 lines are too many to list here

instance "teapot-i" "teapot"
        transform
                0.97  0   0.24  0
                0     1   0     0
                -0.24 0   0.97  0
```

```
                      -5      4 20      1
         material "white"
end instance

instance "cam-i" "cam"
         transform
                 1     0     0     0
                 0   0.97 0.24    0
                 0  -0.24 0.97    0
                 0   -2     0     1
end instance

instgroup "all"
         "cam-i" "light-i" "teapot-i"
end instgroup

render "all" "cam-i" "opt"
```

The *contour_contrast_function_levels* parameters specifies that there should be a contour where the change in depth (Z delta) is greater than 2.0 using the zdelta parameter. The ndelta parameter, which places contour segments at high-curvature areas, is set to 180 degrees to disable curvature contours. Contours are also restricted to differences of primary rays by setting the max_level parameter to 1; outline contours should not show the outlines of the reflections or refractions of other objects in the scene.

The *contour_shader_simple* contour shader in the material definition only has two parameters: the color parameter chooses the RGBA color of the contour, and the width parameter chooses the width of the contour as a percentage of the width (X resolution) of the rendered image. Widths are given as percentages to make sure that the contour scales correctly when the image resolution in the camera changes. It is important to specify the contour color as an RGBA value, with an alpha component (fourth number) greater than 0. A value of 1 draws fully opaque contours, which is desirable most of the time. Values less than 1 draw semitransparent contours.

Color only   Color with contours   Contour only

Figure 10.1: Contours from large depth differences.

Finally, there are three output statements in the camera. The first writes out the rendered color image *before* the contours are drawn (left image of figure 10.1). The second draws the contours on top of the color frame buffer by calling the *contour_composite* contour output shader. The third writes the image *after* compositing (middle image of figure 10.1). (There is also another contour output shader *contour_only* that clears the frame buffer before drawing contours; this results in a contour-only image similar to the right image of figure 10.1.)

10.2 PostScript Contours

The right image of figure 10.1 does not actually show a color image but a true PostScript™line drawing. PostScript output is useful for large-scale paper printouts of the contour image. Cartoon production is often a combination of computer-rendered images and hand-drawn images. The computer "sets the stage" with complex camera motion and perspective computations, but characters may still be hand-drawn. The artists drawing the characters require printouts of the background so they can match their drawings precisely with the rest of the scene. PostScript is faster and more efficient than image galleys for this purpose.

The PostScript file for figure 10.1 was created with the same scene file shown on page 262 but with the three output statements in the camera replaced with the following two:

```
output          "contour,rgba" "contour_ps" (
                    "paper_size"        4,
                    "paper_scale"       1.0,
                    "paper_transform_b" 0.0,
                    "paper_transform_d" 1.0,
                    "file_name"         "wire.ps"
                )
```

No image is drawn before calling the contour output shader *contour_ps*; it would have been identical to the one in figure 10.1. The *contour_ps* shader produces a PostScript file in memory. The `paper_size` parameter selects the paper format as a code number from the following table:

number	paper format
0	letter
1	executive
2	legal
3–6	DIN A3, A4, A5, A6
7–9	DIN B4, B5, B6
10	11×17

A 5% margin all around the paper is unused; printers cannot print too close to the edge of the paper. The `scale` parameter scales the printout; 1.0 is unscaled. The `paper_transform` parameters allow compensation of skewed printouts due to printer imprecision by replacing paper coordinates x (horizontal) and y (vertical) with $x + b \cdot y$ and $d \cdot y$. If omitted or set to 0 and 1, as in the example, no skew correction is done.

The *contour_ps* output shader also has two boolean parameters: `title`, which enables a title line in the PostScript file, and `landscape`, which rotates the output by 90 degrees.

The `file_name` specifies the name of the PostScript file that the contour lines are written to.

All the contour-only teapot images in this chapter, and all wireframe figures on pages 342f. were created as contour PostScript files. The `diff_label` and `diff_index` features of the *contour_* *contrast_function_levels* shader were used to outline triangles. (See appendix E for a complete description of this and the other contour-related shaders.)

10.3   Edge Contours

By changing the parameters of the *contour_contrast_function_levels* contour contrast shader in the example on page 262, the contours can be changed to follow internal edges of the object. The following options block replaces the one in the example:

```
options "opt"
        samples          0 3
        contour store    "contour_store_function" ()
        contour contrast "contour_contrast_function_levels" (
                         "zdelta"     0.1,
                         "ndelta"     60.0,
                         "max_level"  1
                         )
        object space
end options
```

| Color only | Color with contours | Contour only |

Figure 10.2: Contours from small depth and orientation differences.

The small `zdelta` value causes parts of the object that pass in front of other parts of the object, such as the teapot handle, to be contoured (see figure 10.2). The smaller `ndelta` parameter causes contours at sharp edges, such as all around the lid of the teapot: there is a contour where the surface orientation changes by more than 60 degrees.

10.4   Contours on Reflections and Refractions

The `max_level` parameter of the *contour_contrast_function_levels* shader controls whether contours should be drawn around reflections of this or other objects, or around objects visible behind the surface of the frontmost one. This is done by letting the shader consider a difference in trace depth as contrast. If the `max_level` parameter is set to 1, only primary rays (from the camera to the frontmost object at a given pixel) are considered; if it is increased to 2, the first-order reflections and refractions are considered too; greater values also include reflections of reflections. Here is another modified options block for the example on page 262:

```
options "opt"
        samples         0 3
        contour store   "contour_store_function" ()
        contour contrast "contour_contrast_function_levels" (
                        "zdelta"    0.1,
                        "ndelta"    60.0,
                        "max_level" 2
                )
        object space
end options
```

Color only   Color with contours   Contour only

Figure 10.3: Contours from reflections.

Color only   Color with contours   Contour only

Figure 10.4: Contours from transparency.

The material shader was appropriately changed to make the teapot surface reflective and transparent, respectively; see pages 118 and 123 for examples.

Figure 10.3 shows contours around the reflections of the lid button, the handle, and the spout. Figure 10.4 shows that the teapot was modeled such that the spout and the handle penetrate the pot surface, causing contours around the part inside the pot.

10.5 Contours at Color Contrasts

The next example derives contours from object color contrast edges. Since the very soft gradations of the teapot body would not suffice for accurately placing a contour, the example uses a custom-written shader to create some brightly colored stripes depending on the direction of the light source relative to the surface normal. Custom material shaders provide a flexible way to produce contour lines at arbitrary places on a surface, for example cross-hatching implemented as a high-contrast texture.

```
options "opt"
        samples          0 3
        contour store    "contour_store_function" ()
        contour contrast "contour_contrast_function_levels" (
                              "zdelta"    0.1,
                              "ndelta"    60.0,
                              "contrast"  on,
                              "max_level" 1
                         )
        object space
end options

$code
#include "/h/misrc/ray/modules/include/shader.h"
int stark_version(void) {return(1);}
miBoolean stark(miColor *result, miState *state, miTag *light)
{
        miScalar dot_nl = 0;     /* ray 3.3 and later: must set to 0 */
        mi_trace_light(result, 0, &dot_nl, state, *mi_eval_tag(light));
        result->r = dot_nl > .4 ? 1 : .2;
        result->g = dot_nl > .7 ? 1 : .2;
        result->b = dot_nl >  0 ? 1 : .2;
        result->a = 1;
        return(miTRUE);
}
$end code

declare shader "stark" (light "light") version 1 end declare

material "bunt" opaque
        "stark" (
            "light"      "light-i"
        )
        contour "contour_shader_simple" (
            "color"      0.0 0.0 0.0 1.0,
            "width"      0.5
        )
end material
```

The $code block used in this scene example is not the most efficient way of loading a shader; see page 399 for ways of creating a shader library.

The contour.so shader library contains a variety of contour shaders that control contour width and color by considering light source distance and direction, distance, object color, trace depth, curvature, and combinations of these. (See appendix E for details.

Color only   Color with contours   Contour only

Figure 10.5: Contours from color contrast.

10.6   Variable-Width Contours

All the contour lines in the preceding examples had a constant width, 0.5% of the width of the image. Cartoon animations usually require variable contour line widths for a more natural look: contours may be wider in shadow, close to the camera, or around dark parts of the contoured object.

The contour shader in the material definition is responsible for all these effects. This means that different objects, or even parts of objects, may use different approaches to controlling width and color of the contours. For example, a scene with a boat may have heavy dark contours on the boat, and thin or no contours on the water or water spray. The following material definition uses the contour shader *contour_shader_widthfromlight* to change the contour width depending on the surface orientation relative to the light:

```
material "white" opaque
        = "illum"
        contour "contour_shader_widthfromlight" (
            "color"     0 0 0 1,
            "min_width" 0.2,
            "max_width" 2.5,
            "light"     "light-i"
        )
end material
```

Color only   Color with contours   Contour only

Figure 10.6: Variable-width contours from lighting.

The min_width and max_width parameters control the width range. The name of the light source instance name must also be given.

10.7   Glowing Contours

As a final example, a contour line need not be a solid opaque line. The *contour_composite* contour output shader can also draw contour lines with a soft brush. This creates a glow effect around bright objects.

```
output          "contour,rgba" "contour_composite" (
                    "maxcomp"      on,
                    "glow"         on
                )
```

Color only   Color with glow   Glow only

Figure 10.7: Glowing contours.

In addition to enabling the `glow` parameter, the value of the contour `width` parameter of the *contour_shader_simple* contour shader was increased to 10.0. The `maxcomp` parameter ensures correct blending of adjacent contour lines.

10.8   Performance

The speed of contours depends on the choice of shaders and their shader parameters. If only simple outlines of objects are needed, simple shaders like *contour_shader_simple* should be used with *contour_store_function_simple* and *contour_contrast_function_simple* to get fast contour computations. Also, simple material shaders should be used; if only the contours or very simple cartoon-like color images are needed, it may be possible to disable complex illumination, shadows, area light sources, reflection, refraction, motion blur, volume, or texture computations.

Sometimes incorrect settings of contouring criteria such as the `zdelta` and `ndelta` parameters of the contour contrast shaders can cause very many contours to be computed. This leads to increased rendering times, and very poor contour generation performance in the contour output shader when it tries to properly connect huge numbers of contour line segments. If this happens, increase the tolerances, for example by choosing larger `zdelta` and `ndelta` values. When very small values seem to be necessary, this may be an indication that the shader is used for something it was not designed to do. Using another shader, or writing a custom shader as described in the chapter on variable-width contours on page 269, can fix such problems.

Chapter 11

Shaders and Phenomena

Shaders are plug-in modules that are used in materials, light sources, cameras, and other elements to control a wide range of effects, from surface material, volume, and camera lens properties to compositing (figure 11.1). Custom shaders can be custom-written in C or C++ and loaded by the mental ray rendering software at runtime. See page 12 for a list of shader types.

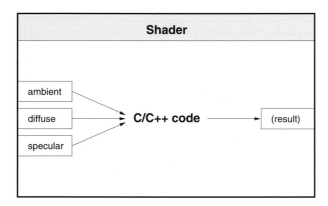

Figure 11.1: Structure of a an example shader.

Phenomenon™ components look like shaders when they are being applied to the scene, but their functionality is implemented in a different way: instead of C or C++, Phenomena™ encapsulate one or more subshader graphs and rendering options which are attached to the appropriate locations in the scene automatically (figure 11.2). Phenomena are "implemented" using standard mi scene definition syntax. No knowledge of any programming languages is necessary to design new custom effects as Phenomena.

Both shaders and Phenomena have *interface parameters* that feed data into them, and *result parameters* that return the result of their evaluation. In the case of the Phenomenon, the result parameters of the Phenomenon are taken from a specific shader that is also called the root shader of the Phenomenon. Phenomena can have more than one root. See page 286 for details.

In the schematic diagrams in this chapter, boxes represent shaders or Phenomena; their interface

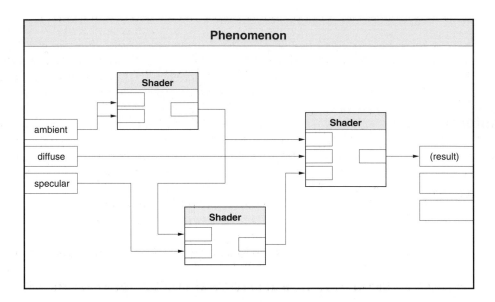

Figure 11.2: Structure of a an example Phenomenon.

parameters (such as "ambient", "diffuse", or "specular") are at the left side and result parameters are at the right side. All Phenomena are defined with .mi scene statements here. In practice, visual tools such as mental images' Phenomenon Creator™ utility are used to build new Phenomena, or the Phenomenon Editor™ utility to create "instances" of Phenomena by assigning values to its parameters. Phenomenon instances are useful as prepackaged effects: a wood Phenomenon, for example, may have parameters that define colors and wood grain turbulence, and different predefined instances of it can supply parameter values to make it look like oak, redwood, birch, or other variations.

This chapter describes the function and use of shaders and Phenomena. Writing shaders in C or C++ is not covered; see volume 2 [PROG] of this series (available in electronic form on the included CD).

11.1 Declarations

When using shaders or Phenomena in a scene, three properties must be known:

- The name of the shader or Phenomenon,

- its interface parameters, and

- its result parameters.

The shader name is identical to the C/C++ function name that implements it. The interface parameters are a set of named values passed to the shader or Phenomenon when it runs. For example, a shader implementing Phong shading would have three interface parameters of type "color" named "ambient", "diffuse", and "specular". The interface parameters can be freely selected by the author of the shader or Phenomenon. Finally, the result parameters of a shader represent the values returned by the shaders. Most of the time, this is a single value of type "color", but other types and structures of multiple values are also possible.

Since the shader or Phenomenon name, its interface, and its result parameters are not hardcoded into mental ray but may be selected by the author of the shader or Phenomenon, they must be made known to mental ray before the shader or Phenomenon is used for the first time. This is called a *declaration*. Declarations specify names and types but not values.

Once a shader or Phenomenon is declared, it can be used in the scene by referencing its name and providing values for some or all of its interface parameters. For example, once the Phong shader is declared, it can be used in many different materials, each assigning different colors to its ambient, diffuse, and specular parameters. The association of parameter values is called the *definition* (or sometimes *shader instance*, which has nothing to do with scene graph instances so the term is avoided here). The optional Phenomenon Creator™ tool creates declarations; the Phenomenon Editor™ tool creates definitions.

Consider the following declaration for the shader "phong":

```
declare shader
    color "phong" (
            color           "ambient",
            color           "diffuse",
            color           "specular",
            scalar          "exponent"  default 50,
            array light     "lights"
    )
    version 1
end declare
```

This scene file fragment can be used in a scene file before the first use of the shader, but by convention such declarations are put into separate files that come with the shader library, and are inserted into the scene file with a $include command in the scene file. Since this is a shader declaration, a shader library must exist and be linked using a link command in the scene file that implements the "phong" shader.

The syntax of shader declarations is

```
declare shader
    [ result_parameters ] "shader_name" (
        [ interface_parameters ]
    )
    [ version version_int ]
    [ options ]
end declare
```

The quoted shader name is the name of the C/C++ shader as it appears in the compiled shader library.

The version number is an integer greater than zero that should be incremented whenever the declaration of the result parameters or the interface parameters changes, perhaps due to a redesign of the shader code. Compiled C/C++ shaders also contain a version number, and mental ray will print error messages when the library version does not agree with the declaration version. This indicates a shader library installation problem that can cause problems when rendering. Version numbers are optional in the language but should not be omitted.

The options specify requirements of the shader, such as the case when a shader will only function if ray tracing is enabled. mental ray will reconcile requirements before rendering begins, enabling or disabling options as required and reporting conflicts. Options are described in detail below (page 284).

Both the result parameters and the interface parameters are comma-separated lists of parameters, each consisting of a quoted parameter name and a type. There are two forms:

[`array`] *simple_type* *"parameter_name"*
[`array`] `struct` *"parameter_name"* { *parameters* }

Additionally, mental ray 3.3 and higher allow adding the keyword `default` followed by a default value. Defaults are allowed only for boolean, integer, scalar, vector, matrix, and color types. The default value is used if a shader is derived from the declaration, and the parameter is left undefined. If no explicit default is supplied, false for booleans and 0 for numeric types is assumed. For example, in the code example above, the exponent parameter, if left unspecified, will default to a value of 50.

The following simple types are supported:

`boolean`	a true/false flag
`integer`	a signed 32-bit integer number
`scalar`	a 32-bit floating-point number
`string`	a string of arbitrary length
`color`	an RGBA color
`vector`	an XYZ vector
`transform`	a 4×4 transformation matrix
`color texture`	a color image file
`scalar texture`	a scalar (grayscale) image file
`vector texture`	a vector texture file
`shader`	a callable shader
`material`	a material
`light`	an instance of a light source
`geometry`	a geometric object or an instance
`data`	a user data block

The parameter name is a quoted string that identifies the parameter, such as "ambient" or "diffuse". Names should not contain periods (.) or colons (:). Parameter names must be unique in any given list; sub-structures count as separate lists with their own separate name space.

The struct keyword requires an extra parameter block enclosed in curly braces after the parameter name. The sub-parameters follow the same rules as the "main" interface parameter list of the shader; they are comma-separated lists of type/name pairs that may also include sub-arrays and sub-structures. Structures are used to collect parameters into groups; they are especially useful when turned into an array. If a shader returns a structure, the name between the struct keyword and the opening curly brace is omitted; see page 281 for an example.

The array keyword turns any parameter except array into an array (an ordered list) of zero or more parameter members. Arrays cannot be nested. The number of members is unlimited. For example, most shaders that calculate illumination accept an array of light sources, and collect the light contribution from all light sources in the list. Arrays of structures are useful for shaders that perform multi-layered texture mapping. To optimize memory usage, the last parameter in a declaration should be the array with the largest type (for example, the struct with the most members).

Result parameters may contain structures but not arrays. If the result parameters are not declared, they default to color.

11.2   Definitions

Once defined, the "phong" shader can be used to control the surface properties of a material, using a material statement such as

```
material "green_mtl"
    "phong" (
            "ambient"       0.0  0.3  0.0,
            "diffuse"       0.0  0.7  0.0,
            "specular"      1.0  1.0  1.0,
            "exponent"      50,
            "lights"        [ "light1_inst", "light2_inst" ]
    )
end material
```

This is an *anonymous shader definition* of the "phong" shader. It is called *anonymous* because the shader/value pair is defined where it is used, without giving it its own name. A *named shader definition* equivalent can be written as

```
shader "green_sh"
    "phong" (
            "ambient"       0.0  0.3  0.0,
            "diffuse"       0.0  0.7  0.0,
            "specular"      1.0  1.0  1.0,
            "exponent"      50,
            "lights"        [ "light1_inst", "light2_inst" ]
    )
```

```
material "green_mtl"
    = "green_sh"
end material
```

This creates the named shader "green_sh", which can then be used in any number of material or other statements that require a shader. Both the anonymous and named versions operate exactly in the same way; there is no runtime performance loss other than the small overhead required for parsing and storing the shader name when the scene file is read. The "=" sign indicates that the name of a named shader follows instead of an anonymous shader definition.

Parameter values are set by giving the quoted parameter name, followed by the value. Parameters can be defined in any order, and must be separated by commas. The form of the values depends on the parameter type, as defined in the declaration:

boolean	one of the keywords on, off, true, or false. on and true are synonymous, as are off and false.
integer	an optional minus signed followed directly by a sequence of numerical digits in the range -2147483648...2147483647 with no decimal point.
scalar	either an integer or an optional minus sign directly followed by a floating-point number consisting of numerical digits, a decimal point, and an optional decimal exponent, in the range $\pm$ 1.175e-38 ... 3.402e+38. The decimal exponent notation xey stands for $x \cdot 10^y$. Examples are 1, 2., .5, 3.1415, 9.10625e-31.
string	a double-quoted string of characters not containing a double quote or a newline. There is no length limit.
color	a sequence of either three or four scalars that describe the red, green, blue, and alpha components of the color. If the alpha component is omitted, it defaults to zero. Color components are normally in the range 0...1, but negative values and values greater than 1 are allowed and often useful.
vector	a sequence of three scalars that describe the X, Y, and Z components of a vector.
transform	a sequence of sixteen scalars that describe a 4×4 matrix in row-major order. Matrices have the form

$$\begin{pmatrix} r_{01} & r_{02} & r_{03} & s_x \\ r_{11} & r_{12} & r_{13} & s_y \\ r_{21} & r_{22} & r_{23} & s_z \\ t_x & t_y & t_z & 1 \end{pmatrix}$$

and must be given in the order r_{01} r_{02} ... t_z 1. The r's specify the rotation and scaling matrix, the t's are the translation, and the s's can be used for skewing.

`color texture`	the quoted name of a texture file previously defined with a `color texture` statement (see page 71).
`scalar texture`	the quoted name of a texture file previously defined with a `scalar texture` statement.
`vector texture`	the quoted name of a texture file previously defined with a `vector texture` statement.
`shader`	the quoted name of a named shader. Note that a reference to the shader itself is passed, this is not a shader assignment unless the "=" sign is used.
`material`	the quoted name of a material.
`light`	the quoted name of an instance of a light source (not the light source itself).
`geometry`	the quoted name of a geometric object, or an instance of a geometric object, depending on the shader.
`data`	the quoted name of a user data block. See section 11.6.
`struct`	an opening curly brace ({), followed by a sub-parameter list, followed by a closing curly brace (}). The sub-parameter list follows the same rules as the main parameter list.
`array`	an opening square bracket ([), followed by a comma-separated list of parameter values, followed by a closing square bracket (]). All parameters in the list have the same type.

Most examples in this book use an array of lights. Arrays of structs are also possible; some shaders that support layered textures use them. The mi language allows omitting color, vector, and array numbers; missing numbers are assumed to be 0. This is how RGB values are provided for RGBA color types: the missing fourth number defaults to 0. It is not recommended to abbreviate `transform` matrices in this way because many shaders assume that a matrix was omitted completely and need not be taken into account if the last (3, 3) element is 0.

Parameters can be set in any order; the definition order need not agree with the declaration order. Parameters can also be omitted completely in a definition; in this case they default to 0, or the default value[3.3] supplied in the shader declaration block.

11.3 Shader Lists

Shaders and Phenomena can be connected to form shader lists by listing more than one shader, either anonymous or named. For example, if the material on page 275 is rewritten as

```
material "green_mtl"
    = "green_sh"
    "phong" (
            "ambient"       0.0   0.3   0.0,
            "diffuse"       0.0   0.7   0.0,
            "specular"      1.0   1.0   1.0,
            "exponent"      50,
            "lights"        [ "light1_inst", "light2_inst" ]
    )
    = "red_sh"
end material
```

a list consisting of three shaders is constructed. The list begins with "green_sh", followed by the anonymous "phong" shader, followed by "red_sh" (which must have been defined previously with a shader statement). The shaders are chained by attaching the anonymous "phong" shader to "green_sh" and "red_sh" to the anonymous shader. This chain is permanent; if "green_sh" would also be used elsewhere in the scene file, the connection to the anonymous "phong" shader is still intact.

When a shader in a shader list is called, this shader and all that follow it in the list are executed in order, each receiving the result from the previous. Shaders that are written to operate with previously computed results (volume shaders and geometry shaders; and possibly others that have been designed for it) are good candidates for shader lists. Also, some shaders are not called for their result but for their side effects; for example the *mib_bump_map* shader used on page 531 applies a perturbation to the current normal vector. Such shaders can be placed at the beginning of a shader list to ensure that later shaders in the list see the perturbed normal.

As a special case, lens shaders, when connected to a list, are not called in order by mental ray, but recursively from within the lens shader — each one uses a special function to call the next explicitly, instead of relying on mental ray to call them sequentially. This allows a lens shader to make modifications before *and* after the next shader in the list is executed. However, this detail is only significant to shader writers.

11.4   Shader Graphs

The previous examples all assigned constant values to interface parameters, such as 0.0 0.7 0.0 to "diffuse". mental ray also allows assigning the result parameter of another shader to an interface parameter. This is called *shader assignment*. For example, a shader performing illumination may have "ambient" and "diffuse" color parameters that define the color of the object. Assigning a constant value to these parameters results in an object that has a uniform color (assuming uniformly colored light sources).

Here is a simple scene from page 84, with the following material referencing an (anonymous) material shader:

```
material "mtl"
        "mib_illum_phong" (
                "ambient"       .3 .3 .3,
                "diffuse"       .7 .7 .7,
                "ambience"      .1 .1 .1,
                "specular"      1  1  1,
                "exponent"      50,
                "mode"          1,
                "lights"        [ "light1_inst" ]
        )
end material
```

All the interface parameters of this shader are constants, so the surface color is constant too (except for lighting effects), as shown in the left image of figure 11.3. The following example uses shader assignment to control the ambient and diffuse colors with another shader that provides texturing information:

```
color texture "pic1" "tex_image.rgb"

shader "coord" "mib_texture_vector" (
        "select"        0,
        "selspace"      1
)

shader "remap" "mib_texture_remap" (
        "input"         = "coord"
)

shader "tex" "mib_texture_lookup" (
        "tex"           "pic1",
        "coord"         = "remap"
)

material "mtl"
        "mib_illum_phong" (
                "ambient"       = "tex",
                "diffuse"       = "tex",
                "ambience"      .1 .1 .1,
                "specular"      1  1  1,
                "exponent"      50,
                "mode"          1,
                "lights"        [ "light1_inst" ]
        )
end material
```

A collection of shaders connected in this way is called a *shader graph* (the technical term is *shader DAG*; DAG stands for Directed Acyclic Graph, meaning that there may be no loops).

The texture lookup shader *mib_texture_lookup* provides both the ambient and diffuse colors, so the image changes as shown on the right of figure 11.3. Clearly, only named shader definitions can be used for shader assignment because a name is needed after the "=" sign.

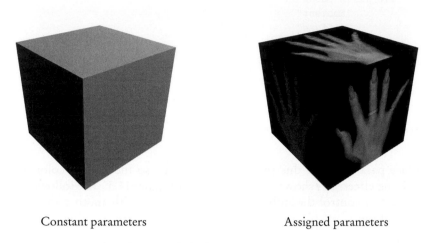

<table>
<tr><td>Constant parameters</td><td>Assigned parameters</td></tr>
</table>

Figure 11.3: Rendering with shaders attached to interface parameters.

The *mib_illum_phong* shader is not "aware" that its interface parameters are being fed by another shader instead of being constant. It uses a C/C++ library function provided by mental ray (*mi_eval*) that handles constant values, shader assignments, and interface assignments (see next section) automatically, and also handles caching: *mib_texture_lookup* is called only once even though it is assigned to two different parameters, "ambient" and "diffuse". mental ray automatically keeps track of multi-level rendering scopes and detects when the result of a shader can be re-used, and when it becomes invalid.

In this example the *mib_texture_lookup* shader itself has another shader, *mib_texture_remap* assigned to its "coord" interface parameter, which controls which point on the texture should be looked up. *mib_texture_remap*, in turn, derives its original coordinate from *mib_texture_vector*. (See figure 11.4; for a detailed description of these shaders, see appendix C.)

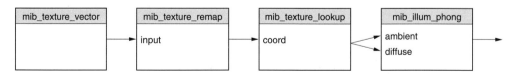

Figure 11.4: Shader graph with attachments.

The ability to combine simple shaders into complex shader graphs greatly reduces the need to write new shaders for new scenes, and allows shaders to remain simple. This is called the *toolbox approach*: a collection of small tools that do one thing well and can be easily combined into arbitrarily complex graphs.

mental ray makes sure that shader assignments use the compatible types. The output of *mib_texture_lookup* can be assigned to the interface parameters "ambient" and "diffuse" of *mib_illum_phong* because they all have the type `color`. The types must match, with the following exceptions:

shader result type	can be assigned to parameter of type
color	scalar
shader	color texture
shader	scalar texture
shader	vector texture

No automatic conversions are done; when assigning a color to a scalar the shader expecting the scalar will see the red component of the color. This is useful for generic shaders computing grayscales. mental ray allows assigning shaders to textures to allow shaders to work with both texture image files and procedural textures.

Arrays must be assigned as a unit. By convention, array members may not be assigned to shaders (or interfaces). In other words, no "=" signs may be used inside angle brackets ([ ]). This convention simplifies writing shaders and improves performance. (Remember that arrays cannot be used in result parameters.) Conversely, structures (type `struct`) cannot be assigned as a unit but only by member:

```
declare shader
    struct {
            color "amb",
            color "diff"
    } "illum" ( ... )
end declare

shader "subshader" ( ... )

material "mtl"
    "phong" (
            "ambient" = "subshader.amb",
            "diffuse" = "subshader.diff",
            ...
    )
end material
```

The *illum* shader is declared to return two colors, "amb" and "diff", that are individually selected by the "phong" shader. Note that the result structure is not named; the opening curly brace ({) directly follows the `struct` keyword. Again, mental ray caches results to ensure that `illum` is not called twice even if result parameter members are used twice.

11.5 Phenomena

A Phenomenon is a scene element containing one or more cooperating shaders or shader graphs, plus various miscellaneous options that control rendering. On the outside a Phenomenon looks exactly like a shader with interface parameters and result parameters, but internally its function is implemented not as a C/C++ function but as internal shaders or shader graphs that have access to the Phenomenon interface parameters. Phenomena are attached at a unique root node which serves as an attachment point to the scene. The internal structure is hidden from the outside user.

From the Phenomenon implementor's point of view the Phenomenon concept is characterized by:

- the generalization of the shade tree concept to the concept of *shader graphs*.

- itm• the introduction of the concept of *cooperation* among these shader graphs,

- the introduction of the new concept of *geometry shaders*, and

- instructions for *automatic integration* of the Phenomenon into the scene at runtime.

Cooperation among shaders is defined as sharing common sub-DAGs by shader parameter reference and mutual access to data built by shaders at runtime or during startup.

Geometry shaders are a special type of shader introduced specifically for use in Phenomena, in addition to the regular rendering shader types. A geometry shader creates geometrical entities in the scene. The name "shader" is used for consistency only. This shader type does not actually shade anything but consists of functions which perform procedural geometric modeling operations. For example, a particle system that is based on the actual creation of geometrically described particles can be used as a geometry shader in a Phenomenon.

Automatic integration into the scene includes specification of control parameters for camera lenses, rendering options, frame buffer specification and postprocessing effects, as well as management of the relevant coordinate space transformations.

The syntax of Phenomenon declarations is

```
declare phenomenon
    [ result_parameters ] "shader_name" (
        [ interface_parameters ]
    )
    [ version version_int ]
    [ options ]
    [ shader definitions ]
    [ materials ]
    [ lights ]
    [ instances ]
    [ material definitions ]
    [ roots ]
end declare
```

This is similar to the shader declaration on page 273, with two exceptions: the declare keyword is followed with the phenomenon keyword, and the syntax allows the definition of shaders, materials, and roots. Shader definitions, materials, light sources, and instances inside Phenomena are exactly identical to similar definitions outside of Phenomena, except that they can be used only inside the Phenomenon. Definitions outside the `declare phenomenon ... end declare` block are not visible inside the Phenomenon, and vice versa.

Since a Phenomenon is not implemented as a C/C++ function, like a shader, its name is not restricted to characters possible in C/C++ function names, namely, a–z, A–Z, 0–9, and _. Only the double quote, period, and colon are not allowed. However, for clarity it is recommended to stick to the legal C/C++ characters.

Version numbers are possible but not necessary — there is no C/C++ function in a linked library whose version number would have to be compared to the declaration version number. Still, version numbers are useful to keep track of Phenomenon revisions.

11.5.1 Phenomenon Interface Assignments

The interface parameters of a Phenomenon have the same function as the interface parameters of a shader: they serve as the gateway to the rest of the scene file using the Phenomenon or shader. But unlike shaders, Phenomena are implemented not in C/C++ but in terms of internal shader and material definitions, so it becomes possible for an internal shader definition to access an interface parameter "from the inside".

This adds a third way of assigning values to internal shader parameters, in addition to the regular constant values and shader assignments:

> "*parameter_name*" = interface " *interface_parameter_name*"

This is called a Phenomenon interface assignment. When the shader executes and evaluates its parameter *parameter_name*, mental ray will provide it with the value of the interface parameter *interface_parameter_name*. Here is an example based on the "phong" shader on page 273:

```
declare phenomenon
        color "phen_mtl" (
                color "spec"
        )
        shader "tex_sh" "tex" (...)

        shader "illum_sh" "phong" (
                "ambient"   .1 .1 .1,           # constant
                "diffuse"   = "tex_sh",         # shader assignment
                "specular"  = interface "spec"  # interface assignment
        )
        root = "illum_sh"
end declare

material "mtl"
        "phen_mtl" (
                "spec"      .7 .7 .7
        )
end material
```

When "phong" is executed, its ambient color parameter will be 0.1 0.1 0.1, its diffuse color parameter will be whatever the "tex" shader returns, and its specular color will be 0.7 0.7 0.7. The root statement will be explained later; it connects the "phong" shader to the Phenomenon body so that mental ray knows to execute "phong" first when the Phenomenon is executed.

Note that the "phong" shader needs to be written correctly for this to work: it must use the *mi_eval* shader interface function when accessing its parameters.

Phenomena can be nested. The shaders "phong" and "tex" can be replaced with Phenomena, as long as they have been previously declared with another declare phenomenon statement. Declarations may not be nested.

11.5.2 Shader and Phenomenon Options

Both shaders and Phenomena may define options anywhere in their declaration blocks. Options have the same form as in the scene options block, but only a subset is available:

scanline off	The shader or Phenomenon works only if scanline rendering is disabled; everything must be rendered by ray tracing. See page 14 for scanline rendering vs. ray tracing.
scanline on	The shader or Phenomenon works only if scanline rendering is enabled (regular or OpenGL).
trace off	The shader or Phenomenon works only if ray tracing is disabled; everything must be rendered with scanline rendering (regular or OpenGL).
trace on	The shader or Phenomenon works only if ray tracing is enabled. This is useful for lens shaders that modify the ray origin or direction, and for material shaders or other shaders that rely on reflection and refraction.
shadow off	The shader or Phenomenon works only if no shadows are rendered.
shadow on	The shader or Phenomenon works only if regular shadow mode is enabled. See page 147 for shadow modes.
shadow sort	The shader or Phenomenon works only if sorted shadow mode is enabled. This and the next option is useful if neighboring shadow shaders and volume shaders along the ray exchange information. For example, some fur shaders use segmented shadow mode to keep track of where rays enter and leave furry space.
shadow segments	The shader or Phenomenon works only if segmented shadow mode is enabled. This is also useful for volume shaders that produce effects such as smoke that gives rise to volumic shadows. Volumic shadows usually require segmented shadow mode.

`face front`	The shader or Phenomenon works only if only front-facing geometry is rendered. See page 124 for details.
`face back`	The shader or Phenomenon works only if only back-facing geometry is rendered.
`face both`	The shader or Phenomenon works only if both front-facing and back-facing geometry is rendered. This is useful if there is solid transparent or refractive geometry. This is a default.
`derivative 1`	The shader or Phenomenon works only if the free-form surface geometry is tessellated with first surface derivatives. This is useful for shaders that require a surface orientation, for example anisotropic material shaders implementing brushed aluminum (see page 104).
`derivative 2`	The shader or Phenomenon works only if the free-form surface geometry is tessellated with second surface derivatives.
`derivative 1 2`	The shader or Phenomenon works only if the free-form surface geometry is tessellated with both first and second surface derivatives.
`object space`	The shader or Phenomenon works only if the scene is defined in object space.
`camera space`	The shader or Phenomenon works only if the scene is defined in camera space. (Not recommended.)
`apply` *list*	This option has a different function than the others, and is not one of the standard options block options. It tells mental ray what kind of shader or Phenomenon is being declared. The *list* is a blank-separated list of the following keywords: the shader or Phenomenon can be used as:

`lens`	lens shader
`material`	material shader
`light`	light shader
`shadow`	shadow shader
`environment`	environment shader
`volume`	volume shader
`texture`	texture shader
`photon`	photon shader
`geometry`	geometry shader
`displace`	displacement shader
`emitter`	photon emitter shader
`output`	output shader
`lightmap`[3.3]	lightmap shader
`photonvol`[3.3]	photon volume shader
`state`[3.3]	state shader

Frequently, shaders can be used for multiple types; for example, material shaders can often also work as shadow shaders and/or photon shaders. For a list of shader types, see page 9. The `apply` flags are not used by mental ray, but by some tools such as the Phenomenon Creator™.

Before rendering, mental ray collects the options of all shaders and Phenomena used in the scene, and adjusts the options read from the scene options block or command line options. Declaration options override the options block and the command line. If declaration options conflict (for example one declaration specifies `trace on` and another `trace off`, mental ray prints an error message and tries to render anyway.

11.5.3   Phenomenon Roots

When a Phenomenon is evaluated during rendering, for example if a Phenomenon is used in place of a material shader in a material and a ray has hit the object that the material is attached to, then mental ray evaluates the shader that is attached to the Phenomenon's *primary root*, called the *root shader*. The primary root is specified in the Phenomenon declaration with a `root` statement:

> `root` *shader*

Typically, the *shader* is an "=" sign followed by the quoted name of a named shader definition. For example, the main root of the Phenomenon on page 283 is attached to the named shader "illum_sh". The result type of the Phenomenon and the root shader must agree. Root statements are only allowed (and required) in Phenomenon declarations but not in shader declarations.

A Phenomenon may also have *secondary roots*. Secondary roots are not called when the Phenomenon is evaluated; they are extracted from all Phenomena used in the scene and are attached to various points in the scene before rendering begins. The following secondary roots are available:

`output`	attaches an output shader or file output statement to the camera. See page 47 for details. Output shaders are often useful if the root shader collects information from the scene, such as where the lights are, and uses an output shader to composite effects like halos on top of the final rendered image.
`lens`	attaches a lens shader to the camera. See page 44 for details. Lens shader roots are also often used to automatically produce local image effects such as lens flares, or to collect image data for output shaders.
`volume`	attaches a volume shader to the camera. See page 166 for details.
`environment`	attaches an environment shader to the camera. See page 108 for details.
`geometry`	attaches a geometry shader to the scene graph instance where the Phenomenon is used. The primary purpose of geometry roots is to automatically insert bounding objects for volume effects.

contour store   attaches a contour store shader to the options block. This is used for contour rendering. See page 261 for details.

contour contrast   attaches a contour contrast shader to the options block, another shader required for contour rendering.

Here is a summary of the syntax for root statements. Typically, these statements are listed last in a Phenomenon, and the *shader* is normally a shader assignment for better readability. As always, shader lists can also be used in place of a single *shader*.

root	*shader*
output	*shader*
output	["*type*"] [*options*] "*format*" "*filename*"
lens	*shader*
volume	*shader*
environment	*shader*
geometry	*shader*
contour store	*shader*
contour contrast	*shader*

Output options are the same as in the camera; see page 301. Finally, priority statements are available to control where output, lens, and volume shaders should be added in the respective shader lists in the camera. Lower numbers sort before higher numbers. Shaders installed directly in the camera definition have priority 0.

output	priority	*priority$_{int}$*
lens	priority	*priority$_{int}$*
volume	priority	*priority$_{int}$*

These statements can appear anywhere in the Phenomenon declaration, and apply to all corresponding shader roots in the Phenomenon.

11.6   User Data Blocks

Sometimes shaders require large amounts of data that is impractical to put into shader parameters for some reason: the size may be too large, or it contains data types that are not supported for shader parameters, or they apply to many shaders and would have to be duplicated many times. For example, a particle database is too large for a shader parameter block. User data blocks[2.1] exist to hold this type of data. They can be defined in three different ways:

data "*name*" [label *label$_{int}$*] *size$_{int}$* [*bytes*]
data "*name*" [label *label$_{int}$*] "*filename*"
data "*name*" [label *label$_{int}$*] "*decl_name*" ([*parameters*])

Each style requires the data block to be named. This name can then be used when defining the value of a shader, instance, or data parameter of type data, and it can be used to attach the data block to

The first style defines the data contents as raw, literal data, listed as strings of single-quoted hexadecimal bytes such as `'4920686174652057696e4e5421'`. Strings may contain up to 1024 two-digit bytes; larger blocks require multiple strings that are being concatenated, such as `'55736520'` `'4c696e7578'`. The total size of the data block must be specified in advance as *size*, which limits the total number of two-digit bytes in the strings. If fewer bytes than this are specified by the strings, the remainder is filled with zeros.

The second style reads the given file into the data block. The data size is the file size.

The third style defines the data block with parameters. Parameters follow the same rules as shader parameters. There must be a matching declaration for *decl_name*. Both shader and phenomenon declarations may be used here (see page 273), or a special form of declaration that specifically exists to declare data blocks:

```
declare data
    "decl_name" ( [ parameters ] )
    [ version version_int ]
end declare
```

Unlike the first two data block styles, parameterized user data blocks work correctly when used on machines with differing byte orders. Since mental ray does not know the type of the contents if the first two styles are used, it cannot swap bytes if necessary. Shaders can query the data block to find out whether the block was created on an incompatible machine, and perform the necessary swapping on the retrieved data.

User data blocks can be referenced in shader parameter lists, options blocks, cameras, geometric objects, light sources, instances, and instance groups using the `data` keyword. In all except shader parameter lists, multiple `data` statements can be specified to chain multiple blocks. Chaining is done by storing a reference to the next block in the previous block. Once this link is stored, it remains intact until rewritten. For example,

```
data "foo" data "bar"
```

stores a reference to *bar* in *foo*, so that wherever *foo* is accessed during rendering it will have a successor *bar*, even where *foo* appeared in the scene definition without being followed with *bar*. Also, if there is another definition in the scene file that assigns a different successor to *foo*, it is undefined which successor ends up being stored in *foo* — it depends on the scene parsing order. This is the same principle as used for shader lists.

11.7   Summary and Performance

A shader is a procedural building block used for a wide variety of purposes — surface shading, light sources, construction of geometry, photon mapping, contour rendering, and many others. A shader is implemented in C or C++, and has a set of user-definable interface parameters (input) and result parameters (output). Available parameter types include simple types such as scalars, colors, vectors, and matrices, as well as structures and arrays of parameters.

A Phenomenon looks similar to a shader but is not implemented in C/C++ but in terms of a set of cooperating shader graphs. Phenomena can be used wherever mental ray expects shaders.

Phenomena can provide various secondary root output nodes that install optional procedural geometry, atmospheres, environments, and others.

Before a shader or Phenomenon can be used, it must be declared, which makes its name and its interface and result parameters known to mental ray. Once declared, it can be defined any number of times, each with a different set of values for its interface parameters.

There are three ways of assigning a value to an interface parameter in a definition:

- by providing a constant value, such as a number for a scalar;

- by shader assignment, which takes the result from another shader ("=" *shader* notation);

- by interface assignment, which takes the value from the interface of the enclosing Phenomenon ("= interface *parameter*" notation). This is only available for shader definitions inside Phenomena.

Shader assignment comes at a cost. Picking up a constant value is fast; it only requires testing a flag in a known place before returning the constant. Shader assignment is slightly more expensive: the shader must be called, introducing a C/C++ function call overhead, and the validity of a result cache must be checked. To optimize performance, a compromise must be found between versatility and size of a shader. A shader that does nothing but add two numbers would never amortize the cost of calling it, and monolithic shaders that are too large to avoid internal shader assignments are inflexible, require frequent recoding, and tend to spend much time checking unused options.

In any case, rendering time is often dominated by shading time. Optimizing the C/C++ shader code, both by mechanical optimization (such as compiler options or register variables) and improvement of the algorithms implemented by the shader (casting fewer secondary rays, for example) has a great impact on rendering performance. See [PROG] for shader writing details.

Chapter 12

Postprocessing and Image Output

The two main uses for image files are textures and output images. Textures are described in detail on page 57. Output images are the result of a rendering operation, usually an RGBA color image containing the rendered image, but it is also possible to generate multiple output images and image types other than RGBA color.

In addition to simply writing the rendered image to a file, it is possible to perform postprocessing to the rendered image before a file is written. This is done by *output shaders*. Output shaders are plug-ins written in C or C++ that operate on entire images and perform operations such as

- compositing, which merges an image with another image,

- motion blurring, which blurs pixels according to their motion and is sometimes preferred to the builtin motion blurring during rendering (see page 237),

- depth of field, which blurs pixels according to their distance to the camera, replacing the standard depth of field that is implemented as a lens shader,

- light halo effects, which are normally added after rendering,

- color correction, which adjusts rendered colors to match colors found in live action footage or special output devices that the image will be used for,

- film grain insertion, which introduces graininess caused by silver halide particles on film stock to make the image blend in and avoid excessive "cleanness" that makes it stand out.

Since output shaders are custom plug-ins, there is no limit on the functionality that can be implemented in an output shader.

Calling output shaders and writing image files is controlled by the output statement list in the camera in the scene file. There are two forms of output statements:

```
output ["type"] "format" [options] "filename"
output "type" shader
```

The first form writes an output image with the name *filename*, and the second calls an output shader. The *shader* consists of a double-quoted shader name followed by parenthesized parameters or a shader assignment using the "=" notation; see page 275 for details. All the statements in the list are executed in the order they are listed in the camera definition, so it is possible to first write the rendered image, then run one or more output shaders over it, and then write the modified image to another file. The options *options* are format-dependent; see below.

12.1 Image Types

Output statements specify a image type. It is optional for file output statements because it can be inferred from the image format (see below) but mandatory for shader output statements. The image type is a comma-separated list of one or more type specifiers, each with an optional "+" or "−" prefix. The following types are supported:

type	comp	bpc	contents
rgba	4	8	RGBA color
rgba_16	4	16	RGBA color
rgba_fp	4	32	RGBA color (floating-point)
rgb	3	8	RGB color
rgb_16	3	16	RGB color
rgb_fp[3.3]	3	32	RGB color (floating-point)
rgbe[3.3]	4	8	RGBE high dynamic range color
a	1	8	alpha channel
a_16	1	16	alpha channel
a_fp[3.3]	1	32	alpha channel (floating-point)
s	1	8	synonymous with a
s_16	1	16	synonymous with a_16
s_fp[3.3]	1	32	synonymous with a_fp
z	1	32	depth channel
n	3	32	normal vectors
m	3	32	motion vectors
tag	1	32	label channel
vta	2	16	low-precision UV basis vector texture
vts	2	16	synonymous with vta
bit	1	1	bitmask channel (1 bit per pixel)

The synonymous types are not separate types but specify alternate conversions when the mental ray rendering software converts one type to another. For example, when writing the rendered color image with an output statement specifying type a or a_16, the alpha channel is written; if type s or s_16 is specified then a grayscale intensity image is generated. Either way, the file ends up with a one-channel image. The bitmask channel and UV vector types are not useful in output statements; they are listed only for completeness.

The *comp* column indicates the number of components; for example, an RGBA color has four (red, green, blue, and alpha). The *bpc* column shows the number of bits per component: 8 is an unsigned byte in the range 0...255, 16 is an unsigned short integer in the range 0...65535 or a signed short integer in the range -32767...32767 in the vector texture case, and 32 is either a floating-point number in the range $-3.4 \cdot 10^{38}$ ... $3.4 \cdot 10^{38}$ (with the exception of the `tag` type, which is stored in a 32-bit unsigned integer in the range 0...4294967295).

mental ray 3.3 has introduced high dynamic range RGBE data types, which compress nonnegative floating-point data into four bytes. This allows very efficient storage of superbright color component values greater than 1, at the cost of losing the alpha channel. High dynamic range is commonly abbreviated HDR. Superbright colors often occur in irradiance maps, such as chrome ball plates that capture the natural light on a set.

Although mental ray internally always works with colors and alpha channels where 0 0 0 stands for black and 1 1 1 stands for white, and where values less than 0.0 and greater than 1.0 are not displayable but are allowed, most of the common image file formats work with byte or integer formats where 0 is black and 255 or 65535 is white. To bring its internal floating-point numbers into this integer range, mental ray clamps values less than 0.0 to 0.0 and values greater than 1.0 to 1.0, and then multiplies by 255 or 65535. The notable exception is the `rgba_fp` type, which allows arbitrary unclipped floating-point values to be stored. This is sometimes useful to preserve super-bright highlights or blacker-than-black colors for special postprocessing, and the `rgbe`[3.3] type, which compresses nonnegative floating-point RGB data to be encoded in only four bytes.

Clamping a color component or alpha to 1.0 normally means that all values greater than 1.0 are replaced with 1.0. mental ray also supports an option to desaturate, which fades colors that contain one or more components with values greater than 1.0 to white. Consider the RGB color (6, 1, 0), which is an extremely bright and slightly yellowish red. Yet, when simply clamping the red component, the result is (1, 1, 0), which is pure yellow. Desaturation results in white instead. Desaturation is enabled by adding the statement

```
desaturate on
```

into the options block in the scene file, or by using the `-desaturate` on option on the command line. No desaturation is done if the target data type can store values greater than 1.0, namely, floating-point and high dynamic range RGBE[3.3] types.

Each type in the list may be prefixed by either "+" or "−". A "+" tells mental ray to smoothly interpolate the frame buffer if there is no sample for a particular pixel, by averaging its neighbors. A "−" does not average but picks an appropriate neighbor and uses its value. This fills in the gaps if infrasampling is enabled by choosing a negative minimum sampling density with the `samples` statement in the options block, which allows mental ray to avoid sampling every pixel in areas where all pixels are similar, and expend samples primarily in areas of high contrast. It also applies to the way oversampled pixels are interpolated. In detail, the meaning of the prefixes when applied to different image types is:

type	*meaning*
-rgba	last color
+rgba	average color
-z	lowest depth
+z	average depth, excluding infinite depths
-n	last normal
+n	average normal, excluding null vectors
-m	last motion vector
+m	average motion vector, excluding null vectors
-tag	last label
+tag	maximum label

In this context, "last" means the last sample taken for the neighboring pixels, which is arbitrary and depends on the sampling direction. If neither "+" nor "−" is specified, "+" is the default for the RGBA frame buffer and "−" for all others.

12.2   Frame Buffers

Before mental ray begins rendering, it collects all the types from all the output statements in the camera, and decides which frame buffers must be maintained during rendering. There are five standard frame buffers, one of which always exists and four optional ones that are created only when required by a type in the output list, and an unlimited number of user-defined frame buffers[1]:

rgba   Contains RGBA colors. It is always created even if no type in the output list requires it, but its type is controlled by the output list: it normally uses 8 bits per component unless the output list contains a type ending in _16, which switches it to 16 bits per component, or type rgba_fp, which switches it to 32 bits (floating-point) per component.

When rendering large images, keep in mind that the master mental ray (not the servers on other hosts) must keep the entire frame buffer in memory at some point, and at a resolution of 4000×4000 pixels (a common slide printer format), a floating-point frame buffer requires $4000 \cdot 4000 \cdot 4 \cdot 4 \approx 244$ MB of memory whereas an 8-bit frame buffer would require only 61 MB.

z   Contains depth values: the distance from the camera to the frontmost object behind a pixel in camera coordinates, after that object's material shader completed (in other words, the material shader can influence what gets stored in the Z buffer). This is not the same as the distance to the camera because only the camera Z axis (which is the negative camera viewing direction) is taken into account and not any vertical or horizontal distances with respect to Z. See page 39 for details on camera coordinates. Infinite distances, where rays through a pixel did not hit any object, are stored as 0.0.

---

[1] mental ray 3.3 and earlier supported up to eight user-defined frame buffers.

n   Contains normal vectors. The procedure is similar to the depth buffer, except that the normal vector and not the depth is stored after the frontmost material shader completes. If there is no object behind a pixel, a null vector is stored.

m   Contains motion vectors. The procedure is again similar to the depth buffer, except that the motion vector and not the depth is stored after the frontmost material shader completes. If there is no object behind a pixel, a null vector is stored.

tag   Contains object labels. Labels can be attached to objects using the `tag` keyword (see page 306). This keyword allows attaching a unique integer to every object, and the label frame buffer will contain the label of the frontmost object behind the pixel. Some output shaders use this for performing special operations only on pixels that show objects tagged in a particular way. Some scene files number objects sequentially; others use the label integer as a bitmap of flags. If there is no object behind a pixel, a null value is stored.

fb0...fb$n$ Up to eight or arbitrarily many[3.4] user frame buffers can be defined with an arbitrary data type. These frame buffers are not accessed by mental ray, but shaders may place sampling data in them during rendering, output shaders can access this data when rendering has finished, and file output statements can write the contents of user frame buffers to disk. User frame buffers, like the predefined frame buffers, have the resolution specified in the camera definition.

For the file output statement, it does not make sense to list more than one type because only one frame buffer can be written to a file, and even this is optional because the frame buffer type can be inferred from the image format (see below). However, output shaders may require more than one frame buffer: for example, a postprocessing depth-of-field shader requires both a depth map and a color frame buffer, so its type would be `"+rgba,-z"`. A postprocessing motion blur output shader might have the type `"+rgba,-m"`.

Before user frame buffers can be used, it must be declared in the options block:

        frame buffer *number* [`"type"`]

The *number* is the user frame buffer *number*, defined to contain data of the type *type*. The first user frame buffer is numbered 0. mental ray 3.3 and earlier were limited to eight user frame buffer; mental ray 3.4 removed that limitation. All standard data types, such as `rgba` or `z`, can be used. If the type begins with a plus sign, as in `+rgba`, the frame buffer is interpolated. If not, or if it begins with a minus sign, it is padded. If the `type` specifier is missing, the frame buffer is deleted. This is useful to remove previously defined frame buffers by incrementally changing the options block. After a user frame buffer is defined, it can be used in output statements. For example:

```
output "fb0,rgba"   "merge" ()
output "rgba" "rgb" "file1.rgb"
output "fb0"  "rgb" "file2.rgb"
```

The first line is an example for an output shader that operates both on user frame buffer 0 and on the standard RGBA color frame buffer. The next line writes the standard color frame buffer to the color image file "file1.rgb", and the last line writes user frame buffer 0 to the image file "file2.rgb". Note that if a shader references a frame buffer that was not properly defined, it will run but all its writes to the missing buffer will be ignored, and all its reads from the missing buffer will result in zeroes (which is transparent black in the color case).

12.3 Image Formats

Image formats are methods of storing data into files on disk. There is a variety of common formats for storage of RGB or RGBA data in file, such as TIFF (Tagged Image File Format) or SGI RGB. File formats are normally identified by a certain file name extension, such as .tiff or .rgb. Some formats have variations, which mental ray considers separate image formats. Each format has a "preferred" data type, such as 8-bit RGBA for TIFF, but some formats also support other data types that must be explicitly requested by naming a data type in the output statement.

Storing high dynamic range RGBE[3.3] data in a file is a problem because HDR is a recent development and there are few file formats available that store it; mostly HDR and OpenEXR[3.3]. For this reason, mental ray 3.3 and higher accept rgbe wherever rgba is listed in the second column in the table below. This will produce an RGBE image file that probably cannot be read properly by image viewers or other tools that expect RGBA data.

The following table lists the image formats that mental ray can write. The first column is the image format name (also the second parameter of the output statement), and the suggested file name extension), and the second column is the data type name (also the first (and optional) parameter of the output statement). If a format accepts multiple data types, the default data type that is used if the the output statement specifies no data type is marked "*".

The *compress* column shows the compression: RLE stands for run-length encoding, which tokenizes spans of identical pixel values and typically achieves a compression of about a factor of two; YUV is a 4:2:2 pixel storage method that encodes luminance (Y) and chrominance (UV) separately, storing one Y for every pixel but only one UV for every two pixels. 4:2:2 encoding is common in the television industry, where video formats like PAL and NTSC (which encode colors as phase angles relative to a color carrier signal) allocate half of the bandwidth to luminance and the other half to color. This exploits the fact that the human eye sees luminance at a higher resolution than color.

format	type	compress	description
pic	rgba	RLE	Softimage color
Zpic	z	—	Softimage depth map (write only)
iff	rgba	RLE	Alias Maya RGBA color[3.3]
	rgb	RLE	Alias Maya RGB color[3.3]
	rgb_fp	RLE	Alias Maya RGB floating-point color[3.3]
	a	RLE	Alias Maya alpha channel[3.3]
	z	RLE	Alias Maya depth map[3.3]
alias	rgb	RLE	old Alias color format
lwi	rgb	RLE	Solidworks color[3.3]
hdr	rgbe	RLE	Radiance high dynamic range color[3.3]
rgb	rgba*	RLE	Silicon Graphics 8-bit RGBA color
	rgb	RLE	Silicon Graphics 8-bit RGB color
	rgba_16	RLE	Silicon Graphics 16-bit RGBA color
	rgb_16	RLE	Silicon Graphics 16-bit RGB color
jpg	rgb	JPEG	JFIF picture
png	rgb	RLE	Portable Network Graphics 8-bit RGB color[3.2]
	rgba	RLE	Portable Network Graphics 8-bit RGBA color[3.2]
exr	a	†	OpenEXR[3.3] 8-bit scalar
	rgb	†	OpenEXR[3.3] 8-bit RGB color
	rgba	†	OpenEXR[3.3] 8-bit RGBA color
	a_h	†	OpenEXR[3.3] half-float scalar
	rgb_h	†	OpenEXR[3.3] half-float RGB color
	rgba_h	†	OpenEXR[3.3] half-float RGBA color
	a_fp	†	OpenEXR[3.3] floating-point scalar
	rgb_fp	†	OpenEXR[3.3] floating-point RGB color
	rgba_fp	†	OpenEXR[3.3] floating-point RGBA color
	z	†	OpenEXR[3.3] depth map
	n	†	OpenEXR[3.3] normal-vector map
	m	†	OpenEXR[3.3] motion-vector map
tif	rgba*	RLE	8-bit RGBA TIFF
	rgba_16	RLE	16-bit RGBA TIFF
	rgba_fp	RLE	floating-point RGBA TIFF[3.x]
	rgb	RLE	8-bit RGB TIFF
	rgb_16	RLE	16-bit RGB TIFF
	rgb_fp	RLE	floating-point RGB TIFF[3.x]
tifu	rgba*	—	8-bit RGBA TIFF
	rgba_16	—	16-bit RGBA TIFF
	rgba_fp	—	floating-point RGBA TIFF[3.x]
	rgb	—	8-bit RGB TIFF
	rgb_16	—	16-bit RGB TIFF
	rgb_fp	—	floating-point RGB TIFF[3.x]
picture	rgb	RLE	Dassault Systèmes CATIA PICTURE
ppm	rgb	—	Portable pixmap, 8-bit P6 binary
tga	rgba	—	Targa color
bmp	rgb	RLE	MS Windows and OS/2 color

format	type	compress	description
qntpal	rgb	YUV	Abekas/Quantel, PAL (720×576)
qntntsc	rgb	YUV	Abekas/Quantel, NTSC (720×486)
rla	rgba	RLE	8-bit or 16-bit Utah/Wavefront color, type A
rlb	rgba	RLE	Utah/Wavefront color, type B
ct	rgba*	—	mental images 8-bit color (3)
	rgba_16	—	mental images 16-bit color (6)
	rgba_fp	—	mental images floating-point color (11)
	rgbe	—	mental images high dynamic range color[3.3](14)
st	a*	—	mental images 8-bit alpha (4)
	a_16	—	mental images 16-bit alpha (7)
	a_fp	—	mental images floating-point alpha[3.3](15)
vt	vta	—	mental images alpha basis vectors (5)
wt	vts	—	mental images intensity basis vectors (5)
zt	z	—	mental images depth map (8)
nt	n	—	mental images normal-vector map (9)
mt	m	—	mental images motion-vector map (12)
tt	tag	—	mental images integer label channel map (10)
bit	bit	—	mental images mask bitmap (13)
map	any	—	mental images memory map
null	—	—	null, deleted on close, write only

[†] OpenEXR[2] in mental ray 3.4 supports the compression modes RLE (default), PIZ (Wavelet-based), ZIP, and PXR24[3]. The first three are lossless; PXR24 is lossy if the written data is stored in full floating-point precision and lossless otherwise. mental ray 3.3 and earlier always use ZIP compression.

Older versions of mental ray (2.0 before 2.0.28 and 2.1 before 2.1.30) did not take the data type named in the output statement into account, and used variants of image format names to control the data type. These pseudo data formats should not be used any longer but are still supported for backwards compatibility:

obsolete format	new format	type	description
tif3	tif	rgb	8-bit RGB TIFF
tif16	tif	rgba_16	16-bit RGBA TIFF
tif16-3	tif	rgb_16	16-bit RGB TIFF
tif16-3u	tifu	rgb_16	16-bit RGB TIFF
tif3u	tifu	rgb	8-bit RGB TIFF
tif16u	tifu	rgba_16	16-bit RGBA TIFF
ct16	ct	rgba_16	mental images 16-bit color (6)
ctfp	ct	rgba_fp	mental images floating-point color (11)
st16	st	a_16	mental images 16-bit alpha (7)

All these formats can store images at any resolution, except the two Abekas/Quantel formats which use the television resolutions according to the CCIR 601 standard only. mental ray will

[2] See page 486 for the OpenEXR copyright notice.
[3] See page 486 for the PXR24 copyright notice.

crop larger images and pad smaller images with black pixels when saving to these formats. Note that the Abekas/Quantel and JFIF/JPEG[4] formats use lossy compression that drops image data during compression; all other formats use lossless compression which does not degrade image quality in any way because all bits are preserved. The JFIF/JPEG format quality defaults to 75%, and mental ray 2.1 and later allow selecting the quality in the range 1...100%. mental ray's implementation of the TIFF format does not support LZW compression due to unacceptable software patent restrictions by Unisys.

Many variants of the formats listed above can be read but not written. For example, `rgb`, `pic`, and `tiff` support different byte layouts that are all accepted, and mental ray can also read but not write the ASCII PPM P3 format and various formats with less than eight bits per component, and several color-mapped formats. The following table lists readable formats, with the number of components (for example, 3 for RGB and 4 for RGBA), the number of bits per component, compression method, and color map capability. Color mapping (cmap) is an alternative to true-color storage that relies on a fixed-size color table that the pixels reference. Since pixels store only an index instead of a full color, the files tend to be smaller, but the very limited range of colors often causes severe aliasing. Note that `Zpic` cannot be read because it contains no format or size information. An asterisk * includes all name variants.

---

[4]This software is based in part on the work of the Independent JPEG Group.

format	description	colormap	compress	comp.	bits/comp.
pic	Softimage image	—	RLE, —	3, 4	8
iff	Alias Maya image[3.3]	—	RLE	1, 3, 4	8, float
alias	old Alias image	—	RLE	3	8
lwi	Solidworks color[3.3]	—	RLE	3	8
hdr	Radiance HDR[3.3]	—	RLE	3	8
rgb	Silicon Graphics color	—	RLE, —	3, 4	8, 16
jpg	JFIF image	—	JPEG	3	8
png	Portable Network Graphics[3.2]	—	RLE, —	3, 4	8
		yes	RLE, —	3, 4	8
exr	OpenEXR[3.3]	—	All	1, 3, 4	half, float
tif*	TIFF image	—	RLE, —	1	1, 4, 8
		—	RLE, —	3, 4	8, 16, float
		yes	RLE, —	3, 4	4, 8
exr	OpenEXR[3.3]	—	various	1, 3, 4	8, 16, float
picture	Dassault Systèmes PICTURE	—	RLE	3	8
ppm	Portable pixmap	—	—	3	8, 16
tga	Targa image	—	RLE, —	1, 3, 4	8
		—	RLE, —	3	5
		—	RLE, —	4	5/1
		yes	RLE, —	3, 4	8
bmp	MS Windows/OS2 bitmap	—	—	3, 4	8
		yes	—	3, 4	1, 4, 8
rla/rlb	Wavefront image	—	RLE	3, 4	8, 16
qnt	Quantel/Abekas YUV image	—	YUV	3	3
ct*	mental images texture	—	—	4	8, 16, float
st	mental images alpha texture	—	—	1	8, 16
vt/wt	mental images basis vectors	—	—	2	16
zt	mental images depth channel	—	—	1	float
nt/mt	mental images vectors	—	—	3	float
tt	mental images tag channel	—	—	1	32
bit	mental images bit mask	—	—	1	1
map	memory mapped textures	—	—	any	any

The Targa format with 5/1 bits per component allocates 5 bits each for R, G, and B, and one bit for A. Lines with comma-separated alternatives allow all possible combinations within that line.

The mental images formats ct ... bit are simple uncompressed formats designed for image exchange with custom utilities. Some of them are used to store data specific to mental images (such as tag and motion vector information). The structure of the files is very simple: the file begins with a header followed by uncompressed image data, pixel by pixel beginning in the lower left corner. Each pixel consists of one to four 8-bit, 16-bit, or 32-bit component values, in RGBA, XYZ, or UV order. The header consists of a "magic number" byte identifying the format (the number in parentheses in the first table above), a null byte, width and height as unsigned shorts, and two unused null bytes reserved for future use. All shorts, integers, and floats are big-endian (most significant byte first).

The map format is a special memory mapped format designed for memory mapped textures. It is recommended for color textures because of its speed and low memory usage. See page 70 for a discussion of memory mapped textures and how to create map files.

When reading image files, mental ray will recognize the image format regardless of the filename or extension. When writing image files, mental ray must be given the image format name and the file name separately:

```
output [ colorprofile "profilename"³·⁴]
       [ "type" ]
       "format"
       [ options ]
       "filename"
```

This allows specification of the image format without being bound to a specific file name or extension. This is particularly useful to optimize performance and memory requirements: the imf_copy tool can convert any file format to the more efficient .map format (-p -r options). The resulting .map files can then be stored under the old names so it is not necessary to change the file names in the scene file.

If specified, the color profile[3.4] controls the color space written to the image file. This option only works if a color profile was also specified in the options block; see page 419. Before a color space name can be referenced, it must have been defined; see page 162 for details.

With mental ray 2.1 or later, the options *options* may specify the JPEG quality if the format is jpg, for example:

```
output "jpg" quality 75 "myfile.jpg"
```

The quality is in the range 1...100. The default is 75. Higher quality settings result in larger picture files. Note that the optional image type was omitted because jpg implies the type rgb. JPEG (Joint Picture Experts Group) is the name of the standard, and JFIF (JPEG File Interchange Format) is the official name of the file format. However, mental ray uses the common convention of using jpg instead of jfif.

mental ray 3.4 or later provides an option to select the compression mode if the output format is OpenEXR:

```
output "exr" compress "mode" "myfile.exr"
```

The available compression modes are none, rle, piz, zip, and pxr24. These mean no compression, run-length encoding, wavelet-based compression, Huffman dictionary compression, and an efficient but lossy (for floating-point data, which loses 8 of 32 bits) rounding method, respectively. The fastest ones are normally RLE or ZIP; PIZ usually achieves better compression but is much slower; if there are many very large textures a scene can render much slower. The OpenEXR manual recommends PXR24 for depth maps. mental ray 3.3 and earlier always use ZIP compression; mental ray 3.4 defaults to RLE.

Chapter 13

Geometric Objects **

Geometry modeling is a complex domain. Normally, special modeling programs are required to create precise geometry data. This chapter provides a detailed description of modeling geometry with simple mi scene file objects, including some underlying mathematical concepts. It can be skipped on first reading.

The mental ray rendering software supports five types of geometry: polygons, free-form surfaces, subdivision surfaces, and two-dimensional and three-dimensional curves. (3D curves are also called space curves). Subdivision surfaces and space curves are supported in mental ray 2.1 and higher. They require an optional modeling library, and are not described here[1]. The basic scene element is the *object*, which contains either definitions of one or more polygons, or one or more free-form surfaces. Both types cannot be combined in a single object. The syntax for polygonal geometric objects is:

```
object " object_name"
    [ tagged        [ on | off ]]
    [ visible       [ on | off ]]
    [ reflection    modeint ]3.4
    [ refraction    modeint ]3.4
    [ transparency  modeint ]3.4
    [ trace         [ on | off ]]
    [ shadow        [ on | off | modeint3.4 ]]
    [ shadowmap     [ on | off ]3.3
    [ caustic       [ on | off | modeint ]]
    [ globillum     [ on | off | modeint ]]
    [ finalgather   [ on | off | modeint ]]3.4
    [ hardware      [ on | off ]]3.3
    [ tag           labelint ]
    [ data          "data_name" | null ]
    [ box           low_vector high_vector ]3.x
    [ motion box    low_vector high_vector ]3.x
    [ max displace  disp ]3.x
```

---

[1] For more information, refer to the documentation of the mental matter™ product.

```
    [ face           front|back|both ]³·⁴
    group
        vector list
        vertex list
        polygons
    end group
    [ more groups ]
  end object
```

Free-form surface objects are similar, but free-form surfaces are listed instead of polygons, and a variety of optional statements describing curves, approximations, connections, and other features are available in the group ... end group block. See section 13.3 for details.

Every object must have a name that is referenced in instance statements (see page 371) for placing the object into 3D space, which is necessary for the object to take part in rendering (unless the object is passed as a shader parameter to a geometry shader that performs extra manipulations before it, or a derived object, is placed into 3D space with an instance).

There is a number of optional flags that can be applied to an object, in any order. Unless otherwise noted, if an on/off-type flag is missing, it defaults to off, and if the flag is present but the on/off argument is missing, it defaults to on.

tagged [on|off]   If on, the object uses tagged material inheritance, which means that its polygons and free-form surfaces specify 32-bit label integers instead of materials. The label integers can either select which inherited material to use, or can be picked up as user data by shaders to perform specialized shading. See page 384 for details on tagged inheritance.

visible [on|off]   If on, the object is visible to primary rays that directly hit it after leaving the camera (or its lenses). This flag does not apply to rays that undergo reflection or refraction before hitting the object, or to shadow rays.

reflection $mode_{int}$³·⁴   If the *mode* is 1, the object can be reflected, and other objects show its reflection, assuming that the materials of the other objects compute reflection by casting reflection rays. If the *mode* is 2, the object is reflecting and casts secondary rays to other objects. If the *mode* is 3, the object both receives and casts reflections. The default for *mode* is 2.

refraction $mode_{int}$³·⁴   Similar to the reflection statement, but applies to refraction. The default for *mode* is 2.

transparency $mode_{int}$³·⁴   Similar to the reflection statement, but applies to transparency. Transparency is a special case of refraction where the index of refraction is exactly 1.0 so that the transparency ray continues in the same direction is the incoming ray; the distinction is important for performance reasons because refraction requires ray tracing while transparency can make do with the faster scanline rendering algorithm. The decision whether to use refraction or transparency is made by the material shader. The default for *mode* is 3.

trace [on|off]

This statement has become obsolete in mental ray 3.4. For backwards compatibility, trace on is equivalent to reflection 3 refraction 3 finalgather 3, and trace off is equivalent to reflection 2 refraction 2 finalgather 2. The default is 2. Effectively, mental ray 3.4 allows finer control over the three types of secondary rays than the old trace statement did.

shadow [on|off|$mode_{int}$ [3.4]]

If the *mode* is 1, the object casts shadows onto other objects, provided that the light shader computes shadows. If the *mode* is 2, the receives shadows from other objects, again assuming that the light shader computes shadows. If the *mode* is 3, the object both casts and receives shadows. The default for *mode* is 2. The numeric modes are available in mental ray 3.4 and higher; for backwards compatibility off is equivalent to 2 (receive only), and on is equivalent to 3.

shadowmap [on|off[3.3]]

This statement has an effect only if the shadow mode is 1 or 3. If set to on, the object casts shadow map shadows; of set to off it will be omitted from the shadow map. The default is on. This is useful if the object is actually fully transparent because it only acts as a bounding hull of a volumic effect, and its shadow shader lets rays pass unchanged. Shadowmaps do not call shadow shaders and would assume that the object is fully opaque, unless prevented from considering the object by setting the shadowmap mode to off.

caustic on|off[2.1]

If on, the object participates in caustic photon tracing. This is the default. If off, caustic photons pass through the object without interacting with it in any way, regardless of what the caustic mode numbers below specify.

caustic [$mode_{int}$]

Specifies how the object deals with caustics (see page 190). The following arguments are supported:

0   The object neither casts nor receives caustics.

1   The object casts caustics but does not receive them.

2   The object receives caustics but does not cast them.

3   The object both casts and receives caustics.

If the `caustic` keyword is missing, the mode defaults to 0. If the `caustic` keyword is present but neither `off` nor the mode integer is specified, the mode defaults to 3. For example, to create caustics on the floor of a swimming pool the water surface object has mode 1, and the floor object has mode 2. See also the `caustic` mode in the options block.

globillum on|off

If on, the object participates in global illumination photon tracing. This is the default. If off, global illumination photons pass through the object without interacting with it in any way, regardless of what the globillum mode numbers below specify.

globillum [*mode*$_{int}$]

Specifies how the object deals with global illumination (see page 198). The modes work the same way as the numeric caustic modes described above, but apply to global illumination photons[2.1].

finalgather on|off[3.4]

If on, the object participates in final gathering. This is the default. If off, final gathering rays pass the object without interacting with it in any way, regardless of the finalgather mode below, or the (obsolete) trace statement.

finalgather [*mode*$_{int}$][3.4]

Specifies how the object deals with final gathering (see page 206). The modes work the same way as the numeric caustic modes described above, but apply to final gathering rays.

hardware on|off[3.3]

If on, the object will be rendered using a hardware acceleration board, if enabled in the options block. If off, the object will always be rendered with software rendering. The default is off, but it can be overridden with a `hardware all` statement in the options block which will behave as if all objects in the scene had their hardware flags set to on. Hardware rendering is extremely fast but has a limited range of shading features.

tag *label*$_{int}$

The object carries a 32-bit label integer *object label*. This is independent of the polygon or free-form surface labels enabled with the `tagged` flag. Object labels are useful to identify objects in the final rendered image if an appropriate output statement was used to enable a label channel image, which shows the label of the frontmost object behind every image pixel. The object label can also be used in shaders to allow special treatment of some objects. If labels are not otherwise used, it is a good practice (but not required) to assign sequential numbers to all objects in a scene.

data "*data_name*" | null

This statement allows attaching user data to the object. User data is not used by mental ray but can be accessed by shaders. See page 287 for details. If the `null` keyword is used instead of the name of a user data block, any existing user data block reference is removed from the object; this is useful for incremental changes. If more than one `data` statement is specified, they are connected to a chain in the order specified.

box *low high*[3.x]

Specifies the bounding box of the object. For a polygonal object, this is simply the three smallest and the three largest vector components of all vertex point-in-space positions (that is, the vectors referenced directly after the v statements but not n, t, and so on). For example, a sphere object with a radius of 1 and centered at the origin would have a *low* of (-1, -1, -1) and a *high* of (1, 1, 1). Free-form surface objects are more complicated because for some bases such as NURBS, the control points are not especially close to the actual surface, so the bounding box derived from them would be too loose. If a bounding box is too large, this will cause mental ray to "see" it too early during rendering and use up more memory, but the scene will render correctly; if a bounding box is too small the object is seen too late and might become truncated. If no bounding box is specified, mental ray will compute one based on the vertex or control point positions.

motion box *low high*[3.x]

This statement must be supplied if three conditions are met: the object has a `box` statement; the object has motion vectors or motion transformations; and motion blurring is enabled. While the `box` statement describes the minimum and maximum points in space, the `motion box` describes the minimum and maximum motion vector components. For example, if there are only two motion vectors, (1, 2, 3) and (4, 0, -1), the *low* would be (1, 0, -1) and *high* would be (4, 2, 3). Motion transformations must be factored in as if the transformation had been created by adding or extending motion vectors. Again, if missing, mental ray computes the motion box based on all motion vectors and transformations for the object.

max displace *disp*[3.x]

Specifies the maximum displacement of the object, which is the maximum absolute value that any displacement shaders applied to the object will return. The bounding box specified by the `box` statement (or mental ray's automatically computed bounding box if there is no `box` statement) will be expanded all around by this value. If missing, it defaults to 0.0. Unlike mental ray 2.1, mental ray 3.x depends on this statement — if it is missing on an object that is known to have displacement shaders, mental ray 3.x is forced to tessellate the object immediately to find its real bounding box, to avoid truncating it during rendering. This is inefficient and defeats the work-on-demand approach of mental ray 3.x.

`face front|back|both`[3.4]   Specifies whether the object will be seen from the front side, the back side, or both. Normally this is determined by the global face mode in the options block, but this can be overridden per object. The default is the face mode specified in the options block.

The most common combination of flags is `visible trace shadow`, which makes all objects visible to all rays, and makes them cast shadows.

It is possible to use multiple `group ... end group` blocks in an object, but this is not recommended. mental ray will automatically subdivide multi-group objects into an instance group with multiple sub-objects, so there is no advantage over creating multiple objects in the scene file. Explicit instance groups also have the advantage that the object instances are controllable individually, and allow finer incremental changes. (See page 371 for more details on instance groups and instances.)

A group may contain either only polygons or only free-form surfaces. For an introduction and definition of polygons and free-form surfaces, see page 6. The following sections discuss their definition in the .mi language. The rest of this chapter is a condensed version of the scene geometry chapter in volume 2 of this series.

13.1   Vectors and Vertices

Both polygons and free-form surfaces are built in three stages: first, an XYZ vector list is given, followed by a vertex list that builds polygon vertices or free-form surface control points from these vectors, and finally the polygons or free-form surfaces themselves.

The *vector list* contains 3D vectors that can describe points in space, normals, texture vertices, basis vectors, or motion vectors. Vectors are anonymous, they are triples of floating-point numbers separated by whitespace without inherent meaning[2]. Vectors are numbered beginning with 0. Numbering restarts at 0 whenever a new object group starts. Vector and vertex lists in different object groups, and in different objects, are independent of each other.

All objects are specified in either camera or object space, depending on the `object space` or `camera space` statements in the options block. In camera space mode, the camera is assumed to sit at the coordinate origin and point down the negative Z axis, and objects are defined using camera space coordinates. In object space mode, the camera location is determined by its instance, and objects are defined in local object coordinates that are positioned in the scene with the object instance. Typically, the object space coordinate $(0, 0, 0)$ is at the center of the object. Object space is recommended since camera space does not permit multiple instancing and is retained only for backwards compatibility with mental ray 1.9.

---

[2]There is a special format for binary vectors that is more efficient (both in the space on disk and the time to read them into memory) than vectors defined by three numbers. A binary vector consists of a backquote ('), followed by twelve bytes forming the big-endian memory image of three IEEE-854 numbers of the C type "float", followed by another backquote. This format is useful for automatic scene translators but is not at all human-readable, and some text editors are unable to work with such files because binary vectors can contain null bytes and other codes that editors may find hard to digest.

Vertices build on vectors. In the mi language, there is no syntactical difference between polygon vertices and control points for free-form surfaces; both are collectively referred to as "vertices" here. All vertices define a point in space along with optional vertex normals, derivatives, motion vectors, and zero or more texture and basis vectors. A single vertex is defined as follows:

    v $index_{int}$
    [n $index_{int}$]
    [d $index_{int}$ $index_{int}$ [$index_{int}$ [$index_{int}$ $index_{int}$]]]
    [t $index_{int}$ ... [$index_{int}$ $index_{int}$]]
    [m $index_{int}$]
    [u $index_{int}$]
    ...

A vertex list is a sequence of such vertex definitions, each beginning with a v reference.

v   specifies the point in space.

n   specifies the vertex normal vector (ignored when the vertex is used as a curve or surface control point). Vertex normals always have length 1 and point away from the front face of the polygon. If missing, polygon meshes have a faceted look because the normal and hence shading changes abruptly at the edges of each polygon; attaching normal vectors to vertices allows smoothing across polygon edges because lighting is based on normal vectors. In typical polygonal geometry, normal vectors are almost always present.

m   specifies the motion vector (the distance the point moves during the shutter open time specified in the options block). This is one of the two methods for creating motion blur; it is useful for objects that change shape rapidly, which requires specifying the motion for each vertex rather than for the entire object as a whole. For rigid moving objects, it is sufficient to attach a single motion transformations to the instance of the object. Up to 15 m statements can be attached to a single v block to define a motion path, where each vector defines the point where the object has moved relative to the v vector of the fraction of the shutter interval [0, 1]. The v vector applies to time 0, and the last motion vector applies to time 1. See pages 237 and 240 for the difference between motion vectors and motion transformations.

t   specifies a texture vector with an optional XY basis vector pair for bump map calculation. There may be up to 64 t statements for any given v statement. (The texture and basis vectors are ignored when the vertex is used as a curve or surface control point. See page 64.)

d   specifies first or second surface derivatives, or both. First derivatives describe the UV parametric gradient of a surface, second derivatives describe the curvature. For surfaces they can be computed analytically but not for polygons, so the d keyword allows explicit specification of derivatives. If d is followed by two indices they are taken to reference the first derivative $\partial S/\partial U$ and $\partial S/\partial V$ (with S being the surface); if three indices follow they reference the second derivative $\partial^2 S/\partial U^2$, $\partial^2 S/\partial V^2$, and $\partial^2 S/(\partial U \partial V)$; and if five indices follow the first two describe the first derivative and the next three the second derivative. Derivatives are not used by mental ray, they are made available to shaders only.

u   specifies a user vector. No constraints are imposed on user vectors. mental ray does not operate on them in any way, they are passed through with the vertex and can be picked up by the shader. There may be up to 255 user vectors in a vertex.

Every vertex begins with a v statement and ends with the next v statement or with the start of the geometry description. If the vertex is used as a control point, it is not meaningful to specify a vertex normal or any other optional vector except motion vectors. All occurrences of *index* index the vector list; 0 is the first vector in this group. Vector definitions of different types (for example, v and n) may not reference the same vector. As stated before, all vectors are 3D. If the third coordinate is not used (as is the case for 2D texture vertices, for 2D curve control points, and for special 2D surface points) it should be set to 0. If both the second and third coordinates are unused (as is the case for special 1D curve points), they should both be set to 0.

Vertices themselves are numbered, independently of vectors. The first vertex in every group is numbered 0. The geometry description is referencing vertices by vertex index, just as vertices are referencing vectors by vector index. This results in a three-stage definition of geometry:

1. List of vectors

2. List of vertices

3. List of geometry

The reason for this three-stage process is to allow both sharing of vectors and sharing of vertices. This is best illustrated with an example. Consider two triangles ABC and ABD sharing an edge AB. (This example will use the simplest form of polygon syntax that will be described later in this section.) The simplest definition of this two-triangle object is:

```
object "twotri"
     visible trace shadow
     group
          0.0   0.0   0.0
          1.0   0.0   0.0
          0.0   1.0   0.0
          1.0   0.0   0.0
          1.0   1.0   0.0
          0.0   1.0   0.0

          v 0
          v 1
          v 2
          v 3
          v 4
          v 5

          p "material_name" 0 1 2
          p 3 4 5
     end group
end object
```

The first three vectors are used to build the first three vertices, which are used in the first triangle.

The remaining three vectors build the next three vertices, which are used for the second triangle. Two vectors are listed twice and can be shared:

```
object "twotri"
    visible trace shadow
    group
        0.0    0.0    0.0
        1.0    0.0    0.0
        0.0    1.0    0.0
        1.0    1.0    0.0

        v 0
        v 1
        v 2
        v 1
        v 3
        v 2

        p "material_name" 0 1 2
        p 3 4 5
    end group
end object
```

The order of vector references is non-contiguous to ensure that the second triangle is in counter-clockwise order. Two vertices are redundant and can also be removed by sharing:

```
object "twotri"
    visible trace shadow
    group
        0.0    0.0    0.0
        1.0    0.0    0.0
        0.0    1.0    0.0
        1.0    1.0    0.0

        v 0
        v 1
        v 2
        v 3

        p "material_name" 0 1 2
        p 1 3 2
    end group
end object
```

The need for sharing both vectors and vertices becomes apparent when vertex normal vectors are introduced:

```
object "twotri"
```

```
        visible trace shadow
        group
             0.0    0.0    0.0
             1.0    0.0    0.0
             0.0    1.0    0.0
             1.0    1.0    0.0
             0.0    0.0    1.0

             v 0     n 4
             v 1     n 4
             v 2     n 4
             v 3     n 4

             p "material_name" 0 1 2
             p 1 3 2
        end group
    end object
```

In this last example, both vector sharing and vertex sharing takes place. The normal vector is actually redundant: if no normal vector is specified, mental ray uses the polygon normal, which in this case agrees with the specified normal vector. Even if vertex normals are explicitly specified, defaulting to the polygon normal is slightly more efficient than interpolating vertex normals.

13.2   Polygonal Geometry

Polygonal geometry was first introduced in page 32 without detailed explanation. This section gives an in-depth description of the definition of polygonal geometry in the .mi language. For efficiency reasons, mental ray distinguishes simple convex polygons from general concave polygons or polygons with holes. Both are distinguished by keyword, c for convex without holes, and p for general polygons:

> c ["*material_name*"] *vertex_ref_list*
> p ["*material_name*"] *vertex_ref_list* [hole *vertex_ref_list* ...]

The c statement is slightly more efficient because mental ray does not need to test for convexity. If the enclosing object has the tagged flag set, mandatory label integers must be given instead of the optional materials:

> c *label_number*$_{int}$ *vertex_ref_list*
> p *label_number*$_{int}$ *vertex_ref_list* [hole *vertex_ref_list* ...]

The results are undefined if the c keyword is used but the polygon is not convex. The p keyword also renders both convex and concave polygons correctly, and allows specification of holes, using one or more hole keywords, each followed by a *vertex_ref_list*. If all polygons within the same object group are simple convex polygons containing three sides (that is, triangles), mental ray will pre-process them in a more efficient manner than non-triangular polygons. See page 7 for an illustration of convex and concave polygons.

A *vertex_ref_list* is a list of non-negative *index* integers that reference vertices in the vertex list of the group described in the previous section. The first vertex in the vertex list is numbered 0. Any vertex index can be used in either polygon or hole *vertex_ref_list*s. A polygon with *n* vertices is defined by *n* index values in the vertex list following the material name. The order of the polygon vertices is important. A counter-clockwise ordering of the vertices yields a front-facing polygon. The vertex list of a hole may be ordered either way. It is not necessary (and not allowed) to list the first vertex index again at the end to "close" the polygon or hole loop. Therefore, an *n*-sided polygon or hole must have *n* vertex indices.

The material name is optional. If specified, it must be defined before the object definition that contains the polygon definition, in a statement like

```
material "material_name"
    ...
end material
```

(See page 49 for details.) Once a material name has been specified for a polygon, it becomes the default material. All following polygons may omit the material name; polygons without explicit material use the same material as the last polygon that does have an explicit material. Omitting materials improves parsing performance. If no material is specified, the material from the closest instance up the scene graph is used instead. This is called *material inheritance*. Tagged objects always inherit their material from the instance.

The triangulation algorithm is different for the two cases: convex polygons without holes (c keyword) and polygons which contain holes or are concave (p keyword). Convex polygons without holes are triangulated by picking a vertex on the outer loop and connecting it with every other vertex except its direct neighbors. If polygons are not flagged by the c keyword and do not have any holes an automatic convexity test is performed and if they are indeed convex they are triangulated as described.

The tessellation of polygons assumes that polygons are "reasonably" planar. This means that every polygon will be tessellated, but the exact subdivision into triangles does not attempt to minimize curvature. If the curvature is low, different tessellations cannot be distinguished, but consider the extreme case where the four corners of a regular tetrahedron are given as polygon vertices: the resulting polygon will consist of two triangles, but it cannot be predicted which of the four possible triangles will be chosen.

For tessellation of the polygon into triangles, a projection plane is chosen such that the extents of the projection of the bounding box of the (outer) loop have maximal size. If the projection of the polygon onto that plane changes the topology the results of the triangulation will be erroneous.

Figure 13.1 shows an example. The shaded polygons are the ones found in the scene file. Choosing the projection plane fails for the right polygon because the polygon vertices A and B are projected onto the same point on the projection plane.

If a textured polygon's material contains a displacement shader the vertices are shifted along the normals accordingly. If an approximation statement is given triangles are subdivided until the specified criteria are met; see page 337 for details.

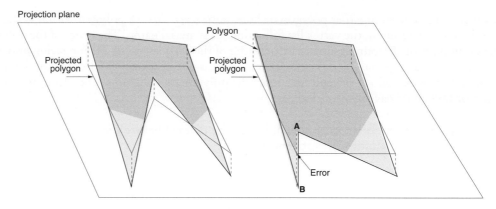

Figure 13.1: Polygon projection.

13.3   Free-Form Surface Geometry

This sections is an introduction to free-form surface definition with the mental ray scene language. The description of the underlying principles sacrifices mathematical precision for readability. Refer to [Bartels 87], [Foley 96], [Farin 97], and [Piegl 97] for the mathematical foundations.

Free-form surfaces are polynomial patches. Supported basis types include Bézier, Taylor, B-spline, cardinal, and basis-matrix form. Any type can be rational or non-rational. Surfaces can be explicitly or automatically connected to one another, or may be defined to contain explicitly defined points or curves in their approximation. Various approximation types including (regular) parametric, spatial, curvature-dependent, view-dependent, and combinations are available. Surfaces may be bounded by a trimming curve, and may contain holes.

Surface geometry, like polygonal geometry, is defined by a series of sections. An object containing only surface geometry follows this broad outline, expanding on the overview on page 303:

```
object "object_name"
    [ ... ]
    basis list
    group
        vector list
        vertex list
        [ list of curves ]
        surface
        [ list of surface derivative requests ]
        [ list of texture or vector surfaces ]
        ...                                        # more surfaces
        [ list of approximation statements ]
        [ list of connection statements ]
    end group
end object
```

Curves, surfaces, approximations, and connections may be interspersed as long as names are defined before they are used. For example, a curve must come before the surface it is trimming, and an approximation must come after the surface to be approximated. Texture and vector texture surfaces must always directly follow the surface they apply to. The individual sections are:

- The **basis list** must be specified at the beginning of the object definition, just before the group begins. Curve and surface definitions specify their degrees and types (such as Bézier or B-spline) by naming the appropriate basis or bases.

- See page 308 for details on the **vector list** and **vertex list**.

- **Curves** are defined in surface UV coordinates, and are used for trimming, holes, and special curves. Trimming a surface means to cut away portions that fall outside the trimming curve; holes cut away portions inside the hole curve. Special curves are always included in the tessellation; they can be used to define features like sharp creases that need to be tessellated consistently. Surfaces may also be connected along trimming curves.

- The **surface** list consists of `surface` statements, much like polygonal geometry consists of `p` and `c` statements. A surface statement may optionally be followed by surface derivative request statements and one or more `texture surface` or `vector surface` statements.

- The **approximation** statements give additional information about how curves and surfaces are to be approximated. Various modes such as parametric, regular parametric, curvature-dependent, and view-dependent approximations can be selected, along with the precision. If there are approximation statements in the options block, they override any approximation statements in the objects; see below.

mental ray distinguishes between *surfaces* and *patches*. A patch is the smallest unit that can be described with a given basis; in the cubic Bézier case this would be the result of a set of 4×4 control points. A surface consists of one or more patches, created by specifying longer parameter vectors and more control points. As described below, control points in surfaces consisting of multiple patches may control multiple neighboring patches. In the simplest case (degree 1 in any basis or Bézier of any degree) the last control point of a patch is also the first control point of the next patch; in other cases (for example, B-spline) the last *degree* control points of a patch are the first *degree* control points of the next patch.

13.3.1   Bases

When surfaces and curves are present in an object, it is mandatory that at least one basis is first defined in the object. Bases define the degree and type of curves or surfaces. Curves and surfaces reference bases by name. Every surface needs two bases, one for the U and one for the V parameter direction. Both can have a different degree, but must have the same type (for example, rational Bézier in U and cardinal in V is not allowed). There are five basis types:

```
basis "basis_name" [ rational ] bezier degree_int
basis "basis_name" [ rational ] bspline degree_int
basis "basis_name" [ rational ] cardinal
basis "basis_name" [ rational ] matrix degree_int stepsize_int basis_matrix
basis "basis_name" [ rational ] taylor degree_int
```

The basis is intimately connected with the `curve` or `surface` statement which references it. The following discussion describes curves but also generalizes to surfaces — curves only have one parameter direction while surfaces have two (U and V), but both are defined with similar bases, parameter vectors, and control points.

Curves and surfaces contain a *parameter vector* (called *knot vector* in the B-spline case), followed by the actual control point (vertex) references. Parameter or knot vectors are lists of monotonically increasing (that is, every number may be equal to but not less than the preceding number) floating-point numbers that specify distances along a curve, and allow control over how large the section of the curve is that a given set of control points controls. Exactly which control points control which section of the curve depends on the basis type.

In the B-spline case, knot vectors whose parameter values increase in constant steps are called *uniform*; if the differences between successive numbers vary the knot vector is called *non-uniform*. If knots are close, the curve shrinks in the corresponding region; larger differences stretch the curve. In the Bézier case, the curve does not change but its parameter space does, which leaves the 3D shape unchanged but in the surface case, textures are stretched. The type of the basis establishes that correspondence between curve sections and control points.

In the free-form surface case, two bases are required, one for the U direction and one for the V direction. Although there is only one basis and one parameter or knot vector per direction, the entire grid of control points must be specified, basically creating a grid of curves.

The following sections describe the different basis types. Again, basis types are described in terms of curves, but the description also applies to surfaces. Surfaces require two bases, one for the U and one for the V direction, and a mesh rather than a sequence of control points.

13.3.1.1 Bézier

The basis type specifies how control points affect the curve. The Bézier basis makes the curve run through the first and last points of each segment. Each segment requires *degree* + 1 control points. If there is more than one segment, the last control point of a segment is also the first control point of the next, such that *n* segments require $n \cdot degree + 1$ control points. For degree 3 (the most common case, also called *cubic*), two segments require 7 ($2 \cdot 3 + 1$) control points, as shown in figure 13.2:

The white points are control points, joined with thin lines to show their order. Note that the curve runs through (or, in technical terms, *interpolates*) control point 0, 3, and 6, and that the edges joining them to their neighbor control points form tangents to the curve. In the diagram, the control points 2, 3, and 4 form a straight line, so that the tangents on both sides of point 3 are equal and the curve does not bend sharply at point 3. The curve is always entirely contained in the *convex hull* of the control points, which is a curve that connects the outermost control points like a rubber band wrapped around them would.

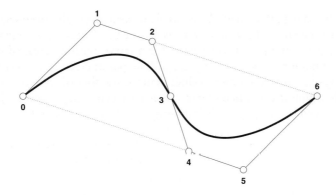

Figure 13.2: Bézier curve of degree 3.

13.3.1.2 B-Spline

The B-spline basis does not cause the curve to pass through the control points in the general case. One could visualize them as magnets that tug at the curve. See figure 13.3 for a degree 3 example.

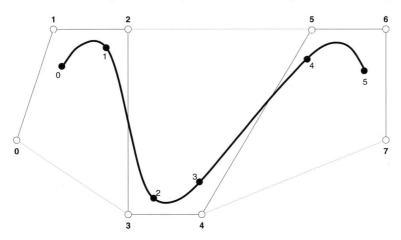

Figure 13.3: B-spline curve of degree 3.

B-splines approximate a series of m control points with a curve consisting of $m - degree$ segments; m must be larger than $degree$. In particular, for $m = degree + 1$ there is just one segment. Segment endpoints are called *knots* and the parameters values at such points are called *knot values*. There is a total of $m - degree + 1$ knots. For $m = degree + 1$ this is equal to 2, and the knots are the initial and final points of the single segment. There are always $degree - 1$ fewer knots than control points.

The first segment, between the first and second knot, is controlled by the first $degree + 1$ control points. The second segment is controlled by the $degree + 1$ control points starting at the second control point, and so on. Another way of thinking about this is that a control point can only influence $degree + 1$ segments.

To specify the B-spline basis affected by the control points for a single curve segment $2(degree+1)$ parameter values are needed. If a curve consists of several segments, the various parameter domains are sequential. The parameter vector for a curve with m control points is given by $m + degree + 1$ parameter values $t_0, \ldots, t_{m+degree}$. The parameter vector is often also called the *knot vector*. It always has $degree+1$ more values than the number of control points. Starting with segment 0, the i-th segment takes parameter values between $t_{i+degree}$ and $t_{i+degree+1}$. Therefore the knot values are given by $t_{i+degree}$ with i running from 0 to $m - degree$.

In the example of the degree-3 curve in figure 13.3 the eight white dots are the control points and the six $(8 - (degree - 1))$ knots are shown as black dots. Its knot vector consists of twelve $(8 + (degree + 1))$ elements -3 -2 -1 0 1 2 3 4 5 6 7 8, that is, $t_0 = -3, t_1 = -2, t_2 = -1, t_3 = 0 \ldots, t_{11} = 8$. We therefore have a parameter domain $[0, 5]$ and knots (black dots) that correspond to knot values 0 1 2 3 4 5. The first segment, between knot 0 and knot 1, is controlled by control points 0...3; the second segment by control points 1...4, and so on. For example, moving control point 5 will only affect the part of the curve between knot 2 and knot 5. The rest of the B-spline section will be examples describing how changes in the knot vector or control points affect the curve.

The example curve in figure 13.3 is open — that is, the endpoints do not meet. It can be closed by repeating the first three control points at the end of the list and add the values 9, 10, and 11 to the knot vector.

Sometimes it is useful to give the same number two or more times in a knot vector. This is called *increasing the multiplicity* of the knot (more precisely, of the knot value) in the knot vector. For example, increasing the multiplicity shrinks a segment of a B-spline curve down to a point, which introduces abrupt bends: the section where the curve would normally have a smooth bend has shrunk to a point. Increasing the multiplicity of a knot value can also be used to bring the curve closer to the control points. See figure 13.4 for an example.

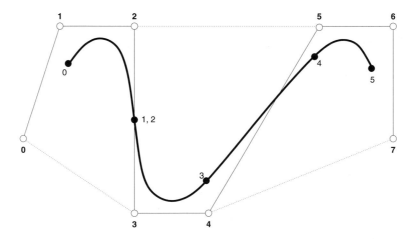

Figure 13.4: B-spline curve, degree 3, knot of multiplicity 2.

The knot vector for this curve is -3 -2 -1 0 1 1 2 3 4 5 6 7, with a new parameter range $[0 \ldots 4]$. Note that this knot vector is no longer uniform because successive values no longer have constant increments — all successive values differ by 1 except one that differs by 0. This constrains the double knot (1, 2) to lie on the line between control points 2 and 3. This line is the intersection of the convex hull of the control points 1, 2, and 3 with the convex hull of the control points 2, 3, and 4.

Further increasing the multiplicity constrains the knot on the curve to a point, as shown in figure 13.5. The knot vector for this curve is -3 -2 -1 0 1 1 1 2 3 4 5 6, with a new range [0 ... 3]. Note that the curve now makes a sharp bend at control point 3 because no control points before 3 can "reach across" the double multiplicity (remember that a control point can only reach over (*degree*) knots).

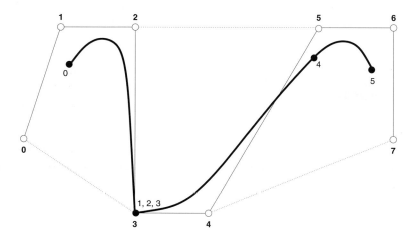

Figure 13.5: B-spline curve, degree 3, knot of multiplicity 3.

Note that integer ranges were used here to avoid fractional numbers in the knot vector. If all values in the knot vector were multiplied by a constant, the parameter range of the curve would be scaled, but its image would not change in any way.

More formally, the range determines the valid coordinates T on the curve or UV on the surface to be approximated. Since the UV coordinates are the basis for trimming curves, hole curves, and texture space mapping by texture surfaces, they should be chosen carefully. More about this below.

13.3.1.3 Cardinal

The cardinal basis always has degree 3. The curve runs through all its control points, as shown in figure 13.6:

Note that cardinal curves, unlike Bézier and B-spline curves, are not bound by the convex hull of the control points. Cardinal curves generally appear less smooth than Bézier and B-spline curves. See [Bartels 87] for details.

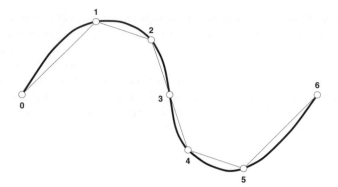

Figure 13.6: cardinal curve.

13.3.1.4   Basis Matrix

Bézier, B-spline, and cardinal bases are all based on the same principle: a set of piecewise polynomials is constructed that control which control points have influence over which points on the curve. In the Bézier case, the polynomials are called *Bernstein polynomials*, and look like figure 13.7.

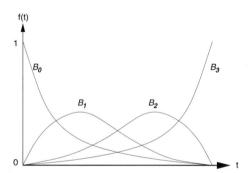

Figure 13.7: Cubic Bernstein polynomials.

If the curve is parameterized with a parameter t that runs from 0 at one end to 1 at the other, the curve point at $t = 0$ is influenced only by the control point attached to polynomial B_0 because all other polynomials are zero at this point. The other end of the curve at $t = 1$ is controlled only by the control point attached to B_3. Between these two points, all four control points have some influence. The curve can be seen as the average of the control point coordinates, each weighted by the corresponding B_n polynomial.

If the polynomials add up to 1 at every point t, and if none of them becomes negative, all segments of the resulting curve are contained in the convex hull defined by their control points. This is the case for the Bézier and B-spline bases, but not for the cardinal basis.

The curves B_n in the figure are cubic curves, which means that they can be expressed as a polynomial equation containing the terms t^3, t^2, t^1, and t^0, multiplied by factors determined by the basis type. The fact that 3 is the highest exponent makes the curve "cubic", another word for the degree 3. A degree-4 curve would also have a t^4. Curves of degree 1 are called "linear"; they connect their control points with straight lines. The factors that are applied to the t^n can be collected into a matrix of size $(degree + 1) \times (degree + 1)$, or 4×4 in the cubic case. This matrix is called the *basis matrix*, and the basis matrix basis type allows direct specification of the factors.

Choosing the right components for the basis matrix goes beyond the scope of this book. For example, a basis matrix basis for cubic Bézier is defined as

```
basis "basis_name" matrix degree_int stepsize_int
    1.0   -3.0    3.0   -1.0
    0.0    3.0   -6.0    3.0
    0.0    0.0    3.0   -3.0
    0.0    0.0    0.0    1.0
```

Note that many books on the subject, such as [Foley 96], multiply their matrices from the other side. To use a basis matrix found in these books, transpose the matrix (swap rows and columns) and then reverse the column order.

The basis matrix type also requires the specification of a *step size* after the degree in the `basis` statement. The step size determines how many control points in a parameter direction the tessellator must step forward when the next patch is begun. If it were 0, all patches would use the same set of control points, like the first 4×4 in the cubic Bézier case. For degree-n Bézier, the step size is n (so the last control point for a patch is also the first control point for the next patch); for a cardinal basis it is always 1.

For more information on bases, refer to [Foley 96], Representing Curves and Surfaces, pp. 471–529.

13.3.1.5   Taylor

Taylor curves are defined by control points that define the coefficients for t^n directly. The control points have no intuitive geometrical meaning. For a degree-n curve, $n+1$ control points are needed for a curve segment; the first is the start point of the segment (multiplied by t^0), the second is the linear segment direction (multiplied by t^1), the third is the quadratic contribution (multiplied by t^2), the third is the cubic contribution (multiplied by t^3), and so on, up to the degree of the curve.

They are supported because they are used by certain client applications for modeling. Their numerical stability is lower than the stability of the other basis types, which can lead to imprecision if the basis degree is very high.

13.3.2   Surfaces

Free-form surfaces are constructed from meshes of curves. The mesh is formed by two sequences of curves that run in independent directions called the U and V directions, as shown in figure 13.8:

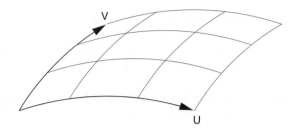

Figure 13.8: UV surface parameter mesh.

Piecewise polynomial surfaces map the 2D (UV) parameter space into 3D (XYZ) space. A free-form surface definition contains one basis for all the U curves and one for all the V curves. This means that they all have the same type, rational flag, and degree. The U basis and the V basis must have the same type and rational flag, but may have different degrees. The control points form a mesh. Each control point is shared by one U and one V curve, which is why the U and V basis type and rational flag must agree. For a cubic Bézier surface, consisting of 3×3 adjoining patches, 100 control points are required (figure 13.9).

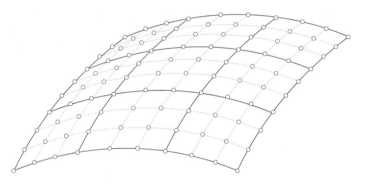

Figure 13.9: Surface control point mesh.

As described above, free-form surface definitions also require parameter vectors (or knot vectors, in the B-spline case), and a range:

```
surface "surface_name" "material_name"
    "u_basis_name" range u_param_list
    "v_basis_name" range v_param_list
    control_point_indices
```

The control point indices begin with the control point at the UV coordinate origin (lower left corner in the following examples), then progresses along the U axis, then proceeds to the next higher V and repeats. If the surface is rational, there may be a weight after each index; see page 326. Each control point index references a vertex (for free-form surfaces, "control point" and "vertex" are synonymous) previously defined with v statements.

Here is a full example that replaces the object and object instance from the simple cube scene on page 32:

```
object "bez_surf"
```

```
visible shadow trace tag 1
basis "bez3" bezier 3
group
        4.0  0.0  4.0    4.0  0.6  3.2    4.0  1.0  2.2    4.0  1.2  1.4
        4.0  1.4  0.6    4.0  1.4 -0.6    4.0  1.2 -1.4    4.0  1.0 -2.2
        4.0  0.6 -3.2    4.0  0.0 -4.0    3.2  0.6  4.0    3.2  1.2  3.2
        3.2  1.6  2.2    3.2  1.8  1.4    3.2  2.0  0.6    3.2  2.0 -0.6
        3.2  1.8 -1.4    3.2  1.6 -2.2    3.2  1.2 -3.2    3.2  0.6 -4.0
        2.2  1.0  4.0    2.2  1.6  3.2    2.2  2.0  2.2    2.2  2.2  1.4
        2.2  2.4  0.6    2.2  2.4 -0.6    2.2  2.2 -1.4    2.2  2.0 -2.2
        2.2  1.6 -3.2    2.2  1.0 -4.0    1.4  1.2  4.0    1.4  1.8  3.2
        1.4  2.2  2.2    1.4  2.4  1.4    1.4  2.6  0.6    1.4  2.6 -0.6
        1.4  2.4 -1.4    1.4  2.2 -2.2    1.4  1.8 -3.2    1.4  1.2 -4.0
        0.6  1.4  4.0    0.6  2.0  3.2    0.6  2.4  2.2    0.6  2.6  1.4
        0.6  2.8  0.6    0.6  2.8 -0.6    0.6  2.6 -1.4    0.6  2.4 -2.2
        0.6  2.0 -3.2    0.6  1.4 -4.0   -0.6  1.4  4.0   -0.6  2.0  3.2
       -0.6  2.4  2.2   -0.6  2.6  1.4   -0.6  2.8  0.6   -0.6  2.8 -0.6
       -0.6  2.6 -1.4   -0.6  2.4 -2.2   -0.6  2.0 -3.2   -0.6  1.4 -4.0
       -1.4  1.2  4.0   -1.4  1.8  3.2   -1.4  2.2  2.2   -1.4  2.4  1.4
       -1.4  2.6  0.6   -1.4  2.6 -0.6   -1.4  2.4 -1.4   -1.4  2.2 -2.2
       -1.4  1.8 -3.2   -1.4  1.2 -4.0   -2.2  1.0  4.0   -2.2  1.6  3.2
       -2.2  2.0  2.2   -2.2  2.2  1.4   -2.2  2.4  0.6   -2.2  2.4 -0.6
       -2.2  2.2 -1.4   -2.2  2.0 -2.2   -2.2  1.6 -3.2   -2.2  1.0 -4.0
       -3.2  0.6  4.0   -3.2  1.2  3.2   -3.2  1.6  2.2   -3.2  1.8  1.4
       -3.2  2.0  0.6   -3.2  2.0 -0.6   -3.2  1.8 -1.4   -3.2  1.6 -2.2
       -3.2  1.2 -3.2   -3.2  0.6 -4.0   -4.0  0.0  4.0   -4.0  0.6  3.2
       -4.0  1.0  2.2   -4.0  1.2  1.4   -4.0  1.4  0.6   -4.0  1.4 -0.6
       -4.0  1.2 -1.4   -4.0  1.0 -2.2   -4.0  0.6 -3.2   -4.0  0.0 -4.0

        v 0      v 1      v 2      v 3      v 4      v 5      v 6      v 7
        v 8      v 9      v 10     v 11     v 12     v 13     v 14     v 15
        v 16     v 17     v 18     v 19     v 20     v 21     v 22     v 23
        v 24     v 25     v 26     v 27     v 28     v 29     v 30     v 31
        v 32     v 33     v 34     v 35     v 36     v 37     v 38     v 39
        v 40     v 41     v 42     v 43     v 44     v 45     v 46     v 47
        v 48     v 49     v 50     v 51     v 52     v 53     v 54     v 55
        v 56     v 57     v 58     v 59     v 60     v 61     v 62     v 63
        v 64     v 65     v 66     v 67     v 68     v 69     v 70     v 71
        v 72     v 73     v 74     v 75     v 76     v 77     v 78     v 79
        v 80     v 81     v 82     v 83     v 84     v 85     v 86     v 87
        v 88     v 89     v 90     v 91     v 92     v 93     v 94     v 95
        v 96     v 97     v 98     v 99

        surface "surf" "mtl"
                "bez3" 0 3      0.0  1.0  2.0  3.0
                "bez3" 0 3      0.0  1.0  2.0  3.0

                99 98 97 96 95 94 93 92 91 90 89 88
                87 86 85 84 83 82 81 80 79 78 77 76
                75 74 73 72 71 70 69 68 67 66 65 64
                63 62 61 60 59 58 57 56 55 54 53 52
                51 50 49 48 47 46 45 44 43 42 41 40
                39 38 37 36 35 34 33 32 31 30 29 28
```

```
            27 26 25 24 23 22 21 20 19 18 17 16
            15 14 13 12 11 10 9 8 7 6 5 4 3 2 1 0

          approximate surface parametric 3.333333 3.333333 "surf"
     end group
end object

instance "bez_surf_inst" "bez_surf"
     transform      6  0  0  0
                    0  6  0  0
                    0  0  6  0
                    0 -1  0  1
end instance
```

Note the definition of the basis "bez3" at the beginning of the group. It is used for both the U and V specifications of the surface statement. After each basis reference, there is a parameter range [0, 3], followed by the parameter vector, (0.0 1.0 2.0 3.0). Since this is a Bézier basis, this parameter vector describes the patch boundaries (solid lines in the diagram above), so there are 3×3 patches — [0, 1], [1, 2], and [2, 3]. Note that the parameter vector *must* be defined using floating-point values containing a decimal point, so that mental ray knows where the second parameter vector ends and the vertex references begin.

The approximation statement is explained on page 337.

Like polygons, free-form surfaces use the two-stage vector and vertex method, but there is exactly one point-in-space vector for every vertex because coinciding control points do not make sense. Vertices used as control points may have motion vectors (a m statement following each v statement), but normals, derivatives, texture coordinates, and so on are ignored. See below for texturing surfaces.

To create a surface of degree d with p patches, the number of parameters in the parameter vector (or knot vector) can be derived from the following table. In the basis matrix case, s is the step size. The table must be used for the U and V directions separately; multiply the U and V control point numbers to arrive at the total number of control points needed in the surface definition.

type	# of parameters	# of control points
Bézier	$p + 1$	$p \cdot d + 1$
B-spline	$p + 2 \cdot d + 1$	$p + d$
cardinal	$p + 1$	$p + 3$
basis matrix	$p + 1$	$(p - 1) \cdot s + d + 1$
Taylor	$p + 1$	$(d + 1) \cdot p$

A Bézier surface of degree 3 in both directions with only two patches in the V direction requires only seven control point rows, and a shorter parameter vector. The following surface leaves off three control point rows at the left edge:

```
surface "surf" "mtl"
```

```
"bez3"  0 3       0.0   1.0   2.0   3.0
"bez3"  0 2       0.0   1.0   2.0

69 68 67 66 65 64
63 62 61 60 59 58 57 56 55 54 53 52
51 50 49 48 47 46 45 44 43 42 41 40
39 38 37 36 35 34 33 32 31 30 29 28
27 26 25 24 23 22 21 20 19 18 17 16
15 14 13 12 11 10 9 8 7 6 5 4 3 2 1 0
```

The U basis contains $p_u = 3$ patches and therefore needs $p_u + 1 = 4$ parameters. The V basis contains $p_v = 2$ patches and only needs $p_v + 1 = 3$ parameters. Since the degrees for the U and V direction are both 3 ($d_u = d_v = 3$), the number of control points is therefore $(p_u \cdot d_u + 1) \cdot (p_v \cdot d_v + 1) = 70$. A similar effect can be achieved by restricting the parameter vector range, here to exclude the first patch and the last 1.5 patches from tessellation, leaving only one-half of the middle row. All control points remain in the surface definition, but the range selects only a subset of the parameter domain:

```
surface "surf" "mtl"
        "bez3"  0 3       0.0   1.0   2.0   3.0
        "bez3"  1 1.5     0.0   1.0   2.0   3.0

99 98 97 96 95 94 93 92 91 90 89 88
87 86 85 84 83 82 81 80 79 78 77 76
75 74 73 72 71 70 69 68 67 66 65 64
63 62 61 60 59 58 57 56 55 54 53 52
51 50 49 48 47 46 45 44 43 42 41 40
39 38 37 36 35 34 33 32 31 30 29 28
27 26 25 24 23 22 21 20 19 18 17 16
15 14 13 12 11 10 9 8 7 6 5 4 3 2 1 0
```

Figure 13.10 shows the rendered images.

V range: 0 3   V range: 0 2   V range: 1 1.5

Figure 13.10: Parameter range and parameter vector.

13.3.3 Rational Surfaces and NURBS

Rational curves extend nonrational curves by adding another value, called a *weight*, to each control point. Effectively, while nonrational curves are defined by XYZ control points, rational curves are defined by XYZW control points. If all the weights W are 1.0, the W "curve" is also 1.0 at all points and the rational curve is identical to the nonrational curve with the same XYZ control points but no weights.

In the .mi language, weights are specified after the control point indices. The example on page 322, written with weights, looks like this:

```
object "bez_surf"
        visible shadow trace tag 1
        basis "bez3" bezier 3
        group
#               ...
                surface "surf" "mtl"
                        "bez3" 0 3      0.0   1.0   2.0   3.0
                        "bez3" 0 3      0.0   1.0   2.0   3.0

                        99 w 1    98 w 1    97 w 1    96 w 1    95 w 1    94 w 1    93 w 1
                        92 w 1    91 w 1    90 w 1    89 w 1    88 w 1    87 w 1    86 w 1
                        85 w 1    84 w 1    83 w 1    82 w 1    81 w 1    80 w 1    79 w 1
                        78 w 1    77 w 1    76 w 1    75 w 1    74 w 1    73 w 1    72 w 1
                        71 w 1    70 w 1    69 w 1    68 w 1    67 w 1    66 w 1    65 w 1
                        64 w 1    63 w 1    62 w 1    61 w 1    60 w 1    59 w 1    58 w 1
                        57 w 1    56 w 1    55 w 1    54 w 1    53 w 1    52 w 1    51 w 1
                        50 w 1    49 w 1    48 w 1    47 w 1    46 w 1    45 w 1    44 w 1
                        43 w 1    42 w 1    41 w 1    40 w 1    39 w 1    38 w 1    37 w 1
                        36 w 1    35 w 1    34 w 1    33 w 1    32 w 1    31 w 1    30 w 1
                        29 w 1    28 w 1    27 w 1    26 w 1    25 w 1    24 w 1    23 w 1
                        22 w 1    21 w 1    20 w 1    19 w 1    18 w 1    17 w 1    16 w 1
                        15 w 1    14 w 1    13 w 1    12 w 1    11 w 1    10 w 1     9 w 1
                         8 w 1     7 w 1     6 w 1     5 w 1     4 w 1     3 w 1     2 w 1
                         1 w 1     0 w 1

                approximate surface parametric 3.333333 3.333333 "surf"
        end group
end object
```

The weights are floating-point numbers introduced by the keyword w. (The w keyword may be omitted, but then the weight must be a floating-point number containing a decimal point to distinguish it from the next control point index.) If an index has no weight, the weight defaults to 1.0. A control point with a weight is also called a homogeneous control point.

Non-uniform rational B-splines are commonly abbreviated NURBS. Non-uniformity means that the numbers in the knot vector are increasing by varying increments; rationality means that weights are present.

The following surface example can be inserted in place of the sphere object geometry definition in the simple sphere example on page 49 and in appendix B:

```
object "sphere1" visible shadow trace tag 1
        basis "bez2" rational bezier 2
        group
                0.5  0.5  0.0    1.0  0.5  0.0    1.0  1.0  0.0
                0.5  1.0  0.0    0.0  1.0  0.0    0.0  0.5  0.0
                0.0  0.0  0.0    0.5  0.0  0.0    1.0  0.0  0.0
                1.0  0.5  0.5    1.0  1.0  0.5    0.5  1.0  0.5
                0.0  1.0  0.5    0.0  0.5  0.5    0.0  0.0  0.5
                0.5  0.0  0.5    1.0  0.0  0.5    1.0  0.5  1.0
                1.0  1.0  1.0    0.5  1.0  1.0    0.0  1.0  1.0
                0.0  0.5  1.0    0.0  0.0  1.0    0.5  0.0  1.0
                1.0  0.0  1.0    0.5  0.5  1.0

                v 0 v 1 v 2 v 3 v 4 v 5 v 6 v 7 v 8 v 9 v 10
                v 11 v 12 v 13 v 14 v 15 v 16 v 17 v 18 v 19
                v 20 v 21 v 22 v 23 v 24 v 25

                surface "surf" ""
                    "bez2" 0.0 1.0   0.0 0.25 0.5 0.75 1.0
                    "bez2" 0.0 1.0   0.0 0.5  1.0

                    0         0        0 w 2   0         0
                    0         0 w 2    0       0         1
                    2         3 w 2    4       5         6
                    7 w 2     8        1       9 w 2     10 w 2
                    11 w 4    12 w 2   13 w 2  14 w 2    15 w 4
                    16 w 2    9 w 2    17      18        19 w 2
                    20        21       22      23 w 2    24
                    17        25       25      25 w 2    25
                    25        25       25 w 2  25        25

                approximate surface parametric 12 12 "surf"
        end group
end object
```

This is a simple rational Bézier surface consisting of four patches in the U direction and two patches in the V direction. Both bases have degree 2. Only 45 control points suffice for a smooth sphere. Some control points are referenced more than once, so only 26 v statements are required to define the 45 control points required for the surface. The material name after the surface name is the empty string ("") to allow material inheritance from the instance of the object. The result is shown in the left image of figure 13.11; the right image shows the same object with the weights removed.

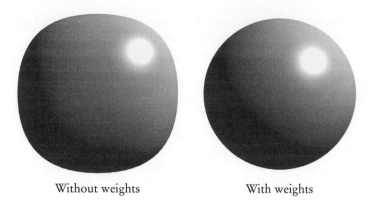

Without weights   With weights

Figure 13.11: Nonrational and rational sphere.

13.3.4   Trimming and Holes

mental ray allows the definition of parametric curves that cut away parts of a surface. The curves must be closed and may not intersect themselves or other curves on the same surface. They may be constructed from multiple curve segments spliced together to form the closed loop. The curves are called *parametric* because they are defined in the surface's UV coordinates — all curve control points have only two coordinates (U and V), while the third component of every vector is null. These UV coordinates must be in the surface range — remember that both the U basis and the V basis have a range used to bound the parameter vector or knot vector. This range delimits the valid range of UV coordinates for all curve control points.

Each surface may have one boundary trimming curve, which cuts away all parts of the surface outside of the curve, and any number of hole curves, which cut away parts inside the hole curve. These curves can be nested: a trim curve inside a hole curve "restores" the patch area inside the inner trim curve. This allows cutting a surface into concentric ribbons, for example. It is necessary to sort the trim and hole list in the surface definition correctly: the trim first, followed by the outermost holes, followed by the inner trimming curve, and so on. A curve that encloses another curve must be listed in the surface statement before that other curve. Curves that do not enclose each other can be listed in any order. Clockwise/counterclockwise ordering is not significant.

The definition of a curve in the scene file is similar to the definition of a surface, except that only one basis is specified, and that the list of control point indices is a one-dimensional list instead of a two-dimensional mesh:

```
curve "curve_name"
     "basis_name" parameter_list
     control_point_indices
```

The parameter list and the control point indices follow the same rules as in the surface definition. This includes weights in the rational case. The exception is that no range is given before the parameter list. The range is instead specified where the curve is used in a trim, hole, or special statement. This allows different pieces of the same curve to be used in different contexts. If the range were "baked into" the curve it would be more difficult to splice curves together.

Once a curve has been defined, it can be applied to a surface. The curve must be defined before the surface, and is referenced by a `trim` or `hole` statement that is appended to the surface definition:

```
trim    "curve_name" min max
        ...
hole    "curve_name" min max
        ...
```

The dots indicate that each trim and hole statement may be followed by more than one curve segment. If there is more than one, all segments are concatenated to form the trimming curve or hole curve. The *min* and *max* numbers provide the range that was missing in the curve statement.

Here is a new version of the surface on page 322 that uses both trimming and nested holes:

```
object "bez_surf"
        visible shadow trace tag 1
        basis "bez3" bezier 3
        group
                4.0  0.0  4.0    4.0  0.6  3.2    4.0  1.0  2.2    4.0  1.2  1.4
                4.0  1.4  0.6    4.0  1.4 -0.6    4.0  1.2 -1.4    4.0  1.0 -2.2
                4.0  0.6 -3.2    4.0  0.0 -4.0    3.2  0.6  4.0    3.2  1.2  3.2
                3.2  1.6  2.2    3.2  1.8  1.4    3.2  2.0  0.6    3.2  2.0 -0.6
                3.2  1.8 -1.4    3.2  1.6 -2.2    3.2  1.2 -3.2    3.2  0.6 -4.0
                2.2  1.0  4.0    2.2  1.6  3.2    2.2  2.0  2.2    2.2  2.2  1.4
                2.2  2.4  0.6    2.2  2.4 -0.6    2.2  2.2 -1.4    2.2  2.0 -2.2
                2.2  1.6 -3.2    2.2  1.0 -4.0    1.4  1.2  4.0    1.4  1.8  3.2
                1.4  2.2  2.2    1.4  2.4  1.4    1.4  2.6  0.6    1.4  2.6 -0.6
                1.4  2.4 -1.4    1.4  2.2 -2.2    1.4  1.8 -3.2    1.4  1.2 -4.0
                0.6  1.4  4.0    0.6  2.0  3.2    0.6  2.4  2.2    0.6  2.6  1.4
                0.6  2.8  0.6    0.6  2.8 -0.6    0.6  2.6 -1.4    0.6  2.4 -2.2
                0.6  2.0 -3.2    0.6  1.4 -4.0   -0.6  1.4  4.0   -0.6  2.0  3.2
               -0.6  2.4  2.2   -0.6  2.6  1.4   -0.6  2.8  0.6   -0.6  2.8 -0.6
               -0.6  2.6 -1.4   -0.6  2.4 -2.2   -0.6  2.0 -3.2   -0.6  1.4 -4.0
               -1.4  1.2  4.0   -1.4  1.8  3.2   -1.4  2.2  2.2   -1.4  2.4  1.4
               -1.4  2.6  0.6   -1.4  2.6 -0.6   -1.4  2.4 -1.4   -1.4  2.2 -2.2
               -1.4  1.8 -3.2   -1.4  1.2 -4.0   -2.2  1.0  4.0   -2.2  1.6  3.2
               -2.2  2.0  2.2   -2.2  2.2  1.4   -2.2  2.4  0.6   -2.2  2.4 -0.6
               -2.2  2.2 -1.4   -2.2  2.0 -2.2   -2.2  1.6 -3.2   -2.2  1.0 -4.0
               -3.2  0.6  4.0   -3.2  1.2  3.2   -3.2  1.6  2.2   -3.2  1.8  1.4
               -3.2  2.0  0.6   -3.2  2.0 -0.6   -3.2  1.8 -1.4   -3.2  1.6 -2.2
               -3.2  1.2 -3.2   -3.2  0.6 -4.0   -4.0  0.0  4.0   -4.0  0.6  3.2
               -4.0  1.0  2.2   -4.0  1.2  1.4   -4.0  1.4  0.6   -4.0  1.4 -0.6
               -4.0  1.2 -1.4   -4.0  1.0 -2.2   -4.0  0.6 -3.2   -4.0  0.0 -4.0

                1.5  0.0  0      2.5  0.0  0      3.0  0.5  0      3.0  1.5  0
                3.0  2.5  0      2.5  3.0  0      1.5  3.0  0      0.5  3.0  0
                0.0  2.5  0      0.0  1.5  0      0.0  0.5  0      0.5  0.0  0

                1.5  0.2  0      2.4  0.2  0      2.8  0.6  0      2.8  1.5  0
                2.8  2.4  0      2.4  2.8  0      1.5  2.8  0      0.6  2.8  0
                0.2  2.4  0      0.2  1.5  0      0.2  0.6  0      0.6  0.2  0
```

```
1.5  0.4  0      2.3  0.4  0      2.6  0.7  0      2.6  1.5  0
2.6  2.3  0      2.3  2.6  0      1.5  2.6  0      0.7  2.6  0
0.4  2.3  0      0.4  1.5  0      0.4  0.7  0      0.7  0.4  0

1.5  0.6  0      2.2  0.6  0      2.4  0.8  0      2.4  1.5  0
2.4  2.2  0      2.2  2.4  0      1.5  2.4  0      0.8  2.4  0
0.6  2.2  0      0.6  1.5  0      0.6  0.8  0      0.8  0.6  0
```

```
v 0     v 1     v 2     v 3     v 4     v 5     v 6     v 7
v 8     v 9     v 10    v 11    v 12    v 13    v 14    v 15
v 16    v 17    v 18    v 19    v 20    v 21    v 22    v 23
v 24    v 25    v 26    v 27    v 28    v 29    v 30    v 31
v 32    v 33    v 34    v 35    v 36    v 37    v 38    v 39
v 40    v 41    v 42    v 43    v 44    v 45    v 46    v 47
v 48    v 49    v 50    v 51    v 52    v 53    v 54    v 55
v 56    v 57    v 58    v 59    v 60    v 61    v 62    v 63
v 64    v 65    v 66    v 67    v 68    v 69    v 70    v 71
v 72    v 73    v 74    v 75    v 76    v 77    v 78    v 79
v 80    v 81    v 82    v 83    v 84    v 85    v 86    v 87
v 88    v 89    v 90    v 91    v 92    v 93    v 94    v 95
v 96    v 97    v 98    v 99

v 100   v 101   v 102   v 103   v 104   v 105   v 106   v 107
v 108   v 109   v 110   v 111

v 112   v 113   v 114   v 115   v 116   v 117   v 118   v 119
v 120   v 121   v 122   v 123

v 124   v 125   v 126   v 127   v 128   v 129   v 130   v 131
v 132   v 133   v 134   v 135

v 136   v 137   v 138   v 139   v 140   v 141   v 142   v 143
v 144   v 145   v 146   v 147
```

```
curve "boundary"
        "bez3"            0.0  0.25 0.5  0.75  1.0

        100 101 102 103 104 105 106 107 108
        109 110 111 100

curve "outerhole"
        "bez3"            0.0  0.25 0.5  0.75  1.0

        112 113 114 115 116 117 118 119 120
        121 122 123 112

curve "innerhole"
        "bez3"            0.0  0.25 0.5  0.75  1.0

        124 125 126 127 128 129 130 131 132
        133 134 135 124
```

```
                curve "innerhole2"
                        "bez3"              0.0   0.25 0.5   0.75   1.0

                        136 137 138 139 140 141 142 143 144
                        145 146 147 136

                surface "surf" "mtl"
                        "bez3" 0 3        0.0   1.0   2.0   3.0
                        "bez3" 0 3        0.0   1.0   2.0   3.0

                        99 98 97 96 95 94 93 92 91 90 89 88
                        87 86 85 84 83 82 81 80 79 78 77 76
                        75 74 73 72 71 70 69 68 67 66 65 64
                        63 62 61 60 59 58 57 56 55 54 53 52
                        51 50 49 48 47 46 45 44 43 42 41 40
                        39 38 37 36 35 34 33 32 31 30 29 28
                        27 26 25 24 23 22 21 20 19 18 17 16
                        15 14 13 12 11 10 9 8 7 6 5 4 3 2 1 0

                        trim "boundary"  0 1
                        hole "outerhole" 0 1
                        trim "innerhole" 0 1
                        hole "innerhole2" 0 1

                approximate surface parametric 3.333 3.333 "surf"
                approximate curve   parametric 6.0    "boundary"
                approximate curve   parametric 6.0    "outerhole"
                approximate curve   parametric 6.0    "innerhole" "innerhole2"
        end group
end object

instance "bez_surf_inst" "bez_surf"
        transform       6  0  0  0
                        0  6  0  0
                        0  0  6  0
                        0 -1  0  1
end instance
```

Note that the curves in the example are all closed. In the Bézier case this is easily achieved by listing the first control point also as last control point in the vertex list; in the B-spline case *degree* control points would have to be replicated. Each curve has its own set of vectors and vertices. Figure 13.12 shows the rendered image, along with the untrimmed image from page 325:

13.3.5   Special Points and Curves

Special points and special curves are points and curves that force the tessellation to include them. Normally, mental ray chooses triangle vertices as it sees fit during the tessellation process. Sometimes, the tessellation quality can be improved by placing special curves on the surface such that they follow sharp creases, texture mapping discontinuities, or features of a displacement map, so it cannot happen that mental ray decides to place triangles that straddle the discontinuity.

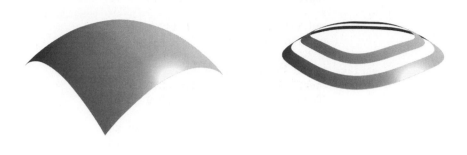

Figure 13.12: Untrimmed and trimmed Bézier surface.

Including special curves and special points in the tessellation allows control over where the triangle vertices are placed. Triangle vertices at sharp discontinuities improve the tessellation quality because they provide normals — if the vertices would be some distance away from the discontinuity their normals would be interpolated across the discontinuity during rendering.

An important application of this is to outline isolines in a displacement maps. Displacement isolines are lines of constant displacement. Since displacement maps are sampled at vertices during tessellation, special curves and points force mental ray to sample the displacement map at these points. However, with properly chosen approximation statements (see below) mental ray usually does a good job tessellating geometry even without special curves and points, but at the cost of creating more triangles because of the recursive algorithms used for surface subdivision.

Special curves are defined just like trimming curves and holes, and special points list a single point, optionally followed by a 3D coordinate index:

```
special          "curve_name" min max
special          control_point_index
special          control_point_index -> 3d_index
```

The first type of `special` statement is listed at the end of `surface` statements, just like `trim` and `hole` statements. The second type places the specified control point, which must be in UV coordinates (that is, the third, Z, component is zero) in the tessellation. The third type enforces that a specific UV coordinate is mapped to a specific 3D object coordinate. The point on the surface with the UV coordinate given by the *control_point_index* index is pulled to the 3D coordinate given by the *3d_index* index. As usual, both of these indices are indices into the vertex table.

Consider the trimming example on page 329. If the outer hole curve is changed to a special curve, and the other trimming and hole curves are removed, like this:

```
surface "surf" "mtl"
```

```
"bez3" 0 3      0.0  1.0  2.0  3.0
"bez3" 0 3      0.0  1.0  2.0  3.0

99 98 97 96 95 94 93 92 91 90 89 88
87 86 85 84 83 82 81 80 79 78 77 76
75 74 73 72 71 70 69 68 67 66 65 64
63 62 61 60 59 58 57 56 55 54 53 52
51 50 49 48 47 46 45 44 43 42 41 40
39 38 37 36 35 34 33 32 31 30 29 28
27 26 25 24 23 22 21 20 19 18 17 16
15 14 13 12 11 10 9 8 7 6 5 4 3 2 1 0

special "outerhole"  0 1

approximate surface parametric 1.0 1.0 "surf"
approximate curve    parametric 3.0    "outerhole"
```

then the tessellation makes sure that the vertices of the special curve are included in the tessellation, as shown in figure 13.13.

Figure 13.13: Tessellation without and with special curve.

Of course, special curves, trimming curves, and hole curves can be combined as long as no two curves intersect.

13.3.6   Texture Surfaces

As described on page 64, certain kinds of texture mapping done by texture shaders require texture vectors. Texture vectors are built into the geometry and control exactly where and how the texture appears on the object. In the polygonal case, texture vectors can simply be provided along with the vertices. This does not work for free-form surfaces because the vertices are not provided in the scene file but instead are computed during tessellation. It would not help to attach them to the control points because most types of surfaces do not pass through all of their control points.

Since the computation of UV coordinates is part of the tessellation of free-form surfaces, mental ray provides a way to specify a mapping from those UV coordinates to texture vectors, using *texture surfaces*. A texture surface is attached to a specific geometric surface simply by listing it after the definition of the geometric surface, much like trimming curves are listed after the geometric surface definition. In the simplest (and most common) case, the texture surface is a parametric grid of control points that each provide not a 3D coordinate, as the control points of the main surface do, but a texture vector.

Whenever the tessellator computes a new vertex for a geometric surface, it takes the UV coordinates of the new vertex and looks them up in the texture surface, and uses the corresponding location in texture space as specified by the texture surface's control points as the texture vector for the new vertex.

If the geometric surface and the texture surface have the same bases and the same number of control points, there exists a one-to-one mapping in which the control points of the texture surface are the texture vectors for the corresponding control points of the geometric surface. In other words, the geometric control points provide the point in 3D space and the texture control points provide the texture vectors. However, this is rarely the case. Texture surfaces are usually parametric grids of degree 1 to ensure that the texture surface passes through all its control points, especially the ones at the edge to ensure a proper texture vector range. Many texture shaders expect their texture vector components to be in the range [0...1), including 0 but excluding 1.

A common case is a texture surface that provides a single patch of degree 1 on both U and V directions. This requires only four control points at the corners. This is useful for making raw UV coordinates available to the shader.

Just as there may be more than one texture vector on a polygonal vertex, there may be more than one texture surface attached to a geometric surface. The first one becomes texture space 0, the next one texture space 1, and so on.

The generic syntax of texture surfaces is:

```
[ volume ] [ vector ] texture
    "u_basis_name" u_param_list
    "v_basis_name" v_param_list
    vertex_ref_list
```

This is similar to the geometric surface definition (see page 322), except that the keyword surface is replaced with the keyword texture, and the addition of two optional keywords:

volume   tells mental ray not to perform seam compensation, which normally makes sure that the texture does not "rewind" on closed surfaces. Suppose that a texture is mapped on a closed surface such as a cylinder, and that the texture is slightly rotated so that the texture vector (0, 0) is not at the geometric surface edge. This may create triangles that end up with a texture coordinate of 0.95 at one end and 0.05 at the other end. With compensation, interpolation runs from 0.95 to 1.0, switch to 0.0, and then to 0.05. This produces a smooth texture map. Without compensation, something else would happen: the texture would rewind from 0.95 backwards to 0.05. However, for 3D texturess (also called volume textures, see page 81), this is actually desirable, so compensation can be turned off with the volume keyword.

vector   adds bump basis vectors to the geometric surface. If present, mental ray will compute a texture space with bump basis vectors. This is equivalent to the situation with polygonal geometry where the t statement is followed by three, not one, vector indices, except that it is not necessary to provide the actual bump basis vectors because they can be computed analytically by mental ray. See page 85 for details on bump mapping.

Both keywords can be combined. Note that the texture surface statement contains no ranges after the basis names. Texture surfaces always use the ranges specified by the geometric surface to which they belong. In addition, there is no material name, and texture surfaces have no extra attributes such as trimming curves or holes.

Here is an example that performs basic UV mapping. It is derived from the simple surface on page 322, plus four vectors, four vertices, and the texture surface definition. The ranges were changed to [0... 1], and the parameter vectors were adjusted accordingly. The material is not shown, it is a simplified version from the texture vector example on page 64.

```
object "bez_surf"
        visible shadow trace tag 1
        basis "bez3" bezier 3
        basis "bez1" bezier 1
        group
                4.0  0.0  4.0    4.0  0.6  3.2    4.0  1.0  2.2    4.0  1.2  1.4
 #              ...
                -4.0 1.2 -1.4   -4.0  1.0 -2.2   -4.0  0.6 -3.2   -4.0  0.0 -4.0

                0.0  0.0  0.0    0.0  1.0  0.0    1.0  0.0  0.0    1.0  1.0  0.0

                v 0      v 1      v 2      v 3      v 4      v 5      v 6      v 7
 #              ...
                v 96     v 97     v 98     v 99

                v 100    v 101    v 102    v 103

                surface "surf" "mtl"
                        "bez3" 0 1       0.0  0.33  0.66  1.0
                        "bez3" 0 1       0.0  0.33  0.66  1.0

                        99 98 97 96 95 94 93 92 91 90 89 88
                        87 86 85 84 83 82 81 80 79 78 77 76
                        75 74 73 72 71 70 69 68 67 66 65 64
                        63 62 61 60 59 58 57 56 55 54 53 52
                        51 50 49 48 47 46 45 44 43 42 41 40
                        39 38 37 36 35 34 33 32 31 30 29 28
                        27 26 25 24 23 22 21 20 19 18 17 16
```

```
                    15 14 13 12 11 10 9 8 7 6 5 4 3 2 1 0

            texture
                    "bez1"            0.0  1.0
                    "bez1"            0.0  1.0

                    100 101 102 103

            approximate surface parametric 3.333333 3.333333 "surf"
        end group
    end object
```

Figure 13.14 shows the resulting image.

Figure 13.14: Surface with UV texture.

13.3.7 Surface Derivatives

mental ray can automatically generate surface derivative vectors if requested. First derivatives describe the UV parametric gradient of a surface; second derivatives describe the curvature. They are computed and stored only if requested by *derivative_request* statements in the surface definition:

    derivative *number$_{int}$* [*number$_{int}$*]

There can be one or more `derivative` statements that request first or second derivatives, or both. Valid values for *number* are 1 and 2, for first and second derivatives, respectively.

mental ray does not use derivative vectors but makes them available to shaders. First derivatives are presented as two vectors ($\partial S/\partial U$ and $\partial S/\partial V$, with S being the surface), second derivatives are presented as three vectors ($\partial^2 S/\partial U^2$, $\partial^2 S/\partial V^2$, and $\partial^2 S/(\partial U \partial V)$). This is the same order that can be explicitly given for polygonal data using the d keyword in vertices. For surfaces, mental ray computes the vertex derivatives analytically, any explicit vertex derivatives given by d keywords are ignored.

13.3.8   Simple Approximations

Approximations control how finely mental ray tessellates free-form surfaces into triangles. They are optional but should always be specified. Approximations can be given for both surfaces and curves. They are listed at the end of the object group definition.

mental ray supports a large variety of approximations. In practice, only three types are sufficient for nearly all purposes:

```
approximate [type] regular parametric u [v] "name" ...
approximate [type] fine length l "name" ...
approximate [type] fine view length l "name" ...
```

The approximation applies to all curves or surfaces (depending on *type*) whose names appear in the trailing name list. The type specifies what the approximation applies to:

surface   Approximate a surface. The name list must consist of surface names.

curve   Approximate a curve. The name list must consist of curve names.

trim   Approximate all curves used in a given surface. The name list must consist of surface names. This is a shorthand in cases where many curves are used and all require the same approximation.

displace   Approximate the displacement map of the surface. The name list must consist of surface names.

—   If no type is given, approximate the displacement map of all polygons in this object. Approximation statements for polygons only make sense if the polygons are displacement-mapped. The name list is omitted in this case because polygons are not named.

The three simple approximation modes are

- **Regular parametric** approximation divides surfaces into a grid of $(u \cdot degree) \times (v \cdot degree)$ triangle pairs. For curves, only u is specified and v is omitted. This is useful for surface approximations and curves, and for trace-only or shadow-only geometry, but it is usually not sufficiently adaptive for displacement.

- **Fine length**[3.1] approximation ensures that no triangle has an edge longer than the length l, in object space. This works well for multiply instanced objects (because they can all share the same tessellation) and camera flythroughs (because camera movements do not cause retessellations). The disadvantage is that a good value of l depends on the largest size of the object in the image. The "fine" keyword puts mental ray in a mode where it can efficiently deal with very large numbers of triangles.

- **Fine view length**[3.1] approximation ensures that no triangle has an edge longer than l pixels. Good values of l range from 0.5 to 0.1. This mode is perfect for complex displacement (see page 94 for an example image), and is also the easiest to handle for surface approximations, unless there is heavy multiple instancing or object or camera movements in the animation. Another advantage is that the size of the rendered image provides a natural bound for the number of triangles generated, which greatly simplifies picking good parameters.

It is possible to provide override approximations in the options block, instead of putting them in every object. mental ray versions older than 3.1 do not support fine approximation modes.

13.3.9   Advanced Approximations *

mental ray supports a large range of additional approximation modes, described in this section. They are only needed for special CAD applications, like rendering class-A surfaces in automotive design. Although these approximations allow fine control over triangle generation, some of them can require much more time to fine-tune than the three simple approximations described in the previous section.

The full syntax of approximation statements is:

```
approximate [type] [style] [fine3.1] [view] [any] technique
            [maximum] [grading] [limits] "name" ...
```

The *type* was describes in the previous section.

style   Three styles are supported:

      `tree`   specifies a hierarchical subdivision that allows local subdivision without affecting other areas.

      `grid`   works on a grid of isolines that allow subdivision only by adding more isolines. Since isolines always run from one edge of the surface to the opposite edge, and since only whole isolines can be added, this produces regular triangle meshes which can sometimes result in many more triangles than necessary. It is not normally necessary to explicitly choose between tree and grid styles.

      `delaunay`[2.1] specifies a mesh refinement style based on Delaunay triangulation, which attempts to maximize triangle compactness and to avoid thin triangles. Triangle vertices are generally not restricted to rectangular isoline grid points like in the previous two styles. The Delaunay is supported only for free-form surfaces but not polygons.

—   If no style is specified, the approximation defaults to grid for the parametric techniques, and tree for all other techniques.

fine[3.1]   This keyword puts mental ray in a mode that can efficiently generate very large numbers of triangles, but creating them in small and short-lived batches that avoid filling up memory. This makes it possible to choose small approximation lengths that would not otherwise be possible. Fine approximation works only with the length, view length, and, for free-form surfaces without displacement, parametric techniques.

view   If the view keyword is specified, the length and distance tolerances are interpreted as fractions of a pixel diagonal in raster space (pixel coordinates on the viewing plane) instead of object coordinates. Effectively, this makes tessellation view-dependent: if the object, or parts of the object, are far away from the camera, fewer pixels on the viewing plane are covered so the tessellation requires fewer triangles. Objects outside the viewing frustum (that is, objects that do not project onto the viewing plane) are approximated much more coarsely.

For example, an ocean object stretching away in all directions greatly benefits from view dependency because it is tessellated finely near the camera and coarsely at the horizon. This is especially true if the ocean has displacement-mapped waves, which must be resolved finely near the camera but are practically invisible near the horizon.

Multiply instanced objects (objects that appear in several different places in the scene) are tessellated multiple times instead of sharing one tessellation if they are view-dependent because the tessellation depends on their position relative to the camera. Here it is necessary to balance the advantages of view dependency and the overhead of separate tessellations. mental ray reports the number of triangles generated; choose view dependency if it reduces the number of triangles significantly.

any[2.1]   Normally, tessellation continues until all *techniques* are satisfied. The any keyword changes this policy to stop tessellation if any *technique* is satisfied. For example, if both angle and length techniques are specified together with any, the angle technique will only create triangles until the triangle edge lengths drop below the limit imposed by the length technique.

technique   A listing of criteria and their parameters that specify when to subdivide a part of the surface, curve, or polygon. If a part of the surface does not meet these criteria, it is subdivided further. mental ray supports two parametric techniques that operate in UV space, and three curvature, length, and angle dependent techniques that operate in 3D space; see below. The following criteria are supported:

parametric *u v*
    Subdivide each patch into $(u \cdot degree) \times (v \cdot degree)$ triangle pairs. For example, with $u = 1.333$ and $v = 4$ a cubic patch would get subdivided into $1.333 \cdot 3 \cdot 4 \cdot 3 = 48$ triangle pairs, or 96 triangles. With $u = 0$

and $v = 0$ a cubic patch would not get subdivided, here meaning that it is just split into two triangles. For curves, v must be omitted. If no approximation statement is given, 0 0 is the default for surfaces, 0 for curves, and 0 0 for displacement-mapped polygons.

regular parametric *u v*

Subdivide the whole surface into $u \times v$ triangle pairs. The tessellation density is constant over the entire surface or curve, unlike `parametric` which tessellates each patch independently. For curves, v must be omitted.

length *l*

Subdivide until no triangle has an edge longer than l. l is measured either in pixels (if view-dependent) or object coordinates. Length approximation is especially useful in conjunction with view dependency.

distance *d*

Subdivide until the resulting triangle mesh is at no point farther away than d from the true mathematical representation. d is measured either in pixels or object coordinates. Small values such as 0.1 work well.

angle *a*

Subdivide until no two normals of neighboring triangles form an angle of more than a degrees. The angle should be chosen carefully — if it is too small, the number of triangles increases very quickly. 45 degrees is a good starting point.

spatial *l*

This is synonymous with `length` *d*, for backwards compatibility.

curvature *d a*

This is synonymous with `distance` *d* `angle` *a*, also for backwards compatibility.

The length, distance, and angle criteria can be combined by listing one or more of them in the same approximation. They are collectively called LDA approximation. If no any keyword is specified, combinations will create at least as many triangles as any of the criteria alone because tessellation continues until all criteria are satisfied. If the `any` keyword is specified, tessellation stops when any criterion is satisfied.

maximum[2.1] Delaunay triangulation is not subject to subdivision limits but continues until a given maximum number of triangles has been created.

max *max$_{int}$*

max_{int} specifies the maximum number of triangles of the surface tessellation. mental ray exceeds this number only if required by trimming, hole, and special curves because every curve vertex must become part of the tessellation regardless of the specified maximum.

The *maximum* specification has no effect on tessellation styles other than `delaunay`.

grading Grading is a technique that allows fading the tessellation density smoothly from the edge of a surface to the interior. It is only supported for Delaunay triangulation and has no effect on other styles. For example, a finely subdivided trimming curve or hole curve might result in a large number of triangles near the curve, which directly connect to only a few large triangles that cover the interior of the surface. Grading avoids neighboring triangles with very different sizes. The grading specification consists of the keyword `grading` and an angle:

`grading angle`
> The *angle* constant specifies a lower bound related to the degree of the minimum angle of a triangle. Values from 0.0 to 30.0 can be specified. Small values up to 20.0 are recommended. The default is 0.0, which disables grading.

limits mental ray subdivides the object until all criteria specified by the techniques are met. The subdivision limit specifies the minimum and maximum number of subdivisions, and can be used to prevent "runaways" where another subdivision does not improve the situation much and causes more and more subdivisions. Locally, a rule of thumb is that every new subdivision quadruples the number of triangles. (Locally means this is true only where the subdivision actually takes place, which can be a small part of the object if the **tree** style is used.)

The subdivision limits consist of two integers, min_{int} and max_{int}, which must be 0 or greater, with $min \leq max$. If missing, they default to 0 and 5, or, 0 and 7 for `fine`, respectively. Good results can often be achieved with a maximum of 3 subdivisions. Subdivision limits should not be used to control the approximation quality; the parameters available for the various techniques are better suited for that because they are more selective. Subdivision limits do not apply to Delaunay triangulation.

name Each approximation ends with a list of surface or curve names that it applies to. More than one may be given. The approximation type (see above) determines whether surfaces or curves are listed, or whether the name list can be omitted.

Here is a simple object with variable curvature (based on the sphere scene on page 335):

```
object "bez_surf"
        visible shadow trace tag 1
        basis "bez3" bezier 3
        group
                -4 -4   4      8 -4   4      4 -8   4      4   4   4
                -4 -4   1      6 -4   1      4 -6   1      4   4   1
                -4 -4  -1      4 -4  -1      4 -4  -1      4   4  -1
                -4 -4  -4      0 -4  -4      4   0  -4      4   4  -4

                v 0      v 1        v 2        v 3        v 4        v 5        v 6        v 7
```

```
                              v 8      v 9      v 10     v 11     v 12     v 13     v 14     v 15

                      surface "surf" "mtl"
                              "bez3" 0 1       0.0  1.0
                              "bez3" 0 1       0.0  1.0

                              0 1 2 3 4 5 6 7 8 9 10 11 12 13 14 15

                      approximate surface parametric 3.3 3.3 "surf"
                end group
        end object

        instance "bez_surf_inst" "bez_surf"
                transform       6.3 0   0   0
                                0   6.3 0   0
                                0   0   6.3 0
                                1  -1.9 0   1
        end instance
```

Here are seven different approximation statements, using the parametric, length, distance, and angle criteria, respectively, and the Delaunay[2.1] versions of length, distance, and angle criteria. Note that the number of triangles in these examples was chosen too low for high-quality shading in order to keep the wireframe images simple.

```
        approximate surface parametric 5.0 5.0 "surf"

        approximate surface length 1.1 "surf"

        approximate surface distance 0.04 "surf"

        approximate surface angle 5.6 "surf"

        approximate surface delaunay length 1.5 "surf"

        approximate surface delaunay distance 0.0175 "surf"

        approximate surface delaunay angle 2.59 "surf"
```

Figure 13.15 shows the tessellation resulting from these approximation statements. All seven images have approximately the same number of triangles. Clearly, angle approximation uses the triangles most effectively, in areas of high curvature. However, angle approximation is also most sensitive to overly small values because if the surface has a sharp 90-degree angle, for example, the angle criterion might force a large number of subdivisions before a solution that satisfies all criteria is found, or the subdivision limit is reached. In these cases the any keyword is useful. The combination of Delaunay and angle creates very small triangles near the front center; in practice this means that a much smaller number of triangles would have been sufficient to achieve good results.

Grading is a method available for Delaunay triangulation[2.1] that allows fading tessellation density between a highly subdivided trimming or hole curve to a coarsely subdivided interior. Normally

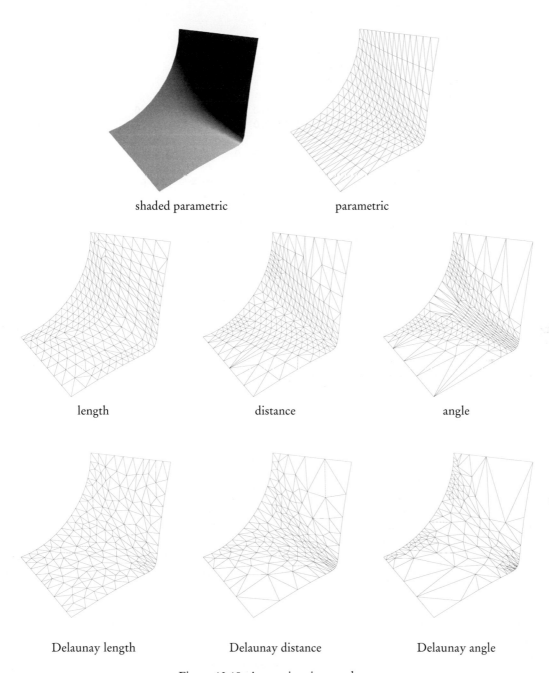

shaded parametric   parametric

length   distance   angle

Delaunay length   Delaunay distance   Delaunay angle

Figure 13.15: Approximation results.

this leads to very small triangles near the edges that directly join large triangles in the interior. If the surface is curved, this can result in visible artifacts because surface normals are stored only at triangle vertices, which means that shading quality abruptly changes near the edge. Consider this object:

```
object "bez_surf"
        visible shadow trace tag 1
        basis "bez1" bezier 1
        basis "bez3" bezier 3
        group
                -3.0 -3.0  0      3.0 -3.0  0     -3.0  3.0  0      3.0  3.0  0
                 1.5  0.0  0      2.5  0.0  0      3.0  0.5  0      3.0  1.5  0
                 3.0  2.5  0      2.5  3.0  0      1.5  3.0  0      0.5  3.0  0
                 0.0  2.5  0      0.0  1.5  0      0.0  0.5  0      0.5  0.0  0

                v 0     v 1     v 2     v 3     v 4     v 5     v 6     v 7
                v 8     v 9     v 10    v 11    v 12    v 13    v 14    v 15

                curve "boundary"
                        "bez3"          0.0  0.25 0.5  0.75  1.0
                        4 5 6 7 8 9 10 11 12 13 14 15 4

                surface "surf" "mtl"
                        "bez1" 0 3      0.0  3.0
                        "bez1" 0 3      0.0  3.0
                        0 1 2 3
                        trim "boundary"  0 1

                approximate surface delaunay length 2.5 "surf"
                approximate curve parametric 20.0 "boundary"
        end group
end object
```

It consists of a simple flat square first-degree surface with four control points, and a very finely approximated trimming curve (much more finely than necessary, for the purpose of this example). The left image of figure 13.16 shows the resulting triangle mesh with 248 triangles, most of which are long and thin and hence difficult to shade correctly. Normally Delaunay triangulation avoids long and thin triangles, but the trimming curve forces a large number of vertices at the edge and leaves it no choice here. The right image of figure 13.16 shows that introducing more triangles by changing the approximation to length 0.5 does not improve matters much — there are now three times as many triangles (758) that exhibit the typical irregular Delaunay distribution in the interior, but the triangles near the edge are still long and thin.

Figure 13.17 shows the effect of grading, using the following approximations:

```
                approximate surface delaunay length 2.5 grading 10 "surf"
                approximate curve parametric 20.0 "boundary"

                approximate surface delaunay length 2.5 grading 25 "surf"
                approximate curve parametric 20.0 "boundary"
```

The grading angles 10 and 25 are the lower limit for the smallest angle of each triangle in normalized UV parameter space. Good choices for grading angles are in the range (5...25). Angles greater than 30 are not allowed. If the angle is chosen close to 30, and if the approximation

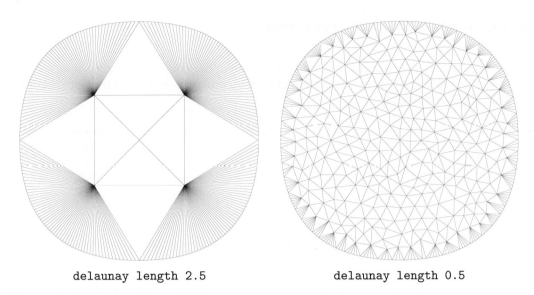

delaunay length 2.5   delaunay length 0.5

Figure 13.16: Ungraded triangulation

has no max statement, it is possible (but extremely unlikely) that there is no solution, causing mental ray to try endlessly to tessellate the surface.

The triangles now grow gradually from the edge to the interior, avoiding those long and thin triangles and thus improving shading quality. The triangle counts are 440 and 778, respectively.

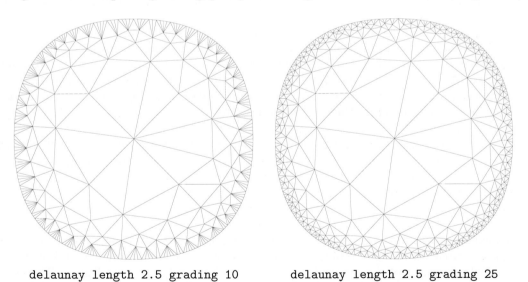

delaunay length 2.5 grading 10   delaunay length 2.5 grading 25

Figure 13.17: Graded triangulation

13.3.10   Triangle Count and Performance *

This section applies to advanced approximations only. The simple approximations are either completely predictable (regular parametric), or have no problems with large triangle counts (fine length and fine view length).

To achieve good performance and low memory usage, it is very important to choose approximations carefully. If the criteria are not strict enough, coarse tessellation results and silhouette artifacts and poor texture vector resolution becomes a problem. If the criteria are too strict, too many triangles are generated and memory usage can go up exponentially. At some point the system memory is exhausted and the machine begins swapping, which has a great impact on performance.

Always begin without approximation statements, or very coarse parametric techniques. Identify the areas that need improvement:

☑ If triangle edges are visible uniformly all over the object, especially near the edges, increase the number of subdivisions.

☑ If the surface is trimmed and triangle edges are visible only at the edges (or hole edges), provide an approximation for the curves. Otherwise do not use curve approximations.

☑ If triangle edges are visible in areas of high curvature but not elsewhere, replace the parametric technique with an angle criterion, or a combination of distance and angle criteria. Begin with large parameters and work down. Keep track of the total triangle count printed by mental ray by starting it with the -verbose on command line option.

☑ If the object is large, and some parts are much closer to the camera than others (such as a large floor), and not instanced too many (hundreds of) times, use view-dependent approximation. The view-dependent length and distance parameters are measured in fractions of pixel diagonals. This requires changing all length and distance approximation parameters, again beginning with large values and working down.

☑ If angle approximation requires a small angle to resolve sharp discontinuities, which causes excessive triangulation in other areas, combine the angle technique with the length technique, and specify the $any^{2.1}$. This effectively puts a lower bound on the size of triangles. This works well with view dependency also; the approximation may specify "subdivide until angles exceed n degrees, but do not create triangles with diagonals shorter than m pixels".

☑ Delaunay tessellation starts with an initial triangulation of the region bounded by the approximated curves and refines this triangulation until the criteria are fulfilled. A gradual refinement of the surface is necessary to achieve a "good" tessellation. Therefore, approximation constants have to be chosen more carefully than for the tree or grid styles. A coarser curve approximation should be used because the curve will be further subdivided during mesh refinement. The distance and angle techniques may not be sufficient if they do not cause enough refinement, for instance, if the surface is nearly flat. Start with the length technique and add distance and/or angle if required.

☑ If the object is displacement-mapped and misses features of the displacement map, begin with a regular parametric approximation for the surface, which provides the sample points for the displacement map, and use an additional `approximate displace` statement for adjusting the displacement approximation (for example using the angle criterion).

☑ If the triangle count shoots up suddenly when tuning parameters, set subdivision limits. It is tempting to do all tuning by adjusting the maximum limit, but this is not a good idea because it is nonspecific and applies the same maximum all over the surface, while carefully chosen curvature-dependent criteria help avoiding triangles in low-curvature "safe" areas. Normally, only a few areas of the surface require maximum tessellation.

☑ If the surface and its texture look good in a still image but begins to flash and "pop" in an animation, the length criterion parameter may need to be reduced. In some close camera flybys, it may be necessary to turn off view dependency.

☑ In an animation it can happen that a surface abruptly switches to a different approximation level because a significant number of triangles exceed some criterion all at once, for example because many triangle edges have slowly grown until they exceed the `length` criterion. If the subdivision is so coarse that reducing the length does not help, Delaunay triangulation helps distributing the triangle density changes more smoothly.

For quick previews, it is possible to specify override approximations in the options block, between the `options` and `end options` statement. Both a standard and a displacement approximation can be given. The displacement approximation has its usual syntax, but the standard approximation is given in a slightly different form:

> `approximate` [*style*] [`view`] [`any`] *technique* [*maximum*] [*limits*] `all`

No type is given, but the approximation applies to all free-form surfaces and curves, and overrides approximations found in object definitions. The `all` keyword replaces the normal name list; it can only be used in the options block.

13.3.11 Connections

Connections may be defined within a group to specify the connection between two surfaces along intervals of their respective trimming curves or hole curves. They may be used in place of or in addition to the edge merging performed on the group level. A connection is defined as:

> `connect` "*surface_name$_1$*" "*curve_name$_1$*" *min$_1$ max$_1$*
> "*surface_name$_2$*" "*curve_name$_2$*" *min$_2$ max$_2$*

This statement connects two surfaces *surface_name$_1$* and *surface_name$_2$* by connecting their trimming curves *curve_name$_1$* and *curve_name$_2$*. The curves are connected only in the range ($min_1 \ldots max_1$) and ($min_2 \ldots max_2$), respectively. They share the same points, but normals, textures and so on are evaluated on the individual surfaces. Only surfaces that have trimming curves can be connected by an explicit connect statement. Trimming curves used in connections must satisfy three conditions:

- The trimming curve or sequence of trimming curves must be closed, as always.

- It does not matter whether the trimming curve is oriented clockwise or counterclockwise, but if a sequence of trimming curves is used all pieces must have the same direction.

- The trimming curves along the connected range must run in the same direction in 3D space.

The range values $min_{1,2}$ and $max_{1,2}$ must not exceed the range of the trimming curve segment as referenced by a `trim` statement of the corresponding surface. The minimum value must be less than the maximum value. It is not possible to satisfy the third condition by inverting the range.

Best results are obtained if the curves to be connected are close to each other in world space and have at least approximately the same length. "Close" means that any gaps are the result of modeling imprecisions; connections should not be used to bridge large gaps. `connect` is not meant to be a replacement for proper modeling. For carefully modeled surfaces it will not be necessary most of the time. Its purpose is to close small cracks between adjacent surfaces that are already very close to each other. Topologically complex situations with several connections meeting in a point are beyond its scope.

13.4   Hierarchical Subdivision Surfaces

A hierarchical subdivision surface definition begins with a triangle or quadrilateral mesh called a *base mesh*. The base mesh can be refined by adding detail, in the form of detail vectors attached to vertices. During refinement, these detail vectors are added to the position which is obtained by applying refinement rules. This effectively creates a finer mesh "on top of" the base mesh. This second hierarchy level can in turn be refined by adding another detail level, and so on.

When all required detail has been added, mental ray takes over and refines the mesh to a final smooth surface called the *limit surface*. This refinement is performed by subdividing mesh faces according to specified rules. Each time a control mesh is refined it creates a mesh at a higher level that better approximates the limit surface. Figures 13.19 and 13.18 show two such mesh sequences.

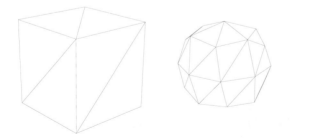

Figure 13.18: Loop refinement: base mesh and levels 1, 2, and 3.

All refinement is based on the *Loop scheme* for triangle meshes and on the *Catmull-Clark scheme* for quadrilateral meshes. The Loop scheme refines triangles into four subtriangles by inserting one vertex on each of the triangle's edges, and the Catmull-Clark scheme refines quadrilaterals

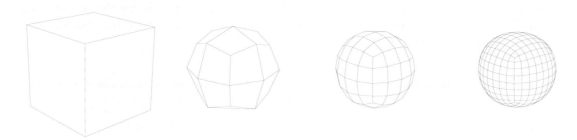

Figure 13.19: Catmull-Clark refinement: base mesh and levels 1, 2, and 3.

into four sub-quadrilaterals by inserting one vertex on each of the face edges and one vertex at the center of the face. Figures 13.20 and 13.21 show Loop and Catmull-Clark refinement, respectively. The subtriangles and subquads are called "children".

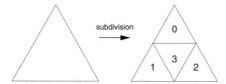

Figure 13.20: Loop refinement into child triangles.

Figure 13.21: Catmull-Clark refinement into child quads.

The main advantages of subdivision surfaces over polygons and freeform surfaces such as NURBS are:

- Works (in contrast to NURBS) with arbitrary-topology meshes
- Built-in smoothness of the generated limit surface
- Convenient access to multi-resolution representation
- Ability to animate at different scales of resolution
- Supports semisharp creases and vertex features such as sharp points
- No gaps and discontinuities across patch boundaries

Uniform subdivision as a way to approximate a limit surface quickly becomes impractical when working with higher levels. At level four there are already 256 times more triangles than on the base level. Therefore, the HSDS library adaptively subdivides the control mesh according to desired precision, which can be user specified with methods provided. The following approximation techniques are supported:

- **length** specifies a maximum edge length, that is, faces with one or more edges longer than this value are subdivided until all edge lengths are below the specified value.

- **distance** specifies the maximum distance face vertices may have relative to the parent face plane.

- **angle** specifies the maximum allowed angle between a face's normal and the normal of its parent face. This is probably the most convenient precision specification.

- **parametric** sets constant subdivision, i.e. the control mesh is uniformly subdivided.

In addition, two flags may be added:

- **view** activates view dependency, in which length and distance criteria are calculated in raster space.

- **any** activates a mode in which a given face is subdivided until at least one of any specified length, distance or angle criteria is fulfilled.

The length, distance and angle criteria can be combined so that refinement continues until all criteria are met. The definition of an HSDS object is very similar to the definition of a polygonal object, except that

- all polygons have either three or four vertices,

- the list of polygons that form a single base mesh is enclosed in `subdivision surface "name"` and `end subdivision surface`,

- and there are approximation statements that reference the name given in the `subdivision surface` statement.

Here is the complete object definition of the triangle-based tetrahedra used in figures 13.22 through 13.24, with an angle approximation of 2 degrees and subdivision limits 2 5:

```
object "tetrabool"
        group
                -1.702979        9.822667        -63.521587
                0.949628         8.403536        -62.511749
                -7.388194        -6.512138       -61.571323
                -14.962239       -10.965755      -57.906708
                -10.040801       -5.093008       -62.581161
                0.527146         -5.064838       -77.005173
```

```
        -7.260269        -6.383899        -58.403168
         1.077554         8.531778        -59.343590
         9.709921        -6.296125        -62.270470
         9.837849        -6.167886        -59.102310
         0.949630        17.499264        -59.701412
        17.667742       -10.553516        -59.240952
        12.234603        -4.811586        -63.492008
         3.474309         9.888076        -63.733288
         0.143369        -2.417650        -85.572861
         9.709921        -9.328034        -63.207249
        -7.388194        -9.544046        -62.508102
         3.051828        -0.548391        -77.289932
        -2.125460        -0.613800        -77.078232
         0.527146        -2.032930        -76.068398

    v 0 v 1 v 2 v 3 v 4 v 5
    v 6 v 7 v 8 v 9 v 10 v 11 v 12 v 13
    v 14 v 15 v 16 v 17 v 18 v 19

    subdivision surface "surf1"
            p 0 1 2            p 4 0 2            p 5 16 3
            p 14 5 3           p 1 7 6            p 2 1 6
            p 13 17 14         p 10 13 14         p 8 9 7
            p 1 8 7            p 1 13 12          p 8 1 12
            p 4 18 14          p 3 4 14           p 9 8 2
            p 6 9 2            p 8 15 16          p 2 8 16
            p 18 19 1          p 0 18 1           p 18 0 10
            p 14 18 10         p 13 1 19          p 17 13 19
            p 5 19 2           p 16 5 2           p 19 18 4
            p 2 19 4           p 14 11 15         p 5 14 15
            p 15 8 19          p 5 15 19          p 17 19 8
            p 12 17 8          p 3 10 0           p 4 3 0
            p 10 11 12         p 13 10 12         p 11 10 7
            p 9 11 7           p 11 3 16          p 15 11 16
            p 6 7 10           p 3 6 10           p 9 6 3
            p 11 9 3           p 17 12 11         p 14 17 11
    end subdivision surface

    approximate subdivision surface angle 2 2 5 "surf1"
        end group
    end object
```

This example contains only one subdivision surface mesh, but any number of them can be specified in a single object. Figure 13.22 shows two example base meshes, one triangular and one quadrilateral.

An angle criterion was used on the meshes shown in Figure 13.22 to refine them and create coarse approximations of the associated limit surfaces. The results are shown in Figure 13.23.

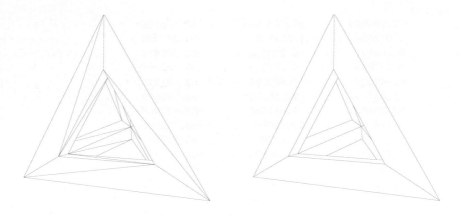

Figure 13.22: Base control meshes (left: 48 triangles, right: 24 quadrilaterals)

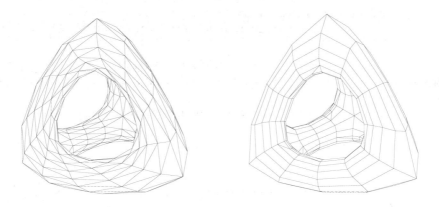

Figure 13.23: Coarse approximations (angle = 25 degrees)

Higher precision settings generate models that approximate the limit surface better. Figure 13.24 approximates the same limit surfaces more finely.

Separate approximation settings can be used for the interior and boundary of the surface or for individual faces. Subtriangles and sub-quadrilaterals inherit the assigned precision setting.

13.4.1   Adding Detail

Adding detail to a base mesh involves subdividing one of its base mesh polygons into four children. (Figures 13.20 and 13.21 show the numbering scheme.) Detail vectors can be assigned to base level vertices and to any vertices present in the subdivision level hierarchy. A vertex that is inherited by child faces in the hierarchy may have multiple detail vectors, one for each level.

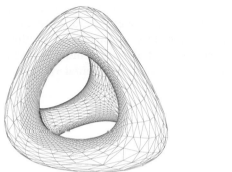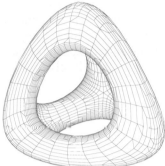

Figure 13.24: Finer approximations (angle = 8 degrees)

A *detail vector* is not a point in space but a distance vector that is *added* to a vertex coordinate. The following example introduces two such detail vectors that are added to levels 2 and 3 of the refined surface:

```
object "quadcube"
        group
                -1 -1 -1
                 1 -1 -1
                 1  1 -1
                -1  1 -1
                 0  0 -.5
                 0  0 1.5

                v 0 corner
                v 1 corner
                v 2 corner
                v 3 corner
                v 4
                v 5

                subdivision surface "surf1"
                        p 0 1 2 3 {
                                child 1 {
                                        child 0 { detail 256 5 }
                                        child 2 { detail 256 5 }
                                }
                                detail 15 4 4 4 4
                        }
                end subdivision surface
                approximate subdivision surface parametric 6 "surf1"
        end group
end object
```

To refine a mesh polygon, a block enclosed in curly braces is appended to the polygon or child to subdivide. Inside the curly braces, each of the four children, numbered 0 to 3, can be referenced and subdivided again. Inserting a `detail` statement at the end of a curly braced block attaches detail vectors to the vertices. The `detail` keyword is followed by a bitmap that specifies which vertices are shifted by a detail vector, and for each bit that was set one vertex index that references a `v` statement is specified. For details of the grammar, refer to the mental ray 3.4 manual. Figure 13.25 shows the refined surface.

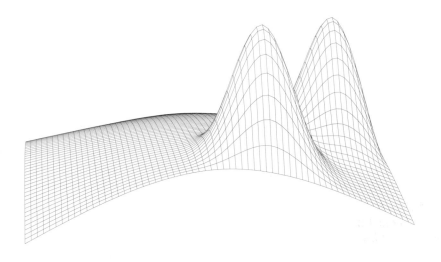

Figure 13.25: Surface with detail refinement.

13.4.2 Smooth Creases

Face edges can be tagged as creases on any level in the hierarchy. All sub-faces sharing a creased edge automatically inherit the feature. Crease edges may have an optional fractional sharpness value between 0.0 and 1.0 assigned. A value of 0.0 gives smooth shapes, while a value of 1.0 produces infinitely sharp creases. Intermediate fractional values give semisharp creases. Adjacent crease edges with different sharpness values are smoothly blended.

Figure 13.26 shows the effect of setting various sharpness values on creases. Here is an object definition that uses `crease` statements to mark all four edges of the polygons that form the roof and floor of a cube as creases:

```
object "quadcube"
        group
                -1 -1 -1
                 1 -1 -1
                 1  1 -1
                -1  1 -1
```

```
              -1 -1  1
               1 -1  1
               1  1  1
              -1  1  1

              v 0 v 1 v 2 v 3 v 4 v 5 v 6 v 7

              subdivision surface "surf1"
                    p 0 1 5 4
                    p 1 2 6 5
                    p 2 3 7 6
                    p 3 0 4 7
                    p 4 5 6 7 crease 15 1 1 1 1
                    p 0 3 2 1 crease 15 1 1 1 1
              end subdivision surface

              approximate subdivision surface parametric 0 "surf1"
        end group
  end object
```

The `crease` statement is followed by a bitmap that specifies which edges of the quad receive a crease value: bit 0 is the first edge between the first and second vertex of the quad, bit 1 is the second edge, and so on. The value 15 means that all four edges (1+2+4+8) have crease values. The crease values are the fractional sharpness values in the range from 0.0 (smooth) to 1.0 (sharp); if there are n bits set in the mask there must be n sharpness values.

Figure 13.26 shows a cube with the top and bottom edges tagged as creases, with the effects of sharpness values 0.0, 0.5, and 1.0 (from left to right, respectively).

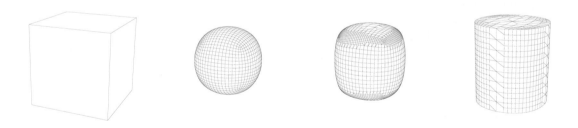

Figure 13.26: Base cube and limit surfaces with sharpness 0, 0.5, and 1.

13.4.3   Vertex Features

A vertex attached to one or more creased edges may be tagged as a *dart vertex*. The limit surface will have a well-defined tangent plane at such vertices. Interior vertices attached to exactly one creased edge are automatically tagged as dart vertices. To mark a vertex as a dart vertex, append the keyword `dart` to the `v` statement:

```
object "octaobj"
        group
                    -1 -1 0
                     1 -1 0
                     1  1 0
                    -1  1 0

                     0 -1 0
                     1  0 0
                     0  1 0
                    -1  0 0
                     0  0 1

                    v 0
                    v 1
                    v 2
                    v 3
                    v 4
                    v 5
                    v 6
                    v 7
                    v 8  dart

                    subdivision surface "surf1"
                            p 0 4 8 7 crease 2 1
                            p 4 1 5 8
                            p 7 8 6 3 crease 2 1
                            p 8 5 2 6
                    end subdivision surface

                    approximate subdivision surface parametric 4 "surf1"
            end group
    end object
```

Figure 13.27 shows the effect on a surface.

Figure 13.27: Base surface, surface without and with dart vertex.

A vertex at which two or more creased or boundary edges meet may be tagged as a *corner vertex*. The limit surface will have no tangent plane at such vertices. The surface is partitioned into smooth patches which converge at the corner vertex and are separated by the creased or boundary lines leading to it. To mark a vertex as a corner vertex, append the keyword corner to the v statement:

```
v 0 corner
v 1 corner
v 2 corner
v 3 corner
v 4
v 5
v 6
v 7
```

Figure 13.28 shows the effect on a surface when the four vertices of the floor of the base box are tagged as corners.

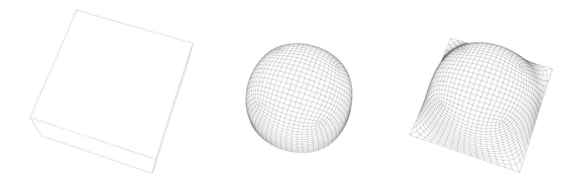

Figure 13.28: Base surface, surface without and with corner vertices.

Any non-boundary vertex may be tagged as a *conic vertex*. The limit surface will have no well-defined tangent plane at such vertices. This is done by appending the keyword conic to the vertex:

```
v 0
v 1
v 2
v 3
v 4
v 5
v 6
v 7
v 8  conic
```

Figure 13.29 shows the effect on a surface that has the vertex at the tip of the pyramid tagged as a conic vertex.

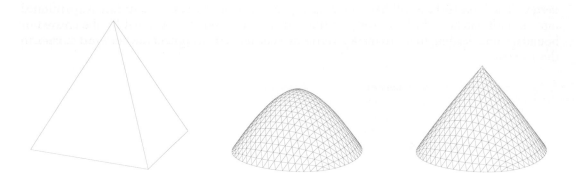

Figure 13.29: Base surface, surface without and with conic vertex.

Any non-boundary vertex may be tagged as a *cusp vertex*. At such a vertex all approaching tangent vectors on the limit surface converge to a single direction, that is, the tangent space collapses to a line. This is done by appending the cusp keyword to cusp vertices:

```
v 0
v 1
v 2
v 3
v 4
v 5
v 6
v 7
v 8   cusp
v 9
```

Figure 13.30 shows the effect on a surface where the tip of the upper pyramid is tagged as a cusp vertex.

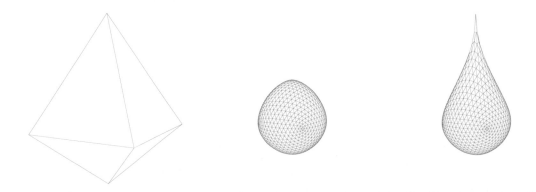

Figure 13.30: Base surface, surface without and with cusp vertex.

13.4.4 Trimming

Trimming allows non-boundary faces anywhere in the mesh hierarchy to be removed by specifying a closed loop of face edges. The region inside the trimming loop is cut out of the surface and refinement ensures that trimmed regions are never omitted from the hierarchy during tessellation. Vertices on the trim edges can be tagged with vertex features.

The following example consists of a single base polygon that is refined twice. The term "child" refers to the four subquads (or subtriangles) that the polygon is refined to. Figures 13.20 and 13.21 show the numbering scheme. A child can be flagged as a trimming child to omit it from the mesh.

```
object "quadcube"
        group
                    -1 -1 -1
                     1 -1 -1
                     1  1 -1
                    -1  1 -1
                     0  0  0
                     0  0  0

                v 0 corner
                v 1 corner
                v 2 corner
                v 3 corner
                v 4 corner
                v 5 corner

                subdivision surface "surf1"
                        p 0 1 2 3 {
                                child 0 {
                                        child 0 {}
                                        child 1 {
                                                trim 3 15
                                        }
                                        child 2 {}
                                        child 3 {}
                                }
                                child 2 {
                                        trim 0 7
                                }
                                child 3 {
                                        detail 272 4 5
                                        trim 1 13
                                }
                        }
                end subdivision surface
                approximate subdivision surface angle 2 "surf1"
        end group
    end object
```

Figure 13.32 shows a refined surface with trimming. The right mesh shows the base polygon where the four corner vertices are tagged with a *corner* feature, so the result shape will be a quad with sharp (not rounded) corners. The base polygon is subdivided once, resulting in four children. Trimming is demonstrated by cutting two holes into the shape, one oval hole consisting of two adjacent level 2 faces, and one circular hole consisting of a single level 3 face. The oval trimmed region is constructed by subdividing the two level 1 children 2 and 3: in child 2 face edges 0, 1 and 2 are trimmed, and in child 3 adjacent to the left edges 0, 2 and 3 are trimmed. Vertices 0 and 3 of this face are tagged with the corner keyword to make them sharp. Figure 13.31 shows the layout.

These two level 2 vertices have a corner feature (and zero detail vector)

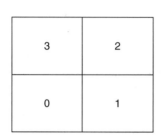
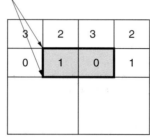
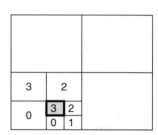

Base quad, subdivided once   A trim region defined by two   Trim region defined by one
                                         faces on level 2.   face on level 3

Figure 13.31: Mesh refinement.

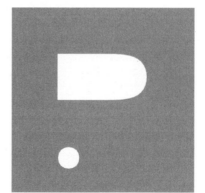

Figure 13.32: Untrimmed and trimmed surface with detail vectors.

13.5 Hair

A hair definition consists of a group of curves, each defined by a series of vertices, followed by an index list defining which vertices belong together. The vertices may form linear, quadratic bezier, or cubic bezier hairs, as specified by the degree statement. The degree must be the same for the whole hair object. Additionally, different kinds of data may be associated with each hair strand or each vertex, such as normals, textures, and so on. The radius of a hair may be specified for the object, for each hair, or at each vertex.

When the hair definition is complete and rendering proceeds, mental ray tessellates the hair strands into short linear segments, as specified by the approximate statement, on a per-segment basis. For example, a hair with a single two-segment strand and an approximate value of 3 will be tessellated as 6 linear segments, regardless of the strand type. The value of specifying the hair definition as cubic bezier versus linear segments, for example, lies in the more compact representation, and the minimal effort required to change the fineness of the tessellation to achieve a higher quality look, via the approximate statement of the hair object.

- **Hair Object Features**
  Several parameters are specified at the hair object level, including the approximate statement, and the degree of the curve. Additionally, a radius may be specified for all hairs, if no finer control is needed. Finally, the hair BSP tree may be tuned via the max size and max depth parameters.

- **Hair Strand Features**
  Additional parameters and data may be specified on a per-strand basis, including a normal, a single per-hair motion vector, texture scalars, userdata scalars, as well as a per-hair radius. The per-hair motion, radius and normal will be overridden by any present per-vertex motion, radii and normals. A per-hair normal turns the hair from a flat, ray-oriented ribbon to a flat normal-oriented ribbon.

- **Hair Vertex Features**
  Further parameters and data may be specified on a per-vertex basis, including normals, a single per-vertex motion vector, texture scalars, userdata scalars, as well as a per-vertex radius. The per-hair motion, radii and normals will override any present per-hair motion, radius and normal. A per-vertex normal turns the hair from a flat, ray-oriented ribbon to a flat normal-oriented ribbon, which can change orientation, ie. twist, from vertex to vertex. This can be useful for simulating grass, for example. The per-vertex radii can be used to splay individual hairs at the roots, and taper them at the tips, for example, for a more realistic look without excessive data.

- **Textures and Userdata**
  Textures and userdata can be used to pass information to shaders, to allow customized renders according to certain criteria. For example, the base colour of a strand of hair can be passed as a per-hair texture. This could then be used to colour hair near temples grey, perhaps combined with another texture scalar specifying the rate of colour change along the hair, while not requiring expensive per-vertex colours. Note that hair uses scalars, not vectors like polygonal and freeform surface objects: for an XYZ vector or RGB color, three scalars are required. This makes storage of UV textures (two scalars) or linear data (one scalar) more efficient because no scalars are wasted; this is important because hair objects

can be very large. (Human heads are typically modeled with some 100,000 hairs, each of which may have ten or more vertices.)

This table summarizes the features that can be attached to the entire object, to hairs, and to vertices:

feature	object	strand	vertex	combining
approximate, degree	●	○	○	—
max size, max depth	●	○	○	—
material	●	○	○	—
radius	●	●	●	override
normal vector	○	●	●	override
motion vector	○	●	●	override
texture scalars	○	●	●	append
userdata scalars	○	●	●	append

Normal vectors, motion vectors, and radii supplied at the vertex level override the corresponding normal, motion, or radius at the hair level, and a hair radius overrides the object radius. Texture and userdata scalars are appended, so that the shader sees both: first all the strand scalars, followed by the vertex scalars.

Here is the scene file syntax, excluding the flags and parameters shared by all geometric objects:

```
object "object_name"
    [ ... ]
    hair
        [ material      "material_name" ]
        [ radius        radius ]
        [ approximate   approx_int ]
        [ degree        degree_int ]
        [ max size      max_size_int ]
        [ max depth     max_size_int ]

        [ hair    n ]
        [ hair    m   hm_count_int ]
        [ hair    t   ht_count_int ]
        [ hair    radius ]
        [ hair    u   hu_count_int ]
        [ vertex n ]
        [ vertex m   vm_count_int ]
        [ vertex t   vt_count_int ]
        [ vertex radius ]
        [ vertex u   vu_count_int ]

        scalar [ s_count_int ]   scalar_list
        hair   [ i_count_int ]   index_list_int
    end group
end hair
```

This syntax is designed to pass large amounts of data with a minimum of syntactic overhead. The hair definition begins with information shared by the entire object: the material (unless inherited from the instance), a shared hair radius, the approximation that specifies the number of linear segments each hair segment is to be divided into (this is equivalent to a parametric freeform surface approximation, the hair curve degree (1, 2, or 3), and the hair BSP parameters for this object (usually the defaults are adequate).

This is followed by a description of the format of each strand of hair: does each strand have a radius or a normal (n), and the number of motion vectors (m), texture scalars (t), and userdata scalars (u). This information is shared by all strands; a missing statement means "none". The description of each vertex of each hair follows.

The list of scalars contains all floating-point data describing each strand of hair. The number of scalars needed for each strand is determined by the preceding hair and vertex statements: three scalars (XYZ) for the hair normal if enabled, then $3 \cdot hm\_count$ scalars (XYZXYZ...) for the motion vectors (hm_count may not exceed 15), then ht_count scalars for the hair texture scalars, then hu_count scalars for the hair userdata scalars, and then the same for the vertex data of each vertex. After all this, the next hair scalars follow. The s_count number, enclosed in literal square brackets, is the total number of scalars in *scalar_list*. Figure 13.33 shows the layout.

Finally, the *index_list* contains one integer per hair strand that is the index into the *scalar_list* where that hair strand definition begins, followed by one extra integer at the end that is the index of the scalar one past the last scalar of the last hair. Typically, the first index is 0 and the last index equals s_count. This method makes it easy to find the number of scalars used for a particular strand of hair: it's the next hair's index minus the hair's index. Again, the number of indices in *index_list* must be specified as i_count in literal square brackets.

13.5.1 Optimizing Hair Usage

Hair does not support object splitting, up to and including ray 3.4. Hence it is important to plan hair objects well, so that they do not cause excessive consumption of memory at tessellation time. Grouping hairs into logical chunks is very important, and should be done in such a fashion that the chunks are as compact in space as possible. Examples would be separate hair objects for legs, tail, ears, face, and so on, for a furry creature.

When rendering with the regular scanline algorithm or raytracing, it can become necessary to tune the hair bsp parameters to obtain optimal performance. When rendering with the rasterizer, the hairs are converted to triangles, which need no separate tuning.

When planning auxiliary data needs for hair objects, it is important to try to push as much data to the hair object as possible, and where this is not possible, to put the data in per-hair storage. Large hair objects with several per-vertex textures and per-vertex radii and normals can quickly consume large amounts of memory.

Careful tuning of the `approximate` statement is also important. It is easy to specify a high value for a high quality look, but there will be a penalty in memory consumption and rendering time, so careful tuning to achieve the minimal value is important. It is crucial to know at what distances

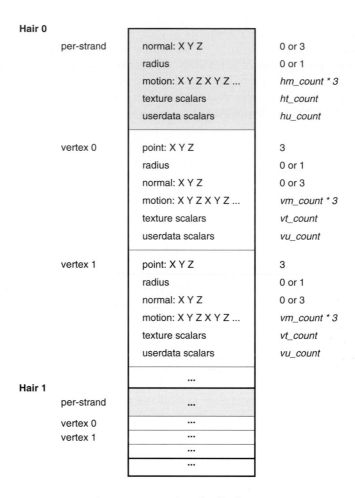

Hair 0

per-strand	normal: X Y Z	0 or 3
	radius	0 or 1
	motion: X Y Z X Y Z ...	hm_count * 3
	texture scalars	ht_count
	userdata scalars	hu_count
vertex 0	point: X Y Z	3
	radius	0 or 1
	normal: X Y Z	0 or 3
	motion: X Y Z X Y Z ...	vm_count * 3
	texture scalars	vt_count
	userdata scalars	vu_count
vertex 1	point: X Y Z	3
	radius	0 or 1
	normal: X Y Z	0 or 3
	motion: X Y Z X Y Z ...	vm_count * 3
	texture scalars	vt_count
	userdata scalars	vu_count
	...	

Hair 1

per-strand	...	
vertex 0	...	
vertex 1	...	
	...	
	...	

Figure 13.33: Hair scalar list layout.

the hair will be viewed to avoid excessive tessellation.

Also related to the distance at which the hair will be rendered is the detail modeled of the original hair object. Modeling a human head of hair with a realistic 150,000 hairs should be avoided for characters which will occupy only small areas of the screen, or which will be motion blurred. Care should be taken to create hair objects whose individual hair overlap each other as little as possible, while satisfying quality criteria. Heavily overlapping hairs can cause long rendering times.

Furthermore, the hair primitive has been optimized to render faster than triangles with certain assumptions in mind. The primary assumption is that the hair is small in screen space, ie. the width of hairs will not exceed 1 pixel by much. As such, highly detailed cylindrical shading will not be necessary, although the intersection information does provide enough information to allow this. Specialized hair shaders are crucial to achieving a high quality look without excessive rendering times, and can eliminate the need for much data, by simulating certain effects.

13.5.2 Example

This is a simple example of a hair object consisting of 25x25 hairs, built from cubic Bézier curves with randomized control points. All vertices have normals to turn the hair into twisting ribbons, and each vertex has a radius to make the ribbons taper to a point. The hair object uses a simple *mib_illum_phong* material.

```
object "hair1Shape"
        visible trace shadow tag 1
        hair
              material      "hairSG"
              approximate 20
              degree        3
              vertex        radius
              vertex        n
              scalar [ 30625 ]
                  # coord X Y Z              radius      normal X Y Z
                  -9.704   0.000  -9.848     0.200      0.705  0.000   0.709
                  -9.842   1.946  -9.975     0.200      0.788  0.000   0.615
                  -9.137   4.972  -9.138     0.200      0.834  0.000   0.552
                  -9.123   6.195  -9.308     0.200      0.927  0.000   0.375
                  # ....4368 lines omitted....
                   9.488   7.850  10.269     0.200      0.998  0.000  -0.065
                  10.291   8.367  10.364     0.200      0.896  0.000  -0.445
                  10.520  11.157  10.107     0.000      0.765  0.000  -0.643

              hair [ 626 ]
                     0 49 98 147 196 245 294 343 392 441 490 539 588 637 686 735 784
                     833 882 931 980 1029 1078 1127 1176 1225 1274 1323 1372 1421
                     1470 1519 1568 1617 1666 1715 1764 1813 1862 1911 1960 2009
                     # ....53 lines omitted....
                     29351 29400 29449 29498 29547 29596 29645 29694 29743 29792
                     29841 29890 29939 29988 30037 30086 30135 30184 30233 30282
                     30331 30380 30429 30478 30527 30576 30625
        end hair
end object
```

Figure 13.34 shows the rendered image.

Figure 13.35 shows a tribble with 30000 cylindrical linear hairs.

13.6 Procedural Geometry

Instead of defining geometric objects with object statements containing polygons and free-form surfaces, they can be built procedurally by *geometry shaders*. A geometry shader is a plug-in written in C or C++ that uses a dedicated shader API (Application Programming Interface) to build scene elements. The shader API is structured in the same way as the mental ray .mi scene

Figure 13.34: Using a hair object to render grass.

language; there is a direct correspondence between language elements and shader API elements. The details of the API are beyond the scope of this book; see [PROG].

Geometry created by geometry shaders is attached to the scene in one of two ways: either attaching it to a Phenomenon geometry root, or by naming it in an instance. For the former, see page 286. Instances name geometry shaders with the geometry keyword:

```
instance "instance_name"
    geometry "shader_name" ( parameters )
    ...
end instance
```

As always, instead of listing an anonymous shader, it is possible to use a shader assignment of a named shader definition. See page 278 for details.

Here is an example using several geometry shaders from the base shader library:

Figure 13.35: 30000 hairs.

```
instance "sphere_inst"
        geometry "mib_geo_sphere" (
                "u_subdiv"      64,
                "v_subdiv"      64
        )
        material "mtl"
        transform       2    0    0    0
                        0    2    0    0
                        0    0    2    0
                       -2   -.8   1    1
end instance

instance "cone_inst"
        geometry "mib_geo_cone" (
                "u_subdiv"      64,
                "v_subdiv"       4
        )
        material "mtl"
```

```
        transform          2.5 0     0     0
                           0   0     0.7   0
                           0  -2.5   0     0
                          -1   1.5  -0.5   1
end instance

instance "cylinder_inst"
        geometry "mib_geo_cylinder" (
                "u_subdiv"      64,
                "v_subdiv"      2,
                "top_capped"    true
        )
        material "mtl"
        transform          6   0     0     0
                           0   6     0     0
                           0   0     1     0
                           2  -3     0     1
end instance

instance "cube_inst"
        geometry "mib_geo_cube" ()
        material "mtl"
        transform          1.3 0     0     0
                           0   1.3   0     0
                           0   0     1.3   0
                           0.5 1     1     1
end instance

instgroup "rootgrp"
        "cam_inst" "light1_inst"
        "sphere_inst" "cube_inst" "cylinder_inst" "cone_inst"
end instgroup
```

Figure 13.36 shows the image.

Since geometry shaders have access to the entire mental ray shader API, they can do much more than this. For example, it is possible to write a geometry shader that has shader parameters of type *object*, which means it can build objects based on other objects, which in turn may be either scene file objects or procedural objects themselves. Geometry shaders may also add instances, lights, groups, even cameras. Everything that can be found in a scene file except the render statement can be created procedurally by a geometry shader. For example, this makes it possible to write a particle system based on animatable density functions in terms of geometry shaders and volume shaders.

Note that geometry shaders are generally not compatible between mental ray 2.0 and 2.1 because the geometry shader interface was extended in mental ray 2.1 to support additional features. Using geometry shaders compiled for the wrong mental ray may crash or have unexpected results. mental ray 3.x introduced further minor changes that might cause geometry shaders for mental ray 2.1 fail when run under 3.x, but most shaders are not affected by this. See [PROG] for details.

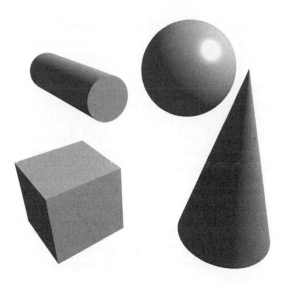

Figure 13.36: Objects created by geometry shaders.

13.7 Demand-loaded Placeholder Geometry

As described on page 431, mental ray 3.x is capable of deferring operations until the time their results are actually accessed. This has a number of advantages, such as avoiding a lot of dead weight in memory for things that are not currently needed, and that might in fact never be needed. It's not uncommon to render a small portion of a large scene, and not having to fit the entire scene including the off-screen parts in memory saves a lot of time and space.

On-demand loading is always done for tessellated geometry, which is under complete control of mental ray 3.x, but it can be extended to object definitions in .mi scene files too. mental ray cannot go back to the scene file later and reload portions of it because scene files tend to be so large that they do not reside on disk but merely as pipelines fed by a modeling or translation tool. However, mental ray 3.x allows object definitions to be merely "placeholders" that do not specify any actual geometry, but a *reference* to another file that does contain the geometry.

A placeholder object contains a `file` statement instead of the usual `group ... end group` statements. It *must* contain `box` and, if required, `motion box` and `max displace` statements, so that mental ray knows when it is getting close enough to the placeholder object to load it:

```
object " object_name"
    ...
    box            low_vector high_vector
  [ motion box     low_vector high_vector ]
  [ max displace   disp ]
    file           "filename"
end object
```

This definition, and all its statements, are the same as for regular objects as described on page 303, except that the box statement is no longer optional, and the new `file` statement. When mental ray enters the specified bounding box of the object, for example because a ray has hit it, it will open the file *filename* and parse it. *filename* is expected to be in regular .mi scene file format, and may contain any legal .mi syntax except `render` statements.

The file must contain a definition for *object_name* that is not a placeholder. It must repeat the placeholder object definition exactly except that the `file` statement is replaced with a `group` ... `end group` block that contains the actual geometry. The file may also contain other top-level objects such as materials or shaders required for the object definition. mental ray will load the entire file and not just pick the parts it needs; only when loading has completed it checks whether the required placeholder has been properly defined (and aborts if not, this is a fatal error).

This means that it is possible to define a whole group of small objects in the demand-loaded file *filename*, and have multiple placeholder objects reference this *filename*. When the first of these is needed, they all get defined. However, this has two disadvantages: more data is loaded than necessary, which defeats the purpose, and if one of the objects is later deleted from the geometry cache but then accessed again, mental ray must load the entire file again, which wastes time and causes redefinition warnings.

It is recommended that placeholder objects are only used for large objects. The `explode` sub-option of the `-echo` command line option will create one file for every object, no matter how small, which is not efficient because the overhead of opening, parsing, and attaching the file contents far outweighs the benefit. (The `explode` mode is still useful for quickly splitting a scene file into its constituents.)

The ray interaction on/off flags (visible, reflection[3.4], refraction[3.4], transparency[3.4], shadow, shadowmap[3.3], caustic, globillum, and finalgather[3.4]) are especially useful here. For example, if a photon enters the bounding box of a placeholder object that has the corresponding flag turned off, the photon will pass right through the box without causing the object to be loaded from its scene file.

Chapter 14

Instancing and Grouping

14.1 Instances

Instances are scene elements that place other elements such as objects, lights, cameras, and sub-groups in the right place in 3D space where they can be rendered. Every instance references exactly one element to be instanced, plus additional information:

- The element to be instanced may either be the quoted name of an object, light, camera, or instance group, or a geometry shader introduced with the `geometry` keyword. In the geometry shader case, the shader is called at scene preprocessing time just before rendering, and is expected to generate an object, light, camera, or instance group with which preprocessing can then proceed. Procedural elements are deleted automatically after rendering.

- The `transform` keyword allows specification of a matrix that converts the parent coordinate space above the instance to the space of the instanced element. This matrix is optional but will nearly always be used because it provides the relation between world space (at the top of the scene graph) and object space (at the bottom of the scene graph). The camera is also placed in 3D space with an instance, so the camera instance transformation matrix converts world space to camera space.

- The `motion transform` statement does a very similar thing, except that it specifies the motion transformation matrix, which gives rise to motion blur. If the motion matrix is omitted, it effectively defaults to an identity matrix. The alternate form `motion off` cancels any motion transformation inherited from above, which effectively nails the instanced element in place in the 3D world, as far as blurring is concerned, even if it belongs to a moving sub-scene. See chapter 8 for details on motion blurring.

- The `tag`[2.1] statement sets a **label** in the instance, which can be used for identification purposes. The mental ray rendering software does not use it but makes it available to shaders, which can alter their behavior based on the label.

- The data[2.1] statement allows attaching user data to the instance. User data is not used by mental ray but can be accessed by shaders. See page 287 for details. If the null keyword is used instead of the name of a user data block, any existing user data block reference is removed from the instance; this is useful for incremental changes. If more than one data statement is specified, they are connected to a chain in the order specified. Shaders can traverse the chain.

- The material statement allows . If the name of a material (not a material shader) is given, it replaces any inherited material with this one and propagates it down the instanced element or subgraph. It is also possible to specify a square-bracketed material list here, for tagged objects whose primitives select inherited materials by index. If the index is too large for the list, the first material of the list is used.

  For this and the other kinds of inheritance, see chapter 15. If the override[3.x] flag is set before the material keyword, this material becomes the final object material even if "lower" instances or the object itself specify other materials.

- The hide statement allows disabling the instance. If set to on, the instance and its contents are ignored, as if it and its reference in the parent instance group had been removed. This is useful for quick preview rendering of parts of the scene without massive changes to the database.

- The visible, reflection, refraction, transparency, trace, shadow, shadowmap, caustic, globillum, finalgather, hardware, and face flags are used for flag inheritance. They are propagated down the scene graph and override similar flags in geometric objects. See page 389 for details. Note that the $mode_{int}$ fields in instances have extra bits for turning flags *off*, where objects only have the bits for turning flags *on*).

- Finally, parameters may attached to an instance much like parameters can be defined for named shaders. If an instance does not require parameters, it is not required — and in fact not efficient — to use an opening parenthesis directly followed by a closing parenthesis as is done in shader definitions because that would store a null parameter block, as opposed to omitting the parameter block. Like shader parameters, instance parameters must be declared. The declaration used is the declaration of the inheritance shader specified in the options block, and it is the same for all instances in the scene.

Here is the complete syntax summary:

```
instance "instance_name"
    [ "item" ]
    [ geometry "shader_name" ( parameters ) ]
    [ transform          a00 a01 a02 a03 a10 a11 a12 a13 a20 a21 a22 a23 a30 a31 a32 a33 ]
    [ motion transform   [ a00 a01 a02 a03 a10 a11 a12 a13 a20 a21 a22 a23 a30 a31 a32 a33 ]]
    [ motion             off ]
    [ tag                label_int ]
    [ data               "data_name" | null ]
    [ material           "material_name" ]
    [ material           [ "material_name" "material_name" ... ] ]
    [ override material  "material_name" ]
    [ override material  [ "material_name" "material_name" ... ] ]
```

```
      [ hide              on | off ]
      [ visible           on | off ]
      [ reflection        mode_int ]^3.4
      [ refraction        mode_int ]^3.4
      [ transparency      mode_int ]^3.4
      [ trace             on | off ]
      [ shadow            on | off | mode_int^3.4 ]
      [ shadowmap         on | off ]^3.3
      [ caustic           on | off | mode_int ]
      [ globillum         on | off | mode_int ]
      [ finalgather       on | off | mode_int ]^3.4
      [ hardware          on | off ]^3.3
      [ face              front | back | both ]^3.4
      [ ( parameters ) ]
  end instance
```

The meaning of the statements is described in the Inheritance chapter on page 379. Flags are described on page page 389 in the same chapter.

14.2 Instance Groups

Instance groups are containers for instances. All scene graphs have an instance group at the top (called the *root group*), which contains the camera instance and instances for lights, objects, and other instance groups. Multilevel scene graphs can be constructed by defining an instance for a sub-group and putting this instance into a parent group. (This is explored in more detail in the next chapter.)

Instance groups are very simple:

```
  instgroup "instgroup_name"
      [ tag      label_int ]
      [ data     "data_name" | null ]
      [ "instance_name" ... ]
  end instgroup
```

The optional label[2.1] and user data[2.1] blocks can be used for identification purposes. mental ray does not use it but makes it available to shaders, which can alter their behavior based on the label and the user data. If multiple user data blocks are specified, they are chained; `data null` detaches an existing data block or data block chain.

The list of instances forms the body of the loop. This list is cleared on every incremental change of the instance group using the .mi language; there are no statements to individually add or delete instances.

14.3   Multiple Instancing

The previous chapters used simple scenes consisting of objects that were instanced once in the scene. However, the power of instances is best exploited when multiple instances refer to the same object. The advantage is that objects that appear in a scene many times need to be defined only once, but appear in the scene at several different places and orientations. Consider an auditorium: it may contain hundreds of chairs that would greatly increase the scene size, but with multiple instancing it becomes possible to define a single chair object and place many instances of it in the auditorium.

Since instance groups can themselves be instanced, this can be taken one step further. Suppose that the auditorium has five rows of ten chairs each. It is possible to create one chair object and 50 instances placing it in the appropriate positions, but it is easier to define ten instances of chairs that make up one row, and place them in an instance group named "row". This row instance group is then instanced five times, using five instances that all reference "row" and are put into the root instance group.

The following scene example simplifies this example — cubes replace chairs, and there are only two rows of two cubes each. The part of example 1 on page 32 up to end object remains the same, but the remainder defining "cube1_inst", "cam_inst", and "rootgrp" is replaced with the following definitions:

```
instance "cube1_inst1" "cube1"
        transform         1     0   0   0
                          0     1   0   0
                          0     0   1   0
                         -0.7   0   0   1
end instance

instance "cube1_inst2" "cube1"
        transform         1     0   0   0
                          0     1   0   0
                          0     0   1   0
                          0.7   0   0   1
end instance

instgroup "row"
        "cube1_inst1" "cube1_inst2"
end instgroup

instance "row_inst1" "row"
        transform         1   0     0   0
                          0   1     0   0
                          0   0     1   0
                          0  -0.7   0   1
end instance

instance "row_inst2" "row"
        transform         1   0     0   0
```

```
                             0   1    0  0
                             0   0    1  0
                             0   0.7  0  1
        end instance

        instance "cam_inst" "cam"
                transform      0.7719   0.3042  -0.5582  0.0
                               0.0000   0.8781   0.4785  0.0
                               0.6357  -0.3693   0.6778  0.0
                               0.0000   0.0000  -4.1000  1.0
        end instance

        instgroup "rootgrp"
                "cam_inst"   "light1_inst"
                "row_inst1"  "row_inst2"
        end instgroup

        render "rootgrp" "cam_inst" "opt"
```

Note how "cube1_inst1" and "cube2_inst2" shift the cube to the left and right, and how "row_inst1" and "row_inst2" shift the rows up and down. The camera instance has been changed slightly to dolly the camera back another 1.5 world space units. The scene hierarchy looks like figure 14.1; figure 14.2 shows the rendered image.

Note that the top right cube appears slightly brighter than the bottom left cube because it is closer to the light. The fact that a single piece of geometry is placed in the scene multiple times instead of defining it individually has no effect on the end result; each visible object is still shaded as if it consisted of unique geometry. Instancing is a scene construction tool, not an image copying operation.

14.4 Coordinate Spaces

Remember that an instance contains a transformation matrix that transforms the parent coordinate space into the local coordinate space of the instanced element. In the previous example, the local coordinate space of the element remains unchanged, with the origin at the center of the element. When a material shader or any other shader attached to the element performs an operation in object space, it will work with the coordinates the element was defined in, no matter where the instances have put it in world coordinates. In this example the cubes go through two coordinate transformations: one when "cube1_inst1" and "cube1_inst2" shift it sideways, and another one when "row_inst1" and "row_inst2" shift it up and down.

The mental ray rendering software distinguishes four 3D coordinate spaces:

- **Object space** is the space objects are defined in, if the options block enables object space computations (which is the standard mode). All vertices, control points, and other vectors that define the object are given in object space coordinates. Typically, the object space origin is at the center of the object.

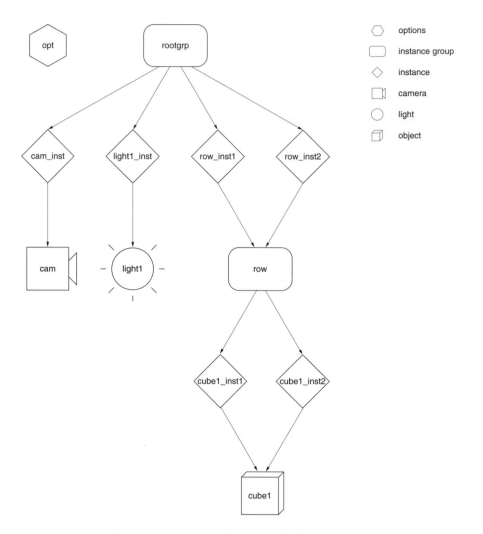

Figure 14.1: Scene graph with multiple instancing.

- **Camera space** is the space with the camera at its origin. The camera looks down the negative Z axis, and the Y axis points up.

- **World space** is the space of the root group that forms the root of the scene graph.

- **Internal space** is an abstraction used internally by mental ray and shaders. It is not relevant for the scene definition, and is listed here only for completeness.

The relation between object, camera, and world space is defined by the transformation matrices in the instances that connect the elements of the scene graph. Instance transformation matrices always specify the transformation from the parent space "above" the instance to the local space of the instanced element. For example, the camera instance in the root group specifies the transformation from world space to camera space. When applied to a world space vector, it generates the camera space vector. If an object is attached to the root group with an instance,

Figure 14.2: Multiple instancing.

the transformation matrix of that instance defines the mapping from world space to the object's object space.

Since it is possible to create a hierarchy of instance groups, like in the example above, in which multiple instances must be traversed from the root group at the top of the scene graph to the object at the bottom, a hierarchy of local spaces can exist, each defined by the instance that connects the instance group or object to the next higher space.

On page 238, motion matrices were introduced. They are also stored in instances, and specify the transformation matrices of the next frame, slightly later. If they differ from the regular instance transformation matrix, motion blurring is computed (if enabled in the options block).

Chapter 15

Inheritance

The previous section introduced multiple instancing, with instances that move a cube to multiple different locations in world space. This is only one of the two main purposes of instances. They also support inheritance. There are four different kinds that can be individually and independently specified in an instance:

- **Material inheritance** propagates materials down the scene hierarchy to objects that do not specify their own materials.

- **Tagged material inheritance** propagates material arrays down the scene hierarchy to objects that specify indices instead of materials. The indices select materials from the inherited material array.

- **Parameter inheritance** allows attaching arbitrary typed parameters to instances, and propagating them down the scene hierarchy in configurable ways.

- **Flag inheritance** propagates the visible, shadow, caustics, and all the other flags specified in instances and objects down the scene hierarchy.

Inheritance operates differently for each kind, but the general idea is that there is information stored in instances that travels down the scene graph, beginning at the root and propagating to the bottom "leaf" nodes. Information stored in instances higher up in the graph can potentially affect more objects than instances lower in the graph, because there are more paths leading down the graph. However, depending on the type of instancing, lower instances can override inherited information before it reaches objects at the bottom of the graph.

15.1   Material Inheritance

Material inheritance is the most common form of inheritance. It allows specification of materials in instances, instead of in the object. Consider the following scene, which builds on the previous scene, but changes all lines after "end camera" to the following description:

```
material "bright"
        opaque
        "mib_illum_phong" (
            "ambient"   0.6   0.6   0.6,
            "diffuse"   0.9   0.9   0.9,
            "specular"  1.2   1.2   1.2,
            "ambience"  0.5   0.5   0.5,
            "exponent"  50,
            "mode"      1,
            "lights"    ["light1_inst"]
        )
end material

material "dark"
        opaque
        "mib_illum_phong" (
            "ambient"   0.2   0.2   0.2,
            "diffuse"   0.5   0.5   0.5,
            "specular"  0.8   0.8   0.8,
            "ambience"  0.2   0.2   0.2,
            "exponent"  50,
            "mode"      1,
            "lights"    ["light1_inst"]
        )
end material

material "flat"
        opaque
        "mib_illum_phong" (
            "ambient"   0.1   0.1   0.1,
            "ambience"  1.0   1.0   1.0
        )
end material

object "cube1"
        visible trace shadow
        tag 1
        group
                -0.5 -0.5 -0.5
                -0.5 -0.5  0.5
                -0.5  0.5 -0.5
                -0.5  0.5  0.5
                 0.5 -0.5 -0.5
                 0.5 -0.5  0.5
                 0.5  0.5 -0.5
                 0.5  0.5  0.5

                v 0   v 1   v 2   v 3
                v 4   v 5   v 6   v 7

                p 0  1  3  2
                p 1  5  7  3
                p 5  4  6  7
```

```
                        p  4   0   2   6
                        p  4   5   1   0
                        p  2   3   7   6
            end group
end object

instance "cube1_inst1" "cube1"
        material        "bright"
        transform       1    0   0   0
                        0    1   0   0
                        0    0   1   0
                        -0.7 0   0   1
end instance

instance "cube1_inst2" "cube1"
        transform       1    0   0   0
                        0    1   0   0
                        0    0   1   0
                        0.7  0   0   1
end instance

instgroup "row"
        "cube1_inst1" "cube1_inst2"
end instgroup

instance "row_inst1" "row"
        material        "dark"
        transform       1  0    0   0
                        0  1    0   0
                        0  0    1   0
                        0  -0.7 0   1
end instance

instance "row_inst2" "row"
        material        "flat"
        transform       1  0    0   0
                        0  1    0   0
                        0  0    1   0
                        0  0.7  0   1
end instance

instance "cam_inst" "cam"
        transform       0.7719   0.3042  -0.5582  0.0
                        0.0000   0.8781   0.4785  0.0
                        0.6357  -0.3693   0.6778  0.0
                        0.0000   0.0000  -4.1000  1.0
end instance

instgroup "rootgrp"
        "cam_inst"  "light1_inst"
        "row_inst1"  "row_inst2"
end instgroup
```

```
render "rootgrp" "cam_inst" "opt"
```

Instead of one material "mtl", there are now three, named "bright", "dark", and "flat". As the names imply, the bright material uses much brighter colors than the dark material, and the flat material assigns a constant color everywhere on the object, regardless of lighting. These materials have been referenced in various instances in the scene, and the old "mtl" material in the object has been removed. Figure 15.1 shows the resulting image.

Figure 15.1: Material inheritance.

Material inheritance allowed the cube, whose geometry was defined only once, to appear with different surface properties in different places in the scene. This example only used different colors, but since materials also control other effects such as transparency, texturing, and volume effects, the range of what material inheritance can do is quite large.

Figure 15.2 shows the scene graph. It is the same as the previous one that introduced multiple instancing, except that all materials are shown in the instances in boldface italics.

Note that the object itself has no material, and neither does the instance "cube1_inst2". The operating principle here is that material references lower in the graph override materials inherited from higher up. A material referenced in the object itself is "lowest" and overrides any inherited instance materials. To see which cube ends up with which material, it helps to follow all the arrow paths from the root group to the cube (the groups were omitted for clarity, they do not participate in inheritance):

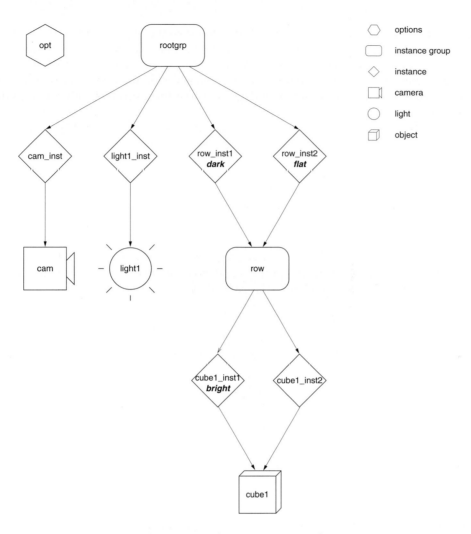

Figure 15.2: Inheritance scene graph.

row_inst1	$\longrightarrow$	cube1_inst1	$\longrightarrow$	cube1
dark		*bright*		*bright*
row_inst1	$\longrightarrow$	cube1_inst2	$\longrightarrow$	cube1
dark				*dark*
row_inst2	$\longrightarrow$	cube1_inst1	$\longrightarrow$	cube1
flat		*bright*		*bright*
row_inst2	$\longrightarrow$	cube1_inst2	$\longrightarrow$	cube1
flat				*flat*

As you can see, in every case the material defined closest to the object "wins". If the object had any materials of its own, this would win over anything inherited from the instances, which is why the object material was removed in the example. It is, however, possible to define materials for some polygons or free-form surfaces and leave others undefined; in this case the polygons without materials use inheritance and the polygons or free-form surfaces with materials do not.

mental ray 3.0 allows a material reference in an instance to be prefixed with the keyword override. This changes the inheritance algorithm such that the override material "wins" over all lower materials, and even the materials defined in the object itself.

15.2   Tagged Material Inheritance

Simple material inheritance works well if a single material is inherited. An object may still use multiple materials, but all of them except the one that is inherited must be defined in the object itself, which means they always look the same regardless of where in the scene they are instanced.

The alternative is to let instances provide not a single material, but a list of materials. Lists of materials are inherited down the scene graph just like simple materials — the lists in lower instances override lists in higher instances. In every case, the entire list is inherited or overridden as a unit; lists are never merged.

If an object inherits a list of materials, each of its polygons or surfaces must be able to specify which material in the inherited list applies to it. This is done by assigning tag numbers (also known as labels) to polygons. (Tag numbers can also be assigned to objects and light sources, but material inheritance only deals with polygon tags.) An object can either specify materials or tags in its polygon or surface definitions, but mixtures are not allowed. Objects that specify tags must be marked with the tagged keyword.

Instances may contain materials or material lists, objects may be tagged, and polygons may contain materials or tags. The following combinations are possible:

instance	object	polygon	result
—	—	material	polygon material
—	—	—	previous polygon material
material	—	material	polygon material
material	—	—	previous polygon material if any, or
material	—	—	instance material if no previous polygon material
material	tagged	tag	instance material
material list	—	—	first instance material
material list	—	material	polygon material
material list	tagged	tag	*tag*-th instance material

All combinations not listed here are not legal because they would leave the material undefined. If this happens, the mental ray rendering software will print an error message during rendering and leave the object black. In the instance column, the inheritance result applies: if the lowest instance does not have a material or material list of its own, the nearest higher instance that does will be used. Instance materials can override instance material lists and vice versa; a single material is the same as a material list with a single member (but very slightly more efficient when rendering).

The table shows the same principle that applies to material inheritance in general — materials defined lower in the scene graph override materials inherited from higher up in the graph. Note that if an object is marked tagged it *must* specify a tag; it is not possible to omit it as is possible to omit materials in untagged objects. Omitting materials in untagged objects specifies that the same material as defined in the previous polygon should be used; inheritance applies only if there is no previous polygon with a material in this object. This avoids long inefficient and space-consuming columns of identical materials in objects with many polygons that do not use inheritance. It also means that untagged objects with both polygons that inherit their materials, and polygons that specify their own, the polygons that should inherit must be listed first because otherwise they would take the material of some previously defined polygon that had one.

All this applies not only to objects defining polygons, but also to objects defining free-form surfaces. Here is an example based on the first single-cube example in this chapter on page 32. All statements after end camera are replaced with:

```
material "flat-bright"
        opaque
        "mib_illum_phong" (
            "ambient"   0.8  0.8  0.8,
            "ambience"  1.0  1.0  1.0
        )
end material

material "flat-dark"
        opaque
        "mib_illum_phong" (
            "ambient"   0.3  0.3  0.3,
            "ambience"  1.0  1.0  1.0
        )
end material

shader "shd-f-t"
        "mib_illum_phong" (
            "ambient"   0.1  0.1  0.1,
            "ambience"  1.0  1.0  1.0
        )

material "flat-transp"
        "mib_transparency" (
            "input"     = "shd-f-t",
            "transp"    0.4  0.4  0.4
        )
end material
```

```
object "cube1"
        tagged
        visible trace shadow
        tag 1
        group
                -0.5 -0.5 -0.5
                -0.5 -0.5  0.5
                -0.5  0.5 -0.5
                -0.5  0.5  0.5
                 0.5 -0.5 -0.5
                 0.5 -0.5  0.5
                 0.5  0.5 -0.5
                 0.5  0.5  0.5

                v 0   v 1   v 2   v 3
                v 4   v 5   v 6   v 7

                p 0    0  1  3  2
                p 2    1  5  7  3
                p 7    5  4  6  7
                p 2    4  0  2  6
                p 1    4  5  1  0
                p 1    2  3  7  6
        end group
end object

instance "cube1_inst" "cube1"
        material       [ "flat-bright",
                         "flat-dark",
                         "flat-transp" ]
        transform      1  0  0  0
                       0  1  0  0
                       0  0  1  0
                       0  0  0  1
end instance

instance "cam_inst" "cam"
        transform       0.7719  0.3042 -0.5582 0.0
                        0.0000  0.8781  0.4785 0.0
                        0.6357 -0.3693  0.6778 0.0
                        0.0000  0.0000 -2.5000 1.0
end instance

instgroup "rootgrp"
        "cam_inst" "cube1_inst"
end instgroup

render "rootgrp" "cam_inst" "opt"
```

There are three materials in this scene: "flat-bright" is assigned to the polygons that form the left and right wall of the cube, flat-dark is assigned to the polygons that form the floor and ceiling, and flat-transp is a transparent material (described later, see page 123) used for the front and back wall. The bright, dark, and transparent materials are listed in this order in the instance material list, which gives them the indices 0, 1, and 2. The polygon statements in the object (beginning with the p keyword) reference them with these numbers.

There is one peculiar polygon containing the tag value 7, even though the instance material list only has three members. mental ray uses the first material in the list for all tags that are out of range, either negative or too large. Incidentally, this is also how tagged objects that inherit a single material and not a list are handled: a single material is like a list with one material in it, which is selected directly by tag 0 and by default by all other tags (which are out of range, only 0 is valid). Effectively, this means that the single available material is always used regardless of the tag. Figure 15.3 shows the result.

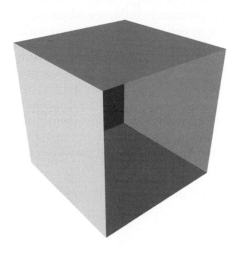

Figure 15.3: Tagged material inheritance.

Note that the light and dark polygons get their color from the material color definitions directly. All materials generate flat (constant) colors and do not take illumination into account. The light is still defined, but it is not included in the rootgrp definition and so does not become part of the rendered scene. All color differences are the result of inherited material selection by polygon tag. Note how the floor and right wall appear darker than the ceiling and left wall, respectively, because the front wall is 40% transparent.

15.3 Parameter Inheritance

Material inheritance and tagged material inheritance propagate entire materials down the scene graph, complete with various shaders and their parameters. In the previous example, the material only contained a single shader ("mib_illum_phong") with its parameters such as "ambient", but a material can specify other shaders too, for example for volume effects. Inheriting materials is convenient and takes care of most problems, but in some cases a more flexible mechanism is needed.

Parameter inheritance propagates neither materials nor shaders, but only simple parameters. Parameters are named values such as the diffuse color or the transparency color in the previous example. There is a large number of parameter types and ways to group and nest them. This is under control of the shader writer. (Refer to volume 2 of this series for details on writing shaders.)

Parameter inheritance has advantages and disadvantages:

- Overriding is under control of a user-written function, much like a shader but with different arguments. This function can decide for every parameter how it is inherited in the scene graph: top-down, bottom-up, or merged in a user-defined way. The inheritance function can also decide that some parameters influence others (such as selecting whether and how they should be inherited), or define boundaries across which inheritance rules change.

- This flexibility comes at a price. A shader writer must write the inheritance function in a programming language such as C or C++, and the function is applied to the entire scene. The structure of the parameters in instances are defined by the parameters the inheritance function is declared with, which means that all instances have the same set of parameters (of course the inheritance function is free to interpret them in any way it wants, even differently for different instances). This makes it difficult or impossible to merge two scenes that rely on different inheritance functions or different parameter structures.

Integration into the scene description is simple. First, the inheritance function is declared with a statement like

```
declare shader "inheritance_func" (
    color           "diffuse",
    integer         "mode",
    boolean         "flag")
end declare
```

This specifies that the inheritance shader expects to find a color, an integer, and a boolean in each instance. Each of them can be omitted, in which case it defaults to zero, or the entire parameter block can be omitted. An instance that specifies parameters might look like this:

```
instance "cube1_inst" "cube1"
    transform       1  0  0  0
                    0  1  0  0
                    0  0  1  0
                    0  0  0  1

    ("diffuse"      0.7 0.5 0.3,
     "mode"         1)
end instance
```

Here, the instance sets a diffuse color and a mode but lets the flag default to false (zero). Defining instance parameters looks very much like defining shader parameters, such as the ones for the shader "mib_illum_phong" in the preceding scene examples, except that no shader name is given.

The inheritance shader must be installed in the options block with a `inheritance` statement. mental ray 3.3 and later also support traversal shaders, which are a variant of inheritance shaders that provide better access to traversal states, such as inherited materials. New projects should use traversal shaders instead of inheritance shaders.

15.4   Object Flag Inheritance

Objects and instances support many flags, described in chapter 13 on page 303. Here is a brief summary. The defaults are 0 for all modes, and neither on nor off for all flags. Note that there is a difference between turning a flag on, turning a flag off, and leaving it unchanged by omitting the statement.

`visible on|off`

> If on, the object is visible directly to the camera (in ray tracing parlance, visible to primary rays).

`reflection` $mode_{int}^{3.4}$

> Controls whether the object casts reflections (its reflection appears in reflective objects), or receives reflections (is itself reflective).

`refraction` $mode_{int}^{3.4}$

> Similar to the reflection statement, but applies to refraction.

`transparency` $mode_{int}^{3.4}$

> Similar to the refraction statement, but applies to transparency. The decision whether something is a refraction or transparency is made by the material shader on the refractive or transparent; transparency is chosen if the index of refraction is 1.0 so that the ray does not change direction, and does not require switching from the scanline rendering algorithm to the slower ray tracing algorithm.

`finalgather` $mode_{int}^{3.4}$

> Similar to the reflection statement, but applies to finalgather rays. See page 206 for information of final gathering.

`trace on|off`

> This statement has become obsolete in mental ray 3.4. For backwards compatibility, trace on is equivalent to reflection 3 refraction 3 finalgather 3 finalgather on, and trace off is equivalent to reflection 12 refraction 12 finalgather off. Note that mental ray 3.3 and earlier did not support disabling ray emission; the chosen on/off mode mappings emulate this behavior.

`shadow` $mode_{int}^{3.4}$

Controls whether the object casts shadows on other objects, or receives shadows from other objects that occlude it.

shadow on|off

This statement has become obsolete in mental ray 3.4. Shadow on is equivalent to shadow 3, and shadow off is equivalent to shadow 6 (because in mental ray 3.3 and earlier there was no way to turn off shadow receiving).

shadowmap on|off[3.3]

Specifies whether an object casts shadows computed with the shadowmap algorithm, provided that the shadow flag allows it. Turning it off is useful for transparent volume bounding hull objects because the transparency is defined by its shadow shader, and shadowmapping does not call any shaders and would cast an unwanted shadow from the transparent hull.

caustics on|off|n

The object generates caustics if n is 1, receives (shows) caustics if n is 2, does both if n is 3, and neither if n is 0. If turned off[2.1], objects below this instance in the scene graph do not participate in caustic photon tracing at all, which improves performance. See page 190.

globillum [on|off|n]

This flag is analog to the caustics flag, but applies to global illumination[2.1]. See page 198.

face front|back|both[3.4] Specifies whether the object will be seen from the front side, the back side, or both.

tagged

Each polygon or free-form surface in the object specifies a tag integer instead of a material. This flag makes the object subject to tagged material inheritance. It cannot be inherited from instances because it describes how the object was defined. See page 384 for details on tagged objects.

tag n

The integer n uniquely identifies the object. It is also called an object label. It can be used to write a label channel image for selection operations, or by shaders that need to identify objects. Since the label is supposed to identify the object, it cannot be inherited.

Object tags and polygon and free-form surface tags should not be confused; both are independent concepts. An object definition that specifies all flags might begin like this:

```
object "cube1"
    visible trace shadow tagged
    caustics 3
    globillum off
    tag 42
    ...
```

The order does not matter, as long as the arguments follow the keywords they belong to. The idea behind the distinction between visible, trace, and shadow flags is that visible object can be defined with great detail, while an object only visible as a reflection or behind glass, or as a shadow, often requires much less detail. These flags allows low-resolution stand-in objects that handle the shadow and trace cases.

Flag inheritance means that instances above the object, higher up in the scene graph, can supply flags of their own. For example, an instance may be defined as:

```
instance "cube1_inst" "cube1"
        visible         on
        trace           off
        shadow          off
        caustics        2
        globillum       3
        transform       1   0   0   0
                        0   1   0   0
                        0   0   1   0
                        0   0   0   1
end instance
```

Propagating flags down the scene graph works just like for materials — a "visible off" lower in the graph overrides an inherited "visible on", for example. If an instance does not define a flag, it accepts the inherited flag, but if it sets the flag either on or off (or sets it to an integer, in the caustics case) the new flag value overrides the inherited value.

For backwards compatibility reasons, objects do not need to specify on or off; if the flag name is given, on is implicit (it would not make sense to set it to off here). However, an inherited "visible off" switches off the object visible flag. In the example, cube1 ends up with visible on (the object and the instance agree), but trace and shadow are off because the instance specified it. The ability to turn a flag off is available only for flags. There is nothing comparable in material inheritance because complete absence of a material is an error — every polygon or surface must have *some* surface properties. Instances have no such default.

The flags that support mode integers (reflection[3.4], refraction[3.4], transparency[3.4], shadow[3.4], caustic, globillum, and finalgather[3.4]) accept the following arguments in objects:

on   the object is visible to the ray or photon type
off   the object is not visible to the ray or photon type
1   the object casts rays or photons of the given type
2   the object receives rays or photons of the given type

The numbers can be added: 3 means that the object both casts and receives. For reflections, refractions, and transparency, "casting" means that the object is visible in mirrors or through refractive or transparent objects, and "receiving" means that the object is itself a mirror or refractive or transparent, and will show other objects on its surface. For shadows, casting means the object casts a shadow and receiving means shadows fall on it (provided the light source supports shadows). For caustics, globillum, and finalgather, casting means that the object indirectly illuminates other objects, and receiving means that it is indirectly illuminated by other objects. In all cases, 0 means that the object neither casts nor receives.

In instances, the same values are used, plus two more:

on	instanced objects are visible to the ray or photon type
off	instanced objects are not visible to the ray or photon type
1	instanced objects cast rays or photons of the given type
2	instanced objects receive rays or photons of the given type
4	instanced objects do not cast rays or photons of the given type
8	instanced objects do not receive rays or photons of the given type

Again, numbers can be added, but 1 and 4, and 2 and 8, are mutually exclusive. For example, 5 is not legal because it turns casting both on and off; mental ray will resolve the conflict by choosing "off". Denying an interaction means that the interaction does not occur even if the instanced object has that interaction enabled. Effectively, 1 and 2 turn an interaction "on", and 4 and 8 turn it "off", and an instance that says "off" overrides an object that says "on". This can be used to disable interactions for an entire sub-scene.

It is more helpful to think of the numbers combining by turning each other on or off, but here is the complete table of combinations:

instance=	object=0	object=1	object=2	object=3
0	–	cast	receive	cast/receive
1	cast	cast	cast/receive	cast/receive
2	receive	cast/receive	receive	cast/receive
3	cast/receive	cast/receive	cast/receive	cast/receive
4, 5	–	–	receive	receive
6, 7	receive	receive	receive	receive
8, 10	–	cast	–	cast
9, 11	cast	cast	cast	cast
12..15	–	–	–	–

After applying this inheritance mechanism, the result is bitwise OR-ed with the caustic mode specified in the options block, which defaults to 3. Since 3 makes all objects both caustic casters and receivers regardless of instance and object caustic flags, a `caustic 0` statement should be added to the options block to use caustics inheritance.

Note that an object that has no visible, trace, reflection, refraction, transparency, shadow, caustics, globillum, or finalgather flags does not appear in the rendered image in any way, but it is still present. All the rays that hit it check the flags and continue on their way in search of another object, which is fast but less efficient than not having the object in the scene in the first place. Also, such objects are still preprocessed (tessellated). To remove objects without these performance penalties, either remove the object's instance (or instances) from their instance groups, such that these instances are not referenced anywhere, or use the `hide` on statement in these instances. Hidden instances behave as if they did not exist, which is often easier than locating and changing all the instance groups where they are referenced.

Chapter 16

Incremental Changes and Animations

An animation consists of a sequence of frames. For example, to make a ball move from the left to the right, a sequence of images must be played in rapid succession, with the ball starting on the left side in the first frame and moving successively farther to the right in each successive image. The previous chapters showed how to generate a single image from a scene file. In principle, an animation can be generated by rendering a large number of such scenes, but this is not the most efficient method.

Typically, animations have a high scene coherence. This means that most of the scene remains unchanged. Some objects or lights may move or change orientation, change colors, or some objects may be replaced, introduced, or deleted, but most of the work needed for the first frame need not be redone for the next frame. Instead, it is sufficient to specify the scene elements that have changed. This type of change is called an *incremental change* to the scene. It is considered a change even if the new definition exactly matches the old one.

At any point in time, the mental ray rendering software stores one single consistent scene in memory, which can be edited by changing, creating, or deleting elements. However, it is possible to define objects that are not needed at first, and make use of them later. For example, to alternate an object's material between red and blue, it is possible to initially specify both a red and a blue material, but only the red one is used in the instance that references the blinking object such that it inherits this material (see material inheritance on page 379). In a later frame the instance can be incrementally changed to reference the blue material instead. This can be repeated any number of times.

As an example, consider one of the simplest types of animations: camera flythroughs. Since the position and orientation of the camera in the scene is determined by the camera instance, only that one instance needs to be incrementally changed from one frame to the next. However, the camera itself should also be changed because it contains the image file name on disk, which should be changed for each frame. To make a three-frame animation of the simple cube example on page 32, append the following lines to the scene file:

```
incremental camera "cam"
        frame           2
        output          "rgb" "out.2.rgb"
end camera

incremental instance "cam_inst" "cam"
        transform       0.7719  0.3042 -0.5582 0.0
                        0.0000  0.8781  0.4785 0.0
                        0.6357 -0.3693  0.6778 0.0
                        0.0000  0.0000 -3.5000 1.0
end instance

render "rootgrp" "cam_inst" "opt"


incremental camera "cam"
        frame           3
        output          "rgb" "out.3.rgb"
end camera

incremental instance "cam_inst" "cam"
        transform       0.7719  0.3042 -0.5582 0.0
                        0.0000  0.8781  0.4785 0.0
                        0.6357 -0.3693  0.6778 0.0
                        0.0000  0.0000 -4.5000 1.0
end instance

render "rootgrp" "cam_inst" "opt"
```

Rendering this scene will result in three files: out.rgb from the original simple cube scene on page 32, out.2.rgb from the first incrementally changed frame, and out.3.rgb from the second incrementally changed frame. Each of the three frames in this simple animation scene differs by the frame number (which is not used by mental ray itself but should be given in case a shader needs it), the image file name, and the translation row of the camera instance transformation matrix, which dollies the camera away by one unit for each frame. Figure 16.1 shows the resulting images.

Incrementally changing a named scene element is as simple as repeating the definition, and prefixing the definition with the "incremental" keyword. The object to be incrementally changed is specified by name. Incrementally changed objects, instance groups, and shaders must be redefined from scratch; all previous information in these elements is lost at the beginning of an incremental change. All other elements retain their previous values, and it is possible to override only some of their previous settings. Overriding is generally done by simply repeating the statement, giving new parameters. For example, the frame statement, if given with a parameter 2 or 3, simply replaces the previous value. The behavior depends on the element type:

options   Retains previous values. It is sufficient to repeat only those statements whose
                 parameters should be changed.

out.rgb   out.2.rgb   out.3.rgb

Figure 16.1: Frames of an animation.

camera	Retains previous values. It is sufficient to repeat only those statements whose parameters should be changed. Cameras can contain lists of output, lens, volume, and environment shaders. Defining any of them deletes that list and begins a new one. To delete a list without beginning a new one, just specify the name (such as lens but omit the shader.
light	Retains previous values. It is sufficient to repeat only those statements whose parameters should be changed. Like cameras, lights can contain lists (of light and photon emitter shaders), which behave the same way as in cameras. In order to redefine the type of a light, the complete combination of origin, direction and spread statements must be specified. A point light (origin only) cannot be "upgraded" to a spot light (origin, direction and spread) by specifying a direction and a spread without respecifying the origin. See page 133 for a description of light types.
object	Does not retain previous values. The entire definition must be repeated.
instance	Retains previous values except the name of the instanced item, which must always be given (just after the instance name). All other parameters, such as the transformation matrix, can be changed by repeating them. If the instance parameters are changed, they must all be repeated.
instgroup	Does not retain previous values. The entire definition must be repeated.
material	Retains previous values. All shader lists in the material (of material, volume, shadow, environment, displace, contour, photon, and photon volume shaders) follow the same rules as the shader lists in cameras and lights.
texture	Does not retain previous values. The entire definition must be repeated.
shader	Does not retain previous values (it does not have any). The entire definition must be repeated.

declare   Cannot be incrementally changed because that would imply a change to existing
                 compiled C/C++ code.

In addition to changing existing elements using the incremental statement, or defining new ones
and attaching them to an existing scene by changing an instance group, it is also possible to delete
elements using the delete statement:

        delete "*name*"

However, before an element can be deleted, all references to it must be removed first. The
order is very important to avoid dangling links. For example, the simple cube scene on page 32
contains a root group named "rootgrp", a light instance named "light1_inst", and a light
named "light1". To delete the light, three steps are necessary:

☑   The root group is deleted or incrementally changed to make sure that it contains no reference
    to the light instance.

☑   The light instance is deleted.

☑   The light is deleted.

This order ensures that there are no "dangling links", references to elements that no longer exist.
For example, if step 3 had been done before step 2, step 2 would have failed because it would have
tried to decrement the reference count of the light, which no longer existed. (Reference counting
is a bookkeeping mechanism in mental ray that keeps track of how often an object is referenced;
this is important for multiple instancing.) The correct order of statements for deleting the light
is:

```
incremental instgroup "rootgrp"
        "cam_inst" "cube1_inst"
end instgroup

delete "light1_inst"

delete "light1"
```

Of course, instead of deleting the light in step 3, it is also possible to create a new light instance
for it and continue to use the light. Also, if the light has multiple instances that reference it, it
can not be deleted without deleting those other instances as well, by repeating the first two steps
as necessary until no reference remains.

mental ray uses point sampling to render an image. If the sample rate parameters are set very
low in the options block (see page 440), this can result is a small amount of noise. During an
animation, small amounts of noise are not normally visible. If the image contains little motion,
the noise pattern normally remains static, as if glued to the object. This is called sample locking.
It is normally beneficial because it avoids flickering.

However, in some situations sample locking can become a problem. For example, if the camera
performs a slow pan and there is little or no other change, the human eye can catch the noise

pattern. In these cases it is helpful to turn sample locking off with a `samplelock off` statement in the options block. This works by artificially disturbing the noise pattern based on the frame number in the options block. This assumes that every successive frame has a different frame number, set with `frame` statements in incremental changes to the options..

Chapter 17

Using and Creating Shader Libraries **

This chapter is advanced material that can be skipped on first reading.

All color, displacement, contour, and other customizable computation in the mental ray rendering software is based on shaders. There are various types of shaders for different situations, such as material shaders to evaluate the material properties of a surface, light shaders to evaluate the light-emitting properties of a light source, lens shaders to specify camera properties other than the default pinhole camera, and so on. The term "shader" originally referred only to material shaders which actually shade something (by computing a surface color), but the term outgrew its origins and is now used for any kind of plug-in C/C++ code module.

Shaders are written in a programming language such as C or C++, which is beyond the scope of this book; see [PROG]. Once shaders are written, they must be loaded by mental ray before they can be used. Figure 17.1 shows a flow diagram.

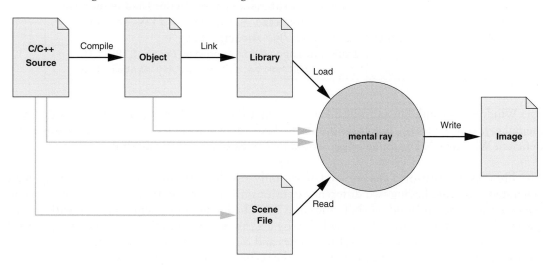

Figure 17.1: Compiling, linking, and loading shaders.

The solid arrows show the normal way of loading shaders, but the shaded arrows are also supported. They are mainly useful for testing; for production rendering mental ray should never see source or object files because mental ray would have to compile and link, which slows down loading significantly. The files have extensions that depend on the file type:

file	Unix	Windows NT
C source	`.c`	`.c`
C++ source	`.C`	`.cpp`
object	`.o`	`.obj`
archive	`.a`	`.lib`
shared library	`.so`	`.dll`
scene file	`.mi`	`.mi`
image file	`.rgb` etc.	`.rgb` etc.

C++ extensions sometimes vary, and image files support a large range of extensions for different file formats (see page 296). Shared libraries are the most common and recommended form of shader libraries because they are very fast to load, but mental ray also supports the archive library format. Shared libraries are normally created with a shell command line that depends on the platform. Here are examples for some of the most common operating systems; for a complete list refer to volume 2.

operating system	command line
SGI IRIX 6.x, 32 bits	`cc -O3 -n32 -shared -o file.so file.c`
SGI IRIX 6.x, 64 bits	`cc -O3 -64 -shared -o file.so file.c`
Linux, 32/64 bits	`gcc -c -O2 -fPIC file.c`
	`ld -export-dynamic -shared -o file.so file.o`
MacOS X, 32 bits	`cc -c -O2 -fPIC -dynamic -fno-common file.c`
	`libtool -flat_namespace -undefined suppress`
	`            -dynamic -lstdc++ -o file.so file.o`
Windows NT, 32 bits	`cl /c /O2 /MD /nologo file.c`
	`link /nologo /DLL /nodefaultlib:LIBC.LIB`
	`            /OUT:file.dll file.obj shader.lib`

The Windows NT link line must be given on a single line. The `shader.lib` file is provided with mental ray. It provides the link from the shader back to mental ray for cases where the somewhat deficient Windows NT runtime linker would lose track of executable module handles.

The libraries are platform-specific and work only on the type of machine where they were generated. To avoid having two different extensions for shader libraries, mental ray also accepts the extension `.so` on Windows NT. Libraries must be loaded into mental ray explicitly, either automatically in the startup file or explicitly by a `link` statement in the scene file. See page 411 for instructions on how to do this if file names and directory paths vary on different machines, without having to edit the `link` statement in the scene file for every machine.

Throughout this book the `base.so` and `physics.so` shader libraries are used in example scenes. The scenes all contain the statements

```
link "base.so"
link "physics.so"
```

The complete path could have been specified, but it is simpler to rely on the library search path, which is a sequence of directory paths, separated by colons (Unix) or semicolons (Windows NT), that is searched by mental ray until the library is found. The search order can be monitored by increasing the mental ray verbosity level to 6 (using the -verbose 6 command line option, for example). The library search path can be set with the -L command line option or the MI_LIBRARY_PATH environment variable. The registry provides more options; again see page 411.

Shader libraries contain the shader implementation. Before mental ray can use any of them, they must be declared. This is because mental ray does not search libraries for anything that could be a shader, rather every shader must be explicitly declared with its name, interface, parameters, version, and other details. See page 272 for details.

mental ray also allows shader object files to be loaded, simply by naming the object file in the link statement instead of a shader library name. It is also possible to use the code statement to name a source file directly. mental ray will then run the compiler and linker automatically, and load the end result as a shared library (except on older HP/UX 9 systems that do not support shared libraries). This is useful for debugging, but is generally less efficient because it happens for every scene, instead of once when the shader is written. However, it is instructive to do this once with the -verbose on command line option so that mental ray prints the exact compiler and linker commands it is using.

When first designing a shader, it is sometimes useful to put the source code directly into the scene file. This can be done with a $code ... $end code block:

```
verbose on
link "base.so"
$include <base.mi>

$code
#include "shader.h"
DLLEXPORT int tex_version(void) {return(1);}
DLLEXPORT miBoolean tex(miColor *result, miState *state, void *paras)
{
        miVector vec;
        mi_point_to_object(state, &vec, &state->point);
        result->r = (int)((vec.x + 1) * 8) & 1 ? 0.2 : 0.8;
        result->g = (int)((vec.y + 1) * 8) & 1 ? 0.2 : 0.8;
        result->b = (int)((vec.z + 1) * 8) & 1 ? 0.2 : 0.8;
        result->a = 1;
        return(miTRUE);
}
$end code

declare shader color "tex" () version 1 end declare

light "light1"
```

```
                "mib_light_point" (
                    "color"        1 1 1,
                    "factor"       0.75
                )
                origin             2 3 2
        end light
        instance "light-i" "light1" end instance
        options "opt"
                samples            -1 2
                object space
        end options
        camera "cam"
                output             "rgb" "out.rgb"
                focal              50
                aperture           44
                aspect             1
                resolution         800 800
        end camera
        shader "cloudy" "tex" ()
        material "mtl" opaque
                "mib_illum_lambert" (
                    "ambient"     = "cloudy",
                    "diffuse"     = "cloudy",
                    "ambience"    0.2  0.2  0.2,
                    "lights"      ["light-i"]
                )
        end material
        object "cube" visible trace shadow tag 1
                group   -.5 -.5 -.5      -.5 -.5  .5      -.5  .5 -.5      -.5  .5  .5
                         .5 -.5 -.5       .5 -.5  .5       .5  .5 -.5       .5  .5  .5
                        v 0   v 1   v 2   v 3   v 4   v 5   v 6   v 7
                        p 0 1 3 2 p 1 5 7 3 p 5 4 6 7 p 4 0 2 6 p 4 5 1 0 p 2 3 7 6
                end group
        end object
        instance "cube-i" "cube" material "mtl" end instance
        instance "cam-i" "cam"
                transform          0.7719   0.3042 -0.5582 0.0
                                   0.0000   0.8781  0.4785 0.0
                                   0.6357  -0.3693  0.6778 0.0
                                   0.0000   0.0000 -2.5000 1.0
        end instance
        instgroup "rootgrp" "cam-i" "light-i" "cube-i" end instgroup
        render "rootgrp" "cam-i" "opt"
```

The DLLEXPORT qualifier is a Windows NT peculiarity. It is ignored on Unix. The shader is a very simple texture shader which computes a stripe pattern from object coordinates, as shown in figure 17.2.

Figure 17.2: Scene rendered with inlined shader sources.

Chapter 18

Parallelism

Parallelism refers to the ability to use more then one processor at a time. There are two types: thread parallelism and network parallelism.

18.1 Thread Parallelism

Thread parallelism, also called multithreading, is the ability to use multiple processors on a single machine. Although there is only one mental ray program running, the program is simultaneously executed by multiple processors, all sharing the same program code and data. This is very efficient because all processors have direct access to the same scene database and other common data without the need for any transmission and copying. mental ray automatically takes advantage of multiprocessor machines by starting one thread per processor.

However, thread parallelism has some limitations. Since more work is done simultaneously, and since each processor needs some temporary memory to perform the work, such as stack memory and intermediate data for tessellation and rendering, the demands on memory increase. This is normally not a problem for small numbers of processors such as eight or less, where per-thread storage does not add up significantly compared to scene and other common data, but as the number of threads grows so does the total process memory consumption. In extreme cases, such as many threads working on highly detailed displacement maps, memory can become a problem even with smaller numbers of threads.

Additionally, on systems with a large number of processors such as Silicon Graphics Origin 3000 systems, the 32-bit mental ray executable can run into another, similar problem of consuming all available address space. 32 bit addresses leave only 2 GB (gigabytes) of virtual memory, and if 16 or 64 processors share it then their stack sizes alone will cause trouble, even if the physical RAM in use does not. The default stack size is 64 MB on these machines. mental ray warns and reduces this to 16 MB, but even then address space can become a problem, especially if there are large numbers of memory mapped textures, which also use up address space even though they may use only very little physical RAM. The best approach is to use the 64-bit mental ray in these cases. The environment variable MI_STACKSIZE can be set to the number of kilobytes to use for thread stacks; 8192 is normally sufficient.

The number of threads running on a machine can be controlled with the -threads command line option:

        ray -threads 8 *scene_name.mi*

will run with eight threads no matter how many processors are available. Although it is possible, it is normally not an advantage to start more threads than there are processors on the local machine.

18.2   Network Parallelism

Network parallelism refers to using multiple machines on a local network in cooperation to render a single scene. Each of these machines may in turn use multiple processors. The mental ray executable on the machine where the operation was started is called the *client* or *master*, and the supporting remote mental rays on other machines are called *servers* or *slaves*. Effectively, mental ray treats all processors on all connected machines the same, regardless of whether the machine is a client or a server. This is achieved with mental ray's *virtual shared database*.

When a processor needs a piece of scene or other data that is stored in the virtual shared database, it uses a token called a *tag* to access the data. The virtual shared database will either return the data immediately if it is stored in local memory, or use a network communication layer based on message passing to find a machine that has a local copy of the data in memory, and then obtain the data across the network. Once the transfer is completed, the virtual shared database returns the transferred data. The result is that any processor on the network can request and receive any piece of data, regardless of the machine where the data resides.

The virtual shared database is complemented by a task manager, which handles jobs that are broken up into many small tasks. Tasks are handed out to available processors until all are finished, using special methods designed to assign tasks to processors that can handle them best. During rendering, the image to be rendered is divided into many small rectangles, each of which becomes a task that assigned to some processor somewhere on the network.

The list of servers to use is specified when the client is started, in one of two ways: the command line option

        ray -hosts castor pollux -- *scene_name.mi*

renders the scene on the local machine along with two servers on the remote machines *castor* and *pollux*. Alternatively, if a file called .rayhosts exists in the current directory or in the home directory on the client machine, it is read and each line is assumed to contain the name of a server machine. A .rayhosts file in the current directory takes precedence over one in the home directory. The first instance of the client machine's name is ignored to allow using the same .rayhosts file on all machines on the network.

A machine name may also contain -threads options. On the command line this requires quoting:

        ray -hosts "castor -threads 3" pollux -- *scene_name.mi*

Now *castor* uses three threads. The double quotes are necessary to group the options with the machine name. In the .rayhosts file, no quotes are required.

When rendering scenes with local textures (see page 69) on the network, the file name of the texture must be valid on all rendering machines. This can be achieved by using network file systems such as NFS to store the texture files in a central location, though this may slow down texture access. It is faster to install frequently-used texture files on all server machines, which prevents NFS from competing for network bandwidth. This is especially true for memory mapped textures. See page 411 for methods to make heterogeneous networks work with file names provided by a client.

Note that Windows NT systems should not be used as a server machine and for interactive work at the same time. Windows NT 4.x is *not* capable of multiuser operation. Running a mental ray server is like another user, and if another user is working on the console, there will be unexpected interactions between both, such as mixed up access permissions and network drive allocations. For example, if the interactive user logs out, the mental ray server may lose its disks. Also, Windows NT parallel process scheduling is very poor. These are known design problems of Windows NT, it is not well suited to be used as a server operating system — unlike, for example, Linux.

For detailed instructions on setting up network parallelism, see the installation notes. Both the client and the server machine must be correctly configured, and both must run the exact same version of mental ray and shaders. Essentially, mental ray becomes a TCP/IP service waiting on a particular well-known (to the machine) port for incoming requests from a client machine.

18.3 Parallelism Efficiency

No matter how large and fast the machines and the network are, every scene has an optimal number of processors that achieves maximum performance. If that limit is reached, adding more processors will yield diminishing returns, and at some point adding machines to the network will even increase rendering time. There are two reasons for this:

- Every rendering operation has parts that are not parallel. For example, reading a scene file from disk allows little parallelism, and there are certain bookkeeping operations during rendering such as collecting finished image data, breaking up jobs into parallel tasks, and other internal steps that do not take much time by themselves but when the parts that parallelize well run faster and faster as processors are added, they gain in relative importance. At some point, rendering time is dominated by these non-parallel tasks, so there will be little further benefit from adding more processors.

- Network parallelism follows the same rules, except there is an additional cost involved in adding another machine, whereas the cost involved in adding another processor on the same machine is negligible. This cost is the time it takes to transfer scene data and other information that the new machines need to perform useful work across the network. (Remember that local processors share memory, so there is no transmission or copying overhead.)

There are many types of networks, such as 10 and 100 Mbit/s Ethernet, 100 Mbit/s FDDI (Fiber Distributed Data Interface, an optical network), ATM (Asynchronous Transfer Mode), token rings, and others. They differ in various aspects and some behave better than others when approaching capacity. In practice, the nominal bandwidth of 100 Mbit/s or similar is never achieved because of protocol overheads, and because CSMA/CD-based networks such as Ethernet experience a condition called a *collision*.

Collisions occur when a machine decides that the network is free to send a message, and mistakenly begins sending a message at the same time as another machine begins sending one. This results in both messages being dropped, and both machines must retransmit after some random backoff time. Most Ethernet hubs and switches have collision lamps that indicate network overload when they turn on continuously. Collisions reduce the bandwidth sharply as the network is nearing its nominal capacity.

The upshot is that mental ray network efficiency is highest if the network is fast, and if there are few machines sharing the local subnet (more precisely, the collision domain). Two sets of mental ray clients and servers, both rendering separate scenes but sharing the same subnet, will delay each other as they compete for network bandwidth.

The fact that efficiency drops with increasing numbers of processors is not a problem specific to mental ray. It is known as *Amdahl's law*, which states that there is a performance limit that is independent of the number of processors used. In other words, the performance gained by adding more processors always converges to zero. In the case of mental ray, the point where Amdahl's law makes adding more processors impractical is determined by the type and size of the scene.

The parallel efficiency is defined as the speedup divided by the total number of processors. On a Silicon Graphics Origin 2000 with 8 processors, typical scenes render about 7.7 times as fast as on a single processor, so the efficiency is about 96%. Tessellation usually achieves somewhat lower efficiencies in mental ray 2.x (but not 3.0), and scene parsing inherently parallelizes poorly because hard disks provide a sequential stream of data (this is where incremental changes become important). Figure 18.1 shows a typical efficiency graph for a moderately well-behaved scene, showing the speedup gained by increasing the number of threads on a single machine (thread parallelism) and the number of machines on a network (network parallelism).

In this example, thread parallelism works very well for small numbers of CPUs such as eight, but 32 CPUs only give a speedup factor of 24. Network parallelism fares worse because of data duplication and network transfer overhead, and the point where adding more CPUs *reduces* performance is reached quickly because too much time is spent on the overhead. Efficiency is significantly better than shown in figure 18.1 if image resolutions are large and shaders are complex, and worse if rendering consists mainly of shuffling large amounts of scene data but rendering only small images with simple and fast shaders.

Finding the optimal number of machines is a matter of testing. Scenes with large amounts of scene data (especially large numbers of triangles) but simple and fast shaders will work better with fewer machines, while scenes with simple geometry but complex shaders (such as fur or similar volumic effects) will work well with larger numbers of machines. As a ballpark measure, begin with three or four machines, and do not expect to efficiently use more than ten on typical low-speed networks.

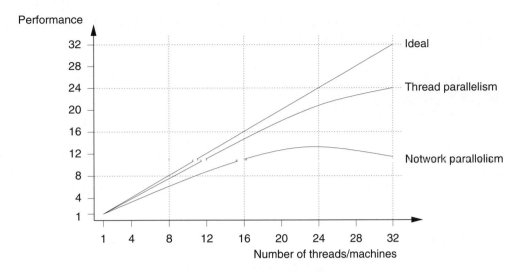

Figure 18.1: Parallel efficiency.

18.4 Balancing Network Rendering

It is also important to run mental ray with verbose messages (using the command line option -verbose on, for example), and look for parallelism statistics. If the client machine is fast and the network is slow, or if the object sizes are very unbalanced, the tessellation report from mental ray 2.x can show that the server machines did very little work:

```
GEO   0.0 info : host triangles    surfaces   polygons   time ms/triangle
GEO   0.0 info :   0     86%         89%         93%      1.42    0.020
GEO   0.0 info :   1      2%          2%          1%      0.05    0.034
GEO   0.0 info :   2      5%          2%          0%      0.09    0.023
GEO   0.0 info :   3      7%          7%          6%      0.43    0.070
```

Here, the client machine got most of the objects tessellated while the other machines were still receiving data across the network. With mental ray 3.0, this situation does not occur because tessellation is done on demand, during rendering. Rendering is often easier to balance because less data needs to be transferred and task complexity is more predictable:

```
RC    0.0 info : host pixels     time ms/ray
RC    0.0 info :   0    20%         41  0.059
RC    0.0 info :   1    10%         17  0.052
RC    0.0 info :   2     8%       16.2  0.052
RC    0.0 info :   3    62%         95  0.052
```

The ms/ray column indicates that all machines roughly had the same amount of work to do per ray, but server machines 1 and 2 contributed much less than server machine 3. Machines 1, 2, and 3 in this example were single-processor Indigo2's, and machine 3 was a 16-processor Origin 2000. Removing machines 1 and 2 improves the balance:

```
RC   0.0 info : host pixels     time ms/ray
RC   0.0 info :    0   12%      30.2 0.059
RC   0.0 info :    1   88%       109 0.051
```

Still, with 16 processors machine 1 only got 7.3 times the amount of work done than machine 0 with one processor. Assuming that all pixels were about equally expensive to render (based on the ms/ray column), this indicates that rendering is too simple in this scene to justify the overhead of sending it across a network, probably because the shaders are very simple. In this case performance can be improved by rendering the scene on machine 1 as the client and not using network parallelism.

In general, networking is more efficient for a single scene file using incremental changes to render multiple frames than for one that does not use incremental changes. This is because incremental changes allow transmitting only the changes to the other machines instead of retransmitting the entire scene. Restarting mental ray for every frame of an animation is especially inefficient on a network because not only is the complete scene retransmitted for every frame, but also the network setup (called the rendezvous) is repeated for every frame.

Animations that use a largely constant scene, such as camera flythroughs, can be extremely efficient on a network because server machines are able to amortize the cost of loading scene data over many frames, to the point where the network is only used to send rendered pixel blocks.

18.5   Rendering Animations

As shown above, the overhead of distributing scene data across the network limits the efficiency of the network, because the client machine gets a head start rendering alone while the servers are busy with network transmissions. However, animations that make use of incremental changes improve the situation significantly because a large fraction of the data only needs to be transferred once for the first frame. After that, it stays on the server machines until explicitly changed, which means that efficiency improves significantly for the second and subsequent frames of the animation.

Consider the extreme cases: if the animation consists of a camera flythrough, the scene database for all frames of the animation is nearly identical because only the camera and its instance change. This means that server machines incur almost no overhead when beginning to render the second and later frames, so efficiency is excellent and approaches the efficiency of thread parallelism. On the other hand, certain types of creature animation where nearly all the geometry changes from frame to frame is much less able to benefit from data caching on server machines, so the second and later frames have little advantage over the first frame.

This means that it is important to use incremental changes when setting up an animation, instead of redefining the entire scene from scratch for every frame. This does not only reduce the time spent for retessellation and other preparations, but also makes better use of the scene caches on server machines and increases network efficiency. Note that a change is considered a change that forces retransmission even if the end result is the same — for example, performing an incremental change on a light to set the energy to the same value that it had before is no different from a complete rewrite of the light in terms of incurred overhead. mental ray does not compare before and after and ignores the change if both match.

18.6   Filename Rewriting

When accessing file names, the scene file or an element in the virtual shared database on a server machine which is received from the client machine, such as a local texture, may contain file paths that are valid on one machine but not another. For example, while the shader library name `/usr/local/lib/shaders/myshaders.so` will be found on a Unix machine, it will not on a Windows NT machine where the corresponding name might be `c:/shaders/myshaders.dll`. If a scene file is started on a Unix client machine that contains a `link` command referencing one of these two, and there is a Windows NT server machine, the shared library will fail to load on one of the two.

This is a concern for

- shared library file names, which are always broadcast from the client to all servers,

- local texture file names, which are also broadcast from the client to all servers, and

- output file names, which are not used on servers because only the client writes output files, however the scene file may have been created on a different machine with different path name conventions.

To address this problem, there are two mechanisms for rewriting file names locally. First, the environment variable `MI_RAY_SUBSTITUTE` can be set to a substitution string list of the form

> /*search*/*replace*/

Instead of /, any character except whitespace may be used that does not appear in either the *search* or *replace* strings. There may be more than one such search/replace pair in the environment variable; they must be separated by blanks. In every file name, mental ray replaces all matches of *search* with *replace*.

The *search* string supports several special tokens: the caret (^) and the backquote (`) stand for the beginning of the file name, the dollar sign ($) stands for the end of the file name, the question mark (?) stands for any character, and a square-bracketed range ([a-z]) stands for any character in the ASCII range a through z. If the `MI_RAY_SUBSTITUTE` variable does not exist, mental ray defaults to the substitution

```
/.dll$/.so/ /.obj$/.o/ /.lib$/.a/ /^[a-z]:// /^[A-Z]:// %\%/%
```

on Unix and

```
/.so$/.dll/ /.o$/.obj/ /.a$/.lib/
```

on Windows NT. Note how the dollar sign was used to make sure that the `.dll` and `.so` extensions are matched only at the end of the file name, the caret was used to remove drive letter/colon pairs only at the beginning, and the percent sign was used instead of the slash to allow replacing backslashes with slashes. (Windows NT accepts both slashes and backslashes as path separators but problems may occur if a path begins with a slash because it may be mistaken for a command line option.) When setting `MI_RAY_SUBSTITUTE`, the defaults are no longer in effect, so it is a good idea to include the above substitutions explicitly.

The more sophisticated alternative uses a mechanism called the *registry*. (This registry is unrelated to the various other registries found on Unix and Windows NT machines.) This method is also more convenient because it does not involve having to set environment variables for all server executables.

Registry entries should not be listed in the scene file because this information would only be read by the client machine and not reach any server machines. mental ray does not transfer registry information to other machines because the purpose of this information is to describe local differences, so the registry must contain different information on all machines and cannot be shared. For this reason there exists a special startup file, using standard .mi language syntax, which is read by all instances of mental ray on the client and all servers.

On Unix, the following startup file names are tried in order:

```
././.rayrc
$HOME/.rayrc
$MI_ROOT/rayrc
/usr/local/mi/rayrc
```

with `$X` standing for the environment variable X. On Windows NT, the following files are searched:

```
./rayrc
%SystemDrive%/rayrc
%MI_ROOT%/rayrc
%SystemDrive%/Program Files/mental images/rayrc
```

Here, `%X%` stands for the environment variable X. When a file is found, it is read and no further file names are checked. The startup file may contain regular .mi scene language statements. `link`, `code`, and `$code` statements are only taken into account on the client side; servers on remote machines take their link and code lists from the client and not their own startup file. Although convenient, it is not a good idea to add long lists of link and code statements to the startup file because linking and especially compiling takes time. The startup file is intended mainly for registry statements of the form

```
registry "{key}"
```

```
        [ value   "value" ]
        [ link    "shader_library_file_name" ]
        [ code    "shader_source_file_name" ]
        [ mi      "scene_file_name" ]
        [ spdl    "spdl_file_name" ]
        [ echo    "text_message" ]
        [ system "shell_command" ]
     end registry
```

When a file name goes through registry substitution (which happens in addition to MI_RAY_SUBSTITUTE substitution), it is searched for brace-delimited keys. If there is a registry entry for that key, the key including the braces are replaced with the registry entry's value. Consider the following registry entries:

```
    registry "{ext}"
        value ".so"
    end registry

    registry "{shaderpath}"
        value "/usr/local/shaders"
    end registry
```

If the scene contains the file name {shaderpath}/myshader{ext}, it will be replaced with /usr/local/shaders/myshader.so on the machine where the startup file contains the registry entries listed above. Another machine with different registry entries in its startup file would apply different substitutions to the file name. If the registry key name (here, {ext}) begins with an underscore after the opening brace, it is considered discretionary and no error message is printed if the registry lookup fails. Apart from the omitted message it behaves exactly like other keys. This is used for certain built-in lookups; see below.

Registry entries are applied recursively, so a *value* string may itself contain braced keys that are looked up in turn. Also, braced strings beginning with a dollar sign are interpreted as environment variable lookups; for example, ${MI_ROOT} is replaced with the value of the environment variable MI_ROOT. Any key must be defined before it can be used.

The $lookup command in scene files takes this one step further. Suppose the scene file uses a shader *myshader*, which is declared (see page 272) in a file mylibrary.mi, and which is stored in a shader library mylibrary.so on Unix machines and mylibrary.dll on Windows NT machines. If the startup file contains the above two entries plus this one:

```
    registry "{myshader}"
        link  "{shaderpath}/mylibrary{ext}"
        mi    "{shaderpath}/mylibrary.mi"
    end registry
```

then the statement

```
$lookup "{myshader}"
```

in the scene file before the first use of *myshader* is sufficient to load the appropriate shader library and declare the shader, regardless of which files are needed to do that and their file names. However, remember that server machines never load locally specified libraries (they always take their library list from the client), so the order of events is:

1. The client looks up {myshader} in its registry.

2. The client looks up {shaderpath} and {ext} in its registry, and loads the shader library and reads the shader declaration file. The declaration is stored in the scene database.

3. The client broadcasts the original shader library file name {shaderpath}/mylibrary{ext} to all server machines.

4. The servers look up {shaderpath} and {ext}, and link the appropriate shader library file.

5. When the servers later need the declaration, they will find it in the scene database where the client stored it.

Note that the servers never look up the registry entry for {myshader}, and never execute a link command in a registry entry (or anywhere else, for that matter, servers always get their library lists from the client).

The registry commands have the following effects:

value	the replacement string for {} substitutions.
link	link the given shader library.
code	compile and link the given source file.
mi	read the given .mi scene file.
spdl	read the given SPDL declaration file.
echo	print a message (assuming verbosity level 5 or higher).
system	execute a shell command.

The first, value, is used during substitutions; all others are used for $lookup statements but not for substitutions, which means they are never seen by server machines because only the client reads scene files. SPDL is a proprietary declaration language used by the Softimage XSI product, which mental ray is integrated into. Note that shell commands executed by the system command uses whatever shell the system uses as the default shell, and the shell command syntax on Unix and Windows NT is quite different.

It is possible to use mi and spdl commands to build deep hierarchies of registries and declarations. However, this is not a good idea because each file opened increases mental ray startup time slightly since the operating system must locate, open, and read data from disk. As described above, this is sequential overhead that has a direct impact on overall execution time.

Two registry variables are of special interest: {_MI_REG_INCLUDE} is at the front of mental ray's standard include path, which is used for evaluating $include commands in .mi scene files, and {_MI_REG_LIBRARY} is at the front of mental ray's standard library search path. To add two directories /usr/foo and /usr/bar to the library search path, add this to the startup file:

```
registry "{_MI_REG_LIBRARY}" value "/usr/foo;/usr/bar" end registry
```

If a library is loaded with a statement such as link "fred.so", mental ray will try to load /usr/foo/fred.so first and then /usr/bar/fred.so.

Chapter 19

The Options Block

Every scene file must have an options block that specifies various operational modes of the mental ray rendering software. More than one options block may exist, but only one can be named in a `render` statement that initiates rendering. This section lists all available options. The page numbers in the tables refer to more detailed explanations in other chapters.

19.1 Feature Flags

option		default	page
trace	on|off	on	14
scanline	on|off|opengl	on	14
lens	on|off	on	44
volume	on|off	on	165
geometry	on|off	on	365
displace	on|off	on	90
displace presample	on|off[3.2]	on	90
output	on|off	on	291
samplelock	on|off	on	396
desaturate	on|off	off	293
premultiply	on|off	on	54, 417
colorclip	alpha|rgb|raw	rgb	417
gamma	*gamma*	1.0	163
colorprofile	*"profilename"*[3.4]	1.0	162
motion	on|off	off	237
motion steps	*steps$_{int}$*	1	237
shutter	[*delay*[3.1]] *time*	0.0 0.0	237
frame buffer	*number* ["*type*"]	—	295

Feature flags enable or disable features of mental ray. Turning normally enabled features off is useful for fast preview rendering, for example to verify geometry without waiting for displacement mapping or depth of field calculations. Turning features off can have unexpected consequences; for example if a Phenomenon scene element consists of two types of shaders, and one of them is disabled with a feature flag, then the entire Phenomenon will not operate, or operate incorrectly. Phenomena may override some feature flags; see page 284.

trace
Allows turning all ray tracing off. In scenes with reflections and refractions, this can save a lot of time because reflection and refraction (unlike plain transparency, which does not alter the ray direction) requires ray tracing. Lens shaders that bend rays, such as fisheye or depth of field lenses, will not work without ray tracing.

scanline
Allows turning off the scanline rendering algorithm. This is mainly useful for testing and if a lens shader needs to divert primary rays. The OpenGL acceleration mode makes use of local hardware, see page 446.

lens
Allows turning off all lens shaders in the scene. Lens depth of field, lens glares, and other lens effects in the scene will disappear.

volume
Allows turning off all volume shaders in the scene. This disables volumetric effects such as fog, fur, smoke, and fire that are implemented as volume shaders.

geometry
Allows turning off all geometry shaders in the scene, so no procedural geometry will be generated.

displace
Allows turning off all displacement shaders in the scene. All geometry will be undisplaced, unless it has been displaced for an earlier frame and is still cached by mental ray.

displace presample[3.2]
Normally mental ray precomputes displacement maps to find optimal bounding boxes. This improves performance significantly, but if the displaced surface is mostly hidden the presampling cannot be amortized. If mental ray spends a lot of time in presampling, and then renders very quickly, try turing presampling off.

output
Allows turning off all output shaders in the scene. Output shaders are used for postprocessing and compositing when rendering has completed.

samplelock
Allows turning off sample locking. This is useful in certain kinds of animations, such as slow camera panning, to introduce artificial flickering to prevent the human eye from detecting momentarily static noise patterns.

desaturate
Allows enabling desaturation of colors that are brighter than peak white (RGB 1 1 1). Desaturated colors are faded to white instead of having their RGB components clipped to 1. This is done if the frame buffer is 8 or 16 bits wide because such frame buffers can only store

numbers in the range 0...1.

premultiply   Normally mental ray works with alpha premultiplication, which means that a white color that is 30% transparent is stored as (0.7 0.7 0.7 0.7) because RGB (1) are multiplied by A (0.7). In this mode RGB can never exceed A (alpha). If premultiplication is turned off, pixels stored in the frame buffer and output image files are not premultiplied. (Color clipping should also be switched to raw mode.) Shaders, however, still see premultiplied colors in this mode; mental ray performs all the necessary conversions internally. This is intended to simplify the life of shader writers.

colorclip   There are three ways to clip colors[2.1] that must be brought into the 0...1 range in order to be stored into 8-bit or 16-bit frame buffers. `rgb` mode tries to preserve the color and brightness, and adjusts the alpha component if necessary. `alpha` mode does the opposite, trying to preserve the transparency even if the color brightness must be reduced. Finally, `raw` mode does not touch RGB or alpha, even if that results in an RGBA color normally considered illegal. This mode also turns off premultiplication mode. It should be used with care because shaders might receive illegal colors. The default is `rgb`.

gamma   Gamma correction can be specified for pixels stored in the frame buffer and output image files by choosing a value other than 1.0.

colorprofile[3.4]   This statement selects a color profile by name. If specified, all shaders will operate in the color space defined by this profile. It will have the side effect of switching the main color frame buffer to floating-point accuracy. The data written to image files can be independently chosen by adding a color profile to the corresponding output statements in the camera. Before a color space name can be referenced, it must have been defined; see page 162 for details.

motion   This option turns motion blurring on or off.

motion steps   This statement chooses the number of motion segments used to approximate motion transformations in object instances. Larger numbers approximate curved paths better but use more memory. The default is 1; the maximum is 15.

shutter   If a time value other than 0.0 is chosen, motion blur is enabled unless disabled with a motion off statement. A value of 1.0 makes the blur length equal to the motion vector length or motion transformation distance; smaller values decrease and larger values increase blurring. mental ray 3.1 and later also support a delay value that defines the time when the shutter opens; the default is 0.

frame buffer   This statement allows defining user frame buffers containing custom pixel types. The first frame buffer is numbered 0. Until mental ray 3.3, only eight frame buffers were available; version 3.4 removed this limitation.

19.2 Rendering Quality and Performance

option		default	page
contrast	$r\,g\,b\,[a]$	0.1 0.1 0.1 0.1	440
time contrast	$r\,g\,b\,[a]$	0.2 0.2 0.2 0.2	237
samples	$min_{int}\,[max_{int}]$	-2 0	440
jitter	$size$	0.0	
filter	box|triangle|gauss|		
	mitchell|lanczos $x\,[y]$	box 1 1	
trace depth	$refl_{int}\,[refr_{int}\,[sum_{int}]]$	2 2 4	122
dither	on|off	off	
approximate	$approximation$	—	337

These options balance rendering quality and performance. They should be carefully selected, as they can dramatically change rendering times and quality. For more information on scene tuning, see page 437.

contrast This is the primary quality tuning parameter. It controls how much two neighboring samples must differ in order to force further oversampling in the area. Reduce the value if aliasing appears in areas of low contrast but not in areas of high contrast, and increase it if no aliasing is visible to reduce the number of samples.

time contrast Independent of normal spatial contrast, this controls temporal contrast (used by motion blur), which can be set higher to save time because in areas where objects move quickly, lower quality settings (that is, higher contrast values) are usually acceptable.

samples The sampling limits are specified in powers of two. 0 means one sample per pixel, 1 means four, -1 means one sample for every four pixels. mental ray chooses the number of samples between the limits set by *min* and *max* depending on the contrast settings. Good values are -2 0 for previews, 0 2 for standard rendering, and 1 3 or 1 4 for very high-quality rendering.

jitter Jittering alters the sample positions slightly to avoid systematic aliasing artifacts such as Moiré patterns and regular staircases. Jittering is enabled with a value of 1.0. If the sampling density is low, jittering works better with ray tracing than scanline rendering because the scanlines impose vertical constraints.

filter Filtering controls the way samples are combined into pixels. The box filter is fastest; other filters can improve quality at a small performance cost. Larger filter sizes make the image softer because more samples are considered, but increase rendering time slightly. The filter shapes determine the influence of a sample based on its distance from the pixel center, as shown in figure 19.1. Good filter sizes are 1.0 for box, 2.0 for triangle, 3.0 for gauss, and 4.0 for mitchell[2.1] and lanczos[2.1]. In mental ray 2.0, this option requires a sampling density of at least 1 1; in mental ray 2.1 and later the sampling density must be at least -1 0.

trace depth   The trace depth specifies how often a ray can be reflected and refracted, separately for the number of reflections and refractions, and for the sum of the two. Sometimes rays are bounced back and forth many times, but after a certain number of bounces the contributions become negligible and can be stopped by reducing the trace depth values. If deep tracing is required, for example because objects are clearly visible behind many glass windows or behind full-transparent helper objects that provide bounding boxes for volume shaders, the trace depth must be increased. If the trace depth is too low, black or dark patches appear in the image, often at the edges of curved glass objects. The defaults are 1 1 1. If the *sum* is omitted, it defaults to the sum of *refl* and *refr*.

dither   Dithering introduces noise into 8-bit and 16-bit color frame buffer and output image files. The noise is normally imperceptibly small (only the lowest bit is changed) but if the image contains very smooth fades such as blue skies that are brighter near the horizon, dithering can avoid Mach banding caused by the color transitions in regular intervals. Mach banding can become a problem if the images are rendered with only eight or sixteen bits per component (see page 292) and are then written out to high-resolution film or slide recorders. Dithering does not affect floating-point color frame buffers or non-color frame buffers.

approximate   This statement provides an approximation statement that overrides all approximation statements found in objects. It is useful for fast preview rendering of objects with approximation statements which would otherwise result in a large number of triangles, by specifying a very simple override approximation technique such as parametric 1 1. See page 337 for details on approximations.

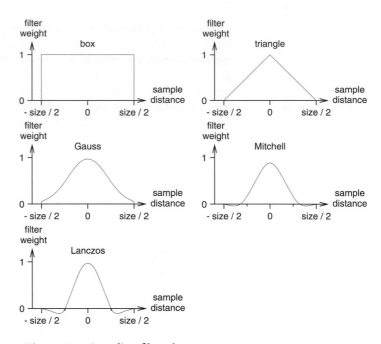

Figure 19.1: Sampling filter shapes.

19.3 Shadows

option		default	page
shadow	off|on|sort|segments	on	147
shadowmap	on|off	off	148
shadowmap	only[3.2]	—	148
shadowmap	motion on|off	on	152
shadowmap	rebuild on|off	off	152

shadow   Selects the shadow mode. If set to off, no shadows are computed. All other modes enable shadows. The correct shadow mode depends on the types of shaders, especially volume shaders, used in the scene.

shadowmap   Shadow mapping is a fast but less precise shadow generation method that uses precomputed shadow maps. In addition to enabling this option, some or all light sources in the scene must be modified to create shadow maps. It is also possible to turn on shadowmapping only, which computes shadowmaps but does not render. This is useful to prepare shadowmaps for an animation before beginning to render final images, but does not work with detail shadowmaps[3.3] because detail shadowmap files only store shadowmap tiles that were needed during rendering.

shadowmap motion   If shadow maps are enabled, this option controls whether the shadows created with the shadow map method are motion blurred if the shadow-casting object moves. This is normally enabled, but if the shadow or motion is very subtle, performance can be increased slightly by disabling it.

shadowmap rebuild mental ray allows storing shadow maps on disk, and re-using them if possible instead of creating new shadow maps for every frame. This option forces mental ray to ignore the files if present and recreate all shadow maps.

19.4   Ray Tracing Control

option		default	page
acceleration	bsp|large bsp$^{3.3}$|grid	bsp	
bsp size	$size_{int}$	10	437
bsp depth	$depth_{int}$	40	437
bsp memory	$megabytes_{int}$	—	437
grid size	$size$	10.0	437

acceleration The acceleration method for ray tracing:

bsp BSP stands for Binary Space Partitioning, an algorithm that subdivides 3D space into a nested set of "voxels", small boxes with triangles in them. This is the default algorithm. It is efficient, but careful attention should be given to the size and depth parameters, which can have a great impact on speed and memory usage.

large bsp[3.3] A variant of BSP that can deal with very large scenes. It is often about 10% slower but is broken up into many small data blocks that do not need to reside in memory at all times.

grid The grid algorithm is an alternative to BSP. It also subdivides 3D space but in a different way. Its memory usage is more predictable, but it may be slower if the geometry is not evenly distributed in the scene.

It is best to stay with BSP unless the size and depth parameters get out of hand and memory usage becomes a problem, at which point the grid should be used. See [Arvo 89] for a detailed discussion of rendering algorithms.

bsp size If BSP acceleration is enabled, the maximum number of triangles in a voxel. If there are more, the voxel is subdivided unless the BSP depth is reached (see below).

bsp depth

If BSP acceleration is enabled, the maximum depth of the BSP tree, that is, how often a voxel can be subdivided into smaller voxels. Small scenes work best with values around 25, typical scenes with 40, and large scenes with 50 or higher. Values over 60 are rarely useful. This parameter can have a great impact on rendering speed, especially if set too small. Before rendering a project, try a few values to find the optimum depth.

bsp memory

Sometimes scenes are so large that BSP preprocessing takes unusually large amounts of memory. This parameter sets an upper limit, in megabytes. It should be used only if the process size (excluding textures and scene data) is too large, because the resulting BSP tree may not be optimal. Do not use this option to control BSP tree building; it is intended for unusual cases where memory usage must be tightly controlled.

grid size

If grid acceleration is enabled, the size of a grid voxel. Smaller values generally improve rendering speed; larger values improve preprocessing speed and reduce memory usage.

19.5   Final Gathering, Global Illumination, and Caustics

option			default	page
finalgather		on|off|fastlookup	off	206
finalgather	accuracy	[view$^{3.x}$] $rays_{int}$ [$rmax$ [$rmin$]]	1000 — —	206
finalgather	falloff	[$start$] $stop^{3.2}$	1000 — —	206
finalgather	file	"$filename$"	—	206
finalgather	file	["$filename$" "$filename$" ...]$^{3.3}$	—	206
finalgather	rebuild	on|off|freeze	on	206
finalgather	only$^{3.4}$		—	206
finalgather	trace depth	$refl_{int}$ [$refr_{int}$ [sum_{int}]]	1 1 1	122
caustic		on|off	off	190
caustic		$mode_{int}$	3	190
caustic	accuracy	acc_{int} [$dist$]	100 —	190
caustic	filter	box|cone|gauss [$size$]	box	190
globillum		on|off	off	198
globillum	accuracy	acc_{int} [$dist$]	500 —	198
photonvol	accuracy	acc_{int} [$dist$]	30 —	212
photon trace	depth	$refl_{int}$ [$refr_{int}$ [sum_{int}]]	5 5 5	232
photonmap	file	"$filename$"	—	232
photonmap	only$^{3.4}$		—	232
photonmap	rebuild	on|off	off	232

finalgather

This flag enables final gathering. Final gathering is a method of sampling irradiance at points to illuminate. It enhances global illumination but can also be used without it. The `fastlookup` mode[1] modifies the interaction of final gathering and global illumination by storing irradiance results inside the photon map.

finalgather accuracy   If final gathering is enabled, this option controls the number of rays for each final gather point, and the minimum and maximum world-space distance to nearby other final gather point where no new final gather point is needed. With the $view^{3.x}$ keyword, the distances are in pixels, so close objects are sampled with higher accuracy than distant objects. This is usually a good idea.

finalgather falloff   If final gathering is enabled, limit the length of final gather rays to *end*. If the ray has not hit anything before this distance, it returns no indirect light. To avoid sharp boundaries, the ray starts to fade out at the *start* distance, which must be less than the *end* distance. Finalgather ray falloff is very important to prevent finalgather rays to pull in distant geometry. Careful use can greatly improve rendering performance and memory usage. It is also useful if final gathering is used for simple ambient occlusion, where only nearby objects are assumed to occlude the illuminated point.

finalgather file   mental ray 3.0 and up can also store final gather points in files, much like photon maps are stored. mental ray 3.3 also allows specifying multiple final gather files in square brackets; in this case mental ray will read all but write only the first. This is useful for keeping precomputed maps small.

finalgather rebuild   This option, if set to on, forces mental ray to rebuild the finalgather maps even if a finalgather map file is found. It is useful if the scene changes, making the map obsolete. The $freeze^{3.3}$ mode suppresses finalgather preprocessing, so that *only* finalgather points from the file or files are used; no finalgather point is ever set during rendering.

caustic   This flag enables caustics. Caustics are caused by indirect illumination from specular reflectors or lenses, such as the light patterns on the bottom of a swimming pool.

caustic   The caustic mode overrides all caustic flags in object definitions. If set to 1, all objects are caustic casters; if set to 2, all objects are caustic receivers; and if set to 3, all objects are both caustic casters and caustic receivers. If set to 0, 1, or 2, the mode can be "upgraded" by object caustic modes that specify 1, 2, or 3.

caustic accuracy   If caustics are enabled, the number of photons considered and the maximum distance in which they are considered in the illumination (shading) computation. Higher accuracies make the caustic sharper but slower. The distance, if specified, overrides the scene-dependent

---

[1] Fast final gather lookup mode is available only in mental ray 3.0 or up.

default and sets a hard limit on the distance of photons in the photon map that are to be considered.

caustic filter   If a caustic is too noisy, this option can be used to apply a cone filter to the photons when shading. The cone and gauss filters create sharper caustics, or blurs them, depending on the filter size. The *size* argument, which is used only if cone or gauss is selected, controls the sharpness: it must be greater than 1.0, and larger values are less sharp. The default is 1.1.

globillum   This flag enables global illumination. Global illumination simulates all indirect light paths in a scene, in addition to specular ones. mental ray supports caustics and global illumination independently. It is also possible to turn on photon mapping only, which computes photon maps but does not render. This is useful to prepare photon maps for an animation before beginning to render final images.

globillum accuracy   If global illumination is enabled, this option works the same way as caustic accuracy but for global illumination, not caustics.

photonvol accuracy   The previous two accuracy options control shading of caustics and global illumination, respectively, on surfaces. This one works for photon volume shaders, which compute light patterns in 3D space, such as volume caustics created by focused shafts of light cast by objects acting as lenses.

photon trace depth   If caustics or global illumination are enabled, this option allows limiting the number of reflections and refractions that a photon can go through before it is absorbed. The assumption is that photons which are re-emitted many times have lost so much energy that their contribution is negligible. Small values increase performance, but physical correctness may be lost.

photonmap file   To avoid unnecessary recomputation, the photon map data structures that contain the results from caustics and global illumination preprocessing can be saved to disk, and reused. This assumes that the scene has not changed in a way that would alter the photon map. Saving and reloading is enabled by specifying a photon map file name with this option. This only works if object space mode is selected. in the options block.

photonmap rebuild   This option, if set to on, forces mental ray to rebuild the photon maps even if a photon map file is found. It is useful if the scene changes, making the photon map obsolete, for example if a light source moves.

19.6   Scene Modeling

option		default	page
camera|object|world space		camera space	308
face	front|back|both	both	124
max displace	*maxdisplace*[3.1]	both	124
contour store	*"shadername"*	—	261
contour contrast	*"shadername"*	—	261
inheritance	*"shadername"*	—	387
traversal	*"shadername"*[3.3]	—	387
data	*"data_name"* | null[2.1]	—	287

The options in this section tell mental ray more about the scene to render. The space options is particularly important because it controls how every vertex and control point in the scene is interpreted.

space
This option specifies whether the scene is defined in object space, camera space, or world space. Object space means that every object, light source, and camera carries its own coordinate origin, usually with the coordinate (0, 0, 0) at the center. Camera space means that the camera sits at the coordinate origin and looks down the negative Z axis. World space also specifies a single coordinate origin, but instead of being attached to the camera, it sits at some arbitrary fixed point in the scene. Note that multiple instancing, and in fact any instance specifying a transformation, only make sense in object space. It is recommended to **always specify object space**. It is not the default to ensure backwards compatibility, but this may change in future versions.

face
This option determines how a ray sees a geometric object. If set to face front, only front-facing surfaces are visible; if set to face back, only back-facing objects are visible, and if set to face both, all objects are visible. Face both is usually required if any kind of volume shaders or photon volume shaders are present that are bounded by transparent helper objects. In simple scenes with little transparency it often improves performance to allow mental ray to ignore back-facing objects by specifying `face front`.

max displace[3.1]
Override the maximum displacement values on all objects. Maximum displacement specifies how much a displaced object can grow in every direction; if set too small the displacement will be truncated and if set too large rendering slows down. This option makes it possible to render scenes with displacement that are so old that they do not contain max displace options on the objects. The value must be given in object space.

contour store	Contour rendering requires a contour store shader to collect selects the information used for contour drawing at the end of rendering.
contour contrast	Contour rendering also requires a contour contrast shader that decides whether a contour is needed based on the previously stored contour information.
inheritance	Some scenes rely on parameters inherited from higher up in the scene graph. The inheritance shader, if specified, controls how parameters in different instances are merged. A scene built with a particular type of parameter inheritance generally requires a particular inheritance shader and will not render correctly without it.
traversal[3.3]	Traversal shaders are an alternative to inheritance shaders that provides more functionality to the shader, such as access to material inheritance. It should be used instead of inheritance shaders in new projects. Traversal and inheritance shaders cannot be combined.
data[2.1]	The data statement allows attaching user data to the options block. User data is not used by mental ray but can be accessed by shaders. If the `null` keyword is used instead of the name of a user data block, any existing user data block reference is removed from the options block; this is useful for incremental changes. If more than one `data` statement is specified, they are connected to a chain in the order specified. Shaders can traverse the chain. Note that once connected, the chain stays intact even when a user data block in the chain is referenced elsewhere in the scene without the remainder of the chain — chaining means storing a forward reference in the preceding user data block.

19.7   Diagnostic Modes

option		default	page
`diagnostic grid`	`off|object|world|` `camera` *size*	`off`	
`diagnostic photon`	`off|density|` `irradiance` *max*	`off`	
`diagnostic samples`	`off|on`	`off`	443
`diagnostic bsp`	`off|depth|size`	`off`	

Diagnostic modes[2.1] overlay statistical or parameter information on top of the rendered image, or even replace the rendered image. Instead of the regular photorealistic output, dots, lines, or other indicators appear that visualize coordinate spaces or sampling and photon densities. The purpose of diagnostic modes is to serve as aids for parameter tuning for optimal quality and performance.

diagnostic grid   This mode draws a colored grid on all objects in the scene that shows object, world, or camera space coordinates. Steps on the X, Y, and Z axes are shown with red, green, and blue grid lines, respectively. The distance between grid lines is *size* units. This is useful to estimate the size and distances between objects in mental ray, or to visualize object space coordinates. Note that grid line drawing is subject to standard sampling, so the minimum sampling limit should not be too low to avoid missing grid lines.

`diagnostic photon` When rendering caustics or global illumination, this option disables all material shaders in the scene and produces a false-color rendering of photon density, or the average of the red, green, and blue irradiance components. Photon density is the number of photons per unit surface area. *max* is the density (or irradiance) that is assigned to 100%, or red. The colors are, from 0% to 100%: Blue, cyan, green, yellow, and red. Higher values fade to white. *max* can be given as zero in which case the appropriate maximum is automatically found. This is done after the whole image has been rendered. This mode is useful when tuning the number of photons in a photonmap and setting the various _accuracy options, since the density (or irradiance) is estimated using those settings.

`diagnostic samples` If set to on, switch to sampling visualization mode and create grayscale images representing sampling densities instead of color images. A black pixel has had no samples, whereas a white pixel has had the maximum amount as specified by the -samples option. In addition, a red grid is drawn indicating task boundaries. See page 443 for details.

`diagnostic bsp off|depth|size`

This diagnostic mode[3.x] can be used to visualize the parameters for BSP tree parameters (see `bsp depth` and `bsp size` statements), to find the reason for unexpected large depths or sizes reported after rendering.

Chapter 20

The Architecture of mental ray 3.x **

This chapter briefly describes the basic architecture of mental ray 3.x. It is designed to overcome a number of limitations with the design of mental ray 2.x:

- **Avoid bounded phases.** mental ray 2.x is split into parsing, tessellation, photon map building, shadow map building, BSP tree building, rendering, and postprocessing phases. A phase cannot begin before the previous one completes, so on a multithreaded system where different processors finish a phase at different times, all but one CPU are idle near the end of a phase. This reduces parallel efficiency, and hence the maximum number of CPUs that can work on a scene. mental ray 3.x has no phases, anything can run at any time.

- **On-demand execution.** Preprocessing all data just in case it is needed later often requires large amounts of time and memory. Therefore, mental ray 3.x builds the data when it is first used, and when memory runs out, the oldest data gets deleted. If that deleted data is needed again, it is simply rebuilt.

- **Avoid unnecessary work.** Frequently, mental ray 2.x does unnecessary work, such as tessellating objects that are not visible because they are behind the camera or behind other objects. mental ray 3.x builds objects on demand, and if there is no demand, no time or memory is wasted on it.

- **Spread out work over time.** Instead of having all hosts on a network do data intensive tasks like BSP tree building at the same time, do things on demand when they are first needed.

mental ray 3.x replaces mental ray 2.x's procedural design with a *dataflow design*. This means that it is not based on pre-coded recipes for what to do in which order. Instead, it is driven by the flow of data. Instead of working down a list of *instructions* to generate data, the *data* is the primary object that carries instructions for its generation. The new design focuses on data, not on procedures.

The basic principle that the dataflow design is based on is the subdivision of rendering into a large number of small interdependent jobs. A job is a simple and small operation such as tessellating a part of an object, loading a texture, casting a bundle of photons, or rendering a screen rectangle. Some jobs can only be performed when other jobs are finished; for example, the job to tessellate an object assumes that the job of parsing the object from the .mi stream has finished. Hence, jobs form a dependency graph that helps mental ray to impose ordering. The dependency graph is dynamic — it is well known that all image rectangles must be rendered before a frame buffer can be built from them, but surprises can happen too, for example when a ray hits an as-yet untessellated object in a different part of the scene. mental ray can efficiently handle and schedule all these cases.

Despite the replacement of the underlying architecture, mental ray 3.x is almost completely compatible with mental ray 2.x, except where noted below.

20.1   Scene Database Caching

mental ray 2.x requires storing all geometry in memory, first as source geometry and then as tessellated geometry, before it can begin to render. Since it is unknown when a piece of geometry will be needed, and since it is impossible to reconstruct geometry once deleted, all geometry must be created up front and none can be deleted before rendering completes.

mental ray 3.x only needs to know the list of objects and each bounding box up front. Source and tessellated geometry can be created on demand. More importantly, such geometry can be deleted at any time because it can always be reconstructed later. Geometry storage is hence based on data that enters memory when needed, and is deleted from memory when it is assumed to be no longer needed and room needs to be made for other data. Such memory is called a *cache*.

mental ray 3.x loads geometry into the cache when it is accessed and not yet available in the cache. The accessing code can never bypass the cache, so data that is used in any way must be loaded into the cache. Unlike a CPU cache, which always loads the cache from a second level of main memory, mental ray's cache can be loaded by following execution recipes. For example, data that represents tessellated geometry is loaded into the cache by tessellating source geometry (which itself resides in the cache). mental ray 3.x uses sophisticated adaptive algorithms to select items to remove from the cache when the total cache size reaches the limit set by the `-memory` command line option.

In a computer graphics context, caches have been used before to keep a working set of geometry in a *geometry cache*. mental ray 3.x's cache is not limited to geometry. All scene data is stored in the cache, including textures, photon maps, flux packets, certain acceleration structures, shadow map fragments, frame buffers, and so on.

20.2   Multithreading and Networking

mental ray 2.x connects to a fixed network of hosts, each with a fixed number of threads. Once mental ray has started, the number of hosts and the number of threads can never change. The first host that initiated the startup is called the master host, and the initial thread on each host is called the master thread. All other hosts are slave hosts.

mental ray 3.x has a dynamic networking and multithreading concept. Threads can be started and stopped at any time, under control of the application that mental ray is built into.

The fact that the number of local threads is not fixed in mental ray 3.x has important implications for shaders. Shaders that use the number of threads to allocate local arrays with one member per local thread will no longer work because that number is no longer available (if it were, it would be unreliable because it might change at any time). This is the primary incompatibility between mental ray 2.x and 3.x.

20.3 Cache Behavior

This section illustrates the effects of the geometry caching performed by the job manager. Figure 20.1 illustrates the memory usage of a scene with many fairly small objects when rendered with mental ray 2.x.

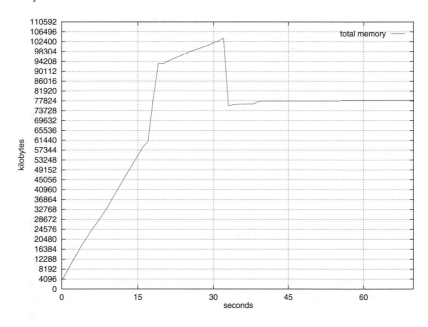

Figure 20.1: memory usage of mental ray 2.x.

mental ray 2.x's phases are clearly visible. The graph begins at about 4 MB, which is mental ray's "idle size" used for the program itself, the program stack, and various other static data that must be present. Then, the source geometry is read from the scene file, and memory usage rises smoothly. Tessellation requires temporary data structures and creates renderable triangle boxes. When tessellation is finished, the temporary data and much of the source geometry can be deleted. Rendering itself adds rather little memory. Peak memory usage is about 104 MB, and 78 MB during rendering.

The same scene rendered with mental ray 3.x shows that there are no more phases (reading, tessellation, rendering), as illustrated by figure 20.2.

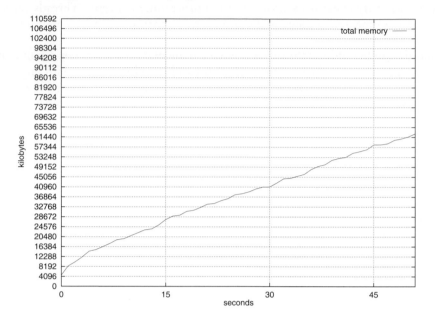

Figure 20.2: memory usage of mental ray 3.x.

Memory usage rises smoothly as source geometry is read, tessellated, and rendered on demand. No scene data enters memory before it is used. Since the geometry is not distributed too unevenly in the scene, there are no significant bumps (typical distribution imbalance is smoothed out because simple areas render faster). Memory usage rises only to about 63 MB, and overall rendering is faster. This is mainly due to the fact that a few objects are invisible and never entered the memory.

Limiting the size of the cache with the -memory command line option reduces memory usage further, as shown in figure 20.3.

Here, mental ray 3.x has flushed data from the cache whenever its size reaches 16 MB. No placeholder objects were used here, so all source geometry was retained. Together with the frame buffer and other unflushable data, this leads to the gap between flushable data size (dotted line) and total size (solid line). The drops in memory usage occur slowly because of the measurement method; memory usage was sampled once per second.

Note that memory usage is reduced significantly without marked increase of total rendering times. In fact, if the scene is much larger than the part that is visible, mental ray 3.x will ignore all extra geometry and not spend time or memory on it. This is especially an advantage for camera flythrough animations, where any given frame rendering will need to spend time and memory only on a small subset of the scene. During successive frames of the animation, new objects will enter the cache and older ones will drop out, while the bulk of the data remains in the cache for reuse.

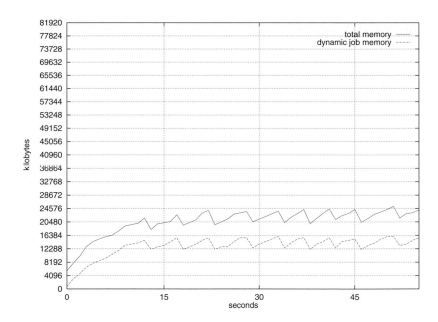

Figure 20.3: memory usage of mental ray 3.x with 16 MB cache limit.

20.4   Controlling Cache Performance

It is important to choose an appropriate cache limit to optimize performance. This is done with the -memory command line option, which expects the total heap memory size[1] in megabytes as an argument. Figure 20.3 was rendered with the option -memory 20. If this option is omitted, mental ray will allocate as much memory as it needs, and never delete any data until it will provably never be used again. In this case, the memory usage of mental ray 3.x will be unlimited, but will not exceed the memory usage of mental ray 2.x (and will in practice stay significantly lower).

If the -memory option specifies a size that is larger than the unlimited case, it will be ignored. mental ray does not preallocate and leave unused memory allocated but empty. The memory limit is simply used as a "high watermark" that, if exceeded, causes a cache flush. If it is set too high, it will never be exceeded, but there is no penalty.

If, however, the cache size is too small, mental ray may be forced to delete data from memory that is needed again shortly after. This is not a problem if it happens rarely because recomputation is often more than compensated for by not having to spend memory (and possibly disk swap time) on data that is unused most of the time, but if it happens too often, runtime increases sharply. Figure 20.4 shows rendering times for various -memory values.

Until mental ray 3.3, frame buffers were always kept in memory because they were frequently written. If the frame buffer is large, or there are many user frame buffers, this could block a

---

[1] mental ray 3.2 and earlier used a command-line option -jobmemory that applied only to the cache (dotted line in the chart); the -memory option applies to all heap data (solid line).

significant chunk of available memory. mental ray 3.4 was modified to page out frame buffer tiles to disk.

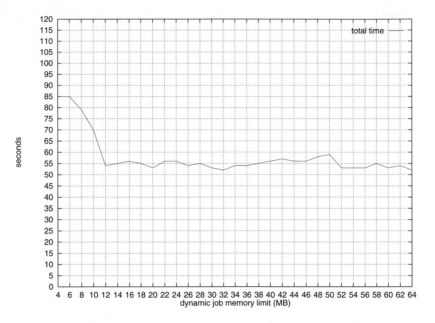

Figure 20.4: mental ray 3.x render time vs. cache limit.

The numbers are wallclock measurements, which causes some variations from the ideal flat curve above 12 megabytes. Below 12 megabytes, runtime increases sharply because data must frequently be rebuilt, a condition called *cache thrashing*. Even so, mental ray will retain essential data in the cache even if this means that the limit is exceeded to prevent extreme or infinite run times.

See page 455 for information on choosing a good cache size.

Chapter 21

Quality and Performance Tuning

This chapter provides guidelines for building high-quality scenes that can be rendered most efficiently with the mental ray rendering software, and provides hints for finding and fixing problems. It assumes familiarity and some experience with mental ray. This chapter can be skipped on first reading.

mental ray offers a range of parameters to control rendering quality and, indirectly, performance. The primary concern is achieving the desired level of quality, but the impact on performance must be considered or rendering time can become prohibitive. Some quality settings, particularly sampling density, directly impact rendering performance (the better the quality, the longer it takes), but by carefully choosing parameters it is often possible to avoid this tradeoff and achieve high quality without proportionally increasing rendering time. A final beauty pass will always take longer than a quick and dirty preview pass, but the impact can be much reduced by focusing mental ray's quality effort on only those areas where it matters, perhaps by increasing sampling density only in small highly detailed areas of the image while letting mental ray's automatic optimizations take care of the low-detail areas.

There are other performance considerations that are completely unrelated to image quality, mostly those concerning memory use. Rendering performance greatly depends on both geometric scene element construction and rendering options. Mistakes can increase rendering times from minutes to hours easily if, for example, mental ray is told to take a hundred samples per pixel or tessellate all objects into many millions of triangles.

21.1   Reading the Message Log *

mental ray can provide detailed messages as it reads and renders a scene. These messages provide the basis for quality and performance tuning, so this chapter begins with an overview over the structure of the message log.

The command line option -verbose (or just -v) and the command verbose in the scene file select the verbosity level. The command line overrides the scene file command. Both require a numerical argument, on, or off. A higher number means more messages; increasing the number by one prints all the messages printed by the lower numbers plus the new message class. The standalone version of mental ray prints all messages to the console (more precisely, the standard error output). Embedded versions of mental ray may send the messages to application-dependent logs.

0   No messages of any kind are printed.

1   Only fatal errors are reported. A fatal error immediately aborts mental ray. There are very few of these; running out of virtual memory is one of them.

2   Also print non-fatal error messages. A nonfatal error indicates that something is wrong with the scene, but it is possible to continue. The rendered result most likely will not be correct. For example, if a shader cannot be found the scene can still be rendered without that shader. This is the default, and equivalent to off because it does not make much sense to go below verbosity level 2.

3   Also print warning messages. Warnings are printed when mental ray notices an inconsistency or inefficient or ineffective settings in the scene, but the situation is harmless or can be fixed automatically so rendering can continue. Warnings should not be ignored because they might indicate real problems, although occasionally perfectly good scenes may produce harmless warnings.

4   Also print informational messages about the scene, such as the number of triangles or the time spent in various phases. These messages are important for tuning performance.

5   Also print progress messages, such as the number of lines in the scene file read or the percentage of the image already rendered. These messages are also useful for tuning; for example, if the rendering phase is stuck between 10.1 and 10.2% for an hour then something may be wrong there. Level 5 is equivalent to on.

6   Also print debug messages. They indicate in detail what mental ray is currently doing. Some of them are very useful for showing which files mental ray is trying to locate and open at a given moment. The number of messages can be very large.

7   Also print verbose debug messages. This level also prints debug messages that are not normally useful and might increase the number of messages to the point where the output becomes impractical to analyze.

mental ray also supports a command line option -xcolor on which colors the messages by level. This is very useful to quickly spotting important messages because red error messages stand out much more than blue debug messages. It is less useful when the output is redirected to a file for later editing because it embeds binary ANSI "escape sequences" that editors or pagers may display verbatim. Not all terminals support color switching.

Since users are often picky about color schemes, the colors are programmable. Instead of the on argument of -xcolor, a seven-character string can be given. The first character controls level 1 (fatal); the last controls level 7 (verbose debug). Each character must be one of "r" (red), "g" (green), "b" (blue), "c" (cyan), "m" (magenta), "y" (yellow), "k" (black), or "." (uncolored). If on is specified, the default is "rrc..gg". A popular alternative is "mrcy.gb".

Messages have the following format:

```
API 0.1 error 301031: file.mi, line 123: call to undeclared function "X"
```

This message consists of a header and a plain-text message:

API   Four characters representing the mental ray module that printed the message. mental ray is a modular program divided into about 50 components. The module name in the header indicates the category of the message. The most important ones are:

module	purpose
API	construction of elements in the scene database
DB	storage management of elements in the scene database
DISP	communication with realtime image viewers
ECHO	print the scene database in .mi format to stdout
GAP	Geometry Approximation (tessellation into triangles)
GEOM	geometry modeling operations
GEOT	geometry conversion for tessellation, a sub-module of GAP
IMG	image file access, disk read/write/map, and conversion
JOB	job control[3.x]
LIB	library of mathematical and other functions
LINK	dynamic linking of shaders and shader libraries
MAIN	startup and interpretation of the command line
MEM	unstructured memory management (*malloc* replacement)
MI	mi scene file parser, converts text file into API calls
MSG	low-level message passing and thread management
PAR	high-level parallel message routing
PHEN	Phenomenon management and evaluation
RC	Rendering Component, front-end management module
RCB	RC sub-module handling triangle boxes
RCC	RC sub-module handling contours
RCGI	RC sub-module handling caustics and global illumination
RCH	RC sub-module handling hair rendering[3.1]
RCHW	RC sub-module handling hardware rendering[3.2]
RCI	RC sub-module handling scanline rendering and ray tracing
RCFG	RC sub-module handling final gathering
RCLM	RC sub-module handling light mapping[3.x]
RCRM	RC sub-module handling the rasterizer[3.4]
SCENE	structured scene database memory management
SURF	Subdivision surface geometry and modeling

0   Two characters (or more) for the number of the machine on the network, if network parallelism is used. Machine 0 is always the client machine where rendering was started.

.   The decimal point separates host number and thread number. It is replaced with a colon if the thread was started by an application that mental ray is integrated into, rather than mental ray itself.

1   Two characters (or more) for the thread number, if thread parallelism is used. Thread 0 is the mainline thread. Thread n is a special network communication thread that keeps contact with other machines if network parallelism is used.

error   Six characters for the message level: `fatal`, `error`, `warn`, `info`, `progr` (progress), `debug`, or `vdebg` (verbose debug).

301031   Seven characters for the fatal, error, or warning code number. The other message classes omit this number. The code number uniquely identifies the message; it is intended for applications that mental ray is built into that need to know about problems without having to analyze an English text string. The number begins with the module ID (30 means API), severity (1 for fatal errors and errors, 2 for warnings), and a sequential three-digit number that is arbitrary but unique for the module and severity.

The remainder of the message is a plain English description. Shader and Phenomenon scene elements do not have their own module ID; if they print messages the message begins with the name of the module that evaluated the shader or Phenomenon.

Messages printed by a server machine (which has a host number greater than 0) are not printed immediately. They must first be sent across the network to the client machine (host 0), where they are printed shortly after by the client thread 0. This means that server messages are often late, and are printed after messages from host 0 that actually occurred later. Another common effect is that mental ray seems to hesitate near the end of rendering because client thread 0 is too busy to print messages.

If a server ray has important messages to print after losing contact with the client machine, it is unable to print the message in the normal way by sending it to the client. In these cases, it writes the message to a file `/tmp/raylib.log` (Unix) or `%temp%/raylib.log` (Windows NT).

21.2   Image Sampling Quality

mental ray is designed specifically to render photorealistic images with the highest possible quality. Controlling the sampling parameters is central to rendering quality. This section explains how these parameters can be used to choose an initial quality level, and how to fix common quality problems that can show up in the rendered image.

Sampling is the process of shooting rays into the scene, and combining the results into pixels.

The actual algorithm is very complex, but the basic principle is simple: start with some widely spaced samples at pixel corners, and if the difference between nearby samples exceeds a certain threshold, take more samples in that area. The definition of "nearby" and "in that area" is where the complexity comes in; additional samples may be taken at corners or centers of the rectangle defined by the differing pixels but may also identify contrast edges and follow them into remote areas of the image (this is called *edge following*). The idea is to achieve the highest possible quality with the fewest possible samples — far fewer than would be possible with simple recursive subdivision of pixels.

Sampling performance and quality is controlled by five parameters, all in the options block of the scene and also available as command line parameters:

contrast or -contrast
>   accepts three or four floating-point parameters that set the contrast threshold above which more samples are required, given separately for the red, green, blue, and optionally, the alpha components. Small values result in higher numbers of samples, improving quality but reducing performance. The highest possible values that still give adequate results should be chosen, usually in the range between 0.2 and 0.05. The defaults are 0.1. Large values can cause Mach banding in soft color gradations such as blue skies, but this is often be more efficiently solved with jittering than with lower contrasts.

time contrast or -time_contrast
>   is similar to the contrast above, but applies only to moving geometry with motion blur. Since motion blur tends to make sampling artifacts less visible, it is often possible to get away with higher contrast values in these cases. This increases performance without degrading quality noticeably. The defaults are 0.2.

samples or -samples
>   has two integer parameters that set the minimum and maximum sampling density, represented as powers of two. A value of n specifies that there should be at least or at most approximately 2^n samples in each direction per pixel. If n is less than zero, fewer samples are taken than there are pixels; this is called *infrasampling* in mental ray terminology. If n is greater than zero, this is called *oversampling*. Undersampling is useful because it often does not matter if initial sampling misses a long thin object because edge following can fix those pixels later if the object is seen by a sample elsewhere.

>   Typical values are -2 0 for fast previews, -1 1 for moderate quality, and 0 2 or 0 3 for high-quality rendering. The useful range is -3...4.

>   The diagnostic samples on option renders a sampling diagram instead of a color image. See Figure 21.1 on page 444 for an example.

filter or -filter
>   determines how the samples are combined into pixels, once all samples in the current image region have been taken. Five filters are available, box, triangle, gauss, mitchell[2.1], and lanczos[2.1] — each with one or two type-dependent floating-point parameters that specify the filter size in the horizontal and vertical directions (see page 420 for a more detailed description). The box filter is fastest, but the triangle and gauss filters are better at removing

soft staircase artifacts. The Mitchell and Lanczos filters have a negative support and may cause "ringing" (dark fringes), but generally the Mitchell filter is recommended for highest quality.

Good filter sizes are 1.0 for box, 2.0 for `triangle`, 3.0 for gauss, and 4.0 for `mitchell` and `lanczos`. Larger sizes make the image softer; smaller sizes make it sharper. Sizes less than 1.0 are not recommended because the filter is so small that some samples are no longer used. If the default box 1 1 filter shows sampling artifacts, try gauss 2 2. You must choose a sampling density of at least 1 1 in mental ray 2.0, or -1 0 in mental ray 2.1 or later.

`jitter` or `-jitter`
>   Sample points normally start out as a sparse mesh imposed by the minimum sampling density, with clusters forming around contrast edges as samples fall on points of a denser grid determined by the maximum sampling density in the regions of high contrast. This means that despite the irregular distribution there is still an underlying order that could cause artifacts if it interferes with image features. This can sometimes be fixed by increasing the maximum sampling density, but it is much more efficient to introduce jittering, which systematically alters sample points in a way that minimizes unexpected clustering. Jittering is enabled if an argument of 1.0 is given, and disabled if the argument is 0.0.

If the rendered image contains staircasing (visible regular "steps" in diagonal lines that should be smooth), cording (thin lines whose width is incorrectly changing in regular intervals), or other aliasing artifacts, the easy approach is often to simply increase the maximum sampling density until the artifacts go away. However, this is a very inefficient method because it usually increases sampling uniformly and substantially everywhere in the image, so performance drops dramatically. A better strategy is to roughly set the sampling density to perhaps 0 2 or 0 3 for high-quality sampling, and then adjust the `contrast` settings such that they cause oversampling in the critical aliased areas but not elsewhere in the image. Contrast settings are the primary means to control rendering quality; the maximum sampling limit only exists to prevent runaway sampling in very noisy areas.

If very low contrasts (less than 0.05) seem to be necessary to avoid soft regular staircasing all over the rendered image (which catch the eye because they appear in regular intervals), the next approach is to try jittering. Increasing the sampling density should be done as a last resort.

To reduce irregular aliasing that is visible on curved edges, a good approach is to use a Gauss or Mitchell filter instead of the default box filter, which has a square "footprint". Either jittering or filtering can allow increasing the contrast or decreasing the maximum sampling density without loss of quality, which improves performance. Progress can be monitored with these messages, printed after rendering completes (for more information on mental ray message logs, see page 437):

```
RC   0.0 info :    212000 pixels    0.043 ms
RC   0.0 info :     66598 samples   0.137 ms   0.31 / pixel
RC   0.0 info :    150600 rays      0.061 ms   0.71 / pixel   2.26 / sample
```

The first line says that 212000 pixels were rendered, and each took 0.31 milliseconds. Only 66598 samples (0.31 per pixel) were needed, and each sample took 0.137 milliseconds. The number of rays is higher than the number of samples because it also includes secondary rays, as shown by these messages:

```
RC   0.0 info :   eye              66598
RC   0.0 info :   transparency        11
RC   0.0 info :   reflection       59938
RC   0.0 info :   refraction       24053
```

The samples taken in the scene correspond to primary rays emitted by the eye (camera), but most of them are reflected or refracted later (incidentally, this message block indicates that it might be a good idea to check if some of these refractions can be turned into transparency by setting indices of refraction to 1, as transparency renders faster than refraction). Sampling parameters only apply to primary rays, what happens next is controlled by material shaders.

The low number of samples per pixel is due to the low sampling parameters -2 0, which did not permit mental ray to properly resolve contrasts. If the parameters are changed to 0 2, the statistics change to

```
RC   0.0 info :   212000 pixels   0.198 ms
RC   0.0 info :   437665 samples  0.096 ms  2.06 / pixel
RC   0.0 info :   887888 rays     0.047 ms  4.19 / pixel  2.03 / sample
```

Although the maximum sampling limit now permits four (2^2) samples per pixel, only 2.06 were needed. Still, this number can be reduced to about 1.5 without loss of quality by increasing the contrast threshold.

With mental ray 2.1 and later, sampling density can also be visualized by using the -diagnostic samples on option on the command line, or the diagnostic samples on statement in the options block:

```
samples -2 1
diagnostic samples on
```

In sampling visualization mode, mental ray no longer renders a color image but a sampling grid. The pixels sampled at maximum density are rendered white, pixels not sampled at all are rendered black, and gray levels indicate partial sampling. On screen rectangle boundaries pixels appear red instead of white. Figure 21.1 shows the visualization for the pool image in figure 7.8 on page 190.

Generally, the brighter an area is, the more time mental ray has spent rendering it. Note how anti-aliasing was performed by oversampling, especially at object and shadow edges, and how areas with little color changes were sampled very sparsely by infrasampling. Brightness is not an absolute indicator of high cost because some samples take longer than others due to differences in shading runtime; for example, the ball, although bright, uses a much simpler shader than the shader attached to the water.

Figure 21.1: Sampling visualization with "diagnostic samples on"

However, if the sky or the ground had been very bright, this would be a hint that the contrast levels were set too low, or the minimum sampling density was set too high, so mental ray had to oversample uninteresting areas of the image. The goal is to expend samples only in areas of high contrast or other visually significant areas.

21.3 Ray Tracing vs. Scanline Rendering *

Unless the trace and scanline options are changed, either explicitly or by a Phenomenon, mental ray always uses scanline rendering for primary rays. The scanline algorithm is a rendering method that can very efficiently deal with rays traveling in a straight line from the standard pinhole camera to the object. It may be accelerated using local OpenGL hardware if available (see below for details). Ray tracing is an alternative rendering method that handles rays that do not travel in a straight line, but change direction due to camera lenses, reflection, or refraction. See page 14 for more details on the differences.

Ray tracing is generally slower than scanline rendering, but it is normally only required for a small percentage of the rendered pixels. This means that in performance tuning, it is best to first avoid ray tracing where it is not necessary, and then where it is needed to adjust ray tracing parameters to ensure optimal performance. If no ray tracing whatsoever is required, turning it off with the trace off statement in the options block brings an extra performance boost because mental ray can skip ray tracing preprocessing such as building a BSP tree.

Scanline rendering has some inherent restrictions that cause mental ray to automatically switch to ray tracing if one of the following is used:

feature	scanline	ray tracing
transparency	●	●
refraction	○	●
reflection	○	●
standard lenses	●	●
ray-bending lenses	○	●
motion blur	●	●
simple volume shading	●	●
ray marching	●	●
caustics and global illumination	○	●
shadows:		
– opaque shadows	●	●
– transparent shadows	○	●
– motion-blurred shadows	(●)	●
– soft shadows	⋆	⋆

In the table, ○ means "not supported, automatically switches to ray tracing", ● means "supported", and ⋆ means "supported in different ways". mental ray identifies ray-bending lenses by a trace flag in their declaration. Scanline rendering computes shadows using shadow maps, which are enabled and configured by adding certain statements to the light source. Shadow map softness is less precise than true ray-traced shadow softness using area light sources, but is much faster. The quality difference can be noticeable where the shadow meets the edge of the shadow-casting object. All shadows are motion-blurred if the shadow-casting object moves and motion blur is enabled, however as a further optimization motion blurring of shadow map shadows can be disabled. The only way to render transparent shadows is with ray tracing.

The goal is to use the features with ○'s in the table only where they noticeable contribute to the quality of the image. Refraction (which bends rays) can often be replaced with transparency (which does not). For example, a glass window pane can be modeled as glass with an index of refraction of 1.33, but since the glass is flat and thin, this is not going to make a visible difference compared with an index of refraction of 1.0. An index of 1.0 can be handled by transparency while any other index requires refraction.

Reflections can sometimes be avoided by using environment maps. Environment maps simulate reflections by calculating how a texture image, often a distant one that wraps all around the scene, would be reflected from the surface. With an environment map, other objects in the scene cannot be seen in the reflections, unless the texture image was carefully designed to contain images of these objects. (See page 108 for details.) This works well for highly curved objects such as chrome pipes or balls where it is hard to identify any reflected objects anyway, but not for large flat reflections of objects such as the reflections of ships on the water surface.

Often, rays are reflected or refracted multiple times, such as rays entering and leaving both sides of a double-walled glass of water. At some point the contribution of later reflections or refractions becomes insignificant because of low reflectivity or transparency. In these cases, it is possible to limit the number of "ray generations" with the `trace depth` statement in the options block:

```
trace depth reflectionsint [reflectionsint [sumint]]
```

This limits the number of reflections, refractions and transparency, and the sum of the two, respectively. The defaults are 2 2 4. Note that some material shaders override these limits. There are also photon trace depth (default 5 5 5) and finalgather trace depth (default 1 1 1) limits.

21.4   OpenGL Hardware Acceleration *

Many systems have specialized 3D graphics hardware built in. 3D hardware offered by different vendors have very different capabilities and speeds — some only offer shaded scanline span shading, others shade triangles, or may support 3D projection transformations in hardware, or support hardware light sources, or hardware texturing with various types of filtering and local storage. The prevalent programming interface for hardware accelerators is OpenGL®, originally invented by Silicon Graphics but today available from nearly all vendors.

mental ray can make use of OpenGL hardware in various stages of its scanline rendering algorithm. Since OpenGL can place triangles very quickly but has only very poor shading capabilities, compared to mental ray's custom shader interface, mental ray never uses shaded pixels from OpenGL but only triangle transformation, projection, and identification features.

OpenGL acceleration is used only on the client host, not the network servers that participate in rendering. Instead, the client transfers the acceleration data it obtained from OpenGL to the servers over the network. If OpenGL acceleration is used for rendering shadow maps, servers are excluded from contributing to the shadow maps because shadow map generation becomes so fast that remote servers cannot contribute useful work, given network transfer delays.

The advantages of OpenGL acceleration are:

- It is extremely fast.

- Shadow mapping especially benefits because it does not require surface shading.

It also has restrictions:

- There are minimum hardware requirements for OpenGL acceleration:
    { Support for at least a 24-bit Z buffer.
    { Support for a 24-bit RGB frame buffer for a maximum of 16 million triangles. 32-bit RGBA frame buffers allow four billion triangles.
    { Support for Silicon Graphics' GLX extension on Unix machines (does not apply to Windows NT because NT does not support remote display networking).

- It does not support motion blurring.

- It does not support transparency directly. Transparency requires that ray tracing is enabled. (Regular scanline rendering can handle transparency without ray tracing.)

- Reduced accuracy. OpenGL itself does not support normal oversampling. mental ray adds oversampling to the intermediate results computed by OpenGL, but at a certain loss of precision at object edges. This is normally invisible but might become a problem in some cases. Also, shadow maps rendered with OpenGL are much more susceptible to self-shadowing, also known as surface acne. When saving shadow maps to a file (`shadowmap file` statement), the OpenGL mode at saving time determines the quality, not the mode at loading and reusing time.

- Efficient OpenGL rendering is restricted to the screen resolution, typically 1280×1024 pixels. If larger resolutions are used, mental ray automatically uses less efficient in core OpenGL modes or falls back on software scanline rendering.

- Maximum speed requires rendering to the frame buffer to make use of the regular hardware pipeline. This means that a window containing strangely colored scene views appears on the screen for short intervals during rendering, and this window must stay on top of all other windows. This is not a problem for a batch render client machine with an OpenGL board but no monitor, but it may surprise interactive users.

The `-strip` command line option can improve OpenGL rendering performance by a factor of two, at a slight performance loss during tessellation.

OpenGL acceleration must be explicitly enabled:

☑ Use a `scanline opengl` statement in the options block or the `-scanline opengl` command line option to accelerate regular image rendering.

☑ Use a `shadowmap opengl` statement in the options block or the `-shadowmap opengl --` command line option to accelerate shadow map rendering.

Both options can be combined or used separately.

21.5 Tuning BSP Ray Tracing Parameters *

If ray tracing must be used, proper choice of parameters has a large impact on performance. For the standard ray tracing algorithm, BSP (Binary Space Partitioning), the parameters to watch out for are `bsp depth` and `bsp size` in the options block. Each takes a single integer parameter. The BSP depth controls the number of allowed levels in the BSP voxel tree, and the BSP size controls the maximum number of triangles in a voxel (a portion of the 3D space in which the scene lives). If a voxel contains more that the maximum number of triangles, it is split into two smaller voxels, generating a new level in the tree until the maximum number of levels is reached. The fewer triangles in a voxel, the faster it can be searched during ray tracing.

Tuning begins with choosing a good BSP tree depth: 30 for small scenes, 40 for larger ones, and 50 or 60 for very large ones. However, motion blurring often benefits from significantly *smaller* depths if the blur length is large compared to the triangle size, because subdividing voxel with many long blurred triangles increases the tree size without realizing an improvement. As a starting point, subtract a value between 9 and 15 from the non-motion blurred depth; or even more if the motion blur is very long.

The message log shows the final size of the BSP tree. Here is the log for a scene rendered with the default tree depth limit of 40 and the default leaf size limit of 10:

```
RCI   0.0 progr: space subdivision
RCI   0.0 info : max bsp tree depth: 40
RCI   0.0 info : max leaf size     : 80
RCI   0.0 info : average depth     : 23
RCI   0.0 info : average leaf size : 7
RCI   0.0 info : leafnodes         : 92163
```

The term "leaf" refers to voxels at the bottom of the tree that have not been further subdivided. Only leaves contain triangles; the non-leaf voxel hierarchy above the leaves is used to find the right leaf but is not used for triangle intersections.

In the example, the BSP tree grew to the full default size of 40 levels, but the much lower average depth of 23 indicates that only a small fraction of the scene required full subdivision. This can have two reasons: either the scene is very nonhomogeneous, large but with a small clump of very detailed geometry somewhere; or that there are many long thin triangles, perhaps created by fast motion blurring, that span many voxels. The average leaf size of only 7, appreciably less than the limit of 10 in this scene, indicates that the former is the case; long thin triangles would increase the leaf size of all voxels they pass through and increase the average if there are many of these. Small leaf sizes increase rendering performance because mental ray has to test few triangles for intersections when passing through the voxel.

If the average leaf size is larger than the limit, the maximum depth should be increased with the `bsp depth` statement in the options block or the `-bsp_depth` command line option, up to the point where further increases do not significantly improve the average leaf size. The following table and figure 21.2 show the results from rendering a scene with 550 000 triangles and an uneven geometry distribution, with different `bsp depth` settings, on a Silicon Graphics Octane:

max depth	max leaf size	average depth	average leaf size	leaf nodes	preproc. time	render time
24	4257	22	15	80309	0:00:31.25	0:36:52.73
26	2423	23	11	128114	0:00:37.28	0:22:41.51
28	1565	25	10	169548	0:00:33.91	0:17:04.16
32	440	27	9	253494	0:00:38.89	0:13:18.00
36	249	30	8	434881	0:00:40.07	0:12:35.78
40	216	34	7	720854	0:00:47.39	0:12:49.09
44	216	36	6	910777	0:00:47.49	0:12:38.70
48	216	36	6	957747	0:00:48.57	0:12:49.79
52	216	37	6	990059	0:00:49.25	0:12:57.01

Clearly, rendering slows down significantly if the tree depth is too small, while too large depths degrade performance slowly (but cause a small memory usage overhead). The table also shows

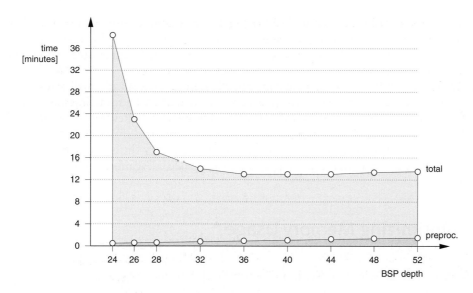

Figure 21.2: Rendering time vs. BSP tree depth.

that an average depth that equals or exceeds the maximum depth is a warning sign; it indicates that mental ray was forced to exceed the leaf size limit in order to meet the tree depth limit. The maximum leaf size also becomes excessive for tree depths of 28 or less.

21.5.1   Using Diagnostics for BSP Optimization *

With mental ray 3.0 or higher, the -diagnostic bsp depth and -diagnostic bsp size command line options can be used to visualize the reasons for unexpected depths and sizes. The primary method is -diagnostic bsp depth, which renders the image and puts a false-color image into the color frame buffer, where colors range from blue to green, yellow, and red to indicate the BSP depth reached in those portions of the image.

Red means that the specified BSP depth has been reached. This is not a problem; there is no need to increase the BSP depth until all red is gone. Instead, large checkered red/orange areas indicate that the BSP depth was chosen well, and is close to the optimum because the BSP tree has reached it just barely.

However, the BSP depth is probably too low if there are large solid red areas. ("Large" usually means solid 25-50% of the image with no orange specks.) That means that the BSP tree got truncated frequently, and likely would benefit from more room. Just tiny specks of orange or red indicate that the BSP depth was chosen too large and was almost never needed, but a few small areas got subdivided very finely. Spending too much effort for very small areas can use up a lot of memory without really paying off because the area is so small.

If increasing the BSP depth does not appear to make much difference, the reason could be a large number of very thin and long triangles, or strong motion blur. In this case a greater BSP depth wastes memory and rendering time because the tree attempts to satisfy a voxel size limit that cannot be achieved. Splitting a bundle of long and thin triangles often results in two bundles, each of which overlaps with as many triangles as the original voxel. This makes it difficult to avoid solid red areas in the BSP depth diagnostic image, and a different strategy should be used.

In these cases, the BSP size is the problem, not the depth. Instead of small sizes such as the default 10, such scenes often benefit from large sizes, such as 30 or sometimes as much as 100, and a *reduced* BSP depth. The goal is no longer to minimize voxel sizes but to distribute the load evenly. The -diagnostic bsp size mode helps identifying the areas where the chosen BSP depth was insufficient (remember that if mental ray cannot satisfy the chosen BSP depth and size limits, it is always the size limit that loses and gets exceeded). Again, the goal is to avoid large solid red areas.

21.6   Optimizing Memory Usage *

When rendering large scenes on typical desktop machines, memory usage is a very important consideration because once the physical memory of the machine is exhausted, it begins to "page" data out to the swap space on disk, which causes a sharp performance drop. (Quality is not affected.) There are two types of memory space:

- **Physical memory** is the RAM built into the computer. It holds the operating system, the mental ray program and its data, and everything else currently in use.

- **Virtual memory** is the memory available to programs, consisting of physical memory plus swap space on disk. If physical memory runs out, the kernel pushes any data that has not been used for a while out to swap space, which allows programs to run that are otherwise too large for physical memory, at a performance penalty that can become very significant.

For this reason, it is important to optimize mental ray's memory usage so that all or most of the process fits into physical memory. The size of the mental ray process can be observed with Unix tools such as top (which shows the top ten running processes). top shows both the process size and the "RSS" (resident set size), which is the part of the program currently in physical memory. This includes the heap, all stacks, the program itself, and all memory-mapped segments. The rest is paged out to the swap space. Both numbers are in pages. The page size depends on the operating system; a typical size for IRIX 6 is 16 KB. If the process size exceeds the RSS by more than perhaps twenty percent, swapping is occurring and steps should be taken to check parameters and reduce memory consumption.

Another method to find out the mental ray memory usage is to turn on verbosity and watch for memory messages like this:

```
MI   0.0 info : wallclock  0:00:06.87 total,  0:00:06.75 for scene file parsing
MI   0.0 info : CPU user   0:00:06.28 total,  0:00:06.19 for scene file parsing
MI   0.0 info : allocated 5735 KB, max resident 10912 KB

SCEN 0.0 info : wallclock  0:00:06.92 total,  0:00:00.04 for scene preprocessing
```

```
SCEN 0.0 info : CPU user   0:00:06.30 total,  0:00:00.02 for scene preprocessing
SCEN 0.0 info : allocated 5861 KB, max resident 10912 KB

SCEN 0.0 info : wallclock  0:00:08.68 total,  0:00:01.75 for tessellation
SCEN 0.0 info : CPU user   0:00:07.73 total,  0:00:01.43 for tessellation
SCEN 0.0 info : allocated 10315 KB, max resident 14224 KB

RCI  0.0 info : wallclock  0:00:13.33 total,  0:00:04.55 for intersection prep.
RCI  0.0 info : CPU user   0:00:11.85 total,  0:00:04.10 for intersection prep.
RCI  0.0 info : allocated 11680 KB, max resident 21232 KB

RC   0.0 info : wallclock  0:00:22.49 total,  0:00:09.14 for rendering
RC   0.0 info : CPU user   0:00:20.31 total,  0:00:08.44 for rendering
RC   0.0 info : allocated 11371 KB, max resident 22800 KB
```

These triples appear at different stages of rendering. The first two lines indicate the time and the phase (file reading, preprocessing, tessellation, or rendering), along with the allocated and resident memory. The "max resident" number is the RSS. The allocated size is not the total size, it only refers to the virtual "heap memory" allocated by mental ray and does not include the program itself, memory mapped textures, thread stacks, shader libraries, and so on. It is a good indicator of the scene complexity. The scene database, acceleration data structures, and all kinds of temporary scratch memory are all part of the heap.

The above lines indicate that it took mental ray 5735 KB to store the scene file in the scene database. Scene preprocessing, which involves traversing the scene tree and calling geometry shaders, increased this to 5861 KB. If the scene had contained geometry shaders, this difference might have been much larger. The next step is tessellation, which converts polygons and free-form surfaces in the scene to triangles. The triangles increased the heap to 10315 KB.

Next, the polygons and free-form surfaces are no longer needed and are deleted (at least in standalone versions of mental ray), and the ray tracing acceleration data structures (such as the BSP voxel tree) are built. As a rule of thumb, the size of the BSP tree is roughly similar to the size of the tessellated geometry, so with the deletion of the polygons and free-form surfaces the heap size increased only slightly to 11680 KB. The scene can now be rendered. After rendering, some temporary data is deleted, reducing the heap size slightly to 11371 KB. The tessellated data is not thrown away but remains cached in case the next frame needs it again.

The following suggests several approaches to decreasing memory usage:

- Try to keep the scene file small, for example by removing objects that are never visible, or at least marking their instances with the hide on flag.

- Use memory mapped textures whenever possible. This not only reduces physical memory usage as only the parts of the texture that are actually needed are read, but it also saves time because the texture does not need to be decompressed. This is such a big win that any scene that uses more than a few hundred KB of texture image files should use memory mapping. See page 70 for a detailed discussion of memory mapping, and how to create the maps without having to modify the scene file.

- If the memory usage increases sharply after tessellation, there may be approximation statements in the scene file that are creating too many triangles, either on the base surface or on a displacement map. Angle criteria with very small parameters are known to drive up triangle counts unexpectedly. See page 346 for help with choosing approximations correctly. A triangle requires about 42 bytes of storage including its position vector, plus 12 bytes for every normal vector, motion vector, texture vector, and other vectors, assuming reasonable vertex sharing.

- Photon mapping also takes up memory, but is more predictable since each light source specifies the number of photons to store, using one of the `photons` statements. The total storage required for photon maps is the sum of the photon counts in all these statements, multiplied by approximately 30 bytes per photon.

- If no ray tracing is needed, the acceleration data structures for ray tracing such as BSP trees do not need to be generated, saving a lot of memory. Otherwise, using smaller BSP tree depths (with the `bsp depth` options block statement or the `-bsp_depth` command line option) decreases memory usage but at a tradeoff as rendering time can increase disproportionally. Using the voxel grid algorithm instead of BSP keeps memory usage more predictable and smaller for large scenes. This may have an effect, positive or negative, on rendering time. See page 423 for more details on ray tracing control options.

- If the rendered image resolution is large, and if many frame buffers are in use, the amount of memory required for frame buffers can become significant. For example, a resolution of 2048 × 2048 requires 16 MB for 8 bits per component, 32 MB for 16 bits per component, 64 MB for floating-point colors, 16 MB for a depth or label buffer, and 48 MB for motion or normal vector buffers. Depth, label, motion, and normal buffers are all optional and depend on output statements in the camera definition. See page 292 for details.

- mental ray 3.0 allows more explicit control over its cache memory size, see below.

After tessellation completes, and before rendering begins, the number of instances and triangle boxes is reported:

```
SCEN 0.0 info : deleted 537 source objects, kept 0 source objects
SCEN 0.0 info : 537 geo leaf instances (115 tessellated, 266 cached, 156 shared)
SCEN 0.0 info : 622 boxes, 1 lights
```

The standalone version of mental ray deletes source object geometry after tessellation because once converted to triangles, the original polygon and free-form surface descriptions are no longer needed. The object element itself is retained in the scene database to allow future incremental changes, but all the attached vectors and polygons and other geometry data are deleted. This frees up space for rendering. However, view-dependent objects cannot be deleted and must be kept in case they need to be retessellated in future frames.

A *leaf instance* is created internally by mental ray for each instance of each object in the scene. They have all transformations and other instance properties fully evaluated down the scene DAG, and form a linear list of things to render. If objects are multiply instanced, there are more leaf instances than objects. In the example, there are 537 leaf instances. 115 of them had to be tessellated, because they were added or incrementally changed since the last tessellation, or because they were view-dependent and some instance transformation change changed the view. 266 did not change and could be re-used from the previous frame without tessellation. 156 were multiple instances of some other instance and were not view-dependent, so the tessellation only needed to be done once and could be shared by the others.

The final number of triangle boxes is larger than the number of instances because the size of a box is limited, so that very large objects are tessellated into multiple boxes. Later, during rendering preprocessing, more information is given about the boxes[1]:

```
RCB  0.0  info :       622 boxes
RCB  0.0  info :    146754 vectors
RCB  0.0  info :     99160 vertices
RCB  0.0  info :     84133 triangles
```

These numbers show the result of vertex sharing and vector sharing (see page 308). This scene uses sharing efficiently: the number of vertices is only slightly higher than the number of triangles (good vertex sharing), and every vertex needs only about 1.5 vectors on average (good vector sharing). If these ratios become significantly less favorable the scene should be checked for possible improvements. A vector requires 12 bytes of memory, a vertex requires two bytes per vector referenced by it (shared or not), and a triangle requires an extra 28 bytes. If motion blurring is enabled, the renderer later adds 36 more bytes per triangle if the triangle has motion vectors, or 48 more if there is a motion transformation. Every box also has a few hundred bytes of bookkeeping information.

More detailed memory usage information can be obtained by inserting `debug "mem summary"` statements into the scene file, typically just before and after the `render` statements. This generates messages like this (assuming that verbosity is enabled):

```
MEM  0.0  info :   module  maxbytes  maxnblks     bytes  nblocks  %bytes
MEM  0.0  info :       DB   9907979      6627   5443871     4074   51.07
MEM  0.0  info :     TASK    156166      1247      4352        1    0.04
MEM  0.0  info :       RC   2504276       231         0        0    0.00
MEM  0.0  info :      GAP    318992        30         0        0    0.00
MEM  0.0  info :      IMG     32846         2         0        0    0.00
MEM  0.0  info :       MI     83137       716     35149      177    0.33
MEM  0.0  info :      API    367060       818      8140      796    0.08
MEM  0.0  info :      RCI   6558496        58   4587676       39   43.04
MEM  0.0  info : overhead                         138176     8636    1.94
MEM  0.0  info :    total                       10658845     8636  100.00
```

The table distinguishes `maxbytes`, which is the maximum reached so far, and the current size. In this example, the scene database (DB), which contains both source geometry (polygons and free-form surfaces) and tessellated geometry (triangles), requires the bulk of the heap. The maximum

---

[1] mental ray 3.0 shows tessellation and BSP statistics after rendering because tessellation and BSP tree building happen continuously during rendering and not before rendering starts, so the complete statistics are not known before rendering completes. There is no way in mental ray 3.0 to see the total number of triangles in a scene because mental ray 3.0 does not create or count triangles for objects that are defined but not needed.

of nearly 10 MB was reached when the database held both source and tessellated geometry at the same time prior to the source geometry being deleted, at which point the database size dropped to about 5.4 MB. The BSP tree required about 4.58 MB, although peak usage exceeded that earlier. The `maxbytes` numbers are not useful for tallying the memory used so far because different modules usually reach their peak usage at different times; use the `allocated X KB` messages described above for that. It is also possible to produce a memory summary from within a shader by calling the *mi_mem_summary* function (no return value, no arguments).

If the amount of memory used by the DB module is mysteriously very large, it can be helpful to produce a database dump using the `debug "db dump"` statement just before or after the `render` statement. This produces a large amount of output: one line for every scene element. Here is partial dump of another scene:

```
DB 0.0 info:host mod       tag      addr     size pins fj refs   type        mi name
DB 0.0 info:    0 API 00000400 10232438      492    0 --      0  1=funcdecl  -
DB 0.0 info:    0 API 00000413 1023c950      640    0 --      0 12=options   opt
DB 0.0 info:    0 API 00000414 10223de8       76    0 --      1  5=camera    cam1
DB 0.0 info:    0 API 00000415 1023bd38      133    0 --      0  2=func      -
DB 0.0 info:    0 MI  00000416 10240c88      272    0 --      1 10=instance  caminst1
DB 0.0 info:    0 API 00000417 10240db8      140    0 --      2  4=light     light
DB 0.0 info:    0 IMG 0000041a 10d1cfc0  9104640    0 -j      0 13=image     tex_0
DB 0.0 info:    0 IMG 0000041b 10223f00       46    0 --      0 29=string    -
DB 0.0 info:    0 API 0000041c 1023c070      228    0 --      0  2=func      obj1
DB 0.0 info:    0 API 00000439 10242180       36    0 --      0  3=material  mtl1
DB 0.0 info:    0 API 000018c8 1094acf0        4    0 --      0 28=tag       -
DB 0.0 info:    0 API 000018cc 1094b760      168    0 --      1  7=object    obj2
DB 0.0 info:    0 API 000018cd 106ee3f8       36    0 --      0  3=material  mtl2
DB 0.0 info:    0 API 000018ce 1070ded8      316    0 --      0  2=func      -
DB 0.0 info:    0 API 00001b6b 107aa960     2200    0 --      0 11=group     world
DB 0.0 info:    0 GAP 00001d86 1099c1c8   109144    0 -j      0  8=box       -
DB 0.0 info:    0 GAP 00001d8a 10725d70     1192    0 -j      0  8=box       -
DB 0.0 info:    0 GAP 00001eaf 10a87968   177780    0 -j      0  8=box       -
DB 0.0 info:    0 RC  00001ff4 10ca5ec8      640    0 --      0 12=options   -
```

For each element, the machine (host) where the element was created is listed, the module which created it, its tag, memory address on the client machine, size in bytes, how often it is currently in use (pins; *pidx* for mental ray 3.0), whether it is scheduled for network broadcast (f), whether it can be built on demand (j, only available with mental ray 3.0), the number of geometric references to it in the scene DAG, the data type, and the name from the scene file if available. The interesting columns are the module, size, type, and name.

This scene has one image file used as texture "`tex_0`", which requires 9104640 bytes. 9 MB is very large, so this is a prime candidate for conversion to a memory mapped texture. It is not unusual for a scene to contain several hundred megabytes of textures like this, so it would be a huge waste of time and memory to keep them in any form other than memory mapped texture files.

Boxes contain triangles. If the scene is dominated by boxes, lower tessellation approximations may help reduce the amount of memory used.

21.7   Optimizing the Cache Size *

This section applies only to mental ray 3.0 and later because caching is not available in mental ray 2.x. See page 431 for information on the architecture of mental ray 3.0.

The size of mental ray's heap memory size, including the geometry cache that holds all scene data that is either permanent or in current use, is controlled with the -memory command line option, whose argument is the cache size in megabytes. The correct -memory value depends on the scene. mental ray's cache, like any cache, exploits scene coherence, which means that mental ray can benefit from keeping a small working set of data in the cache without having to reference other data very often. A non-coherent scene is one where mental ray is forced to jump back and forth all over the place, which causes a large working set that requires a larger cache. There are a number of things that demand a larger memory size:

- Global illumination, by its very nature global in the sense of taking into account many distant parts of the scene while bouncing photons around, is increasing the working set, and requires a larger cache.

- Scenes with a large number of similar-sized small objects behave better than a very small number of very large objects. In the extreme case, if the scene contains only a single huge object, this object can either be in the cache or not, which does not give mental ray a lot of room for optimizing memory usage. (mental ray will attempt to split objects that are extremely large to avoid this situation, but this is not always possible.)

- If there are many large objects, their definition can be stored in separate files that are referenced by placeholder objects in the main scene. This allows mental ray to flush the object definition from the cache after tessellation, because it is possible to reload the object from the file if necessary. Without placeholders, the object definition must remain in the cache at all times, even though it is required only for tessellation and is dead weight in the cache later.

- Large textures stored in image files on disk, in formats such as RGB or TIFF, must be loaded into the cache when referenced. It is much better to use memory mapped textures, which are not stored in the cache, and the ".map" image format, which unlike compressed image formats like TIFF can be efficiently paged.

- Final gathering, like global illumination, casts large bundles of rays in all directions, and pull in much geometry. This can be avoided by specifying a "finalgather ray falloff" in the options block, which keeps finalgather rays short. If the falloww distances are properly chosen, this greatly improves performance and memory usage. Ray falloffs are also available to shaders for other types of rays.

The cache size should be chosen so that cache flushes happen rarely. A *cache flush* is the action of deleting unnecessary or old data from the cache until it is sufficiently below the limit to continue. This is also sometimes called *garbage collection* (although mental ray's garbage collector can safely consider data as garbage that may be used again later, as long as it knows how to rebuild the data). If the verbosity level (see page 437) is set to 5 or higher, messages are printed for cache flushes, and statistics are printed after rendering finishes. A cache flush message looks like this:

```
JOB  0.0 progr: geometry cache flush reduced 16852 KB to 12102 KB, 22 ms
```

means that the memory heap size has exceed the limit set by the -memory option, here set to 16, and reduced the cache size to 12 MB. This took 22 ms, during which the cache was inaccessible to all mental ray threads. If the cache limit is too small, one might see a large number of messages like

```
JOB  0.0 progr: geometry cache flush reduced 4337 KB to 4337 KB, 6 ms
```

which means that mental ray has exceeded a limit that is too small (4 MB) but was unable to find data to evict from the cache because it is all in current use. This is bad for performance because time is wasted on attempting to find data to delete, and because other threads wanting to access the cache finding it blocked during the search, which reduces parallel efficiency. When rendering completes, a summary is printed:

```
JOB  0.0 info : 1150 known jobs, 715 done (3 of these redone), 0 deleted
JOB  0.0 info : 210 geometry cache flushes deleted 254228 KB in 4555 ms
               (21 ms avg)
JOB  0.0 info : cache memory use: current 8227 KB, max 22811 KB, limit
               16384 KB
```

The first line shows how many jobs were flushed but were later accessed, so they had to be recreated (redone). Small numbers are fine because it is sometimes better to flush and rebuild data than to have it clog the cache for a long time, but if it comes close to about 10% of the number of done jobs, the cache size should be increased.

The second line summarizes flushing. The cache limit was exceeded 210 times, and although it was very successful (nearly 250 MB were deleted and only 3 of 715 items had to be rebuilt later) this is a very high number — cache flushes reduce parallelism and take time, so a larger cache should be used to reduce the number of flushes.

The third line shows that at some point the cache limit was exceeded significantly by 6 MB (to a total of 22 instead of 16 MB), which indicates that some very large object existed that pushed the size beyond the limit briefly, which caused a flush and probably displaced a lot of smaller items. Most likely this was a large texture. Textures should be memory-mapped to avoid this situation.

21.8 Address Space Limitations *

On machines with many processors but a small address space (32 bits), virtual memory can also become scarce. Virtual memory does not show up in the above tables. The problem is not the total of the bytes used, but the difficulty in arranging many "segments" into only 2 GB of address space. Every thread requires one segment for its stack, plus every shader library and every memory mapped texture requires a segment. The program itself and its heap require two more segments. If the total size of these segments approaches 2 GB (trouble sometimes starts at 1.5 GB due to gaps in the memory arrangement), rendering fails due to lack of memory even though all the previously mentioned methods indicate that there is plenty of virtual and physical memory available.

If a large number of threads are being used, it is possible to limit the amount of memory used for each stack segment on Unix machines. The shell command

```
limit stacksize 1024
```

sets the maximum stack size to 1024 KB. Most scenes work with just 512 KB. If the stack size is larger than 16 MB, mental ray automatically reduces it to 16 MB, and prints a warning. This shell command can also be added to the ~/.cshrc or ~/.profile shell startup file.

If the total size of all memory mapped textures and shader libraries is too large, and the texture sizes cannot be reduced by using smaller image resolutions, then the 64-bit version of mental ray must be used. The 64-bit version has practically no address space limitations, but not all operating systems support 64-bit address spaces. Linux on Intel EM64T and Opteron CPUs, all Intel IA64 Itanium systems, and Silicon Graphics systems support 64-bit address spaces.

Note that some systems, notably Hewlett-Packard and Compaq Unix machines, have unreasonably low defaults for the maximum data (heap) segment size, such as 64 MB. This should be changed with

```
limit datasize unlimited
limit memoryuse unlimited
limit vmemoryuse unlimited
```

The limit command without arguments prints the current settings. This is standard csh/tcsh syntax; the older sh shell uses ulimit. Some systems do not allow limiting virtual memory use. On Compaq Digital Unix machines it may be necessary to use the *sysconfig* utility to change the following kernel parameters: *per_proc_stack_size*, *max_per_proc_stack_size*, *per_proc_data_size*, *max_per_proc_data_size*, *per_proc_address_space*, *max_per_proc_address_space*, *vm_kentry_zone_size*, *vm_maxvas*, and *vm_maxwire*.

21.9 Summary: Quality and Performance Checklist

This section lists hints to improve quality and performance, with references to more detailed information elsewhere in this book.

21.9.1 Sampling

See page 440 for details.

☑ Use the `sampling` statement only to specify the rough quality range, and work with `contrast` settings instead. Note that motion blur, depth of field, and other sampling methods often need a higher maximum sampling limit, which makes careful contrast selection more important to prevent the maximum rate of sampling from being applied everywhere.

☑ Try to remove artifacts at edges and Mach banding by using jittering and softer filters, not by increasing sampling limits or reducing the contrast too far (below 0.05, usually).

☑ Use `time contrast` to control motion blur quality, and use higher values than for the regular contrast.

21.9.2   Texture Mapping

See page 79 for details.

☑ Use memory mapped textures whenever possible to avoid loading and decompressing texture images into memory, and to reduce cache pressure in mental ray 3.0.

☑ Choose texture resolutions carefully: if they are too small, they appear jaggy unless filtered; if they are too large they use too much space, take longer to access, and longer to load and decompress if they are not memory-mapped.

☑ If using memory mapped textures, or if unsure about the appropriate texture resolution (related to potential image coverage), use pyramid textures. See page 77 for instructions for creating mappable pyramid texture files.

☑ Unfiltered textures are faster than filtered textures, and filtered textures are faster than elliptical filtered textures. However, quality is best with filtered and elliptically filtered textures.

21.9.3   Light and Shadow

See page 161 for details.

☑ Use short light lists in material shaders to reduce the number of lights sampled when a ray hits a surface. The same is true for volumes.

☑ Reduce the number of light sources that cast shadows.

☑ Use shadow shaders only in materials on objects that cast transparent shadows.

☑ Use shadow mapping and shadow map files where possible, and turn off shadow map motion blur if it is not required. Use OpenGL accelerated shadow mapping if possible.

☑ Use area light sources only where necessary, and use small subdivision values.

☑ Remove the shadow flag from objects which do not cast shadows. The objects with shadow flags control the size of shadow maps, and objects with unnecessary shadow flags waste shadow map resolution on areas where no shadow can appear, reducing quality or forcing an increase of the shadow map resolution, which reduces performance.

21.9.4   Final Gathering, Caustics, and Global Illumination

See page 235 for details.

☑ Use final gathering with the `finalgather ray falloff` option to prevent the rays from pulling in too much geometry, and to reduce the number of intersections and shader calls.

☑ If physical correctness is not required, only emit photons from selected light sources.

☑ Begin with small numbers of photons (10000) and increase until the effect is smooth enough. Do not try to fix high-frequency noise by increasing the number of photons; increase the accuracy values instead.

☑ Change the finalgather[3,4], caustic, and globillum default modes in the options block from 3 to 0, and only mark caustic and global illumination transmitters or receivers with the `caustic` and `globillum` object flag, respectively. In particular, assign mode 1 and 3 (casters) only where necessary to make the projection maps more efficient.

☑ When attaching photon shaders to transparent helper objects such as cover polygons or bounding boxes, keep these objects as small as possible.

☑ Make sure that light from the light source can easily reach caustic receivers or materials with a diffuse component to avoid "losing" and re-emitting too many photons.

☑ If the photon map does not change from one frame of an animation to the next, for example in the case where the animation consists of a camera fly-through, use photon map files to avoid having to recompute the photon map for each frame.

21.9.5   Geometry Modeling

See pages 337 and 393 for details.

☑ When creating scene files in mi format from other programs, use binary vectors, not ASCII floating-point vectors. See page 308 for details.

☑ Use conservative free-form surface and displacement map approximations that require a minimum of triangles (see pages 93 and 337).

☑ View-dependent approximation can reduce the number of triangles of distant objects, but if the object is multiple-instanced mental ray must retessellate it for every instance instead of letting all instances share a single tessellation. Carefully evaluate the trade-off between a reduced number of triangles due to view dependency, and the increased number of triangles due to per-instance tessellation.

☑ mental ray deals well with details of extremely large models, however objects that are much larger than the visible area are wasteful and should be avoided. It is not necessary or efficient to model a large airport to render a rivet in the cockpit of one of the aircraft, or to simulate the sky with a huge sphere around the scene instead of using an environment map.

☑ To render an animation, incremental changes should be used whenever possible to avoid redefining, possibly retessellating, and then transmitting across the network elements that have not changed. Fly-through camera animations are an extreme example; if only the camera instance transformation changes mental ray can skip most preprocessing steps.

☑ In mental ray 3.0 and higher, use placeholder objects (see page 369) to store complex objects to permit mental ray to flush them from the cache after tessellation, to make room for more important data.

21.9.6 Shaders and Phenomena

See page 288 for details.

☑ Use optimized shaders. Shading can dominate rendering time, especially in the case of complex volume shaders and ray marching (which evaluates shaders many times for every ray). Note, however, that older Visual C++ compilers for Windows NT have a history of optimizer bugs; make sure you have a new version. The Intel compilers produce significantly faster code than the Microsoft compilers.

☑ When using volume shaders attached to transparent helper objects that bound the effect, make the helper object as small as possible even if that takes a few more triangles.

☑ Avoid connecting too many very small shaders. There is an optimum balance between numbers of shader assignments and shader sizes. Constant values are always fastest.

21.9.7 Networking and Multithreading

See page 407 for details.

☑ Fewer machines with many processors are better than many machines with few processors (in other words, thread parallelism is better than network parallelism unless there is a serious memory shortage). Watch for network collisions that indicate network saturation.

☑ To optimize network parallelism, begin with few machines and add machines until the speedup achieved by adding more machines becomes too small. This is scene-dependent.

☑ Use memory mapped textures or at least local textures on server machines to avoid having to transfer the texture data across the network during rendering.

☑ Watch memory usage carefully and reduce it if a machine begins swapping (see page 450). It often improves performance to use the machine with the most memory and the fastest processors as the client, especially if it also runs front-end applications.

☑ Monitoring rendering progress with a realtime viewer such as `imf_disp` can reduce networking performance because extra data must be transferred.

☑ Higher verbosity levels (especially 6 and 7) can significantly reduce performance on platforms with poorly parallelized I/O systems such as Windows NT.

21.9.8 Memory Management

See page 431 for details.

☑ Avoid situations where a small number of very large geometric objects dominate. Use more and smaller objects.

☑ As mentioned above, use placeholder objects and separate object definition files for large objects.

☑ Choose the memory heap and cache limit (-memory command line option) small enough to keep the machine from swapping, but large enough to prevent frequent cache flushes and frequent rebuilds of memory items.

☑ Use textures in .map format whenever possible, because they can be paged and memory-mapped.. Map images are created with the `imf_copy -p -r` utility.

Chapter 22

Troubleshooting *

This section lists common problems and their solutions.

22.1   Sampling

Sampling artifacts: staircasing, banding, noise
First decrease the parameters of the `contrast` statement in the options block to 0.05 0.05 0.05 or even lower, and use sampling densities such as -1 1 or 0 2 using a `samples` statement. Contrast settings are the primary control; do not try to adjust sampling quality only with increased sampling because that can quickly make performance unacceptable.

Motion blur is grainy
Decrease the parameters of the `time contrast` statement in the options block to 0.1 0.1 0.1 or lower, and make sure that the `samples` statement in the options block specifies at least -1 2. Do not simply increase sampling to large numbers because this can significantly reduce performance.

Soft shadows are grainy or boxy
If the soft shadows were created with area light sources, increase the area light sampling from 3 3 to 5 5 or higher. If the soft shadows were created with a shadow map, increase the shadow map samples or the shadow map resolution.

Speckles instead of soft shadowmap shadow
If a shadow map results in random speckles instead of the expected soft shadow, the `shadowmap softness` parameter in the light source definition is probably much too large. Begin with small values such as 0.05.

22.2 Shading

Flashing textures in animations
Use filtering or elliptical filtering for texture mapping. See the texture mapping chapter for details.

Systematic artifacts appear at edges
Enable jittering by adding the statement `jitter 1.0` to the options block.

Shading is red
This is typically the result of attaching a shader returning a scalar to another that expects a color. Check your Phenomenon declarations.

Displacement maps use too much memory
Displacement map approximation tuning needs some attention. If the mapped surface is large, use view-dependent approximation to avoid increasing the tessellation in areas distant from the camera in order to get closer areas clean. One triangle per visible pixel is normally sufficient. This can be achieved with `displace view length 1` approximations, for example.

Missing surface derivatives
Some shaders and Phenomenon scene elements require surface derivatives, for example to produce anisotropic effects such as brushed metal. If the effect is missing, the normal reason is a missing `derivative` statement in free-form surface objects, or `d` statements in polygonal objects. The shader or Phenomenon sees only null vectors in this case and is unable to determine the parameter directions.

version mismatch: "..." reports version 1, declaration specifies version 0
The version number of the executable shader (which was typically read from a shader library) and the version number of the shader declaration (typically stored in a separate file that is included into the scene file with a `$include` command) do not agree. The most common reason is an incorrect path in the `$include` command. It may also be caused by incorrect software installation. If the declaration specifies version 0, the declaration file may be a leftover from a mental ray 1.9 installation. In any case, mismatches normally cause incorrect images or even cause the shader to crash when it is called.

22.3 Caustics and Global Illumination

Caustics and global illumination: no photons stored
The message "no photons stored after emitting 10000 photons" indicates that photons emitted by a light source do not hit an object that stores energy on the surface or in a volume. This can have several reasons: missing photon or photon volume shaders in the material of the object that casts or receives photons, or incorrect caustic flags in the options block or object definitions, or a light source that emits photons in the wrong directions (if it is a spot or directional light), or a light source that cannot illuminate the photon-storing materials because it is hidden behind other objects such as a large sphere enclosing the scene.

Caustics or global illumination are too weak

Increase the energy of the light sources that create the effect. Remember that unless specified otherwise, energy falls off with the square of the distance, so large energy values that range in the tens of thousands or more are necessary to illuminate distant objects. As a first approximation, begin with light energy values that are the square of the distance from the light source to the illuminated objects.

Caustics are weak and the lens turns into a fireball

The lens that casts the caustic must have a specular component but no diffuse component, or it will scatter too many photons away from the expected caustic pattern. Increasing the brightness of the pattern by increasing the light energy is the wrong approach — the lens will catch too many of the diffuse photons and light up without the desired effect. Instead, remove the diffuse component.

Caustics or global illumination are too soft

Increase the number of photons emitted by the light source creating the effect, or use a caustic filter in the options block.

Caustics or global illumination shows high-frequency noise

If indirectly illuminated surfaces appear mottled or uneven, increase the parameters of the appropriate `accuracy` statement in the options block. Increasing the number of photons rarely helps.

Caustics or global illumination show splatter patterns

Sometimes photons take unlikely paths. For example, in the Cornell boxes used in the global illumination chapter, some light is focused through the sphere on the floor, creating a bright caustic that is again focused by the sphere on the ceiling. Since only a few photons actually reach the ceiling, the density there is too low to create a smooth pattern. Similar situations occur if refractive objects create projections of other parts of the scene on nearby walls. Increase the accuracy or the number of photons.

Caustics do not create the expected sharp bright spots

It takes careful adjustment to get nice sharp caustic patterns, both in the real world and in mental ray simulations. The caustic caster must be shaped like a lens (with varying thickness if double-sided, or curved if one-sided) and must have an appropriate index of refraction such as 1.33 or 1.5, the caustic receiver must have the correct distance, and the light source must have sufficient energy.

22.4   Geometry

Sections of very thin objects are missing

Once found anywhere in a screen rectangle, mental ray uses edge following to resolve thin objects completely, but only up to the edge of the screen rectangle. If there are only a few missing lines and there are few processors and hosts, increase the screen rectangle size by adding a statement like `task size 64` to the options block. If there are many problems, increase the minimum sampling density (the first parameter of the `samples` statement in the options block) from -2 to -1 or 0.

Strobing cracks in surfaces

This happens if objects are very large compared to the size of the part visible to the camera. These artifacts disappear if scanline rendering is disabled with a `scanline off` statement in the options block. Increasing the hither plane value using a clip statement in the camera definition fixes this.

Coplanar geometry

If geometry is closer than the numerical precision limit of floating-point arithmetic, mental ray excludes false matches. This means that if a transparent cube rests on a ground polygon so that the cube floor and the ground are coplanar, there is no guarantee that rays pass first through the cube floor and then hit the ground plane. The same problem occurs if, for example, the wine-glass interface of a wine glass is modeled as two independent surfaces. In these cases, leave a small gap.

Orientation of triangles inconsistent

Very chaotic displacement can cause sections of the surface to flip, that is, make the new normal vector point in the opposite direction from the normal vector of the base surface. If this happens, mental ray prints this error message and ignores the surface. This can be fixed by correcting the displacement shader or its parameters.

Geometry shaders crash

Due to changes in the geometry shader interface in mental ray 2.1 and 3.0 in order to support various additional features, shaders that access mental ray's scene data structures are generally not compatible between mental ray 2.0, 2.1, and 3.0. They must be recompiled with the appropriate `geoshader.h` include file.

22.5   System

Accessing null DB tag

mental ray stores scene elements in a database, where they are referenced by a tag number. A null tag means "does not exist". The most common cause of this is a shader that has a parameter of type "shader", "geometry", "material", or "texture", and accesses this parameter without checking whether it was actually defined in the parameter list of this shader in the scene file. A less common reason for this message is a defective or incomplete scene file, perhaps because of missing shader declarations, in a way that mental ray was unable to repair. In this case additional error messages indicate the problem.

rld: Cannot successfully map soname

The Silicon Graphics run time linker (rld) failed to load a shader library, either because it could not be found or because it has the wrong type. In the first case, either use the -L command line option or the `LD_LIBRARY_PATH` environment variable to specify the correct location. In the second case, there is an installation problem; use the `file` command at a shell prompt to find out the type of the library and of mental ray. ELF 32-bit, ELF 64-bit, and ELF N32 are not compatible.

Out of memory

Memory is used for scene geometry, textures, frame buffers, rendering acceleration data structures and other purposes. In most cases, the reason for memory problems is the size of the textures. Use memory mapped textures to address this (see page 70). On some systems the default limit on memory usage is too low; see page 450.

Plate 1. *Orange Apple Banana*, caustics.

Plate 2. *Dusty Room*: sunlight through a stained glass window scattered off from dust particles in the air lights the room.

Plate 3. light beam in 3D space created by a volume caustic.

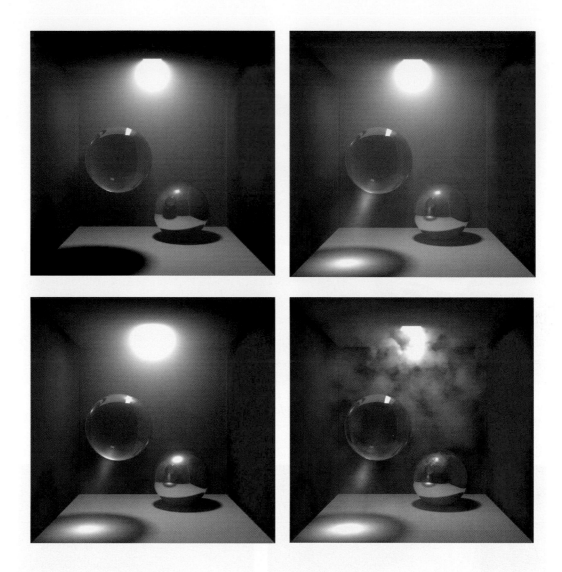

Plates 4–7. *Cornell box*: illumination simulation of a room with fog with direct illumination only (top left), with global illumination (top right), with global illumination and anisotropic fog (bottom left), and global illumination and nonhomogeneous fog (bottom right).

On the facing page, plates 12 and 13 show the effect of very low numbers of photons (1000 caustic and 10 000 globillum, left) and large numbers of photons (50 and 1 000 000, respectively, right), enhanced with false colors. Note the quality of the complex ceiling caustic from a LSSDSSDE path that crosses the refractive sphere twice. In the right plate, also note the sharper floor caustic and the presence of the small caustic on the wall near the bottom left, which is a reflection from the right sphere focused through the left sphere (an LSSSDE path). Higher relative densities affect illumination sharpness, not brightness. $\longrightarrow$

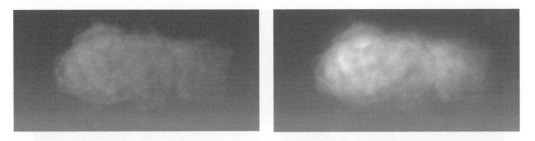

Plates 8 and 9. *Clouds*: Simulation of a cloud with traditional raytracing (left) versus full global illumination using multiple volume scattering (right).

Plates 10 and 11. *Underwater Sunbeams*: Fish under water with sunlight seen from underneath a wavy water surface, using volume caustics.

Plates 12 and 13. Diagnostic modes "photon irradiance 2.5".

Plates 14 and 15 *Matrix Reloaded*, Plate 16 *Matrix Revolutions*.
All images © Warner Brothers 2003.

Plates 17–19. *Star Wars: Episode II – Attack of the Clones.*

Plates 20–22. *The Day After Tomorrow*.

Plate 23 and 24. *Shark Tale*.

Plates 25–27. *Alexander.*

Plates 28–30. *Fight Club*, 100% CG.

Plates 31 and 32. *The Cell*. Only the glass containers and the breathing horse slices are CG.

Plate 33. *Panic Room*.

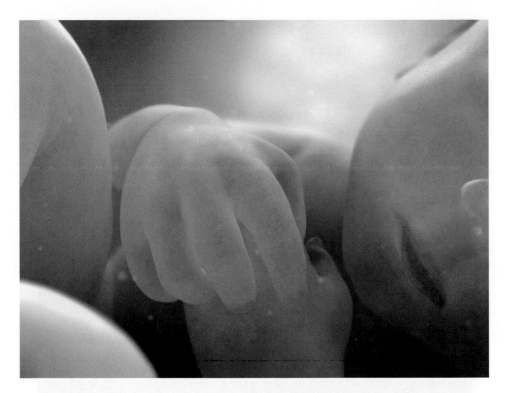

Plate 34. *Baby*. Subsurface scattering.

Plates 35. *La Cité des Enfants Perdus*.

Plates 36 and 37. *HTC Babelsberg*: Architectural design, 1.6 million triangles, without and with global illumination. Both images were adjusted to show similar overall brightness.

Plate 38. *Swimming Pool*: Caustics on a pool floor from a wavy water surface.

Plate 39. *Rough AppRoach* (short movie available at http://www.filmschool.de).

Plate 40. *U-Bahn*: Berlin City Hall subway station rendered with global illumination, final gathering, and elliptical filtered textures on each tile of the back wall.

Plate 41. Mercedes SLK: high-quality modeling with class-A surfaces and volumic layer paint.

Plate 42. Detail of the Mercedes: curvature approximation of folded metal.

Plate 43. Detail of the Mercedes: ray-traced reflections.

Plate 44. *Snowflake*: Translucency, subsurface scattering, image-based lighting, displacement.

Plates 45 and 46. *Apevision*: Simulation of fur using a volume shader.

Plates 47 and 48. *Riven Game*.

Color Plates

Third-Party Copyright Notices

Distribution of OpenEXR requires the following copyright notice:

Distribution of the OpenEXR PXR24 compressor requires the following copyright notice:

Appendix A

Command Line Options

This appendix lists all commands in the mental ray suite. Not all programs are available with all distributions.

A.1 mental ray

When started from a shell command line, the mental ray rendering software accepts a large number of options. Most of these correspond to similar commands or camera or options statements in the scene file. When an option is given on the command line, it overrides the corresponding command or statement in the scene file, which in turn overrides the defaults. The defaults for certain options given in the option list below apply only if the corresponding command or statement is not present in the scene file.

mental ray is started as

    ray [*options*] [*scenefile*]

If no scene file is given, the scene is read from standard input. Scene file names normally end in .mi. If the extension is missing mental ray will read the name as specified, and if this fails, retry with .mi added.

Options can be abbreviated as long as the given substring is unambiguous. mental ray checks for ambiguities and prints an error message listing the choices. For example, -resolution can be abbreviated as -res. For frequently-used options such as -verbose and -filename, short forms are available. The page numbers on the right side refer to the relevant chapters in the main part of this book. The available options are:

-acceleration bsp|largebsp|grid
            Selects the standard binary space partitioning (BSP) algorithm, or the large BSP algorithm that works for far larger scenes at a small performance penalty, or the voxel grid algorithm algorithm. The default is BSP. All these algorithms accelerate

ray tracing.

-approx [*options*] --[3.1]

mental ray 3.1.2 and later allow specifying override approximations on the command line. Override approximations override any object approximations in the scene file. They are primarily useful for fast preview rendering, where approximation accuracy is not required. The following *options* can be specified:

view	view-dependent approximation
fine	fine approximation with microtriangles
sharp	faceted, useful for fine displacement
parametric U V	rectangular grid of $U \cdot V \cdot 2$ triangles
regular U V	rectangular grid that spans patches
length L	triangle edge length less than D
distance D	distance from true surface less than D
angle A	angle between neighboring triangles less than A degrees
any	it is sufficient if any of length, distance, and angle is satisfied
min max	subdivide at least *min* and at most *max* times, default 0 5

Except for any, which must be spelled out, all options can be abbreviated by their first letter. If no options are specified (-approx --), parametric 0 0 is used, which produces a very fast low-quality approximation. See the scene description chapter for detailed information on approximations.

-approx_displace [*options*] --[3.1]

This option is similar to -approx and accepts the same options, but sets the override approximation for displacement. If no options are given, it defaults to parametric 0 0, which is so low that most displacements turn into a vaguely bumpy surface. High-quality displacement requires an approximation like -approx fine view length 0.25 0 7 --.

-aperture *aperture*   p. 39

The aperture is the width of the viewing plane. The height of the viewing plane is *aperture* divided by *aspect*.

-aspect *aspect*   p. 39

This is the aspect ratio of the camera. The default is 1.33. In camera space, *aperture* is the width of the viewing plane, and *aperture* divided by *aspect* is the height. The viewing plane is divided into pixels as specified by the resolution *viewdef*, so the aspect will result in nonsquare pixels if it is not equal to the X resolution divided by the Y resolution.

-bsp_depth *depth*$_{int}$ p. 423

The maximum number of levels in the BSP tree. This option is used only if binary space partitioning is enabled. Larger tree depths reduce rendering time but increase memory consumption, and also slightly increase preprocessing time. The default is 40.

-bsp_memory *memory_int*   p. 423

The maximum memory in megabytes used in BSP preprocessing. A value of zero indicates that there is no limit on the memory consumption; this is the default.

-bsp_size *size_int*   p. 423

The maximum number of primitives in a leaf of the BSP tree. Larger leaves will be subdivided unless the bsp_depth is reached. This option is used only if binary space partitioning is enabled. Larger leaf sizes reduce memory consumption but increase rendering time. The default is 10.

-bsp_shadow on|off[3.1]

mental ray 3.1.2 and later support a separate shadow BSP tree that accelerates raytraced shadows. It can greatly improve speed if shadows are cast by simplified shadow-only objects because it is no longer necessary to populate the master BSP tree with large hero objects. This mode is off by default.

-caustic on|off   p. 190

Enable or disable the generation of caustics in an appropriately defined scene. The default is off.

-caustic_accuracy *nphotons* [*radius*]

The number of photons used to estimate caustics during rendering and the maximum radius to be used when picking up the photons. The number of photons may be set to 0, which means that all photons within the given radius are used. The defaults are 100 and a scene-size dependent *radius*.

-caustic_scale *r g b* [*a*][3.4]

Caustics are multiplied by the specified color. Factors greater than 1.0 make the caustic brighter.

-clip *hither yon*   p. 39

The *hither* (near) and *yon* (far) planes are planes parallel to the viewing plane that delimit the rendered scene for scanline rendering. Raytracing is not affected. Points outside the space between the hither and yon planes will not be rendered. The defaults are 0.001 and 1000000.0.

-code *"filename"* ... --   p. 399

The named *filename* is interpreted as a C source file (ending with the extension ".c") and compiled and linked into mental ray.

-colorclip rgb|alpha|raw   p. 419

This option controls the rules used to clip an RGBA color before quantization to an 8-bit or 16-bit frame buffer. The rgb mode states that RGB are first to be clipped to the range [0, 1] before A is clipped to [$max(R, G, B)$, 1]. This is the default mode.

The *alpha* mode lets A first be clipped to [0, 1] before RGB is clipped to [0, *A*]. Both of these modes ensure that all channels are within [0, 1] and that A is no less than any of R, G, and B, which is is the valid domain of premultiplied colors. The third mode, *raw*, ignores all requirements, and clips both A and RGB to [0, 1]. This is useful to make mental ray modify output colors as little as possible. Because the color output may be invalid, the raw mode overrides the `premultiply off` option if present. Desaturation is always applied if enabled.

-contrast *r g b* [*a*]   p. 420
The contrast controls oversampling. If neighboring samples differ by more than the color *r, g, b, a*, oversampling is done as specified by the sampling options. The default is 0.1 0.1 0.1 0.1. If missing, the default for *a* is the average of *r, g,* and *b*.

-c_compiler "*filename*"   p. 399
If this option is given, the standard C compiler "`cc`" is replaced with *filename*.

-c_flags "*options*"   p. 399
The *options* string replaces the standard options given to the C compiler. The defaults depend on the machine type. If the *options* begin with two plus signs[2.1], such as "`++ -I.`", it is inserted into the default options instead of replacing them.

-c_linker "*filename*"   p. 399
If this option is given, the standard linker "`ld`" is replaced with *filename*.

-desaturate on|off   p. 293
If a rendered sample returns an RGBA color whose components are outside the legal range, mental ray will clip the color into this legal range. This option determines how the clipping of R, G, and B is performed. If desaturation is turned off, which is the default, the components are clipped individually. If turned on, then if any of R, G, and B exceed the allowed range, the color is shifted towards the grayscale axis of the color cube in order to try to maintain the perceived brightness of that color, effectively bleaching out the color. The valid range of RGBA is controlled by the `colorclip` option.

-diagnostic bsp depth|size
This diagnostic mode[1] can be used to visualize the parameters for BSP tree parameters (see `-bsp depth` and `-bsp size` options), to find the reason for unexpected large depths or sizes reported after rendering. This does not work in `-acceleration largebsp` mode because that mode never creates a single BSP tree from which consistent diagnostics could be computed.

-diagnostic grid off|object|world|camera *size*
This diagnostic mode[2.1] is intended for scene debugging. Unless set to `off`, it draws a colored grid on all objects in the scene that shows object, world, or camera space coordinates. Steps on the X, Y, and Z axes are shown with red, green, and blue grid lines, respectively. The distance between grid lines is *size* units. This is useful to

---

[1]The -diagnostic bsp option requires mental ray 3.0 or higher.

estimate the size and distances between objects in mental ray, or to visualize object space coordinates. The `off` argument disables the grid. The default is `off`.

-diagnostic hardware [window|grid]^{3.4}

Hardware rendering diagnostics. Without argument, turns off shading and uses a default gray material. The `window` mode pops up a window on the screen, showing rendering progress. The `grid` mode renders a wireframe scene.

-diagnostic photon off|density|irradiance *max*

When rendering caustics or global illumination, this option disables all material shaders in the scene and produces a false-color rendering of photon density, or the average of the red, green, and blue irradiance components. Photon density is the number of photons per unit surface area. *max* is the density (or irradiance) that is assigned to 100%, or red. The colors are, from 0% to 100%: Blue, cyan, green, yellow, and red. Higher values fade to white. *max* can be given as zero in which case the appropriate maximum is automatically found. This is done after the whole image has been rendered. This mode is useful when tuning the number of photons in a photonmap and setting the various _accuracy options, since the density (or irradiance) is estimated using those settings. The default is `off`.

-diagnostic samples on|off   p. 443

Switch to sampling visualization mode and create grayscale images representing sampling densities instead of color images. A black pixel has had no samples, whereas a white pixel has had the maximum amount as specified by the `-samples` option. In addition, a red grid shows task rectangle boundaries.

-diagnostic finalgather^{3.1}

This mode shows final gathering points, as green dots for initial raster-space final gathering points, blue dots[3.4] for final gathering points from per-object finalgather map files, and red dots for render-time final gathering points.

-displace on|off   p. 337

Ignore all displacement shaders if set to `off`. The default is `on`.

-displace_presample on|off^{3.2}   p. 420

Enables or disables presampling of displacement-mapped geometry. Presampling increases performance by introducing a preprocessing phase before tessellation, and is enabled by default. If turned off, rendering begins earlier but takes longer; this is sometimes useful for preview rendering.

-dither on|off

Ditheringdithering mitigates 8-bit and 16-bit color quantization errors by introducing noise into the pixel such that the round-off errors are randomly distributed. The default is `off`.

-echo "*filename*" [ascii][source][approx][norendercommand][textures][incremental^{3.2}] [omit "*S*"][norecurse "*S*"][explode [*N*]] --

Echo the current scene to the file *filename*. The options specify the format of the echoed file. Allowed options are:

ascii uses ASCII format for the vectors (default is binary),

source prefers source geometry over triangles if available (default),

approx prefers triangles over source geometry if available,

norendercommand disables the echo of the **render** command,

textures includes texture pixel data verbatim.

incremental[3.2] causes multiframe animations to be echoed in a more compact format, by omitting scene elements that did not change since the previous frame.

omit specifies that certain types of elements, specified by S, should be omitted from the output. It is supported by mental ray 3.0 only. Note that both omit and norecurse will produce incomplete and nonrenderable scene files. These options are useful for extracting subsets of a scene.

norecurse specifies that references of certain types of elements specified by S should be omitted from the output. It is supported by mental ray 3.0 only. For example, if S contains icil, instances of cameras and lights would be echoed (unless disabled by omit), but the instanced camera or light would not be echoed first. The S strings of the omit and norecurse attributes are sequences of the following codes:

code	element	affected statement
g	instance group	instgroup
o	geometric object	object
c	camera	camera
l	light source	light
m	material	material
t	texture	texture
p	option block	options
s	named shader	shader
d	declaration	declare
u	user data	data
ig	instance of an instance group	instance
io	instance of an object	instance
ic	instance of a camera	instance
il	instance of a light	instance
is	instance of a geometry shader	instance

Note that triangle echos have displacement mapping already applied to the triangles, but the displacement shaders are not removed from the materials so the echoed file will get displaced twice when rendered. The echo option must be terminated with a double minus.

explode causes all objects with more than N vertices to be written to a separate file with a name beginning with autoload. This file will be referenced by a placeholder object with an appropriate file statement in the main echo file. If omitted, N defaults to 1; a typical good value is 10000 to make sure that the overhead of opening a file is not wasted on really small objects.

-face front|back|both   p. 423

The *front* side of a geometric object in the scene is defined to be the side its normal vector points away from. By specifying that only front-facing triangles are to be rendered, speed can be improved because fewer triangles need to be tested for a ray. The default is face both.

-fb_dir "*directory*"[3.4]

Specifies a directory for temporarily storing memory mapped frame buffer files. mental ray 3.4 and later store frame buffers in files on disk, not in memory, to conserve space. If this option is not provided, the environment variables TMPDIR and TEMP are examined. If they are also not defined the current working directory is used for storing memory mapped frame buffer files.

-file_name "*filename*"   p. 291

Overrides the file name given by the first file output statement in the camera definition in the scene file. The full file or path name must be given, including extension if desired.

-file_type "*format*"   p. 296

Overrides the file format given by the first file output statement in the camera definition in the scene file. File formats include "pic" for Softimage image files, "rla" for Wavefront RLA files, and "ps" for PostScript files if contour mode is enabled.

-filter [clip[3.2]] box|triangle|gauss|mitchell|lanczos *width* [*height*]   p. 420

This option specifies how multiple samples in recursive sampling mode are to be combined. The filter defaults to a box filter of width and height 1. The filter size can also be specified, in pixel units. Good filter sizes are 1.0 for box, 2.0 for triangle, 3.0 for gauss, and 4.0 for mitchell and lanczos. mental ray 3.2 and up also support clip mitchell and clip lanczos to clip the filter result to the sample range under the filter, which avoids ringing in these filters because they contain negative coefficients. In mental ray 2.0, this option requires a sampling density of at least 1 1; in mental ray 2.1 and later the sampling density must be at least -1 0.

-finalgather on|off|only[3.3]|fastlookup   p. 206

Enables or disables final gathering[2.1]. It is disabled by default. Final gathering is a rendering technique used for computing indirect illumination with a one-generation raytracing step. mental ray 3.0 adds a third choice, fastlookup, that enables final gathering and also arranges for irradiance to be stored in the photon map. This slows down photon tracing but greatly accelerates final gathering. mental ray 3.3 adds the only keyword, which computes the finalgather map and skips rendering.

-finalgather_accuracy [view] $nrays_{int}$ [$maxdist$ [$mindist$]]   p. 206

> $nrays$ is the number of rays cast in a final gathering step during rendering. The
> default is 1000. $maxdist$ is the maximum distance within which a final gather result
> can be reused. The default is scene dependent. $mindist$ is the minimum distance
> within which final gather results must be reused. The default is scene dependent.
> Both distances are specified in world space units, or raster space units if $view^{3.x}$ is
> specified.

-finalgather_depth $reflect_{int}$ [$refract_{int}$ [$diffuse^{3.4}_{int}$ [sum_{int}]]]$^{3.2}$

> This option is similar to -trace_depth but applies only to finalgather rays. The
> defaults are all 0, which prevents finalgather rays from spawning subrays. This
> means that indirect illumination computed by final gathering cannot pass through
> glass or mirrors, for example. A depth of 1 (where the sum must not be less than
> the other two) would allow a single refraction or reflection. Diffuse bounces$^{3.4}$ can
> also be controlled. It is not normally necessary to choose depths greater than 2.
> This is not compatible with mental ray 3.1 and earlier, which used the trace depth
> (which defaults to 2 2 4) for final gathering.

-finalgather_display on|off$^{3.3}$

> Allows image previewing during the finalgather presampling stage if the imf_disp
> viewer is attached to the output image file. This is disabled by default. The quality of
> the preview image is very low, but it allows fast detection of illumination problems
> in a scene. This option has no impact on the final image. To improve performance
> it is recommended to disable this option for non-interactive rendering.

-finalgather_falloff [$start$] $stop^{3.2}$

> Limits the length of final gather rays to a distance of $stop$ in world space. If no object
> is found within a distance of $stop$, the ray defaults to the environment color. The
> $start$ parameter defines the beginning of a linear falloff range; objects at a distance
> between $start$ and $stop$ will fade towards the environment color. This option is
> useful for reducing memory usage for the geometry cache.

-finalgather_file "$name$"$^{3.2}$

> Tells mental ray to use the file $filename$ for loading and saving final gather points. If
> the finalgather file does not exist, it is created and the final gather points are saved.
> If it exists, it is loaded, and the points stored in it become available for irradiance
> lookups. If mental ray creates extra final gather points, they are appended to the
> file. This means that the file may grow without bounds.

-finalgather_file ["$name$" "$name$" ...   ]$^{3.4}$

> mental ray 3.4 and later allow attaching a list of finalgather file names instead of a
> single file name from a command line. All files are read and merged. The first file
> is rewritten with the complete map like in the single-file case.

-finalgather_filter $size_{int}$$^{3.2}$

> Final gathering uses an speckle elimination filter that prevents samples with extreme
> brightness from skewing the overall energy stored in a finalgather hemisphere. This
> is done by filtering neighboring samples such that extreme values are discarded in

the filter size. The default is 1; 0 turns speckle elimination off and greater values
remove more speckles and soften contrasts. Sizes greater than 4 or so are not
normally useful.

finalgather_presample_density $T^{3.4}$

This option controls the density of initial finalgather points created during
preprocessing (green dots in the diagnostic image). It increases (decreases if $T < 1$)
the number of precomputed finalgather points approximately T times.

-finalgather_rebuild on|off|freeze$^{3.2}$

If a filename is specified using the -finalgather_file option, it is normally loaded
and used if the file exists. -finalgather_rebuild on causes existing files to be
ignored, all final gather points will be recomputed and an existing file will be
overwritten. freeze is equivalent to on, except that the final gather map, once
created by reading it from a file or building it in the first frame, will never be
modified. Extra finalgather points created during rendering will not be appended,
and the finalgather file on disk will not be modified.

-finalgather_scale r g b $[a]^{3.4}$

The irradiance obtained from final gathering is multiplied by the specified color,
making the irradiance effect brighter for factors greater than 1.0.

-focal *distance*|infinity   p. 39

The focal distance is set to *distance*. The focal distance is the distance from the
camera to the viewing plane. The viewing plane is the plane in front of the camera
that the rendered scene is projected onto; its edges correspond to the edges of the
rendered image. If infinity is used in place of the *distance*, an orthographic view
is rendered.

-gamma *gamma_factor*   p. 417

Gamma correction can be applied to rendered color pixels to compensate for
output devices with a nonlinear color response. All quantized R, G, B, and alpha
component values (ie. not if the frame buffer is floating-point or RGBE) are raised
to *gamma_factor*. The default gamma factor is 1.0, which turns gamma correction
off. The reverse correction is applied to all quantized texture images.

-geometry on|off   p. 365

Ignore all geometry shaders if set to off. The default is on.

-globillum on|off   p. 198

Enable or disable the computation of global illumination$^{2.1}$. The default is off.
To actually compute global illumination, lights must have an energy, and materials
must have photon shaders.

-globillum_accuracy *nphotons*$_{int}$ [*radius*]   p. 198

The number of photons used to estimate global illumination during rendering and
the maximum radius to be used when reading photons during rendering. The
defaults number of photons is 500. If *nphotons* is set to 0, all photons within the

given radius are used. The default radius is scene size dependent.

-globillum_scale r g b $[a]$[3.4]

The irradiance obtained from the globillum photonmap lookup is multiplied by the specified color, making the effect brighter for factors greater than 1.0.

-grid_depth $depth_{int}$[3.1]   p. 423

If the hierarchical grid algorithm[3.1] is used, this option sets the number of recursion levels. If a voxel of a grid contains too much detail, it is subdivided by a subgrid for that voxel, which adds another level.

-grid_resolution $xres_{int}$ $[yres_{int}$ $zres_{int}$ p. 423

If the hierarchical grid algorithm[3.1] is used, this option sets the number of grid voxels in the X, Y, and Z dimensions. If only one number is given, it is used for all three dimensions. The default is 0 0 0, which selects a default computed at runtime.

-grid_size *factor*   p. 423

If the static grid algorithm[2.1] is used, factor is a correction factor for mental ray's internal guess for the grid resolution, so that numbers greater than 1.0 increase the number of voxels in each dimension and numbers less than 1.0 decrease it.

-grid_size $size_{int}$ p. 423

If the hierarchical grid algorithm[3.1] is used, this option sets the maximum number of triangles in a grid voxel. If there are more, and the grid depth permits it, the voxel is subdivided into a subgrid.

-H *"path"*[3.4]

Specifies the directory where hardware shaders are located. This is a shorthand for **-hardware_path** ".

-hardware off|on|all --[3.3]

Specify *which* objects should be rendered with hardware rendering: off disables hardware rendering (this is the default), on uses hardware rendering for all materials that specify a hardware shader, and all uses hardware rendering for all objects and tries to find hardware substitutes for materials that do not specify an explicit hardware shader. The most useful mode is all. Note that this option only selects which objects are eligible for hardware rendering, but mental ray may still fall back on software rendering for objects for which no appropriate hardware shaders are available. This is controlled separately by the following options.

-hardware cg|native|fast* -- [force][3.3]

This option controls *how* hardware shaders are selected for an object that is eligible for hardware rendering, as specified by the previous option. mental ray will try all approaches allowed by this option in turn:

cg means that mental ray will first look for shaders implemented in NVIDIA's Cg 1.2 shader programming language. This is the default.

native looks for shaders implemented in the OpenGL 2.0 native shader programming language, which is less powerful than Cg.

fast uses hardcoded OpenGL materials that do not involve programmable shaders at all. This is limited to simple Gouraud models.

force specifies that the search stops here, and objects that cannot use any of the above methods use a simple gray default material. If force is not specified, mental ray will fall back on software rendering for the object.

The hardware options can be combined. For example, -hardware all cg native fast force -- will render all objects with the best available hardware shading method but never with software; this is useful for fast preview rendering. The option -hardware all cg native -- is best for quality rendering, and so on.

-hardware_echo [error] "*path*"

Write the Cg source code as it is passed to the Cg compiler and the resulting assembly code to disk, to the directory *path*. If the error option is specified, only those files are written for which compilation has failed. This is useful for debugging, and to extract shader code from mental ray for use in game engines or other standalone applications.

-hardware_path "*path*"[3.4]

Specifies the directory where hardware shaders are located. Can also be abbreviated as -H.

-hardware_samples *multi*$_{int}$ *super*$_{int}$[3.4]

Specify the multisampling and supersampling rates to be used for hardware rendering. Multisampling is done by the hardware pixel pipeline, which takes more samples per triangle and writes the result to the frame buffer. Supersampling is done by mental ray, by increasing the frame buffer size and rendering at a higher resolution, and then downfiltering to the requested frame buffer resolution. Multisampling is much faster and does not increase hardware video memory usage (or even exceed the GPU resolution capacity), but supersampling looks better.

-help

Print a summary of all options with their allowed parameters, and terminate.

-hosts "*hostname*[:*portnumber*] [*remote parameters*]" ... --

The machine list overrides the machine list taken from the .rayhosts file, if present. One slave is started on each machine specified. Machine names must be given as expected by the local name resolving method (such as /etc/hosts) or as a numeric IP address (nnn.nnn.nnn.nnn).

-I "*path1:path2:...*"

Overrides the path used to resolve $include commands in the .mi scene file. The default path contains the directories ., {_MI_REG_INCLUDE}, /usr/local/mi/rayinc, /usr/include, and /usr/include/mi. Note that only one -I option can be specified. It may contain a colon-separated (Unix only) or semicolon-separated (Unix and Windows NT) list of directory paths that are tried in sequence if a $include command using angle brackets is used in the .mi scene file. Paths introduced with an exclamation point are special; they are applied to quoted $include paths too, and substitute the entire directory path. This can be used to force mental ray to use a specified path regardless of the path specified in the $include command, for example because that path points to an obsolete (1.9) version of a declaration file. For example, -I /a:/b:!/new tries to find a path <x/y/z> first as /a/x/y/z, then /b/x/y/z, then /new/z.

-imgpipe *fd*_{int}
$$-\texttt{imgpipe}\ \mathit{fd}_{int}$$
Normally mental ray prints connection information into the output image file that let programs like imf_disp connect and display images while being rendered. If -imgpipe is used, the relevant information is printed to the given file descriptor *fd* instead. This can be used for command lines such as "ray -imgpipe 1 scene.mi | imf_disp -". The imf_disp program is a viewer provided by mental images that supports image piping.

-jitter *jitter*   p. 420
The jittering factor introduces systematic variations into sample locations if *jitter* is set to 1.0. Jittering is turned off by default, or by specifying a *jitter* of 0.0.

-jobmemory *mb*   p. 432
The *physical* argument specifies the size of mental ray 3.x's scene cache memory, in megabytes. The default is unlimited for mental ray 3.0 and 512 for mental ray 3.1. (mental ray 3.1 supports fine microtriangle tessellation which depend on the ability to flush obsolete triangles from the cache.) The *virtual* number of megabytes limits the amount of virtual address space available for memory mapping, mostly for memory mapped textures; the default is 1024 (1 GB) on 32-bit machines and 0 (unlimited) on 64-bit machines. This option has been obsoleted by -memory in mental ray 3.2.

-L "*path1:path2:...*"   p. 399
This is an abbreviation for -ld_path.

-ld_libs "*libraries*"   p. 399
The *libraries* string replaces the standard library options given to the linker. The defaults depend on the machine used, typically "-lm -lc". Linker options are machine dependent and operating system dependent and cannot be changed.

-ld_path "*path1:path2:...*"   p. 399
Supply a list of library search paths that mental ray searches for shader libraries containing shader code. The paths given here precede those that can be given by the environment variable MI_LIBRARY_PATH and the built-in search path (consisting of the directories {_MI_REG_LIBRARY}, /usr/local/mi/lib, and ..

-lens on|off   p. 44
Ignore all lens shaders if set to off. The default is on.

`-lightmap on|off|only`[3.4]

> This mode enables rendering of lightmaps. By default, lightmaps are enabled. If this option is set to `only`, only the lightmaps but not the camera images are rendered.

`-link "`*filename*`" ... --`   p. 399

> Like the code command, the link command attaches external shaders to mental ray, which can then be used as shading functions. While the code command accepts ".c" files as *filename*, the link command expects either object files ending in ".o" or ".obj", or shader library files ending in ".so" or ".dll".

`-maxdisplace` *dist*[3.2]

> This option overrides all max displace values in scene objects with *dist* if *dist* > 0. This is useful to render old scene files built for mental ray 1.x or 2.x, which did not support max displace, and so would fail to show any displacement when rendered with mental ray 3.x.

`-memory` *limit*[3.2]

> The *limit* argument specifies the size of mental ray 3.2's total memory usage in megabytes, including heap (non-scene data), scene database, and virtual memory. The default is 512 megabytes. This option replaces `-jobmemory` in mental ray 3.1. Swap space specified with `-swap_limit` is not included. Memory limits have no effect on slave hosts, which do not have a command line.

`-message` *module class_list* `... --`

> Enable or disable individual message classes, per module. The module names are printed at the beginning of every message printed by mental ray; `all` can be used to modify the message classes of all modules. The *class_list* is a comma-separated list of classes to print. Supported message classes are `phase`, `progress`, `vprogress`, `time`, `scene`, `memory`, `render`, `vrender`, `resources`, `network`, `files`, and `debug`. The special words `default`, `all`, and `none` are also supported. A class can be inverted by prepending an exclamation point. For example, to print less verbose RC progress messages and make all modules report every file accessed, specify
>
> `-message rc default,!vprogress all default,files --`
>
> The message codes that perform useful actions are listed in the following table:

module	class	default	action
all	msgtrans	–	network transfers
echo	debug	–	add comments to -echo incremental[3.2] output
gapmi	progress	on	tessellation and displacement sampling
geomi	tessellate	–	triangles created by tessellation
img	files	–	opened files
job	debug	–	job execution, slave transfers, status
job	resources	–	post-render job execution statistics
mi	files	–	opened include files
mi	progress	on	line numbers every 50000 lines
msg	network	–	slave host rendezvous details
msg	progress	on	host list, connecting hosts
phen	debug	–	check shader results for NaN (Not a Number) values[3.2]
rc	phase	on	rectangle rendering begin and end
rc	scene	on	camera/option dump before rendering
rci	debug	–	BSP subtree and grid creation[3.2]
scene	phase	on	preprocessing, geometry shaders
scene	resources	–	postprocessing statistics
spdl	debug	–	echo MI declaration equivalents

-motion   on|off[3.2]

Normally the -shutter option controls whether motion blurring is enabled, and turns it on if there is a nonzero shutter interval. The -motion option overrides this and turns motion blurring on or off explicitly. For example, it is useful to define a zero shutter interval and then (order is important) turn motion blurring on, so that shaders get a correct $state \rightarrow motion$ vector. If motion blurring is turned off, this vector is not computed.

-motion_steps *steps*[3.1]

Approximate instance motion transformations with *steps* segments. This results in a smooth motion path, as if a similar number of motion vectors had been specified. *steps* must be a number between 1 and 15; 1 is the default. If objects with motion transformations also specify motion vectors, the number of motion vectors per vertex must agree with the motion steps value.

-nomaster[3.1]

When rendering with multiple hosts, schedule all jobs on slaves only, if possible. For example, the master host will not render, tessellate, compute shadow maps, etc, if possible; but it will still load textures of the slaves, and will also collect and save rendered images. The master may execute certain rendering jobs only if the slaves run out of resources. This is useful if the master host also runs front-end applications that must remain responsive even under heavy load.

-o *"filename"* p. 291

This is an abbreviation for -file_name.

-offset *x y* p. 39

An offset for the rendered image. The default is 0.0 for both *x* and *y*, which means that the image will be centered on the camera's Z axis. Positive values translate the image up and to the right. The offset is measured in pixel units.

-output on|off   p. 291

Ignore all output shaders if set to off. The default is on. File output statements are not affected.

-photonmap_file "*filename*"

Use *filename* for the photon map, in all frames. If the photon map file does not exist, it is created and saved. If it exists, it is loaded and used. For multiple frames it is only created for the first frame and then loaded for the remaining frames, which can greatly speed up rendering in scenes where the illumination does not change much, such as camera flythroughs.

-photonmap_only on|off[3.4]

If this option is set, only the photon maps but not the camera images are rendered. The default is off.

-photonvol_accuracy *nphotons*$_{int}$ [*radius*]

Controls how global illumination or caustics in participating media are estimated by looking up the photon map during rendering. *nphotons* is the maximum number of photons to examine and *radius* the maximum radius to search. if *nphotons* is 0, all photons are examined up to the *radius* limit. A *radius* of 0 means that a scene size dependent radius will be used. The defaults are 30 and 0.0.

-photon_depth *reflect*$_{int}$ [*refract*$_{int}$ [*sum*$_{int}$]]   p. 232

photon_depth is similar to trace_depth except that it applies to photons. If set to 0, no photons will be reflected; if set to 1, one level is allowed but a photon cannot be reflected again, and so on. The defaults are 5 5 5.

-premultiply on|off   p. 54

Premultiplication means that colors are stored with alpha multiplied to R, G, and B. This is the default. For example, white at 10% opacity is not stored as (1, 1, 1, 0.1) but as (0.1, 0.1, 0.1, 0.1). If turned off, mental ray writes the colors without premultiplication; in this case color clipping should also be switched to raw mode.

-render *begin*$_{int}$ [*end*$_{int}$ [*inc*$_{int}$]]

Render only frames *begin* through *end*[2]. If *end* is omitted, *begin* and all following frames are rendered. If *inc* is given, only every *inc*-th frame is rendered. Frame 1 is considered the first render statement in the scene file; camera frame specifiers are not considered. For example, 4 8 2 will skip the first three frames, then render frame 4, 6, and 8, and omit the rest. It is not an error if the scene file has fewer frames than requested.

-resolution *x*$_{int}$ *y*$_{int}$ p. 39

Specifies the width and height of the output image in pixels. The default is 768 576.

---

[2]The -render option was introduced in mental ray 2.1.36.

-samplelock on|off   p. 396
>	This option selects whether sampling of area light sources, motion blur, and depth-of-field is static or dependent on the frame number. The default is on (static).

-samples min_{int} max_{int} p. 420
>	This option determines the minimum and maximum sample rate. Each pixel is sampled at least ($2^{2 \cdot min}$) and at most ($2^{2 \cdot max}$) times in each direction. If min is 0, each pixel is sampled at least once. Positive values increase the minimum sample rate; negative numbers reduce the sample rate. The default is -2 0.

-samples min_{int} max_{int} $defmin_{int}$ $defmax_{int}$[3.1]
>	mental ray 3.1.2 accepts two optional extra parameters that set the default object sample limits. In mental ray 3.1.2, objects may constrain sampling of the pixels they cover. The $defmin_{int}$ and $defmax_{int}$ parameters apply to pixels where no objects are seen, or all the objects that are seen have no samples limit. mental ray will never take fewer than 2^{min} and more than 2^{max} samples, and in areas with no object sample settings it will further reduce that range to 2^{defmin} through 2^{defmax}. The defaults are –2 0 -128 127; the latter two are markers for "no further restrictions" because they are outside the –2 0 range.

-shading_samples num[3.2]
>	Rasterizer (formerly called Rapid Motion) sampling is controlled by the -shading_samples option. The units are shading samples per pixel, and the default is 1.0.

-samples_collect num[3.2]
>	The rasterizer adds a separate collection phase after tile rendering that combines subpixel samples to pixels. The num argument controls how many shading points should be used for compositing one pixel. Unlike the -samples arguments, the num argument is a linear count per pixel dimension, x and y. The default is 4, which gives 16 samples per pixel. The rasterizer (formerly known as Rapid Motion) no longer uses the -samples option. Rasterizer sampling is not adaptive.

-samples_motion num_{int}[3.3]
>	Determines at how many points in time a moving object is shaded in rasterizer (Rapid Motion) mode. The default is 1, which means that a moving object is sampled once at shutter open time, and this result is blurred across the motion path. Higher values than 1 sample at more points during the shutter interval. This option does not apply to regular scanline rendering because it does not cache shading results.

-scanline on|off|opengl|rasterizer|rapid   p. 417
>	Mode off allows turning off the scanline rendering algorithm to force mental ray to rely exclusively on ray tracing. This will slow down rendering in most cases. The rasterizer mode[3.4] enables a different algorithm that greatly improves motion blurring speed. It is synonymous with rapid[3.2]; the term "Rapid Motion" is deprecated in favor of "rasterizer" because the rasterizer is a full rendering algorithm, not only a motion blurring accelerator. The opengl mode uses local

OpenGL hardware to accelerate rendering, which sacrifice some accuracy for a large speed gain. If shadow mapping is also used, -shadowmap opengl should also be chosen. See page 446 for more information. The default scanline mode is on.

-scanline_collect *num*[3.2]

Rasterizer (formerly known as Rapid Motion) shading is controlled by the second argument of the -samples option, which is also used by all other rendering algorithms. The rasterizer has a separate collection phase that composites samples to pixels. The *num* argument controls how many shading points should be used for compositing one pixel. Unlike the -samples arguments, the *num* argument is a linear count. The default is $2^{max\_samples}$.

-shadow off|on|sort|segments   p. 147

Choose the shadow mode, or disable shadows. The default is on.

off disables all shadows, including shadow maps.

on enables standard shadows.

sort enables shadows and sorts shadow intersections before calling shadow shaders. Some shadow shaders require this.

segments enables shadows and traces shadow rays like visible rays. Some shadow shaders require this.

-shadowmap [on|off|opengl] [only] [rebuild] [reuse] [motion] [nomotion] --

This option can be used to control shadow maps. The option list is a sequence of one or more keywords.

on activates use of shadow maps.

off disables use of shadow maps. This is the default.

opengl enables use of shadow maps, and uses local OpenGL hardware to accelerate shadow map rendering, at a small accuracy loss. See also page 446 and -scanline opengl above; it often makes sense to enable OpenGL in both options.

only causes only shadow maps to be rendered, without rendering a color image. By default the color image is rendered also. This is useful to precompute shadow maps before the actual color rendering passes begin. This does not work with detail shadowmaps[3.3] because detail shadowmap files only store shadowmap tiles that were needed during rendering.

rebuild causes all shadow maps to be recomputed, even if they exist in memory from a previous frame or are found on disk. By default shadow maps are computed only if they are found neither in memory nor on disk.

reuse allow the reuse of shadowmaps. This is the default. If a shadowmap is found in memory or on disk it is used instead of recomputing it. This only works if object space mode is selected in the options block of the scene.

motion activates motion blurred shadow maps. This is enabled by default if shadow maps are turned on.

nomotion disables motion blurred shadow maps. This improves rendering speed.

merge[3.2] specifies that if the shadowmap was saved to disk (using a shadowmap file statement in the light description), this file should be read. Whenever a regular shadowmap computation shows that a shadow-casting object is closer to the light than the shadowmap on disk specifies, the closer value is used; otherwise the shadowmap remains unchanged at that point. This can be used to build up shadowmaps for multipass rendering.

-shutter [*delay*] *shutter*

This option controls motion blurring. The camera shutter opens at time *delay*[3.1] and closes at time *shutter*. The defaults are both 0.0. If *shutter* is equal to *delay*, motion blurring is disabled; if *shutter* is greater than *delay*, motion blurring is enabled. The normal range is (0, 1), which uses the full length of the motion vectors or motion vector paths[3.1]. It can be useful to set *delay*[3.1] and *shutter* both to 0.5, which disables motion blurring but renders with an offset of one half frame, which allows bidirectional post-blurring in an output shader.

-swap_dir "*directory*"[3.2]

Specifies a directory for disk swapping. When mental ray runs out of memory, it can push memory objects to disk, and load them back when they are needed again. mental ray does this much more efficiently than the operating system, which has no semantic knowledge of the data. For example, source geometry is not likely to be needed anytime soon, or at all, after it has been tessellated. The directory should be on a local disk, not a file server. This option should be used together with -swap_limit, and given before -swap_limit on the command line.

-swap_limit *size*[3.2]

Specifies the number of megabytes to write to the swap directory specified with -swap_dir. This space effectively becomes an extension of system memory. The default is 0, which turns off swapping. Good numbers are in the low thousands.

-T "*path1:path2:...*"[3.x]

Specifies a list of directories where texture files will be searched. The default is the current directory. The list is colon-separated (Unix only) or semicolon-separated (Unix and Windows NT). As with the -I option, paths introduced with an exclamation point are special: they substitute the entire directory path of the texture name and keep only the last component (the file name) when searching.

-shutter *shutter*   p. 237

This option specifies the shutter open time. A *shutter* value of 0.0 turns motion blurring off, values greater than 0.0 turn motion blurring on. The standard value for enabling motion blurring is 1.0; larger values increase the blur length. The default is 0.0.

-task_size *task_size$_{int}$*

This option specifies the size of the image rectangles during rendering. Smaller task sizes are convenient for previewing, but also increase the overall rendering time and reduce the effectiveness of edge following. This option can also be used to optimize load balancing for parallel rendering. If the task_size is not specified, an appropriate default value such as 32 is used.

-texture_continue[3.2]

Normally, standalone versions of mental ray abort as early as possible when a texture file cannot be read, to avoid spending a lot of time on unusable images and letting the farm controller know as soon as possible. If this option is specified, mental ray will continue and use transparent black or red-and-black checkerboard defaults (depending on the shader) for missing texture files.

-threads *nthreads$_{int}$*   p. 405

Normally, mental ray starts one thread for each processor in the system. The number of threads can be changed with this option. mental ray will create more threads than specified, but only *nthreads$_{int}$* will perform compute-intensive tasks simultaneously. In mental ray 3.3 and later, this includes threads on hyperthreaded Intel CPUs, which do not consume licenses. For example, a two-processor hyperthreaded Xeon system would run four threads and pull two licenses.

-time_contrast *r g b [a]*   p. 237

The time contrast controls the amount of temporal oversampling for motion blurred scenes. The number of temporal samples is approximately proportional to the inverse of the time contrast value. The default is 0.2 0.2 0.2 0.2. For fast motion blur, an alternative non-adaptive sampling technique can be used by setting the time contrast to 0 0 0 and minimum and maximum sampling to the equal relatively high value, such as 2 2.

-trace on|off

Normally, mental ray will use a combination of a scanline rendering algorithm and ray tracing to calculate samples of the scene. If -trace off is specified, ray tracing is disabled, and mental ray will rely exclusively on the scanline algorithm.

-trace_depth *reflect$_{int}$ [refract$_{int}$ [sum$_{int}$]]*   p. 420

reflect limits the number of recursive reflection rays. If it is set to 0, no reflection rays will be cast; if it is set to 1, one level is allowed but a reflection ray can not be reflected again, and so on. Similarly, *refract* controls the maximum depth of refraction and transparency rays. Additionally, it is possible to limit the sum of reflection and refraction rays with *sum*. The defaults are 2 2 4.

-v on|off|*level$_{int}$*   p. 437

An abbreviation for -verbose.

`-verbose on|off|`*level*$_{int}$ p. 437

> This command controls verbose messages. There are seven levels: fatal errors (1), errors (2), warnings (3), progress reports (4), informational messages (5), debugging messages (6), and verbose debugging messages (7). All message categories numerically equal to or less than *level* are printed. Verbose `off` is equivalent to level 2 (fatal errors and errors); verbose on is equivalent to level 5 (everything except debugging messages).

`-volume on|off`   p. 165

> Ignore all volume shaders if set to `off`. The default is on.

`-window` *x_low*$_{int}$ *y_low*$_{int}$ *x_high*$_{int}$ *y_high*$_{int}$ p. 42

> Only the sub-rectangle of the image specified by the four bounds will be rendered. All pixels that fall outside the rectangle will be left black. This option does not have an affect on the size of the frame buffer or saved image files; it merely suppresses rendering pixels outside the window.

`-xcolor [`"*control*"`]`   p. 437

> Print colored messages. Error messages, for example, are printed in red, which makes them stand out much better in verbose reports. The control string allows customization.

A.2   Inventor mental ray

Inventor is a real-time 3D scene viewing technology introduced by Silicon Graphics. There is a version of mental ray called ivray that has Inventor support built in. It can be used to read scene files and display and manipulate them in realtime on the screen, and rendering and writing them back to disk. Since OpenGL and Inventor do not support custom shaders, very simple shaders are used for the realtime display. Although ivray can be used like a regular mental ray executable, this is not recommended because it is larger and takes slightly longer to start up. ivray up to 3.2 is supported for Silicon Graphics systems only. ivray 3.3 and higher is available for Silicon Graphics and Linux. The following additional command line options are supported:

`-inventor`

> Enables the realtime Inventor viewing window. ivray will read the scene file up to the first `render` command and then create the Inventor window instead of rendering.

`-ivdrawstyle` S_1 S_2

> Static and moving objects will be drawn using styles S_1 and S_2, respectively. Available styles are `shade` (shaded), `wire` (wireframe), and `box` (bounding box). The default is `shade wire`.

`-ivleaf on|off`

> If on, use the leaf instance list to collect objects instead of replicating the mental ray scene graph as an Inventor scene graph. This is useful for scenes with multiple

instancing. The default is off.

-ivout "*filename*"
> Write the scene as an Inventor scene file named *filename*.

-ivrendercache on|off
> Enable or disable Inventor object caching. This is on by default.

-ivstrips on|off
> Enable or disable triangle strips. Strips slightly increase tessellation time but can significantly improve display performance. Strips are enabled by default.

A.3   Environment Variables *

Environment variables can be set from a shell prompt with shell commands such as setenv (see the documentation of your shell) before mental ray, ivray, or the application that mental ray is built into, is started from the same shell. Environment variables set after mental ray is started, or set from a different shell, have no effect. mental ray will work without any environment variables, except that the .rayrc startup script may not be found if MI_ROOT is undefined.

DISPLAY   p. 446
> The Unix X11 display to be used for OpenGL acceleration.

HOME   p. 412
> Unix home directory, for finding the user's local .rayrc file.

HOMEDRIVE   p. 412
> Windows NT home drive, such as C:.

HOMEPATH   p. 412
> Windows NT home directory. mental ray will try to load %HOMEDRIVE%/%HOMEPATH%/rayrc.

MI_CG_FRAGMENT_PROFILE[3.4]
> Pass this profile name to the Cg compiler when compiling hardware shaders, instead of the profile matching the graphics hardware rendered on. This is useful in conjunction with the -hardware_echo command-line option to "cross-compile" shaders.

MI_HWDISPLAY[3.4]
> Overrides DISPLAY. This is useful if mental ray is run on one machine, where all graphical user interfaces are shown (so DISPLAY must point to the local host), but the local host does not have sufficient hardware rendering capacity so mental ray offloads it to another host, pointed to by MI_HWDISPLAY. This kind of remote hardware rendering incurs extra networking overhead but allows multiple desktop clients to share

a fast hardware rendering server. It is not necessary for mental ray to be installed on the server, and no extra license is used. However, both the client and server hosts must have compatible OpenGL and OpenGL extension versions.

MI_IVRAY_OPTIONS   p. 506

Extra options inserted by the Inventor version of mental ray.

MI_LIBRARY_PATH   p. 401

Another search path, used for `link` commands.

SI_LOCATION

The directory of the `linktab.ini` file, which is used by the Softimage|3D application for path mapping.

MI_RAY_SUBSTITUTE   p. 411

An optional list of blank-separated substitution instructions, each in the form `/search/replace/`. Any other character besides / will also work.

MI_RAY_INCPATH   p. 401

A colon-separated or semicolon-separated list of paths to search for files included with the `$include` command.

MI_RAY_OPTIONS   p. 487

Extra options that are inserted by mental ray before the options on the command line. This is commonly used for options such as `-xcolor`.

MI_RAY2_SERVICE   p. 405

The IP service that mental ray uses to contact slaves on other machines. The default is `mi-ray2` for mental ray 2.x and `mi-ray3` for mental ray 3.x. On Unix, service names are defined in `/etc/services` or in the `services` NIS map.

MI_RAY_SERVICE   p. 405

If the previous variable is not defined, this one is used instead. This makes mental ray 2.x compatible with mental ray 1.9 while allowing both to coexist on the same machine. The default is `mi-ray`.

MI_ROOT

The directory that mental ray searches for configuration files such as `rayrc`.

MI_STACKSIZE

New thread stacks will be created with this size in kilobytes if defined. The default is 16384 (16 MB) on Unix and 4096 on Windows NT. 4096 is nearly always sufficient except when very complex recursive shaders are used.

miSWAP_DIR_ENV   [3.2]A swap directory where mental ray can put scene elements when it runs out of memory. This can be useful for large static scenes, where the scene file itself is large. mental ray generally swaps more efficiently than the operating system.

miSWAP_LIM_ENV   [3.2]The maximum number of bytes to write into the swap directory. A value of 0 turns off swapping.

TMPDIR

A directory for temporary code or object files to be compiled or linked. The default is /usr/tmp on Unix and the current directory on Windows NT.

USER

The current user name. It is stored in RLA image file headers, and is optional.

Registry lookups of the form {$*var*} return the value of the environment variable *var*. mental ray 3.4 allows {$?*var*}, which returns 1 if the environment variable *var* exists and 0 otherwise.

A.4   Image Display: imf_disp

The image display and flipbook utility imf_disp is started as

> imf_disp [*options*] [*directory*] [*file ...*]

If the *directory* is present, imf_disp will enter flipbook mode and display a sequence of files as a movie. If no directory is specified, a static image file is displayed. If a single minus sign is given as file name, the image will be read from standard input. This is useful for connecting mental ray and imf_disp:

> ray -imgpipe 1 scene.mi | imf_disp -

If the file to display is still being rendered, imf_disp will open a connection to the mental ray program rendering it, and display rectangles as they are finished. This also works if mental ray and imf_disp run on different machines. Files that are still being rendered can be recognized by their size, which is always 128 bytes. Only one imf_disp can be connected to a running mental ray at any time.

The following options are supported on Unix systems. Many can also be set from pulldown menus. The standard X11 options such as -display or -geometry are also supported. The Windows NT version can only display static images and supports only the -g (gamma) option.

-delaymultiplier *factor*
>   Set timescale multiplier for flipbook playback speed. The default is 1.0.

`-depth` *min max*

> When displaying depth (Z) images such as shadow maps, assign white to the minimum depth *min* and black to the maximum depth *max*, instead of determining the range from the depth map[3]. Infinite depths are always displayed light blue.

`-G` *gamma*

> Set a gamma value. The default is 1.0, or whatever mental ray is using if `imf_disp` is connected to one.

`-help`

> Print a brief option summary.

`-imgtitle` *title*

> Set the window title. Normally the window title displays information about the image file, the operation mode, and the pixel under the mouse.

`-m on|off`

> Display the matte (alpha) channel instead of the color image.

`-mask` *exp*

> Set the file search mask in the file selector dialog to the expression *exp*. The default is *. This dialog is used to select files to cycle through in flipbook mode. The mask is useful to restrict the file listing to similar-named files that are part of a sequence, such as `image*.rgb`. Note that *exp* should be quoted to prevent the shell from evaluating wildcards.

`-pseudocolor on|off`

> If on, `imf_disp` uses a pseudocolor visual that relies on color mapping and dithering. If off, true colors are used. The default is off.

`-reconnect on|off`

> If enabled, `imf_disp` will watch the displayed file. If it is re-rendered, `imf_disp` will connect to the mental ray executable and show the changes as they are finished. If disabled, the displayed image will stay on the display even if rerendered. The default is on.

`-reload on|off`

> This option is similar to the preceding, but checks whether the image was rewritten by means other than rerendering, and reloads it if so.

`-shm on|off`

> Set X11 shared-memory mode. This allows the X11 display server to directly use the process memory of `imf_disp`. This reduces memory usage, but since shared memory is an optional X11 extension, some systems may not support it. Shared memory also cannot be used if the display (as defined by the `DISPLAY` environment variable or the X11 `-display` option) is not on the machine that `imf_disp` is running on. The default is on.

---

[3]This option was introduced with mental ray 2.1.36.

```
-verbose on|off
```
>   Enable or disable verbose messages. The default is off.

```
-vis visual
```

>   Set the visual ID for the display. X11 visuals determine display information such as the color mode, the number of bits per pixel, and so on. Use the X11 xdpyinfo command to determine the visuals supported by the X11 server. Note that *visual* must be a decimal number. The default is the best truecolor visual available.

A.5   Image Copy: imf_copy

The image copying and conversion utility imf_copy is started as

>   imf_copy [*options*] *infile outfile* [*outtype*]

The file *infile* will be copied to *outfile*. The *outtype* specifies the format of *outfile*. If no type is specified, the file name extension of *outfile* is used. See section 12.3 for a list of valid formats. The map format is especially valuable for creating memory-mappable texture images (see page 70 for details). These options are supported:

-h
>   Print a brief option summary.

-p
>   Create a pyramid texture, consisting of a sequence of progressively smaller versions of the same image in one file. This allows better texture anti-aliasing. See page 77.

-v
>   Verbose output prints messages showing what *imf_copy* is doing, and a version banner.

-g *gamma*
>   Perform gamma correction with the gamma factor *gamma*. The default is 1.0.

-q *quality*
>   [3.1]When writing to a JPEG file, set the quality factor to *quality*, in the range 1..100. The default is 75.

-f *filter*
>   [3.2]Useful only if the target format is .map. The filter value is stored in the texture. Memory-mapped texture files always override the filter value specified in the color texture statement or with *mi_api_texture_set_filter*.

-e
>   [3.1]When resampling a format to another with fewer bits per component, perform error diffusion instead of truncation.

-L
>   [3.1]When writing to a memory-mapped .map file, use little-endian byte order. Map files must have the byte order of the rendering host to be effective. Alpha and x86-class processors including Intel Pentium are little-endian; most others are big-endian.

-B
>   [3.1]When writing to a memory-mapped .map file, use big-endian byte order.

-r   [3.2]When writing to a memory-mapped .map file, arrange pixels in rectangles instead of the normal scanline order. This increases cache efficiency and reduces memory usage when rendering. Files created in this way can only be rendered with mental ray 3.2 or higher, which is why it is not enabled by default.

-c   [3.2]When writing to a memory-mapped .map file, collate up to 20 input files to form an image pyramid. This option gives control over the image pyramid, unlike the -p option which automatically creates each successive pyramid level at one-half the resolution of the preceding one, using a box filter. The first input image should have full resolution, the next one approximately one-half width and height, the next one approximately one quarter, and so on. Files created with this option can be read by any mental ray 3.x version.

-x N [3.3]Extract level N from a pyramid .map file. The first (and largest) level is 0; the highest is 19. This can be seen as the reverse operation to -c, but it also works with pyramids created with -p.

-k K [3.4]When writing to an OpenEXR file, set the compression method to K, where K is one of the following: none, piz, zip, rle, pxr24. Default is rle.

A.6   Image Information: imf_info

The image information utility `imf_info` is started as

     `imf_info` [*options*] *file...*

It will display information about all named image files, including resolution, number of color components, number of bits per component, gamma factor if available, top-down or bottom-up line ordering, data type, and the image format. There is only one option:

-v   Verbose output prints messages showing what `imf_info` is doing, and a version banner.

-p   [3.1]Plot a simple pixel intensity histogram.

-m   [3.2]Prints information about multipass sample files.

-l   [3.2]Prints pyramid layer resolutions for memory-mapped texture files.

-L   [3.2]Prints more detailed pyramid layer information, including deviations from the expected resolutions. This is useful for map files created with `imf_copy` -c.

A.7   Image Comparison: imf_diff

The image comparison utility imf_diff is started as

   imf_diff [*options*] *image1* *image2* [*outimage* [*outtype*]]

The files *image1* and *image2* will be compared, and a comparison summary is printed. If *outimage* is specified, a difference image with a histogram is written to *outimage*. The file format of this file is specified with *outtype* if present, or taken from the file name extension if not. The following options are supported:

-a   Ignore alpha channel differences.

-d   Display the difference image and the histogram in a window, by starting the imf_disp program. This works with and without an *outimage* on the command line.

-e   Write an output image even if the compared input images match. Normally the output image is written only if there are differences.

-f   Show differences in false colors, ranging from irrelevant differences in blue, through significant differences in green, red, and white.

-g *gamma*   Perform gamma correction with the given gamma factor.

-h   Print a brief option summary.

-m *thresh*   Set the threshold in the range 0..255. Component differences less than this threshold are ignored. The default is 3. The main purpose is to discard differences introduced by dithering (mental ray's dither option).

-n   Do not add a histogram to the displayed or saved output image.

-s   Magnify the differences such that the largest difference is white and appears at the right edge of the histogram.

-t *thresh*   The difference in percent that causes imf_diff to return the return code 1 instead of 0. The default is 1. This is useful for automated test suites.

-u   Underlay *image1* under the displayed or saved difference image, at 1/10th brightness. This helps locating differences.

-v   Verbose output prints messages showing what imf_copy is doing, and a version banner.

The most common options are -f -u -d (also known as fear, uncertainty, and doubt). Note that the sampling nature of mental ray means that the true image is approximated with appropriately selected samples until the desired image quality criteria are satisfied. This approach ensures consistent quality but it does not necessarily create images that are bit-for-bit identical if rendered under different circumstances, such as different image task sizes, image task assignments to threads or machines, different machines or different networks, or different sampling options. Typically, differences shown in blue in the color histogram are irrelevant.

A.8   Create Shader Skeletons: mkmishader **

The shader skeleton utility mkmishader is started as

> mkmishader [*options*] [*scenefile...*]

This utility is intended for shader writers only. It takes shader declaration files and generates C source code files that implement the shader. The *scenefile*s should only contain shader declarations. One source file per shader is created. If it already exists, it is overwritten. The sources include all necessary includes, declarations, local variables, parameter evaluation statements, and array loops, but the implementation of the actual algorithm is, of course, missing. The body of the shader function usually needs to be rearranged, the local variables, evaluations, and loops are created in no particular order. The following options are supported:

-h   Print a brief option summary.

-i   Also create init and exit shaders.

-r   Read the startup .rayrc file first. This is not done by default because startup files sometimes contain shader declarations, which would cause mkmishader to generate source code.

-v   Verbose output prints messages showing what mkmishader is doing, and a version banner.

A.9   Convert Scenes to C: mitoapi **

The API call generator utility mitoapi is started as

> mitoapi *scenefile*

This utility is intended for writers of geometry shaders, and for integrators of the mental ray library into client applications. It reads a scene file and generates the corresponding C API calls that do the same thing. The resulting source code is an approximation that can not be compiled directly and needs manual rearrangement. In particular, local variables are not distinguished and are listed in the order of recursive descent during scene parsing. However, the resulting source code is a good starting point for implementation. There are no options.

A.10   Finalgather Map Copy: fg_copy **

The finalgather map copying and merging utility fg_copy is started as

   fg_copy [*options*] *infile1 ... infileN outfile*

It reads finalgather map files *infile** created with finalgather file statements in the options block in the .mi scene file, and merges them into a single finalgather file *outfile*. Each file is a collection of finalgather points that represent the irradiance at a specific 3D coordinate.

Optionally, only points in a given region are considered and written. Points that are very close and have similar orientation can optionally be merged to eliminate redundancy and reduce the size of the generated map.

This tool is helpful when rendering animations. Flickering is reduced with moderate computational effort if several key frames are rendered with final gathering saved to files. The -finalgather only command-line of mental ray option allows rendering these files quickly without rendering color images. When all the finalgather map files for the key frames are finished, the *fg_copy* tool can combine them into a single finalgather map file that can be used for beauty-rendering the entire animation. (This does not work for detail shadowmaps[3.3] files.)

This method works well with render farms, where different hosts create finalgather maps for different frames simultaneously.

If the same file is specified several times as an input file, its points appear multiple times in the output map. If point merging is enabled, the points are not duplicated but their importance weights are adjusted.

The following options are supported:

-h   Print a brief option summary.

-f *F*   Merge finalgather points with similar normals within distance *F* into a single one. The value of *F* is related to the minimum radius of the finalgather accuracy statement in the .mi scene file. All finalgather points are tested against all other finalgather points regardless of which file they came from. In particular, *fg_copy* can be used to reduce the redundancy and size of a single input file.

-b *xmin ymin zmin xmax ymax zmax*
            Select and copy finalgather points within the specified voxel only. This may be used for reducing the finalgather map size if only a part of the scene is required.

-v   Verbose output prints messages showing what fg_copy is doing, and a version banner.

Note that the finalgather file statement in the options block of the .mi scene file also allows specifying multiple finalgather map files, enclosed in angle brackets, which will be merged at render time. Using *fg_copy* to precompute a merged map for a list of keyframes for the entire animation is more efficient.

The Sphere and Utah Teapot Models

Many examples in this book use the sphere and teapot models, but omit their definition because of their size. This appendix lists the complete definitions in .mi syntax.

B.1   NURBS Sphere

Here is the NURBS sphere scene file fragment.   It is included in examples with the `$include "sphere.mi"` command, and results in a model `"sphere"` that can be instanced in the scene. The object does not contain a material reference; the instance in which it is used must provide one.

B.2   Utah Teapot

The following scene file fragment defines an instance group called `"teapot"` that can be instanced anywhere in the scene. The Utah teapot was originally created by Martin Newell at the University of Utah. It has become a classic in computer graphics. This version was derived from [Blinn 96], chapter 2. It consists of 32 Bézier patches, each defined by 4×4 control points. The object space size is about ± 3 units. No materials are defined; they must be inherited from external instances.

```
# ----- Teapot body -----

object "bodypart" visible shadow trace tag 100
        basis "bez1" bezier 1
        basis "bez3" bezier 3
        group
            1.4      2.25      0              # row 1 of control points
```

```
1.4       2.25      0.784
0.784     2.25      1.4
0         2.25      1.4
1.3375    2.38125   0           # row 2 of control points
1.3375    2.38125   0.749
0.749     2.38125   1.3375
0         2.38125   1.3375
1.4375    2.38125   0           # row 3 of control points
1.4375    2.38125   0.805
0.805     2.38125   1.4375
0         2.38125   1.4375
1.5       2.25      0           # row 4 of control points
1.5       2.25      0.84
0.84      2.25      1.5
0         2.25      1.5
1.75      1.725     0           # row 5 of control points
1.75      1.725     0.98
0.98      1.725     1.75
0         1.725     1.75
2.0       1.2       0           # row 6 of control points
2.0       1.2       1.12
1.12      1.2       2.0
0         1.2       2.0
2.0       0.75      0           # row 7 of control points
2.0       0.75      1.12
1.12      0.75      2.0
0         0.75      2.0
2.0       0.3       0           # row 8 of control points
2.0       0.3       1.12
1.12      0.3       2.0
0         0.3       2.0
1.5       0.075     0           # row 9 of control points
1.5       0.075     0.84
0.84      0.075     1.5
0         0.075     1.5
1.5       0         0           # row 10 of control points
1.5       0         0.84
0.84      0         1.5
0         0         1.5
0         0         0           # one control point in row 11

v 0       v 1       v 2       v 3
v 4       v 5       v 6       v 7
v 8       v 9       v 10      v 11
v 12      v 13      v 14      v 15
v 16                v 17      v 18      v 19
v 20      v 21                v 22      v 23
v 24                v 25      v 26      v 27
v 28      v 29      v 30      v 31
v 32      v 33      v 34      v 35
v 36      v 37      v 38      v 39
v 40
```

```
                        surface "rim" ""
                                "bez3" 0.0 1.0   0.0 1.0
                                "bez3" 0.0 1.0   0.0 1.0
                                0 1 2 3 4 5 6 7 8 9 10 11 12 13 14 15

                        surface "side1" ""
                                "bez3" 0.0 1.0   0.0 1.0
                                "bez3" 0.0 1.0   0.0 1.0
                                12 13 14 15 16 17 18 19 20 21 22 23 24 25 26 27

                        surface "side2" ""
                                "bez3" 0.0 1.0   0.0 1.0
                                "bez3" 0.0 1.0   0.0 1.0
                                24 25 26 27 28 29 30 31 32 33 34 35 36 37 38 39

                        surface "bottom" ""
                                "bez3" 0.0 1.0   0.0 1.0
                                "bez1" 0.0 1.0   0.0 1.0
                                36 37 38 39 40 40 40 40

                        derivative
                        approximate surface parametric 4.0 4.0 "rim" "side1" "side2"
                                                                    "bottom"
                end group
        end object

        instance "bodypart-1" "bodypart" end instance
        instance "bodypart-2" "bodypart"
                transform -1 0 0 0  0 1 0 0  0 0 1 0  0 0 0 1
        end instance
        instance "bodypart-3" "bodypart"
                transform 1 0 0 0  0 1 0 0  0 0 -1 0  0 0 0 1
        end instance
        instance "bodypart-4" "bodypart"
                transform -1 0 0 0  0 1 0 0  0 0 -1 0  0 0 0 1
        end instance


        # ----- Teapot lid -----

        object "lidpart" visible shadow trace tag 101
                basis "bez3" bezier 3
                group
                        0        3        0              # one control point in row 1
                        0.8      3        0              # row 2 of control points
                        0.8      3        0.448
                        0.448    3        0.8
                        0        3        0.8
                        0        2.7      0              # one control point in row 3
                        0.2      2.55     0              # row 4 of control points
                        0.2      2.55     0.112
                        0.112    2.55     0.2
                        0        2.55     0.2
```

```
            0.4       2.4      0                # row 5 of control points
            0.4       2.4      0.224
            0.224     2.4      0.4
            0         2.4      0.4
            1.3       2.4      0                # row 6 of control points
            1.3       2.4      0.728
            0.728     2.4      1.3
            0         2.4      1.3
            1.4       2.25     0                # row 7 of control points
            1.4       2.25     0.784
            0.784     2.25     1.4
            0         2.25     1.4

            v 0
            v 1      v 2      v 3      v 4
            v 5
            v 6      v 7      v 8      v 9
            v 10     v 11     v 12     v 13
            v 14     v 15     v 16     v 17
            v 18     v 19     v 20     v 21

            surface "upper" ""
                    "bez3" 0.0 1.0   0.0 1.0
                    "bez3" 0.0 1.0   0.0 1.0
                    0 0 0 0 1 2 3 4 5 5 5 5 6 7 8 9

            surface "lower" ""
                    "bez3" 0.0 1.0   0.0 1.0
                    "bez3" 0.0 1.0   0.0 1.0
                    6 7 8 9 10 11 12 13 14 15 16 17 18 19 20 21

            approximate surface parametric 4.0 4.0 "upper" "lower"
        end group
end object

instance "lidpart-1" "lidpart" end instance
instance "lidpart-2" "lidpart"
        transform -1 0 0 0  0 1 0 0  0 0 1 0  0 0 0 1
end instance
instance "lidpart-3" "lidpart"
        transform 1 0 0 0  0 1 0 0  0 0 -1 0  0 0 0 1
end instance
instance "lidpart-4" "lidpart"
        transform -1 0 0 0  0 1 0 0  0 0 -1 0  0 0 0 1
end instance


# ----- Teapot handle -----

object "handlepart" visible shadow trace tag 102
        basis "bez3" bezier 3
        group
                -1.5      2.1      0                # row 1 of control points
```

```
        -1.5      2.1      0.3
        -1.6      1.875    0.3
        -1.6      1.875    0
        -2.5      2.1      0            # row 2 of control points
        -2.5      2.1      0.3
        -2.3      1.875    0.3
        -2.3      1.875    0
        -3.0      2.1      0            # row 3 of control points
        -3.0      2.1      0.3
        -2.7      1.875    0.3
        -2.7      1.875    0
        -3.0      1.65     0            # row 4 of control points
        -3.0      1.65     0.3
        -2.7      1.65     0.3
        -2.7      1.65     0
        -3.0      1.2      0            # row 5 of control points
        -3.0      1.2      0.3
        -2.7      1.425    0.3
        -2.7      1.425    0
        -2.65     0.7875   0            # row 6 of control points
        -2.65     0.7875   0.3
        -2.5      0.975    0.3
        -2.5      0.975    0
        -1.9      0.45     0            # row 7 of control points
        -1.9      0.45     0.3
        -2.0      0.75     0.3
        -2.0      0.75     0

        v 0     v 1     v 2     v 3
        v 4     v 5     v 6     v 7
        v 8     v 9     v 10    v 11
        v 12    v 13    v 14    v 15
        v 16    v 17    v 18    v 19
        v 20    v 21    v 22    v 23
        v 24    v 25    v 26    v 27

        surface "upper" ""
                "bez3" 0.0 1.0  0.0 1.0
                "bez3" 0.0 1.0  0.0 1.0
                0 1 2 3 4 5 6 7 8 9 10 11 12 13 14 15

        surface "lower" ""
                "bez3" 0.0 1.0  0.0 1.0
                "bez3" 0.0 1.0  0.0 1.0
                12 13 14 15 16 17 18 19 20 21 22 23 24 25 26 27

        derivative
        approximate surface parametric 4.0 4.0 "upper" "lower"
    end group
end object

instance "handlepart-1" "handlepart" end instance
instance "handlepart-2" "handlepart"
```

```
        transform 1 0 0 0  0 1 0 0  0 0 -1 0  0 0 0 1
end instance


# ----- Teapot spout -----

object "spoutpart" visible shadow trace tag 103
        basis "bez3" bezier 3
        group
                1.7      1.275    0                # row 1 of control points
                1.7      1.275    0.66
                1.7      0.45     0.66
                1.7      0.45     0
                2.6      1.275    0                # row 2 of control points
                2.6      1.275    0.66
                3.1      0.675    0.66
                3.1      0.675    0
                2.3      1.95     0                # row 3 of control points
                2.3      1.95     0.25
                2.4      1.875    0.25
                2.4      1.875    0
                2.7      2.25     0                # row 4 of control points
                2.7      2.25     0.25
                3.3      2.25     0.25
                3.3      2.25     0
                2.8      2.325    0                # row 5 of control points
                2.8      2.325    0.25
                3.525    2.34375  0.25
                3.525    2.34375  0
                2.9      2.325    0                # row 6 of control points
                2.9      2.325    0.15
                3.45     2.34375  0.15
                3.45     2.34375  0
                2.8      2.25     0                # row 7 of control points
                2.8      2.25     0.15
                3.2      2.25     0.15
                3.2      2.25     0

                v 0      v 1      v 2      v 3
                v 4      v 5      v 6      v 7
                v 8      v 9      v 10     v 11
                v 12     v 13     v 14     v 15
                v 16     v 17     v 18     v 19
                v 20     v 21     v 22     v 23
                v 24     v 25     v 26     v 27

                surface "main" ""
                        "bez3" 0.0 1.0  0.0 1.0
                        "bez3" 0.0 1.0  0.0 1.0
                        0 1 2 3 4 5 6 7 8 9 10 11 12 13 14 15

                surface "rim" ""
                        "bez3" 0.0 1.0  0.0 1.0
```

```
                              "bez3" 0.0 1.0  0.0 1.0
                              12 13 14 15 16 17 18 19 20 21 22 23 24 25 26 27

                    derivative
                    approximate surface parametric 4.0 4.0 "main" "rim"
            end group
end object

instance "spoutpart-1" "spoutpart" end instance
instance "spoutpart-2" "spoutpart"
        transform 1 0 0 0  0 1 0 0  0 0 -1 0  0 0 0 1
end instance

instgroup "teapot"
        "bodypart-1"    "bodypart-2"    "bodypart-3"    "bodypart-4"
        "lidpart-1"     "lidpart-2"     "lidpart-3"     "lidpart-4"
        "handlepart-1"  "handlepart-2"
        "spoutpart-1"   "spoutpart-2"
end instgroup
```

Appendix C

Base Shaders *

The mental ray Base Shader Library is a set of simple shaders designed to form the standard building blocks of Phenomenon™ scene elements. They perform functions useful in many different contexts, and are not tied to specific types of shaders. A base shader is not inherently a material or light shader but can be used to build a Phenomenon used in place of a material or light shader. This means that base shaders must be as generic as possible. They avoid interdependencies that would limit their applicability.

C.1   Overview

Base shaders are designed to form groups, such as the group of geometry base shaders or BRDF functions. Members of a group have similar parameters to make it easy to replace one base shader with another one of the same group. The replacement may have shader-specific extra parameters, but those it shares with other similar base shaders of the same group have the same names and types and the same layout. In general, common parameters come first.

Before any shader in the base shader library can be used, it must be attached to the mental ray rendering software using a statement link "base.so", and the shaders must be declared with the statement $include <base.mi>. See chapter 17 on page 399 for details. All shader names begin with "mib", for "mental images base". Their declarations are given in mi format, as described in chapter 11 on page 271. Here is a summary:

Group	shader	page
Texture Space Mapping	*mib_texture_vector*	529
	mib_texture_remap	529
	mib_texture_rotate	530
	mib_bump_basis	531
	mib_bump_map	531
	mib_passthrough_bump_map	532
(continued on next page)		

(continued from previous page)		
	mib_geo_sphere	555
	mib_geo_cone	555
	mib_geo_cylinder	556
	mib_geo_torus	556
	mib_geo_square	557
	mib_geo_instance	557
	mib_geo_instance_mlist	557
	mib_geo_add_uv_texture	558
Photon	*mib_photon_basic*	558
Light	*mib_light_point*	559
	mib_light_spot	559
	mib_light_infinite	560
	mib_light_photometric	560
	mib_cie_d	561
	mib_blackbody	562
Shadow	*mib_shadow_transparency*	563
Light Mapping	*mib_lightmap_sample*	563
	mib_lightmap_write	564
Lens	*mib_lens_stencil*	565
	mib_lens_clamp	565

C.2   Texture Space Mapping

These shaders take care of selecting, creating, and remapping texture spaces, computing basis vectors, and other tasks necessary before a color or displacement can be applied. Some of these functions have a **select** parameter that has one of the following values:

0..63	selects a texture vector. If this exceeds the number of defined texture spaces, default to -1 (the point in space).
-1	selects the 3D point in space directly, and may apply a space point transformation.
-2	selects the normal vector, and may apply a space vector transformation.
-3	selects the motion vector, and may apply a space vector transformation.
-4	selects the ray direction, and may apply a space vector transformation.
-5..-9	select a surface derivative vector, and may apply a space vector transformation. The values are $\partial\vec{P}/\partial\vec{U}$, $\partial\vec{P}/\partial\vec{V}$, $\partial^2\vec{P}/\partial\vec{U}^2$, $\partial^2\vec{P}/\partial\vec{V}$, and $\partial^2\vec{P}/(\partial\vec{U}\partial\vec{V})$. The object must be defined to contain derivatives.
-10	selects a 2D background plate coordinate with (0, 0, 0) in the lower left corner of the screen, and (1, 1, 0) just outside the upper right corner of the screen. **selspace** has no effect in this mode. The transformation is similar to the one in *mib_lookup_background*.
-11	selects the texture coordinate in the state, where it is typically put by a material shader when evaluating a parameter of type texture, for use by a texture shader.

Space transformations allow transforming the vector that the projection is based on into object, world, or camera coordinates. **selspace** may have the following values:

0	does not apply a transformation, using internal space.
1	converts the vector into object space.
2	converts the vector into world space.
3	converts the vector into camera space.
4	returns the current screen space coordinates in the interval $[0, 0...1, 1)$.

An additional projection[2.1] can be applied to the resulting vector by setting the **project** parameter:

0	disables projections.
1	selects an UV projection if available.
2	selects an orthographic XY projection.
3	selects an orthographic XZ projection.
4	selects an orthographic YZ projection.
5	selects a spherical projection.
6	selects a cylindrical projection. $U = 0$ is at +X, and $V = 0$ is at +Y. Y is also the cylinder axis.
7	selects the lollipop projection, which puts the center of the texture (after texture vector normalization) at X=0.5 Z=1, and the corners at the parameter corners. On a sphere, the texture center is at the north pole and the texture corners are at the south pole, like a lollipop wrapper.

Texture Vertex Generator

Return a texture vector derived from orthographic projections of the 3D point in space (XY, XZ, YZ), non-orthographic projections (spherical or cylindrical); or return a numbered texture vector from the texture vector list.   Optionally, this shader can base its calculations on object, camera, world, or screen space.

```
vector "mib_texture_vector" (
    integer         "select",
    integer         "selspace",
    integer         "vertex",
    integer         "project")
```

select specifies the value to look up, as described above.

selspace allows choosing the source space for projections, as described above. Space conversion is done before the projection specified by the select parameter. If selspace is 4 (screen space), select, vertex, and project are ignored.

vertex specifies the location of the vertex: 0 is the intersection point, and 1, 2, and 3 are the vertices of the intersected triangle. It has no effect if select is -10.

project specifies a projection that is performed after selection and space conversion. It has no effect if select is -10.

Texture Vertex Remapping

Accepts a texture vertex and scales, rotates, translates, crops, and joins textures. The order of operations is transform first, then repeat, alternate, torus, and finally min/max crop. The result is returned (and stored in *state* → *tex*, where it can be picked up by other shaders).

```
vector "mib_texture_remap" (
    vector          "input",
    transform       "transform",
    vector          "repeat",
    boolean         "alt_x",
    boolean         "alt_y",
    boolean         "alt_z",
    boolean         "torus_x",
    boolean         "torus_y",
    boolean         "torus_z",
    vector          "min",
    vector          "max")
```

input is a texture vector from a generator such as *mib_texture_vector* that returns texture vectors. *input* is overridden when this shader is called with a nonzero *arg* parameter in *mi_call_shader_x*. This is useful for remapping multiple texture coordinates when the remapping parameters are identical for all of them.

transform is a general transformation applied to the texture vector before the remaining parameters are applied. If transform[3][3] is 0.0, the matrix is ignored (normally transform[3][3] is 1.0).

repeat contains repetition factors in X, Y, and Z that the texture vector is multiplied with. A value of 2, for example, shrinks the texture such that it fits twice in the $[0, 1)$ interval. Repeating has no effect outside this interval. After the multiplication by the repetition factor, the integer part is removed. This algorithm allows finite repetition in an interval determined by the transform parameter. A repetition value of 0 turns off repetition in the corresponding component, as if the value were 1.

alt_* specifies whether every other copy of the repetition would be reversed such that successive copies of the texture are traversed in alternate, back-and-forth directions. Alternate flags have an effect only if the corresponding repetition component is greater than 1, and also work only in the $[0, 1)$ interval.

torus_* maps the texture space into the range $[0, 1)$ such that values less than 0 and equal to or greater than 1 are put into this range by cutting off the integer part.

min and **max** implement image or volume cropping by specifying the range of the texture to be considered. Portions of the texture outside this range are trimmed off. If repetition is used, the max point of one copy joins the min point of the next copy (unless alternation is turned on). min is inclusive, max is exclusive. If a min component is equal to the corresponding max component, both are ignored.

Rotation of Surface Orientation

An angle is used to rotate the surface orientation around the surface normal. An orthogonal vector pair is returned that, together with the normal which both are orthogonal to, define the rotated orientation. This is especially useful for anisotropic reflection (see below).

```
struct {
    vector          "u",
    vector          "v"
} "mib_texture_rotate" (
    vector          "input",
    scalar          "angle",
    scalar          "min",
    scalar          "max")
```

u and **v** are the returned orthogonal vectors.

input is the texture vector to be rotated. It is expected in internal space.

angle is a scalar that is interpreted as a rotation. A value equal to min specifies no rotation, and a value equal to max specifies a 360-degree rotation. The angle can for example be the intensity from a texture lookup.

min and **max** specify the value limits corresponding to no and full rotation. An angle value α is first mapped to $\alpha \cdot (max - min) + min$. If min and max are both 0, they default to 0 and 0.25, corresponding to 0 and 90 degrees counter-clockwise.

Bump Basis Generator

Given the intersection point, compute a pair of bump basis vectors, based on the projection method (as above: UV, XY, XZ, YZ, spherical, or cylindrical).

```
struct {
    vector          "u",
    vector          "v"
} "mib_bump_basis" (
    integer         "project",
    integer         "ntex")
```

project specifies the projection to perform, as described above. All projections are based on the 3D point in space after conversion to object space. This parameter is used to orient the bump basis.

ntex is the texture space to use, in the range 0...63. It is used only if project is UV (5) or disabled (0 or negative). Otherwise ntex is ignored.

Bump Mapping

Apply a texture to the normal vector by evaluating the texture at multiple points to compute U and V gradients that are multiplied with the basis vectors, combined with the original normal, normalized, and written back. Also return the normal. $state \rightarrow tex$ is left undefined.

```
vector "mib_bump_map" (
    vector          "u",
    vector          "v",
    vector          "coord",
    vector          "step",
    scalar          "factor",
    boolean         "torus_u",
    boolean         "torus_v",
    boolean         "alpha",
    color texture   "tex")
```

u and **v** are the bump basis vectors. They can be generated from another base shader such as *mib_bump_basis*.

coord is the texture coordinate for which the bump should be calculated.

step are offsets to coord. The shader samples three times: at $(coord_x, coord_v)$, at $(coord_x + step_x, coord_v)$, and at $(coord_x, coord_v + step_v)$. The resulting U and V gradients are multiplied by the u and v basis vectors, respectively, then multiplied by the factor, and finally added to the normal, which is then renormalized. If the step components are 0, they default to 0.01.

factor controls the strength of the effect. If it is 0, it defaults to 1.

torus_u and **torus_v** specify that, when step is added to coord, the result (X, Y, and Z) should be wrapped back into the interval [0...1].

alpha, if true, specifies that the alpha component instead of the intensity of the color texture should be used.

tex is a color texture or shader to look up three times. (Only use shader assignment using the "=" notation if the assigned shader returns a shader.)

The following shader is identical to the previous, including the parameters, except that it returns a color instead of a vector. This color is not modified. This allows the shader to be used in material shader lists by prepending it to the actual material shader. In this configuration it is called first and modifies the normal vector in the state before the material shader uses it to compute illumination. At the same time, it does not in any way affect the computed result color.

```
vector "mib_passthrough_bump_map" (
    vector          "u",
    vector          "v",
    vector          "coord",
    vector          "step",
    scalar          "factor",
    boolean         "torus_u",
    boolean         "torus_v",
    boolean         "alpha",
    color texture   "tex")
```

See above for a description of the parameters.

C.3   Environments

These shaders return colors from color textures that are mapped to finite or infinite distances. They are useful for adding background or foreground plates to the rendered scene. Environments must be used for environment shaders, overlays must be used for lens shaders, and textures must be used for texture or material shaders on a plane or other object in the scene.

Spherical Environment

Given a texture shader, assume that the texture it produces is wrapped on an infinite sphere around the scene, evaluate the texture, and return the color. This is useful for environment shaders.

```
color "mib_lookup_spherical" (
    vector          "dir",
    scalar          "rotate",
    color texture   "tex")
```

dir is the direction to sample. If connected to *mib_texture_vector*, a select value of -10 is useful. It should be given in world space. If this is the null vector, the ray direction is used, after conversion to world space.

tex is a texture or shader to look up at the computed coordinate.

Cube Environment

Same as the spherical environment shader, but accept either one or six textures mapped on an infinite cube. This is useful for environment shaders.

```
color "mib_lookup_cube1" (
    vector          "point",
    vector          "dir",
    vector          "size",
    color texture   "tex")

color "mib_lookup_cube6" (
    vector          "point",
    vector          "dir",
    vector          "size",
    color texture   "tex_mx",
    color texture   "tex_px",
    color texture   "tex_my",
    color texture   "tex_py",
    color texture   "tex_mz",
    color texture   "tex_pz")
```

point is the view location.

dir is the direction to sample. If connected to *mib_texture_vector*, a select value of -10 is useful. If this is the null vector, the ray direction is used.

size is the size of the box.

tex is a texture to look up at the computed coordinate. One texture contains all six sides; it has six times the number of scanlines required for a single face, with the sub-textures stacked in the following order, top-down: -x, +x, -y, +y, -z, +z.

tex_** are six textures for the left (mx), right (px), bottom (my), top (py), yon (mz), and hither (pz) faces. "p" and "m" stand for plus and minus.

Cylindrical Environment

This environment shader is most useful for projecting regular patterns onto geometry, for example for surface quality control. The cylinder does not have caps, so it might happen that rays do not hit the cylinder. The cylinder is defined by a transformation which transforms from world to canonical cylinder space, and two scalars that allow cutting off part of the cylinder. If both *begin* and *end* are zero, a full cylinder is selected.

```
color "mib_lookup_cylindrical" (
    transform       "xform",
    scalar          "begin",
    scalar          "end",
    color texture   "tex" )
```

xform transforms from world to canonical cylinder space. The canonical cylinder has the Z axis as the major axis, extends from -1 to $+1$ on the Z axis and has a radius of 1. If tex is a procedural texture, texture coordinates are calculated for the intersection point: $Z = -1$ is mapped to $v = 0$ and $Z = +1$ is mapped to $v = 1$. Texture coordinates for u are calculated counterclockwise around the Z axis where $+X$ is mapped to $u = 0$ and $-X$ to 0.5.

begin specifies the starting angle in radians where the cylinder begins. The angle specification is based on $+X = 0$ radians.

end specifies the ending angle where the cylinder body should end.

tex is a texture or shader to look up at the computed coordinate.

Backgrounds

Given a texture shader, place it in the background of the scene such that the edges of the texture line up with the edges of the rendered image. Factors can be applied to stretch and pan the texture, to allow for lenses that bend rays away from the center. The purpose of this environment is inserting background plates. Returns a color. This is useful in three different types of shaders:

- Environment shaders can place the background plate at infinity.

- Lens shaders can place the plate in front of the entire scene by evaluating the background shader first and casting an eye ray only if the returned alpha is less than 1, and blending the results.

- Material shaders on an XY axis aligned plane in the scene insert the plate at the Z coordinate of the plane if they first evaluate the background shader, then cast a transparency ray only if the returned alpha is less than 1, and blend the results.

```
color "mib_lookup_background" (
    vector          "zoom",
    vector          "pan",
    boolean         "torus_u",
    boolean         "torus_v",
    color texture   "tex")
```

zoom enlarges the texture image by a factor given by the X and Y components of the zoom vector. The Z component is not used. If a component is 0, it defaults to 1.

pan shifts the texture sideways by a fraction of the rendered image size. The Z component is unused. For example, if the X component is 0.1, the left 10% of the rendered image background remain blank.

torus_*, if true, repeats the texture endlessly in the respective direction. If false, transparent black is returned outside the tex image.

tex is a texture or shader to look up at the computed coordinate. It will be sampled in the range [0...1) only.

C.4   Textures

These shaders rely on one of the texture space mapping functions above to produce the **coord** texture vertex, and produce a color for that vertex. Shaders that produce 2D mappings only use the x and y components of the texture vertex.

Most of these return colors. Since colors can be assigned to scalar parameters of other shaders, the shaders can be used in conjunction with blending shaders that select colors from a color spread based on a map scalar. This interacts with the fading and smoothing parameters of the texture shaders.

Image Lookup

Look up a texture image in the half-open interval [0, 1). Points outside this interval are mapped to $R = G = B = A = 0$.

```
color "mib_texture_lookup" (
    color texture   "tex",
    vector          "coord")
```

tex is the texture image to look up.

coord is the coordinate to look up.

This is basically a front-end to the *mi_lookup_color_texture* family of shader interface functions.

Filtered Image Lookup

Lookup of texture image using elliptical filtering.

```
color "mib_texture_filter_lookup" (
    color texture   "tex",
    vector          "coord",
    scalar          "eccmax",
    scalar          "maxminor",
    scalar          "disc_r",
    boolean         "bilinear",
    integer         "space",
    shader          "remap")
```

tex is the texture image to look up. It must be a texture image, not a texture shader; otherwise the texture is looked up unfiltered.

coord is the central texture sampling location.

eccmax is the maximum allowed eccentricity for the ellipse.

maxminor is the maximum number of texture pixels for the minor radius of the ellipse.

disc_r is used in the calculation of screen-to-texture space transformations. A default value of 0.3 is used if disc_r is zero or unspecified. For scenes with highly curved surfaces it may be useful to choose a value in the range (0.0...0.3] if aliasing artifacts appear.

bilinear enables bilinear interpolation of texture samples if set to true. This blurs magnified areas and avoids blocky artifacts.

space is the texture space index in the range [0...63].

remap is a shader that is called for remapping additional texture coordinates.

The shader calls *mi_texture_filter_project* with the given *space* parameter to obtain three corresponding points in raster and texture space. These three texture coordinates are remapped by calling the specified *remap* shader; the actual texture coordinate for remapping is passed as the fourth argument of *mi_call_shader_x* (which means that the called shader must be designed to check its fourth argument). The remapping shader must use it instead of the provided texture coordinate vector in the shader parameters.

The projection transformation matrix required by the filtered texture lookup is calculated by calling the *mi_texture_filter_transform* shader interface function, using the three raster space and remapped texture space coordinates. The translation component in the matrix is set to **coord**. Note that the projection transformation is always calculated for the current raster position, but it is possible to translate the ellipse in texture space using *coord*. This is useful for bump mapping.

This is basically a front-end to the *mi_lookup_filter_color_texture* family of shader interface functions. The elliptical filter parameter *bilinear* is set to false in *mib_texture_filter_lookup*, for *circle_radius* the default value is used. If the projection matrix cannot be calculated properly, or the texture is a shader instead of an image, or the reflection level is not zero, nonfiltered texture lookup is used.

Checkerboard

Divide the unit cube into eight subcubes, each with a separate RGBA color. The width of the left, bottom, and front part is programmable, allowing the use of this shader for generating stripes and two- or three-dimensional checkerboards. This function is also useful for preview shaderball scenes.

```
color "mib_texture_checkerboard" (
    vector          "coord",
    scalar          "xsize",
    scalar          "ysize",
    scalar          "zsize",
    color           "color000",
    color           "color001",
    color           "color010",
    color           "color011",
    color           "color100",
    color           "color101",
    color           "color110",
    color           "color111")
```

coord is the coordinate to texture.

***size** specifies the fraction of the left (x), bottom (y), and front (z) half of the cube in each direction, in the range $[0, 1)$.

color* specifies the colors of the subcubes. The three digits stand for the XYZ coordinates: 000 is front lower left, and 100 is front lower right, and 111 is back upper right.

Polka Dot

Draw a disc with programmable diameter into the unit square, and draw a sphere with programmable diameter into the unit cube. The foreground and background colors are programmable.

```
color "mib_texture_polkadot" (
    vector          "coord",
    scalar          "radius",
    color           "fgcolor",
    color           "bgcolor")

color "mib_texture_polkasphere" (
    vector          "coord",
```

```
        scalar          "radius",
        color           "fgcolor",
        color           "bgcolor")
```

coord is the coordinate to texture.

radius is the radius of the disc or sphere in the unit square or cube, respectively.

fgcolor is the foreground color of the disc or sphere.

bgcolor is the background color around the disc or sphere.

Turbulence

Create a turbulent scalar pattern in a unit cube. One, two, or all three texture vector components may be computed in polar coordinates, causing spherical mapping.

```
scalar "mib_texture_turbulence" (
    vector          "coord",
    scalar          "spacing",
    scalar          "strength",
    scalar          "power",
    integer         "iteration",
    integer         "polar_dim")
```

coord is the coordinate to texture.

spacing is the density of the noise in the unit cube. If it is 0, a default of 1 is used.

strength is a weight describing the strength of the distortion. If it is 0, a default of 1 is used.

power specifies the degree of the turbulence. If it is 0, a default of 1 is used.

iteration sets the number of composed turbulence passes, each of which contributes a diminishing amount of turbulence as specified by the power parameter. If it is 0, a default of 2 is used. The maximum is 8.

polar_dim specifies the number of texture vector components that should be converted to polar coordinates before computing the compound noise value. 0 creates anisotropic noise, 1 creates lines, and 2 creates cylinders.

Waves

Create cosine waves in U, V, and W directions, each with a programmable amplitude. (Frequency and offset can be controlled using a texture remapping base shader.) The result is a grayscale color, R=G=B=A, that can be remapped using a color map base shader. Its range is $[o - s...o + s]$ if s is the sum of the amplitudes and o is the offset.

```
color "mib_texture_wave" (
    vector          "coord",
    scalar          "amplitude_x",
    scalar          "amplitude_y",
    scalar          "amplitude_z",
    scalar          "offset")
```

coord is the coordinate to texture.

amplitude_* is a factor to multiply the generated wave with before adding it to the result. The defaults are 0 (no contribution).

offset adds a constant value to the sum of the weighted cosines. This can be used to shift the result into the positive numbers.

C.5 Sample Compositing

Reflection

Cast a reflection ray of a given color and merge the result with an input color. This can be used to add a reflection effect to a base shader that provides illumination, possibly in conjunction with refractions or transparency added by other base shaders. If no reflection ray can be cast (because the trace depth has been exceeded, or the reflection ray caused a shader to be called that failed, or the **notrace** parameter is set), sample the environment if there is one.

```
color "mib_reflect" (
    color           "input",
    color           "reflect",
    boolean         "notrace")
```

input is the color to composite the reflection onto.

reflect is an RGBA color that blends the reflection onto the input. Transparent black returns the input color without casting a reflected ray; opaque white returns the reflection color without evaluating the input color.

notrace, if set to true, prevents the shader from casting a reflection ray and samples the environment instead.

Refraction

Cast a refraction ray of a given color with an index of refraction, and merge the result with an input color. The indices of refraction can be computed with another base shader, such as *mib_refraction_index*, which is also stored back into the appropriate state variables. This can be used to add a refraction effect to a base shader that provides illumination.

```
color "mib_refract" (
    color          "input",
    color          "refract",
    scalar         "ior",
```

input is the color to composite the refraction onto.

refract is an RGBA color that blends the refraction onto the input. Transparent black returns the input color without casting a refracted ray; opaque white returns the refraction color without evaluating the input color.

ior is the ratio of the indices of refractions; the index of the object being entered divided by the index of the object being exited. This controls the outgoing ray direction. If it is 0, 1 is used, which reduces refractivity to transparency.

Transparency

Cast a transparency ray of a given color and merge the result with an input color. This is like the previous function assuming an index of refraction of 1.

```
color "mib_transparency" (
    color          "input",
    color          "transp")
```

input is the color to composite the refraction onto.

transp is an RGBA color that blends the transmission onto the input. Transparent black returns the input color without casting a transparency ray; opaque white returns the transparency color without evaluating the input color.

Continue[3.3]

Continue a ray of a given color and merge the result with an input color. The purpose is to continue a ray as if the current intersection did not exist. Trace depth, ray type and distance for volume computations are not modified. A typical use is for walls of a showroom where the camera sits outside, so that the room walls must be ignored. This shader was introduced with mental ray 3.3, and will not work with earlier versions.

```
color "mib_continue" (
    color          "input",
    color          "transp")
```

input is the color to composite the continued ray onto.

transp is an RGBA color that blends the transmission onto the input. Transparent black returns the input color without casting a ray; opaque white returns the transparency color without evaluating the input color.

Opacity

Cast a transparency ray of a given intensity and merge the result with an input color. This is like the previous function, except that the opacity is given instead of the transparency. Opacity is defined as 1.0 − *transparency*.

```
color "mib_opacity" (
    color         "input",
    color         "opacity")
```

input is the color to composite the refraction onto.

opacity is an RGBA color that blends the transmission onto the input. Opaque white returns the input color without casting a transparency ray; transparent black returns the transparency color without evaluating the input color.

Dielectric

Another variation of refraction, with the addition of specularity (Snell's law). This shader does only the refraction part of a dielectric material; highlights are left to other illumination nodes.

```
color "mib_dielectric" (
    color         "input",
    color         "absorb",
    scalar        "refract",
    scalar        "ior")
```

input is the color to composite the refraction onto.

absorb specifies the outside absorption coefficients of the surface.

refract blends the refraction onto the input. A value of 0.0 returns the input color without casting a refracted ray; a value of 1.0 returns the refraction color without evaluating the input color.

ior is the ratio of the indices of refractions; the index of the object being entered divided by the index of the object being exited. This controls the outgoing ray direction. If it is 0.0, 1.0 is used, which reduces refractivity to transparency.

Ray Marcher

The ray marcher casts light rays from points on a given ray, and approximates the volumic contribution from light sources sending light through the volume. Instead of using shader interface functions like *mi_sample_light*, it calls a shader given as an input parameter of type *shader*. Ray marching consists of calling the shader for regular points between the start point and end point of the ray, and adaptively subdividing each of these intervals until a given subdivision limit is reached if the color returned by two adjacent shader calls is smaller than a given contrast threshold. The total weighted sum is returned.

```
color "mib_ray_marcher" (
    shader          "shader",
    scalar          "distance",
    integer         "num",
    integer         "subdiv",
    color           "contrast")
```

shader is the shader to call at every sampling point. Its returned color is added to the returned total unless the shader fails (returns false).

distance is the maximum internal space distance between two initial sample points. If the distance is 0, no maximum distance is enforced.

num is the initial number of samples in the given distance. If this number is 0, no initial number is given, and the ray marcher relies on the minimum distance instead. If both are 0, the default number is 4. If the number is not 0, it must be at least 2 (one at each ray end point).

subdiv specifies the number of recursive subdivisions of the initial sample density. A value of 0 (the default) does not subdivide, so the ray marcher is restricted to the initial sample points. Values of 1 or larger make the sampling adaptive; each level of subdivision divides a distance by two. The maximum is 16.

contrast, if exceeded by the absolute difference between two adjacent samples, causes another sample to be taken in the middle. The process then repeats recursively for both sub-segments until the contrast is sufficiently low or the subdivision limit is reached.

Two-Sided

Choose one or the other input color, depending on which side of the geometry was hit. This is commonly used as a multiplexing material shader, with two other material shaders assigned to the front and back parameters.

```
color "mib_twosided" (
    color           "front",
    color           "back")
```

front is returned if the front side was hit.

back is returned if the back side was hit.

Refraction Index

Decide whether the ray is entering or leaving the object it has hit, based on a scan of parent rays (not based on the normal vector; this can be unreliable if the scene contains dubious geometry such as cones with only one axis-aligned normal at the tip). The index of refraction ratio (outgoing divided by incoming) is returned. As a side effect, both incoming and outgoing indices of refraction are stored in the state (*ior_in* and *ior*, respectively), and the current volume shader becomes the refraction volume if the ray is entering.

```
struct {
    scalar           "ior",
    boolean          "enter"
} "mib_refraction_index" (
    scalar           "mtl_ior")
```

ior is the returned refraction index ratio, ready for use by refracting or dielectric base shaders.

enter is true if the ray is entering the object. Most shaders do not need to know this but it makes this base shader more versatile.

mtl_ior is the index of refraction of the material that the ray has hit. It describes the optical properties of the object the ray is entering or leaving, and is returned as the new index of refraction if the ray is found to be entering the object.

C.6   Illumination

Lambert

Perform Lambertian illumination, given ambient and diffuse RGB colors (alpha is ignored), and a light list.

```
color "mib_illum_lambert" (
    color            "ambience",
    color            "ambient",
    color            "diffuse",
    integer          "mode",
    array light      "lights")
```

ambience is a multiplier for the ambient color. The idea is that ambient and diffuse color can be derived from the same subshader result (a texture mapper, for example) and the ambient brightness can be reduced to avoid losing the effect of illumination.

ambient is a constant color offset.

diffuse is added to the result for each light, after multiplication with the color returned by the light and a weight based on the dot product of the incident ray direction and the light direction.

mode controls the meaning of the light list: all, inclusive, or exclusive. All is faster than inclusive, and inclusive is faster than exclusive.

lights is a list of light instances to loop over. If the mode is 0, use every light in the light list parameter. If the mode is 1, use all lights in the global light list that correspond to the lights in the light list parameter (inclusive mode). If the mode is 2, use all lights in the global light list that do not correspond to the lights in the light list parameter (exclusive mode).

Phong

Perform Phong illumination, given ambient, diffuse, and specular RGB colors, a specular exponent, and a light list.

```
color "mib_illum_phong" (
    color           "ambience",
    color           "ambient",
    color           "diffuse",
    color           "specular",
    scalar          "exponent",
    integer         "mode",
    array light     "lights")
```

ambience is a multiplier for the ambient color. The idea is that ambient and diffuse color can be derived from the same subshader result (a texture mapper, for example) and the ambient brightness can be reduced to avoid losing the effect of illumination.

ambient is a constant color offset.

diffuse is added to the result for each light, after multiplication with the color returned by the light and a weight based on the dot product of the incident ray direction and the light direction.

specular provides the color of specular highlights.

exponent controls the width of the specular highlight. Smaller values increase the size.

mode controls the meaning of the light list: all, inclusive, or exclusive.

lights is a list of light instances to loop over. If the mode is 0, use every light in the light list parameter. If the mode is 1, use all lights in the global light list that correspond to the lights in the light list parameter (inclusive mode). If the mode is 2, use all lights in the global light list that do not correspond to the lights in the light list parameter (exclusive mode).

Ward

Perform Ward illumination, given ambient, diffuse, and glossy RGB colors, two shinyness parameters, two direction vectors, and a light list.

```
color "mib_illum_ward" (
    color           "ambience",
    color           "ambient",
    color           "diffuse",
    color           "glossy",
    scalar          "shiny_u",
    scalar          "shiny_v",
    vector          "u",
    vector          "v",
```

```
integer        "mode",
array light    "lights")
```

ambience is a multiplier for the ambient color. The idea is that ambient and diffuse color can be derived from the same subshader result (a texture mapper, for example) and the ambient brightness can be reduced to avoid losing the effect of illumination.

ambient is a constant color offset.

diffuse is added to the result for each light, after multiplication with the color returned by the light and a weight based on the dot product of the incident ray direction and the light direction.

glossy is also added per light. It is the glossy color computed according to Ward's anisotropic glossy reflection model.

shiny_u and **shiny_v** controls the width of the glossy highlight in the u and v directions, respectively. Smaller values increase the size of the highlight.

u is the brushing direction in the anisotropic material. They must be perpendicular to the surface normal and be of unit length.

v is a direction perpendicular to u and to the surface normal. It must have unit length.

mode controls the meaning of the light list: all, inclusive, or exclusive.

lights is a list of light instances to loop over. If the mode is 0, use every light in the light list parameter. If the mode is 1, use all lights in the global light list that correspond to the lights in the light list parameter (inclusive mode). If the mode is 2, use all lights in the global light list that do not correspond to the lights in the light list parameter (exclusive mode).

Ward with surface derivatives

Perform Ward illumination, given ambient, diffuse, and glossy RGB colors, two shinyness parameters, and a light list. The only difference from `mib_illum_ward` is that the brushing directions are taken from the surface derivatives.

```
color "mib_illum_ward_deriv" (
    color          "ambience",
    color          "ambient",
    color          "diffuse",
    color          "glossy",
    scalar         "shiny_u",
    scalar         "shiny_v",
    integer        "mode",
    array light    "lights")
```

ambience is a multiplier for the ambient color. The idea is that ambient and diffuse color can be derived from the same subshader result (a texture mapper, for example) and the ambient brightness can be reduced to avoid losing the effect of illumination.

ambient is a constant color offset.

diffuse is added to the result for each light, after multiplication with the color returned by the light and a weight based on the dot product of the incident ray direction and the light direction.

glossy is also added per light. It is the glossy color computed according to Ward's anisotropic glossy reflection model.

shiny_u and **shiny_v** controls the width of the glossy highlight in the u and v directions, respectively. The u direction is the first derivative of the surface (read from the state), and v is perpendicular. Both u and v are in the plane that is perpendicular to the surface normal.

mode controls the meaning of the light list: all, inclusive, or exclusive.

lights is a list of light instances to loop over. If the mode is 0, use every light in the light list parameter. If the mode is 1, use all lights in the global light list that correspond to the lights in the light list parameter (inclusive mode). If the mode is 2, use all lights in the global light list that do not correspond to the lights in the light list parameter (exclusive mode).

Cook-Torrance

Perform Cook-Torrance illumination, given ambient, diffuse, and specular RGB colors, a roughness, index of refraction for three wavelengths, and a light list. Cook-Torrance illumination has an off-specular peak and a color shift with angles.

```
color "mib_illum_cooktorr" (
    color           "ambience",
    color           "ambient",
    color           "diffuse",
    color           "specular",
    scalar          "roughness",
    color           "ior",
    integer         "mode",
    array light     "lights")
```

ambience is a multiplier for the ambient color. The idea is that ambient and diffuse color can be derived from the same subshader result (a texture mapper, for example) and the ambient brightness can be reduced to avoid losing the effect of illumination.

ambient is a constant color offset.

diffuse is added to the result for each light, after multiplication with the color returned by the light and a weight based on the dot product of the incident ray direction and the light direction.

specular is a factor that the reflected color is multiplied with.

roughness is the average microfacet slope of the surface. It controls the width of the specular highlight.

ior is the index of refraction of the material at three different wavelengths (red, green, blue). Metals typically have a higher index of refraction than glass. Values must be 1.0 or greater; smaller values are clamped to 1.0.

mode controls the meaning of the light list: all, inclusive, or exclusive.

lights is a list of light instances to loop over. If the mode is 0, use every light in the light list parameter. If the mode is 1, use all lights in the global light list that correspond to the lights in the light list parameter (inclusive mode). If the mode is 2, use all lights in the global light list that do not correspond to the lights in the light list parameter (exclusive mode).

Blinn

Perform Blinn illumination, which is a like Cook-Torrance illumination but without the color shift with angles. It only requires one index of refraction.

```
color "mib_illum_blinn" (
    color          "ambience",
    color          "ambient",
    color          "diffuse",
    color          "specular",
    scalar         "roughness",
    scalar         "ior",
    integer        "mode",
    array light    "lights")
```

ambience is a multiplier for the ambient color. The idea is that ambient and diffuse color can be derived from the same subshader result (a texture mapper, for example) and the ambient brightness can be reduced to avoid losing the effect of illumination.

ambient is a constant color offset.

diffuse is added to the result for each light, after multiplication with the color returned by the light and a weight based on the dot product of the incident ray direction and the light direction.

specular provides the color of specular highlights.

roughness is the average microfacet slope of the surface. It controls the width of the specular highlight.

ior is the index of refraction of the material. Metals typically have higher index of refraction than glass.

mode controls the meaning of the light list: all (0), inclusive (1), or exclusive (2).

lights is a list of light instances to loop over. If the mode is 0, use every light in the light list parameter. If the mode is 1, use all lights in the global light list that correspond to the lights in the light list parameter (inclusive mode). If the mode is 2, use all lights in the global light list that do not correspond to the lights in the light list parameter (exclusive mode).

Ambient Occlusion[3.3]

Occlusion is a fast and simple method to simulate the effects of global illumination. Occlusion is the extent to which the area above a point is covered by other geometry. This is achieved by tracing a number of probe rays inside the hemispherical area above the point and testing to what extent this region is blocked.

Occlusion has several uses. One of these is *ambient occlusion*, where the shader is used to scale the contribution of ambient light (which in turn may come from a diffuse environment map shader). For this use, the shader works well when assigned to the *ambient* parameter of a material like *mib_illum_phong*.

Another use of occlusion is *reflective occlusion*, where the shader is used to scale the contribution from a reflection map. For this use, the shader is generally plugged into an environment or reflection shader slot of a material, and the actual environment map image is plugged into the *bright* parameter. An alternative is to allow the return value of the occlusion shader to modulate the strength attribute of a reflection map shader.

A third use is to create files for external compositing, where the occlusion shader is assigned to every object in the scene. The output can be used to modulate other render passes to achieve proper composites in post-production.

```
color "mib_amb_occlusion" (
    integer "samples"              default 16,
    color   "bright"               default 1 1 1 1,
    color   "dark"                 default 0 0 0 0,
    scalar  "spread"               default 0.8,
    scalar  "max_distance"         default 0,
    boolean "reflective"           default off,
    integer "output_mode"          default 0,
    boolean "occlusion_in_alpha"   default off
)
version 2
```

samples is the number of probe rays that will be sent. More rays yield a smoother image. Occlusion mapping will never be as smooth as well-tuned final gathering or photons, but is computationally cheap.

bright is the color used when no occluding objects are found and **dark** is the color used when total occlusion occurs. In most practical cases it is set to black. For partial occlusion, a gradual mix between the two colors is returned.

spread defines how large an area of the hemisphere above the point is sampled. The value defines a cone around the sampling direction which is narrower for small values and wider for large values. It ranges from 0.0, for a cone that is a single direction, to 1.0 for a cone that covers the entire hemisphere.

max_distance is the range within which geometry is probed. If it is zero, the entire scene is sampled. If it is a nonzero value, only objects within this distance will be considered (which makes sampling much faster) where objects outside this range do not occlude at all and objects that are closer occlude more strongly as the distance approaches zero.

If **reflective** is off sampling is performed in a cone area based around the surface normal. If *reflective* is on, the samples are instead distributed around the reflection direction. This generates reflective occlusion which can enhance the realism of reflection mapping greatly.

output_mode defines what the returned color is: 0 enables standard occlusion behaviour; 1 enables environment sampling. This changes the behavior of the shader slightly. As directions are probed for occlusion, the current environment is also sampled and weighted based on how occluded that particular direction is. In mode 1 the output of the function is the gathered weighted environment colors multiplied by the *bright* color, and as a convenience the *dark* color is added.

Setting *output_mode* to 2 enables bent normals. The average unoccluded world space normal direction is calculated and returned encoded as a color where red is x, green is y and blue is z. Setting *output_mode* to 3 is the same as 2 but the normals are encoded in the camera coordinate space instead. Output mode 4 is similar to 2 but the coordinates are in object space.

When **occlusion_in_alpha** is on, the scalar occlusion value is put in the returned colors alpha component, regardless of what *output_mode* is set to. The other color components remain as before.

Bent Normals[3.4]

"Bent normal" is a term used for the average un-occluded direction vector from a surface point. For completely un-occluded surfaces this is the same as the normal vector, but for surfaces occluded by other geometry it points in the direction in which the least amount of occluding geometry is found. Bent normals are used as an acceleration technique for ambient occlusion, allowing very fast rendering that look like global illumination or final gathering lit by an environment at a small fraction of the rendering time.

Ambient occlusion as done by the *mib_amb_occlusion* shader (see page 548) is a ray tracing technique that casts potentially large numbers of probe rays to determine to which extent a surface point is occluded. The speed of this operation depends on the number of rays (**samples**), the reach of the rays (**max_distance**) and the complexity of the scene.

When rendering an animation (or multiple views of the same scene), any object that does not move, does not change shape, or has no moving occluding object nearby will yield the same result for every frame. Therefore one can "bake" (render to a file) the ambient occlusion solution *once* in a first rendering pass, and re-use this result in subsequent rendering passes for any number of frames, with potentially huge performance gains. If one also "bakes" the average un-occluded direction (the bent normal) to a texture, the entire process of lighting the object based on an environment is moved to this second rendering pass, without having to trace a single ray.

By setting the **output_mode** parameter to 2, 3, or 4 on the ambient occlusion shader *mib_amb_occlusion*, bent normals are returned with the vector being encoded as a color where x is red, y is green, and z is blue. If **occlusion_in_alpha** is enabled, the scalar occlusion value is returned in the alpha channel. This color can be baked into a texture, for example with the help of *mib_lightmap_write* (page 564) by putting *mib_amb_occlusion* into its **input** parameter and rendering.

Once the texture file is generated, *mib_bent_normal_env* can be assigned to a surface shader (for example to the **ambient** parameter of *mib_illum_phong*) to look up an environment to light the object based on the baked bent normal texture, which is placed in the **bent_normals** parameter of *mib_bent_normal_env*.

This allows an extremely low-overhead simulation of global illumination-like effects for rigid objects and is especially suitable for animations. The technique does not work on deformable objects since their occlusion, shape, and normals can vary from frame to frame. For deformable objects, it is better to apply the occlusion shader directly, without baking its output.

```
color "mib_bent_normal_env" (
    color       "bent_normals"        default 0 0 0 1,
    boolean     "occlusion_in_alpha"  default on,
    color       "occlusion"           default 1 1 1,
    scalar      "strength"            default 0.2,
    shader      "environment",
    integer     "coordinate_space"    default 2,
    integer     "env_samples"         default 1,
    scalar      "samples_spread"      default 0.0,
    transform   "matrix"              default 1 0 0 0
                                              0 1 0 0
                                              0 0 1 0
                                              0 0 0 1
)
```

bent_normals is the bent normal data output by the occlusion shader. It should be baked to the object. This is usually attached to a node that does the texture lookup such as *mib_lookup_color_texture*. The texture mapping used for generating the texture must match with the one used for lookup.

occlusion_in_alpha specifies whether the scalar occlusion value is already baked into the alpha channel of the "bent normals" pass. This uses slightly less memory but many "bake to texture" functions of OEM integrations of mental ray do not bake the alpha channel.

occlusion is the separate occlusion channel, to be used if it was not already baked into the alpha channel.

strength is a simple scalar multiplier for the effect.

environment is the environment shader to look up. If none is provided, the environment from the material is used. To avoid image noise, it is often desirable to use a separate, highly blurred environment map with no high-resolution detail.

coordinate_space defines the coordinate space of the bent normal:

- 0 is "unmodified". The bent normal data is assumed to be in mental ray's internal space.

- 1 is "by matrix". The bent normal data is transformed with the passed transformation matrix.

- 2 is world space.

- 3 is camera space.

- 4 is object space. This is often the most useful mode. If the map is both created and used in object space, it will automatically follow the object as it moves through an animation.

The coordinate space numbers match the output_mode parameter values of the ambient occlusion shader, where 2 is world space, 3 is camera space, and 4 is object space.

env_samples is the number of samples to take from the environment map. Normally, a highly-blurred environment map is used where only one sample is sufficient, but it is possible to multi-sample the environment map by setting a non-zero value.

sample_spread is the spread factor for each individual environment sample. The range is from 0.0 (infinitely thin rays – a single sample) to 1.0 (the entire hemisphere is sampled).

matrix is an explicit transformation matrix applied to the normal data when coordinate_space is 1. This allows arbitrary transformations.

C.7   Data Conversion

Color to Grayscale

Convert a color to RGBA grayscale, either by extracting the alpha component, by averaging RGB, or by weighting RGB according to a physiological color model that emphasizes green and deemphasizes red. The resulting grayscale value can also be used as a scalar. The returned R, G, B, and A components all have the same value.

```
color "mib_color_alpha" (
    color           "input",
    scalar          "factor")

color "mib_color_average" (
    color           "input",
    scalar          "factor")
```

```
color "mib_color_intensity" (
    color          "input",
    scalar         "factor")
```

input is the color that is converted to a grayscale.

factor is a factor that the result is multiplied with. It should be set to 1.0 for correct alpha, average, and intensity values; a value of 0 will not evaluate **input** and return black.

Color Map Interpolation

Given a scalar or a color, perform a lookup and interpolation of a multicolor map. The map is a set (not array) of up to 8 colors. The actual number of colors is specified by a parameter.

```
color "mib_color_interpolate" (
    scalar         "input",
    integer        "num",
    scalar         "weight_1",
    scalar         "weight_2",
    scalar         "weight_3",
    scalar         "weight_4",
    scalar         "weight_5",
    scalar         "weight_6",
    color          "color_0",
    color          "color_1",
    color          "color_2",
    color          "color_3",
    color          "color_4",
    color          "color_5",
    color          "color_6",
    color          "color_7")
```

input is the scalar to be looked up.

num is the number of colors in the color list. The value must be at least 1 and at most 8.

weight_* specifies the locations of colors 1..6 in the color spread. A value of 0 puts a color at the low end and 1 at the high end. The weights must be monotonically increasing. Color 0 always has a weight of 0, and color $num - 1$ always has a weight of 1. Only the weights between these two must be specified (that is, two fewer than colors, or $num - 2$ weights).

color_* specify the color spread. Only the first num colors are defined. If the input is ≤ 0, only color_0 is evaluated; if the input is ≥ 1, only color_$(num - 1)$ is evaluated. If the input is exactly equal to a weight within numerical precision, only the corresponding color is evaluated. In all other cases, exactly two neighboring colors are evaluated and interpolated.

Mix

Accepts a base color and up to 8 inputs (the exact number is determined by a parameter), each of which consists of an input color, a weight scalar, and a mode. The inputs are evaluated in sequence, each operating on the result of the previous one (the first begins with the base color, which defaults to transparent black). The following modes are supported:

mode	operation	
0	Blend	$R = A \cdot (1 - B_a) \cdot w + B \cdot w$
1	Mix	$R = A \cdot (1 - w) + B \cdot w$
2	Add	$R = A + B \cdot w$
3	Bounded add	$R = bound(A + B \cdot w, 0, 1)$
4	Multiply	$R = A \cdot B \cdot w$
5	Bounded multiply	$R = bound(A \cdot B \cdot w, 0, 1)$
6	Replace alpha	$R_{rgb} = A_{rgb} \cdot w; R_a = B_a$

R is the next result, A is the previous result, B is the current color, and w is the current weight. The subscripts r, g, b, and a are red, green, blue, and alpha components. Note that mode 6 does not ensure that the resulting alpha value is valid, that is, not less than red, green, or blue. mental ray will correct alpha when storing the color in the frame buffer unless premultiplication is turned off.

```
color "mib_color_mix" (
    integer         "num",
    integer         "mode_0",
    integer         "mode_1",
    integer         "mode_2",
    integer         "mode_3",
    integer         "mode_4",
    integer         "mode_5",
    integer         "mode_6",
    integer         "mode_7",
    scalar          "weight_0",
    scalar          "weight_1",
    scalar          "weight_2",
    scalar          "weight_3",
    scalar          "weight_4",
    scalar          "weight_5",
    scalar          "weight_6",
    scalar          "weight_7",
    color           "color_0",
    color           "color_1",
    color           "color_2",
    color           "color_3",
    color           "color_4",
    color           "color_5",
    color           "color_6",
    color           "color_7",
    color           "color_base")
```

num is the number of valid inputs. The minimum is 1 and the maximum is 8.

mode_* are the compositing modes as described above.

weight_* are the compositing weights w as described above.

color_* are the composited colors B as described above.

color_base is the base color.

Spread

Fan out one color input to up to 8 color outputs (the exact number is determined by a parameter). Each output is equal to the corresponding input, multiplied by a weight, with a given conversion (color, scalar derived from alpha, alpha derived from average intensity, alpha derived from weighted intensity, or red component). The equation is

$mode$	operation
0	$R = w \cdot A$
1	$R = w \cdot A_a$
2	$R = w \cdot \frac{A_r + A_g + A_b}{3}$
3	$R = w \cdot (0.299 \cdot A_r + 0.587 \cdot A_g + 0.114 \cdot A_b)$
4	$R = w \cdot A_r$

R is the current (one of up to eight) result, w is the current weight, $mode$ is the current conversion, and A is the input color shared by all outputs. Mode 4 is intended for converting a scalar to a grayscale color.

```
struct {
    color           "out_0",
    color           "out_1",
    color           "out_2",
    color           "out_3",
    color           "out_4",
    color           "out_5",
    color           "out_6",
    color           "out_7"
} "mib_color_spread" (
    color           "input",
    integer         "num",
    integer         "mode_0",
    integer         "mode_1",
    integer         "mode_2",
    integer         "mode_3",
    integer         "mode_4",
    integer         "mode_5",
    integer         "mode_6",
    integer         "mode_7",
```

```
color            "weight_0",
color            "weight_1",
color            "weight_2",
color            "weight_3",
color            "weight_4",
color            "weight_5",
color            "weight_6",
color            "weight_7")
```

num is the number of valid outputs to compute. The minimum is 1 and the maximum is 8.

mode_* are the modes *mode* as described above.

weight_* are the weights w as described above.

C.8   Geometry

Cube

Generates an axis-aligned unit cube with volume 1 centered on the origin.

```
geometry "mib_geo_cube" ()
```

There are no parameters.

Sphere

Generates a polygonal sphere with a given number of U and V subdivisions, centered on the origin. The sphere is subdivided with *v_subdiv* subdivisions in the Z axis (longitude) and *u_subdiv* subdivisions in the XY plane (latitude).

```
geometry "mib_geo_sphere" (
    integer          "u_subdiv",
    integer          "v_subdiv")
```

***_subdiv** specify the number of subdivisions in each parameter range. The shader uses default values for the subdivisions if *u_subdiv* is less than 3 or *v_subdiv* is less than 1.

Cone

Generates a polygonal cone centered on the Z axis with the apex at Z=0 and the base at Z=-1. The cone has a radius of 1 at the bottom and a height of 1. The cone bottom disc is subdivided into *u_subdiv* subdivisions, the cone side in *v_subdiv* subdivisions in the Z axis direction. A parameter controls whether the cone base is capped.

```
geometry "mib_geo_cone" (
    integer          "u_subdiv",
    integer          "v_subdiv",
    boolean          "capped")
```

*_subdiv specify the number of subdivisions in each parameter range.

capped, if true, creates a cap that closes off the cone at the base.

The shader uses default values for the subdivisions if *u_subdiv* is less than 3 or *v_subdiv* is less than 0.

Cylinder

Generates a polygonal cylinder centered on the Z axis with the bottom at Z=-1 and the top at Z=0. The cylinder has a radius of 1 and a height of 1. The two cylinder discs are subdivided in *u_subdiv* subdivisions, the sides in *v_subdiv* subdivisions in the Z axis direction. A parameter controls whether the bottom or top is capped.

```
geometry "mib_geo_cylinder" (
    integer          "u_subdiv",
    integer          "v_subdiv",
    boolean          "bottom_capped",
    boolean          "top_capped")
```

*_subdiv specify the number of subdivisions in each parameter range.

bottom_capped, if true, creates a cap that closes off the cylinder at the base.

top_capped, if true, creates a cap that closes off the cylinder at the top.

The shader uses default values for the subdivisions if *u_subdiv* is less than 3 or *v_subdiv* is less than 0.

Torus

Generates a polygonal torus lying in the XY plane, centered at the origin. The torus is defined by two circles: the smaller one revolves around the center of the larger circle. This shader was introduced with mental ray versions 3.0.1 and 2.1.47.38.

```
geometry "mib_geo_torus" (
    scalar           "radius",
    scalar           "thickness",
    integer          "uSpans",
    integer          "vSpans")
```

radius is the radius of the large circle.

thickness is the radius of the small circle.

uSpans, vSpans specify the number of subdivisions in each parametric range.

If omitted (set to 0), parameters default to the following values: *radius* 2.0, *thickness* 1.0, *uSpans* 32, *vSpans* 32.

Square

Generates a square with area 1 centered on the origin, with the normal pointing up the positive Z axis.

```
geometry "mib_geo_square" ()
```

There are no parameters.

Instance

Given one of the geometry shaders above, construct an instance that translates, scales, and rotates the geometry, and return a group with the instance of the source geometry as its only member. If the result was nonzero because the base shader is part of a list, do not create a new group but add the instance to the result group (this is normal geometry shader behavior).

```
geometry "mib_geo_instance" (
    geometry        "object",
    miMatrix        "matrix",
    material        "material")
```

object is the object to be instanced.

matrix is the transformation matrix of the new instance. If it is a null matrix, use the identity matrix.

material is an inheritance material to store in the instance. It may be null.

Instance with Material List

This instance shader is the same as the previous but accepts a material array, which is converted into a material list in the new instance if the array has more than one member. Material lists are useful if the instanced object is *tagged*, meaning its polygons or surfaces carry integers that index into the material array.

```
geometry "mib_geo_instance_mlist" (
    geometry        "object",
    miMatrix        "matrix",
    array material  "material")
```

object is the object to be instanced.

matrix is the transformation matrix of the new instance. If it is a null matrix, use the identity matrix.

material is an inherited material list to store in the instance. It may be null.

Add a Texture Surface

This shader returns a copy of the input object, which must be of freeform-surface type. It loops over all faces and adds a Bézier texture surface of degree 1 to each face as the last texture surface. The parameters and control points of the texture surfaces are chosen in such a way that there is an exact mapping of the parametric uv coordinates of the geometric approximation to the texture vertex coordinates, i.e. the texture coordinates of the triangle vertices are the uv coordinates of the triangle vertex positions. The Bézier basis is always added to the copy of the object.

```
    geometry "mib_geo_add_uv_texsurf" (
        geometry        "object")
end declare
```

object is the freeform surface object that will be copied.

C.9   Photon

Basic

The basic photon shader supports diffuse reflection and specular reflection and transmission/refraction.

```
    color "mib_photon_basic" (
        color           "diffuse",
        color           "specular",
        color           "transp",
        scalar          "ior_frac")
```

diffuse is the diffuse color.

specular is the specular color, which controls reflectivity.

transp is the fraction of light transmitted.

ior_frac is the refraction index ratio. It is used if the photon material is transparent.

C.10   Light

Point

This is a simple point light shader emitting light uniformly in all directions.

```
color "mib light_point" (
    color           "color",
    boolean         "shadow",
    scalar          "factor",
    boolean         "atten",
    scalar          "start",
    scalar          "stop")
```

color is the light color.

shadow, if true, enables shadows. The light will be diminished or blocked by occluding objects between the light and the illuminated object.

factor only has an effect if shadows are enabled, and blends from the shadow color (0, the default) to the light color (1). Effectively, values greater than 0 let the light penetrate occluding objects. At 1, no shadows appear.

atten, if true, enables distance attenuation such that the light intensity begins to fall off at the distance *start* and fades up the distance *stop*, where no light remains.

start only has an effect if distance attenuation is enabled. It specifies the distance from the light where attenuation begins.

stop only has an effect if distance attenuation is enabled. It specifies the maximum distance reached by the light.

Spot

The spot light is similar to the point light, except that it also supports angle attenuation based on the light direction. It takes the light direction and the spread (the cosine of the outer boundary angle) from the light definition.

```
color "mib_light_spot" (
    color           "color",
    boolean         "shadow",
    scalar          "factor",
    boolean         "atten",
    scalar          "start",
    scalar          "stop",
    scalar          "cone")
```

color is the light color.

shadow, if true, enables shadows. The light will be diminished or blocked by occluding objects between the light and the illuminated object.

factor only has an effect if shadows are enabled, and blends from the shadow color (0, the default) to the light color (1). Effectively, values greater than 0 let the light penetrate occluding objects. At 1, no shadows appear.

atten, if true, enables distance attenuation such that the light intensity begins to fall off at the distance *start* and fades up the distance *stop*, where no light remains.

start only has an effect if distance attenuation is enabled. It specifies the distance from the light where attenuation begins.

stop only has an effect if distance attenuation is enabled. It specifies the maximum distance reached by the light.

cone specifies the cosine of the angle of the inner cone that illuminates with full intensity, in degrees. The value must be in the range 0 (hemisphere) to 1 (null diameter). The cone cannot exceed the spread angle from the light definition.

Infinite

Infinite (directional) lights cast parallel rays in the light direction. Up to mental ray 3.3, the origin is always infinitely far away. Starting with mental ray 3.4, an origin may be specified to define a plane whose normal is aligned with the light direction, and from which light is emitted (all points behind this plane are not lit by the infinite light). In all cases, there is no distance attenuation.

```
color "mib_light_infinite" (
    color          "color",
    boolean        "shadow",
    scalar         "factor")
```

color is the light color.

shadow, if true, enables shadows. The light will be diminished or blocked by occluding objects between the light and the illuminated object.

factor only has an effect if shadows are enabled, and blends from the shadow color (0, the default) to the light color (1). Effectively, values greater than 0 let the light penetrate occluding objects. At 1, no shadows appear.

Photometric

This is a variation of a simple point light shader emitting light according to the distribution determined by a light profile. This shader also honors the decay rate.

```
color "mib_light_photometric" (
    color          "color",
    boolean        "shadow",
    scalar         "factor",
    boolean        "atten",
    scalar         "start",
    scalar         "stop",
    lightprofile   "profile")
```

color is the light color.

shadow, if true, enables shadows. The light will be diminished or blocked by occluding objects between the light and the illuminated object.

factor only has an effect if shadows are enabled, and blends from the shadow color (0, the default) to the light color (1). Effectively, values greater than 0 let the light penetrate occluding objects. At 1, no shadows appear.

atten, if true, enables distance attenuation such that the light intensity begins to fall off at the distance *start* and fades up the distance *stop*, where no light remains.

start only has an effect if distance attenuation is enabled. It specifies the distance from the light where attenuation begins.

profile is a light profile describing the intensity distribution of the light with respect to the emission direction. If no light profile is provided the light behaves like a uniform point light.

C.11   Light Utilities

All light shaders take an argument determining the color of the light source. Here we describe some light utilities that may be used to determine a color. They can be attached to the color parameters of other light shaders.

CIE D Illuminant

The Comission Internationale de l'Eclairage (CIE) has standardized several illuminants. The most well known of these is called D65, but there is an entire range of CIE D illuminants. The number 65 refers to the associated color temperature of 6500 Kelvin. This illuminant describes the color of daylight with an overcast sky. This specific illuminant is widely used to define the color white, and indeed its sRGB coordinates are (1,1,1). The other CIE D illuminant differ from D65 by the associated color temperature. This implementiation supports color temperatures from 4000 Kelvin to 25000 Kelvin.

```
color "mib_cie_d" (
    scalar          "temperature",
    scalar          "intensity")
```

temperature gives the associated color temperature of the CIE D illuminant in degrees Kelvin. The allowed range is from 4000 to 25000 Kelvin with a default value of 6500 Kelvin.

intensity determines the intensity of returned color. By default the intensisty is set to 1.

Blackbody Radiator

An ideal material absorbing all light directed at it is called a blackbody, since it is obviously devoid of any color. However, every material, when sufficiently heated, will also emit electromagnetic radiation. For a blackbody the spectral distribution of this radiation depends solely on the temperature of the material, and on no other material property. There is a specific color associated with each temperature of such a body. With increasing temperature this color ranges from red over white to blue. However, the intensity of this radiation will also increase strongly with temperature – an effect that is ignored here by normalizing the color to a provided intensity.

```
color "mib_blackbody" (
    scalar          "temperature",
    scalar          "intensity")
```

temperature gives the temperature in degree Kelvin to be used for the calculation of the blackbody radiation spectrum. The smallest temperatures provided should be near 1000 Kelvin.

intensity. The shader only computes the color corresponding to the provided temperature, but it does not compute the associated intensity. Instead this intensity parameter, with a default value of 1, is used.

C.12   Shadow

Shadow shaders can only be attached to `shadow` statements in material statements, directly or indirectly in a Phenomenon. They are called when a shadow ray hits an occluding object; the shadow shader of the occluding object controls how much light is transmitted. Shadow shaders are special in that their result color is also an input color, which means that the output cannot be attached to another shader parameters because such attachments are one-way, output-to-parameter only. In a Phenomenon, shadow shaders can only be attached to a material inside the Phenomenon, or to the Phenomenon root if the Phenomenon is attached to a material's shadow shader.

Transparency

The transparency shadow shader can be used to assign a (possibly transparent) color to an object, and to make it transparent for shadow rays. Either a color alpha < 1 or a nonzero transparency cause shadow rays to be transmitted through the object.

```
color "mib_shadow_transparency" (
    color           "color",
    color           "transp",
    integer         "mode",
    array light     "light")
```

color is the RGBA color of the object, which becomes a multiplier for the light color being transmitted.

transp is an RGB transparency. Value 0 is opaque; value 1 is fully transparent. Internally, the transparency RGB components are multiplied by the alpha value of the color before being used.

mode controls the meaning of the light list: all (0), inclusive (1), exclusive (2), or no light dependency (3).

light is a list of light instances to loop over to detect whether the current light (for which shadows are being evaluated) does cause a shadow to be cast from this object. This lets a material control which lights it casts shadows for. If the mode is 0, consider every light in the light list parameter. If the mode is 1, consider all lights in the global light list that correspond to the lights in the light list parameter (inclusive mode). If the mode is 2, consider all lights in the global light list that do not correspond to the lights in the light list parameter (exclusive mode). If the mode is 3, the light list is ignored and a shadow is always cast (which is more efficient than mode 2 with an empty light list).

C.13   Light Mapping

mental ray 3.0 supports light mapping. This is a two-stage process that runs on certain objects (whose materials contain a lightmap shader) to compute illumination or other information, and write the result into a texture or elsewhere. The first stage calls the lightmap shader in *vertex mode* once for every vertex of the object, and collects the returned information. The second stage calls the lightmap shader in *output mode* to use the collected information to paint a texture or other output data by looping over all triangles of the object.

The lightmap shaders in the base shader library collect direct and indirect illumination, and create a writable texture map from it. Although mental ray knows only about one lightmap shader, the base lightmap shader is split into the main shader that handles the output stage, and a separate shader for the vertex stage that is called by the main shader. This makes it easier to substitute only one stage with another user-written shader.

Illumination Sampling

The lightmap illumination sampling shader is a simple color shader that samples the surface light influx density. It gathers direct illumination and optionally indirect illumination. It should not be used in a material; instead, it should be assigned to the **input** parameter of the *mib_lightmap_write* shader.

```
color "mib_lightmap_sample" (
    boolean         "indirect",
    integer         "flip",
    array light     "lights"
)
```

indirect tells the shader to sample indirect illumination too.

flip is an integer value, selecting the side of the geometry to be illuminated. A value of 0 selects the direction of the normal (front side), 1 selects the opposite direction (back side) and 2 selects that illumination be sampled from both directions and combined.

lights is the array of lights from which direct illumination should be sampled.

Lightmap Generation

The lightmap generation shader is the main lightmap shader. It gathers geometric information and texture coordinates on the triangle vertices and then writes a triangular region of texture for each triangle. For each pixel of the texture that the triangle covers, a sampling function is called and the results are written to the shader. The lightmap shader is attached to a material using the lightmap keyword.

```
struct {
    vector          "point",
    vector          "normal",
    vector          "tex"
} "mib_lightmap_write" (
    color texture   "texture",
    vector texture  "coord",
    color texture   "input"
)
```

texture is the writable texture where the lightmap will be written. It must have been declared with the writable keyword.

coord is a shader that returns the texture UV coordinates at the current particular point, such as *mib_texture_remap*.

input is a shader returning the data to be written to each texture pixel. For example, using mib_lightmap_sample here is useful to gather illumination to write into the light map.

C.14   Lens

Lens shaders may not only be used to change the direction of eye rays. They may also be used to manipulate colors and even the apparent shape of the rendered images.

Stencil

The stencil lens shader may be used to block out portions of an image by overlaying a stencil texture. Only if the returned value of the provided scalar texture is between the prescribed floor and ceiling value an eye ray will be cast. If the texture value is below the provided floor value, then the floor color will be used, if the texture value is above the ceiling value, then the ceiling color will be used. If the texture value is between the floor and the ceiling value, then the returned color will be blended with the floor color with the weight provided by the relative texture value with respect to the floor and ceiling values.

```
color "mib_lens_stencil" (
    scalar          "floor",
    scalar          "ceiling",
    color           "floor_color",
    color           "ceiling_color",
    scalar texture  "stencil")
```

floor: if the value of the scalar stencil texture is below this value, then the current sample color is replaced with the floor color. The default floor value is 0.

ceiling: if the value of the scalar stencil texture is above this value, then the current sample color is replaced with the ceiling color. The default ceiling value is 1.

floor_color is the color used for samples where the scalar stencil texture value is less than the floor value. The default value is black.

ceiling_color is the color used for samples where the scalar stencil texture value is greater than the ceiling value. The default value is black.

stencil is a scalar-valued 2D texture acting as a stencil overlaid over the camera lens.

Clamp

This lens shader maps color components lying between a floor and a ceiling value to the unit interval. Values below and above those limits are clamped to 0 and 1, respectively. If the mode of the shader is set to luminance, then the sample colors with a luminance below the floor value are replaced by the floor color and sample colors with a luminance above the ceiling value are replaced by the ceiling color. Color values with luminance between those bounds are linearly scaled to luminances between 0 and 1.

```
color "mib_lens_clamp" (
    scalar          "floor",
    scalar          "ceiling",
    boolean         "luminance",
    color           "floor_color",
    color           "ceiling_color")
```

floor is the lower bound. Color coponents below this value are set to 0 if luminance is false. In luminance mode, color samples with luminance below this value are assigned the floor color. The default value is 0.

ceiling is the upper bound. Color components greater than this value are set to 1 if luminance is false. In luminance mode, color samples with values greater than this value are assigned the ceiling color. The default value is 1.

luminance: if true, the shader operates in luminance mode. If false, the shader operates in color component mode.

floor_color: in luminance mode all color samples with a luminance below the floor value will be assigned this color. The default value is black. This parameter is ignored in color component mode.

ceiling_color: in luminance mode all color samples with a luminance greater than the ceiling value will be assigned this color. The default value is black. This paramter is ignored in color component mode.

Appendix D

Physics Shaders *

This shader library provides a collection of shaders that implement caustics, global illumination and other functions that support physical correctness.

Before any shader in the physics shader library can be used, it must be attached to the mental ray rendering software using a statement `link "physics.so"`, and the shaders must be declared with the statement `$include <physics.mi>`. Declarations are given in mi format, as described in chapter 11 on page 271. Here is the summary:

group	shader	page
Lens	*physical_lens_dof*	567
Light	*physical_light*	568
Material	*dgs_material*	569
	dielectric_material	570
Photon	*dgs_material_photon*	571
	dielectric_material_photon	571
Participating Media	*parti_volume*	572
	parti_volume_photon	574
	transmat	574
	transmat_photon	575

D.1 Lens Shader: physical_lens_dof

This lens shader simulates depth of field by casting multiple eye rays into the scene such that an object at the focal distance is sharp and in focus, while objects at other distances are blurred. This shader is available only with the physics shader library included with mental ray 2.1.

```
color "physical_lens_dof" (
    scalar          "plane",
    scalar          "radius")
```

plane is the focal distance at which objects appear in focus. More precisely it is the negative Z coordinate of the focus plane in camera space. It must be a positive number.

radius is the radius of confusion at the camera's focal distance. Larger numbers increase the blurring effect. Note that typical values are small, and large values can reduce the entire scene to a noisy cloud.

D.2   Light Shader: physical_light

The light shader *physical_light* models physically correct light sources. As for ideal point lights, the light intensity falls off with the inverse square of the distance. If physical correctness is not important, this falloff can be modified by changing *exponent*; in general the falloff is $1/e^d$ where e is the falloff exponent and d is the distance between the light source and the illuminated point. For directional lights there is no falloff since the light rays are parallel.

```
color "physical_light" (
    color           "color",
    scalar          "cone",
    scalar          "threshold",
    scalar          "cos_exp")
```

color specifies the light energy. Since this shader is physically correct, its energy is distance-dependent and not normally in the range 0...1. This is normally a copy of the light source energy, but keeping it separate makes it possible to adjust direct and indirect illumination separately.

cone is the cosine of the opening angle of the inner solid cone, if the shader is attached to a spot light source.

threshold is for optimization: if the illumination is less than threshold, the illumination can be discarded and no shadow rays need to be cast. The default is 0.

cos_exp is for flat area lights only (rectangle and disc): the default cosine illumination distribution is made more narrow by taking cosine to the cos_exp power. The default is 1.

The shader reads the direction, spread, and exponent parameters directly from the light source.

D.3   Materials

The material shaders *dgs_material* and *dielectric_material* implement different physically based models of reflection and refraction.

Diffuse-glossy-specular Material Shader: dgs_material

The *dgs_material* material shader can simulate mirrors, glossy paint or plastic, anisotropic glossy materials such as brushed metal, diffuse materials such as paper, translucent materials such as frosted glass, and any combination of these. This shader cannot be used as a shadow shader because shadows can only be computed along straight light rays, which does not agree with the definition of DGS materials. Use global illumination to illuminate objects in partial shadow from DGS objects.

```
color "dgs_material" (
    color           "diffuse",
    color           "glossy",
    color           "specular",
    scalar          "shiny",
    scalar          "shiny_u",
    scalar          "shiny_v",
    scalar          "transp",
    scalar          "ior",
    array light     "lights")
```

diffuse is added to the result for each light, after multiplication with the color returned by the light and a weight based on the dot product of the incident light direction and the light direction.

glossy provides the color of glossy highlights.

specular provides the color of mirror reflections.

shiny determines the width of the isotropic glossy reflection, in a manner similar to the Phong reflection exponent: 5 is very wide and 100 is very narrow. If shiny is nonzero, the following five anisotropic parameters are ignored.

shiny_u and **shiny_v** are used for anisotropic glossy reflection. The specify the width of the glossy reflection is in the first derivative U and V directions. (Derivatives must be enabled or specified on the polygons or free-form surfaces that this shader is applied to.) The regular shiny parameter must be undefined or set to 0.

transp specifies transparency (if ior is 1) or refractivity (if ior is not 1). It also indirectly specifies reflectivity, as 1 − *transp*. Specular transmission is the same as refraction, while glossy and diffuse transmission is known as translucency.

ior is the index of refraction of the material. Metals typically have higher index of refraction than glass.

lights is a list of light instances that illuminate the material.

For isotropic reflection, use the shiny parameter and leave the shiny_u and shiny_v parameters undefined. If the shiny parameter is undefined or zero, the shader will check whether shiny_u and shiny_v are defined and nonzero, and if so, compute anisotropic reflection. The surface U direction is used as the anisotropic brushing direction.

Dielectric Material Shader: dielectric_material

The *dielectric_material* shader is a physically based material shader which can be used to simulate dielectric media such as glass, water, and other liquids. The shader uses Fresnel's formulas for dielectric interfaces. This means that most light is transmitted through the surface for perpendicular incident directions while most light is reflected by the surface for grazing incident angles, simulating the behavior of real dielectric materials. The shader also uses Beer's law for absorption of light that passes through a medium. This means that the light is subject to an exponential falloff as it is transmitted between two surfaces with dielectric material.

Two types of dielectric interfaces are supported: dielectric-air simulates the interface between a dielectric material and air, such as glass-air, and dielectric-dielectric simulates the interface between two dielectric materials, such as glass-water.

Two achieve physically correct simulations it is important to use the correct surface interfaces. When modeling a glass of cognac three different interfaces are required: glass-air, glass-cognac, and cognac-air. The dielectric material uses the normals of the surface to distinguish the media on either side of the interface. For a dielectric-air interface the normals point into the air. For a dielectric-dielectric interface the normal point into a dielectric material which is "outside". To use the dielectric material the model normals must be oriented correctly unless the ignore_normals parameter is set to true. This shader cannot be used as a shadow shader.

```
color "dielectric_material" (
    color           "col",
    scalar          "ior",
    color           "col_out",
    scalar          "ior_out",
    boolean         "ignore_normals"
    scalar          "phong_coef",
    array lights    "lights"
)
```

The components of the declaration are:

col is the "persistence" coefficient which corresponds to the fraction of light which is left after traversing one unit of material. Thus 0.9 means that 10% of the light is absorbed per unit length of the material. Lengths are measured in world coordinates.

ior is the index of refraction of the dielectric material.

col_out: if specified, the material is a dielectric-dielectric interface and col_out is the persistence coefficient of the outside dielectric material.

ior_out is used in combination with col_out to describe the outside dielectric material.

ignore_normals: normally the decision whether a ray enters or leaves the object is based on the direction of the normal (towards or away from the incident ray). If the object is poorly modeled and the normals cannot be trusted, this flag can be set to make the dielectric material shader count the number of times the ray has entered and left the object before instead of relying on the normal direction.

pcoef is a phong coefficient used to compute *normalized phong highlights* which again is used to generate a fake impression of an area light source. If this component is zero there will be no fake highlights and only the reflected rays can create highlight effects if they hit something bright.

lights is a local list of light instances specifying just those light sources which should be used with the normalized phong highlight. If this list is omitted, the global list of light instances is used (that is, all light sources in the scene graph).

D.4 Photon Tracing

Caustics and global illumination are computed by photon tracing. Each object needs a photon material shader for photon tracing. A photon shader will usually have the same name as the corresponding material shader, but with "_photon" appended. When using one of these photon shaders in a material that uses the corresponding material shader (which has the same name but without "_photon"), omitting all photon shader parameters causes mental ray to pass the material shader parameters to the photon shader. This avoids having to specify all parameters twice.

Diffuse-glossy-specular Material Photon Shader: dgs_material_photon

The photon shader *dgs_material_photon* is used for photon tracing of objects that have the *dgs_material* material shader. It has the same parameters as *dgs_material*.

Dielectric Material Photon Shader: dielectric_material_photon

The photon shader *dielectric_material_photon* is used for photon tracing of objects that have the *dielectric_material* material shader. It has the same parameters as *dielectric_material*.

D.5 Participating Media

Fog, clouds, silty water, and similar media scatter some of the light that travels through it. In other words, these media participate in the light transport (see [Jensen 98]). A volume shader is needed to simulate participating media.

Volume Shader: parti_volume

The volume shader *parti_volume* can simulate homogeneous (uniform density) and nonhomogeneous participating media with isotropic (diffuse) or anisotropic scattering. *parti_volume* and *parti_volume_photon* use a two-lobed scattering model, which means that light scatters both forward and back in the incoming light direction. This scattering model is invented by Ch. Schlick and can model real scattering from dust, mist, rain-drops, etc.

Any medium (other than a vacuum) is assumed to contain suspended particles which scatter light traveling through it. Scattering plays an important role in the shading of volumes, and it is the size of the particles in relation to the wavelength of light which determines the type of scattering. If the particle radii are much smaller than the wavelength of light, there is no discernible scattering and the light is absorbed. Particles only slightly smaller than the wavelength of light produce what is known as Rayleigh scattering (cigarette smoke and dust). Particles roughly the same size as the wavelength of light give rise to Mie scattering (water droplets or fog). The Mie model can account for both sparse and dense particle densities, referred to as Hazy Mie and Murky Mie respectively. When the particle size is much larger than the wavelength of light, geometric optics comes into effect (normal solid surfaces). Glassner suggests the following values:

function	r	g1	g2
Rayleigh	0.50	-0.46	0.46
Hazy Mie	0.12	-0.50	0.70
Murky Mie	0.19	-0.65	0.91

```
color "parti_volume" (
        integer    "mode",
        color      "scatter",
        scalar     "extinction",
        scalar     "r",
        scalar     "g1",
        scalar     "g2",
        scalar     "nonuniform",
        scalar     "height",
        scalar     "min_step_len",
        scalar     "max_step_len",
        scalar     "light_dist",
        integer    "min_level",
        boolean    "no_globil_where_direct",
        array light "lights")
```

mode: in mode 0, the participating medium fills the entire volume. In mode 1, there is only participation medium below the given height, and there is clear air or vacuum above.

scatter is the color of the scattering medium. This determines the color of the direct and indirect light that is scattered by the medium. It also acts as a multiplier of the photon energy for the photons in the photon volume map. It inversely depends on the extinction coefficient.

extinction is the extinction coefficient of the medium. It determines how much light is absorbed or scattered in the medium. 0 means clear air or vacuum. The higher the coefficient, the denser the medium (and the more photon scattering). Note that a high extinction coefficient does not allow photons to enter deep into the volume, as they are already scattered after a short distance.

r, g1, and **g2** control scattering. If both g1 and g2 are zero (the default), isotropic scattering is modeled: all scattering directions have equal probability. This is sometimes also called diffuse scattering. Anisotropic reflection is modeled by a two-lobed scattering model. Each lobe can be either backscattering ($-1 < g < 0$), diffuse (isotropic, $g = 0$), or forward scattering ($0 < g < 1$). The first lobe is weighted by r, the second lobe by $1 - r$.

nonuniform determines if the medium is homogeneous (uniform density) or nonhomogeneous (cloud-like density variation). It is a number between 0 and 1. A value of 0 makes the medium is completely homogeneous and depends only on the extinction parameter. A value of 1 creates a cloud-like Blinn density variation. Values between 0 and 1 give a mix between the two extremes.

height determines the height above which there is clear air or vacuum if the mode parameter is 1.

min_step_len and **max_step_len** are used to determine the step length for ray marching. Usually keep the min value at 10 percent of max. The smaller the max is, the more accurately, though slowly, the volume steps will be sampled for visibility. The same parameter is used in mib_parti_volume_photon for volume photon lookup.

light_dist is used for optimization of the sampling of area light sources. It is used if the area light source has the optional lower sampling, as in for example

```
rectangle  0.5 0.0 0.0   0.0 0.0 0.5   10 10 3 2 2
```

For efficiency, *parti_volume* always uses the lower number of samples (here 2 2). This is usually sufficient since the direct illumination is computed at many points along each ray during ray marching. However, the higher number of samples (here 10 10) should be used near an area light source. The light_dist parameter determines how far away from a light source the higher number of samples have to be used.

min_level is ignored (it is used by the corresponding volume photon shader).

no_globil_where_direct tells the shader to compute direct illumination only, but no global illumination for the volume effect. This parameter is for optimization if the global contribution is not required. When set to 1 (on), the parameters relative to the directionality of the scattering effect, **r, g1**, and **g2**, are not taken into account for the indirect illumination, but they are evaluated for direct illumination.

lights is an array of light instances.

D.6   Photon Tracing in Participating Media

In order to compute volume caustics and global illumination in participating media, the media need volume photon shaders. A volume photon shader will usually have the same name as the corresponding volume shader, but with "_photon" appended. Details on photon tracing in volumes can be found in the mental ray manual.

Volume Photon Shader: parti_volume_photon

parti_volume_photon is the volume photon shader that matches *parti_volume*. It has the same parameters.

```
color "parti_volume_photon" (
        integer    "mode",
        color      "scatter",
        scalar     "extinction",
        scalar     "r",
        scalar     "g1",
        scalar     "g2",
        scalar     "height",
        scalar     "nonuniform",
        scalar     "min_step_len",
        scalar     "max_step_len",
        scalar     "light_dist",
        integer    "min_level",
        boolean    "no_globil_where_direct",
        array light "lights")
```

scatter is the color of the scattering medium. It determines the color of the indirect light that is scattered by the medium. It also acts as a multiplier for the photon energy for the photons in the volume photon map. Note that in mental ray there are three data structures where photon can stored: the GI, the caustics and the volume photon photon map. The first two can be independently color corrected.

min_level is the minimum refraction level at which photons are stored. This is handled differently for caustic and GI photons. For GI photons the maximum level is set with the global option `photon_refraction_depth`. Caustics photons storage is very different. It depends on more variables. First the global option `photon autovolume` can be set or not. If it is not set then caustic photons are only stored after at least one refraction or reflection. If it is set, and the light source is inside the volume then caustic photons can be stored. If the light source is outside the volume, then caustic photons are only stored after at least one refraction or reflection.

light_dist, **no_globil_where_direct**, and **lights** are ignored since there is no direct illumination in the photon shader.

All other parameters, especially **extinction**, need to be identical to the parameters of *parti_volume*, to preserve consistency.

Material Shader: transmat

This is a material shader for a helper surface of a participating medium. It simply traces a ray further in the direction it came from. Helper objects are used to enclose volume effects such as participating media implemented as volume shaders, without being visible themselves.

```
color "transmat" ()
```

There are no parameters.

Photon Shader: transmat_photon

transmat_photon is the material photon shader that matches *transmat*. It has the same parameters. It simply traces a photon further in the direction it came from.

```
color "transmat_photon" ()
```

There are no parameters.

D.7 Physically Correct Subsurface Scattering

The *misss_physical* shader simulates subsurface scattering in a physically correct way, attempting to simulate reality trough the same (but simplified) mechanism which happens in the natural world. Its goal is to provide subsurface scattering simulation in the situations where the *misss_fast_** shaders might encounter difficulties, for instance when photon tracing comes into play: consider a situation where photons from the environment need to interact with an object with subsurface scattering, as well as when photons coming out from such an object and need to interact with the surroundings. Another example is light scattering trough geometry, as in a fiber channel.

One of the design goals of the *misss_fast_** shaders is to provide a way to efficiently render human skin. They are most suitable for shallow (near surface) scattering. While they do support "through" scattering it is not truly volumetric and most suitable for translucency of relatively thin objects such as ears. For true volumetric results the physical shader is recommended.

The Physical shader is recommended for:

- jade, emerald, and other highly translucent minerals.
- milk, blood, ketchup, ivory soap.
- thick slabs of translucent materials.
- anything where light scatters deeply.
- when rendering accuracy is important.
- users that have experience with setting up scenes for global illumination.

The Fast shader is recommended for:

- leaves, grass, plastic, wax, butter.

- human skin, such as backlit ears.

- when rendering speed is important.

- when memory is important.

- materials into which light does not penetrate deeply.

The shader library exports a shader which must be used both in the material shader and photon shader slots of a material. In addition, a material Phenomenon is provided. It internally connects the *misss_physical* shader both to material and photon slots.

Type	name	page
Shader	*misss_physical*	578
Phenomenon	*misss_physical_phen*	579

D.7.1   Scene Requirements

In order to work correctly with the *misss_physical* shader, it is necessary to set up the scene following these requirements:

- Version: this shader will not work with version of mental ray prior to 3.3.

- Link/include: link the subsurface shader library and include the subsurface.mi shader declaration file in the .rayrc file, or in the scene file itself, if this is not handled automatically by the modeling package that mental ray is built into.

- Raytracing must be activated.

- Caustics and/or global illumination must be enabled. (Caustics only is preferred to global illumination only.)

- A light, preferably focused on the subsurface-scattering media object must specify an energy value as well as emit caustic and/or globillum photons.

- The *misss_physical* shader must be used both as a material and a photon shader, or the material Phenomenon must be used. It must have a light that emits photons in its lightlist.

- Subsurface-scattering objects or their instances must be flagged as receiving and casting caustics and/or global illumination.

The following .mi scene fragments ensure that the conditions are met:

- At the beginning of the scene file:

```
min version "3.3.0.7"
link "subsurface.so"
$include "subsurface.mi"
```

- In the options block:

```
trace on
caustic on
globillum on
```

- In the light definition (example):

```
energy 10000 10000 10000
caustic photons 250000
globillum photons 250000
```

- The shader and material definition:

```
shader "myshader" "misss_physical" ("lights" [ "lightinstancename" ])
material options
material "materialinstancename"
    = "myshader"
    photon = "myshader"
end material
```

- In the object or its instance definition:

```
caustic 3
globillum 3
```

The shader provides useful feedback when executed, using info messages. In any case verbosity level 5 is suggested to debug your scene. The shader statistics reports are especially valuable to estimate correct values for the following parameters:

- depth: look for information in "channel 0 1 2" and "photon statistics".

- max_radius and max_photons. Look for information in "multi-scatter photon per samples statistics".

D.7.2   Shaders

D.7.2.1   misss_physical

The *misss_physical* shader performs three kinds of calculations which can be used together or independently, as described here:

- Multiple-scattering estimation, the most accurate, uses a strictly deterministic simulation of photon tracing to record sites in an internal photon map. These sites are looked up at render time and an optimized ray marching technique estimates multiple scatter irradiance.

- Single-scattering approximation is based on light intensities, which is independent from photon mapping.

- Diffusion theory is applied to evaluate the contribution of photons in the deep layer.

This is the shader declaration:

```
declare shader
    "misss_physical" (
        color   "material",
        color   "transmission",
        scalar  "ior",
        vector  "absorption_coeff",
        vector  "scattering_coeff",
        scalar  "scale_conversion",
        scalar  "scattering_anisotropy",
        scalar  "depth",
        integer "max_samples",
        integer "max_photons",
        scalar  "max_radius",
        boolean "approx_diffusion",
        boolean "approx_single_scatter",
        boolean "approx_multiple_scatter",
        array light "lights"
    )
    version 3
    apply material, photon
end declare
```

This shader integrates subsurface scattering seamlessly into mental ray, and supports these features:

- Simulate subsurface scattering materials both in still images and animations (although the *misss_fast_** shaders are more suitable for animation).

- Receive and continue subsurface scattering media caustics from the outside world.

- Cast caustics from the subsurface scattering media to the outside world.

- Specify both absorption and scattering coefficients. The resulting image will simulate correctly areas of absorption and areas of scattering. This is very important to get subtle color changes for example in milk from blue to yellow.

- Perform scattering along the geometry.

The shader must be used both as material and photon shader. Otherwise use the following phenomenon.

D.7.2.2   misss_physical_phen

This is a Phenomenon that allows the user to avoid setting up shading graph connections both to the material and photon slots. It has the same characteristics of the *misss_physical*.

D.7.3   Optical properties

The optical properties controlling the subsurface scattering shader are surface color, transmission color, refractive index, scattering and absorption coefficients, and the scattering function:

material provides the material shader which determines the appearance of the material and the shading model to apply at a surface level.

transmission is the transmission color or texture shader that filters light as it enters the object.

ior is the index of refraction of the material, which determines how light changes direction as it enters or leaves the material.

absorption_coeff is a measure of light attenuation as it passes through a turbid medium. Usually expressed in units of inverse length such that the product of the absorption coefficient and path length of a photon's travel through the medium, it is dimensionless and the probability of transmission is $e^{-u_a L}$ where ua is the absorption coefficient and L is the path length. When using a coefficient that has been experimentally obtained, it is important to specify a correct scale conversion ratio between coefficient units and world units. Absorption is wavelength dependent.

scattering_coeff is the scattering coefficient is a measure of light scattering as it passes through a volume. This is usually expressed in units of inverse length so that the product of the scattering coefficient and path length of a photon's travel through the volume, is dimensionless and the probability of transmission without redirection is $e^{-u_s L}$.

When using a coefficient that has been experimentally obtained, it is important to specify a correct scale conversion ratio between the coefficient units and the world units. Scattering is wavelength dependent.

The table below gives suggested scattering and absorption coefficients (based on empirical data) for several materials.

Material	Scattering_coeff	Absorption_coeff	ior
Jade	0.657 0.786 0.9	0.00053, 0.00123, 0.00213	1.3
Ketchup	0.18 0.07 0.03	0.061 0.97 1.45	1.3
Marble	2.19 2.62 3.00	0.0021 0.0041 0.0071	1.55
Skim milk	0.70 1.22 1.90	0.0014 0.0025 0.0142	1.3
Whole milk	2.55 3.21 3.77	0.0011 0.0024 0.014	1.3

scale_conversion is a transform between the world coordinate system and the units used to represent the scattering and absorption coefficients. For example, if the world coordinate system is expressed in inches and the coefficients are in millimeters, then the correct scale factor is 25.4 (mm/inch).

scattering_anisotropy is a measure of the degree of scattering. Specifically, it is the average dot product between the incident light direction and the scattered light direction. Most turbid materials do not scatter light uniformly. Values may range from -1 to 1. Where -1 corresponds to back scatter only and 1 corresponds to forward scatter only. The value 0 indicates uniform scattering in all directions.

The following simplified diagram traces the role of the scattering function:

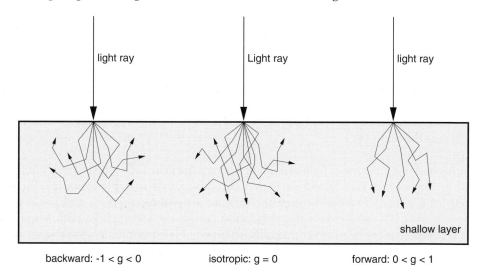

Schematic display of different values of g

D.7.4   Tuning

Properties of the algorithm control the quality and complexity of the rendering. The calculation of subsurface scattering is broken into three components: single scatter, multiple scatter, and diffusion. Depending on the optical properties of the material, the contributions of each component may dominate or be negligible. An important factor in determining this is the mean free path length of the material. This is the average distance a photon will travel in the material without scattering or absorption and is equal to the reciprocal of the sum of the scattering and absorption coefficients.

depth The shader uses two different ways to scatter photons. After a certain number of scatterings a photon is scattered less precisely, yet faster. The depth determines how many scattering events are done using the precise scattering. The precise scattering is also called "shallow layer". The depth determines the end of the shallow layer and the begin of the deep layer.

max_samples is the maximum number of samples evaluated by the single and multiple scatter components. Typical values range between 10 and 30.

max_photons is the maximum number of photons to sample per lookup. It is similar to the global illumination accuracy parameter. Typical values range between 100 to 1000. Values up to 5000 are useful for scenes with uneven photon distribution.

max_radius is the maximum radius of a sphere centered at a sample point from which to collect photons. It is similar to the global illumination accuracy radius. Typical values are a small percentage of the total size of the object.

approx_diffusion: this switch turns the diffusion component of the calculation on or off. Usually it should be on.

approx_single_scatter: this switch turns the single scatter component of the calculation on or off. Usually it should be on.

approx_multiple_scatter: this switch turns the multiple scatter component of the calculation on or off. Usually it should be on.

lights is the light list array that specifies which lights in the scene will contribute to the illumination of the material.

D.7.5   Attributes Correlations

The shader decouples subsurface scattering in the following three types of calculations:

- single scattering
- multiple scattering
- diffusion

The figure below shows how each of the three above types contributes to the overall effect:

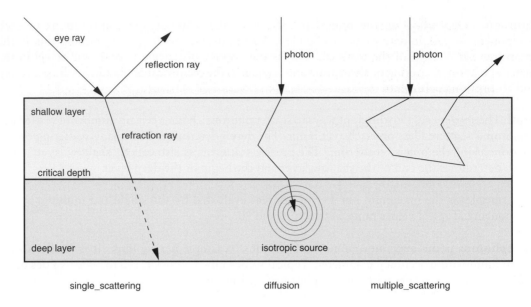

single_scattering   diffusion   multiple_scattering

Simplified diagram of single, diffuse and multiple approximation

Any of these three computations can have a dominant influence under differing optical parameters. For example, single scattering has dominance under low scattering conditions, whereas multiple scattering and diffusion approximation dominate under high scattering conditions, for example, where the scattering coefficient is much larger than the absorption coefficient.

Many parameters of the shader affect all three components, while few parameters act on specific components only. The table below shows a summary.

Parameter	Diffuse	Single	Multi
Depth	yes	no	yes
Max_samples	no	yes	yes
Max_radius	no	no	yes

The other two parameters which are correlated are the max_photons and max_radius. Photon averaging can be forced by increasing lookup radius. The figure below shows a series of images from the milk tutorial, where max_radius and max_photons parameters are increased to force photon averaging.

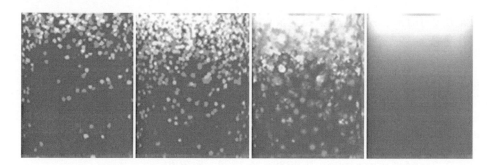

max_radius and max_photons increase from left to right.

Each instance of the *misss_physical* shader reports information about its rendered results.   A sample information report is as follows:

```
PHEN 0.2 info : "SkimMilk|Shader" channels 0  1   2
PHEN 0.2 info : albedo: 99.80 99.80 99.26
PHEN 0.2 info : coefficient of extinction: 0.70 1.22 1.91
PHEN 0.2 info : mean free path length: 1.43 0.82 0.52
PHEN 0.2 info : reduced albedo: 99.01 98.99 96.40
PHEN 0.2 info : reduced coefficient of extinction: 0.14 0.25 0.39
PHEN 0.2 info : reduced mean free path length: 7.07 4.06 2.54
PHEN 0.2 info : critical depth: 0.00 0.00 0.00

PHEN 0.2 info : "SkimMilk|Shader" photon statistics
PHEN 0.2 info : received: 41328
PHEN 0.2 info : channels 0 1 2:
PHEN 0.2 info : stored: 44335 44932 43903
PHEN 0.2 info : stored: 2155 2412 2566 isotropic
PHEN 0.2 info : propagated: 2526 2266 2101
PHEN 0.2 info : scatter depth:
PHEN 0.2 info : min: 1.00 1.00 2.00
PHEN 0.2 info : max: 69.00 82.00 64.00
PHEN 0.2 info : mean: 12.75 12.78 12.66
PHEN 0.2 info : variance: 59.85 64.61 57.77

PHEN 0.2 info : "SkimMilk|Shader" multi-scatter component
PHEN 0.2 info : samples: 79364
PHEN 0.2 info : channels 0 1 2:
PHEN 0.2 info : minimum: 0.0000, 0.0000, 0.0000
PHEN 0.2 info : maximum: 19.9112, 31.2088, 53.3636
PHEN 0.2 info : mean: 4.4254, 5.9017, 6.6080
PHEN 0.2 info : variance: 12.2979, 28.7988, 50.9151

PHEN 0.2 info : "SkimMilk|Shader" multi-scatter photons per sample
PHEN 0.2 info : photons: 476184
PHEN 0.2 info : minimum: 0.0000
```

```
PHEN 0.2 info : maximum: 512.0000
PHEN 0.2 info : mean: 503.7983
PHEN 0.2 info : variance: 3104.0889

PHEN 0.2 info : "SkimMilk|Shader" isotropic scatter component

PHEN 0.2 info : samples: 39682
PHEN 0.2 info : channels 0 1 2:
PHEN 0.2 info : minimum: 0.0000, 0.0000, 0.0000
PHEN 0.2 info : maximum: 6.4335, 8.1329, 5.3061
PHEN 0.2 info : mean: 3.1183, 3.1236, 1.5807
PHEN 0.2 info : variance: 2.1284, 3.0800, 1.3180

PHEN 0.2 info : "SkimMilk|Shader" results
PHEN 0.2 info : minimum: 0.1085, 0.1059, 0.1020
PHEN 0.2 info : maximum: 32.8014, 35.6229, 29.9977
PHEN 0.2 info : mean: 4.0739, 4.4873, 3.7535
PHEN 0.2 info : variance: 6.6836, 9.3765, 10.9592
PHEN 0.2 info : "SkimMilk|Shader" sampled 79364 single scatter sites
```

The seven main categories contained in the report are:

- Optical properties of the medium that are derived from the shader parameters.

- Photon statistics:
  – Number of photons received from all sources, global illum and caustics.
  – Number of photons and photon type stored per color channel.
  – Number of photons propagated back into the scene.
  – Scatter chain depth.

- QMC scatter component statistics and irradiance.

- Isotropic scatter component irradiance.

- Final results.

The list below provides explanation for some of the photon statistics.

- `PHEN 0.2 info :  "SkimMilk|Shader" photon statistics:`
  `PHEN 0.2 info :  received:  41328`
  Provides the number of photons that hit the object and invoked the shader.

- `PHEN 0.2 info :  stored:  44335 44932 43903`
  The number of photons that were stored in the shallow layer for each color channel.

- `PHEN 0.2 info :  stored:  2155 2412 2566 isotropic`
  The number of photons that were stored in the deep (isotropic) layer for each color channel.

- `PHEN 0.2 info :  propagated:  2526 2266 2101`
  The number of photons that re-emerged from the object back into the scene for each color channel.

D.7.6   Known Issues and Limitations

Issue or limitation	Workaround
The shader does not work with mental ray core version prior to 3.3, this is due to a newer and required version of the KD tree.	Use 3.3 or later.
SDS (SubDivision Surfaces) are not supported yet	Convert to polymeshes or NURBS.
Network parallelism is not supported yet.	None.
Absorption and scattering coefficients may require 4 or more digit numbers after the comma, some OEM UI's show only 3 digits in regular field numbers. However, extra digits are interpreted correctly.	None.
Objects should have an entering and exiting surface in order to store photons correctly, open surfaces/meshes/sds (when supported) may cause storage problems.	Model with an eye on the storing process, think volumetrically.

Contour Shaders *

The contour shader library contains a number of contour shaders that are useful for rendering cartoon-type images. For details on contour rendering, see chapter 10.

Before any shader in the contour shader library can be used, it must be attached to the mental ray rendering software using a statement link "contour.so", and the shaders must be declared with the statement $include <contour.mi>. Declarations are given in mi format, as described in chapter 11 on page 271. Here is the summary:

group	shader	page
Contour store	*contour_store_function*	588
	contour_store_function_simple	588
Contour contrast	*contour_contrast_function_levels*	588
	contour_contrast_function_simple	589
Contour shader	*contour_shader_simple*	589
	contour_shader_curvature	590
	contour_shader_widthfromcolor	590
	contour_shader_factorcolor	591
	contour_shader_depthfade	592
	contour_shader_framefade	593
	contour_shader_widthfromlight	594
	contour_shader_widthfromlightdir	594
	contour_shader_layerthinner	595
	contour_shader_combi	596
Contour output	*contour_only*	598
	contour_composite	598
	contour_ps	599

E.1   Contour Store Shaders

Contour store shaders decide what kind of information to store at an image sample location. This information allows the contour contrast shader to decide whether two samples are different enough to place a contour line between them. The contour store shaders have no shader parameters.

```
"contour_store_function" ()

"contour_store_function_simple" ()
```

The *contour_store_function* shader returns the intersection point, normal, material tag, object label (tag), triangle index, color, and the refraction and reflection level.

The *contour_store_function_simple* contour store function only stores the material tag. It can be used for very fast contour computations if only the outlines of objects need to have contours (and if they should only have simple contours).

E.2   Contour Contrast Shaders

There are two built-in contour contrast shaders. Contour contrast shaders specify where there should be a contour by comparing the information stored by the contour store shader during sampling. The two contour contrast shaders are designed to be paired with the standard and simple contour store shaders described above, respectively.

contour_contrast_function_levels

```
"contour_contrast_function_levels" (
    scalar          "zdelta",
    scalar          "ndelta",
    boolean         "diff_mat",
    boolean         "diff_label",
    boolean         "diff_index",
    boolean         "contrast",
    integer         "min_level",
    integer         "max_level"
)
```

The following parameters are available:

zdelta is the minimum depth difference required to cause a contour, measured in coordinate units.

ndelta is the minimum angle difference between normal vectors required to cause a contour, measured in degrees.

diff_mat, if set to on, causes a contour between different materials.

diff_label, if set to on, causes a contour between different object labels. It can be used to outline objects.

diff_index, if set to on, causes a contour between different triangles. It can be used to draw triangle wireframes.

contrast, if set to on, causes a contour between colors that exceed the contrast threshold specified in the options block. In the case of semitransparent object, contrasts caused by other objects behind the semitransparent object are taken into account.

min_level and **max_level** limit contours to ray generations of at least min_level and at most max_level. Every reflection and refraction counts as one level. For example, to exclude contours around reflections and refractions, set max_level to 0.

contour_contrast_function_levels_simple

This shader can be used for very fast contour computations along with *contour_store_function_simple* if only the outlines of objects need to have contours (and if they should only have simple contours). This shader has no parameters.

```
"contour_contrast_function_simple" ()
```

E.3   Material Contour Shaders

After the contour contrast shaders have decided where contours should be drawn, contour shaders decide on the contour color and width (and optionally motion, normal, material tag, and label).

Simple contours: contour_shader_simple

A material gets a simple contour of constant color and width if it references the *contour_shader_simple* contour shader.

```
"contour_shader_simple" (
    color          "color",
    scalar         "width"
)
```

The following parameters are available:

color is the color of the contour.

width is the width of the contour, in percent of the image width. Percentages allow scaling of the image without changing the relative contour width.

Curvature-dependent Width: contour_shader_curvature

This shader draws contours whose width depends on the curvature (the difference in surface orientation). If θ is the angle between two surface normals, the width is computed by the formula $(W - w)(1 - \cos\theta)/2 + w$, where w is the parameter min_width and W is the parameter max_width. So if two normals are in nearly opposite directions, there is a contour of width close to max_width between them. When the angle between them decreases, the width of the contour decreases down to nearly min_width. (The width will never reach min_width completely, since the contour contrast function will not create any contours where the surface curvature is less than ndelta degrees, and ndelta can not be set to zero without getting contours in the interior of all objects.

At the edge of an object, where the depth difference is large, the maximum contour width is used. The minimum width would theoretically occur at 0 degrees and the maximum width at 180 degrees.

```
"contour_shader_curvature" (
    color          "color",
    scalar         "min_width",
    scalar         "max_width"
)
```

The following parameters are available:

color is the color of the contour.

min_width is the minimum contour width, in percent of the image size.

max_width is the maximum contour width, in percent of the image size.

Color-dependent Width: contour_shader_widthfromcolor

With the contour_shader_widthfromcolor contour shader, a material gets contours whose thickness depends on material color. The thickness depends on the maximum m of the red, green, and blue color bands. (m is clamped to 1 if it is larger than 1.) The width is computed as $(W - w)(1 - m) + w$, where w is the parameter min_width and W is the parameter max_width. When the color is bright no contour is visible, and when the color gets darker the contour gets wide. The minimum width is used at bright colors and the maximum width is used at black.

```
"contour_shader_widthfromcolor" (
    color          "color",
    scalar         "min_width",
    scalar         "max_width"
)
```

The following parameters are available:

color is the color of the contour.

min_width is the minimum contour width, in percent of the image size.

max_width is the maximum contour width, in percent of the image size.

For example, to get black contours that are thick where the material is in shadow and thin where the material is brightly illuminated, specify

```
contour "contour_shader_widthfromcolor" (
    "color"        0 0 0 1,  # solid black
    "min_width"    0.5,      # min width
    "max_width"    1.5       # max width
)
```

Note that for semitransparent materials, the material color is not just the color of the object material under the given illumination; the color of the objects behind the material is also taken into account.

Color from Material Color: contour_shader_factorcolor

This shader draws a contour whose color matches the color of the object being contoured, only with a different brightness (usually much darker).

```
"contour_shader_factorcolor" (
    scalar          "factor",
    scalar          "width"
)
```

The following parameters are available:

factor is the multiplier for the material color. If the factor is 0, a black contour results. If the factor is between 0 and 1, a dark contour (of the same hue as the material) results. If the factor is 1, the contour gets the same color as the material at that point. If the factor is larger than 1, bright contours of the same hue as the material result.

width is the contour width, in percent of the image size.

For example, to get contours that are half the material color and two percent wide, specify:

```
contour "contour_shader_factorcolor" (
    "factor"    0.5,    # factor of material color
    "width"     2.0     # contour width (in %)
)
```

Like the previous shader, this shader takes the color of objects behind semitransparent materials into account.

Depth-fading Contours: contour_shader_depthfade

Contours are drawn whose color and width are linearly interpolated between two values as specified with the near and far parameter sets. If a contour point is more distant than far_z, the contour gets color far_color and width far_width. If a point is nearer than near_z, the contour gets color near_color and width near_width. If the depth is in between, the color and width are linearly interpolated.

```
"contour_shader_depthfade" (
    color           "color",
    scalar          "near_z",
    color           "near_color",
    scalar          "near_width",
    scalar          "far_z",
    color           "far_color",
    scalar          "far_width"
)
```

The following parameters are available:

near_z is the minimum distance.

near_color is the color at and below the minimum distance.

near_width is the width at and below the minimum distance.

far_z is the maximum distance.

far_color is the color at and below the maximum distance.

far_width is the width at and below the maximum distance.

For example, to get contours that are interpolated between two percent wide red at depth -10 and half a percent wide blue at depth -25, specify

```
contour "contour_shader_depthfade" (
    "near_z"        -10,
    "near_color"    1 0 0 1,
    "near_width"    2,
    "far_z"         -25,
    "far_color"     0 0 1 1,
    "far_width"     0.5
)
```

Animated Contours: contour_shader_framefade

This shader draws contours with a color and width that depends linearly on the frame number. Two frame numbers, colors, and widths are specified. If the frame number is less than the first frame number, the first color and width is used. If the frame number is higher than the last frame number, the last color and width are used. If the frame number is in between, a linear interpolation of the two colors and widths are used.

```
"contour_shader_framefade" (
    integer         "frame1",
    color           "color1",
    scalar          "width1",
    integer         "frame2",
    color           "color2",
    scalar          "width2"
)
```

The following parameters are available:

frame1 is the minimum frame number.

color1 is the color at and below the minimum frame number.

width1 is the width at and below the minimum frame number.

frame2 is the maximum frame number.

color2 is the color at and below the maximum frame number.

width2 is the width at and below the maximum frame number.

In the following example, the contour will be fully opaque white before frame 3, and then disappear gradually until frame 10. After frame 10 the contour is completely transparent.

```
contour "contour_shader_framefade" (
    "frame1"        3,
    "color1"        1 1 1 1,
    "width1"        1,
    "frame2"        10,
    "color2"        0 0 0 0,
    "width2"        0.2
)
```

Width from Light Direction: contour_shader_widthfromlight

Contours are drawn whose width depends on the angle θ between the surface normal and the direction to a light source. The width is computed by the formula $(W-w)(1+\cos\theta)/2+w$, where

w is a parameter min_width and W is a parameter max_width. Therefore the thickness increases gradually from min_width when the surface is directly facing the light direction to max_width when the surface is facing exactly opposite the light direction.

```
"contour_shader_widthfromlight" (
    color          "color",
    scalar         "min_width",
    scalar         "max_width",
    light          "light"
)
```

The following parameters are available:

color is the color of the contour lines.

min_width is the minimum width of the contour.

max_width is the maximum width of the contour.

light is the light.

For example, consider the case where the name of the light source is light_0. To get black contours that are two percent wide where the surface is facing away from the light source, decreasing down to zero width where the surface is facing the light source directly, specify:

```
contour "contour_shader_widthfromlight" (
    "color"        0 0 0 1,        # contour color
    "min_width"    0.0,            # min width (%)
    "max_width"    2.0,            # max width (%)
    "light"        "light_0"       # light name
)
```

Width from Light Direction: contour_shader_widthfromlightdir

This shader is a variation of the previous one. It accepts a direction directly, instead of a light that implicitly provides the direction.

```
"contour_shader_widthfromlightdir" (
    color          "color",
    scalar         "min_width",
    scalar         "max_width",
    vector         "light_dir"
)
```

The following parameters are available:

color is the color of the contour lines.

min_width is the minimum width of the contour.

max_width is the maximum width of the contour.

light_dir is the direction to the main light source.

Width from Layer: contour_shader_layerthinner

With this contour shader, the width of a contour will change depending on how many levels of materials are on top of it. If the material is on top, its contour will be of a width specified by a parameter. For each material on top of it, its width will decrease by a factor that is also controllable with a parameter.

```
"contour_shader_layerthinner" (
    color           "color",
    scalar          "width",
    scalar          "factor"
)
```

The following parameters are available:

color is the color of the contour lines.

width is the width of the contour at the top layer.

factor is the factor to make the contour thinner for each layer.

For example, to get red contours that are 2 percent wide when the material is on top, 1 percent wide when the material is behind one other (semitransparent) material, 0.5 percent wide when the material is behind two materials, and so on, use the following:

```
contour "contour_shader_layerthinner" (
    "color"         1 0 0 1,        # contour color
    "width"         2.0,            # width at top layer (%)
    "factor"        0.5             # factor pr. layer
)
```

Combination: contour_shader_combi

This is a combination of the *depthfade*, *layerthinner*, and *widthfromlight* contour shaders. The width of the contour fades into the background (from near_width to far_width), and the color fades from near_color to far_color. The contour width and color changes with a ramp function between distances near_z and far_z. For each layer the ray has passed through, a factor is multiplied on to the width. If no factor is specified, the width will not depend on the layer. If a light source is specified, the width also depends on the surface normal relative to the light source direction.

```
"contour_shader_combi" (
    scalar          "near_z",
    color           "near_color",
    scalar          "near_width",
    scalar          "far_z",
    color           "far_color",
    scalar          "far_width",
    scalar          "factor",
    light           "light",
    scalar          "light_min_factor"
)
```

The following parameters are available:

near_z is the minimum distance.

near_color is the color at and below the minimum distance.

near_width is the width at and below the minimum distance.

far_z is the maximum distance.

far_color is the color at and below the maximum distance.

far_width is the width at and below the maximum distance.

factor is the factor to make the contour thinner for each layer. Leave this undefined to disable layer dependency.

light is the light source; leave undefined for no light dependency.

light_min_factor specifies the minimum factor that the light-dependency decreases the contour width.

For example, for contours that are interpolated between two percent wide red at depth −12 and one percent wide blue at depth −18, and get half as wide for each layer of material above this material, and where the width also depends on the direction to the light source named *mylight*, specify

```
contour "contour_shader_combi" (
                                    # interpolate from
    "near_z"        -12,            # this depth,
    "near_color"    1 0 0 1,        # color (red),
    "near_width"    2,              # and width (in %)
                                    # to
```

```
    "far_z"         -18,         # this depth
    "far_color"     0 0 1 1,     # color (blue)
    "far_width"     1,           # and width (in %).
                                 # optional:
    "factor"        0.5,         # factor pr. layer
    "light"         "mylight",   # light name
    "light_min_factor" 0.5
)
```

Contours only on Silhouette: contour_shader_silhouette

This shader only puts contours at the silhouette of objects — even if the contour contrast function has decided that there might also be contours internally on objects.

```
"contour_shader_silhouette" (
    color           "color",
    scalar          "width"
)
```

The following parameters are available:

color is the color of the contour lines.

width is the width of the contour.

Contours with Maximum Material Color: contour_shader_maxcolor

This shader takes the maximum (in each color band) of the two material colors on each side of the contour.

```
"contour_shader_maxcolor" (
    scalar          "width"
)
```

The following parameter is available:

width is the width of the contour lines.

E.4   Contour Output Shaders

Contour output shaders are called after the regular image has been computed.

Contour Image: contour_only

The contour output shader *contour_only* generates a contour image with a given background color in the color frame buffer, discarding the rendered color image.

```
"contour_only" (
    color           "background",
    boolean         "glow",
    boolean         "maxcomp"
)
```

The following parameters are available:

background is the background color (default black).

glow, if set to on, makes all contours become darker and more transparent near their edges, creating a glow effect.

maxcomp, if set to on, specifies that when a contour is over another contour, the maximum of the two colors (in each color band) should be used. If maxcomp is not specified (or set off), normal alpha compositing is used.

Composited Contour Image: contour_composite

This contour output shader generates a contour image composited over the rendered color image.

```
"contour_composite" (
    boolean         "glow",
    boolean         "maxcomp"
)
```

The following parameters are available:

glow, if set to on, makes all contours become darker and more transparent near their edges, creating a glow effect.

maxcomp, if set to on, specifies that when a contour is over another contour, the maximum of the two colors (in each color band) should be used. If maxcomp is not specified (or set off), normal alpha compositing is used.

PostScript Contours: contour_ps

The contour output shader *contour_ps* creates PostScript code with black contours. The PostScript code can be written to a file with a separate output statement that specifies the file type ps. This shader does not touch the rendered color frame buffer.

```
"contour_ps" (
    integer         "paper_size",
    scalar          "paper_scale",
    scalar          "paper_transform_b",
    scalar          "paper_transform_d",
    boolean         "title",
    boolean         "landscape",
    vector          "ink_stroke_dir",
    scalar          "ink_min_frac",
    string          "file_name"
)
```

The following parameters are available:

paper size is an integer, with 0 indicating "letter" size, 1 indicating "executive", 2 indicating "legal", 3–6 indicating "a3", "a4", "a5", "a6", 7–9 indicating "b4", "b5", "b6", and 10 indicating "11x17".

paper_scale scales the PostScript output. The default is 1.

paper_transform_b and **paper_transform_d** transform the Postscript coordinates according to the matrix $\begin{pmatrix} 1 & b \\ 0 & d \end{pmatrix}$, where b and d are the parameters paper_transform_b and paper_transform_d. This allows compensation of printers that print with a slight skew.

title, if set to on, determines whether a title (consisting of file name and frame number) and a frame around the image are written.

landscape, if set to on, makes the output be in landscape mode rather than portrait mode.

ink_stroke_dir, if set no a non-zero vector, makes the thickness of each contour line segment depend on its orientation; this gives an ink pen look. The contour lines are widest in the stroke direction.

ink_min_frac specifies how thin the "ink look" contour lines should be (relative to the maximum thickness) in directions perpendicular to ink_stroke_dir.

file_name specifies the name of the PostScript file that the contours are written to.

For example, to get a PostScript file in A4 paper size with full scale, use the following statements in the camera definition:

```
output "contour,rgba" "contour_ps" (
    "paper_size"        4,
    "paper_scale"       1.0,
    "paper_transform_b" 0.0,
    "paper_transform_d" 1.0,
    "title"             on,
    "landscape"         on,
    "file_name"         "contourimage.ps"
)
```

Glossary

Terms that are specific to mental ray and not to computer graphics in general, or are used by mental ray in a certain specific sense, are marked "ᵐʳ".

3D texture: a ▷texture that does not define a flat wallpaper but the volumic properties of a three-dimensional solid that the mapped object will appear carved out of.

adjacency detectionᵐʳ**:** a technique for automatically finding ▷connections.

aliasing: artifacts caused by insufficient sampling, for example staircase patterns on diagonal lines or Moiré patterns on small regular texture details. Avoiding aliasing is called anti-aliasing.

alpha component: the opacity of a color. An alpha of 0.0 means fully transparent, and 1.0 means fully opaque. See ▷premultiplication.

ambient color: a common material ▷shader parameter that adds a constant contribution to the color of the object surface to simulate an ambient light level that equally reaches all points of the ▷scene. For correct ambient lighting, ▷global illumination must be used instead.

ambient occlusion: a kind of simplified ▷final gathering that considers only how much an illuminated point is close to other objects that are assumed to block mostly uniform ambient light. It gives a fast but very inaccurate simulation of

▷global illumination.

animation: a computer-generated or hand-drawn film consisting of a sequence of ▷frames, each rendered independently.

anisotropic shading: a form of shading that behaves differently when rotated around the normal vector. For example, brushed aluminum looks different when seen in the brushing direction than when seen perpendicular to it.

anonymous shaderᵐʳ**:** a ▷shader instance defined with its parameters in-place where it is used, as opposed to a ▷named shader that is given its own name to allow re-use.

aperture: the opening width of a camera lens. The greater the aperture, the greater the field of view (and the greater the perspective distortion).

approximationᵐʳ**:** a description of how to ▷tessellate a geometric object into less complex primitives, usually triangles. The goal is to faithfully represent the object with the lowest possible number of triangles.

area light source: a ▷light source that has a nonzero size, with the entire surface uniformly emitting light. This causes

▷soft shadows because a point can be partially in shadow.

array: a finite, ordered list of items of the same type, such as pixels. Two-dimensional arrays are like row-column lists.

ASCII (pronounced as-key): American Standard Code for Information Interchange, a seven-bit set of control codes and printable characters. It was integrated with minor changes into the eight-bit ISO 8859 Latin-1 alphabets that are used by all modern computers.

aspect ratio: a width divided by height, usually applied to the rendered image. It is used to account for image display technology that works with nonsquare pixels, such as television.

ATM: Asynchronous Transfer Mode, a high-speed networking technology that originated with telephony applications but is often used to transfer computer data using ▷TCP/IP. Mostly obsolete now.

atmosphere: a volumic effect that simulates reduced visibility at large distances.

back culling: a technique that ignores geometry seen from behind. This can improve performance because less geometry needs to be considered, but it does not work well with transparency.

base shader^{mr}: a generic small monolithic ▷shader designed to work well in concert with other shaders, typically inside a ▷Phenomenon.

basis: the definition of a curve or surface type, such as ▷B-spline, ▷Bézier, ▷cardinal, and others.

Bézier curve: a type of smooth curve defined by control points. The curve

passes through some points, and others define tangents, which makes Bézier curves easy to handle.

big-endian: a ▷byte order defined by the microprocessor architecture or operating system that stores the high bytes first. 0x12345678 is stored as 0x12 0x34 0x56 0x78. The opposite of ▷little-endian.

Blinn shading: a technique for computing the illumination of a point on an object surface, with special attention to grazing viewing directions. Normally implemented in a ▷material shader.

BRDF: Bidirectional Reflectance Distribution Function. It describes how much light is reflected based on incoming and reflected light direction. All ▷material shaders implement a BRDF.

BSP: Binary Space Partitioning, a technique for fast ▷ray tracing that recursively subdivides 3D space into voxels.

B-spline curve: a type of smooth curve defined by control points. The curve does not usually pass through the control points.

bump map: a surface shading technique that simulates surface roughness by perturbing the ▷normal vector of the surface point.

byte order: either ▷big-endian or ▷little-endian. (Other byte orders are no longer in use.)

camera: a description of the viewpoint from which the ▷scene is rendered.

camera offset^{mr}: shifts the viewing plane of the ▷camera sideways and up or down.

camera space: a coordinate system in which the ▷camera is at the coordinate origin (0, 0, 0) and (in mental ray) looks down the negative Z axis.

cardinal curve: a type of smooth curve of degree 3 defined by control points. The curve passes through all control points.

caustics: a light pattern created by specular reflection or refraction of light, such as the patterns on the bottom of a swimming pool. mental ray simulates caustics with the ▷photon map method.

coherent noise: a mathematical function that generates deterministic pseudo-random values based on a coordinate, with identical coordinates producing identical values, and similar coordinates producing similar values. Also known as ▷Perlin noise.

color: a data type consisting of red, green, blue, and optional ▷alpha components.

color bleeding: a ▷global illumination effect that causes colored diffuse reflectors to tint neighboring surfaces. Color bleeding causes a white wall close to a red wall to appear pink because it receives red light from the wall.

command line: a line typed in at a shell prompt. A shell is an interactive command processor that ships with most operating systems.

compositing: a layering technique that pastes one image on top of another, properly taking transparent pixels (see ▷alpha) into account. Compositing utilities usually assume ▷premultiplication.

concave polygon: a polygon with edges that "cave in". A rubber band tightly wrapped around a concave polygon would not touch all its edges. Opposite of ▷convex polygon.

connection^{mr}: a specification that two surfaces are connected, causing mental ray to eliminate gaps caused by modeling imprecisions. Also see ▷edge merging.

contour: lines around certain prominent features of objects, such as edges or sharp creases. Contours are used in cartoon animation.

contrast ^{mr}: the difference of two colors, defined as RGB or RGBA difference thresholds.

control point: a 2D (UV) or 3D (XYZ) ▷vertex that helps defining a curve or ▷free-form surface.

convex hull: a convex object that fully encloses an object or other 3D entity, without caving in on itself.

convex polygon: Opposite of ▷concave polygon.

Cook-Torrance shading: a shading model similar to ▷Blinn shading. It simulates surface roughness by assuming that the roughness is caused by a random distribution of microscopic facets.

coordinate space: a way of expressing points and vectors in 3D space relative to a coordinate origin, which can be at the camera (▷camera space), in the current object (▷object space), or an arbitrary position in the ▷scene (▷world space).

Cornell box: a physical box with colored walls built at Cornell University to conduct lighting experiments and compare the results with ▷global illumination simulations.

CPU: Central Processing Unit, the part of the computer that executes program instructions.

DAG: Directed Acyclic Graph. A hierarchical data structure similar to a tree except that its edges can join such that a child node has multiple immediate parent nodes. Scene and shader graphs in mental ray are DAGs.

darklight: a ▷light source with negative light contribution, also called "light sucker". It is a trick to remove unwanted light during shading.

declaration^{mr}: a description of a ▷shader and its parameters in a form that mental ray needs to properly call the shader.

Delaunay: a ▷tessellation technique that maximizes the internal angles of the triangles to avoid very thin and long triangles.

depth frame buffer: an image in memory whose pixels contain the Z coordinates of the frontmost object visible at that pixel.

depth of field: an effect observed in cameras that are not ▷pinhole cameras that causes blurring of objects that are not in focus. Depth of field can be simulated by mental ray using either ▷lens shaders during ▷rendering, or using ▷output shaders during ▷postprocessing.

desaturation: a technique that fades colors that are too bright to be represented towards white, which prevents color aberrations.

DGS^{mr}: an abbreviation indicating that Diffuse, Glossy, and Specular effects are handled.

dielectric: a material property, and a light propagation mode in certain standard mental ray shaders that correctly accounts for reflection and refraction on and in materials such as glass.

diffuse color: an idealization of a surface color used by many ▷material shaders, as opposed to ▷ambient and ▷specular colors. It is used for diffuse reflection of light.

direct illumination: light reaching a given point on a surface or in a volume on a direct and straight path, from a light or through a transparent shadow-casting object without reflection or refraction. Opposite of ▷indirect illumination.

directional light: a ▷light source that emits parallel light rays in a single direction. For all practical purposes the sun is a direction light on Earth. Also called an infinite light.

displacement map: a technique that deforms a geometric surface based on the results of a displacement shader, often producing extra triangles. It is used when ▷bump mapping is not sufficient.

dynamic linking^{mr}: the attachment of a ▷shader library containing executable ▷shader code to mental ray, which is required for calling the shader.

edge following^{mr}: a technique that improves ▷sampling quality by ensuring that high-contrast edges are properly resolved even if they are so small that they are missed by sampling at regular intervals.

edge merging^{mr}: the process of closing a gap between to nearby surface edges as a result of a ▷connection specification or ▷adjacency detection.

elliptical texture filtering: an algorithm that samples an elliptical area of a ▷texture, which results in a higher quality than point sampling or rectangular filtering but requires more knowledge about the viewing angle.

environment map: a ▷texture conceptually wrapped around the ▷scene without requiring a geometric object. It can be seen by the camera and can be seen as reflections and refractions. It is often used as a cheap replacement for ray tracing, and works well for chrome effects and skies.

environment variable: a variable maintained by the ▷command line processor (shell). mental ray queries certain environment variables to modify its configuration.

Ethernet: a popular networking technology that connects computers at speeds of typically 100 Mbit/s or 1 GB/s, using ▷TCP/IP. Also see ▷ATM.

FDDI: an obsolete fiber-optic token-ring based alternative to ▷Ethernet operating at 100 Mbit/s.

field: interlaced images (video) consist of two fields that must be rendered independently and combined into one ▷frame. All the odd lines of the frame come from one field, and all the even lines from the other.

field of view: the amount of the ▷scene visible to the camera, defined as the camera's ▷aperture divided by its ▷focal length. Wide-angle lenses have a larger field of view.

file format: the storage method of data in a file. In the context of this book, it describes image file storage formats such as TIFF or OpenEXR.

film grain: the effect of uneven distribution of silver halide particles on film stock, causing a grainy appearance at high magnification.

final gathering: a technique to discover immediate ▷indirect illumination by sending rays in a hemisphere and accumulating the colors found at the endpoints of the rays. No secondary rays are cast. Works in conjunction with or independently of ▷global illumination.

focal length: the distance from a ▷camera lens to its focal point.

frame: every image in an animation sequence. See also ▷field.

frame buffer: an image stored in memory, consisting of a two-dimensional array of pixels. Each pixel may hold color, depth, label, motion, or normal values.

free-form surface: a geometric object defined by a mesh of curves defined by ▷bases and ▷control points, as opposed to a geometric object consisting of ▷polygons.

gamma correction: a technique to equally distribute representable color component values physiologically. Monitors and printers have a logarithmic response curve which must be compensated with gamma correction.

geometry shader[mr]: a procedural function that creates geometry procedurally at runtime, as opposed to loading geometry from a ▷scene file. Geometry shaders are often used to automatically create helper objects that are used as bounding volumes.

global illumination: the simulation of light transport from ▷light sources to illuminated surfaces or volumes, including paths that involve diffuse, glossy, and specular reflection and transmission from other objects. mental ray uses the ▷photon map method to simulate global illumination. Opposite of ▷local illumination.

glossy: the reflection or transmission predominantly but not exclusively in a certain direction, causing blurring. Examples are rough metals and frosted glass.

high dynamic range (HDR): colors whose components exceed a value of 1.0, and are packed in a four-byte ▷RGBE storage format. HDR images can capture superbright highlights or irradiance without the storage overhead of 16-byte floating-point storage.

hither plane: the close clipping plane perpendicular to the viewing direction of the ▷camera. No geometry in front of the hither plane is rendered. See ▷yon plane.

homogeneous control point: a ▷control point with a weight, defined as XYZW. Weights are used by ▷rational surfaces.

illumination: the computation of the color of a point on a surface or in a volume based on its ▷ambient, ▷diffuse, and ▷specular colors in conjunction with the light arriving from ▷light sources, and based on ▷global illumination if available.

image resolution: in this book, the height and width of an image, measured in pixels. (Outside computer graphics, the word "resolution" is often used to measure the density of pixels, not the absolute number.)

incremental change^mr: a change to an existing ▷scene database to prepare for ▷rendering the next ▷frame or ▷field. Replacing only the changing ▷scene elements rather than rebuilding the entire ▷scene database from scratch improves performance.

index of refraction: the ratio of the optical density of a transparent material relative to the optical density of air.

indirect illumination: light reaching a given point on a surface or in a volume on an indirect path, after reflections or refractions. This requires ▷photon mapping and/or ▷final gathering. Opposite of ▷direct illumination.

infinite light: another term for ▷directional light.

infrasampling^mr: taking less than one sample per pixel to improve speed. See ▷oversampling.

inheritance: the propagation of ▷materials, parameters, and flags down the ▷instances in the ▷scene graph hierarchy.

instance: a node in the ▷scene graph that defines the location and transformation of the instanced element, as well as ▷inheritance. See ▷multiple instancing.

instance group^mr: a node in the ▷scene graph that permits grouping of ▷instances at a point. All nodes of the ▷scene graph except the leaves are either instances or instance groups.

jittering: a technique that perturbs the sample points during ▷rendering to avoid aliasing caused by regular sample grid distances.

keystone distortion: the distortion resulting from the camera viewing plane being shifted in XY directions.

knot vector: another name for ▷parameter vector if the ▷basis is ▷B-spline.

label^mr: a 32-bit integer value that can be attached to a geometric object or ▷light source. ▷Shaders can use labels for identification purposes.

Lambert shading: a technique for computing the illumination of a point on a purely ▷diffuse object surface with no ▷specular component.

LDA approximation^{mr}: Length, Distance, Angle; a generic ▷approximation technique.

leaf instance^{mr}: a member of the linear instance list that mental ray derives from the ▷scene graph before ▷rendering begins. Leaf instances have all transformations and ▷inheritance fully resolved.

lens shader^{mr}: a type of ▷shader that controls the characteristics of the rays cast by the ▷camera.

light emitter shader^{mr}: a type of ▷shader that controls how ▷light sources emit ▷photons for ▷indirect illumination.

light shader^{mr}: a type of ▷shader that controls how ▷light sources emit light rays for ▷direct illumination, and also handles shadowing.

light source: a ▷scene element that represents a point light, spot light, or ▷directional light that provides illumination for surfaces and volumes. It is connected to the ▷scene graph with an ▷instance.

Linux: a popular Open Source variant of ▷Unix.

little-endian: a ▷byte order defined by the microprocessor architecture or operating system that stores the high bytes last. 0x12345678 is stored as 0x78 0x56 0x34 0x12. The opposite of ▷big-endian.

load balancing: the operation of distributing jobs over a number of processors such that they all have an equal amount of work.

local illumination: another term for ▷direct illumination; opposite of ▷global illumination. It is called local because no other objects are taken into account.

local texture: a ▷texture that is read from the local disk and not read over the network by ▷server machines.

lossless/lossy compression: lossless compression reduces the file size by eliminating redundant information without loss of quality; the original can be restored exactly. Lossy compression achieves better compression by losing less relevant information; examples are QNT and most JPEG image formats.

Mach banding: stripe artifacts caused by pixel quantization in color gradations, for example, blue skies that cause integer RGBA steps in regular intervals.

material: a ▷scene entity attached to ▷polygons, ▷free-form surfaces, or ▷instances that control the shading and other programmable aspects of geometric objects.

material shader: a type of ▷shader that controls the illumination of a surface.

memory mapping: a technique that makes a ▷texture image available to mental ray without loading it all into memory and decompressing it. This has great performance and memory usage advantages.

mip-map texture: Multim Im Parvo, a technique using successively smaller versions of the same texture (also called a texture ▷pyramid) for fast filtered lookups.

motion blur: the blurring of objects that move during the opening time of the ▷camera ▷shutter.

motion transformation[mr]: a transformation (providing position, orientation, and scaling) in an ▷instance that describes the situation at the end of the opening time of the ▷camera ▷shutter. This causes ▷motion blur.

motion vector: a vector that describes how a ▷vertex moves during the opening time of the ▷camera ▷shutter. This is another way of creating ▷motion blur.

multiple instancing: if more than one ▷instance references the same ▷scene element (geometric object, ▷light source, ▷camera, or ▷instance group), that element appears in multiple places in the ▷scene without having to be defined multiple times.

multiple volume scattering: a ▷global illumination effect caused by ▷photons bouncing back and forth in volumes, such as clouds.

multiplicity: the count how often a given ▷control point appears in a ▷parameter vector of a curve or ▷free-form surface in sequence.

multithreading: running with multiple threads by having multiple processors on a single machine executing the same program simultaneously in the same address space.

named shader[mr]: a shader instance with parameters that was assigned a name. Opposite of ▷anonymous shader.

network parallelism: multiple machines on a network contributing to the same ▷rendering operation. A less efficient alternative to ▷multithreading.

NFS server: Unix Network File System server that makes directory trees (file systems or parts of file systems) available to other hosts, where the file system appears just like a local file system.

normal vector: a vector that defines the perpendicular direction on a surface. It may be orthogonal to the surface, but can be adjusted for smoothing the shading of adjacent ▷polygons, or for ▷bump mapping.

NURBS: Non-Uniform ▷Rational ▷B-spline, a type of curve ▷basis.

object: a geometric object defined by one or more ▷polygons or ▷free-form surfaces.

object space: the local coordinate space of an object. Every object has its own. Typically, the coordinate origin is at the object center, but this is not required.

OpenEXR: a lossless compressed image file format designed by Industrial Light & Magic that is widely used in film production.

OpenGL®: a 3D programming interface invented by Silicon Graphics that is widely used for fast hardware 3D rendering.

options block[mr]: a ▷scene element that contains a large number of ▷rendering options and parameters, such as whether ▷ray tracing is enabled or disabled.

orthographic camera: a camera that casts parallel rays so that no perspective distortion is created.

output shader: a type of ▷shader that performs postprocessing operations after ▷rendering completes.

oversampling: taking more than one sample per pixel to avoid ▷aliasing. See ▷infrasampling.

parameter vector: a sequence of ▷control point references that define the shape and number of ▷patches in a ▷free-form surface.

participating media: volumes that interact with light, such as fog or smoke. They are simulated with ▷volume shaders or ▷photon volume shaders.

patch: the smallest unit of a ▷free-form surface. Free-form surfaces may connect many patches in a two-dimensional grid.

Perlin noise: ▷coherent noise, named after the inventor Ken Perlin.

Phenomenonmr (plural *Phenomena*): a package that looks like a ▷shader from the outside, but is not implemented in C or C++ but in terms of cooperating shader ▷DAGs, materials, and other elements.

Photon Mapmr: a three-dimensional data structure holding photons, which represent the flux of light. Used for simulating ▷caustics and ▷global illumination.

photon shadermr: a ▷shader that controls the interaction of photons with surfaces.

photon volume shadermr: a ▷shader that controls the interaction of photons with volumes.

photorealism: the attempt to achieve physical correctness as would be shown by a real camera, by rigorously simulating the physics instead of tweaking parameters until the ▷scene "looks good".

physical memory: the RAM chips installed in the computer.

pinhole camera: a simple camera-obscura type of ▷camera that provides perspective without ▷depth of field blurring. This is

the default in mental ray.

point light: a ▷light source that emits light uniformly in all directions.

polygon: a geometric primitive consisting of a set of boundary ▷vertices connected with straight edges, optionally containing holes.

postprocessing: the processing of the ▷frame buffers by ▷output shaders after ▷rendering finishes.

PostScript: a description language for printed documents, invented by Adobe Systems.

premultiplication: RGBA ▷colors stored as (red·A, green·A, blue·A, A). RGB may not exceed A. This simplifies many operations on colors and is standard practice in computer graphics.

primary ray: a ray that originates at the ▷camera.

primary rootmr: the main attachment point and result node of a ▷Phenomenon.

pyramid texture: a general term for multiresolution textures that store successively smaller versions of the same texture. See ▷mip maps.

radiosity: diffuse-only ▷global illumination.

RAM: Random Access Memory, fast chips that store information such as running programs and data, as opposed to slow long-term storage on disks.

rational surface: ▷free-form surfaces whose ▷control points have weights.

ray marching: a technique that samples points along a ray in a volume, integrating over the results to determine what happens to the light as it travels through the volume.

ray tracing: a ▷rendering technique that can deal with ▷reflections and ▷refractions, as opposed to ▷scanline rendering which cannot (but is faster). mental ray combines both adaptively.

recursion: see ▷recursion.

reflection: the evaluation of a mirror reflection by casting a ▷secondary ray. This requires ▷ray tracing.

reflection map: another name for ▷environment map. Despite the name, no ▷reflection (and hence no ▷ray tracing) is involved.

refraction: the evaluation of a glass-like transmission by casting a ▷secondary ray into the glass material, at some angle determined by the ▷index of refraction of the glass, which is a value not equal to 1.0. (If the index is 1.0, the ray does not change direction, and it's called ▷transparency instead of refraction.)

Relay library^{mr}: a library by mental images that acts as a proxy between an application program and a mental ray renderer.

rendering: the process of computing, pixel by pixel, one or more 2D images from 3D scene data, from the viewpoint of a simulated ▷camera.

RGB, RGBA, RGBE: color data types: red, green, blue; RGB with alpha (opacity), and RGB with an exponent that allows ▷high dynamic range colors whose RGB component values exceed 1.0.

root group^{mr}: the topmost ▷instance group of the ▷scene graph.

sampling: the process of repeatedly computing function values at distinct points to approximate the function result.

scanline rendering: a ▷rendering technique based on projecting and sorting triangles. Unlike ▷ray tracing it cannot deal with reflections, refractions, and other scattering effects, but is very fast.

scene: a description of all ▷objects, ▷light sources, ▷cameras, ▷materials, ▷textures and everything else required to render an image. Scene elements are stored in a scene graph describing the hierarchical relationships.

secondary ray: a ray that continues a ▷primary ray after undergoing ▷reflection, ▷refraction, or ▷transparency.

self-shadowing: a concave object casting shadows onto itself.

server machine^{mr}: another machine on the network that contributes to ▷rendering. Also called slave machine. The machine where ▷rendering was started is the client (also called master) machine.

shader: a procedural plug-in written in C or C++, usually loaded into mental ray in the form of a shader library. Originally, shaders computed only surface shading, but the term stuck as new types of shaders were invented that had nothing to do with shading.

shader assignment^{mr}: the attachment of the result of one shader to an input ▷shader parameter of another. Shader assignments are used to build shader graphs in Phenomena, for example.

shader declaration^{mr}: see ▷declaration.

shader instance^{mr}: a shader together with its ▷shader parameters, which are either constant or assigned.

shader library: a file containing one or more executable ▷shader plug-ins that permits ▷dynamic loading. Shaders are normally packaged into shader libraries for easy loading.

shader list^{mr}: the concatenation of shaders into a linear list, such that every shader in the list operates on the result of its predecessor. This is commonly done for ▷lens shaders.

shader parameter^{mr}: custom input values to shaders that control its behavior. A ▷material shader, for example, typically has parameters for its ▷ambient, ▷diffuse, and ▷specular colors and a light list.

shadow map: a fast but less precise technique for ▷rendering shadows without requiring ▷ray tracing that relies on precomputed depth maps.

shadow mode^{mr}: the method for computing shadows with ▷ray tracing: standard, sorted, or segmented.

shadow ray^{mr}: a ray sent from an illuminated point to a light source to find out whether there are occluding objects that cast shadows.

shadow shader^{mr}: a type of ▷shader that is called to determine object transparency when a ▷shadow ray hits an occluding object.

shutter time: the time that the ▷camera shutter is open and the "film" is exposed. If a nonzero time is specified, moving objects cause ▷motion blur.

special curve^{mr}: a curve on a ▷free-form surface that is included in the ▷tessellation.

specular color: the highlight color used by many ▷material shaders, as opposed to ▷ambient and ▷diffuse colors. It is normally multiplied by the light color.

spot light: a variation of a ▷point light where the light emission is restricted to a cone.

startup file^{mr}: a file called `.rayrc` or `rayrc` that is read by mental ray when it starts up. It is used for initialization, such as loading of standard ▷shader libraries.

surface acne: artifacts caused by incorrect ▷self-shadowing where a ▷shadow ray starting on the surface mistakes that same surface for an occluding shadow-casting object.

surface derivative: optional vectors that define the local UV coordinate system on a surface (first derivative), and the rate of change (second derivative).

swap space: a hard disk partition that together with ▷physical memory limits the maximum amount of memory that can be allocated. If physical memory runs out and the system begins to use the swap space, performance degrades.

swimming texture: ▷textures not anchored to a surface that shift around during an animation.

TCP/IP: Transmission Control Protocol/Internet Protocol. The dominant connection-oriented method for sending and receiving data over a network.

terminator: the line that divides an object into the part that points towards a ▷light source and can be directly illuminated by it, and the part that points away.

tessellation: the process of subdividing ▷polygons and ▷free-form surfaces into triangles for ▷rendering.

texel: a single pixel of a ▷texture image.

texture: an image or ▷shader that is mapped on an object like wallpaper (in the 2D texture case), or that the object appears to be carved out of (in the ▷3D texture case). Textures can also be used for many other purposes, such as projector lights or ▷anisotropic shading.

texture, 3D: ▷3D texture.

texture, elliptical filtering: ▷elliptical texture filtering.

texture filtering: a method of sampling not a single point but an area on a ▷texture to avoid ▷aliasing.

texture flashing: an effect caused by insufficient ▷texture filtering. During animations, poorly resolved texture features flash in and out. Also called strobing.

texture, local: ▷local texture.

texture, mip-map: ▷mip-map texture.

texture, pyramid: ▷pyramid texture.

texture shader[mr]: a type of ▷shader that evaluates or samples a ▷texture.

texture vector[mr]: a vector that can be attached to ▷vertices, or computed by texture surfaces, to anchor a ▷texture to a surface.

TIFF: Tagged Image File Format, a common image ▷file format with countless variations.

total internal reflection: ▷refractions normally cross the boundary of the refracting object, but at grazing angles the refraction can turn into an internal reflection.

trace depth: an option that allows limiting the number of ▷reflection and ▷refraction and ▷transparency interactions that a ray can undergo.

translucency: glossy or diffuse ▷refraction or ▷transmission.

transmission: either ▷refraction or ▷transparency.

transparency: a variant of ▷refraction with an ▷index of refraction of 1.0, which means that the ray does not change direction. This is more efficient because it does not require ▷ray tracing.

triangulation: see ▷tessellation.

trimming curve: a curve that can be put on a ▷free-form surface. Everything that falls outside the trimming curve is cut away.

Unix: a professional operating system, offered by various workstation vendors. See ▷Linux.

Utah teapot: a simple geometric object built by Martin Newell from ▷free-form surfaces that has become so popular in computer graphics that it is sometimes called the sixth Platonic solid ("teapotahedron").

UV coordinates: two-dimensional coordinates on flat surfaces that are useful for mapping two-dimensional ▷textures.

vector sharing[mr]: the practice of referencing the same vector in more than one place in the ▷vertex list, reducing redundancy and memory use.

vertex (plural: vertices): a point in 3D space with optional normal vectors, motion vectors, texture vectors, and other information, that ▷polygons and ▷free-form surfaces are built from. In the free-form surface case, they are called ▷control points.

vertex sharing[mr]: the practice of referencing the same vertex in multiple ▷polygons to reduce redundancy.

virtual memory: the sum of ▷physical memory (fast) plus ▷swap space (slow).

virtual shared database[mr]: the technology that mental ray's ▷scene database is based on. It allows transparently sharing the database across multiple processors and networked machines.

volume: a bounded or unbounded section of 3D space. ▷Volume shaders can create procedural effects in volumes.

volume shader[mr]: a type of ▷shader that controls what happens to rays that travel through a ▷volume, for example using ▷ray marching.

voxel: a building block of ▷ray tracing acceleration techniques such as ▷BSP trees, dividing 3D space into boxes containing renderable geometry.

Windows NT, Windows 2000: operating systems from Microsoft Corp. This book uses "NT" but all statements equally apply to Windows 2000.

world space: a coordinate system in which all coordinates are measured relative to an arbitrary single coordinate origin.

yon plane: the distant clipping plane perpendicular to the viewing direction of the ▷camera. No geometry behind the yon plane is rendered. See ▷hither plane.

Bibliography

[Arvo 89]   J. Arvo, D. Kirk, "A survey of ray tracing acceleration techniques". In: A. S. Glassner (ed.), An introduction to ray tracing. Academic Press, London.

[Bartels 87]   R. H. Bartels, J. C. Beatty, B. A. Barsky, *An Introduction to Splines for use in Computer Graphics and Geometric Modeling*. Morgan Kaufmann, Los Altos, Calif., 1987.

[Blinn 96]   J. Blinn, *Jim Blinn's Corner, a trip down the graphics pipeline*. Morgan Kaufmann, San Francisco, 1996.

[Farin 97]   G. Farin, *Curves and surfaces for computer-aided design*, 4th edn. Academic Press, San Diego, 1997.

[Foley 96]   J. D. Foley, A. van Dam, S. K. Feiner, J. F. Hughes, *Computer Graphics: Principles and Practice*, 2nd edn. in C. Addison-Wesley, Reading, Mass., 1996.

[Glassner 89] A. S. Glassner (ed.), *An Introduction to Ray Tracing*. Academic Press, London, 1989.

[Glassner 95] A. S. Glassner, *Principles of Digital Image Synthesis*. Morgan Kaufmann, London, 1995.

[Hanrahan 93] P. Hanrahan, "Rendering Concepts". In: M. F. Cohen, J. R. Wallace, *Radiosity and Realistic Image Synthesis*. Academic Press Professional, Boston, 1993.

[Hall 89]   R. Hall, *Illumination and Color in Computer Generated Imagery*. Springer, New York, 1989.

[Heckbert 90] P. S. Heckbert, "Adaptive Radiosity Textures for Bidirectional Ray Tracing". In: *SIGGRAPH 90, Proceedings of the 17th Annual Conference on Computer Graphics and Interactive Techniques*. Association for Computing Machinery, New York, pp. 145–154, 1990.

[Herken 94]   R. Herken, R. Hödicke, K. J. Schmidt, "High Image Quality, Interactive Rendering on Scalable Parallel Systems. An Interim Report on ESPRIT Project 6173 (DESIRE)". In: J. C. Zuidervaart and Dekker L. (eds.), *Proceedings of the 1994 EUROSIM Conference on Massively Parallel Processing*. Elsevier, Amsterdam, 1994.

[Jensen 96]   H. W. Jensen, "Global Illumination Using Photon Maps". In: X. Pueyo, P. Schröder (eds.), *Rendering Techniques '96*. Springer, Wien New York, 1996.

[Jensen 98]   H. W. Jensen, P. H. Christensen, "Efficient Simulation of Light Transport
                 in Scenes with Participating Media using Photon Maps". In: *SIGGRAPH
                 98, Proceedings of the 17th Annual Conference on Computer Graphics and
                 Interactive Techniques*. Association for Computing Machinery, New York,
                 pp. 311–320, 1998.

[LeFrançois 05] M.-K. LeFrançois, "Implementing the mental images Phenomena Renderer
                 on the GPU". In: M. Pharr (ed.), *GPU Gems II*. Addison-Wesley, Upper
                 Saddle River, N.J., pp. 201–222, 2005.

[Piegl 97]   L. Piegl, W. Tiller, *The NURBS Book*, 2nd edn. Springer, Berlin, 1997
                 (Monographs in visual communication).

[PROG]   T. Driemeyer, R. Herken (eds.), *Programming mental ray*, 3rd edn. Springer,
                 Wien New York, 2005.

[Ward 92]   G. Ward, P. Heckbert, "Irradiance Gradients". In: A. Chalmers, D. Paddon,
                 F. Sillion (eds.), *Proceedings of the Third Eurographics Workshop on Rendering*.
                 Consolidation Express, Bristol, pp. 85–98, 1992.

[Whitted 80]   T. Whitted, "An Improved Illumination Model for Shaded Display".
                 Communications of the ACM 23, pp. 343–349, 1980.

Index

SpringerComputerScience

Thomas Driemeyer, Rolf Herken (eds.)

Programming mental ray®

Third, completely revised edition.
2005. XVI, 825 pages. With CD-ROM.
Softcover **EUR 129,–**
(Recommended retail price)
Net-price subject to local VAT.
ISBN 3-211-24484-0
mental ray Handbooks, Volume 2

This book is the definitive reference manual for mental ray version 3.4. It starts with a brief overview of the features of mental ray and continues with the specification of the mental ray scene description language, the mental ray shader interface, and the integration interface for third-party applications. All material is presented in reference form, organized by grammar elements and C function call, rather than by feature set. The book is intended for translator writers, shader writers, and integrators who are familiar with the C and C++ programming languages. This third, completely revised edition was extended to cover the new generation of mental ray, version 3.4, throughout the book, and also includes the mental ray integration manual. The enclosed CD contains a demo version of the mental ray stand alone and the mental ray library, as well as example shaders with source code and demo scenes, for a variety of computer platforms.

Description of the contents:
Chapter 1 gives a brief overview of the functionality of mental ray. Chapter 2 describes the scene language in detail. This chapter is organized by language unit. Chapter 3 explains how custom shaders and Phenomena™ are written and documents the shader call interface. Chapter 4 describes the extended geometry shader interface. Chapter 5 describes the integration interface of the library version of mental ray. This chapter is useful only for application developers, and not part of the standard mental ray manual. Chapter 6 contains porting guidelines for users and shader writers upgrading from mental ray 3.x to mental ray 3.4. Appendix A describes the command-line interface of mental ray. Appendix B contains the source code of mental ray's scene language parser.

SpringerWienNewYork

P.O. Box 89, Sachsenplatz 4–6, 1201 Vienna, Austria, Fax +43.1.330 24 26, books@springer.at, **springer.at**
Haberstraße 7, 69126 Heidelberg, Germany, Fax +49.6221.345-4229, SDC-bookorder@springer-sbm.com, springeronline.com
P.O. Box 2485, Secaucus, NJ 07096-2485, USA, Fax +1.201.348-4505, orders@springer-ny.com, springeronline.com
Eastern Book Service, 3–13, Hongo 3-chome, Bunkyo-ku, Tokyo 113, Japan, Fax +81.3.38 18 08 64, orders@svt-ebs.co.jp
Prices are subject to change without notice. All errors and omissions excepted.

Springer and the Environment